The Art and Science of Music Therapy:
A Handbook

The Art and Science of Music Therapy: A Handbook

Edited by

Tony Wigram
Institute for Music and Music Therapy
University of Aalborg, Denmark

Bruce Saperston
Utah State University, USA

Robert West
St George's Hospital Medical School, UK

 harwood academic publishers
Australia • Canada • China • France • Germany • India • Japan
Luxembourg • Malaysia • The Netherlands • Russia • Singapore
Switzerland

First published 1995
Second printing 1996
Third printing 1999

Amsteldijk 166
1st Floor
1079 LH Amsterdam
The Netherlands

British Library Cataloguing in Publication Data

Art and Science of Music Therapy: Handbook
   I. Wigram, Tony
   615.85154

   ISBN 3-7186-5634-5 (hardback)
   ISBN 3-7186-5635-3 (paperback)

Contents

Acknowledgements

We are grateful to the staff at the Ciba Foundation for their hospitality and most especially to Dr Margaret Christie, Chair of the Applied Psychology Research Group who helped organise the event and who provided part of the funds to enable it to take place. We would also like to thank Jo Ryan and Joy Searle for their secretarial help. Funding for the Ciba seminar was also kindly provided by the Music Therapy Charity, the British Society for Music Therapy and the National Research in Music Therapy Centre.

Foreword

It may be said that music therapy has a long history, but a short past. Indeed the oldest account of medical practices, the Kahum papyrus, provides an account of the use of incantations for healing, and references to the therapeutic uses of music are continually found throughout eastern and western history. However, the emergence of music therapy as an organised profession has occurred primarily during the past 50 years.

Music therapy has developed as a profession to a greater or lesser extent in approximately 50 countries. In several of these countries (e.g. Hong Kong, Cyprus, Korea, Iceland), there is only one practising music therapist; in other countries, such as the United States, there are more than 3,000 trained music therapists. Although music therapy practice was in existence prior to these times, formal professional associations were formed in the United States, Austria, and Great Britain during the 1950s; in the Netherlands, Argentina, Brazil, Japan, Denmark, Norway and Uruguay during the 1960s; in Israel, Columbia, France, Finland, South Africa, Canada, Australia, Italy, New Zealand, Puerto Rico, and Spain during the 1970s; in Belgium, Switzerland, Poland, Scotland, Hungary and China during the 1980s; and in Greece during the early 1990s.

The rapid or slow development in various countries has been linked with a number of factors, a significant one being the cultural or societal viewpoints regarding the importance of music in general and specific preferences with regard to music. Logically then, music therapy practices have embraced these viewpoints and preferences, and thus music therapy is very distinct and different from country to country.

In addition, there may be complex and even contradictory relationships between these societal and cultural views and the development of music therapy as a science. For instance, in some cultures music is widely acknowledged as a 'healing' medium, and the terms, 'music' and 'therapy' are considered redundant. While this cultural viewpoint may support its widespread use, it may often delay or prohibit its scientific development. Conversely, in societies where music is less embedded in traditional healing practices, its regard as a science may be enhanced.

Of course, numerous other factors have influenced the development of music therapy in different countries, such as specific historical events, various music therapy pioneers, political and financial issues, the organisation of higher education, various health care approaches and definitions of therapy. As these factors are unique to each country, they have provided either a nurturing or unsupportive context for the development of music therapy and have literally shaped its past and present clinical characteristics.

In addition, given the breadth of potential clinical applications of music therapy as a treatment (i.e. as a medical, psychotherapeutic, educational, rehabilitative, palliative, diagnostic, etc. intervention) coupled with the numerous theoretical and clinical orientations to treatment in each of these areas and prevalence of one or more of these theories in each country, it is relatively easy to comprehend the multiple influences on music therapy which account for its current diversity.

Thus, some music therapy approaches have emerged from psychoanalytic traditions, some from humanistic tradition, some from behavioural traditions, some from special education philosophy, etc. In addition, one or more of these traditions may dominate music therapy practice in a single country, or there may be eclectic or integrated approaches to music therapy in others (e.g., developmental/humanistic, behavioural/medical, etc.).

As can be expected, methodologies for music therapy practice are mildly to vastly different among countries. These have been developed based on a particular theoretical orientation or combination of orientations. Also, for a variety of reasons they may emphasise one or more of the experiences within music (improvisation, reception, composition, performance, activity, combined arts) (Maranto, 1993). Aspects of and requirements for the client-therapist relationship as well as the level, breadth and depth of the therapeutic intervention are likewise related to the theoretical orientation and type of music experience used.

Furthermore, because the types of patients (e.g., medical, psychiatric, handicapped) and the ages of patients who are primary recipients of music therapy may vary in different countries, it is difficult to speculate on whether this phenomenon is the cause or result of a particular theoretical orientation and experience within music.

For the reasons stated above, diversity both in national and international music therapy practice is a distinct reality which is considered both necessary and healthy within the discipline and profession. Thus, diversity is considered a positive outcome of the breadth of music therapy applications and the need for music therapy practices that are relevant to clinical needs within each country. However, such diversity makes music therapy difficult to define, although several definitions are becoming more widely accepted, and several taxonomies of music therapy practice have been published. Continued international dialogue and collaboration particularly through its official international organisation, the World Federation of Music Therapy, will undoubtedly bring about a greater knowledge and acceptance of the diverse practices within music therapy and perhaps offer a distinct paradigm that will embrace them.

At the present, music therapy is seen as both an art and a science. Its practices, although well-developed on a clinical level, have not always yielded to traditional models of quantitative research. Specifically, music itself is difficult to quantify, the music therapy process is difficult to quantify, and their effects on the complex aspects of the human being are even more difficult to analyse in a quantitative manner. Thus, there is a continuous search for models of research that will address these inherent difficulties. For this reason, qualitative research methods as well as combinations of quantitative and qualitative methods may in the future provide more insight into and documentation of the clinical effects of music therapy.

Research models must be relevant to diversity within music therapy practice as well. Some music therapy methods and theoretical orientations are more aligned with quantitative methodology, e.g. behavioural methods. Within this orientation, overt behaviours (as dependent variables) may be specified objectively and musical stimuli or reinforcements may also be defined in such a manner. Thus, quantitative effects of treatment are more direct and observable, and there is an abundance of literature on these effects. This is certainly not the case however, in attempting to examine the treatment effects of improvisationally-oriented music therapy processes or the effects of music therapy on individuals with psychiatric difficulties, to name just a few situations.

Additionally, in the area of music and medicine, quantitative research is increasing. Specific effects of music therapy on various psychological and physiological parameters have been identified with some consistency. This type of research is necessary to meet the rigorous requirements of the medical community as to the effectiveness of music therapy with regard to medical treatment. However, given the most recent research and theories regarding the mind-body relationship, psychoneuroimmunology, and behavioural medicine, qualitative aspects of the music experience, e.g., the meaning of the music to the patient, the relationship of the patient to the music and the influence of the patient's thinking on physiological processes warrant further investigation using new research paradigms. Implications of the integral mind-body relationship and the influence of music therapy on all parameters of a person's health (i.e., physiological, psychological, social, etc.) must be taken into consideration and examined in all diverse methods of music therapy, not just those in the areas of medicine.

The reader may gain a perspective of the art and science of music therapy as well as its potential for diversity in the present text. In the case studies and research articles contained herein, one can obtain: a keen insight into the variety of theoretical orientations upon which music therapy is based, a description of various experiences within music (receptive, improvisatory, etc.) which are at the heart of the therapeutic process, a sense of the various aspects of the therapeutic relationship which develops through music, and a knowledge of the variety of clinical groups that benefit from music therapy treatment. In addition, the reader can derive a breadth of ideas concerning the diversity of music therapy methodologies, for assessment, treatment and evaluation.

The value of such text is in presenting this diversity in an accessible way for music therapy students and practitioners, as well as for students and therapists from other disciplines. From both its editors and contributors, who represent a broad range of countries and perspectives, the reader is challenged to contrast, compare, and go deeper into the possibilities for music therapy practice, and emerge stimulated and open for new ideas and future potentials.

The diversity of the art and science of international music therapy is at once illuminating, enlivening and thought-provoking. I am honoured to have been asked to write a foreword for this international forum for ideas and hope that this text will provide the basis for much future discussion.

Cheryl Dileo Maranto, PhD, RMT-BC
Professor and Co-ordinator of Music Therapy
Temple University, Philadelphia, Pennsylvania, USA
President: World Federation of Music Therapy

References

Maranto, C.D. (Ed) (1993). Music Therapy: International Perspectives, Pipersville, PA; Jeffrey Books.

Preface

The therapeutic value of music has been evident for centuries, and the last 50 years has seen the development of a music therapy profession. It has now taken its place in the clinical field alongside professions such as physiotherapy, occupational therapy, speech therapy and psychology in the paramedical services provided by health authorities in many countries.

Music therapists are usually first and foremost musicians, and probably for this reason the dominant approach to the field has been subjective and founded in artistic and literary traditions. The medical model of therapy, however, demands scientific evaluation based on rigorous measurement of process and outcome. Therefore, to gain wider acceptance among the medical community, a blending of the artistic and scientific traditions will have to be found - the artistic traditions inspiring the development of treatment methods and science providing a means of finding out which methods work with which clients and in what circumstances.

This book aims to provide a broad overview of the state of the art in music therapy today and to provide a basis from which it can develop and grow into a more effective method of treatment and gain more widespread acceptance among health professionals as a treatment of choice in a variety of conditions, both psychological and physical.

The reader will observe that the range of approaches and client groups is diverse, from controlled studies of the effects of music in augmenting medical treatment to a case study of the use of music therapy with an autistic child. The writing styles of the contributors are similarly diverse and we have undertaken only light editing of the chapters so as to provide the reader with a greater insight into the ways that different music therapists conceive of their work.

Therefore this book contains chapters by many of the world's leading music therapists and should provide practising music therapists and music therapy students with a unique opportunity to learn about the methods used by the individuals who have developed those methods. Music therapy often runs parallel to, or augments, other forms of therapy such as psychotherapy, and this book should be invaluable to clinicians in these other areas who are interested in referring patients to music therapists.

The styles of work, approaches and techniques employed in music therapy may depend on the training and methodological stance of the music therapist, or on the needs of a particular client group. Many of the chapters represent one of the more typical styles of music therapy, the use of active and creative music-making to build a therapeutic relationship between an individual or group of clients, and the therapist. The use of free or structured improvisation in an interactive way by skilled therapists is described in case material in 11 of the chapters. The process by which a client expresses emotional, physical or psychological needs and difficulties in creative improvisation either on their own, or in dialogue with the therapist forms one of the most common approaches in music therapy.

Receptive forms of music therapy are also well documented, ranging from the use of music in guided imagery, vibroacoustic therapy, and physiologically interactive music to the use of popular classical music to elicit feelings, memories, associations and desires.

Music therapists work with individuals or groups for different reasons. There is a wealth of literature on single case studies, both from a clinical and a research standpoint. While many of the chapters in this book contain individual case examples, four of the chapters focus on group music therapy, and the dynamics of group process.

The development of assessment procedures has grown alongside the profession in response to the demand that music therapy as a clinical intervention should fulfil this function in medical, educational and social milieu. Four chapters look specifically at assessment from both a diagnostic point of view, and from the requirement to assess the needs a client or group of clients may have for either music therapy or for some other form of intervention. All music therapy approaches contain elements of assessment either during the initial stages of therapy, or as part of sustained treatment, and the many case studies reviewed in this book give some insight into this process from either analytical, medical, remedial, psychotherapeutic, education or purely musical standpoints.

Research is assuming an increasingly important place in music therapy, where the focus can vary from evaluating the outcome of music therapy, to analysing more specifically the significant elements in music and sound and their influence on the therapeutic process. Empirical data is evident in many chapters, but eight chapters concentrated on recording and discussing specialised research. The first chapter in the book gives an overview by means of a meta-analysis of music used in medical and dental situations.

Music Therapy can benefit a wide variety of people, from both clinical and non-clinical populations. The effect of music therapy on a large range of clients with mental or physical illnesses and disabilities is documented here. In addition there are chapters that focus on issues that can affect all of us, such as those on stress and grief counselling. Key words used in the indexing include any chronic or acute clinical conditions mentioned in this book in relation to music therapy intervention, and will enable the reader to use this book as a reference.

This book is part of a series emanating from symposia held annually at the Ciba Foundation in London and organised by the Applied Psychology Research Group based at Royal Holloway and Bedford New College, London University.

Tony Wigram
Bruce Saperston
Robert West

Contributor Details

John Bean trained at the Royal Academy of Music, City of Manchester College of Higher Education and Guildhall School of Music and Drama, London. He was a Professional cellist in a symphony orchestra for eight years and a cello teacher. He is currently a peripatetic music therapist for Special Schools in Leicestershire. He has frequent lecturing engagements in the UK, and also in Europe Switzerland and Spain. He was awarded Churchill Fellowship to investigate music therapy in the treatment of cerebral palsy; Switzerland, 1985.

Ruth Bright has worked in Music Therapy for over 30 years. Her work has involved many populations over a wide range of ages but she is known around the world for her work, lecturing and books about geriatrics and on grief counselling in music therapy. Ruth Bright's reputation extends beyond the field of music therapy; she has served as chairman of the New South Wales branch of the National Association for Loss and Grief, has been President of the Gerontology Foundation of Australia since 1988 and is a long-standing Director of Maranatha, a training group home of Developmentally Disabled young adults. She was founding President of the Australian Music Therapy Association and was President of the World Federation of Music Therapy from 1990-1993. In the Queen's Birthday Honours, 1992, she received Membership of the Order of Australia for services to community health in music therapy.

Alicia Ann Clair is a Professor of Art and Music Education and Music Therapy, the Director of Music Therapy at the University of Kansas, Lawrence, Kansas and a research associate at Colmery O'Neil Veterans Affairs Medical Center in Topeka, Kansas. She is a past president of the National Association for Music Therapy and has served that Association in many other capacities. Dr Clair teaches graduate and undergraduate courses in music therapy and is involved in ongoing music therapy clinical practice research with persons who have dementia, primarily of the Alzheimer's type. Dr Clair's research concerning persons with dementias and with other populations of elderly persons is published widely. She served on the Editorial Boards of the *Journal of Music Therapy* and the *International Journal of Arts Medicine.*

Alice-Ann Darrow is Associate Professor of Music Education and Music Therapy at the University of Kansas, Lawrence, Kansas, where she also holds a courtesy appointment in the Department of Speech and Hearing. Dr Darrow has organised and implemented music education and music therapy programs in the Miami public school system, a cultural arts centre for inner city students, a federal prison, a state psychiatric hospital, and a state institution for the mentally retarded. Related to Dr Darrow's research interest in the music perception of hearing-impaired individuals, she has produced several instructional videotapes. She presently serves on the Editorial Boards of the *Journal of Research in Music Education* and *Update: Application of Research in Music Education.* Dr Darrow has been the recipient of a research award given by the National Association of Music Therapy.

Steve Dunachie was educated at St Mary's College, Crosby and Churchill College, Cambridge. At present he is Senior 1 Music Therapist at Lea Castle Hospital, Caterham, having qualified from the Guildhall School in 1981. He also lectured at the Guildhall School on the Music Therapy course for two years. In addition to therapy, he is also involved in performing, recording and composing.

Frances Smith Goldberg is a graduate in music from Indiana University and clinical psychology from Lone Mountain college. She is Associate Clinical Professor, Department of Psychiatry and former Director, Rehabilitation Therapies, Langley Porter Psychiatric Institute, University of California, San Francisco. A fellow of the Association for Music and Imagery and a Licensed Marriage, Family and Child Therapist with more than 30 years as a music therapist, she also maintains a private practice and teaches with the Bonny Institute for Music-Centred Therapies and her own Therapeutic Arts Psychotherapy and Training Institute in the United States, Canada, Sweden, Denmark, Germany and Switzerland. Ms Goldberg has published several articles on music psychotherapy, including research on music group psychotherapy and has presented at numerous national and international conferences. She serves on the Editorial Boards of *The Arts in Psychotherapy, Music Therapy Perspectives,* and the *Journal of the Association for Music and Imagery.*

Roy Grant has been a faculty member in the University of Georgia Developmental Disabilities Program since 1972, supervising clinical practicum experiences and internships, developing programs for clients with developmental disabilities, and teaching Principles of Music Therapy in the School of Music. Previous work included adult psychiatric clients, corrections, mentally retarded children and adults, emotionally disturbed children, forensics, and geriatrics in the states of Kentucky, Alabama, and Georgia. He has served on numerous regional and national committees, has served as Council Chairperson and member of the Executive Board and Assembly of Delegates of the National Association for Music Therapy, and has served as president of the regional chapter for two terms. He has published numerous articles and has co-authored three musicals for special education students.

Suzanne Hanser is research scientist at the Department of Veterans Affairs Medical Center in Palo Alto, California. She performed her research in Alzheimer's disease at Stanford University School of Medicine as a Senior Postdoctoral Fellow, sponsored by a National Research Service Award from the National Institute of Ageing. For twelve years, Dr Hanser served as Professor and Chairperson of the Department of Music Therapy at University of the Pacific in Stockton, California. She is currently President Elect of the National Association for Music Therapy. Dr Hanser is the author of the *Music Therapist's Handbook* and numerous articles in stress reduction, cognitive-behavioural approaches to music therapy, and clinical applications of music therapy (e.g. childbirth, dental patients, emotionally disturbed children, nonverbal psychotherapy, etc.).

Margaret Heal Hughes is Senior Music Therapist and Head of the Music Therapy Department for the Learning Disability Care Group of the Forest Healthcare Trust, London, England. She was born in Canada, and holds a B.A. and a B.Mus. from Queen's University (Canada) and a Postgraduate Licentiate Diploma in Music Therapy from the Guildhall School of Music and Drama, London. She is an approved supervisor for the Association of Professional Music Therapists, Great Britain and lectures and publishes on the use of a psychoanalytically - informed approach to music therapy when working with people who have learning disabilities. She is currently completing an M.A. in Observational Studies (Tavistock Clinic, University of East London). She is co-editor of *Music Therapy in Health and Education*, Jessica Kingsley Publishers.

Pixie Holland was a gold medallist of the Associated Board of the Royal Schools Music and a scholar at the Royal Academy of Music, London. She trained as a concert pianist and has accompanied, lectured and performed music for most of her life. She is a freelance music therapist working at various hospitals and day centres and schools. She has also worked extensively with the media and has held several music therapy sessions 'on air'. She is a committee member of the International Stress Management association, and Vice Chairman of the British Society for Music Therapy. She is an Honorary Research Associate of Royal Holloway College, London University, where she is researching "The Role of Music Therapy of The Effective Use of Stress".

Robin Howat holds a BA in music (Exeter University); Diploma in Education (London University) 1980; and a Diploma in Music Therapy (Nordoff-Robbins) 1977. He is currently Head of the Training Course at the Nordoff-Robbins Music Therapy Centre, London. His previous posts include being part-time music therapist at Helen Allison School for Autistic Children (1977-80); St Thomas's Psychiatric Day Hospital with children under five (1980-83); Ravenswood Village with children and adults with special needs (1985-88); Nordoff-Robbins Music Therapy Centre (1978-88).

David John studied music at Cambridge College of Arts and Technology and trained as a music therapist at the Roehampton Institute. Since then has worked in the field of adult Mental Health firstly with patients suffering from a severe degree of mental and physical handicap and since 1985 at Fulbourn psychiatric hospital, Cambridge. His main interest is in working with a psychoanalytic model specialising in work with adults who suffer from a severe degree of mental illness. He is currently a student member of the British Association of Psychotherapists.

Chris Lawes obtained his PhD from Leeds Polytechnic where he was the Dalzell-Ward Memorial Research Fellow. He has since qualified as a clinical psychologist. He is currently working with children and adults with head injuries and neurological problems at the Department of Psychology, Essex County Hospital, Colchester, Essex. Prior to this he worked with people with learning disabilities.

Paul Nolan is the Director of Music Therapy Education in the Creative Arts in Therapy Program and Director of The Creative Arts Therapy Centre at Hahnemann University, Philadelphia, Pennsylvania. He is past Vice-President of the American Association for Music Therapy, a member of the General Advisory Board and Editorial Board for the *Arts in Psychotherapy* a member of the Editorial Board for *Music Therapy* and a member of The Advisory Board of the *International Journal of Arts Medicine.* He has served on numerous committees for the National Association for Music Therapy, the American Association for Music Therapy, and the Certification Board for Music Therapy and has lectured and presented throughout the United States, Canada and Great Britain. His clinical experiences include psychiatric, oncology, forensic, general medical, chronic pain, developmentally disabled, and eating disorders. He has published in the areas of eating disorders, improvisation, music in medicine, Guided Imagery and music, oncology, forensic psychiatry, and education in music therapy and the creative arts in therapy.

Helen Odell-Miller is a music therapist and therapy services manager in the mental health services in Cambridge. She trained in the mid 1970s as a music therapist at The Guildhall School of Music in London, and subsequently completed an MPhil in music therapy research with elderly mentally ill people, at City University in 1988. She has clinical experience with people with learning difficulties, and has now specialised in working with adults with mental health problems of all ages. She has also been involved nationally and internationally with Arts Therapies developments, and music therapy specifically, as an adviser, lecturer, conference delegate and organiser in conjunction with various bodies, e.g. Association of Professional Music Therapists, and Standing Committee for Arts Therapies Professions. She has lectured in and taught music therapy in Canada, the USA, France, Spain, Italy and Great Britain.

Amelia Oldfield completed the Guildhall Music Therapy Course in 1980. Since then she has been working as a music therapist for the Cambridge Health Authority in mental handicap, child development and child and family psychiatry. In 1986, she obtained an M. Phil. degree for a music therapy research project with profoundly mentally handicapped adults. She has published many papers on various aspects of her clinical work and is co-author of the book *Pied Piper - Musical activities to develop basic skills.* She is a past chairperson of the Association of Professional Music Therapists and is now on their advisory council and on the advisory editorial panel of the *Journal of British Music Therapy.* She runs numerous workshops and gives lectures both in Great Britain and abroad.

Mercedes Pavlicevic trained at the Nordoff-Robbins Music Therapy Centre in London in 1980 and worked as a music therapist in Scotland for ten years, first with mentally handicapped adults, and then with adult psychiatric patients and psychogeriatrics. She has also practised privately, with children and adolescents, and with people suffering from cancer. She completed her doctoral thesis entitled 'Music in Communication: Improvisation in Music Therapy' at the University of Edinburgh, Department of Psychology and Music and recently returned to South

Africa to pursue special interests in cross-cultural music communication and in the use of music therapy to alleviate traumatic stress syndrome. She now works at the Nordoff-Robbins Music Therapy Centre in London.

Mary Priestley trained at the Royal College of Music and the Geneva Conservatoire. In 1969 she qualified as a music therapist from the Guildhall School of Music. She also spent two years at the Institute of Group Analysis. For the past 20 years she has practised as a music therapist and trained students from 18 countries in her techniques. She has lectured in the UK and abroad and made many radio and television appearances. She is author of *Music Therapy in Action* and *Analytische Musiktherapi* and has published widely in professional journals.

Penny Rogers obtained her first degree in music from Manchester University where she majored in performance and studied the cello. Following work as a freelance cellist, she obtained her diploma in Music Therapy from the Guildhall School of Music & Drama, London. Since qualifying, she has specialised almost exclusively in the field of Mental Health developing a special interest in work with the sexually abused. Penny's interest in Health Service management led to a post as the District Business Manager for North East Essex Health Authority before her return to full-time work as a Music Therapist. She is currently Research Fellow at City University, London, where she is hoping to obtain a PhD looking at the use of Music Therapy with the sexually abused. She has previously obtained an MSc in Cognitive Neuropsychology from London University. In addition to her research interests, she has been an executive committee member of the Association of Professional Music Therapists for the past four years; played an active role in a number of associated forum, as well as lecturing in Estonia, USSR on Music Therapy in Mental Health.

Bruce Saperston is Director of Music Therapy, Associate Professor of Music, and Head of the Department of Music at Utah State University, Logan, Utah. Prior to his academic appointment, Dr Saperston practised clinical music therapy for 16 years with various populations (i.e. mentally retarded, autistic, emotionally disturbed, multiply handicapped) and supervised the music therapy clinical internships of 48 students. Internationally renowned as a clinician and researcher, Dr Saperston has lectured in Hong Kong and London as well as throughout the United States. Dr Saperston is a member of the Editorial Board of the *Journal of Music Therapy* and has served for several years as a member of the National Research Committee of the National Association for Music Therapy (NAMT). His numerous publications include original clinical techniques and research, and a video documentary of his work, *Music Therapy: Health Vibrations*, was produced by the NAMT as part of a national in-service programme.

Olav Skille trained as a teacher and music teacher and specialised in teaching children with brain injuries. He has worked as a music therapist, teacher and consultant on many projects. He has carried out extensive research, developing and evaluating methods of assessing musical behaviour and for developing vibroacoustic therapy. He has lectured in many countries including

Norway, Finland, Sweden, Denmark, Germany and in the UK, Italy, Yugoslavia, Estonia, and Austria.

Henk Smeijsters received a masters degree in social science and a doctors degree in musical science from the University of Nijmegan. He works as a researcher into music therapy at the Music Therapy Laboratory Nijmegen, as a lecturer in music psychology and music therapy at the Hogeschool Nijmegen and the Hogeschool Enschede and as a visiting lecturer at the University of Nijmegen. He is co-ordinator of the five year full-time training course for music therapy at the Hogeschool Enschede, a member of the research group for music therapy of the NVKT, and a member of the board of the Stichting Muziektherapie. He has written various papers in journals and has published several books about music psychology and music therapy.

Jayne Standley is Professor of Music Therapy and Director of Music Therapy at The Florida State University in Tallahassee, Florida from which she holds Bachelor's, Master's and Doctoral Degrees. Prior to her academic appointment, Dr Standley had completed 10 years of clinical music therapy experience in agencies serving mentally retarded clients. An active researcher with emphasis on medical/clinical applications of music, Professor Standley is widely published in the field and is a frequent guest lecturer. She is the 1989 recipient of the prestigious Publication Award bestowed by the National Association for Music Therapy is the author of *Music Techniques in Therapy, Counseling, and Special Education,* and is editor of the *Journal of Music Therapy.*

Esmé Towse trained as a pianist at the Royal College of Music, London and as a music therapist at the Guildhall School of Music. She is Senior Music Therapist at Withington Hospital, Manchester. She holds the N.W. diploma in dynamic psychotherapy and is a member of the N.W. Institute. She has presented papers in London and abroad.

Auriel Warwick is a graduate in music from Auckland University, New Zealand. She trained as a music therapist at the Guildhall School of Music and Drama before taking the position of peripatetic county music therapist for the Oxfordshire Education Authority. Her work covers children with severe and moderate learning difficulties, but over the past ten years she has developed her interest in children with autism. She is an experienced lecturer and workshop leader with overseas experience; Paris, Genoa, Portugal, Holland, Spain and New Zealand. Currently, she is an examiner in music therapy at the Guildhall School of Music and Drama. She is a vice-president of the British Society for Music Therapy.

Robert West obtained his PhD in psychology from University College London and has since worked as a research fellow at the Institute of Psychiatry, then as Lecturer and Senior Lecturer at Royal Holloway and Bedford New College, London University. He is currently Reader in psychology at St George's Hospital Medical School, London University. He has published many papers on music psychology and co-edited two books. He also carries out research into addiction, driver behaviour and the use of computers in psychology.

Tony Wigram BA (Hons) LGSM (MT), RMTh is Associate Professor in Music Therapy in the Institute for Music and Music Therapy, Department of Humanities, University of Aarlborg, Denmark. He is also Head Music Therapist at the Harper House Children's Service, Hertfordshire, Enland. He is chairman of the British Society for Music Therapy; co-ordinator of the European Music Therapy Committee; chair of the Commission on Government Accreditation, World Federation of Music Therapy; member of the ISME Research Commission for Music Therapy and Music in Medicine. He read Music at Britsol University, undertook post-graduate study in Music Therapy at the Guildhall School of Music under Juliet Alvin, and more recently took a qualifying degree in Psychology at London University where he is undertaking his doctorate. He is Visiting Lecturer in Music Therapy, Child Assessment and Learning Disability in universities and music therapy programmes in Italy, Spain, USA, England, Estonia and Holland. He is former chairman of the Association of Professional Music Therapists, and a Churchill Fellow of 1985.

John Woodcock studied piano at the Royal Northern College of Music and trained as a music therapist at Roehampton Institute. He has worked in various fields as a music therapist and is currently joint Head of Music Therapy of a Learning disabilities unit and joint course convenor of the P G Diploma in Music Therapy at the Roehampton Institue, London.

Section 1: The Biological and Medical Effects of Music

1

Music as a Therapeutic Intervention in Medical and Dental Treatment: Research and Clinical Applications

Jayne Standley

Introduction

If given an option, would most pregnant women elect to reduce the length of labour by an average of two hours? Would the patient in the surgical recovery room choose to awaken from the anaesthesia sooner, with fewer side effects and less pain? Would persons with chronic pain prefer to use less analgesic medication, thereby reducing possible side effects? Would those undergoing consequential medical treatment opt for reduced anxiety during its course? Research shows that music provides the above medical benefits and more, and that most people perceive their preferred music to be relaxing and beneficial to their recovery.

Despite the volume of research demonstrating the value of music in a variety of medical and dental treatments, there is little consensus on which techniques or procedures are most effective. Further, the profession of music therapy is still evolving as a viable component in the array of medical treatments. As medical music therapy develops, its methodology will have to conform to the specifications of the medical model, i.e. *a priori* treatment protocols dictated by specific diagnoses and proven options, predictable outcomes for a known frequency and duration of applications, and systematic documentation procedures to readily identify positive or negative health consequences. A formal summary of the research literature which provides a quantitative synthesis of the available data could assist the evolution of accountable music therapy techniques in applied health practices.

A meta-analysis is a procedure which provides quantitative synthesis of research data through formal statistical techniques. Specifically, it is the application of a variety of formulae to the results of a body of homogeneous research to compute effect sizes, i.e. quantitative summaries of the properties and findings of individual studies. Effect sizes can then be compared and contrasted across multiple variables (Glass, et al., 1984) and these overall results, to some extent, generalised.

The purposes of this chapter are to use the results of a meta-analysis of existing research in music and medicine to identify and authenticate effective music therapy techniques and to develop these techniques into clinical procedures which meet the criteria of standard medical protocols.

While empirical studies on the effects of music in medical treatment continue to accumulate, by the mid-1980s there existed a sufficient quantity for reasonable and relevant analysis. An initial study screened over 98 references on this topic and identified 30 empirical studies which were amenable to a comprehensive meta-analysis of characteristics and results (Standley, 1986). Recently, additional references published since 1986 were reviewed and analysed, resulting in a pooled meta-analysis of 55 studies utilising 129 dependent variables (Standley, 1992).

Procedures and Results

Studies qualified for inclusion in the two meta-analyses by containing empirical data; by utilising actual, not simulated pain stimuli; by utilising music as an independent variable; by utilising subjects who were actual patients with medical or dental diagnoses; and by reporting results in a format amenable to data analysis. The procedures followed the three basic steps outlined by Getsie, Langer and Glass (1985): 1) a complete literature search was conducted to find all possible members of the defined population of studies whether published or unpublished; 2) the characteristics and findings of the collected studies were identified, described, and categorised; and 3) the composite findings were statistically analysed and standardised effect sizes computed.

Table 1 shows that the resulting estimated effect sizes ranged from 3.28 to.59, meaning that the music condition was sometimes more than three standard deviations greater in desired effect from the control condition without music. Only 4 of the 129 variables had a negative value, indicating that for those dependent measures the music condition was less beneficial than the non music one. (It should be noted that several of these negative results were from studies where other dependent measures showed a positive reaction to music.) The overall mean effect size for all 129 dependent measures was .88. Therefore the average therapeutic effect of music in medical treatment was almost one standard deviation greater than that without music.

Table 1. Mean music effect size for each dependent variable analysed

Reference	Dependent variable	Effect size
Bob	Podiatric Pain	>3.28
Ammon	Paediatric Respiration	3.15
Oyama et al.	Pulse-Dental Patients	3.00
Monsey	Use of Analgesia-Dental	2.49
Martin	EMG-35 Min. of Music	2.38
Gardner & Licklider	Use of Analgesia-Dental Pts.	2.36
Oyama et al.	Blood Pressure-Dental Pts.	2.25
Rider	Pain-(*Debussy*)	2.11
Siegel	Medication-Paediatric Surgery	2.11
Martin	EMG-26-30 Min. of Music	2.10
Schuster	Distraction-Hemodialysis	2.08
Rider	EMG-(*Entrainment*)	2.03
Chetta	Observed Paediatric Anxiety	1.97
Cofrancesco	Grasp Strength-Stroke Pts.	1.94
Rider	EMG-(*Metheny*)	1.90
Tanioka et al.	Cortisol-Surgical Recovery	1.80
Bonny	Perceived Anxiety-Cardiac Pts.	1.77
Budzynski et al.	EMG-Tension Headache	1.76
Budzynski et al.	Pain Intensity-Headache	1.76
Rider	EMG-(*Crystal*)	1.56
Rider	Pain-(*Reich*)	1.55
Rider	EMG-No Music	1.52
Ward	Pain-Debridement of Burns	1.52
Rider	Pain-(*Entrainment*)	1.51
Locsin	Post-operative Pain	1.49
McDowell	Attitude Toward Music	1.34
Tanioka et al.	Adrenalin-Surgery	1.33
Winokur	Relaxation-Obstetrical	1.32
Siegel	Pulse-Paediatric	1.28
Tanioka et al.	Anxiety-Surgery	1.28
Schieffelin	Crying-Debridement	1.23
Bonny	Pulse-Cardiac	1.22
Martin	EMG-18-25 Min. of Music	1.22
Roberts	Intracranial Pressure - preferred vs sedative music	1.21
Jacobson	Perceived Pain-Dental	1.19
Rider	Pain-(*Metheny*)	1.16
Bonny	Perceived Pain-Cardiac	1.15
Spintge & Droh	Choice of Epidural Anaesthesia-Surgery	1.12
Sanderson	Preoperative Anxiety	1.02

Epstein et al.	Migraine Headache	1.00
Winokur	Length of Labour-Childbirth	.99
Goloff	Perceived Satisfaction	.98
Levine-Gross & Swartz	State-Trait Anxiety	.98
Winokur	Use of Medication-Obstetrical	.98
Froelich	Verbalizations	.97
Rider	Pain-(*Crystal*)	.96
Rider	Pain-(No Music)	.96
Shapiro & Cohen	Pain-Abortion	.96
Gfeller et al.	Helplessness-Dental Pts.	.94
Staum	Walking Speed-Stroke Pts.	.94
Staum	Gait Improvement-Stroke	.94
Rider	EMG-(Preferred Music)	.91
Hanser et al.	Observed Childbirth Pain	.90
Sanderson	Pain Relief-Surgical	.89
Crago	Relaxation-Open Heart Surgery	.88
Crago	Pain-Open Heart Surgery	.87
Scartelli	EMG of Spasticity	.85
Behrens	Exhalation Strength	.83
Hoffman	Blood Pressure-Hypertension	.83
Locsin	Blood Pressure-Surgical	.82
Kamin et al.	Cortisol-20 Min. after Extubation	.80
Tanioka et al.	Cortisol-1 hr. of Surgery	.75
Brook	Pulse-Obstetrical	.73
Brook	Neonate Apgar Score	.73
Lininger	Neonate Crying	.72
Shapiro & Cohen	Pain-Abortion	.71
Caine	Neonate Weight Gain	.71
Schneider	Pain-Paediatric Burn Pts.	.70
Curtis	Contentment-Cancer Pts.	.67
Kamin et al.	Cortisol at Anaesthesia	.67
Roberts	Intracranial Pressure - preferred music vs silence	.67
Burt & Korn	Perceived Effect-Obstetrical	.66
Chapman	Neonate Hospitalization	.65
Curtis	Perceived Cancer Pain	.63
Frank	Anxiety-Chemotherapy	.63
Codding	Perceived Childbirth Pain	.59
Epstein et al.	Pain Intensity-Headache	.59
Rider	Pain-(Preferred Music)	.59
Sanderson	Pain Verbalization-Surgical	.58
Caine	Neonate Hospitalization	.56
Locsin	Pulse-Surgical	.56

Sanderson	Blood Pressure-Surgical	.55
Brook	Cervical Dilation Time	.52
Goloff	Physical Comfort	.51
Rider	EMG-(*Reich*)	.50
Sanderson	Analgesics-Surgical	.50
Ward	Pulse-Burn Pts.	.50
Roberts	Blood Pressure - preferred music vs silence	.49
Ward	Perceived Pain-Debridement	.48
Corah et al.	Autonomic Sensations-Dental	.47
Frank	Emesis Intensity-Chemotherapy	.47
Crago	Music Listening-Open Heart	.45
Kamin et al.	Cortisol-15 Min. after Incision	.44
Sammons	Music Choice	.44
Bonny	Blood Pressure-Cardiac	.42
Crago	Sleep-Open Heart Surgery	.42
Kamin et al.	Cortisol-10 Min. Before Anaesthesia	.42
Spintge	Epidural Anesthesia	.42
Crago	Anxiety-Open Heart Surgery	.41
Burt & Korn	Use of Analgesia-Obstetrical	.39
Metzler & Berman	Pulse-Bronchoscopy	.39
Frank	Nausea Length-Chemotherapy	.36
Burt & Korn	Amount of Analgesic-Obstetrical	.35
Bailey	Perceived Anxiety-Cancer	.34
Clark et al.	Perceived Anxiety-Obstetrical	.34
Clark et al.	Perceived Pain-Obstetrical	.33
Frank	Emesis Length-Chemotherapy	.33
Rider	EMG-(*Debussy*)	.33
Crago	Analgesic-Open Heart Surgery	.30
Roter	Perceived Benefit-Patients	.28
Lininger	Neonate Crying - instrumental vs no music	.26
Roter	Perceived Benefit-Families	.26
Livingood et al.	Perceived Anxiety-Families	.23
Owens	Neonate Movement	.19
Lininger	Neonate Crying - vocal vs instrumental music	.15
Chapman	Neonate Movement	.14
Clark et al.	Perceived Length of Labour	.14
Clark et al.	Childbirth Attitude	.10
Schuster	Blood Pressure-Dialysis	.10
Owens	Neonate Crying	.06
Caine	Neonate Relaxation	.05

Roberts	Blood Pressure - preferred vs sedative music	.03
Owens	Neonate Weight	.02
Siegel	Respiration-Paediatric	.01
Frank	Nausea Intensity-Chemotherapy	.00
Tanioka et al.	ACTH Level-Surgery	-.17
Corah et al.	Anxiety-Dental	-.39
Crago	Hospitalization-Open Heart	-.51
Caine	Neonate Formula Intake	-.59

N= 129 Overall mean effect size of music = .88

After each study was evaluated and categorised according to its unique characteristics and a value on a linear scale of effect was calculated for each dependent variable incorporated, then multiple comparisons were made, i.e. subjects' diagnosis, age or sex; type of experimental design or sample size; and independent or dependent variables.

Since a primary concern of a meta-analysis is the acceptability of generalised results based on the soundness or inherent bias of research procedures as judged by peer review, studies were compared on this issue. The analysed variables proved to be primarily from published (N=77) vs. unpublished (N=52) sources. It was found that published sources which were not refereed yielded the same effect size (1.0) as published refereed studies. Unpublished, refereed studies, such as theses and dissertations undergoing stringent faculty review, were few in number and yielded the smallest effects (.69). It was concluded that music results included in the meta-analysis were neither biased by the publication/referee process nor inflated by the lack thereof.

A secondary concern about the viability of the research included for analysis was the impact that design variables might have had on reported results. Studies which used a research design with experimental and control groups were in the majority and yielded a much more conservative effect (.70) than did those using subjects as their own control (1.14) or those with post-test measures only (1.14). It was concluded that research included in the pool for analysis seemed to be of predominantly sound procedure and design with a tendency toward conservative measures of the effect of music. Subsequently, multiple comparisons of study demographics, including sex, age, presence of pain, type and frequency of dependent measures, diagnosis, and type of music, were conducted and are summarised in Tables 2, 3 and 4.

Table 2. Meta-analysis results: generalisations from the research literature about the use of music in medical treatment

SEX	Women (ES=.70) respond to music with somewhat greater effect than do men (ES=.57)
AGE	Children and adolescents respond with greater effect (ES=1.12) than do adults (ES=.86) or infants (ES=.47).
PAIN	Music has greater effect when some pain is present (ES=.95) than when it is not a usual symptom of the diagnosis (ES=.70), though music seems to become less effective as the pain increases.
TYPE OF DEPENDENT MEASURE	The most conservative measure of music's effect is patient self-report (ES=.76) while systematic behavioural observation (ES=.94) and physiological measures (ES=1.0) result in relatively equivalent effect sizes.
DIAGNOSES	Music is less effective when severe pain is a usual symptom or the diagnosis has serious implications. Effects vary widely according to diagnosis. Effects are greatest for dental patients and those with chronic pain, i.e.migraine headaches. Minimal effects are reported for obstetric, coma and cancer patients.
MUSIC	Live music presented by a trained music therapist (ES=1.10) has a greater effect than does recorded music (ES=.86).
DEPENDENT MEASURES USED	Effects vary greatly according to the specific dependent measure used . Greatest effects are reported for respiratory rate, EMG, amount of analgesic medication, and self-report of pain. Smallest effects are measured by length of labour in childbirth, amount of anesthesia, days of hospitalization, and measures of neonate behaviour.

ES= Effect Size

Table 2 lists the generalisations that can be made from the meta-analysis results about the uses of music in medical treatment. Analyses by sex showed that women reacted more favourably to music than did men, even though obstetric studies with severe ischemic pain represented a large portion of the research on females. Adolescents had a stronger reaction than did adults or children. Infants had the least response.

Across the diagnoses, which are cited in Table 3 in order of music's benefit, it appears that effects were differentiated by issues of severity, including level of pain, degree of anxiety, and prognosis. When pain was the only diagnostic characteristic considered, the effect size was greater (ES=.95) than when pain was not a usual symptom of the diagnosis (ES=.70). Further comparison clarifies the extent to which music specifically alleviates physical distress. When the pain was temporary (as with dental problems and headaches) and not the 'deep' pain of ischemic muscle tissue (as in childbirth, surgery, or cancer), then music proved to be more effective.

Even though the number of empirical studies using live music was small (N=12), these data do suggest that there is a more pronounced medical impact when adapting the musical event to meet the specific needs of the patient as opposed to results obtained with the use of commercial, pre-recorded selections.

Table 3. Mean music effect size by patient diagnosis

Diagnosis	Mean Effect Size	Variables Analysed
	1.54	8
Chronic Migraine Headache	1.54	7
Respiratory Problems	1.46	3
Chronic Pain	1.26	14
Physical Impairment	1.17	4
Cardiac	1.14	4
Kidney Dialysis	1.09	2
Burn	.89	5
Abortion	.84	2
Surgery	.78	30
Obstetric	.64	17
Coma	.60	4
Families of Patients	.44	4
Cancer	.43	8
Neonates	.24	12

N= 124

Results for specific dependent measures used in more than one study are listed in Table 4 in order of effect size recorded. Respiration rate was first, followed by EMG and amount of analgesic medication used by patients. Again, especially low effects were achieved when infant behaviours were monitored (movement, ES=.17; crying, ES=.30; and weight gain, ES=.46).

Table 4. Mean music effect size by dependent measure and number of variables analysed

Dependent Measure	Mean Effect Size	Variables Analysed
Respiratory Rate	1.58	2
EMG	1.39	13
Analgesic Amount	1.31	7
Pain (Self-Report)	1.16	16
Pulse	1.10	7
Relaxation	1.10	2
Pain (Observed)	1.01	10
Intracranial Pressure	.94	2
Attitudes	.87	7
Stress Hormones	.76	8
Anxiety	.72	12
Blood Pressure	.69	8
Length of Labour	.57	2
Infant Weight Gain	.46	3
Anaesthesia Amount	.36	2
Infant Crying	.30	4
Emesis/Nausea	.29	4
Days in Hospital	.23	3
Infant Movement	.17	2

N=114

Music therapy medical techniques

In this section, the results of the meta-analysis are summarised by the delineation of specific techniques of the use of music in medical treatments. For each technique the following information is provided: the intended function of the music and specific therapeutic objectives, expected results by diagnosis with indication of the duration of music treatment as documented in the research literature, general procedures for utilising the technique effectively, and suggested ways of documenting effects through behavioural, physiological, and self-report means. Some clinical music therapy examples are also provided.

Technique 1. Passive Music Listening (Alone or Paired with Anaesthesia, Analgesia, Suggestion, Relaxation Techniques or Imagery)

Music Function:
To serve as an audioanalgesic, anxiolytic or sedative.
Therapeutic Objectives:
Reduction of pain, anxiety, or stress.
Enhancement of chemical anaesthetic/analgesic to reduce amount of medication required, duration of use, and aversive side effects.

Reduction in length of hospitalisation.

Diagnoses:

Surgery - Music used pre-operatively to reduce anxiety and to reduce amount of anaesthesia required (1/2 to 1 hour); used during surgery, especially with local anaesthesia, to reduce anxiety and mask operating room sounds (several hours); used post-operatively in the recovery room to promote wakefulness and reduce discomfort (1/2 to 1 1/2 hours); used for first 48 hours following surgery to reduce amount of analgesic and aversive effects of anaesthesia (e.g. vomiting, headaches, restlessness, etc.).

Kidney dialysis - Music used to reduce discomfort and serve as a distraction during this frequent, long term, lengthy, uncomfortable (pain, nausea, restricted movement) procedure (2 to 3 times per week for 4 1/2 to 5 hours across months or years).

Burn - Music used to reduce pain and anxiety in hydrotherapy, intravenous fluid therapy, skin grafts, etc. (daily for each medical procedure or as requested across weeks or months).

Cancer - Music used to reduce pain and enhance analgesic effects of medication (1/2 hour twice per day across weeks or months).

Coma - Music used to decrease intracranial pressure (1/2 of each hour, ongoing).

Neonates - Music used with premature or sick infants to promote weight gain, to reduce pain or stress, and to reduce length of hospitalisation (1/2 hour 2 or 3 times per day for 5-6 weeks).

Office Treatments - Music used during stressful office treatments such as dental procedures, abortions, and podiatry treatments to reduce amount of self-administered anaesthesia and analgesia (treatment duration).

Documentation:

Record one or more of the following measures:

Physiological: Blood pressure, pulse, amount of medication used, blood analysis of stress hormone levels.

Behaviourally observed: Overt pain/anxiety responses, time in recovery room, length of hospitalisation, number of anaesthetic/analgesic side effects experienced.

Self-Report: Ratings of pain/anxiety, State-Trait Anxiety Scale (Spielberger et al, 1970), pain/anxiety adjective selection.

Procedure:

Use patient's preferred music and equipment with quality reproduction capabilities.

Begin the music prior to the pain/fear-inducing stimuli.

Use earphones when possible or a pillow speaker as an alternative.

Suggest that music will aid pain relief, comfort, anxiety, etc.

Maintain a pain-free association by not assisting medical staff with pain-inducing procedures, especially when working with children.

Allow the patient to control as much of the procedure as possible: volume, cassette manipulations, starting and stopping music, etc.

Reinforce overt signs of relaxation, co-operation, and verbalisations with no pain or anxiety content.

Technique 2. Active Music Participation

Music Function:
To serve as a focus of attention and/or to structure exercise (tempo, repetition, duration, force, or fluidity).
Therapeutic Objectives:
Reduction of pain from physical movement or muscle contractures.
Increased joint motility.
Increased motor abilities (duration, strength, co-ordination).
Shortened labour using Lamaze childbirth exercises.
Increased respiration ability (capacity, strength).
Diagnoses:
Childbirth - Music used during pregnancy to structure Lamaze exercises and to reinforce focusing of attention (1 hour session per week in 8th & 9th months plus daily practice for 1/2 hour). Used in labour and delivery to focus attention, to structure breathing, and to reduce pain perception (avg. of 8-12 hours). Selected music used at birth to enhance joy in the event. Music and prescribed exercises used after birth to reduce pain from contractures and to help uterus return to normal size while rehabilitating abdominal muscles (1/2 hour per day across weeks).
Chronic Pain - Music paired with appropriate exercises for involved muscles (1/2 to 1 hour per day across days or weeks).
Respiratory Deficiencies - Music used to structure deep breathing exercises or therapeutic coughing to relieve congestion (5 minutes several times per day). Music performance (singing, piano, harmonica) used to structure breathing and enhance lung capacity (1/2 hour per day across days or weeks).
Patients Prescribed for Physical Therapy (PT) - Music used to structure PT regimen for stroke, burn, orthopaedic, cerebral palsied, and paralysed persons (1/2 to 1 hour daily across weeks or months).
Gait Disturbances - Music paired with walking and gait training to increase duration and to improve gait length, width, and rhythm (1/2 to 1 hour daily across weeks).
Documentation:
Record one or more of the following:
Physiological: Amount of analgesic medication used, electromyographic (EMG) muscle response, exhalation strength (spirometer), degrees of movement in joints (goniometer).
Behaviourally Observed: Frequency and duration of exercises, pain-free verbalisations; length of labour in childbirth; overt pain responses; walking distance; gait length, width, and/or duration.

Self-Report: Ratings of improvement, ratings of pain, personal log of exercises completed.

Procedure:

Select exercises appropriate to diagnosis or as prescribed by a physician or physical therapist.

Evaluate patient's baseline capacity for exercise in terms of speed, duration, repetitions, etc.

Select style of music which matches above traits and also desired *kind* of motor movement (i.e. disco music for forceful movements, waltz music for fluid movements).

Model appropriate movements and teach patient to match them to music.

Change music in successive approximations as patient progresses. In this category, patient's music preference is important but is secondary to the music's properties for matching the desired exercise.

Teach focusing (if exercise routine requires it) by pointing out musical elements for which the patient might listen.

Reinforce exercising (see Example 1), pain-free verbalisations, matching the exercise to the music, focusing attentiveness, and overt signs of patient's motivation to succeed or progress (see Example 2).

Example 1

PINPOINT: An 8 year old male in traction with a broken leg is beginning to contract bed sores from limited movement. He refuses to co-operate in using traction pull to increase movement.

RECORD: Patient was asked to use the traction pull and he refused, covering his face with the sheet and replying, 'I'm tired.'

CONSEQUATE: Therapist played and sang a song, then made music contingent upon use of the traction pull.

EVALUATE: By the third session, the patient used the traction pull 100% of requests at a 90° angle to prone position. Verbal and motor responses to music had increased.

Jama King, RMT (1982)

Example 2

PINPOINT: Female (age in mid-60s) had Parkinson's disease and rigidity on left side due to recent stroke. Patient was non responsive during physical therapy and with visitors.

RECORD: No response was noted to recorded instrumental music, live singing with guitar, or placement of music instruments in right hand. Family interview revealed that the patient formerly played the piano.

CONSEQUATE: First session: Poulenc's Piano Concerto for Two was presented prior to physical therapy. Patient immediately opened her eyes and reached for the recorder with her right hand and began answering yes/no questions.

Subsequent sessions: Piano music was played for 1 minute prior to PT to arouse the patient, who was then told that music would be contingent upon her eyes being open and her attempting physical movement.

EVALUATE: Patient's awareness responses (open eyes and physical movement) increased to 2-3 minute intervals throughout PT sessions after 1 month. Verbal responses also increased. Patient was discharged to a long-term care facility.

Dawn Ferrell, RMT (1984).

Technique 3. Music and Counselling

Music Function:
To initiate and enhance therapist/patient/family relationships.
Therapeutic Objectives:
Reduction of distress/trauma/fear related to terminal or serious illness or injury to self or significant others.
Acceptance of death, permanent disabilities, or scarring. Enhancement of effective interpersonal interactions in times of distress.
Management of illness and personal affairs, i.e., selection of treatment options and making personal or family decisions.
Diagnoses:
Patients or families in distress, including those with traumatic injuries or illness, permanent disabilities or disfigurement; terminal prognoses; hospitalised children; organ transplant patients, etc. Music used to initiate and maintain counselling interaction (1/2 hour daily across days or weeks).
Documentation:
Record one or more of the following:
Physiological: Amount of analgesic or sedative medication used, blood pressure, pulse, stress hormone levels.
Behaviourally Observed: Verbalisations free of distress or fear, actions implementing decisions, overt signs of distress/fear, family interaction patterns.
Self-Report: Ratings of attitudes such as satisfaction/contentment, diary of feelings, attitude scales.
Procedure:
Use live music listening or participation to offer *opportunities* for pleasure, reminiscence, verbalisation, closeness, etc. Use song content for initiating discussion (see Example 3). (The therapist's presence and warmth are crucial, so the use of earphones or the patient listening to music alone are contraindicated.) Identify source of any patient distress by listening or by watching patient reactions.
Help patient identify decisions that can or must be made, all possible options, consequences of each option, preferred option, and actions to implement selected option (see Example 4).
Serve as an advocate for the patient or family who has made a firm decision about the course of treatment by being supportive and giving assistance in communicating with the medical staff.
Teach effective interpersonal relationship abilities, i.e. positivism, avoidance of guilt for self or imposition of guilt on others, openness in stating feelings, avoidance of blame.
Assist terminally ill persons who wish to get closure on some aspect of their life, such as drafting a living will, selecting music for the funeral, recording a song to leave to a loved one, etc.
Assist permanently disabled persons to identify and develop assets and abilities.

Reinforce reality-based (acceptance) verbalisations and those free of blame, bitterness, guilt, regrets, etc. Also reinforce verbalisations about the present rather than the past.

Provide music and leave the room if the patient is uncommunicative. Continue offering opportunities for communication during later visits.

Example 3.

PINPOINT: A 15 year old male with terminal abdominal cancer and paralysis of lower extremities was referred for counselling due to depression and failure to co-operate with other therapies, including homebound instructional programme.

RECORD: In the initial interview, patient was moody, withdrawn, and non communicative until the guitar was presented. Immediate interest was then displayed.

CONSEQUATE: Patient was given guitar lessons to increase interest, motivate co-operation, reduce loneliness.

1st Day: Patient learned 2 chords and sang several songs. He asked how much a guitar costs.

3rd Day: Patient was loaned a guitar and folder of songs for use in the hospital, and given a focused attention musical listening task for use when in pain.

2 Weeks: Patient's eye contact and verbalisation increased, while great motivation to learn more about guitar and singing was demonstrated. He reported the focused music listening helped him cope with pain. The patient was also reinforced for plans to do more school work.

3 Weeks: Guitar lessons were continued. The patient also revealed he had fear and tension when given shots for nausea from chemotherapy. He was given relaxation techniques and recorded music to listen to during those times. Patient was discharged.

5 Weeks: The music therapist visited the patient's home to continue guitar lessons. Patient reported excitement over guitar and interest in school work via homebound instruction. The music therapist talked with his family about a guitar as a Christmas present.

8 Weeks: Patient was re-admitted to the hospital and guitar lessons were continued. Patient played a Christmas concert for the medical staff and patients on the paediatric ward and was excited by their reaction. He received a guitar for Christmas.

Next 6 Months: Patient was periodically re-admitted for chemotherapy. Guitar lessons were continued at home and in the hospital.

9 Months: Patient was constantly in the hospital, too ill for schoolwork or playing the guitar. The music therapist visited daily and played and sang for him. Counselling for acceptance of death was intensified.

13 Months: Patient was in ICU semi-comatose but continued receiving MT visits.

14 Months: Patient died. The last MT session had occurred the prior day.

Sue Sanderson, RMT (1984)

Example 4.

PINPOINT: A 21 year old male, paraplegic as result of trauma, was in need of counselling for depression and decisions about long-term care.

RECORD: Patient was asked in the initial interview to describe one good thing that had happened to him that day. His response took 5 minutes to formulate, with frequent interruption of eye contact, use of vague comments, and switching of topics.

CONSEQUATE: Pop/rock music was added to the patient's weight training during PT using some of his personal tapes from home. Relaxation routines to music were conducted after PT sessions. Finally, a discussion was held each day of 'good things' and 'bad things' happening and options for long-term care. Patient was reinforced for positive, motivated verbalisations and for decisions communicated to the music therapist.

EVALUATE: The patient chose a plan for long-term care and became very motivated in PT. He was able to verbalise 'good things' that happened to him each day. Patient was discharged to a long-term care facility.

Dawn Ferrell, RMT (1984)

Technique 4. Music and Developmental or Educational Objectives

Music Function:
To reinforce or structure learning.
Therapeutic Objectives:
Prevention of developmental regression due to hospitalisation.
Increased academic learning.
Diagnoses:
Hospitalised children (birth to 18 years) and their families
Music used as reinforcement for attentiveness to educational tasks, as reinforcement for learning, and as a structure to provide academic information. Music activities used with family members to teach parents the importance of helping children maintain developmental milestones and avoid regression (1/2 hour daily across days).
Documentation:
Record one or more of the following:
Physiological: Not applicable.
Behaviourally Observed: Number of academic tasks completed, correctness of academic work, time spent on task, amount of information learned, incidence of independent self-care (i.e. feeding self, toileting independently, walking instead of being carried, etc.), positive verbalisations.
Self-Report: Log or checklist of independent self-care tasks performed daily.
Procedure:
Use child's preferred music activities to reinforce or structure desired developmental maturity (see Example 5).
Tell child ahead of time the criteria for participation if music is to be a reinforcer. At music time, determine if educational or developmental criteria were met and provide music contingently.
Determine the teacher's specific educational objectives for the child and materials being used, and develop educational music activities accordingly.
Leave activities or music 'assignments' with the child that will structure independence and increase positive interactions with others in the environment.
Invite parents to participate in a music activity with the child. Tell them ahead of time that you will be cueing them to reinforce the child for independence and co-

operation. Leave parents a checklist of age-appropriate developmental milestones which they might reinforce during the hospital stay.

Reinforce children for on-task behaviour, learning, assignments completed, independent self-care.

Reinforce families for positive interactions and for allowing children to be independent.

Example 5.

PINPOINT: A 7 year old male was admitted for asthma and reported as crying all day following several occurrences of medication administered by hypodermic.

RECORD: Patient was hysterical when the therapist entered his room.

CONSEQUATE: The therapist played the guitar and sang one song. The patient became quieter. Music continued and the patient was reinforced for sustained interest and positive responses.

EVALUATE: The patient began to strum the guitar and sing along with the therapist. The music therapy session was terminated after 30 min.

Lawson Miller, music therapy student (1984)

Technique 5. Music and Stimulation

Music Function:

To stimulate auditorily and increase awareness of other forms of stimuli.

Therapeutic Objectives:

Increased overt responses to stimuli (auditory, sensory, olfactory, and visual).

Reduced depression/anxiety due to sensory deprivation in sterile environments.

Diagnoses:

Comatose or brain damaged patients/stroke victims/premature neonates - Music used to elicit physiological and overt responses which are then increased through reinforcement (1/2 hour daily across days, weeks, or months).

Patients in sterile environments (such as burn victims, organ transplant patients and those with contagious diseases) or long term hospitalisation - Music used to reduce depression or anxiety due to deprivation and to increase patient awareness and pleasure (1/2 hour 3 times per week, across weeks or months).

Documentation:

Record one or more of the following:

Physiological: Vasoconstriction (plethysmograph), respiration rate, pulse, blood pressure.

Behaviourally Observed: Overt gross or fine motor responses such as sucking, eye blinks, head movement, mouth movements; auditory responses; pleasure responses, such as smiling; positive verbalisations.

Self-Report: Ratings of depression/anxiety.

Procedure:

For elicitation of response:

Use patient's preferred music, which might be ascertained through family interviews. With infants, lullabies are traditional and effective.

Use pillow speaker so that music source may be moved in space for maximum stimulation.

Combine music with pleasurable multi-stimulation activities which include physical stroking, moving visual stimuli, pleasurable olfactory stimuli, and other auditory stimuli such as patient's name and family voices.

Watch for and identify overt responses. If no overt responses occur, use physiologic measures to determine any response to selected stimuli.

Discontinue non-contingent stimulation when response begins to occur. Give selected stimulus, wait until patient emits response, then reinforce immediately with other multi-stimulation activities.

Pair eliciting stimulus with verbal command so that patient will begin to respond to the human voice.

Begin moving the patient's body in an overt response timed to coincide with any physiologic events that are apparent.

Continue with these procedures and lengthen the chain of events to which the patient will respond (see Example 6).

For reducing deprivation:

Use patient's preferred music.

Combine music with age-appropriate multi-stimulation activities, such as looking at slides or pictures to music, reminiscing about memories related to smells (e.g., flowers, vanilla flavouring, lemons, etc.), or touching a variety of surfaces (e.g., velvet, sandpaper, or fur). Use variety of puppets and toys with children. If sterile conditions prohibit use of real materials such as these, use guided imagery techniques with music to imagine multi-sensory events.

Reinforce pleasure responses and creative thinking (imagination).

Example 6.

PINPOINT: A 13 year old male automobile accident victim appeared comatose and failed to respond to stimuli following prefrontal lobotomy.

RECORD: The patient responded inconsistently with upper extremity movement to a variety of music stimuli after 5 to 10 second delay.

CONSEQUATE: The patient was presented with a variety of music stimuli paired with verbal commands and all responses of any type were noted and reinforced by verbal approval and stroking. As the patient began to respond consistently, music and commands were varied and visual stimuli were added. Progress was noted in all response modes.

EVALUATE: The patient was discharged after 4 1/2 months with vastly improved abilities to respond. His final statement to the music therapist was, 'music makes me happy.'

Dawn Ferrell, RMT (1984)

Technique 6. Music and Biofeedback

Music Function:

To serve as reinforcer or structure for physiological responses.

Therapeutic Objectives:

Increased awareness, self-control, and monitoring of physiological state.

Diagnoses:
Epilepsy - Music used to reduce frequency of seizures by inducing relaxation as reaction to stress or prior to fatigue (total of 5-6 hours across days or weeks).
Coronary - Music used to lower blood pressure, heart rate, tension responses (total of 5-6 hours across days or weeks).
Habituated Tension Responses - Music used to lower blood pressure, lower stress hormone levels, and to relax muscle tension (total of 5-6 hours across days or weeks).
Migraine Headaches - Music used to reduce frequency through relaxation responses to stress rather than tension responses (total of 5-6 hours across days or weeks).
Poor Circulation - Music used to increase blood flow to extremities through temperature measurement (total of 5-6 hours across days or weeks).
Documentation:
Record one or more of the following:
Physiological: Blood pressure, pulse, vasoconstriction, stress hormone levels, EEG waves, EMG muscle tension, temperature (internal and peripheral), seizure frequency, migraine frequency, etc.
Behaviourally Observed: Overt signs of relaxation, verbalisations free of content about stress.
Self-Report: Log of relaxation practice and incidence of physiological problem, ratings of improvement.
Procedure:
Use patient's preferred music.
Use headphones if possible.
Pair music with selected biofeedback procedures for specific physiological problem. Non contingent background music may be used to enhance patient's ability to relax or contingent music may be used as reinforcement for patient maintaining desired physiological response.
Transfer ability to relax from the biofeedback clinic to other locations through the use of procedures that can be paired with music in any setting (home, work, car, etc.).
Reinforce relaxation, desired physiologic state, and positive verbalisations about improvement.

Technique 7. Music and Group Activity

Music Function:
To structure pleasurable and positive interpersonal interactions.
Therapeutic Objectives:
Reduction of depression/anxiety due to isolation.
Increased pleasure and feelings of well-being.
Diagnoses:

Patients capable of joining a group and desiring to do so, especially children and persons with long-term hospitalisation - Music used for pleasure, group interaction and to reduce stress of hospitalisation (1 hour twice per week, ongoing).

Documentation:

Record one or more of the following:

Physiological: Pulse (self-monitored).

Behaviourally Observed: Pleasure responses, such as smiling or laughing; positive verbalisations free of 'illness' content; time spent in group and out of hospital room.

Self-Report: Ratings of pleasure or feelings of well-being.

Procedure:

Use variety of age-appropriate activities that maximise time in music. Match types of activities to areas in which they are conducted, i.e. quieter activities in areas for the seriously ill.

Identify meeting space for group which is deemed by staff as being compatible with medical routine, i.e. not disruptive.

Combine focused listening and participation activities to reduce fatigue.

Give patients name tags which they might label and attach, then refer to each by name.

Perform live music for audience pleasure, taking requests if possible.

Invite patients, visitors, staff, volunteers, etc. to participate.

Feature medical personnel and staff in music 'solos' such as playing the kazoo or spoons or leading group singing.

End session with relaxation/guided imagery to music to reduce discomfort and prepare patients for rest. Suggest patients try similar techniques at night when falling asleep.

Reinforce pleasure responses, 'non-sick' verbalisations, music participation, spontaneous contributions to musical activities, and musical talent of participants.

Other Reported Techniques

Other music therapy techniques have been reported in the medical literature, though not yet in a format amenable to or sufficient for meta-analysis. Foremost among these is music paired with vibrotactile stimulation to increase the awareness of comatose patients (Grundy, 1990) and to enhance physical therapy objectives (Skille, Wigram, and Weeks, 1989). This technique would seem to have great potential for medical treatment and further research is warranted.

Music Therapy Programs for the General Hospital

Patients in hospital settings are extremely diverse in age, medical diagnosis, and treatment. These differences range in magnitude from those who are terminally ill to others hospitalised for a 'rest' or to women giving birth and considered to be participating in a 'wellness' event. Patients also differ in length of stay, prognosis, and responses to the illness. Medical treatment is, therefore, very individualised with ongoing documentation of effect often determining its course. Benefits, both medical and psychosocial, must be readily observable as contributing to each individual's recovery. This meta-analysis has shown that music therapy services in the medical setting can include specific objectives relevant to the medical diagnosis, treatment protocol, and discharge timeline.

The music therapy discipline will continue to develop and document viable techniques through its reliance on an aggressive research program. As research continues, future meta-analyses may provide the definitive answers we still seek: What type of music is most effective and is this differentiated situationally or by diagnosis? Can principles of composition which predictably and reliably structure physiological entrainment be developed? When and how is the presence of a qualified music therapist crucial and different from the use of recorded music stimuli provided by other professionals or the patients themselves?

Whether or not these answers are achieved quickly, there is substantial documentation to show that music techniques in current use make a distinctly positive and therapeutic difference in the treatment of persons with medical problems. Such benefits are authenticated both in the research literature and in the awareness of medical professionals who cite the increased humanisation brought to health care through the addition of music and music therapists.

Note: Portions of this paper have appeared previously and are included here by permission (Standley, 1986; 1992)

2

The Effect of Music, Vocalisation and Vibration on Brain and Muscle Tissue: Studies in Vibroacoustic Therapy

Olav Skille and Tony Wigram

In considering the effect of music and the elements that constitute music, and in fully understanding the processes involved in music therapy, the physiological effect of sound on the body should be taken into consideration. There have been many exciting developments in the last two decades in the use of sound and sound technology in treatment techniques. Although this is not a new concept, and history has thrown up evidence both in past civilisations and in different cultures in the use of sound as a means of treating physical disabilities and pain, it is only in the latter part of this century that developments have occurred resulting in the use of such treatments as ultrasound (Forster & Palastange, 1985) and interferential therapy (Savage, 1984), a form of low frequency electrical stimulation. At the same time that these developments were occurring, the growth of music therapy as a form of treatment mainly concentrated on the use of music and improvisation in interactional work with people with communication disabilities. It has been by the building of a relationship through music by means of musical interaction that music therapists have been able to demonstrate breakthroughs in achieving both physical, emotional and cognitive response from people who had seemed inaccessible to other forms of intervention. This was evident in the work of Juliette Alvin (1975, 1976, 1978) and Nordoff and Robbins (1971, 1977) with handicapped children and adults, and subsequently by many music therapists trained in these approaches in England, the Americas, Europe, Canada and Australia; although the approaches differ in terms of the means of developing interaction with clients through music, the ethos that music therapy is a process involving the perceptual, cognitive and intellectual response of individuals to music is common. However, it has also been realised that whereas music achieves an intellectual response when listened to, music and sound also cause a significant and frequently measurable physical response when sound waves enter the body. The appreciation of music, and the emotional impact of a particular piece may also stimulate a physical reaction - it may be one of elation or depression, sadness or happiness. The components of a sound or combination of sounds, in particular their pitch, volume and timbre, will have a significant physiological and biochemical effect on the body. Muscular energy will increase or decrease depending on the rhythm, and breathing will accelerate or change its regularity. Fatigue can be reduced or induced and voluntary activity may be increased. In addition, a marked variable effect on heart rate, blood pressure and the endocrine function is produced, and changes in metabolism and the biosynthesis of various enzymatic processes may be induced. These and further physiological reactions to sound and music were investigated and summarised by Dr Benenzon, a music therapist and psychiatrist working in Argentina (Music Therapy Manual, 1981).

The idea of vibroacoustics (VA) developed out of a conversation between Skille and Juliette Alvin in London in 1968 while discussing the common denominators of music - the culturally independent variables of the effects of music on human beings. They agreed upon the basics: Such effects must be described using quantitative parameters, and not by using the usual qualitative evaluation of music.

They isolated three so-called universals of music. Three specific principles involved were highlighted:

1. Low frequencies can relax
2. Rhythmical music can invigorate
3. Loud music can create aggression

and, of course, the opposites of these universals may create the opposite effects.

The conversation started a process of research and development, until in 1980 the first so-called 'Music Bath' was built. Skille was then working in a day centre for multiply handicapped retarded children. The theoretical speculations were then ripe enough to be tried out in practical work.

Physical problems presenting to a music therapist working with cerebral palsy clients will often include flexor or extensor muscle spasm; the dichotomy in a treatment process involving interactional work is that, whereas one can see a development in the responsiveness of the individual to the therapist, the increased level of activity will often stimulate a spasm. Looking at ways of reducing the high muscle tone created by this spasm, there is evidence of the effect of mechanical vibration (Stilman, 1970, Carrington, 1980) where a motor within an object or on a base unit will set up a physical vibration that is indiscriminate in terms of frequency. In the early 1980s work began to look at the effects of low frequency sound on high muscle tone and spasticity. The idea of using a pure sinusoidal tone at a low frequency has been known for thousands of years, and in primitive cultures instruments and sounds were used to treat psychosomatic disorders. (In Shamanistic music, physical vibrations were often used.) With more specific problems in mind, the possibility arose of finding a specific range of frequencies that could be coupled with relaxing, unrhythmic music to produce an effect directly into the body of physically handicapped people (Skille, 1982a; 1982b; 1985).

Our first patient was an 8 year old, spastic girl with contracting spasms and Skille did not do the observations himself because of the possible bias, being the inventor of the new method. One of the other teachers did the observations and, after only three minutes, he observed a marked reduction of the spasms. The reduction of spasms were later used to include movement facilitating exercises during the treatment session.

This initial success led to further empirical research and in 1982 the first articles of the 'Music Bath' - now called vibroacoustics (in Finland: fyysioakustiikka - Physioacoustics), were published in Norway, Sweden, Finland and Denmark.

The first attempts in using vibroacoustic therapy were conducted in Norway in 1980. The method was then tentatively named the 'Music bath' and 'low frequency sound massage'. The music bath is trying to create an environment whereby the body is 'bathed' in sound and vibration. During 1981/82 several test units were built in Norway, where there are over 200 units at present in daily use. Further developments have led to research projects in Finland, England, Germany and Estonia. The process of vibroacoustic therapy was described at the first International Symposium for Music in Medicine in Lüdenscheid in 1982. The equipment (patented on a world-wide basis) consists of a bed/bench or chair with several built-in loud speakers. This is connected to a signal unit with six channels containing a cassette player which can run various tapes.

The process of vibroacoustic therapy involves lying a client on the bed so that the sound is being transferred by air directly to the body of the client. Sound may also be transferred through a mattress or some other means which can conduct the sound waves directly to the body. The body vibrates according to the different sound waves, and at 100 Hz, 2% of the energy is absorbed by the client (Broner 1978). As one might expect, the sound waves also have a substantial effect on the autonomic system.

The pioneers of music vibration

In 1962, Dr H R Teirich wrote an article on therapeutics through music and vibrations. In this article he describes work done by himself, Pontvik and Jaedicke, where music is combined with autogenous training (AT). He describes that this is possible in three ways:

a) with records or tape
b) with 'live' music by the therapist himself
c) by providing patients with vibrational sensations.

He drew on the work of Pontvik (1955) suggesting that transmission of musical vibrations by actual contact between the sound source and patient is a process which has the right to be described as a musical sensation. Therapeutic use of this phenomenon had, until then, only been used in the case of mentally defective deaf-mutes. Teirich gives many examples of how music is enjoyed by patients lying on a couch which permits the sound to enter the body in the back, in the region of the solar plexus. He used four loudspeakers, giving a range of 20 Hz to 10 kHz.

He reports on the use of this instrument on 51 neurotic patients. The patients felt an increased and prolonged sensation of heaviness and warmth, and he concludes that music does not directly lead to 'mastery of life' but that it has at least an alleviating function, which logically follows suitable diagnosis, and that the effect is usually much longer lasting than might be expected.

It seems that these pioneers of music therapy in Europe mainly concentrated their work on auditory reception of music and that they were very fixed on the qualitative aspects of music. The thorough study of the quantitative elements of musical vibrations and their effect on physical functions in man was forgotten.

Alongside the development of the music bed, Olav Skille found it necessary to develop taped programmes that would be varied and effective in treating different problems. Cassette tapes were made up with a mixture of music and rhythmical pressure waves which are in harmonic relation to the music. A pulsed tone is created by placing two tones very close together, i.e. 40 Hz and 40.5 Hz. This rhythmical pressure wave will cause a synchronisation of nervous impulses through the body, including the central nervous system. This comprehensive stimulation contributes to a harmonisation of a body which has come out of phase with itself because of defects or traumas caused by external or internal conditions. This process is influential in treating a number of disorders and handicaps, and this paper describes its therapeutic benefit. The music used is recorded over a pulsed, low frequency tone, and is invariably gentle, improvised and without a pronounced rhythm. Music has been written specifically for this therapeutic process, e.g. an improvisation on the tone E by the Finnish composer, Otto Romanovski. In addition, existing 'New Age' music by composers such as Don Campbell and Steven Halpern has been used. As far as the use of specific tones is concerned, subjective tests have indicated that the most significant frequencies range between 40 Hz and 80 Hz. The lowest frequencies, 40 Hz to 55 Hz will predominantly set up a resonant response in the lower lumbar region, pelvis, thighs and legs. As one moves through the frequency range so the sound is resonated in the more dense tissues of the body in the upper chest, neck and head.

The first years of development in Norway

Through vibroacoustic therapy and by the use of technical equipment which was unavailable in the late 1950s, the work Skille did in 1980-1982 investigated the effects of musical vibrations and it became a field of specialised study. His first studies were done with multiply handicapped children with severe learning difficulty.

The first results showed a remarkably positive effect on spasticity. A study on the effect of a spastic girl aged 12 years, done by a student from a school for nurses, showed an improvement of 7 to 21 degrees in the open angle of three measure points. When the vibroacoustic stimulation was accompanied by movement patterning, the increase was measured to be between 41 and 79 degrees. The study was performed over an 8 week period.

Encouraged by these results, Skille tried the method on other children and other conditions - including autism -and we found new indications leading to other possible fields of use.

In Norway, vibroacoustic therapy concentrated particularly on the benefit of treating people with muscle spasm, pain or pulmonary conditions. Low frequency sound waves had been found to have a spasmolytic effect on muscle tissues. This effect has been used in the treatment of children with cerebral palsy at the Health Centre in Sonjatun and with the pre-school group at Fagerheim School; also at Moan School and Day Centre, Norway. Similarly, it had been used to reduce muscle spasm in patients at Lebenschilfe in Berlin, Germany and Harperbury Hospital, England. Bjerkely School has used vibroacoustic therapy with their multiply handicapped spastic children since 1985 with good spasmolytic effect, as has Österbo Central Institution since 1982. The head injuries unit at Sunnaas Hospital has been using vibroacoustic therapy to reduce muscle spasm in their patients since September 1986.

Users of vibroacoustic therapy consistently report relief of pain. A chief community nurse at Kåfjord has treated patients with rheumatism and at Sonjatun Health Centre, patients with polyarthritis and Morbus Bechterew have been treated since October 1986. All report decrease in pain. In conditions which have an acute phase followed by periods of remission, e.g. rheumatoid arthritis, Morbus Bechterew, use of low frequency sound waves in the acute stage may cause an increase in pain. It should, therefore, be given in the non-inflammatory period and avoided in the acute stage.

Moan School and Day Centre reported relief of stomach and colic pain. Österbo Central Institution reports relief of both muscular and menstrual pain. Therapists treating sports injuries have found vibroacoustic therapy a useful method of relieving pain. In over-use syndromes, low frequency sound waves are reported to relieve pain and reduce the length of the rehabilitation period.

Using the laboratory of the SEAS loudspeaker factory in Moss, Norway, we found that the sound penetration through the body was strongest at 60 Hz, with another, nearly as high, peak at 80 Hz. The sound pressure was equivalent to 0.2 G when an effect of 8V was applied to the loudspeaker.

Musically, these two Hz values are interesting, as we see a harmonic connection between the values. 80 Hz is one octave above 40 Hz and 60 Hz is one-fifth above 40 Hz and one-fourth lower than 80 Hz. It seemed that the physical forces of sound penetration of the human body were following the laws of harmonics according to classical musical theory and the Pythagorean scale. Consequently, the following table may be applied when choice of frequencies is possible.

Table I: Values for calculating harmonic Hz values from a basic value

	Interval factor	Opposite value
Prime	1.000000	1.000000
Minor second	1.066667	0.937500
Major second	1.125000	0.888889
Minor third	1.200000	0.833333
Major third	1.250000	0.800000
Perfect fourth	1.333333	0.750000
Chr. tritone	1.414214	0.707107
Perfect fifth	1.500000	0.666667
Minor sixth	1.600000	0.625000
Major sixth	1.666667	0.600000
Minor seventh	1.800000	0.555556
Major seventh	1.875000	0.533333
Octave	2.000000	0.500000

When establishing a basic Hz value for a condition, one can use Table 1 to calculate a series of harmonic Hz values, which can theoretically be used for the same condition. We soon found that 40 Hz and 60 Hz were basic values for reduction of spasms. Other basic values followed after empirical work, and the basis for a therapeutic method was laid.

While working with sinusoidal tones alone and music alone, using only one of the stimuli was not satisfactory. The effect of the music alone was too uncontrolled, and the use of sinusoidal vibrations alone was too uncomfortable for the patient (vertigo, nausea, cold sweat and anxiety may occur). The combination of both music and sinusoidal vibrations appeared to be more effective and the unwanted side-effects of sinusoidal vibrations alone were considerably reduced. The range of the vibroacoustic frequency area was set to between 30 Hz and 120 Hz, although there may be considerable effect from sounds beyond this range.

The reason for choosing this range was very simple: below 30 Hz sinusoidal vibrations are mostly felt and not heard. Above 120 Hz the vibrations are more heard than felt. Research on infrasound has also showed negative effects of infrasound exposure to the human organism and therefore I wanted to stay clear of the infrasound range (< 20 Hz).

The range of the human auditory receptors is between 16 Hz and 24,000 Hz, i.e. 10 octaves. The two defined octaves of the vibroacoustic area cover only a tiny fraction of the possible areas, for which we have vibration receptors in our body but it covers the important area where two senses overlap each other - the vibration receptors in our skin and the auditory receptors. The sensitivity of the ear decreases by about 20 dB/octave in the range below 100 Hz. It is impossible to make a division between sound and vibration in this frequency area, as all sound will be perceived by the skin as vibrations and by the ears as sound/music.

In this context the work of Dr Karel Jindrak and Dr Heda Jindrak show us that it is interesting to look upon the human skull and compare it with a musical instrument, for example, a violin. In Figure 1 we see the mandible and the shape of the tongue when we are pronouncing the vowel 'i' (as in see) and the vowel 'a' (as in park). When pronouncing these vowels we can put the tips of our fingers on the top of our skull and feel the difference of skull vibration between 'i' and 'a'. In 'i' much more of the energy used to produce the sound is used to vibrate the brain than in pronouncing 'a'.

Figure 1: Position of the mandible and shape of the tongue during pronunciation of 'i' (as in see) and 'a' (as in park).

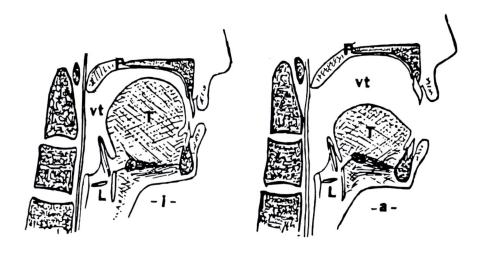

In the first vowel, the mandible is very high, lifted up by the muscles which are attached to the base of the skull, and the tongue (T) is also raised, filling to a major extent the oral cavity. It leaves only a narrow space under the soft and hard palate (P). This lifting up of the mandible and contraction of the muscles in the floor of the mouth pulls at the hyoid bone and stretches the thyrohyoid membrane. All this facilitates transmission of laryngeal vibrations onto the skull base. In the vowel 'a' the mandible is lowered, mainly due to its own weight. All the muscles in the mouth floor are relaxed, together with the tongue. The relaxed muscles cushion very effectively the larynx (L) so that its vibrations are not transmitted onto the skull base through the muscles but only indirectly. The vocal tract (VT) is getting progressively wider from the larynx to the oral cavity. On the other hand, in 'i', the vocal tract is narrowed in its distal half, between the tongue and the hard palate and between the teeth and lips.

It is the shape of the vocal tract that determines which vowel will be generated. To produce a shape, certain muscles have to be stretched and others relaxed. This then determines in which vowel the mandible will vibrate and in which it will not. The vowels 'i' and 'a' are the extremes of possible variations in this respect.

In an instrument (Figure 2) the vibrations are used to make the air vibrate and to produce as effective a sound to the environment as possible.

Figure 2: Spread of vibrations from the strings through the violin.

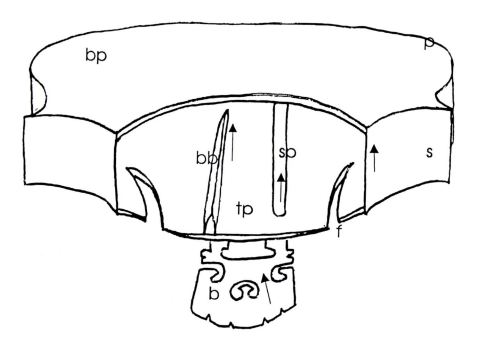

Vibrations of the strings are transmitted through the bridge (b) to the top plate (tp). From there, the vibrations get to the back plate (bp) in a complicated way. The sound post (sp) transmits the vibrations of one leg of the bridge directly to the back plate. The bass bar (bb), a longitudinal bar running on the underside of the top plate, transmits the vibrations of the bridge to the ends of the top plate. The sides (s) also transmit the vibrations of the margins of the top plate onto the margins of the back plate.

In the skull, the conditions are similar, except that the sound post is replaced by the tentorium and falx. The bass bar is represented by petrous bones. The sutures between individual skull bones resemble the purflings (p), marginal grooves on both plates, filled with thin strips of wood. They make the connection of individual parts of the violin less rigid and facilitate their vibrations. Even the F-holes on the top plate (f) resemble to some extent several openings in the bony wall of the skull base.

The vibrating skull does not produce sound as the violin does. The sound's massaging effect on the brain is evident. In the brain (Figure 3) the vibrations we feel do not produce any external sounds - the watery contents and the skull vibrate for some other reasons. Sound energy needs solid matter, liquids or gases to be spread around.

Figure 3: Transmission of vocal vibrations onto the skull.

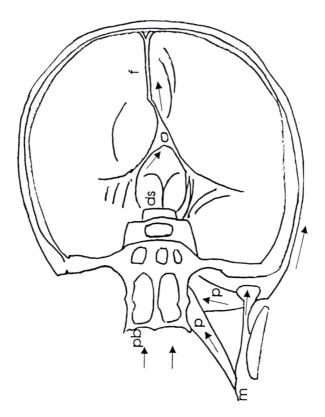

The vibrating air in the vocal tract shakes the walls of the pharynx and mouth, here represented only by palatal bones (pb). Vibrations of the mandible (m) are transmitted directly on the temporal bone and indirectly through the pterygold muscles (p) onto the sphenoid bone. From there the vibrations get in a complicated way from the processes of the sella turcica through the tentorium and falx on the parietal bones (only the posterior clinoid processes with the dorsum sellae are depicted here). Some vibrations are also transmitted through the temporal bones.

This complicated spread of vocal vibrations through the skull resembles to some extent the spread of vibrations from the strings in the violin, as shown in Figure 2.

Fractal music - the special music for vibroacoustics

In vibroacoustic therapy, the mixture of music and sinusoidal sound vibrations is very important. Although it is possible to use any kind of music in any kind of sound furniture, the vibroacoustic equipment and therapy tapes are specially constructed for therapy purposes, not for general relaxation or entertainment. This also applies to the music which may be specially composed for vibroacoustic use.

Using the fractals of the Pythagorean scale (Table 1), one can construct music programmes from the basis of one frequency. Otto Romanowski's composition E-vib is a good example of how this fractal music sounds. The effect of this kind of music will give a sense of total relaxation and implies a harmonic synchronisation of nerve impulses in the whole body.

Composing fractal music means that the composer must use just one frequency, or a harmonic sequence of frequencies as a base for the composition. From this base, single tones or tone clusters will emerge. The musical frequency range is not limited to the vibroacoustic range and the composer therefore will have an extensive degree of freedom in his/her work.

Fractal music does not contain melody lines in the way we usually think of melodic structures. It is important that the music is free from associations with other pieces of music known to the patient. Thus, the time in the therapy chair will also give the patient a possibility to be free from associations with everyday life, and will be able to concentrate on the processes taking place inside his/her body. The patient loses the sense of time and will often feel the effect of treatment very much like the feeling one has when awakening from a long night's sleep.

Vibroacoustic therapy and 'normal music'

For stimulating purposes, one can also use music in the normal sense. There have been research tapes made with music plus sinusoidal vibrations ranging from classical music to hard rock. Usually one does not use music containing vocal elements as this may have a disturbing emotional effect.

The choice of normal music is often dependent on the patient's needs and the time of the day. If a patient is to go directly to work from the therapy room, one must not make the patient too drowsy. This will make it unpleasant to start working. In such situations we use stimulating music which will make the patient fit for work. This means that fractal music is to be avoided.

For brain damaged patients, where recognition of songs and themes is an important part of the therapeutic procedure, one of course can choose well-known music. We often make special customised tapes for patients with special needs. These music programmes are often chosen by the patient, or the patient's family, and the sinusoidal vibrations are added when the tapes are sent to Olav Skille in Norway.

Vibrations and liquids - cell vibration

The human body consists of about 66% water. The brain contains about 80% water. Water is an excellent conductor of sound, and sound travels about 4.5 times faster in water than in air. The sound waves are also 4.5 times longer in water than in air. The length of the sound waves of the vibroacoustic area is roughly between 5 meters and 30 meters inside the body. The physical effect of sound entering the body has the energy equivalent of about 1 watt.

There is very little absorption of acoustic energy by man (2% by 100 Hz for example) due to the mismatch between the airborne acoustical energy and the body. The sound pressure level decreases by 6 dB when the distance from the sound source is doubled.

For vibroacoustic therapy this means that the body should be placed as near the sound source as possible, in order to avoid too much energy loss. The use of earphones has very little physical effect on the patient at all.

The cell may be compared with a closed vessel filled with water. Cell metabolism is dependent on diffusion processes and the electric cell membrane potential.

Diffusion may be a very ineffective mechanism for transporting energy to the cell and transporting waste products out of the cell.

Diffusion may be considerably helped by vibration. Diffusion is an incessant displacement, change of position, of each individual molecule of a liquid or a gas and all molecules which may be dissolved in that fluid. These molecules move in all possible directions, hit each other and transmit kinetic energies to the molecules they hit, the direction and speed of their progress changing with each encounter.

One can, for example, visualise a container with a liquid in it as a billiard table, across the surface of which many balls are permanently rolling in all directions, hitting each other and changing their directions with each contact but maintaining a constant total in kinetic energy. The speed of the balls will vary within a certain range but the average speed maintained will be constant. Let us assume that we place a bowling ball among these constantly rolling billiard balls. This big ball will be frequently hit by the smaller balls but it will not move at the same speed. Mathematically expressed, the speed of the balls will change inversely with their mass, or with the third power of their diameters. However, the probability that the balls will be displaced on their erratic path in any specific direction for a specific distance will change inversely with the fourth power of their diameters. That means that a molecule 1,000 times heavier than other molecules of the system will move 1,000 times slower but the distance for which it actually will be displaced will be 10,000 times shorter.

In biology, the main diffusion systems are water solutions or suspensions of various substances. The molecular weight of water is 18. In biological systems we regularly encounter molecules with molecular weights of 100,000, one million, or more, as a matter of course.

When it comes to giant particles such as viruses, it can be calculated that it would take 100 years before a particle the size of a herpes virus would travel the distance of four millimetres, which is approximately the thickness of the brain cortex, had it to rely on diffusion only (Jindrak and Jindrak, 1986).

Additional mechanisms are needed for assisting the mechanisms of solute transport.

Vibrating the contents of the cell may be compared with shaking or tilting the billiard table used in our visualising experiment above. This makes it possible to make the exchange of fluids more rapid, and in muscle tissue this means that waste products can be transported into the blood system and the lymphatic system more easily. It also means that substances harmful to the body cells may be transported out of the body in a more effective way than is possible without vibration.

Vibroacoustic therapy transfers low frequency sound vibrations directly to the human body, giving an effect much like massage. The human body measures only a fraction of one wavelength of sound in watery substances, and this means that every cell in the human body will be gently massaged by this therapy method.

A holistic approach in massage has been impossible until now, as manual massage and the use of ultrasound will only have local effects.

The choice of frequencies may be symptom-related but the actual treatment will have an effect on the whole body.

Cleaning brain cells by vibration

The brain has no lymphatic system and is totally dependent on other mechanisms to get rid of substances, identified by the brain as being 'not self'. The brain floats in the cerebro-spinal fluid (CSF) and this fluid also surrounds each brain cell. The blood-brain barrier (BBB) prevents infections from other parts of the body to spread into the brain. The CSF fills the subarachnoid space (SAS), and the intercellular spaces between the glial cells and neurons are narrow, but continuous with the SAS. In the brain, an antigen has to stay longer than in muscle cells because of the BBB and lack of lymphatics. It gets very slowly into the blood and usually does not stimulate an immune response. If it does, the response will destroy both the antigen and the brain as well.

The CSF is renewed every four hours and the exchange of fluid is mainly dependent on diffusion (Scientific American, 1989). If one can vibrate the brain, the flow of the CSF will be greatly enhanced, just as the diffusion of sugar in a cup of tea is helped when we stir the fluid with a spoon. When the speed of the CSF is speeded up, this fluid can 'wash' the surfaces of the brain cells, carry away metabolic waste products and waste products from synaptic activity. Figures 4 and 5 show which parts of the brain would be expected to benefit most from vocal vibration.

Figure 4: Midline section through the skull and the brain showing the areas of the brain affected by vibrations of the sphenoid bone (s) and the parietal bone (p).

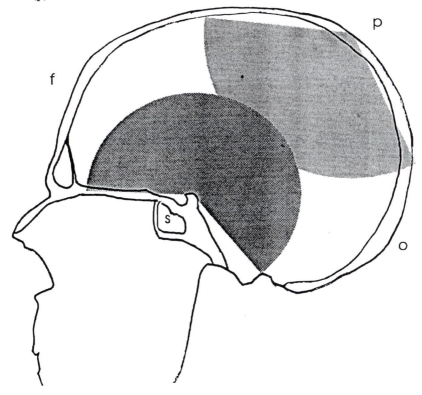

The vibrations extending from the sella turcica (s) affect part of the frontal and temporal lobes and the entire brain stem. Vibrations of the parietal bone (p) affect the entire parietal lobes and portions of the frontal (f) and occipital lobes (o).

Figure 5: Section through the brain showing the distribution of sound in white and grey matter.

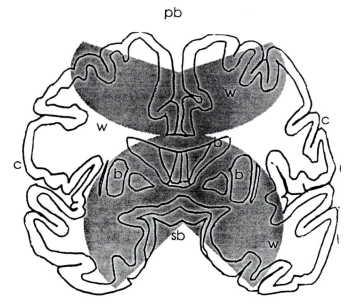

The folded layer on the brain is the cortex (c). Deep inside the white matter (w) are the basal ganglia (b). The shaded areas represent parts of the brain which receive the greatest benefits from the vibrations of the sphenoid bone (sb) and from the parietal bones (pb) at their midline junction in the sagittal suture. While the lower area is almost spherical, because the source of vibrations is the sella turcica, the upper area is elongated in the anterioposterior direction, because the source of vibration is linear, the sagittal suture. The areas of the brain which are not shaded are also vibrated. However those vibrations are 'secondary' in the sense that they are waves which have bounced off the walls of the cranial cavity. At present it is very difficult to figure out the intensity of these secondary vibrations in individual parts of the brain.

It is interesting to note that we see an area of overlapping between vibrations from the skull base and from the parietal bones. In this area lies the choroid plexus - an organ which functions much like a kidney system for the CSF.

The sphenoid bone (Figure 6) is situated very near this structure. The sphenoid bone articulates with all the bones of the cranium, and five of the face, and is attached to 11 pairs of muscles. The falx cerebri is also connected with the sphenoid bone, thereby transferring vibrations to the greater part of the cortex.

Figure 6: Sphenoid bone. In humans, the sphenoid bone, besides being a part of the skull, has also assumed a new, unexpected function as a transmitter of vocal vibrations onto the brain.

The hypophysis is attached to the sphenoid bone. Falx and tentorium are stretched according to the forces applied to the sphenoid bone, and this mechanical vibration will give a gentle massage to the cortex. The fibrous structure of the skull vault 'milks' the arachnoid granulations penetrating the BBB. The pressure applied makes it possible for the CSF to escape into the superior sagittal sinus and the lateral lacunae. By speeding up the flow of the CSF, its renewal is increased and elution of substances from the brain is facilitated. (The effect of vocalisation and the figures illustrating this effect belong to the 'Jindrak postulate' (Jindrak and Jindrak, 1986).

Dependent upon the localisation of loudspeakers the effects of vibroacoustic therapy may be described according to the 'Jindrak postulate'. Although this postulate is mainly concerned about the effect of vibrations on the brain, the same effect of vibrating cell contents and 'washing' the surfaces of the cells may also apply to any cell structure in the human body being exposed to sound vibrations. As vibroacoustic therapy gives sound exposure to the whole body, the effect of this therapy will have both a symptom related effect and a general effect on the patient.

Early findings

Having worked with the multiply handicapped children for some time, the staff also wanted to try the effect of this treatment. We soon found which frequencies were best for neck/shoulder pains and menstruational cramps/pre-menstrual tension/dysmenhorrea. The results were very encouraging, and soon people with various problems came and wanted to try the equipment. By empirical work, we found frequency areas which appeared to be better than other areas for the specific symptoms, and by 1987 the following list of symptoms/illnesses were included in the list of cases where it is possible to expect some kind of positive effect on the patient.

The duration of the effects is considerably varied - from complete healing of an acute wry-neck after 1 to 2 treatments, to a feeling of well-being only during the actual therapy sessions. The findings are anecdotal and indicate areas where vibroacoustic treatment has shown effective results with single subjects or with small numbers of subjects, predominately in Norway, and also in Finland, England and Estonia.

Conditions responding well to treatment (Skille, 1989)

Autism

Autistic children become so engaged by the vibration effect that they may permit the staff to give them more skin contact/skin stimulation than they were permitted to in other situations. We may see the outline of a therapy setting where contact training during vibroacoustic therapy may be transferred to situations where the music could be gradually withdrawn.

Asthma/cystic fibrosis

Problems of excretion of lung secretion may be eased by using frequencies in the middle range. The effect may last 1 to 2 days. In serious asthmatic conditions, the use of the equipment up to 15 times per day may be necessary.

Abdominal pains/colic pains

Several observations have been made where effective reduction of such pains has been obtained by using the lower frequency range of 40 to 50 Hz.

Cerebral palsy and other spastic conditions

With spastic conditions following CP, vibroacoustic therapy has demonstrated a considerable effect. Alone, or in combination with physiotherapy, the method has given very good results in reducing muscle tone.

Constipation

In some cases there has been observed spontaneous relief of constipation in institutionalised patients in whom natural mobility has been impaired. It is possible that the mechanical vibrations given by vibroacoustic therapy are giving new vigour to the natural processes in the digestive system.

Neck/shoulder pains

Such pains - caused by occupational myalgia or as a result of stress of various causes, were considerably relieved by using frequencies in the upper middle area. Repeated treatments over 1 to 3 weeks (up to 10 x 30 minutes) gave relief which lasted for a long period.

Menstrual pains/pre-menstrual tension

Such pains and tension conditions have been relieved by using frequencies in the lower middle region and using calm, harmonic music. Treatment every day in the 'acute' phase and once per week in the middle phase repeated over 3 to 4 cycles may give an effect of long duration.

Low back pains

Pains in the low-back area were relieved by use of frequencies in the low middle region. Acute back pains because of sprained muscles or muscle cramps are relieved by daily treatments for 2 to 5 days. Pains from muscular tensions of diverse causes have been reduced by treatments 2 to 3 times per week up to 4 weeks.

Stress-induced depression

Relief may be observed after the first treatment session. The positive effect is dependent on the right choice of both frequency and music. The choice of music must be made in co-operation with the patient, and the therapist must have a varied choice of relaxing music. Often 'New Age' music may have a good effect. At the end of the treatment period, various frequencies and activating music are used.

When dealing with general stress and discomfort, if the client is placed in a sheltered environment - protected as much as possible from external influence - a 30 minutes' vibroacoustic programme containing slow pressure waves and 'floating' music will alleviate stress symptoms and give the client new vitality.

Sport injuries

Several cases have been treated with positive results. Both acute muscle traumas and post-operative convalescence have shown positive reactions to harmonic frequency sequences which are built on a basic tone in the low frequency area.

Generally, low frequencies are given to the big muscles and we move upwards in frequencies when we are treating smaller muscle masses. Thus, the thighs need lower frequencies than the shoulders. It is recommended to use multi-frequency tapes in order to avoid too much stress placed on a single type of muscle tissue. Muscles and sinews are more easily stretched after tough muscular efforts.

By muscular over-use syndrome pains, vibroacoustic therapy will contribute to shorten the restitution period and reduce pains. The frequencies in the first half of the normal octave are recommended. <u>Vibroacoustic therapy is NOT to be used during external or internal bleeding.</u>

Insomnia

Patients easily fall asleep during treatment and they have reported that after treatment they have less difficulty falling asleep at their normal time for retiring and the duration of sleep is longer than they normally experience. This has led to specific use as therapy for insomnia. Treatment for insomnia has best effects when it is carried out in the late afternoon.

Morbus Bechterew

The effective diminishment of pain and discomfort from this rheumatic condition has been reported by several institutes. However, in the active phase of this disease, one may find an increase of discomfort. Therefore vibroacoustic therapy should be used with caution when the inflammations are active.

Polyarthritis

Physiotherapists using vibroacoustic equipment have reported some relief of symptoms in patients suffering from polyarthritis, especially in the smaller joints of the hands and feet.

Circulatory and pulmonary deficiency

Patients suffering from severe circulatory deficiency in the extremities may find effective relief of this condition. These observations have been made by policlinical patients as well as by institutionalised patients with oedema. There have been reports of very encouraging relief of symptoms in patients suffering from pulmonary emphysema.

Fibromyositis/fibromyalgia

Patients suffering from this pain syndrome seem to obtain some relief of pain when they are exposed to single frequencies in the lower frequency range, directly followed by a multi-frequency tape.

Multiple sclerosis and Parkinsonism

Reduction of rigidity and considerable palliative effect has been reported.

Research and development

Much of the work done to date has been in the use of vibroacoustic therapy as a treatment. There are between 25,000 and 30,000 hours of work recorded, the majority of which is substantial in quantity but does not come strictly within the criteria of objective evaluation and research. Much of the recorded material is observed response, and in some institutions in Scandinavia vibroacoustic therapy has been in daily use for up to 8 years. Many of these institutions are small and it is difficult to find subjects who have matching pathologies, making it difficult to set up control groups if one were to undertake a between-groups design study. Also, many of the staff using the equipment are nurses who have not established ethical guidelines to set up experimental situations where a patient may be denied treatment which has proved to be beneficial in order to determine whether or not it is having a true and lasting effect.

Consequently, many of the reports sent to the International Society for Vibroacoustic Therapy (ISVA) are anecdotal.

This section of the chapter will review four of the most significant research studies that have been undertaken, three of which were made by the authors of this chapter.

Study l: The effect of low frequency sound and music (VAT) on muscle tone and circulation (Wigram and Weekes, 1989)

Vibroacoustic therapy treatment began at Harperbury Hospital, Radlett, Hertfordshire, in England in 1988. Harperbury Hospital is a large long-stay Mental Handicap Hospital, and the Mental Handicap Unit funded the initial construction and purchase of equipment and the project to look at the effect of this new treatment on physically handicapped clients with high muscle tone (spasticity) and elderly clients. A secondary interest of the original study was to look at the effect of this treatment on oedema, heart rate and blood pressure. The study was set up as a joint venture between the Music Therapy Department and the Physiotherapy Department at Harperbury Hospital, and was the first such study of its type in Great Britain using this equipment. Up until this point, the equipment had only been constructed in Scandinavia (Norway) and it was only at the beginning of 1988 that it began to become available commercially.

Following the construction of vibroacoustic therapy equipment for treatment and research in England, during 1988 over 40 clients at Harperbury Hospital had regular sessions of vibroacoustic therapy. These sessions were started primarily as treatment sessions and although notes were taken of the effects, these were not clinical trials. However, some very interesting results came out of this work which highlighted the value of this therapy for a variety of different conditions. One elderly lady who was treated is severely spastic with a kyphosis and a scoliosis. She has extensive spasm of her hips, one elbow, some of her fingers and her tongue, which makes speaking very difficult. She has flexor spasms of her trunk, one arm and most of her fingers. She has some very painful joints and also suffers from asthma.

She had vibroacoustic therapy twice a week for two years and she relaxes to the extent that she very often falls asleep during treatment. She is a frail, thin, intelligent lady with a very keen sense of humour. When her tongue thrust is relaxed, she is able to talk more clearly. At the beginning of the treatment session, she will be extremely spastic with distressed, rasping breathing. By the end of the thirty minutes she will often be breathing peacefully and drifting off to sleep.

In looking at the deeply penetrating effect of low frequency sound waves as an effective means of improving circulation, we also worked with a client who had chronic oedema. His oedema was so severe in both legs that from the point below his patella down to his toes, his skin was stretched and shiny and the tissue fluid had organised, i.e. the legs felt very hard. His legs were swollen and he frequently had sores and the condition caused him serious discomfort. He enjoyed the treatment session and in using a frequency of around 40 Hz, we measured the circumference of his ankles before and after the treatment. Typically, we found a reduction of between ½ and 1 inch in size over the course of a half hour treatment.

Objectives of the research

The research we have been engaged with looks at the use of this treatment to reduce muscle tone in spastic patients. We designed a research project that set out to differentiate between the effect of music alone, compared with music combined with low frequency sound. One might expect a reasonable degree of relaxation and reduction in muscle tone simply as a result of lying on a comfortable unit and having gentle music played; therefore we asked ourselves the question as to whether low frequency sound combined with music would have a greater effect than a placebo effect of music alone.

Method - subjects and materials

Three male and seven female subjects resident in Harperbury Hospital took part in trials to determine whether muscle tone could be reduced by introducing low frequency sound at 44 Hz or 55 Hz into a treatment programme involving music. The subjects' ages ranged from 28 to 77 years and their level of functioning ranged from very profoundly handicapped to moderately handicapped. All the subjects had measurably high muscle tone which affected each of them in individually differing ways, although there were some affected muscle groups that were shared by all or some of the subjects. The subjects were identified by the therapists involved in the project as being those who may benefit from a treatment designed to reduce muscle tone. The average age of the male subjects was 51 and the average age of the female subjects was 44. The overall average age of the 10 subjects was 46.

Two male subjects and one female subject were also involved in an experiment to evaluate whether the condition of chronic oedema could be alleviated, and the size of the limbs reduced by the use of low frequency sound with music, as opposed to music alone.

The subjects were all residents of a Mental Handicap Hospital and their average age was 52. The subjects all suffered from a condition of chronic oedema in their legs. The experimental conditions designed to test the effectiveness of low frequency were the same for the subjects who had oedema as for the subjects who had high muscle tone, although the measurements taken were different. The list of measurements will be tabulated separately at the end of the Design section, and the description of the design for these clients will be the same as the design used for the clients suffering from high muscle tone.

The equipment which was used in the experiment was modelled on the 'Music Bath' and 'Music Bed' which were developed by Skille in the late 1970s and early 1980s (Skille 1982a; 1982b; 1985). A frame of a sprung bed was used and two 18 inch speakers were mounted in boxes underneath with springs, with the cones directed upwards. The speaker boxes contained ports for acoustic balance, and the cone of the speaker was approximately 2 inches from the springs of the bed. On top of the springs was a single polythene sheet (in the event of incontinence) and on top of this was a 1 inch pile of sheepskin. One half of the bed was made so that it could be lifted up to an angle of approximately 30 degrees from the horizontal, although this technique was not used in the trials. The speakers were connected to an amplifier with 120 watts output per channel (rms) and with the ability to increase and decrease the bass volume. When the clients were treated with low frequency sounds and music, the bass and master volume were set at 7. When the clients were treated with music alone, the master volume was set at 7 and the bass volume was set at 0. When the subjects were treated horizontally, the speakers were in such a position for the sound waves to pass directly into the body of the subject.

The equipment was isolated electrically and taped recordings were used so that the style of music, frequency of the tone and intensity were all constant for each treatment. Two tapes were used for the clients with high muscle tone, one tape with a single tone of 44 Hz throughout, and another tape with a single tone of 55 Hz throughout. For the subjects of the oedema trial, a further tape with a single tone of 40 Hz was used throughout the trials.

Design

The experiment to determine the effect of low frequency sound on muscle tone was set up as a repeated measures design across two experimental conditions. Each subject undertook a minimum of 12 trials, 6 in each condition. Condition A was when the subject had a 30 minute session on the vibroacoustic unit and received music and low frequency sound, and Condition B was when the subject received music alone.

In the muscle tone trials, the dependent variables were the measurements taken on the subjects of their degree of extension before and after each trial. Each subject had a different set of measurements, although there were some measurements that were common to many of the subjects. The dependent variables measured for the muscle tone trials were coded and are as follows:

1. Left shoulder to right shoulder
2. Right shoulder to right radial artery
3. Left shoulder to left radial artery
4. Right elbow to side
5. Left elbow to side
6. Nose to navel
7. Right side greater trochanter to right side lateral malleolus
8. Left side greater trochanter to left side lateral malleolus
9. Base of right patella to base of left patella

For each subject in each trial, an independent evaluator measured the maximum possible extended range between each of the two points in the dependent variables pertinent to each subject, and then was not present during the course of the trial. When the trial had finished, the independent evaluator proceeded to take the measurements again, without knowing whether or not the client had been treated in Condition A or Condition B. This ensured that the evaluators were 'blinded' for the trials.

In repeated measures designs, particular problems often arise from the fact that experiences change individuals, and the subjects may have learnt what was happening and begun to habituate to the stimuli. In this experiment, the subjects may have learnt from the experience of the trials conducted with low frequency sound (LFS), and the muscle tone reduction may have been greater in the trials without LFS as a result. In addition to the possibilities of conditioning to the stimuli, there may also have been a cumulative effect. The trials were carried out twice a week over a period of six weeks. In order to control for order effects, subjects were not all treated on the same days of the week, and there were occasionally larger gaps between some subjects than between others. In addition, the course of the trials was randomly decided individually for each subject.

As the measurements that were taken were common to many of the subjects, some consideration will be given in the Results section to evaluation of these measurements between subjects.

Oedema group

In the case of the three subjects who were being monitored for oedema, the same design was used in the trials, and the same number of trials in the two conditions was undertaken. The dependent variables in the case of these subjects were:

a. Base of right great toe
b. Base of left great toe
c. Instep of right foot
d. Instep of left foot
e. Right ankle round the heel
f. Left ankle round the heel
g. Circumference of right leg 3 cms above lateral malleolus
h. Circumference of left leg 3 cms above lateral malleolus
i. Circumference of right leg 10 cms above lateral malleolus
j. Circumference of left leg 10 cms above lateral malleolus
k. Circumference of right leg 20 cms above lateral malleolus
l. Circumference of left leg 20 cms above lateral malleolus

Blood pressure and heart rate

Three further dependent variables were measured before and after each trial in both conditions. Systolic and diastolic blood pressure were measured as was the heart rate. Not all of the ten subjects in the muscle tone group or the three subjects in the blood pressure group had their blood pressure taken. One subject in the oedema group had tight flexor spasm in his arms and it was impossible to gain accurate readings. One subject in the muscle tone group also had tight flexor spasm in his arms, a further subject in the muscle tone group consistently recorded errors in her blood pressure readings due to the difficulty in measuring her very short arms, and the third member of the muscle tone group had such thin arms it was difficult to take her blood pressure readings.

Procedure

Each subject in both groups was placed on one of the VAT units. They had a foam rubber pillow (sound dampening material) under their head, and where necessary their body was supported by pillows containing polystyrene beads (polystyrene beads have been found to be a good conductor of sound wave energy). After a resting period (3 minutes), a blood pressure reading and pulse rate were taken and then measurements were taken as specified for each subject. The evaluator taking these measurements then left, and the therapist responsible for treating the clients began the tape. On the 2-speaker vibroacoustic unit (VAT(X)), the master volume control was increased to 7. In conditions where the low frequency tone was being used, the bass control was then also increased to 7. Where the low frequency tone was not being used, the bass control was left at 0.

The treatment then proceeded and, where necessary, the therapist would remain with the client sitting quietly in the room. At the end of the treatment, the therapist would turn all the controls to 0 and the independent evaluator would be asked to come in. Blood pressure readings were again taken and the independent evaluator would measure again the joint extension measurements relevant to each individual. Finally, the measurements were all entered on to a form which also recorded the day, time, and whether or not the subject had received the LFS tone.

It was also possible to record any further information on the forms arising out of the treatment session.

During the course of each treatment, a client was undressed to the point of absolute necessity to take the measurements, and was always covered with a blanket.

Where necessary, clients were reassured verbally while measurements were being taken, especially blood pressure measurements.

Results

The raw data we obtained was a series of difference measures in centimetres. This in itself was not particularly meaningful, as one could be describing an improvement in one trial of the range of movement in one subject of perhaps 4 or 5 centimetres. What we needed to determine from the figures was what the total possible range of movement for that client was. This we calculated by taking the minimum possible measurement the client was capable of in each of the measurements we took (i.e. in measurement 9, the right patella to the left patella, this measurement would be taken where the legs were completely together), and subtracting that from the best possible extension or range of movement that we got in each of our measurements over the course of the whole twelve trials.

By this means we were able to calculate the best possible range of movement each individual had for each of their measurements. Following this, we were then able to see the different measurements in each trial as a percentage of the maximum potential range of movement, and normalise all our data accordingly. Therefore, in one trial we obtained a difference measurement of 5 centimetres within a total possible range of 25 centimetres, and we were able to conclude that the subject's range of movements had improved by 20%. We calculated the means of all the data we had and having normalised it we came up with some evidence of a difference between using low frequency sound with music, compared with using music on its own in the treatment. The results we obtained showed clearly in all of our subjects, that when low frequency sound is combined with music one can expect a greater range of movement, indicating a reduction in muscle tone, than when music is used on its own. In Table 2, the upper figures in each box represent the condition when we used a low frequency sound as well as music, the lower figures in each box represent the condition when we used only music. The averages of each subject's scores (representing a percentage improvement in their range of movement) are on the right hand column, and, for example, Subject 2 shows a 22% improvement in range of movement when we used low frequency sound and a 3% deterioration when we did not. Other subjects show equally impressive results, and using a sign test gave us significant results of $p<.0004$. On a related T-test, the result was $p<0.01$.

Of particular value for us were the results with certain subjects in certain measurements. For example, Subject 9 has severe abductor spasm, and the ninth measurement we took from her, the one where she had a 31% improvement in her range of movement when we used low frequency sound, indicated that abduction was much easier after this treatment, thus lessening the danger of a fixed deformity which may well lead on to dislocation of the hip. This treatment was therefore welcomed both from a long-term preventative point of view and from a short-term treatment one.

Table 2: Mean scores of increased or decreased range of movement within minim and maximum ranges, shown as percentage scores for both conditions

Subj	1	2	3	4	5	6	7	8	9	Mean
S1		+8.2	+2.6				+4.6	+3.8	+14.3	+7
		-3.7	-1.0				-6.2	-1.0	-4.0	-3
S2		+15.3	+23.5						+27.0	+22
		-5.0	-2.0						-2.0	-3
S3		+11.5	+14.8				+22.3	+4.7		+13
		+0.5	-1.1				+5.0	0		+1
S4		+16.0	+21.0	+26.7					+11.5	+19
		-13.3	-3.0	-0.5					+0.5	-4
S5	+4.5			+15.8	+25.8					+15
	-7.7			+6.7	+10.3					+3
S6			+1.0				+1.3	+1.7	+25.8	+7
			-2.8				+0.4	+1.2	+5.4	+2
S7		+11.4	+1.0					+1.1	+8.4	+5
		+3.8	+1.3					+2.0	+2.0	+2
S8		+20.0	+9.8							+15
		+2.0	+5.3							+4
S9	+31.7	+22.5	+9.5				+9.0	+11.6	+31.5	+19
	0	-0.3	+0.6				+6.1	-0.6	-0.8	+1
S10			+2.8			+26.8	+5.5	+21.0	+17.5	+11
			+1.6			+15.8	-0.4	+1.0	+2.8	+4
Mean	+18	+15	+10	+21	+26	+27	+9	+4	+19	+13
	-4	-2	+1	+3	+10	+16	-1	0	+1	+1

We ran trials at the same time on subjects who had chronic oedema and, although the results showed a reduction, it was not at a significant level, and we decided that it would be necessary to treat the clients on a daily basis. When we monitored blood pressure, we discovered that our clients were not typical of the population at large. However, in the group we treated we found that we had a significant result in the reduction of systolic blood pressure after vibroacoustic therapy. In conclusion, these were objective, blind trials and gave a very positive result in favour of the use of low frequency sound to reduce muscle tone. The evidence from them was sufficient to support further research and current trials involve the use of surface electromyography and skin conductance (electrodermal activity) as a means of measuring reaction of the automatic nervous system. These psychophysiological measures will evaluate the effect of the activity of the muscles, and also the level of arousal of individuals. In addition, a mood adjective check list can be used before and after the treatments to evaluate the emotional and psychological effect on subjects. We are also interested in exploring the cumulative and long-term effect of this treatment, as indications from current treatment results suggest that it is not only effective immediately after treatment, but also for several hours thereafter.

In the blood pressure tests, we saw a statistically significant reduction of systolic blood pressure when low frequency sound was used in the trials as opposed to when low frequency sound was not used, but largely fluctuating results for diastolic pressure and heart rate. The results were taken from a very small sample, and although the systolic graphs indicated a reduction of pressure when low frequency sound was used, we would need to include more data from a greater number of subjects to have any conclusive comments to make about this.

A very small sample consisting of three subjects was run for the oedema trials and although twelve different measures were taken overall, there were only two measurements that were common to all the subjects. The indication we had from this trial was that the measurement became smaller as the oedema lessened when low frequency sound was used, but the graphs indicated a very small difference and this would not indicate a significant result.

Discussion

The outcome of the trials on clients with high muscle tone showed consistently that when low frequency sound (either 44 Hz or 55 Hz) was used with the music, a greater reduction in muscle tone and an improved rate of motion was achieved than when music alone was used. The result obtained from measuring blood pressure fluctuated quite considerably, and only the regular drop in systolic pressure gave any level of significance. The oedema difference scores, although very small, also gave significant indication of improvement due to low frequency sound.

The trials gave a very positive result in favour of the use of low frequency sound to reduce muscle tone. However, there were a number of problems which need to be addressed in future work. Firstly, the equipment used needs to be carefully assessed in terms of the resonance of the speaker cavities. It was evident that the resonant frequencies of one of the units caused it to increase the energy output between 54 Hz and 57 Hz. The units need to be calibrated in order that this variable can be taken into consideration. Secondly, background, skill and confidence of the people undertaking the evaluation varied quite substantially. Some were experienced in the handling of the subjects, and maintained consistency, whereas others began handling in a more tentative manner and then grew in confidence, which would mean the early results reflected a less significant result than later results. Thirdly, some of the evaluators used additional encouragement, for example, verbally encouraging the subject, and may have obtained an artificially improved level of extension. Other evaluators continued with the pressure they were applying until they achieved an artificially improved level of extension. Other evaluators did not apply enough pressure. Fourthly, although strenuous efforts were made to keep all the variables across the condition constant, occasionally subjects did not come for their trials and were therefore treated on a different day. Consistency was not always possible and, in addition, it would have been easier if the clients could have attended more frequently.

Other factors cropped up as the trials proceeded to cause additional problems. After the fourth week of trials, it became necessary to change the batteries once a week on both of these machines. The blood pressure results were not conclusive and many problems arose in obtaining accurate blood pressure readings from the clients. The best the results offer is an indication that it would be worth continuing either with the smaller group of samples but many more treatments to draw on for data, or with a much larger sample of subjects. The oedema trials also suffered from the sample group being small.

In conclusion, therefore, one might comment that besides the very obvious benefits of this treatment for this and other disorders, one of the most valuable parts of the treatment is that it is extremely pleasurable for the patients who have it. For example, maintaining the range of movement and preventing the onset of fixed deformities in spastic clients has to date required patient, lengthy and sometimes strenuous effort, and sometimes uncomfortable physical treatment. We find that we are obtaining good results through this treatment because it is a deeply penetrating and relaxing sound which sets up a vibration right inside the body. The treatment does not claim to cure chronic or long-term disorders like spastic muscles but it provides some relief from pain and discomfort.

Study 2: Variations in blood pressure and pulse during vibroacoustic treatment - pilot study (Skille and Brönstad, 1988-89)

In Norway, vibroacoustic therapy treatment has been going on for a longer period of time and has become available to the general public at centres. These centres have been established and are called TRILAX CENTRES, and there are two such centres in Steinkjer and Trondheim. Clients can self refer themselves to these centres for treatment and may be seeking this for a number of different reasons.

In the Trilax Centre in Steinkjer, routine measurements of blood pressure (BP) and pulse (P) were taken to evaluate the effects of the treatment on the clients there. A sample of 82 measurements were randomly chosen for evaluation from clients who came for treatment during the Autumn of 1988. The overall distribution of patients was 30% men and 70% women.

This study was not intended as a study comparing the effects of vibroacoustic therapy with other relaxation or resting processes in terms of its evaluation of blood pressure and pulse. All the clients who came were exposed to vibroacoustic therapy and this study looks more carefully at the effect on the blood pressure of these subjects.

The age distribution of the subjects was as follows:

Table 3: Age distribution

20-29	years:	6%
30-39	years:	17%
40-49	years:	16%
50-59	years:	18%
60-69	years:	20%
70-79	years:	14%
80-89	years:	3%

Measurements

In this study it was decided to take a measure of blood pressure and pulse when the subjects arrived, after they had had five minutes rest, and then at the end of the treatment. The result of this is that there are three separate measurements which can be looked at and compared. The equipment in use for this trial was a MultiVib Chair VA 115 or a TRILAX Bed VB 555 and a signal unit SU 225 was available from vibroacoustics A/S. The therapy programmes were made by Vibrosoft A/S and were supplied on C-60 cassette tapes. On these tapes, there is music and low frequency sound, mixed. The composer Otto Romanowski from Finland composed music specifically for this treatment system.

No singular specific frequency was used in these trials and some of the tapes had several frequencies, ranging between 40 Hz and 80 Hz. The tapes that we used for the treatment normally lasted between 20 and 29 minutes. A digital electronic Blood Pressure Monitor from Select A/S was used as a measuring instrument.

Table 4: Basic values

SBP at arrival: m = 138,09 sd= 14,37
DBP at arrival: m = 86,72 sd= 7,69
P at arrival: m = 76,54 sd= 16,01
SBP after 5 minutes rest: m = 127,54 sd= 18.08
DBP after 5 minutes rest: m = 79,84 sd= 15,49
P after 5 minutes rest: m = 72,44 sd= 13,95
SBP after therapy session: m= 124,15 sd= 16,90
DBP after therapy session m= 77,05 sd= 11,41
P after therapy session m= 67,77 sd= 11,60

Table 4 shows an overall mean result of the 82 subjects in these trials. On average, the systolic blood pressure reduced from 138 mm Hg to 127.54 mm Hg after 5 minutes' rest and then to 124.15 after the therapy session. Diastolic blood pressure also fell from 86.72 mm Hg to 79.85 mm Hg after 5 minutes' rest and then down to 77.05 after the therapy session. The heart rate fell from 76.54 to 72.44 after 5 minutes' rest and then down to 67.77 on average after the therapy treatment.

Table 5 : Changes in the values at different points in the treatment - subject distribution

Grp	No Change	Rise	Mean rise	SD	Fall	Mean fall	SD	Total	SD
ASBP	1	24	8.92	9.94	57	-9.98	7.65	-4.34	7.65
ADBP	3	21	8.86	10.58	58	-9.09	7.66	-5.35	7.69
AP	9	18	4.78	4.16	57	-8.43	5.08	-4.49	7.20
BSBP	4	16	7.06	3.51	62	-12.74	9.44	-4.29	9.44
BDBP	5	22	7.41	7.73	55	-8.51	9.92	-4.23	10.67
BP	12	19	5.32	5.69	51	-7.14	5.06	-3.16	7.18
CSBP	3	12	8.33	6.09	67	-16.75	9.35	-12.20	12.94
CDBP	5	14	6.00	7.59	63	-11.38	10.03	-7.98	11.23
CP	2	13	5.40	5.84	67	-9.86	5.54	-7.40	8.25

Group A = Values measured after 5 minutes rest and at the end of the session
Group B = Values measured at arrival and after 5 minutes rest
Group C = Values measured at arrival and at the end of the session
SBP = Systolic Blood Pressure
DBP = Diastolic Blood Pressure
P = Pulse

Group A shows the values measured after 5 minutes' rest at the end of the session (ASBP, ADDP, AP). Group B shows the values at arrival and after 5 minutes' rest (BSBP, BDBP, BP) and Group C shows the values measured on arrival and at the end of the session (CSSBP, CDBP, CP). This table gives us some idea of the effect of the 5 minute rest period, and then the effect of vibroacoustic therapy. The most significant information that is drawn from this is from Group A which records the actual effect of vibroacoustic therapy.

The study shows that a significant majority of the 82 subjects experienced a fall in their systolic and diastolic blood pressure as well as a fall in their heart rate.

Discussion

The study did not evaluate the effect of the treatment against giving the subject nothing at all, or giving the subject a placebo treatment. Bearing this in mind, the statistical information in these results can only give us an indication of what one can expect the effect to be on blood pressure and heart rate as a consequence of this treatment. The results cannot be directly compared with other studies, as all the subjects were exposed to vibroacoustic therapy. The subjects who reacted to the therapy with a rise in the measured parameters were reported by the experimenters to have the same subjective feeling of stress reduction, muscular relaxation and well-being after the end of the therapy session as those clients in whom the same values are falling. Therefore, the rise in values seems to have no correlation with any evidence of physical discomfort. There is around a 75% probability for a fall in blood pressure and heart rate in subjects who are exposed to this treatment according to this study.

Study 3: The localisation of low frequencies in the body (Wigram, 1990)

Much of the treatment and research carried out so far into the effect of vibroacoustic therapy has looked at the effect of a combination of music and low frequency sound. The range of frequencies used, between 40 Hz and 80 Hz, has been seen to have a general effect on the whole body, but also a specific effect on certain parts of the body. In his summary of conditions responding well to treatment, Skille has identified more specifically the effect of a limited frequency range, such as 40 Hz to 50 Hz in the treatment of abdominal pains/colic pains. The tapes that have been made up for use in vibroacoustic therapy, have included tapes with only one frequency underneath a piece of music lasting for half an hour, and also tapes where a succession or sequence of frequencies is used. The effect that has been noted with tapes where a succession of frequencies is used, is that of the sound 'moving up the body' as the frequency is raised. Other trials have indicated that people being treated will feel a localisation of effect as the treatment progresses. In other words, the initial effect when the treatment starts is of a general relaxing vibration throughout the body, and as they relax and become sensitive to the effect, the vibration can be felt in one particular part of the body.

This may appear surprising, considering the quite small frequency range that is being used, whereas it is not surprising over the whole spectrum of frequencies, as people with profound hearing loss will clearly identify their sensitivity to different pitches in different parts of their body. It does also give an additional and important significance to the prescriptive value of vibroacoustic therapy, if one can be sure that across a whole range of randomly selected individuals, different frequencies between the range of 20 Hz to 80 Hz will be felt consistently in specific areas of the body. Treatment systems using mechanical vibration often demonstrate the general effect which begins on the surface of the skin and is transmitted down through the tissue from the point at which the body is in contact with the vibrating instrument. A sound wave can be felt within the body, and the potential value of being able to 'target' a frequency at a specific area of the body gives greater flexibility to the use of vibroacoustic therapy.

This study was undertaken as a pilot study to test out the hypothesis that different frequencies are felt in different parts of the body.

Design

Thirty-nine subjects undertook a short ten minute trial where a range of frequencies were presented to them and they were asked to identify where they felt the vibration effect strongest. It was decided to use a sequence of pure sinus tones between 20 Hz and 70 Hz in a specific order which was uniform for each subject. The order of the frequencies presented was as follows:

40, 50, 60, 70, 50, 40, 30, 20, 40.

The frequencies were produced by a function generator, and sent directly into a vibroacoustic unit consisting of two 18 inch bass speakers set into a bed. The subjects lay on the bed, suspended over the speakers on ordinary bed springs. Their bodies were not in contact with the speakers, and they were lying approximately 2 inches above the two speakers. The sound was generated equally in mono mode to the speakers, which were situated approximately 2 feet apart. As the subjects were lying on the bed, one speaker was centred under their thoracic area, and one speaker was centred under their thighs/knees. Their head was supported by a foam pillow.

Procedure

The procedure of administering the test was standardised for all subjects. When the subjects were comfortably settled on the vibroacoustic bed, they were advised that they were going to be played a sequence of nine frequencies, and that they should identify where in the body they felt the effect or vibration from the frequency strongest. In the event that they did not know the exact name of the part of the body where they were feeling the vibration, they were also asked to point to the place on their body as well as verbally explaining where they felt it. A form was devised covering the following areas of the body:-

Feet, Calves, Thighs, Sacrum, Lumbar, Thoracic, Cervical, Shoulder and Head.

Each frequency was played from the function generator for approximately ten seconds, during which time the subject was asked to identify where they felt the effect. Moving from one frequency to another was done, wherever possible, by a smooth manipulation of the fine control, gradually increasing to the new frequency. There were two points in the test where this was not possible - the move from the fourth to the fifth frequency (70 Hz to 50 Hz) and the move from the seventh to the eighth frequency (30 Hz to 20 Hz).

The sequence of frequencies contained one frequency that was repeated three times (40 Hz) and one frequency that was repeated twice (50 Hz).

With some subjects, besides identifying the areas of the body where they felt the frequency strongest, they were permitted to identify areas of the body where they also felt the effect less strongly, but still at a significant level.

No specific explanation was offered to any of the subjects prior to the trial as to what they might expect to experience, or why the effect changed when the frequency was changed. Following the conclusion of the test, some information was given to the subjects about what they had experienced, and they were asked to make any additional comments.

The subjects were all randomly selected from health care staff working at the hospital, and also from visitors coming into the vibroacoustic therapy department.

The subjects were from a wide range of backgrounds, and had varying ages of between 18 and 60.

In addition to identifying the area of the body where they felt a specific frequency, if the subjects were not able to specify a localised effect, but had a more generalised effect, this information was also scored.

Results

Table 6 shows the spread of identified, localised, effects over all the subjects. The scores on Table 6 refer only to the area in the subjects' body which they identified as the primary and strongest area of receptivity to these different frequencies. This indicates that the majority of subjects felt 40 Hz in their calves/thighs, or legs; 50 Hz in their thighs/sacrum and lumbar area; 60 Hz in their sacrum/lumbar and thoracic area;: 70 Hz in the upper half of the body; 50 Hz between the thighs and the lumbar region; 30 Hz in the calves and thighs and 20 Hz in a wide band range between the calves and the lumbar area.

Table 6: First choice - localisations of the frequencies in all 39 subjects - distribution by subjects.

	Hz								
	40	50	60	70	50	40	30	20	40
Feet	6	1	-	1	2	6	-	5	6
Calves	22	4	-	-	3	26	22	6	22
Thighs	8	1	2	-	3	4	7	15	8
Sacrum	2	6	5	1	15	1	2	4	2
Lumbar	1	11	6	1	4	-	-	6	-
Thoracic	-	7	18	10	4	-	-	-	-
Cervical	-	4	2	4	2	-	-	-	
Shoulder	-	2	2	2	1	-	3	1	-
Head	-	1	2	11	-	-	-	-	-
General	-	2	2	9	5	2	5	2	1

Table 7 shows more clearly the localised effect of these different frequencies. Each time we came back to 40 Hz we had a recurrence of the effect of this frequency on the legs, calves and thighs. 30 Hz is near enough to join this category of frequency effect. As the frequency range moved up through 50, 60 and 70 Hz, so the subjects consistently indicated that the localisation of the effect was further up their body, with typical experiences of 60 Hz being felt in the thoracic region, and 70 Hz in the upper chest and head.

There was a definite consistency in the effects felt at 50 Hz and at 40 Hz.

Table 7: Localisation of effect in percentages

Frequency	Localised area	%
40	Calves, thighs	77
50	Thighs, sacrum and lumbar	61.5
60	Sacrum, lumbar and thoracic	66.6
70	Lumbar, thoracic, cervical and shoulder	69.2
50	Thighs, sacrum, lumbar	59
40	Calves, thighs	77
30	Calves, thighs	74.3
20	Calves, thighs, sacrum, lumbar	79
40	Calves, thighs	77

Discussion

At each frequency, a significant proportion of the subjects felt a localised effect. There was a definite correlation between the frequency of 40 Hz and its effect on the calves and thighs. 50 Hz was also localised at a highly significant level among all the subjects in the thighs and sacrum. 60 Hz and 70 Hz showed a less significant localised effect, and nine subjects found 70 Hz giving them a general overall effect. Nearly half of the subject group experienced 60 Hz most strongly in their thoracic area, and 30 Hz was typically felt in the legs. Some subjects reported quite unusual sensations to 20 Hz. In fact, subjects often found it quite a different sensation from the other range of frequencies, a very unusual overall vibration, which some of the subjects did not find particularly pleasant. This supports evidence that extremely low frequencies, from 23 Hz downwards, can cause feelings of nausea or mildly unpleasant physical sensations, and should be avoided.

As a pilot study, this gives some interesting evidence supporting the theory that the body is receptive and resonant to individual frequencies, a theory which has grown out of empirical studies undertaken with vibroacoustic therapy. There are some areas of the design of this study which need to be considered in the next evaluation of the localised effect of low frequency sound. Firstly, more data needs to be taken on subjects involved, including their age, weight and height. Although this data was not taken in this study, we were interested that the overall effect seemed to be consistent across subjects despite differences in weight, which may indicate that the effect is the same, irrespective of body mass and proportion of fat tissue to muscle.

Secondly, in a subsequent study it would be important, in order to control for order effects, to randomise the sequence in which the frequencies are played. One could produce three or four tapes with the frequencies in four different orders. Using cassette tapes would also ensure a tighter control over the variables that may have been present due to individual differences in the way the frequencies were presented - in particular the amount of time allowed on each frequency was not totally uniform each time the trials were done.

Thirdly, factors such as the resonant frequency of the room and the resonant frequency of the equipment need to be taken into consideration to identify any exaggerated power effect at specific frequencies.

However, the study seems to support the growing evidence that frequencies are specific and can be used specifically to focus on particular areas of the body, and further studies replicating this particular study are already underway.

General conclusion

This chapter has tried to give a general overview of the diversity and current application of vibroacoustic therapy, as well as advancing some quite detailed theoretical points relating to the effect of vibration on brain and muscle tissue. To the critical observer, there is no doubt much in the anecdotal and the research material that is open to analysis and criticism. The questions most commonly posed by people experiencing or observing this treatment for the first time are related to the amount of time the treatment lasts in terms of its effect, and whether the treatment achieves anything significantly more effective than lying on a unit and relaxing without having music and low frequency sound, or perhaps having music alone. Some studies (Wigram and Weekes) have been undertaken to examine the effect of this treatment against a placebo, and further studies are at present underway. However, more sustained and extensive research needs to be undertaken to support the evidence that already exists that there is some significant effect.

Insofar as this treatment is perceived as part of music therapy, it is perhaps another resource or technique of effective applications that can be placed alongside the present range of quite diverse applications. There is no doubt that in more conventional music therapy work where, through the medium of instrumental improvisation an engagement with a client and a relationship with a client is built up, the physical effect of the sounds created on both the client and the therapist must be seriously taken into consideration, and are sometimes not given enough emphasis. While most of the music therapist's attention is focused on the elements of client therapist interaction that indicate the nature of the relationship and the nature of the client's response, the way in which sound waves can physically effect an individual are a highly relevant component of the therapeutic process.

This treatment is passive, and although it still requires a relationship between the therapist and the client at the beginning and at the end, the therapeutic effect is generated from the low frequency sound and the music alone, rather than anything the therapist does. However, its potential is not only that of a treatment in itself, but also a pre-treatment. There is already evidence that the nature of the relaxation that occurs is enormously valuable in preparing clients with muscular difficulties for subsequent treatment of a more physical nature, and there is further evidence that clients with emotional problems and anxiety relax to the extent that they find is easy and often necessary to talk with the therapist after a treatment period.

This chapter has attempted to summarise some of the detailed material that already exists in this area, and has gone some way to covering the area of vibroacoustic therapy which has largely grown up over the last eleven years due to the imagination and innovative approach of Olav Skille, and the subsequent efforts of a small group of researchers.

3

The Effects of Consistent Tempi and Physiologically Interactive Tempi[1] on Heart Rate and EMG Responses

Bruce Saperston

Trends In Music-Based Physiological Research

Although numerous studies throughout the past century have explored the effects of music on a variety of physiological responses, comprehensive reviews of these investigations have demonstrated that little has been established regarding such phenomena (Dainow, 1977; Hodges, 1980). Hodges analysed existing research findings with respect to whether music which was categorised as stimulating or sedative according to Gaston's (1951) definitions influenced various physiological parameters in a predictable manner. Hodges discovered that research findings were inconsistent and concluded that while music does appear to influence physiological responses 'the data do not show clear support for the nature of this influence' (p. 396).

During the past 15 years, researchers interested in human response to music have somewhat abandoned studies in which music and physiological responses were employed as the only variables. Instead, new areas of inquiry have evolved, primarily related to the utility of musical stimuli in reducing stress. These studies have utilised either music alone or music in conjunction with various behavioural medicine techniques as the independent variables, while dependent variables have included psychological measures of anxiety as well as physiological responses.

Research in which both psychological measures of anxiety and physiological measures were studied demonstrated that exposure to music resulted in significant reductions in A-State Anxiety Inventory Scores (Jellison, 1975; O'Connell, 1984) and notable reductions in stress as evidenced by verbal reports (Hanser et al., 1982). However, no concomitant decreases were observed in the various physiological parameters measured during these investigations (e.g. pulse rate, blood pressure, muscle tension, galvanic skin response). More recently, Davis and Thaut (1989) assessed the effects of subjects' preferred music for relaxation on psychological and physiological measures of anxiety. Their findings were consistent with those of previous investigators; state anxiety was significantly reduced while reductions in physiological responses were not observed.

---

[1] A patent has been issued for Dr Saperston's 'Physiologically Interactive Music', US Patent No 5,267,942.

The emergence and expansion of the field of behavioural medicine in the 1970s generated new research paradigms germane to the influence of music on physiological processes. Behavioural medicine is 'a broad field that deals with the application of behavioural science knowledge and techniques to problems related to physical health' (Weiss and Billings, 1988, p. 574). Researchers began to explore the effects of music when it was presented in conjunction with behavioural medicine techniques including imagery, biofeedback training, and relaxation procedures. Music and imagery research has demonstrated that music is effective in stimulating imagery (Peach, 1984; Quittner, 1980), intensifying feelings experienced during imagery (McKinney, 1990), and enhancing perceived levels of relaxation (Peach, 1984). Relevant to physiological parameters, researchers have found that music facilitates more relaxed skin temperature responses when combined with imagery (Peach, 1984) and relaxation procedures (Kibler and Rider, 1983), and more relaxed levels of muscle tension when combined with EMG biofeedback techniques (Scartelli, 1982, 1984). Rider (1985) demonstrated that music combined with relaxation and imagery procedures resulted in significant electromyographic EMG reductions in a group of spinal pain patients.

Authors of music-based behavioural medicine strategies have reported that musical stimuli can also be utilised in assisting individuals to improve their performance of behavioural medicine techniques. Clark et al. (1981) and Saperston (1989) used music to control rhythmic and deep breathing, focus attention, and reinforce participation during relaxation procedures. Saperston (1989) reported the use of music in helping clients with cognitive deficits to remember relaxation instructions.

Research during the past 15 years has therefore indicated that music can be useful in altering perceived levels of anxiety, and, when combined with behavioural medicine techniques, can facilitate more relaxed physiological responses. In addition, other contemporary studies have provided evidence that music and/or music-based behavioural medicine strategies can influence biological changes. Goldstein (1980) reported that thrill responses elicited by listening to music may influence endorphin production. Rider et al., (1985) found that a treatment consisting of music, imagery, and progressive muscle relaxation resulted in the re-entrainment of body temperature and corticosteroid circadian rhythms.

Tsao et al., (1991) studied the effects of music alone, imagery alone, and music and imagery combined on an immune response (i.e. secretory Ig-A) in university students. The music condition and the imagery condition each resulted in significant S-Ig A increases, while the no treatment control condition elicited a significant S-Ig A decrease. Somewhat surprising was the finding that the treatment combining music and imagery did not result in a significant S-Ig A increase. An explanation provided for this finding was that it was possible that the music and imagery as a combined stimulus were not complementary.

Collectively, the existing body of research clearly demonstrates that music can serve significant functions in newly emerging clinical models designed to meet a variety of mental and physical health needs. However, the fact remains that the role of the professional music therapist in contemporary treatment models would be greatly enhanced if it could be determined that specific types of music or methods for presenting music would alter physiological responses in a predictable manner. While the argument exists that the literature is already replete with studies which provide evidence that music listening alone will not predictably influence physiological responding, there is support for a rationale which indicates that an abandonment of such studies may be premature at this time.

A Rationale for Further Physiological Research

The pursuance of additional music listening based physiological studies is supported by three factors. First, methodological problems associated with much of the previous physiological research indicates that attempts to combine these findings in the formulation of meaningful conclusions are questionable. Secondly, the emergence of new technologies provides contemporary researchers with various means for circumventing previous methodological problems associated with the systematic presentation of musical stimuli and the reliable measurement of physiological responses. Thirdly, most previous studies have utilised musical selections in a traditional manner by presenting pieces as they were originally composed to meet the artistic and aesthetic needs of the performers and listeners. New methods for presenting music to influence physiological responding have not been fully addressed. Each of these three factors will be discussed prior to a delineation of the purposes of the present investigation.

Previous Methodological Problems

Dainow (1977) and Hodges (1980) authors of comprehensive reviews, have reported consistent conclusions regarding the methodological problems associated with previous physiological studies. One of the problems noted by these reviewers concerned the musical stimuli utilised as the independent variables. The independent variables in previous research have been categorised (either by the investigators or by reviewers) according to Gaston's (1951) definitions. Gaston stated that stimulating music 'is based on such elements as strong rhythms, volume, cacophony, and detached notes' while 'sedative music is of a sustained melodic nature, with strong rhythmic and percussive elements largely lacking' (p. 143). Musical selections are highly complex stimuli comprised of various elements (e.g. timbre, tempo, rhythm, meter, etc.) as well as various styles and instrumental combinations.

Dainow (1977) recommended that 'future research should consider some standardisation of musical stimuli' (p. 217), and Hodges (1980) concluded that 'the definitions of stimulating and sedative music may be too general and not allow for a clear enough distinction between two kinds of music' (p. 396).

The conclusion that Gaston's definitions may be too general for experimental purposes can be corroborated by the diverse musical stimuli which have been grouped together according to these definitions. Heart rate studies in which bongo drum solos (Shatin, 1957), recurring 60-cycle tones (Lovell and Morgan, 1942) and metronomic clicks (Johnson and Trawick, 1938) were employed as independent variables, have been included in reviews of the effects of stimulating and sedative music (Dainow, 1977; Hodges, 1980). Other frequently cited heart rate studies have compared the effects of musical stimuli which differed greatly along various dimensions (i.e. elements, style, orchestration). Such studies have compared Sousa marches with classical selections (Coutts, 1965; Washco, 1948), jazz with classical selections (Ellis and Brighouse, 1952; Gilliland and Moore, 1924) , and classical with baroque selections (De Jong et al., 1973; Zimny and Weidenfeller, 1963). In order to ascertain whether music can affect predictable alterations in specific physiological responses, research is needed in which the individual components of musical stimuli are systematically controlled.

Another methodological problem noted by Dainow (1977) and Hodges (1980) concerned the quality of the measurement techniques used in previous physiological studies. As these studies have spanned several decades, the methods employed in measuring physiological responses have undergone considerable change. Germane to the present investigation, a more specific review of the heart rate/pulse rate literature clearly serves to illustrate this point. Researchers have used a variety of measurement techniques in measuring heart rate/pulse rate including an electroencephalogram (EEG) connected to the wrist (Johnson and Trawick, 1938), manual pulse rate (Shatin, 1957), electrodes placed on the chest and attached to a telemetric transmitter (Barger, 1979) , and a photoelectric cardiotachometer attached to the earlobe (Zimny and Weidenfeller, 1963). The diversity of these measurement techniques and the obtrusive nature of the earlier approaches have yielded findings which, in some cases, may be unreliable, inaccurate, and difficult to generalise. As it would not be appropriate to compare the results of more contemporary studies with those of older studies, no firm conclusions can be made from the existing body of research.

The final methodological problem for discussion relates to the variation in quality of the reproduction equipment used in presenting musical stimuli during physiological investigations. No studies or reviews were found which specifically addressed this issue. Across the decades a wide variety of reproduction equipment has been used in heart rate/pulse rate studies including monaural earphones (Johnson and Trawick, 1938), tape recordings presented through a television speaker (Shatin, 1957), 12-inch records played on a high-fidelity phonograph (Ellis and Brighouse, 1952) and tape recordings presented through stereophonic headphones (De Jong et al., 1973). The variability between the reproduction equipment employed from study to study suggests that subjects have been exposed to qualitatively different stimuli.

The methodological problems previously discussed provide evidence as to why the body of existing research has yielded highly discrepant findings. The need exists for new investigations in which these methodological problems are addressed.

Technological Solutions

Recent technological advancements provide the contemporary researcher with new means for overcoming the methodological problems associated with previous studies. For example, the need for research in which the individual components of musical stimuli are systematically controlled could be addressed through the utilisation of synthesised music. While the use of synthesised music would have been questioned from an aesthetic perspective a few years ago, such a contention would receive little support today, largely due to two factors. First, synthesised musical sounds have undergone vast qualitative changes in recent years. Secondly, contemporary society has been conditioned to synthesised music through repeated exposure to these sounds in popular music recordings and motion picture and television soundtracks.

Synthesised music provides researchers with the capacity to alter one element of music (e.g. tempo, timbre, rhythm, etc.) while holding other elements constant. Such investigations could lead to information which might be useful in formulating more precise definitions of sedative and stimulating music and/or in developing individualised music-listening profiles for prescribing certain types of music to alter the physiological responses of specific clients. In addition, synthesised music could be used in developing new models for presenting music to alter physiological responding, such as the physiologically interactive music' model presented and researched in the present investigation.

Other technological advances, including less obtrusive physiological instrumentation, computer programs designed to record physiological data automatically and reliably, and high quality musical reproduction equipment serve to eliminate many of the methodological problems encountered in earlier studies. An abandonment of music listening based physiological studies would be unfortunate until more investigations are implemented in which state-of-the-art technologies are employed and new models for presenting musical stimuli are more thoroughly explored.

Special Methods of Presenting Musical Stimuli

Most researchers interested in physiological responses to music have presented musical selections in a traditional manner. Research is generally lacking relevant to special methods for presenting musical stimuli to influence physiological responding. Two such methods will now be addressed. First, the 'iso-moodic' principle will be discussed with regard to its utility in altering physiological responses. Secondly, an explanation of physiologically interactive music, an hypothesised approach to be tested in the present investigation, will be provided.

The Iso-Moodic Principle

The iso-moodic or 'iso' principle was originally developed by Altshuler (1948) to alter the moods of psychiatric patients. The iso principle refers to matching musical stimuli to an individual's existing mood and then changing the musical stimuli in the direction in which the individual's mood is to be influenced (Altshuler). Early research demonstrated that this approach was effective with both psychotic and normal subjects (Altshuler, 1948; Orton, 1953).

More recent studies have indicated that use of the iso principle may also affect physiological changes. Rider (1985) presented various styles of music (i.e. minimalist, jazz, impressionistic entrainment, preferred music) along with a progressive muscle relaxation induction and imagery script in a randomised counter-balanced design to spinal cord injury patients. A no music condition was incorporated within the design. Rider's 'entrainment' music was based on the iso principle and exhibited a mood shift from unpleasant to pleasant. According to Rider, 'the rhythm of the unpleasant section was in an accelerating 7/8 meter, while that of the pleasant melodic section was in a comfortable 4/4 meter (andante)' (p. 186). Findings demonstrated that the iso-moodically based entrainment music was the most effective in reducing muscle tension (EMG activity), although three of the other four music conditions (minimalist, jazz, preferred music) and the no music condition resulted in significant EMG reductions.

Pignatiello et al. (1989) recently developed a 'musical mood induction technique' in which music was presented to influence three mood states; neutral, elated and depressed. The iso principle was utilised in presenting music to elicit the elated and depressed mood responses. Findings demonstrated that the three types of mood music elicited significantly different systolic blood pressure responses (p<.05), with means of +9.6%, +0.9%, and -4.4% for the elated, neutral, and depressed groups respectively. Although heart rate differences were nonsignificant, the elated and neutral music groups demonstrated increases in heart rate responses while the depressed music group experienced heart rate decreases. Pignatiello et al., attributed the bi-directional heart rate and systolic blood pressure responses to the musical elements of tempo and rhythm in the iso-based musical selections.

Saperston (1989) presented a music-based stress reduction model which incorporated the iso principle in teaching clients to utilise psychophysiological control skills. Case study data were provided which demonstrated that a behaviourally disturbed mentally retarded client consistently achieved greater reductions in EMG activity when presented iso-structured music than when presented sedative music or no music.

Research is needed which both investigates the effects of iso-structured music on various physiological parameters, and explores new models for presenting musical stimuli in a more systematic manner within the iso model. The musical stimuli presented in previous iso-related studies have been sequenced in order to reflect a general shift in mood, not in physiological responding. While an interaction exists between emotional and physiological responses, perhaps musical stimuli presented in conjunction with a specific ongoing physiological response would result in a more direct influence over that physiological response.

The author has developed a model referred to as 'physiologically interactive music' to explore this possibility. As this model is based on Huygens phenomenon (entrainment) from the field of physics, a brief explanation of this phenomenon will precede a description of the physiologically interactive music model.

Huygens Phenomenon (Entrainment)

In a letter to his father in 1665, Christian Huygens, a Dutch scientist, reported that two pendulum clocks mounted on the same bracket could pull each other into synchrony (Pippard, 1978). Huygens' subsequent investigations of this phenomenon resulted in the first explanation of what contemporary scientists call 'entrainment'. For a simple definition, entrainment is 'the locking into phase of previously out-of-step oscillators' (Halpern, 1978, p. 4). An 'oscillator' is 'anything that vibrates in a regular, periodic manner between two points of rest' (Halpern, p. 4). According to Leonard (1978) this phenomenon is universal.

> *Whenever two or more oscillators in the same field are pulsing at nearly the same time, they tend to lock in so that they are pulsing at exactly the same time. The reason, simply stated, is that nature seeks the most efficient energy state, and it takes less energy to pulse in co-operation than in opposition (p. 12).*

Leonard (1978) provided a common example of entrainment in describing what occurs when one adjusts the vertical or horizontal knobs on a television set.

> *When you turn the knobs, you're adjusting the frequency of your set's oscillators to match the frequency of the station's oscillators. Fortunately, you don't have to create a perfect match. When the frequencies come close to one another, they suddenly lock, as if they 'want' to pulse together (p. 13).*

It is important to note that, in order for entrainment to occur, it is essential that the two oscillators are pulsing at nearly the same time. This critical range within which oscillations must occur for entrainment to take place has been described in the fields of physics (Pippard, 1978) and physiology (Wever, 1979).

Entrainment mechanisms have been identified and researched in various disciplines including physiology (Minors and Waterhouse, 1981) psychology (Brown and Graeber, 1982) and music therapy (Rider et al., 1985). Physiological studies have largely dealt with 'circadian rhythms' which have been defined as 'relating to biological variations or rhythms with a period of 24+/-4 hours' (Minors and Waterhouse, 1981, p. 320). Physiological responses which change in a circadian rhythm include body temperature, adrenal hormones, blood pressure, blood sugar, and concentrations of essential biochemicals throughout the nervous system (Luce, 1971). Relevant to circadian rhythms, entrainment has been defined as 'the coupling of a biological self-sustained (endogenously generated) rhythm with an external rhythm (Zeitgeber), with the result that both rhythms run synchronously with the same period' (Minors and Waterhouse, 1981, p. 321).

Sometimes physiological processes which are normally entrained begin to exhibit changing time relationships. This results in states of 'external' or internal desynchronisation. External desynchronisation occurs 'when a biological rhythm persists with a period different from that of an environmental time cue' while internal desynchronisation is present 'when different biological rhythms within one organism or different components of the same biological rhythm, exhibit different periods' (Brown and Graeber, 1982, p. 461). Physiological studies of entrainment have demonstrated that states of desynchronisation may be indicative of physical health-related problems (Luce, 1971; Minors and Waterhouse, 1981) and psychological studies have reported that desynchronisation can affect task performance (Graeber, 1982; Wever, 1979; Wilkinson, 1982), and the behaviours of individuals with affective mental disorders (Wehr, 1982).

The re-entrainment of desynchronised circadian rhythms through the use of a music-based behavioural medicine strategy was studied by Rider et al. (1985). These researchers reported that a treatment comprised of music, progressive muscle relaxation, and imagery resulted in the re-entrainment of corticosteroid and body temperature circadian rhythms.

In a subsequent study, Rider (1985) again employed music, progressive muscle relaxation, and imagery to influence the pain perceptions and EMG responses of spinal cord injury patients. One type of music utilised in this study was referred to as 'entrainment music.' For the purpose of clarification, Rider's entrainment music (described earlier in this chapter under 'The Iso-Moodic Principle'), should not be confused with the physiologically interactive music model which is also based on the entrainment concept.

Physiologically Interactive Music

Both musical stimuli and physiological responses are comprised of vibrations which occur in a regular, periodic manner. Therefore, musical stimuli and physiological responses consist of oscillations. Given that entrainment is 'the locking into phase of previously out-of-step oscillators' (Halpern, 1978, p. 4), it is possible that musical stimuli could be systematically presented as a synchroniser (zeitgeber) to influence predictable changes in physiological responses through entrainment.

Only a few studies were found which investigated the utility of auditory or musical stimuli in entraining physiological responses. However, all of these studies demonstrated that such stimuli did entrain physiological parameters. Lovell and Morgan (1942) found that respiration rates approximated the rates of a regularly recurring tone, while a more recent study at the New York University School of Medicine (Hass et al., 1986) demonstrated that the respiratory patterns of a majority of subjects could be entrained by pre-recorded rhythmic music. Bason and Celler (1972) reported that subjects' heart rates were entrained through the presentation of audible clicks at a precise time in the cardiac cycle measured from each R-wave of subjects' ECGs.

No studies were found in which music was systematically manipulated in relation to ongoing physiological responses in order to entrain such responses. The physiologically interactive music model was developed by the author to provide a basis for such research.

Physiologically interactive music is an hypothesised approach in which one or more elements of music (or combinations of the same element of music) are continuously presented in a systematic relationship to an organismic rhythm within the periodicity limits necessary for entraining the organismic rhythm. As the organismic rhythm changes, either in the desired direction (i.e. towards the musical synchroniser) or away from the synchroniser, the musical synchroniser is again presented within the new periodicity limits necessary for entrainment. The process is repeated in a continuous manner.

The process is 'interactive' because of the hypothesised interdependent relationship which is set up between the musical stimuli and the physiological response, An example of this approach would be the use of 'physiologically interactive tempi' (PIT) in altering heart rate. First, the tempo of the music is dependent upon the heart rate, as the music is presented at a tempo just under the heart rate. Secondly, if the tempo is within the periodicity limits necessary for entrainment, the heart rate is influenced by the tempo. Thirdly, the tempo is once again influenced by the heart rate, as it is presented just under the new heart rate.

Summary and Statement of Purpose

The information presented thus far has established two basic needs relevant to music listening based physiological research. First, there is a need to investigate the effects of musical stimuli in a more systematic manner in order to ascertain whether such stimuli can affect predictable changes in various physiological parameters. Secondly, there is a need to explore new models for presenting musical stimuli which may be useful in predictably altering physiological responses. The present study was designed to address both of these needs.

The primary purpose of this study was to assess the effects of one element of music, tempo, on two physiological responses (i.e. heart rate and EMG). Synthesised music was utilised so that subjects in each of two experimental groups could be presented music which was identical in all respects (i.e. elements, style, orchestration) except for tempo. One group was presented music at a slow consistent tempo (M.M. = 48) while the other group listened to music at a faster consistent tempo (M.M. = 86).

The secondary purpose of this study was to investigate the efficacy of an approach for presenting musical stimuli to influence physiological response based on Huygens phenomenon (entrainment) and referred to by the author as physiologically interactive music. Subjects in a third experimental group listened to the same synthesised music presented to the subjects in the two consistent tempo groups, with the exception that this music was presented using physiologically interactive tempi (PIT). Therefore, each subject in this group was continuously presented music at tempi approximately one beat below their ongoing heart rates in an attempt to entrain and/or influence their heart rates.

Physiological data were automatically recorded for the subjects in the three music listening groups and a no music control group.

Two experimental hypotheses were tested in this study. Each hypothesis stated that there would be no significant treatment effects for heart rate (Hypothesis 1) and EMG (Hypothesis 2).

Method

Subjects and Groups

Sixty-four undergraduate students (32 males and 32 females; mean age = 21.7 years) from two general education music classes and one sociology class at Utah State University served as subjects. Two hundred and twenty-four students originally volunteered to participate in the study. Each of these students completed a questionnaire designed to determine whether previous musical training or current physically related problems would preclude their participation. As musicians may respond differently from nonmusicians to musical stimuli (Hodges, 1980), only non musicians were eligible to serve as subjects. Non musicians were defined as individuals who had not received formal music training and/or had not actively performed music after the eighth grade.

Ninety-eight students were deleted from the original pool due to prior musical training and three students were deleted due to physical problems (i.e. heart disease, hearing impairment, and a nervous system disorder). The remaining 123 volunteers provided the pool from which 64 subjects were randomly assigned to one of four experimental groups: tempo 1, tempo 2, physiologically interactive tempi (PIT), and a no music control. Each group was comprised of eight males and eight females (n = 16).

The initial questionnaire was also designed to obtain information relevant to each subject's music preferences. While it was necessary to determine each subject's style preference for relaxation music, care was taken not to sensitise the subjects to the purposes of the study. Therefore, other extraneous music preference items were included on the questionnaire.

Baroque music was employed in this study. As subjects' music preferences can affect their psychological responses to music (Stratton and Zalanowski, 1984), it was necessary to have an equal number of subjects in each group whose preferred relaxation music was of a classical nature. The group assignments of 6 of the 64 subjects were adjusted to create this balance (i.e. five subjects with a classical preference in each group).

Independent Variables

All of the subjects in the three music listening groups (i.e., tempo 1, tempo 2, PIT) listened to the same Bach Three-Part Inventions (Sinfonias) presented in the same sequence (Numbers 8, 1, 12, and 14). Each invention was repeated once before the next invention was begun. The selections were recorded using a Kawai K-1 Digital Synthesiser and an Alesis MMT-8 Multitrack MIDI Sequencer Recorder. The music was slightly altered, as an additional quarter note bass part was provided one octave beneath the original bass part in order to create a consistent pulse pattern.

The musical selections were presented to the subjects using the aforementioned synthesiser equipment amplified through a Yamaha A460 Amplifier. Subjects listened to the music through stereophonic headphones (Sennhieser, HO-450). All music was presented using the 'piano 2' pre-setting on the synthesiser to control timbre. The volume controls on the synthesiser and amplifier were taped in a fixed position to control the intensity of the music presentations. The intensity levels of the presentations ranged from 68 to 82 dBs (Realistic Sound Level Meter No. 33-2050).

All subjects were presented with nine minutes of music. The tempo 1 group listened to music at a slow consistent tempo (M.M. = 48) and the tempo 2 group was presented music at a faster consistent tempo (M.M. = 86) . The PIT subjects were presented music at tempi approximately one beat below their ongoing heart rates which required special procedures.

PIT Implementation Procedures

The process of presenting the PIT music required an experimenter to manipulate tempo changes manually throughout each musical presentation for each subject. The ongoing tempi of the music were adjusted through the use of the Alesis MIDI Recorder (AMR). The AMR provided a digital display of the tempo in whole number beats per minute (e.g. 62, 63, etc.). In order to change the tempo, an experimenter would depress a 'tempo' button and simultaneously depress either a 'plus' or 'minus' button which would rapidly increase or decrease the tempo.

The heart rate instrument (Thought Technology, HR 101 T) was positioned on the AMR so that the digital displays of heart rate (HR) and tempo were only 6.3 centimetres apart. This permitted the experimenter to monitor both digital displays simultaneously. The HR display was provided in tenths of a beat (e.g., 71.4). The experimenter adjusted the tempo in whole number increments one beat below the whole number HR reading. Therefore, while the PIT condition was described as music presented approximately one beat below ongoing HR, the difference between tempo and HR could range from 1 to 1.9 beats.

This manual process was easier to employ than was first anticipated. While normal HR activity manifests beat by beat changes which would have been difficult to follow (i.e. 62.4, 66.3, 61.2, etc.), the HR 101 T was designed to smooth out HR data by providing moment by moment (about every half-second) readings based on 3-second averages. Therefore, HR data were presented in a more linear manner (i.e. 62.3, 62.5, 62.8, 63.1, etc.). The experimenter could anticipate tempo increases and decreases by monitoring the direction of the HR changes in tenths of a beat prior to changing the tempo to one whole number beneath the HR reading.

PIT Reliability Procedures

Reliability procedures were implemented to determine the efficacy of the manual PIT approach prior to the onset of the experimental sessions. The experimenter for all PIT sessions was initially provided with five 30-minute practice sessions in which no reliability data were recorded. Following these practice sessions, the experimenter began to conduct pre-study PIT sessions in which reliability data were recorded.

Reliability data were recorded by videotaping the HR and AMR digital displays during the pre-study sessions. A Quasar Newvicon VHS videocamera was utilised. The videotapes were then transformed to a slower speed (i.e. from SP to EP), which enabled independent observers to create clear still frames of the digital displays when the 'pause' button of a videocassette recorder (VCR) was depressed.

Reliabilities were computed through a random sampling microanalysis type of technique. An independent observer was seated in front of a VCR (Hitachi, No. VT-71A) and video monitor. The videotaped session data had already been placed on pause so that the first HR and tempo displays of data were presented as a still frame on the monitor. The observer was instructed to depress the pause button two times in rapid succession without looking at the monitor. This resulted in the presentation of another still picture of the HR and tempo displays. If the tempo display was one beat below the HR whole number display an agreement tally was recorded. A frame in which the tempo display was not one beat beneath the HR reading was scored as a disagreement. The independent observer continued this process until the entire 9-minute videotaped session was observed.

Two independent observers followed these procedures in obtaining reliability data. Reliabilities (percent of agreement) were calculated by dividing the total number of agreements by the sum of the total number of agreements and disagreements for each session (Huck et al., 1974). An a priori criterion for percent of agreement was established as 85% for three consecutive pre-study simulation sessions.

Inter observer reliability ratings (average percent of agreements) for the first three pre-study sessions were 92%, 95%, and 92% respectively (range 90.5% to 95.6%) . Therefore, the pre-study criterion was reached during the first three pre-study sessions. The average number of observations per 9-minute session was 245 (range 222 to 273) or one observation on the average of every 2.2 seconds for 540 seconds.

In order to ensure the reliability of experimental data, periodic inter observer reliability checks were made every fourth session during the implementation of the PIT experimental sessions. These data are reported in the 'Results' section.

Dependent Variables

Heart rate and muscle tension (EMG) were the only dependent variables. A plethysmograph (Thought Technology, HR 101 T) was employed in measuring heart rate. Frontalis muscle responses were measured through the use of an EMG myograph (Autogenic Systems Inc., Autogen 1100). A biofeedback computer interface system (Bio-Track, RMX-1; Apple IIe computer) was utilised for data acquisition and computation purposes.

Setting

Sessions were conducted in a room (4.26 m x 4.87 m) with white walls and no decorations. A recliner was positioned in the centre of the room. The instrumentation used in the study (i.e. physiological instrumentation, computer, synthesiser, etc.) were positioned behind the recliner. The video camera used for reliability data was also positioned behind the recliner. Lighting in the room was moderate, as it was felt that either dim or bright lighting could influence subject responses. Some general office furnishings (i.e. file cabinets, bookshelves) were present.

Procedures

Each subject participated in an individual 30-minute session. Upon arrival, the subject was seated in the recliner in an upright position and was presented with a copy of the informed consent form. The consent form was carefully worded so that procedures were clearly delineated without sensitising the subject to the specific purposes of the investigation. The subject was informed that certain of his or her physiological responses were being measured while they listened to music. Each subject agreed to wait until the conclusion of the entire study before being informed of the specific physiological measures which were monitored. This procedure was considered necessary to ensure that subjects who had completed their sessions would not share this information with other subjects prior to their sessions.

Each subject was informed that the music preference information that they had provided on the initial questionnaire would be useful to the experimenter, but did not have a bearing on the music that they were to be presented with. The subject was informed that all subjects, with the exception of the control group subjects, would listen to the same musical selections.

Upon completion of the informed consent procedures the subject was placed in a reclining position. The HR receptor was attached to the subject's index finger (right hand) by slipping an elastic band around the finger. The subject's arms were placed comfortably on the arm rests of the recliner. The EMG electrode receptors were then attached to the subject's forehead (frontalis muscle) using Spectra 360 electrode gel. The procedures utilised for attaching the EMG electrodes and testing the quality of the electrode placements (impedance testing) were those detailed in the *Instruction Manual for the Autogen 1100* (Autogenic Systems Inc., 1975). The stereophonic headphones were then placed on the subject. Subjects in the no music control group also wore headphones.

The subject was asked to close his or her eyes and find a comfortable position. Once comfortable, the subject was asked to remain still and simply listen to the music when it was presented in another 6 minutes.

At this point of the session the subject had already been sitting in a reclining position for at least 5 minutes. Another 3-minute period of silence was now provided to ensure that the subject would achieve a resting HR prior to the acquisition of baseline data.

Physiological data (i.e. HR and EMG) were recorded during a 3-minute baseline period and three subsequent 3-minute periods comprising the 9-minute treatment condition for each subject. The Bio-Track computer programme calculated means for each dependent variable for each of the four 3-minute periods (i.e. baseline and the three 3-minute treatment periods).

Immediately following the 3-minute baseline period subjects in the tempo 1, tempo 2, and PIT groups were presented the appropriate nine minutes of music. Subjects in the control group sat in silence. One experimenter was present to monitor the session and to present the PIT music to subjects in that group.

Results

PIT Reliabilities
Periodic inter-observer reliability checks were made every fourth PIT session. The inter-observer reliability ratings (average percent of agreements) for these sessions were 91%, 94%, 95%, and 92% (range 90.3% to 99%). The average number of observations per 9-minute session was 216 (range 197 to 249) or one observation on the average of every 2.5 seconds for 540 seconds.

Heart Rate
Correlated tests were performed comparing baseline means with means from each of the three 3-minute periods comprising the 9-minute treatment conditions. This provided information relevant to the amount of HR change that occurred over time.

Data in Table 1 indicates that no significant differences in HR occurred during Period 1. However, the PIT group evidenced the greatest HR change, yielding the only value to approach a level of significance (p=.06). During Periods 2 and 3 (see Table 1) significant HR decreases were demonstrated by the PIT group (p<.001) and the control group (p<.05) with the greatest decreases occurring in the PIT group. The HRs of the tempo 1 (slower tempo) group decreased minimally and nonsignificantly while the HRs of the tempo 2 (faster tempo) group increased minimally and nonsignificantly during Periods 2 and 3.

Treatment effects were analysed for each of the three periods by performing a separate one-way analysis of variance (ANOVA) on the change of HR from baseline for each period. No significant treatment effects were observed in the ANOVA performed on Period 1 data (F=1.5; df=3,60; p=.22). An ANOVA examining Period 2 data revealed significant treatment effects (F=4.08; df=3,60; p=.01). Fisher's LSD test was utilised as a follow-up procedure to determine where significant between-group differences occurred. The LSD test determines whether groups are significantly different at the .05 level. Fisher's LSD test confirmed that the HR decreases demonstrated by the PIT group were significantly different (p<.05) from the HR responses of subjects from both the tempo 1 and tempo 2 groups during Period 2. The HR responses of the control group were significantly different (p<.05) from those of the tempo 2 (faster tempo) group.

Table l: Mean comparisons for heart rate (*p < .05 ** p < .001)

Group	Baseline	Period 1	Period 2	Period 3
No music				
M	64.2750	64.0500	63.1688	62.6688
SD	7.445	7.786	7.579	6.702
t	---	.43	2.38*	2.17*
Tempo 1				
M	67.7062	67.8687	67.6563	67.1375
SD	9.550	9.155	9.186	8.930
t	---	-.49	.10	.87
Tempo 2				
IT	61.5625	61.7313	61.8000	61.7125
SD	7.777	7.795	7.809	7.572
t	---	-.55	-.75	-.35
PIT				
M	65.2750	64.3688	63.7063	63.1500
SD	10.895	11.320	11.000	10.536
t	---	2.03	4. 40**	3. 89**

Significant treatment effects were also observed in the ANOVA performed on Period 3 data (F=2.87; df=3,60; p =.04). Fisher's LSD test demonstrated that HR data for the PIT group and the control group were each significantly different (p<.05) from the tempo 2 group's data but not from the tempo 1 group's data.

As significant treatment effects were substantiated for Period 2 and Period 3 data, Hypothesis 1, stated in the null form, was rejected. Descriptive data presented in Figure 1 shows the numbers of subjects in each experimental group that demonstrated HR increases and decreases, as well as the range of HR changes demonstrated within each group. These data indicate that the PIT condition was the most effective in eliciting HR decreases. Range data demonstrates that the greatest HR increase for a PIT subject was less than half of the greatest increases demonstrated by subjects in the other experimental groups. The greatest HR decrease for the PIT group was also notably below the greatest decreases demonstrated by subjects in the other groups.

EMG

Correlated t- tests were performed comparing baseline means with means from each of the three 3-minute periods. No significant differences in EMG were evidenced by any of the four groups during each of the three periods (see Table 2). During Period 1 the tempo 1 and tempo 2 groups demonstrated slight increases in EMG, while the PIT and control groups demonstrated slight decreases. The largest decrease occurred in the control group.

Data presented in Table 2 demonstrates small EMG decreases for all four groups during Period 2. The tempo 1 and tempo 2 groups decreased the least, while the PIT group demonstrated a decrease that was twice that of the control groups.

During Period 3, the tempo 1 and tempo 2 groups continued to evidence small decreases in EMG activity. The PIT group maintained the greatest decrease from baseline. The control group increased to a level that minimally exceeded baseline.

Table 2: Mean comparisons for EMG (microvolts)

Group	Baseline	Period 1	Period 2	Period 3
No Music				
M	1.9881	1.8713	1.8769	2.0613
SD	.627	.784	.815	1.271
t	---	1.14	.77	-.27
Tempo 1				
M	1.8750	1.9625	1.8431	1.7350
SD	.695	.657	.694	.797
t	---	-1.35	.39	.95
Tempo 2				
M	2.0950	2.0894	2.0319	1.9750
SD	.770	.796	.880	.994
t	---	.05	.64	.48
PIT				
M	2.0144	1.9350	1.7919	1.7963
SD	.534	.688	.679	.823
t	---	.89	1.73	1.21

Across all three periods, the control group demonstrated a slight non-significant increase in EMG and the three music groups demonstrated slight nonsignificant decreases in EMG. The PIT group's decrease was almost twice that of the other two music groups.

Treatment effects were analysed for each of the three periods by performing a separate ANOVA on the change of EMG from baseline for each period. No significant treatment effects were observed in data from Period 1 ($F=.94$; $df=3,60$; $p=.43$), Period 2 ($F=52$; $df=3,60$; $p=.67$), or Period 3 ($F=.32$; $df=3,60$; $p=81$); therefore, Hypothesis 2, stated in the null form, was accepted.

Figure 2 shows the numbers of subjects in each experimental group that demonstrated EMG increases and decreases and the range of EMG changes demonstrated within each group. These data indicate that all three music conditions elicited similar EMG responses, with 68.7% of the tempo 1 subjects and 75% of the tempo 2 and PIT subjects demonstrating decreases. Only 43.8% of the control group subjects demonstrated EMG decreases.

In comparing the EMG data from the present study with data from other investigations it is important to know that the microvolt readings of different manufacturers' EMG instruments are not equivalent. The microvolt readings from the Autogen 1100 utilised in the present study may seem somewhat low to individuals who are familiar with other EMG instruments. For data comparison purposes, EMG amplitude conversion information may either be obtained from the *Instruction Manual for the Autogen 1100* (Autogenic Systems Inc., 1975) or from the present investigator.

Discussion

The primary purpose of the present study was to provide an initial investigation into the effects of different consistent tempi on HR and EMG responses. The present findings appear to indicate that the same music presented at different rates of consistent tempi will not significantly alter HR and EMG responses in a predictable manner. However, these findings should only be considered with respect to certain limitations imposed by the present research methodology which include the particular musical selections presented, the specific tempi employed, and the duration of time over which responses were measured.

While results from this study clearly demonstrated that specific Bach Three-Part Inventions presented at a slow tempo (M.M.=48) and at a moderately rapid tempo (M.M.=86) did not significantly influence HR and EMG responses, it would not be valid to infer that the same results would be obtained with other musical selections. Such an inference would only serve to perpetuate the over-generalisations which have plagued this area of inquiry in the past. Musical selections are comprised of highly complex stimuli and it is possible that certain structural characteristics of the Three-Part Inventions employed were also responsible for the present findings. Hass et al. (1986) found that respiratory entrainment occurred less frequently with more complex rhythms. Perhaps the rapidly moving melodic lines of the Three-Part Inventions elicited responses which would have been different if less complex pieces had been presented. Additional tempo studies employing a variety of musical selections which differ in style and rhythmic complexity, are necessary before firm conclusions regarding the effects of tempo can be substantiated.

Responses were measured in the present study over three 3-minute periods in order to ascertain when physiological changes may have occurred during the 9-minute treatment phase. While future studies should continue to break down treatment phases in a similar manner, slightly longer overall treatment phases should also be considered.

The present study provided a preliminary investigation into the effects of consistent tempi upon the physiological responses of groups of subjects. However, individual differences in the response patterns of specific subjects were not explored. Thaut (1990) has proposed that each person may respond to a particular musical stimulus with an idiosyncratic but consistent physiological response, due to his or her own unique biological system.

Data presented in Figures 1 and 2 demonstrated that individual subjects in the present study responded differently to the same musical stimuli. For example, Figure 1 shows that, although a majority of subjects responded with increases and decreases in HR responses to the faster and slower tempo conditions respectively, several subjects' HR changes were in an inverse relationship to the specific tempo presented.

Figure 1: Baseline/Period 3 comparisons: number of subjects demonstrating heart rate (HR) increases, and decreases for each experimental condition. Ranges of HR changes were: Tempo 1: +3.7 to-5.0; Tempo 2: +3.6 to -2.7; PIT: +1.4 to -7.3; No music: +3.9 to -5.9

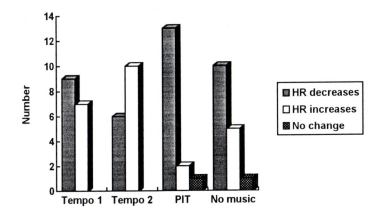

While the present study provided a necessary first step in investigating the possibility of a more universal type of response to one element of music, future studies should be designed to ascertain whether individual subjects would continue to respond in the same idiosyncratic manner to the same element(s) of music. A series of studies which systematically explores the physiological responses of individual subjects to specific elements and combinations of elements of music might lead to the development of efficient methods for generating individualised music listening profiles. These profiles might then be utilised in prescribing particular musical stimuli to alter the physiological responses of specific individuals.

Figure 2: Baseline/Period 3 comparisons: Number of subjects demonstrating EMG increases, and decreases for each experimental condition. Ranges of EMG changes were: Tempo 1: +1.2 to 1.5; Tempo 2: +2.3 to -1.7; PIT: +1.9 to -1.2; No music: +3.3 to -1.6. EMG data are in microvolts

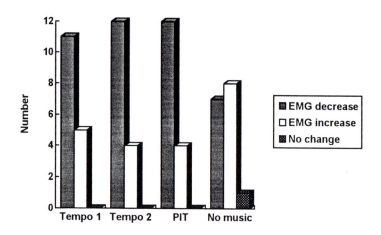

Many authors, including the present investigator, have noted that psychological factors probably play a role in physiological response to musical stimuli (Dainow, 1977; Hanser, 1985; Harrer and Harrer, 1977; Pignatiello et al., 1989; Saperston, 1989; Thaut, 1990). Precautions were taken in the present study to minimise the influence of psychological factors on subjects physiological responses. Obscure musical selections (for the 'non musician') were employed to reduce the possibility that musical stimuli would elicit prior associations. No psychological tests were utilised as dependent measures, as it was felt that such instruments would sensitise subjects to the nature of the study. Care was taken during the experimental sessions to ensure that the physical environment (e.g. lighting, room decor) and the instructions provided to subjects were devoid of cues relevant to how they were supposed to respond.

As subjects' music preferences have affected their psychological responses to music (Stratton and Zalanowski, 1984), this factor was addressed in the present study. An equal number of subjects preferring classically oriented relaxation music (i.e., five) were assigned to each of the experimental groups. This ensured that any significant differences between group data could not have been due to preference. However, it is possible that findings may have been different if all subjects had been exposed to their preferred music. Future research should attempt to address preferred music while systematically controlling the different elements of music.

Findings relevant to the primary purpose of this study have contributed initial data which, when combined with findings from future studies, might serve to substantiate conclusions regarding the role of one element of music in influencing physiological response. In addition, this study has offered methodological procedures which may be utilised as a model for future studies directed towards systematic music research. The more significant findings obtained during the investigation of the secondary purpose of this study will now be discussed.

The secondary purpose of this study was to assess the efficacy of the PIT approach in predictably influencing physiological response. Findings demonstrated that the PIT music elicited the earliest HR decreases and was the only music which elicited significant HR decreases ($p<.001$). Moreover, significant treatment effects ($p<.05$) were found for the PIT condition over both of the other music conditions during Period 2 and over the tempo 2 condition during Period 3. These findings appear to indicate that music presented according to the PIT model can predictably influence HR responses.

Although EMG findings for the PIT condition were non-significant, group mean data demonstrated that the PIT condition elicited decreases which were almost twice as great as the decreases elicited by the other music conditions. While this does not provide evidence that the PIT approach directed at HR influenced another physiological parameter, it does demonstrate that the PIT subjects manifested the most relaxed physiological responses in both parameters.

Future studies should continue to explore the effects of the PIT technique on physiological responses other than the primary response upon which the music is based. However, such studies should probably include physiological responses which are more closely related than HR and EMG (e.g. HR and respiration or blood pressure).

The fact that the control group also demonstrated significant HR reductions is not surprising and for several reasons does not minimise the PIT findings. First, PIT HR reductions were greater than those of the music condition during all time periods. Secondly, the no music condition actually resulted in EMG increases. Therefore, the PIT subjects demonstrated the best overall relaxation profiles. Thirdly, the PIT procedure was developed for future behavioural medicine applications with clients manifesting a variety of psychological disorders including anxiety and cognitive deficits. The present study was designed to obtain normative data prior to implementing PIT procedures with these various client populations. While normal subjects would be expected to demonstrate decreases in HR responses when reclining in silence, this may not be the case for subjects with various psychological disorders.

Finally, research provided earlier in this chapter demonstrated that music can serve a variety of functions in enhancing the effectiveness of various behavioural medicine strategies. Some of these functions include stimulating imagery, intensifying feelings during imagery, altering perceived levels of relaxation, and facilitating more effective participation in biofeedback training. As music will continue to be presented within behavioural medicine paradigms for a variety of purposes, the present findings suggest that physiologically interactive music may be the best type of music for certain applications.

Future studies should address limitations inherent in the PIT procedures employed in the present study. While reliability data indicated that the manually-operated PIT procedures were efficient, there is no doubt that an automated approach would have been more desirable. The rationale for initially employing a manually-operated process as opposed to a computer-automated system was based on the expense required in the development of such a system. Due to the exploratory nature of the PIT technique, it was felt that data from a pilot study was first needed to provide indications as to whether the development of a computer-automated system would be justified.

The author is currently developing a computer-automated system with the help of bio-engineers. Such a system is essential in refining and expanding various aspects of the PIT and PIM models. Future studies will first address specific limitations inherent in the present investigation's PIT procedures. These limitations generally relate to defining the critical range or ranges within which a tempo must be presented to entrain HR.

Entrainment models from other disciplines have demonstrated that it is essential that oscillations occur within a specific range in order for entrainment to take place (Pippard, 1978; Wever, 1979). The PIT music in the present study ranged from 1 beat to 1.9 beats beneath HR. It is probable that entrainment only occurred periodically during the PIT condition. As the PIT music followed a subject's HR responses, it may have occasionally entered some critical range necessary for entrainment.

The computer-automated PIT system currently being developed will automatically present synthesised music at tempi within one-hundredth (.01) of a beat per minute in relation to the subject's HR. Future research will be directed towards determining whether a universal critical range exists for all subjects or whether each individual has his or her own critical range for HR entrainment.

During the present study it was essential for HR responses to be smoothed out, in order to utilise a manual process. As previously described, normal HR activity manifests beat-by-beat changes which would have been impossible to follow manually. The HR 101 T smoothed out HR data by providing moment-by-moment (about every half-second) readings based on 3-second averages. Reliability data and findings from the present study indicates that this type of process was effective. The use of computer-automated systems in future studies would allow researchers to use exact beat-by-beat ECG data as well as smoothed-out HR data.

It should also be noted that the music preference issue addressed earlier in this discussion should also receive some attention in future PIT studies. The fact that the subjects in the PIT group demonstrated significant HR reductions despite the fact that 68.75% of these subjects were not exposed to their preferred music indicates that preference may not be an important factor within the PIT model. However, it would be interesting to know if preferred music would enhance the PIT procedures.

While findings have provided evidence that the PIT model can predictably alter HR responses, these findings should only be considered as preliminary evidence. Future studies are necessary in order to validate and refine this model further. In addition, research is needed in which other elements of music are directed at other physiological systems within the physiologically interactive music model.

If the physiologically interactive music model continues to demonstrate its validity in future studies, it could be utilised in conjunction with a wide range of existing behavioural medicine applications designed for meeting the psychological and physical needs of various client populations. In addition, the need exists for special behavioural medicine strategies which could be implemented with individuals manifesting severe behavioural and cognitive deficits, such as the mentally retarded, dementia patients, and the severely emotionally disturbed. These individuals are frequently unable to benefit from more traditional approaches as a result of their cognitive and behavioural problems. Saperston (1989) has advocated the use of respondent techniques in helping such individuals achieve better states of relaxation, prior to the use of operant techniques directed at teaching these clients to perform relaxation skills more independently. The physiologically interactive music model may eventually provide a new means for these populations to experience more relaxed physiological states.

Section 2: Music Therapy in Psychiatry

4

Approaches to Music Therapy in Psychiatry with Specific Emphasis upon a Research Project with the Elderly Mentally Ill

Helen Odell-Miller

This chapter will give an overview of music therapy approaches in Great Britain and elsewhere, with a summary of historical perspectives in order to show how work in the Cambridge Mental Health Services fits into the field as a whole. Primarily, it will describe a research project carried out in the mid-1980s entitled 'An Investigation of the Effects of Music Therapy with Elderly Mentally Ill People' (EMI), and the conclusions and developments reached by me as therapist and researcher following the work.

The project was set up along scientific lines and caused me some struggle as it meant looking at the therapy work in a different way. It forced me to separate out different components of the therapy e.g. activity and observable behaviour. In retrospect, I feel that the research was justified, and hope the reader considers the discussion points raised at the very end of the chapter, which highlight the benefits and difficulties of carrying out such a project in music therapy.

Rationale for Project

Clinical experience in Cambridge had shown prior to this study, begun in 1982, that patients in the advanced stages of senile dementia could be treated effectively by music therapy. In particular, clinical aims such as increasing interaction, awareness, physical and mental stimulation, appeared to be fulfilled during music therapy group sessions. In addition, such responses seemed to have continued after the sessions.

In Great Britain, in the early 1980s the use of music therapy with this population was not widely documented. Work in this area was not one which therapists have specialised in and, therefore, there seemed a need for a systematic study of the subject. The primary aim of the research project was to investigate how effective music therapy is in achieving observable changes in behaviour during group sessions. These changes were systematically compared with those in reminiscence therapy sessions. Other aims of the project were to investigate the importance of frequency of sessions and to monitor effects after sessions.

It is recognised that many other processes which are not necessarily observable were taking place for clients, and that within the therapy, these interpersonal and intrapsychic phenomena were central to how the therapists/group members relationships developed. However, in the project, only observable components were considered for observation and measurement. This does not mean that other factors are any less important.

This chapter will hopefully show how, in the early 1980s, such an approach was necessary in order to enable the author and the profession to develop further and improve research ideas. The advantages and disadvantages of the approach will be discussed.

The chapter may also enable an understanding of the usefulness of a more scientific approach, thus addressing the resistance and hostility felt by many arts therapists described by Payne And Gilroy (1989) in a report of the First Arts Therapists Research Conference in Britain:-

'There was considerable resistance and hostility towards these scientific models which seemed to be perceived as methods that were quantitative, and which sought to reduce the elusive phenomena within the processes of the Arts Therapies to measurable characteristics that could produce finite answers'.

History and Background

Diversity of Approaches

The diversity of music therapy approaches both in Great Britain and elsewhere is such that it is important to spend time discussing some historical background and different approaches. Music therapy in the field of learning difficulties is more fully discussed elsewhere in a historical context (e.g. Bunt, 1985; Oldfield, 1986) and this chapter will concentrate on music therapy in psychiatry and specifically on recent trends. Music therapy with the elderly, particularly with the EMI population will be discussed in detail later in connection with the research project mentioned above.

Music therapists in Great Britain emphasise two main features of music therapy. These features are 'live music' and 'interaction with the therapist' (Odell, 1988). These points are emphasised because elsewhere there has been a trend towards the use of recorded music. In my opinion, this, by definition, cuts down the intensity of the interaction between patient and therapist, i.e. the relationship, and thus misses what I regard as a central key to the success of the treatment (see Odell, 1988; p.53). Dickens and Sharpe (1970) and Reinhardt (1982) describe the use of recorded music in group music therapy, and other recent examples following observations of American music therapists, are discussed elsewhere (Katsch and Fishman 1984; Odell, 1985; Bruscia, 1987). Others are critical of the use of recorded music in an explicit way (e.g. Priestley, 1975: p.15). Priestley writes 'to reach out only for records or cassettes is to cheat oneself of a profound inner experience of strengthening growth'. As early as the 1960s, Gaston writes in his book 'The therapist uses his speciality to focus the patient, and moves in the desired direction at the most suitable rate in both the activity and the relationship'. (Gaston, 1968). It is interesting that he does not specify what type of music is being used, but an interactive relationship is implied. Bruscia discusses improvisation styles in detail in his book, devoted entirely to the subject of improvisation (Bruscia, 1987).

Interaction and Relationships

The importance of an interactive relationship using music is borne out by paying attention to psychoanalytic theory and practice. Priestley (1975), Rudd (1980), and Feder and Feder (1981), pay such attention when discussing music therapy. Here, it is important to mention a third component within the musical interactive relationship - that of the inclusion of verbal material and links between music and meaning. These aspects are covered in the literature both by music therapists and others, but at the time of the study no conclusive overall theory of the links between music and other human elements in music therapy was developed (see Meyer, 1956; Noy, 1966; 1967). Katsh and Merle Fishmann use verbal material within Metaphoric Improvisation Therapy and see it as important in their Gestalt-based method. Priestley (1975) pays attention to analytic music therapy extensively, and also to counter transference specifically (Priestley, 1976).

The verbal element is of importance here. These anecdotal writings give some answers to theoretical questions posed about the meaning of music within music therapy, such as how much can be understood about a person through their music? Is there a symbolic language in music which can be built upon by music therapists? Storr (1976) and Ruud (1980), begin to discuss and ask such questions.

One answer to these theoretical arguments is optimistic and possibly contentious:- 'although sharing at times certain concepts and attitudes of the psychoanalysts, music therapy will eventually reach the stage when it will be able to step outside of existing models and orientations. It will be regarded as a unique discipline in its own right' (Bunt, 1985, p.50). Bunt, and others, will have more to say about this in this book.

At the time of setting up the research, it seemed that music therapy was involved in an oscillation in this country between theories built upon a more musical basis (e.g. Nordoff and Robbins, 1971) and those following other theoretical concepts (e.g. Priestley, 1975; 1976; Woodcock, 1987).

Musicianship and Improvisation

In Britain, music therapy has its roots in music, and as a result, concepts have developed through live musical methods where the music therapist is a skilled musician. This is of paramount importance (see Odell, 1988: p. 54), and as a result, improvisation has become the most prevalent element in the interaction between client and therapist in Britain. Elsewhere, and indeed in some areas in Britain, precomposed music is used as a predetermined concept (Bright, 1972). Precomposed music is used within improvisation, but what separates out difference in approach is whether the therapist adapts the music because of the therapeutic process, or expects the music to be adapted to by the patients involved in the process. Examples of the latter are found in many American articles about music therapy with the elderly, as shown later in this chapter.

Many therapists work on the basis that musical interactions and behaviour are a reflection of what is happening internally for the patient. Some would say that a patient's music is understood as a metaphor, (e.g. Katsh and Fishmann, 1984; Odell, 1985). However one interprets the sounds and music, it seems clear that in Britain music therapists respond to the patient's music by using music themselves, emphasising the need for skilled musicians to do the work.

This is illustrated by the following case summary:

'J' is a lady of 40 years old with a diagnosis of manic depression. In the past she has had several admissions to hospital, but for the last three years has not needed to be admitted. She lives at home and attends the Day Centre for treatment at particular times during the week, in addition to which she has a part time job. She chose to refer herself to the weekly music therapy group which is set up for those who feel they can benefit by using music as a means towards coping with various problems, and who do not find verbal ways of doing this easy or appropriate. She has had no previous musical ability or training, and her own job is hairdressing. During the two years of attending the present music therapy group, 'J' has often arrived looking angry, upset and feeling helpless. One of her main problems is of feeling worthless, and unable to assert herself. However, she has been able to use the session to explore how to deal with these feelings, particularly by unleashing angry feelings previously unexpressed. A pattern for her now is that she will be able to talk about what is worrying her after loud, often violent playing on the bass xylophone, drum or cymbal, where I support and encourage musically from the piano. Gradually, I have been able to withdraw my musical intervention for longer periods, and sometimes she can assert herself with no help from me or other group members. She has become more confident in herself by being able to lead with an instrument while others follow, thus feeling a sense of importance in a safe setting. This she has been able to use outside the group by finding she can now have the upper hand with her sons, who previously she has felt have had too much control over her (Odell, 1986). A later version of this case study is found in Odell (1988).

The music cannot, therefore, be predetermined or prescribed just as changes in the relationship cannot.

In *Music Therapy and Mental Health* (Scott, Odell and John, 1986), music therapists working in psychiatry defined music therapy as follows:

'Music therapy in the field of mental illness concentrates on the use of music as a means of communication and interaction, and can be defined as: 'The use of music as a means of communication to fulfil therapeutic aims for the patients or client.'

Music therapists work alongside other professionals in the multi-disciplinary team. Approaches vary according to the particular setting, treatment philosophy, client population and immediate patient needs. Emphasis is placed on the 'here and now', working on the principle that personal growth and development happen through meaningful interaction and socialisation. Sessions involve practical music-making for which previous musical ability is not necessary for the client, but imperative for the therapist.

Other chapters in this book will show how practice has developed further in psychiatry in Britain since 1986.

It should be clear from these definitions and the case study that understanding of the patients' music (i.e. what it might mean within the therapeutic relationship), leads to an understanding of what is important for the patient at the time of the session and subsequently in the continuing processes.

Procedure and Background for the Research

During the setting up of the project, a full literature search was carried out in the areas of music therapy, music therapy research, and care of EMI people. This is discussed fully in the thesis submitted for M.Phil., (Odell-Miller 1988), and will be briefly summarised here.

The following Case Study Summary (Scott, Odell, and John, 1986:) shows the authors' general approach in the early 1980s with a severely disturbed elderly man.

'H' was suffering from senile dementia, was hemiplegic as a result of a stroke and had lost the capacity to speak. He was referred to a group music therapy session as a result of becoming restless and aggressive on the ward, in order to help him express himself and communicate with others. At first he refused to play instruments, often becoming upset, but after six months of attending weekly sessions aiming to meet his needs through instrumental work, relaxation and movement, he began to beat the drum loudly in his own rhythm. The music therapist was able to support his playing by improvising on the piano during his drumming and gradually this led to 'H' playing rhythmically and musically with the rest of the group rather than in an opposing aggressive way.

The music therapy session enabled him to relax, sit for longer periods of time than usual, smile a great deal, release aggression and subsequently, as a result of being able to do this, express himself appropriately with others rather than against them. He became part of a group accepted and respected by others, although he could not speak. On the ward he showed less aggressive behaviour and appeared more relaxed for a short time after sessions.

This anecdotal account provides an important rationale for seeing patients in groups, so that feedback, listening, and sharing can be encouraged.

The music therapy of relevance, therefore, involves using live interactive methods where improvisation is used as a focus to make relationships with patients which are meaningful and which reflect their current states. The music therapist is a skilled musician, trained as a music therapist. Group work is the setting for the therapy, yet this approach has been dismissed by some music therapists as not suitable for the elderly mentally ill (e.g. Liederman, 1967; Bright, 1972; Alvin, 1975). The assumption seems to have been (contrary to this author's finding), that group work with the 'risks' of improvisation with the confused and disturbed elderly mentally ill will lead to chaos, or increase chaos already in existence. There seems to be little faith in the therapist having the therapeutic and musical skills to ensure a safe environment in which clinical aims can be reached and 'chaos' worked through.

Music Therapy Research

The wealth of music therapy research in the USA demonstrates some interesting work with EMI people. However, each study investigated showed that the music therapy approach was different to that taken by this author. For example there is emphasis upon the therapist 'teaching' and the patients learning (Schoenberger and Braswell, 1971; Palmer, 1977). Schoenberger and Braswell discuss patients sitting in rows learning instruments and there is no mention of improvisation or therapeutic process. Palmer describes teaching techniques for the elderly also, although the aims of the therapy resemble aims of music therapy treatment in Britain. For example, there is mention of 'restoring self-concepts' and 'building the ego'.

A similar pattern is found elsewhere (Shapiro, 1969). Aims here are to 're-motivate, re-vitalise, re-activate'. Words such as 'emotional release' are used and also the phrase 'feeling of accomplishment through a dynamic activating, rather than a mutual pacifying use of musical therapy.' It then, however, becomes clear that patients sit in rows and 'practice until they can do it well.' This would not be relevant within the approach taken in this study, because Shapiro's theory is one of teaching rather than therapy.

Others have found music to be effective with the elderly in systematic research projects (e.g. Cassity, 1976; Kartman, 1977; Riegler, 1980). However, none of these studies seemed to indicate relevance for the type of group music therapy treatment with the elderly mentally ill at Fulbourn Hospital at the time of setting up the study.

Riegler compares a reality orientation (RO) programme for geriatric patients with and without music. The music-based reality orientation group showed more improvement. However, the patients were able to be questioned before and after using questionnaires, indicating a more 'able' group than in this study.

Cassity and Kartmann talk about the music as an applied teaching aid and the patients' music as an accompaniment' to the therapist respectively. The latter immediately suggests that the patients are fitting in with the therapists' music rather than vice versa.

Australian author (Bright, 1972) discusses an approach using live music and some improvisation methods which are similar to those in this study, but the fact that these were not used with elderly people who are also mentally ill, was important in prompting the author to set up this study.

A survey of the British literature before 1986 showed no systematic documentation about music therapy with EMI people. The British Journal of Music Therapy had published four articles specifically about music therapy with the elderly since its inception in 1969. One was by Bright, 1972; one by an

American: (Greenbaum, 1970); one more about therapeutic music (Byrne, 1971); and one describes a general approach with the elderly (Allen, 1975). All are anecdotal studies of therapeutic programmes.

Priestley (1975) devotes two paragraphs out of her whole book to the elderly, and one of these showed the need for more work in this area.

'I would like to think that one day peripatetic music therapists would be employed to go round helping to light up the lives of some of these older members of society by giving them a form of expression in sound and words, adding dignity and purpose to their rich store of years and breaking down their isolation from the rest of the community.' (Priestley, 1975).

Some physiotherapists are beginning to discover the importance of working with music (Mason, 1978) and specifically with music therapists (Milligan, 1986) with the elderly mentally ill. The conclusions of Milligan and Pickett's work were that, although a scientific study could not back up the objective and subjective results, all their observations led them to believe that 'physiotherapy and music therapy is likely to motivate and mobilise the elderly severely mentally ill.'

Other music therapists have found that music therapy helps physical problems in areas of special need such as with Parkinson's disease and Huntington's chorea (Hoskyns, 1982; Cosgriff, 1986; Dawes, 1987) and since this study (Swallow and Sutton, 1993). These findings, although not specifically with EMI people, are relevant here because of the physical similarities in the resulting problems associated with senile dementia, e.g. loss of control of limbs, fast agitated movements, and general limitation of bodily movement. All these findings indicated that further investigation into specific music therapy treatment with the elderly mentally ill was necessary, and thus the author's research project was set up.

Rationale and Discussion on the Treatment of EMI People

A brief description of possible interventions prior to the study is now discussed. Many studies in Britain have shown that increased staff interaction with residents, or changes in seating arrangements increase the level of engagement of elderly patients, (e.g. Felce and Jenkins, 1979; Davies and Snaith, 1980). Whilst Davies and Snaith carried out an intervention study at meal times, others have concentrated on the introduction of other organised activities such as reality orientation, general activity programmes, reminiscence groups and gardening, (e.g. Brook et al., 1975; Felce and Jenkins, 1979). Felce and Jenkins comment that because staff intervention raised the level of engagement so much, it became apparent how low the levels of engagement were before the materials were introduced, and after members of staff had departed after clearing up materials. The study seems to indicate that the type of activity which takes place is not important; as a wide variety of activities were introduced.

Furthermore, studies indicate that levels of engagement are raised when indoor gardening activities are introduced. The longer-lasting effects of reality orientation have been investigated (e.g. Powell-Procter and Miller, 1982), and what emerges is that short amounts of group sessions do not change the behaviour of EMI people with dementia. However, Woods (1983) using a single case study design showed that verbal skills could be improved with more intensive sessions; and Holden and Woods (1982) show that many generalised changes can happen as a result of RO programmes which help ward settings move towards more human care attitudes in the care of the EMI people, whether or not there are definite signs of behavioural changes. These studies are important because they indicate that in an institution where there is little time for staff-patient interaction (often because of shortage of staff), any concentrated period of interaction raises levels of engagement such as awareness, stimulation and interaction. It is also important to note that most of these studies involve periods of activity rather than actual therapy sessions. This all implies that to find out what effect music therapy has with EMI people, it is important to compare it with another form of therapy rather than with no planned group at all, or activity. Reminiscence therapy was chosen as the form of treatment to be compared with music therapy.

In order to separate out the specific effects of music therapy, so that benefits could be attributed to music therapy rather than other factors such as a general group milieu or environmental conditions, a comparison seemed necessary using a traditional research methodology. A critical discussion of this research model will take place later in this chapter.

In summary, reminiscence therapy was chosen for comparison because it was an already researched successful form of treatment involving as many similar processes as music therapy in a group as possible, e.g. materials to handle, movement, speech. Choosing an already accepted and effective way of working with this population meant that any results would have more relevance and show more worthwhile conclusions than if a less recognised form of treatment had been chosen, such as Art Therapy or Dramatherapy.

Method

There were two parts to the study.

In Part I, eight reminiscence therapy and eight music therapy group sessions took place over a period of sixteen weeks. The same criteria were used to measure the impact of both treatments so that effects could be compared.

The main hypothesis in Part I was that elderly mentally ill people would show a greater level of engagement when they were seated in a circle with the music therapist and nurses, in a music therapy session, than they would when sitting in a circle with the music therapist and nurses talking with them, in a non-music therapy setting.

In order to test this, eight music therapy (MT) and eight reminiscence therapy (RT) sessions were held weekly, on Monday afternoons at the same time each week. These were held in random order so that any differences that were found could be validly attributed to treatment effects, rather than to any other factors (Edgington, 1980). The sessions took place in a special room on the ward. Observations were taken during all sessions, by a specially trained observer, who stood as unobtrusively as possible, recording type of engagement. The system worked so that the time sampling method never took longer than 45 minutes, which was the maximum time the therapy sessions lasted. The sessions, therefore, carried on without any intrusion or interference from the observer, the idea being that the therapists and group members were as unaware of the observer as possible.

In Part II, twelve weekly music therapy sessions took place in order to measure the cumulative effect of weekly music therapy. Also, measurements were taken 30 minutes after sessions on music therapy days, and at the same time on a day when no session had taken place; in order to determine whether there were any longer-lasting effects of music therapy. These will be called the 'after' sessions.

The two hypotheses in Part II were:-

(a) 'When participating in a block of 12 music therapy sessions, EMI people would show a greater level of engagement during the last few sessions than they would during sessions one to three'.

(b) 'There would be a higher level of engagement 30 minutes after a music therapy session than there would be during the same time on a non-music therapy day'.

The Population

The subjects were drawn from one of the nine wards for the elderly mentally ill at the time of the study, within the Cambridge Mental Health Service. All the subjects on the chosen ward were elderly, and confused, and the average age was eighty years. Some were suffering from senile dementia, and others from multiple effects of ageing in addition to functional mental illness such as depression. All had been in hospital for at least a year, and the majority for longer. Thus, most showed signs of institutionalisation, e.g. accustomed to having much responsibility for welfare taken by members of staff. Common problems which were prevalent for most people were sleep disturbance, incontinence, shouting, depression and inability to converse using spoken language. Those with senile dementia suffered from poor short-term memory. Although family history and other psychological phenomena were central to understanding the subjects; only superficial characteristics are mentioned here for the purposes of the research project.

Table 1: Description of subjects

Subject	Diagnosis	Prominent characteristics	Communicat-ion skills	Noticeable behaviour patterns
1	Senile dementia	Small excitable lady with rapid mood swings from tears to laughter	Some communicating language which sounded like meaningful babble, although words not clearly distinguishable	Mood swings often seemed in response to external stimuli Active when encouraged to do something on the ward but often asleep in chair if left on her own
2	Senile dementia	A thin, pale-looking gentleman with a tense, anxious countenance Often had an expression of anguish, but sometimes this changed when interacting with others	No distinct speech, but he often looked up if people moved around near him, or tried to interact with him	Often seemed in pain and suffering from severe constipation which may have been related to his anguished behaviour
3	Senile dementia	A gentleman, often seeming content, with a benevolent smile whilst he also made nervous movements with his head Needed help to walk by end of project	No apparent identifiable speech remaining Quiet and not able generally on ward to communicate his needs very well	Needed help with feeding and dressing and holding objects. Often wandered around in an unsteady way

4	Features of confusion, possibly related to effect of long term institutionalis-ation	A gentleman described frequently as 'stubborn'. Reasons seemed to be frustration owing to institutionalis-ation often expressed by stubborn aggressive behaviour	Seemed to stare blankly ahead rather than look at others on ward. However, his ability to walk around and get to where he wanted, e.g. shop; showed he could communicate when he wished. Some speech but hard to decipher words	Anger and resistance seemed to reflect frustration at not having total control over his life. Preferred to remain isolated on ward and resisted contact with other unless an outing to the shop was offered
5	Long-term chronic behaviour problems. History of differing diagnoses	A lady who seemed frustrated and restless on the ward. Mobile; walking with a limping gait and clumsy movements	Spoke to communicate often in a loud shouting voice	Although full of energy seemed affected by institutionalisati on and often sat for long periods shouting in order to get attention
6	Confused pseudo-dementia and suffering from long term institutionalis-ation effects	A gentleman apparently stone deaf who was quite aware of things around him. He could read, and often seemed upset, which could have been related to being aware of his situation and frustrated by his living conditions	Able to communicate using speech, often gruff and unclear owing to his poor hearing. Others communicated with him mainly by writing things down	Mobile and sometimes tried to initiate contact with others. Upset when frustrated perhaps because of lack of response from other residents on the ward

7	Mildly mentally retarded and pseudo-dementia	Partially-sighted lady with an awkward gait as the result of a stroke Excitable lively personality	Few words, used in a slow sing-song manner. Communicated mainly by using gestures or with facial expressions	Sought much attention from others on ward. Liked playing with fluffy toys during the day
8	Senile dementia	A gentleman usually isolated and withdrawn Walked around with a Parkinsonian shuffle. Occasionally laughed but often had a blank stare	A few inarticulate sounds. Described by ward team as non-communi-cative	Dribbled constantly and seemed not to want or notice external contact with others
9	Severe depression	Extremely thin, frail and isolated lady, doubly incontinent and needing to be fed by staff. Appeared resistant to contact initiated by others	Showed her will and ability to communicate generally being forcefully resistant No communication apparent.	Curled up all day in chair head down; showing little spontaneous response to anyone or events
10	Pseudo-dementias and personality problems	A large energetic bald-headed gentleman with thick set features. Commanding much power on the ward. In a wheel-chair most of the time owing to arthritis	Able to speak and often roared his comments in a loud voice when he wanted to say something usually complaining or abusive	Aggressive and shouting for his immediate needs Could be very belligerent and physically violent. Also periods of humour when he liked a person he was with

| 11 | Senile dementia History of heavy drinking | Friendly active gentleman who talked about the war, and marched a lot as if in the army Restless in nature and shouted and argued when distressed. Intelligent in the way he presented. | Verbally able but the content was often muddled and confused. Socially skilled in his interactions when content | Sudden mood swings and outbursts, and constantly on the move. At times relaxed, warm and sociable |

Subjects were chosen in an unbiased way, and none had been involved in music therapy before. Eleven members is higher than the usual number for a music therapy group of this kind; between six and eight being a more ideal number. However, to allow for the possibility that some people from this type of population might die in the course of the study, or be too physically ill to attend, or refuse to attend; this number was chosen.

Engagement

The aims during music therapy treatment for clients vary from person to person, according to personal need. However, at the time of the study, the music therapist had noted during her work with EMI people that one of these constantly recurring could collectively be termed 'Engagement' as defined by the Wessex Regional Health Authority Publication (Jenkins et al., 1978). The definition of engagement for this study is shown below:

(a) Eye-direction   (E) Looking at other patients or the music therapist, or assistants, or observer (i.e. NOT looking vaguely out of the window).

(b) Verbalising   (V) Verbalising towards another person.

(c) Use of materials   (M) Those activities particular to music therapy (i.e. singing or vocalising as a result of the music; tapping hands or feet rhythmically with the music; clapping hands; playing an instrument or dancing, or getting up and moving as a direct result of the music).

(d) Use of materials (RT) Looking at or handling materials
in talking sessions specifically used in RT sessions
such as photographs, objects, etc.

(e) Smiling (S)

(f) Asleep (Z)

(g) Absent (X)

Brief Description of Sessions

(a) Music Therapy

Sessions lasted for approximately 45 minutes, and the music therapist led the session with two nursing assistants helping, judging the overall structure in a flexible way according to the needs of the patients at the time.

Instruments used were tuned and untuned percussion, piano, violin and voice. The instruments were set up before the session began, and not all were used each week. The therapist used clinical judgement as to what equipment to use each time, both according to the previous sessions, and taking into account patients' needs at the time. For example, the violin was not offered to all patients, or even available every week, because of the inappropriateness of its timbre at certain stages and because of the difficulty some patients would have had in using it. However, one patient began to improvise on it following its use in a communication dialogue with the therapist, where the therapist noted a definite response to its timbre. The patient was hard of hearing, but appeared to notice, and respond rhythmically to, the violin sounds. It, therefore, was a successful way of communicating with him.

As stated previously, the main rationale for music therapy was to use music to make contact with patients in order to achieve clinical aims such as increased interaction and awareness, communication, socialisation, and stimulation both emotional, physical and intellectual. For this reason, the music was improvised throughout, and when pre-composed elements were used within improvisations such as familiar songs, hymns, Sousa marches; it was as a result of discovering musical or expressive needs and potential for patients, and building on this. Thus, pre-composed music was introduced in response to vocalisation or rhythmic pulses expressed by the clients if the therapist felt that this way of working through music would help the patient develop in the ways mentioned above. The music would be adapted and improvised always following the patients' responses and reactions. A more detailed summary of events which took place, and the approach, can be found below.

(b) Reminiscence Therapy

Reminiscence Therapy is based on the concept that recalling memories of past events can 'bring to mind experiences which are personal to us in a vivid and alive fashion'. (Norris, 1986). A different topic was chosen each week, and appropriate materials prepared in order to evoke associations and memories, and to act as a form of stimulation. The music therapist prepared the materials, and led the reminiscence sessions. Topics covered were Families; Occupations; Places of Residence; World-wide Landmarks; Food; Animals; War; Local Landmarks and Flowers. The overall pattern of RT sessions was as similar to that of MT sessions as possible. Materials used were:

(a) Photographs - both prepared from magazines and reminiscence packages; and some were also compiled involving patients' own photographs and life history by ward staff prior to sessions.

(b) Objects - such as those associated with particular hobbies or occupations.

(c) Food - a variety according to what was being discussed.

(d) Animals - a live dog was brought in for the RT sessions about animals.

The equipment was used in many ways:

(i) As a tactile and sensory stimulation e.g. stroking the animal; handling objects and food, also eating the food.

(ii) As a stimulus to conversation and interaction e.g. passing photographs round, or placing one photograph or object in the centre so as to help group interactions.

(iii) As a stimulus to movement e.g. encouraging people to take materials to others by walking around the group.

In this way, materials were intended for use in a concentrated way as instruments were in the MT sessions.

Structure and Format for Music Therapy and Reminiscence Therapy Sessions

In order to meet personal needs at the time, a flexible approach was taken and the exact method of approach cannot be given in a systematic order for each week. However, within such flexibility, the format for MT and RT was approached in as similar a way as possible, so that results would not be biased. Also, so that continuity and structure were present for the clients - this being clinically essential when so many were often confused and disorientated.

There were always three main parts to each session which, although fluidly running into each other depending upon moods, needs and group dynamics that day, gave an overall constant structure. The therapist kept in mind this format and it can be described as a curve, giving shape and form to sessions throughout the study.

Each section varied in length, within a 45 minute limit, depending upon needs of the group that day. The therapeutic method was consistent with usual clinical practice, and not adapted for the research project. Sessions took approximately 45 minutes and always ended by the end of that time. All this took place, regardless of the observations, and the therapist was unaware of what stage in the observations the observer had reached.

The three sections can be summarised as follows:

(a) Introductions - Introducing the group members, building relationships through the appropriate media, i.e. music in MT sessions, and subject matter or talking in RT sessions.

(b) Central Part - Explorations and development of interactions built up during introductions using music, instruments and sound in MT and talking and materials in RT Movement could be developed through either media. Improvised ways of using music in MT and talking and materials in RT were explored.

(c) <u>Final Part</u> - Culmination of the group session in an appropriate way according to what had taken place during the session for group members.

Further Detailed Description of Sessions

(a) <u>Introduction</u>

The therapist emphasised each individual's presence and importance by spending time relating to each person, using personal names either speaking and shaking hands (MT and RT) or through music using voice and/or instruments (MT). For some people in the group, a name seemed to be the only word they could immediately identify with. An additional reason for this approach was that in both treatments, the media or subject matter were introduced. In RT the topic and some materials were introduced after the personal introductions, or sometimes during, depending upon the responses that day of the members. It was important that a relationship between therapist and group members and group members themselves was established.

Musically, in MT sessions, members had the chance to chose their individual way of using a particular instrument, or musical way of introducing themselves usually with the therapist's support, to the rest of the group. Sometimes, in both sessions, other elements would be introduced verbally (RT), or in song form (MT) in order to help orientate members, e.g. the day, date and time. This was done with a short improvisation following the patient's rhythm (MT); or verbally and visually (RT). In MT if a particular musical structure was thought necessary by the therapist, the piano was used sometimes appropriately improvising using familiar harmonic structures and adapting words to suit the occasion. Exceptions to this method of approach in the Introduction Section in MT took place on occasions when it was necessary to reflect the atmosphere of the beginning of the group through music played by the therapist before introducing each person. This was particularly when it seemed that the music would enable members to settle and be more focused on what was happening. The exact point of moving into the middle section varied and was gradual in both RT and MT.

(b) <u>Central Part</u>

During RT sessions, this part of the session involved encouraging interaction, awareness and movement by using as many non-musical materials as possible and helping members relate to their past experiences in discussions. A different topic was chosen each week, and the therapist and helpers developed themes as they arose with individual members, and with the group as a whole by structuring the use of materials, e.g. passing objects and photographs around; sharing in pairs; placing one object in the centre for all to see or touch.

In the MT sessions, this part of the session involved encouraging interaction, awareness and movement using instruments and voice building improvisations from the sounds and music expressed by group members. At times, this involved developing well-known material such as songs, or original material, in improvisations between different members in pairs, threes, small groupings, or as a whole group. For example, if a member began humming or beating in a particular way, the therapist would interact using the same instrument or a different one in order to build on this. This could lead to helpers encouraging others to join in, or remain as a dialogue between the therapist and one member. This depended upon what seemed to be necessary at the time for the members, e.g. support in a duet; the feeling of leading the whole group; or freedom of expression with the therapist taking a musically 'containing role'. This could mean the therapist played firm harmonic rhythmic chordal notes in the bass whilst the member improvised in a free way, perhaps aggressively drumming in irregular rhythms, to give one example.

The types of structures set up varied depending upon needs and moods of the members at the time, but included sharing instruments in pairs, using one instrument in the centre of the circle for members to move towards in turn when they wanted to, (physically helped to the centre if necessary), and free improvisations. These were solos; in pairs with the therapist, helper or other members; or movement with improvised music to follow and stimulate body rhythms. This could encourage emotional expression and encourage energy to be released generally through vocal, bodily or instrumental means.

The therapist identified needs of the clients at the time by observing and getting to know clients as the treatment progressed, and as the relationships developed. Different types of musical interactions were made according to assumptions about what would be helpful. For example, when a client who had previously shown withdrawn frightened behaviour began to beat in a triplet-type rhythm quietly on a metallophone, the therapist immediately saw this as something which could be encouraged musically and perhaps lead to the client feeling more able to communicate in other ways, or feel more relaxed. The musical intervention by the therapist was, therefore, made in a way which would help this, i.e. in this instance with soft but firm melodic improvised phrases in triplet-time, following the client's rhythm, but not repeating it exactly, which could have been intrusive and not encouraging. Another example of how the therapist made assumptions about what seemed necessary and helpful at the time was as follows. A client who often seemed angry and resistant to playing instruments, and also to being in the group, frequently shouted and was abusive towards the other members. During one session, the client began to hit the tambour very aggressively and loudly when it was passed to him. The therapist decided that this way of expressing himself may help in relieving some of the tension he seemed to feel and perhaps lead to him being able to interact with the other members in a less abusive way, thus being able to feel more accepted. The therapist, therefore, actively encouraged the powerful loud beating by sharing the tambour, and loudly beating also, thus accepting the client's expression of anger. Following this, the therapist noticed that the client seemed more relaxed, and suggested that he became a leader for others to follow his beating, and share playing music as a group with him. Thus, the whole group were encouraged to join in, leading to more -'give and take' within the music so that the client felt able to express himself <u>with</u> others rather than upsetting them. These types of assumptions were part of the therapist's rationale throughout the treatment, so although the work was flexible and intuitive, every part of the guiding role within improvisations was thought through, in a rational way with a view to what would be more helpful.

In RT sessions, similar rationale was in operation, such as not thrusting objects or materials at clients if they seemed particularly withdrawn or 'not ready' for this type of contact. Or, at another time, noticing a flicker of interest in someone's eyes and, therefore, gently presenting an idea or object to them, or making a quiet acknowledging comment.

(c) <u>Final Part</u>

It is impossible to be specific about this part. The therapist helped the group move towards finishing in an appropriate way by guiding events to an ending. In RT this involved saying good-bye, and consolidating the group experience by using the materials in a final structure involving any of the methods described for the central part.

In MT improvisations continued, often incorporating good-bye songs for each member, built up according to mood at the time. Sometimes, a group good-bye song would be improvised, or a group improvisation would move towards an ending with the therapist guiding the music either harmonically, or slowing down or speeding up according to the atmosphere at the time. Occasionally, relaxation seemed necessary, and the therapist improvised music, which seemed to be responded to in a calm way by members. This could have involved a slow unaccompanied reflective song in lullaby style, often in triple time, or a slow waltz-like piece on the piano, to give two examples. Sometimes the ending section involved the therapist sharing an instrument with each member, and improvising in a dialogue. This could involve members using their chosen instruments, or sometimes passing round the same one, e.g. a tambour, to encourage a sense of sharing the ending together.

<u>Clinical Reviews</u>

After each session, the therapist and assistants reviewed the session in the usual way. This meant that they spent some time discussing the clinical benefits for each group member, making relevant notes in ward files and in the music therapy file, based on their observations during the sessions. They also reviewed the procedure of working with the group with a view to the sessions in the future. All this was considered normal practice in therapy work at the hospital.

Results

There was no significant difference between the amount of engagement in the MT and RT conditions (Part I) by Analysis of Variance by Ranks (see Meddis, 1980). However, there was more engagement in MT in Part II compared with Part I ($z=2.6$, $p<.05$, see Figures 1 and 2).

From this, and an examination of the profile of individual patients, it was also concluded that:

(a) Music therapy taking place at regular weekly intervals is more effective than music therapy taking place intermittently.

(b) The relationship built up between clients and therapists during Parts I and II developed so that the levels of engagement were higher towards the end of the study.

(c) Involvement in MT in Part I may well have had a sustained effect between Parts I and II, despite the fact that there was a month's break. Subjects had become involved in and accustomed to MT. This could also be due to Part I as a whole, and further discussion of this point will take place later.

One of the hypotheses was that there would be higher levels of engagement in sessions 9 to 12 than in sessions 1 to 3 when a block of 12 weekly music therapy sessions were held. From analysis of the profiles of individual patients, a pattern seemed to emerge showing higher levels of engagement overall during the second part of Part II. Also, seven out of nine subjects involved in both parts started with high scores (higher than in Part I at the beginning in most cases).

There was no evidence that engagement was greater in the period after music therapy sessions than on days when no music therapy was provided. However, levels of engagement were significantly higher in music therapy sessions than after these sessions.

Clinical Notes - Examples for Three Subjects

It was mentioned that clinical notes were made by the therapist and assistants after each session, and some conclusions drawn in the usual way about how clients were benefiting from the treatment. Notes on three subjects as they were written at the time, were collected, together with scores from the data. The three subjects were chosen because each had a different diagnosis and background (Table 1) and each showed a different pattern of responses, which together gave an overall impression of the types of clinical notes made.

There are many different ways this anecdotal information can be looked at and understood, and this point will be expanded upon later.

Although the project was concerned with group statistics, it is important to show examples of individual's case notes, particularly because each subject is so different. Subject number 9 showed little response and little change throughout, whereas subjects 5 and 2 showed a great deal of changes and responses. The clinical conclusions regarding these three clients are as follows:

(a) Subject Number 9 remained at very much the same level of interaction and awareness throughout the study. She was a severely withdrawn person generally, with little apparent desire to participate with others. This remained the same both in and out of the sessions. Thus, she does not even show the expected higher levels of engagement during a planned activity than in no session at all.

(b) <u>Subject Number 5</u> built up a relationship with the therapist during both MT and RT and particularly became more involved in using instruments. She seemed to gradually realise how much enjoyment through interactions with others could be gained, particularly in MT sessions. Her concentration and conversation expanded and she became relaxed and able to trust the group. She was very involved when music therapy sessions were regular in Part II and seemed to show sustained benefits throughout Part II in movement; levels of awareness; language; socialisation; relaxation and integration with the group members, particularly the therapist and assistants.

(c) <u>Subject Number 2</u> was able to benefit most in areas of independence, communication and movement. For example, in Part II he began to improvise using instruments spontaneously (Session Number 3) which was a new thing for him. He seemed to gain an independent sense of self in the group which became apparent in Part II. His levels of communication were much higher in sessions than out of sessions and seemed to develop as the treatment progressed. In RT and particularly in MT because of the non-verbal emphasis, he could interact and involve himself with others in a way which was not possible outside sessions. Ward staff also commented that he showed higher levels of awareness and interaction generally than he had done before treatment begun.

The anecdotal clinical notes show so much detail, that the brief summaries are only able to cover treatment results superficially. However, the important points are able to show the main individual benefits.

<u>Further Outcome</u>

Further interesting outcome results were found comparing the mean average scores in MT and RT for each subject. Whilst it is recognised that these results cannot be statistically significant, they show trends towards a possible relationship between background and diagnoses in this population, and effective treatments.

Table 2 shows the mean scores averaged as percentages of possible obtainable scores. The table shows that within Part I, Subjects 2, 7 and 8 show fairly-marked tendencies towards higher scores in MT than in RT and Subjects 1, 6 and 10 show slight tendencies towards higher scores in MT than in RT Overall, therefore, six out of ten subjects show higher mean scores in MT than in RT The remaining four subjects (Numbers 3, 4, 5 and 9) show marked tendencies towards higher RT scores. It is interesting to note that all six showing marked tendencies towards higher scores in MT have a diagnosis of dementia or pseudo dementia. Out of the four others who had higher scores in RT only one has dementia and the rest have functional illnesses such as depression, or show long-term effects of mental illness and institutionalisation. Out of these subjects, only Subject 5 went on to show markedly higher scores in Part II MT.

Some questions arise from these findings. Is MT more effective, therefore, with EMI people suffering from dementia, or is this a confirmation that the group was too large or not able to cater for varying individual needs?

What can we learn from a closer examination of the process between therapist and client-group about how methods are adapted and changed as a result of following individual client's overall needs? There is clearly a need for further examination of these questions by other researchers.

Table 2: Average scores of overall engagement in Part I expressed as percentages

Subject	% Score in MT	% Score in RT
1	98.7	97.5
2	80	70
3	81.7	90
4	80	90
5	61.2	70
6	80	78.6
7	98.7	91.2
8	48.7	41.2
9	6.2	10
10	72.5	70

Summary of Findings

1. Regular sustained music therapy sessions increase engagement for EMI people significantly more than when music therapy sessions are intermittent.
2. Music therapy is an effective treatment for EMI people.
3. Music therapy increased levels of engagement for EMI people more than when there is no planned activity, and also more than at meal times.
4. Constancy of therapist and group members within safe boundaries (i.e. regular time, place and approach) are important in achieving therapeutic benefits for EMI people.
5. Relationships between therapist, assistants and group members built up over a period of time help to achieve benefits for EMI people.
6. MT using methods involving improvisation within group interactions is successful in achieving therapeutic benefits for EMI people.
7. Diagnosis and background are important factors in determining how to help EMI clients through music therapy.

The analysis of data, and study of clinical notes, showed a need for these conclusions to be discussed further.

Discussion

Various elements of the research design have been critically analysed, and clearly much has been learned from this. The overall design could have been more powerful in the areas of measurement (more refined measures), frequency of sessions (so that MT and RT were compared by each being held weekly), and number of subjects. However, the design did provide a systematic way of studying MT and comparing responses in this and another treatment (RT).

Some critical comments on procedures are necessary. For example, the method of time sampling, whilst effective in obtaining group statistics in a non-biased way, could be said to be contradictory in its application to music therapy treatment of this kind. The whole individual process is important for each patient, and the process between patient and therapist. It could be argued, bearing this approach in mind, that just because a response recurs a significant number of times, it is not necessarily more significant in therapeutic terms, i.e. one different isolated response can be very significant in therapy. The anecdotal case-notes show another side of the story, and clients must be seen in the context of their individual difficulties and diagnosis in order to make some sense of, and understand what the observations and responses might mean. This does not invalidate the measurement procedures used in this study, but raises some questions. For example, how important is it that the therapist's observations sometimes coincide with the objective scores?

The relationship with the therapist primarily through music is central to the therapy in this method and, therefore, it could be argued that observations from an external observer using the time-sampling method, whilst objective in one sense, only give one part of the picture.

The therapist remaining the same throughout MT and RT sessions also raises important issues in addition to the one of continuity.

The higher results in MT Part II could point towards the music therapist being more skilled as a music therapist than as a reminiscence therapist - one would think this is likely! This also shows the problems again of setting up the comparison of RT and MT in this way. On the one hand, it meant that the project compared the therapies rather than different therapists, but on the other, it is difficult to sort out how this affected the clinical judgement of the therapist.

It would be interesting to examine in a further study whether benefits gained by clients are directly related to what is happening musically between client and therapist.

We have learned from the literature that others had found that any concentrated period of interaction between staff and patients of this population is likely to raise levels of engagement.

In the first instance, what emerges from these results is that music therapy is an equally valid treatment method for doing this as reminiscence therapy. The clients chosen for the project were primarily those not deemed suitable for referral to OT or other forms of treatment, but clearly many group members improved over Parts I and II and showed particular responses in MT not shown elsewhere. Figure 1 shows engagement levels in Part I and Part II for three subjects. It is clear that levels were higher when there was weekly MT.

Figure 1: Overall engagement in Part I (MT sessions randomly interspersed, left graph) compared with Part II (weekly MT right graph) for three subjects

a) Subject 5

b) Subject 6

c) Subject 10

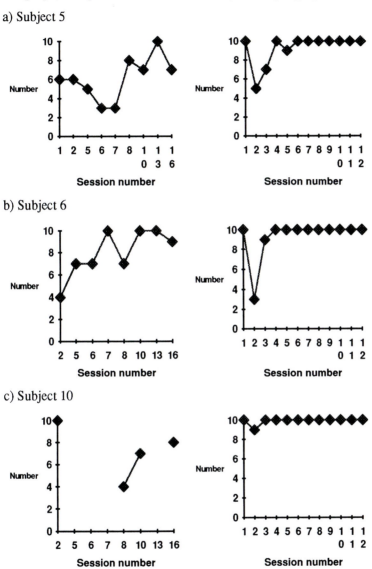

Results of 'after' session data show this too. For example, Figure 2 shows engagement levels during and after MT sessions for three subjects illustrating the finding that engagement during MT was much higher than afterwards. This could imply that where resources of occupational therapists and psychologists are scarce in this field, music therapists are a valuable addition in the team.

No subjects became progressively worse in that no engagement levels deteriorated markedly. Furthermore, in Part II, subjects' levels of engagement either remained constant or improved overall (see Figure 3) where only MT was included. This is significant in looking at this population, many of whom are expected to deteriorate mentally, physically and intellectually.

Figure 2: Number of engagements during MT (diamonds) compared with on same day after MT sessions (squares). Gaps indicate non-attendance.

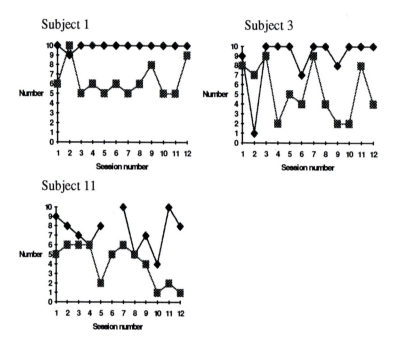

Figure 3: Engagement in MT of the subjects during Part II

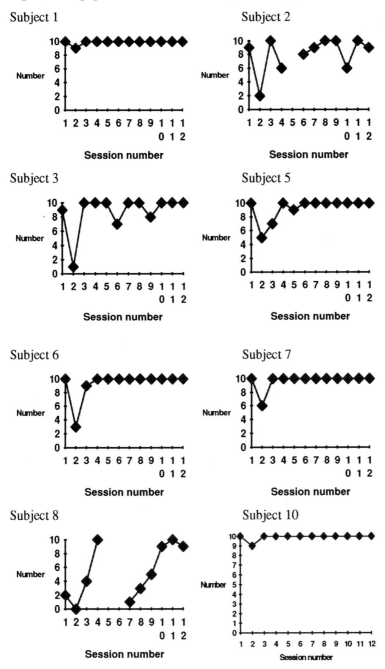

Subject 11

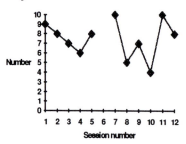

In Part I, when music therapy was compared happening in an irregular pattern (i.e. randomised sessions) with reminiscence therapy also happening in an irregular pattern, most subjects show irregular patterns of responses in comparison with those in Part II, despite the constancy of group members and therapist. In Part II, as the graphs show, levels of engagement were largely raised early on, and remained at consistently high levels towards the end of Part II. The influence of on-going regular music therapy i.e. that of Part I influencing Part II, emerged. The scores in Session 1 in Part II were higher in many cases than those in the first session of MT in Part I. This points towards the continuity and permanence of the group, firm boundaries, and the building of relationships with the therapist and members, being of great importance over a long period. Furthermore, looking at the graphs, seven out of the nine subjects who completed both parts of the project had scores as high, or higher in, Session 1 Part II compared with Session 16 (the final one) in Part I, despite a month's break in between the two parts, which also indicates the importance of an ongoing therapeutic process.

As has been noted, little research exists substantiating the claim that this MT method, using improvisation is effective with this population. Some authors even discourage this method with EMI people. For example, Liederman, (1967), states: 'The only contra-indication against group participation is a severe, acute medical or psychiatric disability'. All the subjects involved in this study would have come under the label 'psychiatric disability'; and yet most seemed to benefit from this group situation. Certainly in Part I, the treatment is as effective as RT and in Part II, the levels of engagement in music therapy were significantly higher than those during MT in Part I. This is an important finding, and points towards the particular effects of this method of MT.

In this study, we gathered statistics to look at group effects, and chose not to look at statistically individual case studies. However, during the process, some individual cases were looked at in more depth, for example, Subject Number 10. Some of his refusals to attend in Part I could reasonably have been attributed to the inconsistent nature of randomly interspersed treatment. Certainly, results for him point towards music therapy as an effective treatment in stimulating him to enjoy socialising with, communicating, interacting with, and tolerating others, especially in Part II.

Subject Number 9 was suffering from severe depression and showed the least response to treatment throughout, which shows the variability between subjects. Music therapists often indicate that prerequisites for successful treatment can be poor communication skills or severe withdrawal. Clearly, looking at Part II overall, nearly all subjects showed some benefits (i.e. consistent raised engagement levels) and all subjects had communication difficulties. The study, therefore, in addition to showing the unpredictability of this population, does show particular benefits in improving communication skills, and this led on to an indication for research needs in the future - that of an investigation of how to determine which EMI patients might benefit from MT in a referral and assessment procedure. This is particularly important when resources are scarce.

Future directions

Following the setting up of this research project, there has already been a move away from this particular type of design in Britain, i.e. looking at outcome (see also Bunt, 1985; Oldfield, 1986), towards a more process-oriented approach. This has been partly because of the findings of the above researchers, and although no additionai specific projects have been completed concerning music therapy with EMI people in Britain, much discussion along the lines described here has taken place by music therapists and others. Discussions have focused around various issues including measurement problems (Adams, 1987), musical process models (Steele and Dunachie, 1986), general theoretical issues (Bunt, and Hoskyns. 1987), culminating in the conference at City University discussing the single case study Sloboda (1988), tackles exactly some of the questions discussed here. He writes 'Can we isolate the necessary or sufficient events associated with these events (contributed by either therapist or client)'? His solution is one which I fully endorse as the way forward:

'There is no one way to get to causes, but one technique involves taking detailed records of client and therapist behaviour (say by videotape) over a series of sessions and making exhaustive coding of session features present or absent in each session. Some measure of client improvement should also be taken after each session. It is then possible, with the many powerful statistical techniques available to discover what session features seem to correlate most highly with improvement. This can then guide theorising about effective causes; and maybe more controlled studies in which the features identified are increased or withheld.' (Sloboda, 1988)

These comments are particularly important in the light of what this project implies in connection with method, and whether different approaches can be defined in terms of the problem presented or 'diagnosed'.

In the method section of this paper, we learned that the EMI people involved as subjects were not those who had been referred to other therapies. Since the project, referral procedures have moved towards more informed referrals often including those not expected to benefit from other treatments by clinical teams, and this project shows that in the future, this population can generally benefit from music therapy.

Furthermore, it seems that a single case design study looking at fewer clients in much more depth is the way forward with this population

Research where more subjects are looked at individually and in groups for much longer periods is clearly necessary. No attempt was made in this study to do this, although the inclusion of clinical notes shows that there is much left to be discovered about this way of working through closer analysis using audio and visual methods.

In summary, this project shows clearly the need for more research projects into music therapy with the elderly mentally ill as a result of many questions raised. This population, for whom the prognosis is poor, and for whom other treatments are often deemed not suitable, can benefit from music therapy as shown in this project. What is needed now is a better understanding of exactly how this can be developed further for the benefit of mentally ill people.

This last discussion section has hopefully shown the reader some of the difficulties and benefits of carrying out such a scientifically designed research project. However, I would like to conclude by adding some more personal comments, following more objective critical appraisal. The whole process taught me many things and for a while afterwards, I concentrated on developing my clinical work in other areas gradually into a more psychoanalytically informed approach particularly with younger long-term psychiatric patients. This clearly presented me with a conflict, as I was forced to look at external observable phenomena in the research, but what really is the focus of my clinical work is a much more intangible process of developing relationships and internal processes within client/patient groups. However, to work under such close detailed scrutiny was an experience I would not have missed. It has enabled me to value close self observation of all my work, and above all to learn through the work.

In addition, the research led to a heightened awareness of the value of music therapy with the elderly mentally ill, and to an increase in posts within the Mental Health Services in Cambridge. In fact, at the time of writing there is more emphasis upon the use of all the various therapies in the psychiatric services for the elderly, and other music therapists are continuing to develop ways of working specifically with this group of people. Although for a time after the completion of the project, the discrepancy between my current clinical practice and the statistical approach was apparent, the project was of value in itself. It set out primarily to look at certain observable 'outcome' phenomena. If others can learn from this, and move on to different areas of research, then this too is important. For me, it has enabled me to move on and encourage others to move on too, into an approach which values an acceptance of the patient as they are, rather than impressing external structures upon the patient. This is of fundamental importance to music therapy at present in Britain, which is struggling to understand the particular role of music, as well as to understand how this relates to other theories and practices. The importance of listening, waiting, and not bombarding the patient with the therapists' own music is now an increasing awareness amongst music therapists.

Prior to this study, it seemed common to regard the EMI population as one who needed a sing-song approach, with familiar music played to them, rather than using interactive improvisatory methods as described in this chapter. I know that many others share my view that whilst a more structured approach may be necessary for those who are confused, a willingness to give space to the patient is essential and a willingness to work with the confusion and respect the negative, as well as positive aspects within the music therapy relationship is of paramount importance.

Acknowledgements

I would like to thank all colleagues and patients involved in the study and particularly the three research supervisors, Malcolm Adams, Linda Powell-Procter and Leslie Bunt.

5

The Bonny Method of Guided Imagery and Music

Frances Smith Goldberg

The Bonny method of Guided Imagery and Music (GIM) is a depth approach to music psychotherapy in which specifically programmed classical music is used to generate a dynamic unfolding of inner experiences. The music facilitates a consistent, continuous dialogue with the unconscious in which the ego holds its own reality while allowing the unconscious to do the same (Hanks, 1985). The therapist provides grounding by maintaining an active dialogue with the listener throughout the session. The work of the therapist is to focus and encourage, as emotions, sensory images, physical sensations, memories and thoughts emerge. Music and therapist are co-therapists: supporting, reflecting and facilitating the creative experience. In the nearly two decades since its inception, GIM has gained increased recognition as an independent vehicle for psychotherapy and personal growth. This chapter will present GIM therapy, its history, practice and theoretical basis. Clinical examples will be provided to illustrate the GIM process.

The Bonny method of GIM was developed in the early 1970s by Dr Helen Bonny, a music therapist, at the Maryland Psychiatric Research Centre (USA). In her research, Bonny found that when subjects listened to a carefully selected programme of classical music while in a relaxed state, powerful feelings and symbolic images were evoked, leading to significant insights into therapy issues.

The idea of imaging to music is not new. Many people spontaneously experience mental images while listening to music. This is evident in Eduard Hanslick's review of the premiere of Tchaikovsky's Violin concerto in D Major with the Vienna Philharmonic. Hanslick (cited in Grunefeld, 1974) wrote

> 'The violin is no longer played. It is yanked about. It is torn asunder. It is beaten black and blue. [The Finale] puts us in the midst of the wretched jollity of a Russian kermis. We see wild and vulgar faces, we hear curses, we smell bad brandy.' (p.6)

This exemplifies the types of sensory images that are possible while listening to music and that are also characteristic of GIM sessions. The strong emotional component is apparent. It will come as no surprise that Hanslick's review of Tchaikovsky's concerto was brutal. Music may be superior to other methods in evoking mental images (Quittner, 1980). Examples of music evoked imagery can be found throughout history.

GIM represents a modern incarnation of elements that have been associated with medicine and healing since ancient times: music, imagery and altered states of consciousness. Their association with medicine and healing has been traced back 20,000 years (Furst, 1977). Music, in the form of chanting, drumming or playing gongs, cymbals or flutes was central to the rituals of the shaman, priest or medicine man in cultures as widespread as Tibet, Africa, Asia, Northern Europe, South America, and the Native Americans of North America (Hamel, 1979). Much of the power of these healers came from their ability to enter altered states of consciousness and experience mental images. From these images shamans gained information and insights which enabled them to perform their healing functions.

The Aesculapian oracle rituals of ancient Greece used music and other arts to induce a trance state and hypnogogic imagery, which facilitated catharsis, insight and integration (Meier, 1967). Pythagoras, Plato, Aristotle, Plutarch and Aristedes believed that music was profoundly important in maintaining health, which was equated with harmony. The Greek god, Apollo, leader of the Muses, was the god of music and considered the founder of medicine (Tyson, 1981).

Achterberg (1985) points out that although shamanic lore is generally considered too untenable for contemporary science, shamanic health practices have continued alongside mainstream medical practices. As with folk medicine, where scientific investigation has verified the healing elements of many popular herbs, so has scientific inquiry begun to unravel mysteries associated with imagery and healing. Areas of investigation in which imagery is employed include hypnosis, autogenics, biofeedback and the placebo effect. Research is also underway on the use of imagery for pain control, stress reduction and the treatment of autoimmune disease (Achterberg, 1985).

Bonny's research focused on finding a way to induce a therapeutic experience similar to that developed by researchers in hallucinogenic drug psychotherapy without using the drugs. Music had been used in drug research to help the patient relinquish his or her usual controls and enter more fully into the inner world of experience, facilitate the release of intense emotionality, contribute to a peak experience, provide continuity in an experience of timelessness, and structure the experience (Bonny, 1980). The drug therapy had proven to be a profound therapeutic catalyst. Bonny reasoned that if the researchers were correct that music enhanced the sensory experience (Godfrey, 1967) and facilitated the action of the drug (Eisner and Cohen, 1959; Sherwood et al., 1962) then music alone might be just as effective (Bonny, 1980). The result was her finding that subjects were able to experience the inner images and emotions of the unconscious with music and without the drug.

In further developing the GIM method, Bonny was influenced by Freud, Jung and Maslow, as well as imagery techniques of Assagioli (1965, 1969) and Desoille's 'Waking Dream' (1968).

Bonny introduced a relaxation phase prior to the start of the music, based on techniques developed by Jacobson (1938) and by Schutz' and Luthe's Autogenic Training (1959). This seemed to increase the subject's initial focus, an idea suggested to her by Leuner's (1969) method called Guided Affective Imagery.

Bonny was also influenced by Leuner's ideas regarding imagery in psychotherapy. Leuner (1969) refers to catathymic imagery as, 'an experience of quasi reality' with its concomitant feelings and associated affects, occurring within a state of altered consciousness. This enhancement of emotions is the most important component of the therapeutic process. By no means is it to be explained simply in terms of abreaction' (p.6).

Initially, Bonny incorporated Leuner's ten standard imagery situations into her work by programming a tape using music suggestive of some of these situations: the meadow, exploring the house as a symbol of the self, following a brook upstream to its source, following a brook downstream to the ocean and climbing a mountain and describing the view (Bonny, 1980). Unlike Leuner, who suggested these themes verbally and worked without music, Bonny used the music to suggest these themes to the listener. While some people had images suggestive of these themes, others did not. It soon became apparent that the uniqueness of the music experience was that it allowed whatever was important to the listener to emerge during the experience.

The Bonny method of GIM is distinguished from these and other imagery methods (including the now popular method of playing music in the background during verbally guided imagery experiences) by the use of music, not the therapist, to evoke and direct the imagery experience.

The success of GIM in psychotherapy brought the recognition that this was a safe method for people who were seeking self-actualisation, 'persons who were normal and healthy, but who sought fuller experience and insight into the areas of the humanistic and transpersonal' (Bonny, 1975, p.129). GIM proved to be an excellent medium for exploring consciousness. 'The multidimensional qualities of musical sound allow it to touch many levels of consciousness both simultaneously and/or in sequence...The movement of music, the rise and fall of dynamics brings about a wide sweep of those levels or layers of consciousness' (Bonny, 1975, p.130). The Bonny method of GIM is holistic, humanistic and transpersonal, allowing for the emergence of all aspects of the human experience: psychological, emotional, physical, social ,spiritual, and the collective unconscious.

Bonny found GIM to be effective in groups. The dyadic approach, however, where the client relates the inner experience to the therapist as it unfolds, is far more intense and is an effective independent psychotherapy method.

Bonny developed what is now the standard four-phase GIM procedure. This consists of (1) the preliminary conversation, (2) the induction (relaxation and focus), (3) the music listening phase, and (4) the post-session integration (Bonny, 1978a). The preliminary conversation sets the stage for the unfolding drama of the GIM session. This is the time to discuss any insights from the last session or to gather history if this is the first session. The therapist notices not only what the clients says, but how he says it, his nonverbal communications. The therapist looks and listens for clues to the client's here and now state as a basis for selecting music for the session and the method of relaxation.

For the induction and music phases the client reclines on a couch or a mat. Based on knowledge of the client's history and a formulation of the therapeutic issues, the therapist selects a taped music programme which supports the client's current mood and issues for the GIM session and begins the induction. The induction consists of physical relaxation and psychological focus. The method of relaxation may be physical, for example, tensing and releasing muscle groups, or imaginal, imaging a soft, white light moving over the body, bringing with it a deep sense of relaxation. For some people, the relaxation process brings sufficient focus; for others the therapist must provide more, such as imagining there is a stairway before them, and beginning to climb the stairs.

After the induction, the music is started. During the music phase, the therapist is the listener's connection with normal reality, providing a grounding that allows the client to let go of normal controls and to experience fully the inner self. The music forms a matrix which allows the client to be with his or her inner reality while maintaining contact with outer reality. The client is encouraged to share all perceptions and experiences within the music with the therapist, who writes them down. The therapist must be completely attuned to the client and the co-therapist, the music, at all times. The role of the therapist is to observe, listen and verbally reflect the process, serving to encourage, help and comfort as the client moves through the experience. It becomes a close interactional one-to-one communication in which an inner flow of dynamic personal material is amplified by music evoked imagery, crystallised at intervals by verbal statements and descriptions (Bonny and Tansill, 1977).

After the music phase the therapist helps the client integrate the experience. The period of integration may extend over days, weeks or months. Immediately following the music session, it is important to address whatever images and feelings seem to stand out. This may be done through discussion, art work, journal writing, or any combination of these. Most clients have a need to discuss their GIM experience and, although there is some clinical evidence of behavioural change without verbal processing of the images (Goldberg et al., 1988), cognitive understanding usually plays an important role in the therapeutic process.

The Practice of GIM

The Bonny method of GIM has been employed successfully in a wide variety of settings. In addition to Bonny's work on self-actualisation with normal, healthy people, GIM has been applied to other non-clinical uses, such as with normal children (McClure, 1983; Summer, 1988), for religious and spiritual development (Houts, 1981) and to facilitate creative written expression (Keiser, 1979). GIM has been effectively used with medical conditions, such as fibroid tumours (Pickett, 1987-88), parasitic infection (McDonald, 1986), sickle cell crisis and brain tumour (Hanks, 1985), and chronic pain (Stokes, 1985), as well as with those experiencing death and dying (Hanks, 1985; Wylie and Blom, 1986).

People who have suffered traumatic brain injury present special problems in dealing with the psychological effects of their catastrophic injuries because of their impaired cognitive ability and sometimes difficulty with fluent verbal expression. There are indications that GIM may be an appropriate and effective approach to these problems. Goldberg et al. (1988) reported the use of GIM with an adult brain damaged patient to decrease 'rage attacks', that included screaming and throwing magazines. Through GIM sessions, it was revealed that the patient was fearful of hospital staff and of her own death, fears brought on by having watched her father die in a hospital. The GIM sessions helped her to address these fears, as well as her anger and depression regarding her physical condition. Her ability to verbalise coherently was markedly improved during her music sessions. Vance (1989) used GIM with such patients resulting in insight into a dysfunctional coping style in one patient and producing in another higher energy levels, increased motivation, brighter affect, and dramatically improved motor functioning.

GIM has also been used in the treatment of autistic (Ventre, 1981) and emotionally disturbed children (Herman-Friedlander, personal communication, November 27, 1988), forensic psychiatric patients (Nolan, 1983) and substance abuse (Bonny and Tansill, 1977; Summer, 1985) and in couples therapy (Weiner, 1985) and pastoral counselling (Houts, 1981). In addition, it has been effective with patients who have obsessive compulsive and borderline personality disorders, phobias, anxiety, depression and problems of sexual identity or dysfunction (Bonny, 1980). Nolan (1981) developed a clinical assessment scale of depression using GIM, which he correlated with the Beck Depression Inventory, and conducted an experimental study using his GIM Depression Scale for diagnostic purposes.

Hanks (1985) reported her work with a depressed 50-year-old woman who was unable to express anger or be assertive and who seemed to function out of a negative masculine orientation. Over the course of treatment the client went from 'gut wrenching tears' as soon as the music started to positive self images, positive masculine images, feminine symbols and healing images in the form of a Christ image. Hanks summarised this therapy: 'The music, her belief in it and its use has given her permission to move from an outer to an inner world, to release herself from rigid ego control, and to have and express feelings' (p.9).

GIM has been used successfully in the treatment of trauma: war veterans suffering from post traumatic stress disorder (Blake, in press), people with multiple personality disorder (Pickett and Sonnen, 1993) and women who have been physically and sexually abused (Bishop and Blake, in press; Borling, 1992; Tasney, 1993). Adult children of alcoholics (ACOAs) have many of these issues to address in therapy including physical and psychological abuse, incest, anxiety and depression. Erich Bonny (1988) found that GIM enabled his ACOA clients to return to childhood experiences, rediscover the helplessness they experienced as children, and understand the survival function of their current need to control. They were able to acknowledge underlying feelings and situations that were blocked in verbal therapy. This was the consequence, Bonny states, of lower anxiety within the music experience that resulted in an increased ability to process difficult material. His clients were able to transcend past experiences and connect with a 'Higher Power'. This spiritual connection is an important component of the Alcoholics Anonymous 12-step programme for the treatment of substance abuse,

ACOAs and related problems. GIM seems to be particularly suited for connecting with the spiritual aspects of oneself.

Altered States of Consciousness

Both relaxation and music contribute to the altered state of consciousness during the GIM experience. Tart (1969) defines an altered state as one in which the person feels a qualitative shift in his pattern of mental functioning, not just a quantitative shift, such as more or less alert, but that 'some quality of his mental processes are different' (p.2). Bonny (1975) represents consciousness as concentric circles. A small circle in the centre is the ego, the normal conscious self. Those layers nearest the centre comprise the preconscious state described by Freud: dreams, daydreams and intense concentration. Further out, in ever expanding rings, are less accessible conscious states, forgotten associations and memories, suppressed feelings, deep dreams, creativity, high religious states, the collective unconscious, bliss and experiences of expansion or oneness.

Bonny urges one to imagine that circles expand on and on. Then notice how small the ordinary conscious mind is, when it is compared to the places it can travel to in an altered state. The GIM experience enables exploration of all these places for the purpose of psychotherapy or self-actualisation. The images and feelings are the experience of this exploration.

The Music

Standard GIM practice calls for an affectively contoured programme of classical music that slowly builds to a peak, has interspersed plateaux, and then returns to a stable resting point (Bonny, 1978b). The music must have no sudden change in dynamics, rhythm or tempo. It must have sufficient variation in these elements, however, and also in melody, harmony, pitch and timbre, to provide movement in the images. The overall music programme should have an integrated and focused mood . Standard music programmes are 30 to 40 minutes long. The music is from the Western classical music tradition and includes the works of Bach, Mahler, Vaughan Williams, Vivaldi, Sibelius, Debussy, Copeland and Puccini, to name a few.

Programmes designed to these specifications by experienced GIM therapists are the primary source of music used in GIM sessions. These programmes fall into two categories. Those for general use are programmed to be used in a great variety of situations. Specific programmes are designed to facilitate affective expression, such as anger or deep sadness. All programmes are designed to be used repeatedly, each use bringing a new creative experience.

Music, Emotion and Imagery

The GIM experience evolves from a complex interaction between music and the listener's current emotional state and life experience. The affective component of music seems to be a primary factor in GIM. According to Meyer (1956), music arouses affect primarily through the form and structure of music as it deviates from the listener's expectation, and secondarily through the mediation of either conscious associations or unconscious image processes, which he characterised as learned associations to music.

In GIM sessions, memory images and associational images frequently occur. There are also images, such as those of death and rebirth, that seem to emanate from a source beyond the memory and associational dimensions. The music used in GIM sessions is Western art music, commonly referred to as classical music. This is music which has transcended both time and cultures, music that may be an archetypal representation of emotion, born of creative genius, and therefore able to touch deep unconscious layers of emotion in the listener. The interaction of archetypal music with the profound depth of human consciousness may produce archetypal images.

Langer's (1980) approach to music and emotion fits clinical observation. She considers the most important function of music to be that it can be 'true to the life of feeling in a way that language cannot; for its significant forms have that ambivalence of content that words cannot have' (p. 243). Musical forms, moving dynamically over time, as feelings do, can capture the quality of emotion in a way that is unmatched by any other medium. Music exists in the here and now, keeping the listener in the here and now of the emotional experience. In GIM sessions, that means the here and now deep within the psyche.

A core concept of music as psychotherapy is that music symbolises, reflects and evokes the ambiguous, fleeting and conflicting inner life of feelings and images. The images in the GIM experience, whatever form they may take, (in any of the senses, body sensations, kinaesthetic or visceral) are manifestations of the inner emotional life, providing a bridge between internal and external, feeling and thinking, the self and the collective unconscious.

The Affect-Image

There are many references in the literature to the close connection between image and affect. Perry (1974) refers to the 'affect-image', and describes a process characteristic of GIM sessions where the affect and image are bound and one may lead to the other. Meyer (1956) describes the process, often observed in GIM sessions, whereby an initial image is produced by music and subsequent images proceed apparently independent of the music being more related to the initial image. This phenomenon is indicative of the reciprocal relationship between the image and emotion. Image contents are influenced by affective states, and imagery experiences in turn evoke further emotions (Horowitz, 1978; Mandler, 1984; Plutchik, 1984; Tomkins, 1962). One imagery study found significantly more imagery in emotional than in non- emotional experiences (Lyman et al., 1980), another phenomenon readily observed in GIM sessions.

Imagery

Image formation is a form of thinking (Achterberg, 1985; Horowitz, 1983; Samuels and Samuels, 1975) that is emotionally laden and facilitates conceptual and emotional change. Imagery is postulated to govern all of our mental life, including problem solving (Mandler, 1984). Since experiences are encoded both verbally and in images (Mandler, 1984; Morrison and Cometa, 1980), issues that are unresolved and repressed or avoided can be retrieved or elicited through the encoded images (Goldberg et al., 1988). In addition, images and their attendant emotional responses are very close to sensory perception (Horowitz, 1978; Sheikh, 1978; Singer and Pope, 1978). In GIM sessions these qualities of the imagery experience and the dynamic movement of the images which are facilitated by the music contribute to a sense of actually living through the sequence of experiences. Such aspects of GIM sessions contribute to emotional and cognitive learning and change within the context of the music experience itself. People often emerge from a GIM experience with new insights and solutions to problems.

In GIM sessions, images are stimulated in all sensory modes (visual, auditory, tactile, kinaesthetic, olfactory) as well as feelings, fantasies, memories, thoughts and physical sensations. GIM therapists tend to refer to all these phenomena as images (Summer, 1985). The images may be symbolic or concrete representations of life situations, and often involve a sequential series of events similar to dreams.

Music-evoked images come from within the listener and tend to represent whatever personal issues are currently important to the listener. There is an authenticity to the GIM experience because the images are self-generated in a personal hierarchy, that is, the images represent feelings and situations in an order in which the individual needs them to occur (Goldberg et al., 1988). In a series of GIM sessions images symbolic of important feelings and issues tend to recur in various forms until the listener is psychologically ready to integrate them. The experience of these images, in turn, facilitates this integration.

A Gestalt Formulation of the GIM Experience

This formulation of GIM is based on the theory that in GIM, image formation is a function of the affective response to music. The music evokes emotion, conscious or unconscious, which, in turn, evokes the image. Subsequent images flow from the first as long as emotion connected with that sequence of images remains. As that emotion is spent, the affective influence of the music returns and a new series of images ensues (Goldberg, 1983). The GIM experience is like that described by Gestalt field theory (figure/ground) which refers to the differentiation of a part of the field of awareness into a place of central importance without losing touch with the rest of the field (Latner, 1974; Perls et al., 1951). The field (music) is always present, but may recede in conscious importance or seem to disappear momentarily as the gestalt (affect and/or image) comes into the centre of attention. The gestalt represents whatever is 'spontaneously dominant' and is the top of the hierarchy of urgency at that time (Latner, 1974).

In GIM sessions, the music field evokes emotion which represents whatever is emotionally spontaneously dominant in the person's life situation, producing a series of images. Even though the music may recede from conscious awareness, it continues to exert its influence by providing focus, emotional support, structure for the experience, and dynamic movement to the images. The music builds a field of sound which sustains focus on the inner experience and serves both as a catalyst for creative image formation and as a container for the gestalt of feelings and images. Image and emotion interact, one stimulating the other until emotion connected with the initial image is diminished. The music again becomes the gestalt and evokes further emotion in a new gestalt, producing its own series of images and emotions and a new cycle begins (Goldberg, 1992). This process works with lightning speed.

The emotions which may be conscious or unconscious give rise to the image. If the initial emotion is unconscious, the image will appear to emerge first. Sometimes the emotion-image sequences lead to strong emotion contrary to that evoked by the music (e.g. when anger gives way to sadness) and the music no longer supports the experienced emotion. The process begins to break down and the client is likely to experience confusion or dissatisfaction. It is standard GIM practice to be alert to this type of affective shift and to provide different music accordingly. The cycle then begins again.

The New Dimension of Musical Experience

The music-emotion-imagery interaction during the GIM experience compounds the impact of each. Stokes (1985) refers to this enhanced experience as synergy. Summer (1988) calls it the music/imagery synergy. Synergy, from the Greek synergia, 'a working with,' describes the capacity of two or more forces to optimise one another and achieve mutual enhancement.

Classical music, such as that used in GIM sessions, is a complex and powerful force, composed of 'vast structures consisting of nothing but tones, [and] overwhelming manifestations of energy' (Zuckerkandl, 1973, p. 53). This vibrating energy reaches deeply to touch human emotion at its core. Images are manifestations of emotional energy released by this music. They are larger than life representations that carry an energy far greater than the simple form in which they present themselves. In a GIM session the energy forces of music, emotion and imagery combine in a synergistic experience that becomes a creative leap into a new dimension for the listener.

This new dimension in GIM is one in which a new meaning is revealed by the creative leap to a higher dimension, where the elements of music, imagery and emotion form a whole, a unity, while maintaining their identities as elements of the GIM process. Zuckerkandl (1973) uses the term 'new dimension' in relation to the synergy of words and music in song and states; 'once the unification has been effected, the new dimension is created, and the potential has become actual' (p.45). The GIM experience actualises a new dimension of musical experience and meaning for the listener.

He also speaks of music as having the capacity to integrate opposites by virtue of its source. Music and word, subjective and objective, all things related to the inner life of the person, as well as all things related to the outer life of things, come from a common source that feeds each individual thing, a place where all things have their roots. His example of a song in which the same melody perfectly expresses the word 'beware' and the word 'rejoice' demonstrates the existence of a dimension of reality in which 'unity shines through diversity' (p.42).

This new dimension, in which new meaning is revealed, opposites are integrated, archetypes are born and the collective unconscious is touched, is actualised by the GIM process. It is in this dimension that the GIM experience lives, and in this dimension that new layers of reality and meaning are opened.

Indications and Contraindications

The value of GIM therapy is in the depth, speed, and relative ease of the work. It enables clients to wrestle with deep-seated conflicts more quickly than in most other therapies by bringing these conflicts to conscious awareness in a manner that they can tolerate. Many issues are worked through in the context of the session itself. GIM therapists frequently comment that feelings and situations that were blocked in verbal therapy have been acknowledged and worked through by their clients in GIM therapy. The holding environment created within the music experience lowers anxiety and allows clients to deal with deeply repressed or highly conflicted material.

How is this so? Nolan (1989) speaks of music as a transitional object in his work with bulimic patients. A transitional object is one that is used to comfort or protect against anxiety by mediating inner states of tension. This term was introduced by Winnicott (1953) to describe the process by which the infant masters the transition from the sense of omnipotent control to control by reality testing. It bridges the infant's fantasy world and the world of reality. The transitional object can be a thing, such as a blanket, or the sound of the infant's own babbling. Music may serve as a transitional object, a mediating bridge between the person's inner world and the world of reality during the GIM experience. Music may bring sufficient support and comfort to the experience to allow the client to use the music to manage the inner tension created by the confrontation with highly conflicted material.

GIM was first used with people who had good, healthy ego strength. These clients kept tension and anxiety at a manageable level by deflecting conflicting images and affect, representing them in symbolic form, transforming them, and, perhaps most importantly, generating images of protection and guidance. These phenomena are observable through the images and are called defensive manoeuvres. Clinical populations have difficulty both in forming defensive manoeuvres and in managing anxiety. Their images are likely to be concrete representations of their conflicts rather than symbolic in form. They require more support from both the therapist and the music.

A useful way to consider this difference between normal and clinical populations is from a self-psychology model (Kohut, 1971). Self-psychology focuses on the narcissistic phase of development in which the self, or ego, develops through two healthy narcissistic configurations: the grandiose self and the idealised parent imago. Most psychiatric patients and many healthy clients, who have sustained a narcissistic blow, function in a narcissistic way in an effort to repair a wounded sense of self (Lonergan, 1982). This fragile sense of self may be threatened with disintegration when confronted with inner conflict.

Using a self-psychology approach to wounded self-esteem, narcissistic defences are mobilised and supported by allowing clients to use GIM for their narcissistic needs. This means supporting the client's need to move away from certain images, and nurturing their grandiose self with less demanding and more supportive music choices. The goal is to help them to feel worthwhile and maintain psychic homeostasis. Sometimes these clients disclaim any responsibility for their sessions by crediting the therapist with wonderful therapeutic powers. This is a manifestation of the idealised parent imago. This narcissistic defence can also be seen in these clients in the form of recurring idealised images.

Bonny (1980) noted that her borderline clients needed much more structure and direction than her healthier clients. Erich Bonny (1988) made the same observation in his work with adult children of alcoholics. He cautioned that regular GIM sessions will sometimes overwhelm the client and block the treatment process. This is true for other patients dealing with major emotional situations such as those with post-traumatic stress syndrome and dissociation disorders. People who are seriously depressed, have suffered loss through death or divorce, or are seriously ill have suffered a narcissistic blow and may also be overwhelmed by the GIM experience. If, after very careful evaluation, the decision is to proceed with GIM therapy with these clients, both the guiding and the music selections must be carefully managed. The therapist must offer extra support and guidance during the session through reassuring verbal interaction and supportive, rather than evocative, music.

Some clients are not suited for GIM treatment. Psychotic patients will carry their psychosis into their experience; the GIM process will then reinforce their psychotic thinking at best, and, at worst, may push them further into psychosis. GIM therapy with these patients is dangerous.

Clients who are suitable for GIM therapy are those who are able to reality test, able and willing to report their experience to the therapist, free of illicit drugs and alcohol, and can understand the language of images (abstract thought).

Research

Research in GIM therapy is just beginning. Hanks (1992) completed a cross-cultural study employing both Western and Chinese classical music in GIM sessions with Chinese subjects in Taiwan and Western subjects in the USA. In a phenomenological analysis of the session transcripts she found that subjects from very different cultures with radically different musical traditions tended to respond in similar patterns. They all produced imagery at three distinct levels - personal, cultural and archetypal. Her conclusion was that the data strongly suggests that the human psyche has a propensity for acting according to patterns of archetypal affect and/or imagery in response to music, regardless of the cultural tradition of the music employed.

Bishop (1993) studied the efficacy of GIM therapy with hospitalised physically and sexually abused women. She found that subjects who were treated with three or more GIM sessions improved on the Global Assessment Scale (as determined by other hospital staff) significantly more than others.

While these studies tend to confirm clinical observation, much more research is necessary to address the function of music in GIM therapy and the efficacy of GIM treatment.

Clinical Vignettes

Three clinical vignettes will be presented. Each case will illustrate a different type of client or approach to treatment.

Clinical Vignette 1

Lynette, a corporate executive, was a tall, attractive divorced brunette who came for help in dealing with her panic and sadness about being childless. At 39 years old, she realised that time was short for her to have children. Although she dated regularly, none of these men were prospective husbands. The following is one session that illustrates several aspects of GIM.

Music: Begins with Ein Heldenleben by Strauss, then excerpts from Brahms and Beethoven symphonies, ending with the Andante from Brahms 2nd piano concerto.

Sitting under a tree, city in the background, the sun is shining, the tree splits open, the sun comes in on me. The sun pulled the scene away from the city. I'm walking. A pastoral scene. Sitting in a green spot on the hill. Very nice. I'm taking care of myself. Feels lovely and warm. I'm now getting up and swaying. It's getting colder and darker. I don't have a coat. Gave myself a shawl, wrapped it around me. I'm walking through the forest on a path. It's dark. I don't know where I'm going. As I turn the corner I see more of the path and trees. I'm walking and walking.

Off to the side is the ocean. Still on the path except in my mind's eye I see myself playing. Footprints in wet sand, I'm playing. But I'm still on the path seeing myself play. Seagull comes and lands on my hand. Telling me something. I don't know what it is. Telling me to leave this place. Something's going to happen. I get away from the water and the beach. There is the bird. I'm not sure I want to leave, don't know where to go. I'm surrounded by rocks, don't know how to get out. The bird can't tell me where to go. He's sitting there and I'm sitting there looking out at the water. A car with no driver drove onto the beach in front of me. I get in the driver's seat. The bird sits on the back of the seat next to me. We're just sitting, not moving. Starting to see the road. We're driving. The bird tells me to go for it. The road is clear and wide open. We're going down the highway.

All of a sudden a big building appears, I know it. High school, not where I went to school. Big old grey steps. Been there years and years, attached to modern gymnasium. Totally empty. Standing looking and thinking about kids. Not at high school where I went. I love this older building. Sitting on steps remembering times in high school. The building symbolised part of life. Like this music, very regal, quiet, and modern. A feeling of old...building has had a lot going on it. Very regal. Changed from high school to Community College. It gave up certain life when it changed. I feel like the building is smiling. Older and wiser. Can't help it that it changed. Thinking I don't belong in this building. But I can reflect back on it and I miss it. Walking down steps away from it.

Back in the car. Resisting leaving it. Turn right to go home; turn left to go away from home. Sitting at a corner trying to decide. Not moving anywhere. Feeling sad. (Tears).

I'm standing there waving good-bye to my family like on opposite sides of a shore. Can't touch them. My niece is saying to come with them. Voices getting distant. Further and further away. Like I'm being pulled from behind. We're all waving, further and further away.

They're totally gone. I'm in blackness. Peaceful. Nothing there. Peace.

Feels okay. Floating up there among the clouds. Sitting on a rock. I see myself as a puppet dancing on toe shoes in front of myself. I want to stop dancing, my body is exhausted. I keep dancing. My feet are moving, my body is limp. Now I start stretching. Movements change. I feel like truly dancing, not as a puppet. Slow, stretching, beautiful movements. Ballerina in a long dress. Body feels good. Slow, yet easy.

Someone holding me toward their chest. Bigger than me. Don't know if it's a man or a woman. Mother, or a man?

Lynette is grieving the loss of her potential to have a family and a child. In this session she is grieving the loss of her family of origin, who live in a distant city. They stand for both that loss and her current sense of loss. This came near the end of the session. There were early signs that she was approaching a difficult issue: it became dark and cold; the bird gave her a warning; she was stuck in the rocks; and initially she couldn't see the road to drive.

The old school building was a symbol of herself growing old. It was older and wiser, and, like herself, couldn't help that it had changed. She expressed love for the building, herself. After saying good-bye to her family, she found herself in blackness, experienced a peaceful interlude, and then she was out of control. She became a puppet dancing and dancing, even though she was limp and exhausted, gradually gaining control. The session ended with her being nurtured by 'mother or man.' This sequence represented her real out of control feelings coming under control. This kind of metaphoric representation of mastery is common in GIM sessions.

Lynette was insightful regarding the relationship between her earlier feelings and her current situation. She began to deal more directly with her panic about being childless and possibly growing old alone; and, as in her session, she regained a sense of control over her panic and her life.

This session demonstrates Lynette's ego strength. She readily solves each problem as it comes. She found a way out of each dilemma, moved away from, or disguised through symbolism the more painful aspects of herself and her life and generated images of guidance (the bird) protection and nurturance. She mobilised defensive manoeuvres, and at the same time did the work she needed to do.

The hierarchical emergence of images is also demonstrated here. The client needed to deal with her earlier losses before she could confront her current situation. Within the session, she first approached her issues symbolically and then in a concrete representation of her family. The duality that is common in GIM sessions was apparent in the section where she is on the path and playing in the sand at the same time, and again, when she dances in front of herself.

Clinical Vignette 2

Jim was a 21 year old single gay man who was admitted to the psychiatric intensive care unit, a short-term inpatient treatment programme, after an overdose of his anti-depressant medication.

This was the second hospitalisation for this young man, the first one having been one year earlier. On admission, he was neatly groomed, had little eye contact, his mood was sad and his affect depressed. He was preoccupied with wanting to die, but said that he 'blew it', so he would have to go on living. There was no evidence of psychotic ideation.

After his last hospitalisation of three weeks, Jim had returned to his clerical job and continued in outpatient treatment. He was not aware of any major stressors in his life that might account for his depression.

Session 1

Music: Beethoven piano concerto No. 5, Adagio.

I'm lying under a tree, relaxing. There's a river, flowers. My friend is here. Men are running, running toward me. They're on the other side of the river. I feel uptight.

I'm in a park now, with my dog. I'm a little boy. There's my father. He's asking where my dog is. I'm just staring at him.

Jim abruptly stopped the session. He was frightened and shocked to see his deceased father in his image, and was very tearful as he spoke of his father's death. He had died shortly before Jim's 19th birthday. Jim said his brothers told him he should not cry; he should be a man. He was so overwhelmed by this experience that he expressed doubt about continuing GIM sessions.

That night Jim dreamed that he and his father walked together in the park. He considered the dream a continuation of his GIM session and asked for another one.

Session 2

Music: Britten, Simple Symphony, sentimental saraband; Vaughan-Williams, Prelude on Rhosymedre; Berlioz, L'Enfance du Christ, Shepherds Farewell, Chorus; Puccini, Madam Butterfly, Humming chorus.

I'm in the park where I used to go with my sisters. Singing. Walking by myself through the tunnel, reading graffiti. Now I'm in the same place as before. (Where he saw his father in the previous session.) It's colder. Squirrels running around. I'm at the pond. Feels like the future. Really quiet, cloudy. I'm just sitting, telling myself I should have come here before. I'm by the pond now. I want to see what it looks like.

I haven't been here since I was little. I was here so many times. (Tears). When he died I couldn't cry. I didn't want him to die.

I'm at the house where we were raised. I can hear my dad upstairs. I still can't talk to him.

I'm at the river with my friend. He's comforting me.

Jim began to confront the reality of his father's death by returning to the places in the park where he had spent time with his father and sisters. He expressed his pain at his father's death and discussed his wish for his father's approval of his gay lifestyle.

Session 3

Jim went to his father's grave, talked to him about himself, told him that he loved him and said good-bye. His sisters and brothers joined him and they all left feeling better.

Jim was quite relieved finally to express his feelings about his father and looked much brighter after the last session. The root of Jim's depression was evident after the first session. Prior to this, he had not connected his depression to his father's death, and, therefore, he had given no information about the anniversary of his father's death. Both of Jim's hospitalisations had occurred on or around his birthday. Through the GIM sessions, he began to mourn and to make some peace with his father. His visit to his father's grave was particularly significant, because he had never been there in real life. By the end of the series Jim had developed quite a bit of insight regarding his relationship with his father, his mourning process, and his guilt. Although he still had work to do regarding these issues, he was no longer suicidal and could continue therapy as an outpatient.

Although care was taken to provide a great deal of support through supportive music and verbal interventions during the first session, Jim's vulnerability was evident in his inability to suppress or transform overwhelming affect and images through defensive manoeuvres. His images were concrete representations of his issues. His only defence was to stop the session. He was overwhelmed by the image of his father and the related feelings and he considered terminating GIM treatment. The dream motivated him to continue with GIM.

This case is an example of the emergence of information during GIM sessions that is crucial to the patient's treatment. It also illustrates concrete rather than symbolic representation of issues and the potential for overwhelming feelings to block the treatment process. Jim's ego strength, however, improved markedly over the course of treatment. This was apparent in the increase in defensive manoeuvres, for example, comfort from his friend at the end of the second session and family support at the cemetery. For the more vulnerable patient, like Jim, each hurdle surmounted makes the next one easier.

Clinical Vignette 3

GIM has been adapted for group work, particularly in hospital settings and in a workshop format for normal, healthy people. Group GIM sessions are not as intense as dyadic sessions; however, since the therapist cannot monitor the clients' experiences nor any concurrent problems, care must be taken in the selection of group members to ensure safety. There are many modifications in the method for hospital groups of this type. Clients sit in chairs. The induction is highly structured and the music is less complex and of much shorter duration. A very small window of free imaging is allowed (2 to 3 minutes) and clients are asked to write their images before the music ends. The entire music session is about 10 minutes long, (Goldberg, in press).

Following is the case of a client in a GIM group on a psychiatric intensive care unit. The GIM groups were part of an ongoing group that met daily.

June was a 32-year-old woman admitted for depression and suicidal ideation. She was a very rigid woman who looked older than her stated age. She was withdrawn and resistant to other patients' efforts to engage her on the unit.

June's image in her first group session to the music of the Pachelbel canon in D was of a walled garden. It was a beautiful garden, full of flowers. June talked about how comfortable and safe it felt to be in her garden. The next group was not a GIM group, but June used her image to communicate to the group her need for protection. The following day June had the same image, except there was a gate in the wall. June did not make anything of the gate; however, other patients in the group noticed it immediately. June was not sure she was ready to go out or let anyone else come in. She did agree that she could talk to others over the gate. Concurrent with the evolution of June's image, she became more social on the ward and was visibly more relaxed. In the last group session, 5 days after admission, the gate in the wall around June's garden was open. Unlike previous groups where the image was addressed only in the metaphor, she was beginning to integrate the image as a representation of herself. She realised she had cut herself off from others, thereby eliminating the possibility of support from friends and family or treatment from professionals. She was also insightful regarding fears of being hurt by others that led to her withdrawal and the subsequent escalation of her depression.

This case demonstrates the value of a very brief version of the GIM method adapted for group therapy in a short-term treatment setting. Others have adapted GIM for clinical therapy groups. For example, Summer (1981, 1988) has worked with the elderly in nursing homes and with hospitalised alcoholics and E. Bonny (1988) has adapted GIM for therapy groups with adult children of alcoholics.

Training and Certification

An in-depth psychotherapeutic method such as the Bonny method of GIM requires experience and expertise of its practitioners. Extensive training and supervision are necessary in order to qualify to practice GIM. Standards for training and certification are established and regulated by the Association for Music and Imagery (AMI). Those who complete the three-level training in a programme accredited by AMI are eligible to apply for the status of Fellow of the Association for Music and Imagery.

The didactic and experiential training includes concepts and elements of GIM at the introductory, basic and advanced levels, reading, case reports, consultations, supervised experience with dyadic and group work and personal GIM therapy. The introductory and basic levels are one or two week programmes. The advanced level typically requires two years to complete.

AMI standards of practice and code of ethics designate completion of advanced-level training as the level of competency required to practice GIM independently. Training is available in the United States at five training institutes and three university programmes. In addition, training is available in Canada, Sweden, Denmark, Germany, Australia, England, and New Zealand.

The Bonny Method of Guided Imagery and Music is a music-centred psychotherapy with great power to help clients actualise their own growth and healing potential when in the hands of a GIM trained therapist. Music therapists are encouraged to consider training in GIM. This work will only enhance the quality of treatment.

6

Linking Sound and Symbol

Mary Priestley

At the time when I was studying music therapy under Juliette Alvin at the Guildhall School of Music and Drama, music was being used in therapy in a relatively simple and straightforward way. Sometimes it was used as a passive therapy to soothe, elevate and delight the patients, sometimes the patients were encouraged to use the instruments themselves as a channel for the expression of their feelings, as a medium for describing a mood picture in sound or as an aid to concentration, relationship and self-discipline, and sometimes they would form a little vocal group and sing the songs that reminded them of happier times or sadness shared.

As I was in analysis with Dr Wooster at that time, I was being made aware of subtler, more problematic, and often more conflicting workings of the psyche, with conscious and unconscious moving in different directions sapping the vital energy and causing confusion in the thinking and subsequent behaviour. Enlightening this were the various Kleinian concepts such as splitting, and projective identification along with the better-known Freudian concepts of the ego defences, and especially, repression, displacement, the Oedipus complex and the language of dreams.

Wishing to explore ways in which patients could obtain more insight into the maladapted functioning of their whole selves, two colleagues at St Bernard's Hospital: Marjorie Wardle, Peter Wright and I decided to meet for two hours weekly to undertake music therapy experiments on each other before using these techniques on the patients. This was the only way of realising how extraordinarily powerful this therapy could be and thus established the kind of parameters that needed to be laid down in order to provide a reasonably informed background to the work. I have made it a personal rule not to use therapeutic techniques on the patients that I have not tried out on myself with colleagues first. When I occasionally break this rule through impatient enthusiasm, I always regret it.

At the time of our experimental sessions Peter Wright was in Jungian analysis, he was the son and brother of Methodist Ministers, with a very wide knowledge of esoteric subjects. Marjorie Wardle was not yet having Jungian analysis but started this shortly after we finished our experimental work. We had 98 experimental sessions over two years, often starting (with Marjorie quailing slightly) with Peter calling on the Archangels Raphael, Michael, Uriel and Gabriel for protection at the start and myself serving hot chocolate 'mit schlabogers' (with whipped cream on it) at the end. This is not a frivolous remark. The rituals concerning these ancient archetypal beings at the start and the maternal feeding at the end had an important place in the shape of the work.

I called our sessions Intertherapy. When, some months later, Constable publishers commissioned a book on music therapy from me, everything, in true Priestley fashion, became grist to the mill, and we realised that the particular kind of music therapy we had developed could be dignified with a separate name. Peter, who had by then left his analyst, wanted us to call it Analytical Music Therapy. I did not feel so easy about this, but the book had to be written to a looming deadline at weekends in between doing music therapy at home and in St Bernards hospital, being a single parent to my three sons, undergoing my analysis and taking courses at the Institute of Group Analysis. As I could not suggest an alternative title, this became the title.

The name of Analytical Music Therapy continued to cause a certain amount of dissonance in analytical circles, especially in Germany, although there are three German courses partly based on this approach; one is actually part of a music therapy training specifically for doctors, and my second music therapy book 'Analytische Musiktherapie' (Klett Cotta 1981) is so far only available in the German translation. On hearing of this dissonance I nervously bent under the pressure and started calling it Exploratory Music Therapy until Dr J W T Redfearn, my Jungian analytical supervisor of 11 years, said he thought, that as it had been in my book 'Music Therapy in Action (Priestley, 1975), he saw no reason not to stick to the original name. Someone would always object but that need not affect the work that we actually did. However, the upshot of this is that today the many music therapists in this country now using their own analytical experience as a background to their music therapy, are calling their work by different names, one even being totally in the clear by using the title 'Analytically-informed music therapy'.

Then what is Analytical Music Therapy? It is hard to say exactly, as a form is always an imperfect representation of the force that gave it birth. Basically it is music therapy practised by a therapist who has had, or is about to have, some analytical psychotherapy or analysis and has had some experience of this therapy as a client of an analytical music therapist. Analytical music therapy aims at creating a time and mind-space in which the patient or client can feel safe enough to attempt the uniting of her thinking, emotion, action and the often unspoken spiritual side of her nature in order to produce a flow of being which can help her to move forward into experimenting, via music and sound expression, with rehearsals of different ways of approaching situations and relationships and reflecting on the life she has led so far, in a relatively smooth way. That is to say, without too many damaging sforzandos of traumatic confrontation; creating a session like a seamless garment with neither sterile rationalisation unaccompanied by meaningful emotion and subsequent relevant action, nor dangerous mindless emotion acted out in dissonant ways.

The patient explores new pathways symbolically in the world of imagination but with the bodily-expressed emotion in sound which gives her a safe toe-hold in the world of everyday reality. I am aware that doctors would say that all emotion is expressed physically or it would not be emotion, nevertheless there is a great difference in the agony of barely containing the seemingly inexpressible pain of anger, sadness or jealousy and the actual process of sobbing, or sobbing on the violin or clarinet, or kicking the waste paper basket round the room or beating out a violent rhythm on a noble drum or vast responsively-resonating gong.

Hearing our improvised musical duet and then reinterpreting and expressing the emotion through bodily movement (sometimes we can actually describe this as dance), brings the client's emotion to a more fundamental level. It is also important that she now uses the lower half of the body and her contact with the ground. One must remember that in instrumental playing or vocalising, it is mainly the hands, arms and the upper part of the body that are used expressively. To take a step with the foot on the ground represents a more concrete level of commitment and realisation than sitting in a chair talking about feelings or waving the arms about to express musically one's deepest emotion.

This use of movement has been a later development in connection with analytical music therapy, although I led a Psychodynamic Movement session for 20 years at St Bernard's Psychiatric Hospital. Heinz Kohut found it necessary to build his own Psychology of the Self on the infrastructure of Freudian theory, because of the situation of the over-close, over-stimulated middle-class childhood of the early part of this century. This approach must now adapt to cater for the present under stimulated, under-mirrored childhood in today's nuclear families with two busy working parents. We now see too many car, desk, or chair-bound individuals in our society, with too much activity and excitement in the head and too little in the feet where the basic healthy rhythm of life can be realised. This regenerating rhythm of effort and relaxation in the action of the two feet can be experienced as a model for a healthier and more holistic life-style. Perhaps today's rich harvest of heart attack patients with their Type A personalities would benefit by applying these ideas to their tortuous and pressured way of living.

The analytical music therapist acts very much as a container, giving a time-space, a geographical space, and a space in the world of feelings and imagination into which the patient can enter and make her explorations. Therapists all have their own unique ways of functioning. Even if they are kidding themselves that they are being a Freudian mirror, the earlier-mystified patient is usually an extremely sensitive reader of body language and even the best-trained therapist gives away a great deal more about what he is thinking and feeling than he realises in this way. Therefore I think that the analytical music therapist should present himself as an honest human being who can give the patient space to be herself and find her own solutions, but who can also be a model of a resonating, flowing person who may well have strong views about certain aspects of life while not in anyway insisting that the patient should be like him.

I think it essential that the patient is aware that her analytical music therapist is himself journeying hopefully and exploring and experimenting, that he is not a static, dogmatic creature who has 'got there' and knows all the answers. Equally, the therapist should also at all times respect the basic dignity of the individual with whom he is working and her right to start from where she is, and find her own serious purpose which makes life meaningful and worth living to her and also, when necessary, worth defending against either internal or external potentially disintegrating forces.

When a client has strong conflicting dissonant emotions locked up inside herself, usually producing unbearable physical tensions, or psychosomatic symptoms or the escape towards psychosis as a result of this inner state, she is able to clarify the direction of the conflicting energies within herself through sound. Using a simple, symbolically or aurally powerful instrument, a way forward can be facilitated via the following means:

1. Playing the instrument releases some of the tension.
2. Hearing the recording of this music promotes reflection and communication.
3. It turns the client into an agent of the expression and no longer the victim via the result of the long term tension.
4. It provides instant mirroring (Kohut, 1985) such as the client may never have had experienced before.
5. It makes the painful experiences shareable and thus more able to be realised.
6. The client feels more easily that her emotions are really responded to empathically via the therapist's accompanying music.
7. It provides something physical (as sound vibrations are) as a symbolic representation of the energies of the inner state which can later on be listened to in a calmer, more reflective mood with the therapist, and built on creatively, possibly in another art form.
8. It promotes verbal communication where this was difficult, or even impossible, previously.
9. It brings the salutary realisation that even the most awful and murderous- feeling rage, when expressed in this way and shared, does not cause any terrible guilt-evoking damage either to oneself, the instruments (not often) or the therapist (not once in 20 years' work) but does give the patient, if she is oriented that way, the insight into who or what she is, what she was angry about and also what was the deep root of this feeling.
10. Being a dynamic musical expression realised in the accommodation of passing time, it lets the rage to die down as the hands and arms get tired and can - if the patient is ready for this - reveal clearly the underlying pain or sorrow that is beneath it. Thus opening up the path towards being motivated to start the search for alternative ways of meeting and dealing with the pain-producing situations. Often it gives

a very clear insight, through a visual memory, into at what age the experienced pain began, producing in the client a more tender, self-mothering attitude to her weaknesses with deep healing involved.

This does not mean that an analytical music therapist does not make interpretations regarding the underlying archaic impulses affecting certain feelings and subsequent behaviour. Where this seems possible and appropriate, he may do so verbally or even via the music; for example, expressing musically the sadness underlying the patient's manic behaviour or brittle stance in a certain area where she feels extremely vulnerable. In this way, something that might be rejected if presented as a thought in words, may be able to be accepted at an emotional level through a poignant melody, against which the patient may not feel the need to defend herself. The meaning may then take some time to filter through to any verbal concept and understanding, and when it does, the patient may, happily, feel that it is her own spontaneous and original insight.

It is very important for the analytical music therapist to have had a minimum of twelve individual sessions of this type of work with a more experienced analytical music therapist, whether or not he has undergone a psychoanalysis or had some analytical psychotherapy. This is so that he does not have the shock of first experiencing the savage dynamism of his own sometimes explosive deeper emotion with his patient, whose emotion he is supposed to be containing and responding to with some degree of outer and inner awareness and subtle control. Also, if he is another type of person, it may be salutary for him to experience the kind of deadness and inability to let the feelings flow and the images unroll in the inner eye, which is the situation with a smaller number of heavily sedated hospital patients or slightly schizoid intellectuals.

The form of the original Analytical Music Therapy (AMT) was roughly as follows. The therapist should seat himself firmly and try to achieve a certain emptiness or 'Accommodating capacity' in his psyche, a process I later discovered that the Japanese call 'mushin'. In short, an inner space for the patient to fill. Patients who are able and willing to speak will usually start the session by talking about anything at all that they want to share, often things that they have not been able to talk about to anyone else. This communication can be at any level: imagination, dreams, emotion-evoking situations, problems - nothing is considered irrelevant. Out of this comes an image or a subject which either the therapist or the patient or both would like to use as a focus for their musical duet improvisation. The music is a purely spontaneous sound expression on simple instruments and, contrary to general supposition, most patients, though totally innocent of any musical training, find no difficulty in this. There are no expectations or instructions, but as they discover the flow of their present emotion through sound, patients experience relief, satisfaction, and often pride and delight.

I have almost never found difficulty in getting patients or clients to improvise musically, the exception being two or three people suffering from agitated depression who often find just remaining in one place an agony beyond endurance. The therapist usually (but not necessarily) on the piano, can accompany, complement, argue musically with, tease, fight or make love to the client in their music as the needs arise.

Some therapists respond somatically to counter-transference (awareness of the client's deeper feelings) which can be a very disturbing phenomenon when it is first encountered. I do not recall that any kind of counter-transference was discussed in my year of training at the Guildhall School of Music (1968/69). I am confident that this subject is now adequately covered in the Psychodynamics Group on this course. Being unusually sensitive to this kind of message from my patient's unconscious, in my early days of practising AMT I was troubled occasionally by acute choking sensations (this meant unconscious anger or deep sadness in the patient). On one occasion I experienced, with some alarm, a kind of creeping paralysis of my hands which turned out to be some feelings that the patient had 'killed off' and not allowed to surface, to be spoken about or even to be expressed in sound between us. In a recent session doing some passive music therapy with a stroke patient who had lost her short term memory, I experienced a total memory block twice running in a piece of Bach which I knew and had performed many times without any trouble. Luckily I could use this happening in my understanding of her difficulties in this area. My analyst was able to explain these phenomena and I became more expert at quickly translating my somatic experiences into recognisable emotion which could be dispersed by feeding it back into the patient's conscious mind, so that latterly counter-transference emotion has been experienced as the raw emotion.

'How do you know if it is your own or the patient's feelings?' is a frequent question asked at talks or workshops. Well, given a good analysis which goes deep into the feelings, plus a period of personal AMT you do know. The inner experience is quite different, aided by certain checks with one's conscious mind. My own reachable emotions I experience as physically global whereas those picked up from patients I feel in an area around the solar plexus or Manipura chakra. This experience is not limited to therapists of today. Laurens Van Der Post described how certain primitive African tribesmen who had had no access to telephones or fax machines had to rely on telepathy, and the hypersensitive members of the tribe said that they sent messages through the head and received them through the heart.

While one always regards the first session with a client as an assessment session (in the case of a private client it may well be a mutual assessment session), I have, during the twenty years of my music therapy practice, never felt that I needed to turn anyone down, not even the private client who came in very drunk to his first session. And I have been privileged to work with an astonishing range of ability and disability. In the hospital I have worked with psychotic patients in the state of catatonia and mutism, coaxing them into musical and then verbal exchange, and with schizophrenic patients in the lively world of symbolic action and florid emotion expressed fluently on instruments, sometimes in dance and then in words. Having had a totally non-scientific education and childhood in an artistic family I have easy access into the levels of fantasy, dreams and symbolism but sometimes have to refer certain patients to staff in other disciplines to help them with the bricks and mortar of the world of everyday reality with its factual limitations and frustrations.

It is very important for the analytical music therapist - or in fact any therapist to be aware of his weaknesses and remaining blocks, and have contacts for any further referral-on that may be necessary either for selective expert help and advice or because the therapist's own areas of weakness and woundedness begin to resonate too strongly and uncontrollably with one or more of those of his patient. An analytical supervisor is of great help in such situations.

On the level of high ability and achievement, I have carried out AMT with consultant psychiatrists, writers, actors and film directors, with some of my talented and brilliant colleagues from twelve different countries and some highly gifted children. But, as far as results generally are concerned, we must remember that, as in the early days of Freudian analysis, music therapists, with their very ancient orally and musically-transmitted profession with its very minute body of the written and generally available unifocussed type of knowledge that medicine has accumulated, tend to have had referred patients who have proved totally problematic, unlabellable or mentally unsuitable for psychotherapy or for much else in the hospital's therapeutic armoury.

The same goes for psychiatric or medical referrals to private practice where emotional and psychosomatic disorders are concerned. No doubt this situation will improve as more music therapists continue to produce positive results with the kind of careful, detailed research that is in line with the scientific minds of today. The new therapies will then have to struggle with the therapeutic dropouts and mystery-mongers of their professional youth. They have my sympathy. Nevertheless, in a rough survey, which we carried out in St Bernard's Hospital, we estimated that 87% of the patients that came to us as individuals or in groups, either reported or evinced (or both) benefit from their music therapy sessions. They often started off in the direction of a more hopeful mood and a feeling that the world was perhaps a slightly more tender and compassionate place to live in than they had hitherto believed, and therefore felt that it was worthwhile being prepared to make some effort to alleviate their situation, sometimes with us but sometimes turning to art therapy or psychotherapy. A questionnaire to nursing staff revealed that they noticed improvements in their patients after their music therapy mainly in the area of communication both to the staff and to fellow patients. Understandably this communication could sometimes express a long-suppressed rage and indignation in appropriate ways and then it was necessary, but not always possible, to discuss this temporarily disturbing situation, which had increased the burden on our already harassed nursing colleagues, in a multi-disciplinary meeting.

It is interesting that most forms of therapy or healing which rely on stimulating the patient's own innate self-healing potential are known to produce either physical or emotional crises of this kind, for examples fevers, skin rashes, diarrhoea and vomiting, and acutely active physically expressed phases of mourning or indignation or the sudden emptying of a large pocket of pus. With regard to the latter, more technologically-primitive societies have devised ways - often through dance and rhythmic music - of containing and detonating these strong emotions on a group level, while allowing them the time they need for full expression and enantiodromic transmutation. Even on an individual basis we frequently see on television a grieving relative from further east than the United Kingdom totally giving way to their emotions which sweep through them torrentially in physical expression while they are physically and emotionally supported by a male on either side. Our own widows and sorrowing mothers are called 'being good about it' when they suppress their emotion, and go about their daily lives as if nothing had happened, only to produce an incapacitating illness which then forces society to care for them totally, even if it is only by professionals, later on within the two year mourning period. Although our powerful modern psychotropic drugs have a useful and valid place in the therapeutic armoury, and much of our therapy could not take place without their aid, they cannot, in every case, wholly take the place of the empathic human support that cathartic suffering requires. Nor is it right, in my opinion (based on experience), to eliminate the need for the patient or his carers to tolerate, understand and transmute a certain bearable level of suffering on the way to health and wholeness. I leave others to debate the finer points of this thesis.

While I am on the subject of problems and difficulties in analytical music therapy but which are also common to most of the more thorough-going therapies, I would like to write about two special difficulties which bring up very deep ethical issues, one not so rare and the other more rare. The first concerns joint sessions with either husband and wife, or with other partners in a mutually committed longer term relationship. In the partnerships with which I have worked, one person has initially come into therapy as the designated patient, even if the couple at once opt to come to therapy as a dyadic unit, which in my experience they seldom have. Nevertheless, the therapist is faced with the questions. 'Am I treating the partnership, which dies if they decide to part, or the designated patient, whose optimum chance of a fulfilled life may well lie in leaving a partner who is totally resistant to personal change in the way of growth or the rebalancing of dynamic exchange or repression?'

In fact, that situation seldom arose as it was generally the husband who decided to leave his wife when he saw, with alarm, that she was now quite capable of expressing her own newly-discovered (or uncovered?) feelings and was not prepared any longer to take on the burden of his unexpressed fears and anxieties and rages by proxy. Personally, I believe that the patient has the right to know her therapist's fundamental beliefs about such issues as the indissolubleness of marriage and the right to choose whether to go through with an unwanted pregnancy; because although he may not influence her in a directly verbal manner, many little non-verbal messages will creep into the relationship to influence her, possibly against her own deepest held beliefs.

The other, much rarer, problematic and traumatic situation is when a patient in the second half of life, in the course of therapy, suddenly, and sometimes quite unexpectedly to the therapist, finds herself inwardly confronted with the realisation that her life, which has been totally reactive, or self-annihilatingly placating or based solely on giant defences, has been utterly meaningless at the core, and in order to continue she will have to make changes that seem to her altogether too challenging, and the making of them will only confirm how disastrously and tragically she has wasted so many valuable years. At such a time I have known a patient actually come up with the visualisation of a cross-roads with one signpost leading to the termination of her life in a not necessarily specified way and the other leading her to a road of impossible challenge and difficulty. Sometimes this devastating realisation will lead to a sudden and violent suicide, sometimes it will lead to the more socially-acceptable option of a terminal illness with death taking place just two years after the end of their therapy. Suicide at this time of life has quite a different meaning from that enacted by those who have not had the support needed to launch themselves into life or have managed to do this with great difficulties but then felt faced with impossible odds.

Both situations point to the necessity for the patient to be encouraged to spend some time in working out the deep and ultimate purpose her life, or marriage or work has for her, right at the start of therapy, even though she may seem quite unready for this and has not brought this kind of material to the session. In this way a possible third option could be created for those who reach this testing cross-roads, so that when, on one level, the option seems to be death or unbearable dishonour, she can descend to a deeper, already prepared path where life can take on a different and more fundamental meaning, if her environment and significant others do not prevent this.

It was in order to prevent this kind of disaster, though here produced in a violent external manner, that forced Dr V. Frank to develop his logotherapy in the concentration camp where he was interned. The choice between a savagely tortured unliveable life and quick death by electrocution against the surrounding fence, had urgently to be supplemented by a third choice: that of hammering out a new meaning through choosing one's attitude to the impossible situation. In normal life the situation can be far less obvious and therefore totally unexpected. Suddenly the older patient can find herself at this fateful cross-roads where there only seem to be two choices and the situation is desperate and urgent. The situation is rare, but far less rare than it would appear as the illness produced by such a state may be regarded merely as 'unfortunate' or 'normal' and may have progressed too far physically for help by the time the patient seeks therapeutic intervention on an emotional level. This is something for the music therapist working with an individual (especially a newly-retired man or a lady recently widowed) to be prepared for and recognise, without too much guilt if it should carry off one of his ex-patients or patients.

One has also to distinguish between patients who are actually willing to struggle and evolve and those who are just seeking a reasonably comfortable life with some of their misery eliminated. With some patients the discovery of music in themselves is a wonderful kind of opening up inside with new possibilities of singing in the local choir, and going to concerts, and privately dancing to the music of their mood in their homes. It is also a great gift that they can give to their children and grandchildren, bridging the generation gap. With others it is a tool to be used during the time with the therapist and discarded when that time is over, moving on to other interests and forms of expression. Neither way is right or wrong, the patient must just decide what use music was for her and act accordingly.

7

Short-Term Verbal and Musical Memory in Schizophrenia: Implications for Theories of Working Memory and Cerebral Dominance

Penny Rogers and Norman Smeyatsky

This chapter describes a study which investigated the processing of musical and verbal information in normal and mentally ill subjects by comparing short-term musical memory with short-term verbal memory. It aims to shed light on two quite separate areas of research, first of all the cerebral localisation of schizophrenia and secondly, Baddeley's model of working memory.

This basis for the study to be described was a clinical observation that psychotic clients' involved in music therapy were able to interact at a more sophisticated level within a musical framework than a verbal framework. This was demonstrated by an apparent increase in the level of initiated gestures (musical), increased levels of concentration whilst involved in clinical improvisation, and increased levels of interaction and awareness of others. Colleagues within the multi-disciplinary setting in which I work, often saw videotapes of clients participating in music therapy within review meetings and case conference, and supported these observations.

The need for music therapists' to examine the processes involved in their work has resulted in a number of research approaches being used in recent years, including 'New Paradigm' methods amongst others, and a detailed perspective on the varieties of research methodologies in music therapy is provided by Bunt and Hoskyns (1987). It is however notoriously difficult to design rigorous, tight clinical trials of music therapy. This study sought to avoid the inherent problems in designing such a trial by evaluating two small components - that is a musical and comparable verbal task involving short-term memory.

The Processing of Musical Information

The study focused on areas of perceptual function and cognitive ability in relation to the short-term memory of music. Thus, other such relevant factors as the aesthetic, emotional and creative aspects of music were omitted.

'Music' is organised sound containing the components pitch, timbre, harmony, rhythm, duration, volume, and dynamics. In order to compare musical skill with a verbal skill where all other parameters were similar, a pitch span task was compared with a digit span task. The digit and pitch span tasks were identical in terms of volume, duration and dynamics, and only varied in terms of pitch and timbre.

Cerebral specialisation for the perception of music has been the focus of considerable interest. A detailed review of the literature clearly demonstrates that the majority of research into this area has focused on studies of musically gifted subjects and the localisation and processing mechanisms of specific musical talents.

Experimental studies with reference to cerebral specialisation for the perception of musical passages have largely indicated a superiority for the right hemisphere (non-dominant). The first study of this kind came from Kimura (1964). Subjects in this study were presented with portions of baroque melodies and subsequently asked to recognise the melodies. It was found that more passages were correctly identified when presented to the left rather than the right ear. This was interpreted as a left ear advantage, and hence a non-dominant hemisphere superiority for the perception of melodies. A non-dominant hemisphere superiority for the perception of musical passages and their recognition has been subsequently confirmed by various studies (Kimura, 1967, King and Kimura, 1972; Spellacy 1970), using passages of unfamiliar solo violin music and by Spreen et al. (1970) using similar material. In contrast to this finding is the consistent finding on dichotic listening tasks of a right ear (dominant hemisphere) advantage for musically experienced subjects. This observation, first reported in a study by Cook (1973) using a comparison control group of non-musically experienced subjects (who demonstrated a left ear superiority) was replicated in a later study by Bever and Chiarello (1974). Additional confirmation for non-dominant processing of musical information in normal subjects has been obtained with other methods of investigation. McKee et al. (1973) recorded bilateral alpha activity in the temporo-parietal regions of the two hemispheres while the subjects were engaged in either a musical task or one of three linguistic tasks of varying difficulties. Results demonstrated left/right ratios of alpha activity being greater for the musical task, tending to decrease progressively with increasingly difficult linguistic tasks.

Clinical studies have also provided evidence of non-dominant hemispheric specialisation for the perception of melodies. Evidence has been derived from studies of patients with unilateral lesions of the brain. Shankweiler (1966) employed the dichotic listening technique and presents data indicating impairment of the perception of melodies following removal of the right temporal lobe. Gordon and Bogen (1974) found similar results with the use of the dada technique. They investigated patients with transient hemiplegia after carotid injection of sodium amylobaritone. Gordon and Bogen found that after right carotid injection singing but not speech was markedly deficient. By comparison singing was relatively undisturbed by left carotid injection in contrast to speech. These findings were replicated in a number of studies by Borchgrevinck (1988).

In essence it can be seen that differential patterns of cerebral specialisation for the perception of musical passages have been found for musically sophisticated and musically naive subjects, and secondly that the non-dominant hemisphere would appear to be the locus for the processing of musical information in the musically naive subject.

Studies of musical memory have in general not focused on recall but on recognition (e.g. subjects have had to judge whether two melodies are the same or different). This results from the anticipated difficulties in using recall because subjects may have no adequate response mode. The use of musically privileged structures and relationships (such as intervals, scales, keys and chords) to provide a framework for the study of musical pitch perception is now quite widespread; for example in the work of Deutsch and Feroe (1981) and Dowling (1978). Again, these studies have focused on the recognition of melodies and pitches rather than on free recall.

These tasks require the subject to repeat sequences of random digits immediately after presentation by the tester. Any one musical note may be realised by a large number of sounds differing widely in their frequency composition although they generate the same pitch percept. Research carried out on pitch perception has shown that the clearest and least ambiguous pitch percepts are generated by harmonic complex sounds having several low successive harmonics (DeBoer, 1976) such as trains of periodic short impulses (Schouten, 1940). Currently successful models used to predict pitch perception embody some form of matching of the incoming sound to harmonic complex templates (Goldstein 1973; Terdhart, 1974; Wightman 1973). Schubert (1980) found that the auditory system provides an extremely accurate representation of the frequency of tones; a frequency difference of 5% of a semi tone can be reliably discriminated by a practised subject . Even when the sound is made more complicated by embedding the target tone within a longer sequence of tones, frequency discrimination is of comparable accuracy as long as there is no uncertainty about the temporal location and frequency range of the target range Watson and Kelly, 1981). Such tasks characterise musical ability tests of the type developed by Bentley (1966).

There is evidence that children immersed in a musical culture such as our own internalise structures that are implicit in the bulk of the music they hear (Gardner, 1981; Zenatti, 1969). It therefore follows that the majority of adults conceive of music in terms of these structures; if this is reflected in recall then it would be expected that performance recall for tonal music would be better than recall for atonal music. A previous study (Rogers, unpublished data) examined recall on short-term auditory stimuli involving tonal pitches and contrasted this with short-term auditory memory for atonal pitches in a single subject. The results clearly demonstrated that opaque structure was utilised in the recall of pitches (it is easier to remember a tonal rather than an atonal sequence of notes). In the present study, pitch strings were all tonal in orientation and thus it would be presumed that all subjects would utilise some opaque structure in their recall. By utilising tonally oriented strings, the investigators were able to avoid some of the arguments that digit strings are a more familiar medium to the subjects (e.g. in telephone numbers) than pitch strings utilising random atonal sequences.

Accuracy in responding to a pitch recall task does not depend solely on the degree of change of any one tone, but is crucially dependent on the relationship between tones; therefore the auditory system draws on certain principles of perceptual organisation that interact with the interrelationships or structure of the input.

Schizophrenia and the Laterality Hypothesis

There has been increasing evidence over the past two decades of an association between abnormal lateralisation and schizophrenia. The first major work in this area (Flor-Henry, 1969) investigated patients with temporal lobe epilepsy and a co-existing psychosis. It was found that the patients with a left-sided temporal focus to their epilepsy had a predominantly schizophrenia-like psychosis, while those with a right- sided focus exhibited an affective psychosis. Thus, this pointed to an association between left hemisphere dysfunction and schizophrenia and right hemisphere dysfunction and affective disorder.

Since the above study a variety of techniques have been used to investigate schizophrenia and laterality further. In perceptual studies, auditory stimuli have been presented to each ear individually or dichotically, to assess the functioning of the contralateral hemisphere. Monaural and dichotic listening tasks (Gruzelier and Hammond, 1979) have been reported as evidence for impaired left hemisphere function in schizophrenia. Similar results have been obtained from studies using visual stimuli. Using tachistoscopic presentations (Beaumont and Dimond, 1973) showed that schizophrenics had abnormally great difficulty in processing items presented to the right visual half field (VHF) (using the left hemisphere), compared with items presented to the left VHF. Gur (1978) obtained similar results in a nonsense syllable identification task. Schizophrenics had difficulty identifying tachistoscopically presented right VHF syllables as compared with left VHF syllables whereas normal subjects displayed much less disparity.

Bilaterally recorded evoked responses (Buchspaun, 1977), as well as resting electroencephalograms (EEG) (Flor-Henry and Koles, 1980) have pointed towards left hemisphere impairment in schizophrenia. Connolly et al. (1983), using visual evoked potentials showed that there was a smaller wave generated in the left hemisphere compared with the right (non-dominant hemisphere).

Electrodermal activity response studies (EDA) have been used as a technique for measuring hemispheric dysfunction. These studies have consistently shown that Skin Conductance Responses (SCRs) recorded from the left-hand of schizophrenics tended to be lower in amplitude than right-hand SCRs, while the amplitude of controls' SCRs tend to be bilaterally equal. (Gruzelier and Venables, 1974).

Evidence from computerised tomography scans also indicate that some schizophrenics have 'altered left hemisphere brain organisation ' (Naeser et al., 1981). Recently further evidence for dominant hemisphere dysfunction in schizophrenia has come from studies using positron emission tomography (PET).

Using 18-F-fluorodeoxyglucose in PET studies of 12 schizophrenics and 12 matched controls (Gur et al., 1987a) showed that there was dysfunction in the dominant hemisphere in schizophrenics compared with normals. Moreover, in a subsequent study (Gur et al., 1987b) they showed that there was reduction in the differences between the hemispheres on clinical improvement.

Neuropsychological tests have also been used to study laterality in schizophrenia. Most investigations have shown that schizophrenics perform less well on cognitive tasks involving the dominant hemisphere compared to the non-dominant hemisphere (Abrams and Taylor, 1981). Other studies, however, have failed to show a difference between the two hemispheres (Silverstein and Meltzer, 1983) and some have even shown an impairment of the non-dominant hemisphere in schizophrenia (West, 1984). Methodological problems such as inappropriate comparison groups, sampling difficulties and exhaustion of patients when faced with large batteries of tests have been cited as reasons for these inconsistencies (Gruzelier, 1981).

The present study makes use of a novel neuropsychological technique (pitch span) to investigate schizophrenia and laterality further. The validity of neuropsychological tests is based upon studies of patients with localised neurological lesions, thus short-term verbal memory (as measured by digit span) has been localised to the dominant hemisphere (Miller, 1966), while short-term musical memory has been localised to the non dominant hemisphere (Borchgrevinck, 1987). Therefore if this study demonstrates that the schizophrenic sample does better on the pitch span task compared to the digit span task, this would provide further evidence that schizophrenia is at least partly characterised by dominant hemisphere dysfunction.

Working Memory

Some of the most influential developments in the study of human memory in the late 1960's were compatible with the view that human memory comprises two major components: a short-term store of limited capacity, which relies on phonemic encoding and a long-term store of much greater capacity which depends heavily on semantic encoding, (Atkinson and Shiffrin, 1971). Subsequently, theorists have distinguished some separable components within this short-term store, and in particular Baddeley and Hitch (1974) initiated what has become a long and productive research effort into the nature and function of what they call working memory.

The principle impetus for the hypothesis that there are separate sub-systems for sensory, short-term and long-term storage (see for example Baddeley, 1984) stems from the mass of evidence illustrating different patterns of performance in various laboratory tests of memory in normal subjects. Neuropsychological evidence has also been a powerful influence in distinguishing between the sub-systems responsible for short and long-term memory. Thus, patients suffering from classical amnesia could be characterised as having intact short-term memory (as measured by their normal digit span), and impaired long-term memory

(Baddeley and Warrington, 1970). In contrast, the opposite dissociation, that is patients with severely impaired digit spans (short-term memory) but essentially normal long-term memory, as in certain types of conduction aphasia have been found, (Shallice and Warrington, 1970). Such double dissociations are powerful evidence for the separation of sub-systems.

The term 'working memory' refers to the temporary storage of information in connection with the performance of cognitive tasks such a reading, problem solving or learning. Baddeley (1974), conceptualises working memory as a limited capacity central processor, the central executive of which employs a number of subsidiary slave systems. Two such sub-systems are described in detail by Baddeley: the articulatory loop, which stores and manipulates speech-based material, and the visuospatial scratch-pad, which is responsible for creating and maintaining visual imagery.

Short term auditory memory has traditionally been assessed through digit span tasks. The capacity of such a system was widely thought to be reflected in a typical memory span of about seven items, the number of items that can be recalled in the correct sequence immediately after presentation. Information held in this unitary, limited capacity system could be refreshed or transformed by active control processes such as sub-vocal rehearsal provided the capacity of the system was not exceeded. These tasks require the subject to repeat sequences of random digits immediately after presentation by the tester.

Performance on this task is thought to be related to age (Winnie and Schoonover, 1976), with children capable of repeating increasing numbers of digits as they grow older. Normal adults are typically able to repeat seven digits (Zimmond and Cicci, 1969). Nicholson (1981) suggests that the increase in memory span is due to the greater speed with which older children can articulate; or in terms of the working memory model, the older children are able to maintain more items in the articulatory rehearsal loop under the control of the central executive than are younger children. Performance on digit span tasks is also thought to be related to intelligence, at least in the course of development. Neuropsychological evidence has, however, illustrated that memory span can be selectively impaired without a corresponding deficit in intellectual performance. Hitch and Halliday (1983) also examined the short term memory of children and suggested that children utilise the visuospatial scratch pad before utilising the articulatory loop.

The working memory model hypothesises a slave system (the articulatory loop) through which a digit span task would be processed. However it does not explain how musical stimuli would be processed and does not propose any other 'loop' for auditory stimuli apart from the articulatory loop. If the results of this study illustrate that two separate processing systems are being utilised, one for the digit span task and a second for the pitch span task, then it would appear that a third 'loop' for musical stimuli may be required.

To assess the capacity of individual components of the working memory model, one of the techniques adopted was to study the effect of loading a person with a task of remembering irrelevant digits whilst simultaneously engaging in an activity such as the articulation of irrelevant words such as 'the-the-the' during the memory task (Murray, 1968; Baddeley et al., 1975). If the digits occupy a common working memory they should lead to interference, i.e. if both components are utilising a common space there should be greater interference on the item to be memorised, than if the two components are utilising separate components. Thus it would be hypothesised that if all auditory information is processed via the articulatory loop, then interference would be equal whatever the mode, e.g. musical suppression or verbal suppression. If however a separate loop processes musical information, then interference would be greater when the two components were the same i.e. musical suppression would impair the retention of musical information to a greater degree than verbal information. The converse would be true for the articulatory loop when verbal suppression would interfere with the retention of verbal information to a greater degree than musical information. If this could be demonstrated, then it would be strong evidence for separate processing mechanisms for verbal and musical information, and thus the existence of a separate 'music' loop in addition to the articulatory loop in the working memory model.

It is the converging effects of phonemic similarity, word length and articulatory suppression that suggest the concept of a speech-based store associated with sub-vocal rehearsal - the articulatory loop. The articulatory loop has a time-based rather than item based capacity (Baddeley et al., 1975). The findings concerning the articulatory loop are fairly straightforward when materials are presented visually. For auditory materials however, articulatory suppression removes the effect of word length on recall but not that of phonemic similarity. The asymmetry between presentation modalities led Salame and Baddeley (1982) to propose the subdivision of the articulatory loop into two components, maintaining that articulatory suppression disrupts subvocal rehearsal but not the passive phonological store. Such an assumption can account for the dependence of articulatory suppression effects on presentation modality and the further finding that the disruptive effect of hearing irrelevant speech when the subject is engaged in articulatory suppression. Thus the articulatory loop is hypothesised as being linked to the perception and comprehension of speech whilst the articulatory control process is associated with the mechanisms of speech production.

In summary therefore, the study aimed to compare short-term auditory memory for verbal information (digits) with short-term auditory memory for musical information (pitches) in a group of schizophrenics. It brings together various disparate lines of enquiry in support of the theory that there is dominant hemisphere impairment in schizophrenia by showing that schizophrenics perform less well on a dominant hemisphere task (short-term verbal memory as assessed by digit span) when compared to a non-dominant hemisphere task (short-term musical memory) as measured by pitch span.

The study also relates these findings to Baddeley's concept of working memory (following an earlier study). A dissociation between the recall of verbal and musical information would appear to suggest that different processing mechanisms operate in the recall of verbal and musical information and thus that both of these mechanisms would not be processed solely by the articulatory loop.

Two control groups were included in this study of the processing of musical and verbal information in short-term memory tasks by schizophrenic subjects. Normal volunteer subjects formed the first control group, and a second control group of depressed subjects was included on the expectation that, if depression, unlike schizophrenia, is associated with a non-dominant hemisphere dysfunction (e.g. Gruzelier and Flor-Henry, 1979), a dissociation would be found between the two groups. Thus it would be expected that the schizophrenic subjects would attain a higher level of performance on the musical task and the depressed subjects a higher level of performance on the verbal task; speech commonly being localised to the dominant hemisphere (Kimura, 1961). If no dissociation were found between the two psychiatric groups, but there was a generalised performance deficit, then this could simply reflect a failure of task involvement or motivation.

Method

The subjects for the trial were randomly selected from a group of inpatients at Severals Hospital, Colchester, a large psychiatric hospital. Depressed and schizophrenic patients were diagnosed according to the American Psychiatric Association. These patients were diagnosed by a qualified psychiatrist. The normal controls were drawn from members of staff at Severalls hospital who had no evidence of psychiatric disorder and no family history of any psychiatric disorder. It was essential to rule out a family history of psychiatric disorder amongst relatives of controls as there have been suggestions that some neuro-physiological abnormalities such as evoked potentials, rapid eye movement sleep latency, and eye tracking tests, in schizophrenia and depression, are trait markers rather than state markers.

After the exclusion criteria were applied to the group of patients, 10 schizophrenic patients and 10 depressed patients were eligible. Ten normal subjects who were matched for age and sex were selected as controls. The inclusion and exclusion criteria for patients and normals are summarised below.

Inclusion Criteria

1. Patients had to satisfy the DSM III (R) criteria for depression and schizophrenia respectively.
2. Ages between 20-55.
3. All subjects were right-handed.

Exclusion Criteria

1. Evidence of, a history of, or a family history of any other psychiatric disorder.
2. Evidence of any neurological disorder.
3. Evidence or a history of alcohol dependence.
4. Patients whose medication had been changed in the period of 2 months prior to the trial.
5. Patients who had received electroconvulsive therapy (ECT) in the past year or were scheduled to during the course of the trial.
6. Patients who had undergone any psychosurgery, e.g. leucotomy.
7. Patients who had received musical training.
8. Patients with diagnosed hearing difficulties.
9. Patients with any diagnosed organic brain damage.
10. Those who were unable to comply with the test procedures.
11. Any subject who was referred to the music therapy department.

Some of these exclusion criteria were necessary as the fields of neuro-psychological and neuro-physiological tests in psychiatric illnesses are relatively new, and the effects of variables such as medication, ECT etc. on these tests has not been adequately studied.

Following the inclusion in the trial various measures were taken. These include:

1. The Neale Adult Reading Test (NART) for intelligence.
2. Handedness was determined using the Edinburgh Inventory. This in turn was used to determine cerebral dominance (Oldfield, 1971).
3. Schizophrenic symptoms were measured on the Brief Psychiatric Rating Scale (Overall and Gorman, 1962).
4. The severity of depression was assessed using the Hamilton Depression Rating Scale (Hamilton, 1970).

These measures are widely used in psychiatric practice and have been shown to be reliable. Besides these measures, length of illness as determined by the patient's first contact with psychiatric services was also determined and the dose of medication was calculated in terms of chlorpromazine or amitriptyline equivalents (Freedman et al., 1976).

Subjects

Three groups of subjects participated in the study. There were 10 subjects in each group. All the psychiatric patients were already hospitalised and were tested for diagnosis on the basis of the DSM III (R). All subjects complied with both the inclusion criteria and exclusion criteria. All subjects were right-handed as assessed by the Edinburgh Inventory. The mean age of the normal subjects was 32.5 years (range 24-45 years). The mean age of the schizophrenic subjects was 37.3 years (range 22-47 years). The mean age of the depressed subjects was 38.2 years (range 27-52 years). Each group contained five female and five male subjects.

Procedure

To eliminate bias in the examination procedure, the investigator assessing the subjects' short-term memory was unaware and therefore 'blind' as to the diagnosis of the subjects (either patients or controls) in the trial. All subjects were unknown to the investigator.

A standardised examination procedure was devised which was used for all subjects whether a patient or normal control. This consisted of five practice sessions to enable subjects to familiarise themselves with the procedure and to feel at ease with the test situation.

Each subject was required to complete three different experimental procedures. These procedures are identified as follows:

1. A digit / pitch span task.

2. A digit / pitch span task utilising articulatory suppression in four conditions: Span task:

i) Pitch + verbal articulatory suppression.

ii) Pitch + musical articulatory suppression.

iii) Digit + verbal articulatory suppression.

iv) Digit + musical articulatory suppression.

3. A recognition task.

The Digit/Pitch Span Task

Prior to the test both the randomised digit span and the randomised pitch span tasks were recorded onto high fidelity audiotape. The digit span consisted of seven series of numbers. The order of digits in each series was taken from the WAIS (Matarazzo, 1972). No digit was repeated in any given series. The number of digits presented at each test ranged between 3 and 9. A one second delay was administered between each digit, and vocal inflection was dropped on the last digit (Hagen, Thomas and Shannon, 1977).

The pitch task span was identical to the digit span task in terms of the number of series used and the number of items in each series with a single pitch being used in place of a digit. The pitches were recorded from a piano onto audio tape prior to testing. There were nine possible digits and therefore nine pitches were used (C, D, E, F, F#, G, A, Bb, B). The sequence of pitches used were all tonal in orientation, with the majority of intervals between notes being either Maj 2nd, Maj 3rd, Min 3rd, Perfect 4th, Perfect 5th. Therefore the following intervals were excluded; Augmented 4ths, Diminished 5ths, Major 6ths, Major and Minor 7ths.

The subjects were presented with a digit span task followed by a paired pitch span task or vice versa. The choice of order was randomised, but presentation was comparable with that for the digit span task component of the WAIS. The subject was asked to listen to the audiotape and repeat as many numbers or pitches as they could recall after one hearing. Pitches were recalled by singing or vocalising the pitches. Unlike the WAIS task, digits were only administered forwards and not backwards. Two trials of each item were administered. The task was discontinued after failure on both trials of any item.

Each subject was cued verbally at the end of each presentation series so that they would know when the series was completed and when to begin to recall either the pitches or the digits. To establish and maintain the subject's motivation, verbal praise was given regularly by the music therapist on a noncontingent basis and given equally regularly to both parameters. The same instructions were given on each presentation, in as neutral a manner as possible.

The highest pitch span scores and digit span scores were obtained for each subject and these were utilised in the analysis of the data.

The Articulatory Suppression Task

Each subject was presented with this task in four conditions.
Span task:
i) Pitch + verbal articulatory suppression.
ii) Pitch + musical articulatory suppression.
iii) Digit + verbal articulatory suppression.
iv) Digit + musical articulatory suppression.

The method of presentation was identical to that of the earlier digit/pitch span task. The items in each string differed to those utilised in the previous task and the shortest string now contained only two items (as opposed to three in the first experiment).

Whilst listening to the string which the subject was to recall, subjects were asked to articulate irrelevant verbal or musical material during the memory task. Where this articulatory suppression was verbal, subjects articulate 'the-the-the' during the task (Murray, 1968; Baddeley et al., 1975), whilst where the articulatory suppression was musical, subjects sang 'la-la-la' on a monotone. It was not specified to subjects that they should remain on a monotone, but it was demonstrated in this manner by the investigator.

The highest pitch span scores and digit span scores were obtained for each subject and these were utilised in the analysis of the data.

Recognition Task

Subjects were presented with a string of digits or pitches. Each string consisted of 5, 6 or 7 items. Each condition, both pitch and digit contained items of all 3 lengths.

Each string was presented on high fidelity audiotape and was then repeated after a delay of 15 seconds. In the second presentation approximately 70% of strings had been randomly altered by one item. The subject was asked to state whether the two strings were identical or different. If the subject stated that the string was different he was asked to identify whether the change had occurred at the beginning, middle or end of the string.

The presentation of the two conditions (pitch and digit) was altered at random for different subjects and praise was given on a non-contingent basis.

Results

Subjects' responses in all three experiments were audiotaped. Whilst the analysis of the verbal responses required a clear right or wrong response, the musical task relied on the discretion of the investigator. Many subjects responded to the musical task correctly but began their response on a slightly different pitch, then continued retaining the correct pitch intervals between the notes. It was decided that such responses would be considered correct. The same stringent criteria were used with all subjects, and as the investigator was blind to the diagnosis of the subject, it was hoped that this would eliminate any unintentional bias on the investigator's part.

The Pitch Span/Digit Span Task

Table 1: Mean scores for each subject group

	Pitch span		Digit span	
Subject group	**Mean**	**SD**	**Mean**	**SD**
Normals	7.3	0.9	6.7	1.6
Schizophrenics	5.9	1.2	4.0	1.8
Depressed	3.9	1.1	5.8	1.5

In an ANOVA a significant main effect of group was found, $F(2,27) = 13.78$, $p<0.01$ with no effect of task and a significant interaction between task and group, $F(2,27) = 12.65$. $p<0.01$.

To look in more detail at the interaction, separate ANOVAs were run for each subject group. For the normal subject group, no significant effect of task was found. For the schizophrenic group, a significant effect of task was found, with performance on the pitch span being significantly better than the digit span $F(1,9) = 12.45$ $p<0.01$. For the depressed group, a significant effect of task was also found, but in the opposite direction, with digit span being significantly better than pitch span $F(1,9) = 12.45$ $p<0.01$.

The mean scores for each group are given in Table 1. It is clear from the results that the schizophrenic subject group achieved a significantly larger mean span on the musical task than the verbal task with the inverse being found in the depressed subject group who achieved a significantly larger score on the digit span task. Comparisons between the mean scores of the normal subjects and the mentally ill subjects also show that the normal subjects attained greater scores on each task as would be expected.

Articulatory Suppression

The results were analysed by way of a mixed design ANOVA, with two within-subject factors (task and suppression) and one between-subject factor (group).

A significant main effect of group was found F(2,27) = 17.87, p<0.01. No significant effects of either task or suppression were found. A significant two-way interaction was found, however, between group and task F(2,27) = 24.14, p<0.01 and between task and suppression F(2,27) = 32.7, p<0.01. There was also a significant three way interaction between group, task and suppression, F(2,27)= 4.35, p<0.025.

This significant three way interaction was decomposed by using separate analyses for each subject group. For the normals there was a significant two way interaction between suppression and task, F(1,9) = 15.94; p<0.01. This was also true for the schizophrenic subject group, F(1,9) = 24.52, p<0.01, but did not occur for the depressed subjects, F(1,9) = 2.5. That this two way interaction was not found for the depressed subject group can probably be explained as a floor effect, as the numeric values for this group were so low.

These results demonstrate that there is greater interference when the two modalities are the same (e.g. a pitch span task with musical suppression), as opposed to when the modality of the suppression is different from that of the material which is to be recalled (e.g. a pitch span task with verbal suppression). These results thus show a dissociation between the two modalities. The mean scores for each of the subject groups in each condition are given in Table 2. All three subject groups achieved lower mean span scores on this task than on the previous task which did not involve articulatory suppression. The difference between the schizophrenic group and the depressed group is seen most clearly in Table 3.

Table 2: Mean scores and standard deviations for each subject group using articulatory suppression tasks

	Pitch span				Digit span			
	C1	SD	C2	SD	C1	SD	C2	SD
Normal	4.8	1.2	3.7	1.3	3.7	1.2	4.8	1.0
Schiz	4.9	1.4	2.8	1.4	1.4	1.2	2.5	1.6
Depr	1.8	1.0	2.0	1.1	2.6	1.5	3.4	0.8

Table 3: Mean scores tabulated over both conditions for each group

	Pitch span	Digit span
Normals	4.25	4.25
Schizophrenics	3.85	1.95
Depressed	1.9	3.0

The mean scores for each modality reflect directly the earlier finding that musical material is recalled to a greater degree by the schizophrenic subjects than verbal material (with the inverse correlation of this found in the depressed subjects), and there is a direct correlation in the mean scores of the normal subjects (Table 1). These findings, again, clearly suggest a dissociation between the processing of musical information and verbal information.

Recognition Task

The results were analysed using chi-square comparisons between the tasks for each subject group. The normal subject group demonstrated no significant effect of task, chi-square = 0.33. The depressed subject group also demonstrated no significant effect of task, chi-square = 1.67. The schizophrenic group did, however, show some significant effect of task, chi-square = 4.31, $p<0.05$.

Discussion

The aims of the study described in this chapter were two-fold, firstly to examine whether Baddeley's theory of working memory was sufficient to explain short-term musical memory, and secondly to assess short-term verbal and musical memory in schizophrenia and relate the findings to the theories of laterality and dominance in schizophrenia.

The initial result of this study replicates an earlier finding in a single case study (Rogers, 1988) of a dissociation between short-term auditory memory for verbal information and short-term auditory memory for musical information.

The ability of the schizophrenic subjects to attain a significantly greater pitch span than digit span reveals that the ability to recall auditorily presented information is not a generalised ability related to sound, but a specific and specialised ability related to music, or more specifically pitches. None of the subjects in this study had any musical training, indeed this was one of the exclusion criteria for the study, and thus the subjects were equally motivated for both the musical task and the verbal task. Indeed it could be argued that all subjects found the pitch recall task more difficult, as singing is a less familiar medium and tended to evoke some embarrassment in the subjects.

The concept of perfect pitch was also an issue in the research. All the subjects participating in the research were able to sing roughly in tune. Initially this was not one of the inclusion criteria, and it was perhaps fortunate that all the subjects were able to do this. In any future study, decisions would need to be made about the implications of only using those subjects who were able to sing in tune. In this study further clarification of the apparent differences in processing between the two tasks was sought by the subsequent use of a recognition task. This evaded the potential difficulties inherent in any task involving musical recall. The results of the recognition task still, however, illustrate an apparent dissociation between the two modalities, the schizophrenic subjects again showing superior skills on the musical task (recognition of strings of pitches) than on the verbal task (recognition of strings of digits).

That the schizophrenic subjects were able to process the musical information more easily than the verbal information in all three conditions, with the inverse being found in the depressed subjects, has implications for the studies of laterality effects.

The 'laterality' hypothesis of schizophrenia (Flor-Henry, 1969; 1979) which was formulated on the basis of the association of schizophrenic symptomatology with epilepsy and organic lesions of the dominant temporal lobe and concordant with the disturbances of language and auditory functions which are characteristic of the disorder, has been supported by evidence from psychophysiological, electroencephalographic and experimental psychological studies (see Gruzelier and Flor-Henry, 1979). More complex models of hemispheric asymmetries of function in psychopathology are being postulated, but continue to support the view that the primary disturbance in schizophrenia arises in the dominant hemisphere (see Gruzelier, 1981).

The dominant hemisphere plays a greater role in the processing of speech and language than the non-dominant hemisphere (Kimura, 1961; Springer, 1977). The converse is true of the non-dominant hemisphere which plays a greater role in the processing of musical information and has been identified as controlling pitch and tonality in singing (Borchgrevinck, 1977; 1980a, b; Kimura, 1964). There is clinical evidence for a speech perception deficit in schizophrenia, but a detailed library search has revealed little data on the processing of musical information in schizophrenia. It is however worthy of note that music therapists are generating an increasing amount of literature identifying and evaluating the usefulness of music therapy as a diagnostic tool in schizophrenia.

The finding in the present study of a higher level of performance in what would be regarded as a dominant hemisphere task for the schizophrenic subjects (the musical task) and conversely a higher level of processing in what would be regarded as a non-dominant task for the depressed subjects (the verbal task) thus has considerable implications for studies of laterality. The findings suggest that musical recall in short term memory is processed using a different mechanism from that used in the digit span task.

In view of this finding, the working memory system as hypothesised by Baddeley (1983) may need to be revised. Whilst it would be expected that the digit span task involved usage of the articulatory loop; the ability of the schizophrenic subject group on the musical task suggests that an alternative 'loop' may be involved in the processing of the musical stimuli. Like the articulatory loop, this would also be able to use structure and would be a slave of the central processor. This could explain not only the large differences in the schizophrenic groups' performance on these tasks, but also the dissociation and reverse affect observed in the depressed subjects. Further research will however be necessary before such a statement can be confidently made.

In the past it has been suggested that short-term memory was synonymous with sub-vocal rehearsal. Baddeley's (1983) working memory model restricts phonological encoding to one of the subsidiary slave systems, the articulatory loop. The loop is assumed to comprise two components; that is, a phonological store (input) and an articulatory rehearsal process involving sub-vocal speech. This relatively simple model is made to account for various findings including:

(i) The phonological similarity effect (Conrad and Hull, 1964).

(ii) The word length effect memory span decreases with increased word length and is a simple function of spoken duration rather than number of syllables. When a subject's span is measured in terms of spoken duration, it works out at approximately 1.5 seconds, regardless of the lengths of the words (Baddeley et al., 1975b)

(iii) The unattended speech effect. This effect is seen when examining memory for visually attended items with the simultaneous presentation of spoken material which the subject is instructed to ignore (see Salame and Baddeley, 1982).

(iv) The articulatory suppression effect. This effect consistently impairs immediate memory span. Suppression also interacts with three previous phonological variables. The unattended speech effect disappears, the word length effect becomes insignificantly small and the phonological effect disappears when presentation is visual, but not when it is auditory.

Baddeley argues that the phonological store can be accessed either by sub-vocal speech, an optional strategy, or directly through auditory speech input, an obligatory process. Thus with auditory presentation (as in the present study), registration in the store is obligatory regardless of whether the subject is engaged in sub-vocal rehearsal. If all auditory material were processed through the same articulatory loop, then it would be assumed that similar results would have been obtained for both the digit span task and the pitch span task in all conditions. Such a finding was not observed in the present study.

The dissociation in the present study on the articulatory suppression tasks suggest that when the stimuli to be recalled are the same as the mode of articulatory suppression, then performance can be expected to decrease. This would imply that significantly greater interference is occurring. The inverse finding that short-term memory span is less impaired when the articulatory suppression is in the opposite condition (i.e. the subject is asked to recall a digit span whilst generating a musical articulatory suppression task) again supports the idea of a dissociation between the two modes. It can thus be concluded from this double dissociation that the articulatory suppression task generates further arguments in favour of a separate 'loop' to Baddeley's model of working memory ; the 'music' loop.

Hypothesised Addition to the Working Memory Model

The findings in the present study of reduced memory span (short-term) on the digit span task, with verbal articulatory suppression replicate earlier and well documented findings (Levy, 1978, 1981). It has been suggested that articulatory suppression suppresses not the reading process but the transfer of information to memory, and it may well be that similar findings would be found on further study with regard to the 'music' loop.

The recognition task was included in the study to examine further whether a dissociation would be observed in the processing of musical and verbal information in all three subject groups, but particularly the schizophrenic subject group. By using a recognition task, the inherent problems involved in a music recall task were avoided. It was also possible to incorporate some materials on which substantial amounts of data have already been generated; for example the 'Seashore Measures of Musical Talent' (Seashore, 1938) and the 'Bentley Measures of Musical Talent' (Bentley, 1966). The results of this task again clearly demonstrate a dissociation between the processing of musical and verbal information. As in the other tasks, the schizophrenic subjects attained a higher level of performance on the musical task, with the inverse being true of the depressed subjects, who attained higher levels of processing on the verbal task (recognition of verbal material). No dissociation was observed in this task for normal subjects.

Some analysis was made of the mistakes generated in the recognition task. Where mistakes were made, they were made more frequently with the longer strings, irrespective of whether the material to be recognised was verbal (a digit string) or musical (a string of pitches). The beginnings and ends of strings were more easily recognised than the middle of strings, with the least number of mistakes occurring in the recognition of the ends of the strings. This result was as expected in view of the well known recency effect (Murdock, 1962).

The majority of experiments used in the literature to create models for auditory memory present words or phonemes as auditory stimuli. The present study would perhaps suggest that the use of musical stimuli should also be examined by neuropsychologists. The data generated from the above experiments show clear dissociations between the processing of an inherently musical phenomena and an inherently verbal phenomena. Such dissociations have implications not only to current theories concerning working memory, but also to the theories concerning schizophrenia and depression. If, as hypothesised (Gruzelier, 1982), schizophrenia is primarily a disorder of the dominant temporal lobe, and the processing of musical information, particularly pitch information, is localised primarily to the non-dominant hemisphere (Gorden and Bogen, 1974), then the results of this study which show that musical information is processed to a superior level than verbal material in schizophrenic subjects, must be of profound interest not only to the neuropsychologist but also to the neuropsychiatrist. The data generated in this study would appear to add weight to the earlier findings of Gruzelier (1981), and Wexler (1987) amongst others. That an inverse correlation was found (to a lesser extent) on examination of the data of the depressed subjects would also appear to add weight to the hypothesis of Gruzelier and Flor-Henry (1979) that depression may be a disorder of the non-dominant hemisphere. It also casts doubt on the argument that the findings of an impaired digit span in schizophrenia is simply as a result of a general lack of motivation by the subjects.

One of the arguments against any such strong claim would be that there is still insufficient evidence to state conclusively that any one task is the sole process of a single hemisphere. Indeed it is highly unlikely that such a clear distinction could be made. Detailed examination of the psychological literature regarding the field of music reveals that whereas the elucidation on some aspects of inter-hemispheric differences in the localisation of musical processing have been made (e.g. that pitch is processed by the non-dominant hemisphere, Borchgrevinck, 1977, 1980a, b, Gorden and Bogen, 1977), other questions have arisen. These concern the suggestion of a differential pattern of cerebral specialisation for the perception of musical passages and the perception of the components of musical talent; and secondly the suggestion of a differential pattern of cerebral specialisation and hemispheric interaction for musically sophisticated and musically naive subjects (Whyke, 1984).

Whilst the above study shows a clear difference in the processing of musical and verbal material on short-term memory tasks with auditory presentation for various subject groups, further research is obviously called for. The schizophrenics in our small sample were heterogeneous, selected from acute and long-stay wards. They represented a spectrum from acute to chronic, mild to severe, and positive to negative symptomatology. It is interesting to be currently investigating the performance of sub-groups of schizophrenics on musical tasks. The more chronic schizophrenics in our sample performed less well on both tasks, but the numbers were too small to examine statistically. It is possible that pitch span, or pitch/digit span ratios may have a diagnostic value, and at the present time the authors of this chapter are engaged in more detailed research of this fascinating and largely under-researched area. Future research thus involves musical tasks involving other components as well as pitch; much larger groups of subjects, but defined much more rigorously e.g. chronic or acute patients; positive or negative symptomatology; and a greater use of recognition tasks thus avoiding the inherent difficulties encountered in asking subjects to recall musical material.

The findings of this small study are of great importance to the practising music therapist in that the schizophrenic subjects in this study demonstrated a greater ability to process musical information (or a small part of musical information), than verbal information. This implies that this client group could be expected to use a musical medium in their expression of emotions and communication more easily, thus facilitating clients' participation in a therapeutic relationship in which the therapist seeks to understand, interpret and reflect issues of particular relevance for the client.

8

The Therapeutic Relationship in Music Therapy as a Tool in the Treatment of Psychosis

David John

Introduction

This paper focuses on the use of music therapy in the treatment of psychosis. The relationship between patient and therapist is seen as central and its therapeutic value is considered using concepts derived from the British object relations school of psychoanalysis. The psychotic condition is discussed with particular reference to Kleinian and post Kleinian concepts and a general theoretical view of individual music therapy is considered in this light. Finally a case is described which reflects the application of such concepts to clinical experience.

Most of my work in the Cambridge Mental Health Service has been with patients who suffer from a severe degree of mental disorder; patients who tend to fall into the psychiatric diagnostic categories of schizophrenic, psychotic or borderline personality disorder.

I noticed early on in my experience that these patients seemed to become involved in a music therapy process quite readily and that often a patient would engage in music therapy when other interventions had failed. I knew that there was something of significance for the patients in musical improvisation but found it difficult to conceptualise or clearly describe the work in a way that I found satisfying.

At Fulbourn Hospital there had been a tradition since the 1950s of social therapy which was vigorously implemented by David Clark. (Clark, 1981). The relative proliferation of arts therapists and occupational therapists can be related to the development of social therapy models and my work at first was in tune with this model. A kind of Rogerian Encounter Group Theory permeated my work and it seemed enough that my patients were being active, relating and letting off steam.

I had always worked with the view that the relationship with the therapist was the mutative factor for the patient and felt strongly that theories in this area needed to be developed. The relationship between patient and music seemed less important, in fact 'music' seemed to be something different to the sounds that were created in music therapy, different perhaps because the music seemed to be a by-product of the particular forms of relating that occurred in the therapy.

Supervision with two psychoanalysts and a music therapist over five years contributed greatly to my development of thought as regards the meaning of the musical and non-musical interactions and I began to work less with groups of psychotic patients and more on a long-term individual basis.

The debate over whether or not to talk with patients never really preoccupied me and I came to see myself, my room and the instruments as a total environmental provision made available for patients to use.

With this change in focus came the feeling that it was very appropriate to be working with psychotic patients in the two-person relationship. Negotiating the relationship then became the task and I began to conceptualise the elements of my experience and the experience of the patient using ideas and theories derived from psychoanalysis, namely object-relations theory as expounded by Klein and developed by Bion and Winnicott.

Psychosis

The World Health Organisation's International Classification of Diseases defines Psychoses as 'Mental disorders in which impairment of mental function has developed to a degree that interferes grossly with insight, ability to meet some ordinary demands of life or to maintain adequate contact with reality' (ICD 9th Revision). Other psychiatric classification mentions the presence of thought disorder, delusional systems and severe impairment of social and ego functions.

These definitions tell us how to recognise psychotic states and make reference to the social manifestations of them but are inadequate when considering what might be happening in the mind of an individual who is using primarily psychotic processes. Psychoanalysis has offered some insight here.

It is suggested that the development of an integrated and strong ego that mediates between inner and outer worlds is the result of an infant successfully negotiating the individual environment set-up. Klein, mainly through her work with children, offers a theory that conceptualises the mental processes that occur on this heroic journey. She proposed that an infant passes through a psychotic stage of development where the mechanisms used to survive psychologically are projection and splitting - this she termed the paranoid-schizoid position (Klein, 1952).

This is a mental state which is dominated by terrible anxieties, threats of annihilation and the use of omnipotent fantasy. Destructive impulses are projected out into a world which is experienced emotionally in polarised terms. Mother (the Breast) is split into part objects which are idealised or denigrated, heavenly or demonic. At this point, there is no perception of absence of a good object, there is only the good or the bad object. The defence mechanism of projective identification is of primary significance especially when one realises that the bad object contains not only the bad experience which is inflicted by the environment but also a projected part of the infant himself.

It should be emphasised that the paranoid-schizoid position is, as Symington says, 'both a stage and a position, a residue that remains in the personality and to which a person can revert in later life, given certain emotional triggers' (Symington, 1986). This position can be seen as central when considering psychotic breakdown.

The development of the ego and the movement to the next stage is dependent on the infant's management of anxiety. The depressive position is where good experiences are introjected and retained and where some integration occurs in the ego. This is referred to by Winnicot as the 'stage of concern' - it is here that the capacity to feel guilt appears and thus the development of social functions. He says the infant:

'realises that both his love and hate are directed towards the same object - the mother - becomes aware of his ambivalence and concern to protect her from his hate and to make reparations for what damage he imagines his hate has done' (Winnicott, 1975).

In a nutshell, the process of successful early emotional development is described by Hannah Segal as a benevolent circle - 'the stronger the ego of the infant, the less he feels threatened and the less he projects; as he projects less so his objects become less threatening' (Segal, 1983).

An understanding of the role of the environment-mother in helping the infant manage these states and become an individual is central to the task of providing a therapeutic environment for people whose mental processes are primarily psychotic.

It is here that I find Bion's concept of mother's reverie as most useful. It is a metaphoric language of container and contained and has been described by Nini Herman as 'the cornerstone of sanity'. She poetically describes the process thus:

'With the maternal reverie the mother strives to contain the confusions and anxieties, which include the fear of dying, that her infant will communicate; she takes them into her own mind with her sharpened intuitions, filters them of their distress and returns them to the infant in a far less threatening form, so that the infantile mind can begin to digest them. The baby will discover, bit by bit, what he is able to contain and digest unaided and what help (without which he feels overwhelmed or threatened with disintegration) is needed' (Herman, 1987).

It is as if the infant makes use of the mother as an auxiliary ego that manages projected anxieties and contributes to the infant's feeling of 'being contained'.

If this environmental provision fails in relation to the infant's needs, we may find a person in constant search of a containing mother with the infant part of a self yearning for a symbiotic union with another, free from anxieties of isolation, separation and emptiness.

In psychosis, satisfactions seem to be hallucinated and in Bion's terms it is as if the psychotic destroys the mechanism to apprehend reality to rid himself of feelings (Bion, 1957). Symington suggests that 'mad is a better word than psychotic in that it is more immediately linked with the idea of fury and rage and hatred, for these are always a component of madness' (Symington, 1986).

Music Therapy

For the psychotic patient, in my view, music therapy can be seen as an experience oriented rather than an insight oriented form of therapy, the aim of which is to help the individual manage their internal world in such a way as to develop ego-strength. The therapist is presented as a usable object and there is the opportunity for action. This action (playing instruments or singing) is seen as being in relation to the therapist.

This somewhat careful description of music therapy betrays my feeling that the act of playing is not the focus (though it becomes the focus if we feel the need to show the singular usefulness of music therapy in relation to other therapies). The focus is the relating and its meaning. The relating goes on whether there is playing or not, and the clue to the meaning is not hidden somewhere in the music but in the shared experience of the therapist and patient.

Having said this, however, it is to my mind worth focusing on the usefulness of playing experiences but I wish to emphasise that the playing is, of course, only part of the therapeutic endeavour.

In my work, patients are encouraged and in some cases (given the severity of the super-ego in the transference) given permission to use the instruments and improvise freely with them. Sometimes form is decided beforehand but mostly evolves and can be perceived only in retrospect. I either listen or respond on other instruments. This process is akin to free association in that the patient is encouraged to release a stream of sounds which have varying degrees of organisation and which may carry varying degrees of affect.

Thus the patient is given the chance to find their pre-verbal 'voice' and to use it to communicate to and discharge into a containing holding object. It could be said that the primitive feelings of rage that otherwise might threaten to overwhelm and destabilise a weak and vulnerable ego can be brought into focus and become mastered and more under conscious control. This process occurs through the patient channelling their sounds (which are often produced by the action of hitting) into the environment-therapist who acts as a receiving object that contains and helps to give form and emotional meaning to their musical utterances.

The situation which stimulates projection and transference and destructive feelings towards the therapist can be symbolically managed in improvisations. (The survival of the therapist is a key feature for the patient who is attacking in fantasy.)

A belief in a good object in the inner and outer world can develop in the patient as the experience of the therapist's responsiveness and capacity to contain is introjected.

Some playing reveals a lack of self object differentiation - the therapist might be doing the same thing as the patient -responding sensitively as if trying to give the patient the experience of being merged with them. Bits of this experience are central to our task in that separation can be introduced gradually as the therapist plays less 'in tune' with the patient and perhaps not at all. Failure to respond as wished for can create frustrations, the primary blue print of this being the 'no-breast' experience and that frustration can, in turn, be experienced, tolerated and modified through improvisation.

Thus music therapy offers the patient a degree of gratification and pleasure together with little bits of what is needed. It seems that what is yearned for is a state of symbiotic union with the therapist and what is needed is an agglomeration of experience that helps the patient develop the capacity for containing split-off and projected parts of the personality.

The Transformational Object

The use of music in therapy is an interesting phenomena that requires further exploration. Alongside this it is also worth considering the *use* of music in general. In the community of the mental health unit where I work the use of music is strikingly manifest. Many patients, in my experience, are musical i.e. they either make music themselves or seem to have an intense bond with music.

I am sure it is true to say that music offers something to all who have ears to hear, it has its uses so to speak, and I would like to suggest a link between the use of music and the concept of the transformational object as described by Christopher Bollas.

Bollas describes the transformational object as 'an object that is experientially identified by the infant with the process of the alteration of self experience'. He goes on, 'The mother .... is experienced as a process of transformation and this feature remains in the trace of this object - seeking in adult life, where I believe the object is sought for its function as signifier of the process of the transformation of being.'

This transforming quality seems to be at the core of music, in that we expect music to do something to our self-experience.

It could be stated then that the offering of music in music therapy as in a teenagers' finding of music in the form of an electric guitar bears the trace of the search for the transformational object, which is, in itself, as Bollas says 'a particular object relation that is associated with ego transformation and repair'.

A Case Study: The Case of Miss M

Miss M is a middle-aged woman who has had a long history of schizophrenia with marked paranoid features. I saw her for weekly music therapy sessions over a five year period and in that time learned much about psychotic processes and how music can be put to use in individual therapy. The case is a useful one for the purposes of this paper for, apart from my learning, Miss M's condition seemed to improve and I feel it is worth reflecting on the process and on some of the therapeutic factors that seemed to have made change possible.

Throughout the work with Miss M, I received supervision in two settings, firstly with a music therapist and subsequently in group supervision with a Jungian analyst. It was possible, through discussion of the work, to gain insight into and understand some of the unconscious processes active in our relationship, indeed without the accompanying supervision process I feel my learning from the experiences with Miss M would have been limited. Supervision helped me contain my anxieties and develop my thinking, it acted like a life line that offered a way through the often times confusing situations in the therapy.

Miss M was 46 when I first met her. I already knew some history, notably that she had her first psychotic breakdown in her early twenties while working away from home for the first time. This marked the first in a series of admissions to hospital that increased in frequency until they became virtually annual in the early 1980s. The three features of her early history that I stored as significant were firstly, that she was born two and a half months premature, secondly, had lived abroad until she was six and thirdly the first signs that something was wrong came when Miss M was depressed over academic work while away at boarding school.

Miss M is a cultured woman from an academic background. She lives in a flat in the community with support from a community psychiatric nurse and attends a hospital-based day-centre twice per week. She is actively creative in the arts of painting, poetry and music. She sings (mostly German Lieder), composes her own songs and plays the piano with a limited technique.

When we first met, Miss M appeared as a slim untidy woman who dressed rather oddly - sometimes wearing layers of clothes that didn't match and having a bunch of keys dangling from her wrist. She wore horn-rimmed spectacles (sometimes two pairs at the same time) and would often peer out over them much in the manner of a disapproving school Ma' am. Miss M looked older than her age with the general appearance of a rather eccentric old woman.

Her personality seemed to consist of fragments. By this I mean parts of her self were expressed in different ways that seemed to lack any cohesion. These parts were interchangeable and expressed themselves in relation to me in such a way as to suggest that to Miss M, I was a split object.

One part was her general demeanour of haughtiness and grandiosity, at times making me feel rather insignificant, or at least as if I was expected to behave towards her with a great degree of social decorum. This had a very distancing effect and created an atmosphere of 'polite society' in which it was very difficult to make anything but superficial contact with her.

In contrast to this was another part of Miss M which I began to see as being the 'wounded victim' in her. She would often limp into the room at the start of a session and tell me in a weak voice that she had just been attacked by men or shot at out of the window of a van. This element of Miss M also seemed quite hyperchondriacal, she would tell me of her physical problems which were usually related to her eyesight. Most commonly she would say that she had been blinded or that her legs were broken. There was a feature to this that Miss M felt lucky to be alive and needed to be cared for, but in her behaviour towards me gave me the impression that I was insufficient to this task.

Miss M would indeed behave as if I was extremely neglectful and would accuse me of not having been there for months when, in fact, we had met the week before. She would also at times place me in a position of malignant authority and often acted out a drama in which she seemed to be turning up for a piano lesson with a teacher who had unreasonably high expectations. She would say things like 'don't badger me this week' or 'how do you expect me to play this?' while looking at a piece of music that I might have left on or near a piano.

The first part of our work was characterised by Miss M's ambivalence towards the therapy. I remember the time as being generally quite stormy, with Miss M expressing her raging feelings mostly through indignation but occasionally through an act of violence like pulling over a pile of chairs. The other side of Miss M's attitude seemed to show in her hopeful and creative involvement in the musical elements which became the core of the therapy.

Miss M's ambivalence was also reflected in her use of the time boundaries of the sessions. Sometimes she would arrive late and leave early, either with the excuse of another appointment elsewhere, or suddenly without warning. Sometimes she would arrive early and wait outside the room where she could be seen sitting just outside the window in 'wounded victim' mode. Sometimes she would interrupt a session beforehand and when I reminded her of our time would return on time and be angry that I had rejected her.

I was often left in a state of bewilderment at the fragments of Miss M's personality that I encountered and found the impact of her transference to me quite difficult to tolerate. At times, my counter transference reactions were to feel overwhelmed, flattened and switched off.

It was in the music part of the therapy that I felt the negative and destructive elements were managed and metabolised and where Miss M, through her relating to me could both find some satisfaction of her enormous need and achieve some new integration in her personality.

There were several music/relation structures which I shall attempt to describe - all of these were initiated by Miss M.

Miss M would sing and play the piano, usually a Victorian type parlour song ('When You Come To The End Of A Perfect Day' for example) and she would accompany herself using Tonic-Dominant in G Major. I often felt cut off and expected to listen when Miss M did this and it felt like she was expressing the rather aloof and dignified part of herself referred to earlier. This was a common feature of the beginnings of sessions and remained throughout the work.

Miss M would choose to sing a Schubert song, some of which she knew well and asked me to accompany her. This structure also lasted throughout the work but changed in its affective features. Miss M at first would sing in a rather superficial grandiose fashion and deny our relationship in the music by turning away as soon as she had finished. Her singing was sometimes accurate and sometimes disorganised and reflected her state of confusion or organisation. She was able to sing more accurately as the work progressed and seemed to choose more and more difficult songs. By our fourth year of working together, Miss M sang with much more fluidity, emotion and sense of contact with me.

Miss M often composed her own music which was written on scraps of manuscript paper which she eventually wrote into one book. These pieces were often songs - settings of her own or someone else's poems and tended to be extremely difficult to read. Miss M liked me to play her pieces and seemed to be sensitive to my reactions to them and it became a tense moment when she put her piece on the piano. The pieces themselves varied enormously - some were easy to read and quite musically well organised others were impossible to read or play. Miss M brought fewer and fewer pieces and then stopped bringing them altogether after a session in which I played through the collection she had made and committed them to tape. The style of the pieces varied but they tended to be tonal and written as short songs with piano accompaniment. Mostly they were in a minor key with a rather melancholic feel and stylistically reflected Schubert.

Spontaneous improvisations occurred on a variety of instruments. Tuned and untuned percussion, guitar, violin, autoharp and two pianos. Miss M at first avoided any drums and only played high tinkling music on glockenspiels and metallophones. She was very spontaneous on the instruments and played with a great degree of rhythmic vitality but never very loudly. The 'being together' in these improvised pieces seemed quite significant in that the atmosphere of them was of intense listening. Miss M would obviously respond to my responsiveness and allowed a degree of symbiotic intimacy in the music. She was sensitive to the endings of pieces of music and although she would stop suddenly would often criticise my 'having the last word' as she said. Most striking of all though was the dissonance that Miss M gradually came to use in her playing and tolerate in mine. She vigorously professed her hatred of modern music and perhaps detecting a liking of it in me, would tell me what a dreadful noise it was - indeed Miss M seemed ambivalent about it. She expressed this eloquently when she told me that there was some Stravinsky (the 20th Century archetype of the primitive) on the radio that evening and she was *not* going to listen to it.

I began to realise that Miss M's liking for Victoriana, her avoidance of drums and her rejection of any aspect of primitive musical elements was in itself an attempt to rid herself of her primitive impulses and remain 'pure' and full of 'good things'.

However, Miss M made her own strides towards reclaiming that part of herself and it seemed to happen by using me as the container for her gradually more intense and impulsive music. In one session, Miss M asked me to play the Grieg piano concerto on one piano while she improvised on the other. This seemed to be her way of taking something out of me and expressing it herself at the same time. She banged the piano with dramatic clusters during the opening and launched into a crashing about that lost its usual sense of caution. An improvisation followed that marked the beginning of two piano work. Playing two pianos became a regular feature of the sessions from then on and the improvisations, although often having tentative beginnings, became atonal and fluid. The experience seemed both to reveal and consolidate Miss M's ability to be in a relationship of contact with me and to share the emotional management task with me.

Miss M came to the sessions with prepared forms that could be used for improvisation. For example, she would organise her movement from one instrument to the next and the whole improvisation seemed to allow the different fragments of her personality which were expressed differently to co-exist. A striking example was when Miss M organised changing instruments from a piano to a glockenspiel to a drum and back to the piano. I accompanied this on another piano and found that she used each instrument to reflect a different aspect of her personality which required a different response from me. Miss M played the piano tonally at first (Victorian type) and as she moved through the other instruments and back to the piano she became more vigorous and finally approached the piano a second time with a more fluid and expressive attitude. The quality of the music became different and new improvisations became longer and Miss M seemed to find a new freedom in relation to me. Overall she seemed less cautious and more confident in her playing.

The Use of the Relationship

To translate, as it were, out of our musical behaviour, I would say that generally my task became primarily one of tolerating and metabolising the feelings of anger, anxiety, frustration and hopelessness which were projected into me and understanding these in relation to the patient. The experience of relating musically with Miss M and having supervision helped me deal with these feelings. As the work progressed I became aware of the gradual development of something in Miss M's personality that seemed to help her contain her experiences. She was able to reflect on her internal world and would try to tell me about her 'voices' and delusions which were remembered and reported as if they were a dream. Also, she was better able to tolerate some of the anxieties that the situation produced and would stay to the end of sessions which, in turn, became more tolerable to her. She also developed a sense of concern for me - asking me how I was and being chatty and interested in me. This new attitude reflected her relatedness to me as someone with a separate identity who is not a part of her.

Her conversation, although always having a symbolic content, became more understandable and the victim part of the personality (although not the somatising hyperchondriacal part) vanished altogether. The overall feeling for me was that Miss M became easier to be with and more able to become involved in a verbal discourse. It would seem that Hannah Segal's benevolent circle is relevant here; through the management of Miss M's emotional states she was better able to incorporate 'something that manages' into her mind. This introjection helped the development of Miss M's sense of self and thus her feelings of being less threatened by me. It could be said that the process facilitated her withdrawing the split-off projected parts of herself from me and thus I became less threatening and easier to relate to. I should also add that Miss M had only one admission to hospital (which occurred during a break) throughout the course of the therapy and has demonstrated her more integrated personality by successfully negotiating some stressful experiences in her life.

I feel the essence of the management process referred to is in the metaphor of the containing environment made up of me as a usable human object, the boundaries of the work and the channels of communication and ways of relating that were available to us.

The channels of communication were both verbal and non-verbal, but to my mind the non-verbal musical elements seemed to have special usefulness for Miss M.

Summary

In my work with psychotic patients I have gradually brought the relationship between patient and music therapist more into focus, and in doing so have made use of psychoanalytical concepts as an aid to my understanding of the relationship. Melanie Klein's descriptions of splitting and projective identification (Klein, 1952) as primitive defence mechanisms characteristic of an early stage of infantile development, have offered a great deal when considering the nature of psychosis. I have also found Bion's concept of maternal reverie useful when thinking about the therapist's task as providing a container for the patients emotional life.

I have viewed the use of music as a way of facilitating the therapeutic relationship and, with reference to Bolus' concept of the transformational object, have attempted to describe some of the theory upon which my music therapy work with psychotic patients is based. The case which concludes the chapter highlights the difficulty of using transference as a clinical tool, and suggests that musical improvisation is used primarily for two reasons, firstly to help the patient manage their emotions and secondly to offer experiences through which the patient can internalise the responsive and containing function of the therapist.

9

Interpersonal Processes in Clinical Improvisation: Towards a Subjectively Objective Systematic Definition

Mercedes Pavlicevic

Introduction

When I read Isenberg-Grezda's article (1988), which communicated the bewildering array of models attempting to assess music therapy, as well as the confusion of the professional community in the face of so many models, my reason agreed and my heart sank. Now, a few months later, my sense is that it is not so much the plethora of assessment models which is the confusing issue, as the absence of attempts to clarify and define the musical relationship between therapist and patient, upon which the therapeutic processes depends. Moreover, I suspect that the bewilderment of our professional colleagues is, in part at least, a reflection of our own lack of clarity about the nature and texture of the musical/therapeutic improvisation.

In his review of papers that have appeared in the *British Journal of Music Therapy* since 1968, Bunt (1985) found that papers falling into the category of research which he described as structured and objective, accounted for only 9% of total papers. Other categories include case studies, discussions of techniques and activities without data collection (21%), position papers which discuss the current needs of the profession (12%), and reports of meetings, news and profiles (64%).

In their review of music therapy research in Britain, Bunt and Hoskyns (1987) describe two trends. The first comprises studies which examine the efficacy of music therapy by assessing the relationship between music therapy as an intervention, and changes in non-musical behaviour such as eye movement, speech, and stereotypical behaviour. Such studies tend to ignore the musical process in the session. Adams (1987) gives support to this strategy, cautioning against the assumption that the effects of music therapy can be observed through changes in musical behaviour. He suggests, rather, that the efficacy of music therapy might be more effectively assessed by ignoring the musical material, and by applying measurements to whichever behaviour the therapist is wanting to alter.

The second trend of research comprises reports which, contrary to the approach advocated by Adams (op. cit.), examine the musical process itself. These, however, tend to appear in the form of anecdotal reports (Bunt and

Hoskyns, op. cit.), which do little to enhance the profession's status as a rigorous discipline.

My own interest tends towards the second trend of research, as described above. This is not so much in order to demonstrate the efficacy of music therapy, but rather in order to comprehend more fully the complex musical processes that generate and enrich the therapeutic setting. Music therapists of all persuasions do share, after all, an understanding that the musical experience is the focus or pivot of the music therapy session, whether the music is used as therapy or in therapy (Bruscia, 1987).

In this chapter I attempt a definition of the inter-musical, therapeutic processes which neither ignores nor apologises for the highly subjective nature of the therapy situation. Rather, I attempt to be systematic, as well as intuitive and objective, in defining these processes as I understand them. I suspect that these three attitudes are reconcilable with one another, and that they may contribute in some small way to embodying the richness and complexity of processes which risk being limited by verbal language. I also suspect that a sound definition may offer directions towards evaluating music therapy, and this may invite colleagues to understand more precisely how we work, and how the music works (and plays) with us.

Clinical Improvisation: Towards a Definition

My understanding of the role of clinical improvisation in music therapy is that it provides the space for a highly dynamic and reciprocal interaction between the therapist and the person (Nordoff and Robbins, 1971; 1977). Thus, rather than being a 'purely musical' event, the improvisation has communicative significance and is focal in the therapeutic process (Pavlicevic, 1990). Clinical improvisation offers the musical partners the opportunity to apprehend one another directly through the music: they share a sense of themselves in relation to one another, without the intrusion and potential diversion of intermediary objects, such as, for example, language (or the non-clinical use of music). David Aldridge makes a case for the direct experience which clinical improvisation offers. He writes:

'A person is invited to improvise music creatively with a therapist. It may be inferred from his playing that one is hearing a person directly in the world.....This experience requires no verbal translation as in psychotherapy. What can be heard is the person being in the world.' (Aldridge, 1989, p. 96)

Theorising about Direct Human Communication

The concept of 'basic' or 'direct' communication has been extensively documented in studies on non-verbal communication, and mother-infant interaction in particular. Here, the inequality of the partners, the non-verbal nature of the interaction, as well as its highly musical character suggest parallels with clinical improvisation in music therapy which seem worth exploring. A very brief diversion into the literature of non-verbal communication will, I hope, clarify some of the interactive features of direct human communication, and provide a useful theoretical construct for attempting to define the inter-active features in clinical improvisation.

Studies which examine the interactive features in mother-infant dyads share a common theme: they demonstrate the sensitivity and susceptibility of mother and infant to one another (Beebe et al., 1985; Papousek and Papousek, 1981; Stern et al., 1985; Tronick, Als and Adamson, 1979) . They also suggest that the mother adapts her 'normal' or 'adult' way of communicating in order to engage her infant. Thus, parents respond to their infants' vocalisations as though these are communicatively meaningful, and this encourages and invites infants to develop their capacity to use their voices in a communicative sense (Papousek and Papousek, 1981).

Both partners' utterances are interactional, rather than self-centred, in that they take into account the quality of the other person's utterances. Trevarthen's concept of 'primary intersubjectivity' describes the direct meeting of mother and new-born infant, and their apprehension of one another through the inter-co-ordination of timing of their acts and vocalisations, and without the use of intermediary objects, such as language or physical objects (Trevarthen, 1984-1986, 1987). Feldstein and Welkowitz (1978) emphasise the psychological importance of time in interactive human behaviour, so that the pacing, duration and timing of spoken utterances within an interaction reveal the characteristic patterns of the individuals, as well as information about the nature or quality of the interaction itself. They noted, and measured, the inclination of empathic adult speakers to develop what they call 'congruence' or interpersonal influence regarding intensity, frequency and durational values of utterances in their conversations.

It is the quality of the persons' acts, rather than the acts themselves, that reveals the communicative dynamics of the interaction. Thus, it is not whether the infant is smiling (or not) that is the critical communicative feature, but the timing, the intensity, the duration of the smile in relation to the timing, intensity and duration of the mother's gesture, act or vocalisation. It is this inter-timing, inter-intensity and inter-duration that reveals how attuned each partner is to the other. It seems to me that the key issues in direct human communication can be summarised as follows:

(i) the susceptibility of a person to the other, or a capacity to be influenced by the other;

(ii) the capacity to 'read' the meaning of the other's acts, so that a movement or vocalisation is experienced as being more than merely that: it is experienced as saying something about the other's inner motivational state. This implies the capacity to co-ordinate the other's various movements and acts into a form which has communicative significance both for the self and for the other;

(iii) flexibility within the self in order to co-ordinate a responsive act which is appropriate both on one's own behalf and within the interactive context; and finally,

(iv) the imagination and capacity to sustain and extend one's self so as to remain within, and share in the interactive intention.

These key issues can only be revealed within the context of human communication (I shall elaborate on this below), and it is precisely this communicative context that the therapist endeavours to create jointly with the person in clinical improvisation. Moreover, it is precisely these capacities which the therapist is constantly addressing and evaluating during the therapeutic processes: these capacities offer critical nuances about how the person is 'being in the world'.

Damaged Interactions in Human Communication

Psychologists have shown that mental illness interferes with the capacity to participate reciprocally in direct, or basic, human communication. Mothers who are mentally ill are unable to provide their infants with an environment which is interactively receptive: they fail to respond to their infants in a manner sufficiently sensitive to provide their infants with experiences of being known intimately (Murray, 1988) . Thus, for example, the qualities of their acts in relation to their infants might be grossly exaggerated in intensity or duration, or the timing might be inappropriate. Murray's perturbation studies with 'normal' mothers showed that infants whose mothers were asked to assume 'blank face' conditions became distressed: they increased their attempts to engage their mothers and eventually, they withdrew and began to disengage from their mothers (Murray and Trevarthen, 1985) . Their responses to their mothers were a clear indication of their alertness to the inappropriateness of their mothers' responses to them.

Another strong case for the link between mental illness and the capacity to organise and adapt gestures and acts in communication, has been made in a famous study by Condon and Ogston (1966) . Their analysis of recordings of conversations between 'normal' and mentally ill people demonstrated that mentally ill adults showed an incapacity for what they call 'self-synchrony', that is, the temporal features of their own speech and body motions were not synchronised with one another, in contrast to those of the 'normal' adult speaker. They noted the 'semi-frozen' body motion of these patients, their limited range of prosodic features and the absence of variation in their head movements. They also found that those parts of the patients' bodies which showed 'self-desynchrony' could not enter into 'interactional synchrony' with the normal partner, whereas those parts of their bodies which were self-synchronised could do so.

Brown and Avstreih (1989) lend support to this view in their paper entitled 'On Synchrony'. They discuss the shared rhythmicity of behaviour which they see as fundamental to sustaining rapport in social encounters. They also suggest that in psychotic patients, the innate capacity for 'interactional synchrony' may be constitutionally impaired.

These studies provide music therapists with a powerful theoretical basis for making the link between the manifestation of mental illness (and emotional disorders) in human interaction and in clinical improvisation. The link can be explained thus: if the therapist is providing an interactive context through the use of clinical improvisation, then any disturbance in the person's susceptibility and response to the other, as well as any disorder or damaged capacity to organise the self in order to engage intimately with another, will be revealed directly within the musical improvisation (Pavlicevic, 1991).

Reporting and Interpreting: A Distinction

It is at this profound and basic level that the person is engaged in clinical improvisation, and to offer interpretations about the nature and texture of this inter-engagement invites confusion. Rather, we can look to the improvisation itself in order to glean essential information about the fluctuating quality of the partners' communication.

The psychological studies above have shown that this kind of engagement can be described in great detail, so that it seems to me that a systematic definition of the levels or dimensions of musical emotional communication and of their dynamic nature is more appropriate. Such a definition, once refined, offers fundamental concepts which potentially enrich music therapists' own understanding of their work, and which might facilitate reporting on their work to their professional colleagues (in contrast to offering interpretations about their work) and provide the basis for evaluation. This definition need not reduce or limit the meaning of the improvisation, although it might be acknowledged that this can never be fully apprehended in the first place. (The apprehension of meaning of the clinical improvisation requires a sound and imaginative intuition, but this is a separate matter altogether.)

Whether its meaning is explored and shared verbally by therapist and person depends to a great extent on whether a verbal communication is appropriate, after the improvisation, and on the degree of the person's insights and access to their inner states. I would like to suggest, hypothetically, that there exists a fairly stable relationship between the degree of a person's insight, and their apprehension of their own internal states as revealed in clinical improvisation, irrespective of their musical experience or sophistication.

I was fascinated to note, in my data collection for a study with schizophrenic patients, that not one of these patients saw the music therapy session as being anything other than an opportunity to play music. Their comments all pointed to their curiosity about the musical acts themselves (e.g. they would comment on the tunes we played, on the speed or the dynamic level of our improvisations), but never about what the acts might mean. My understanding of this phenomenon is that it reflects an incapacity to 'read' the communicative significance of gestures or acts, and a tendency to remain at the level of the acts themselves. In other words, they seemed only able to apprehend the medium through which we worked, and not the significance of its interactive application. In contrast, (and at the other end of the interactive spectrum), people who do not suffer from a mental illness make the connection between their inner states and the improvisation immediately. For example, they might comment that they became stuck in a rhythmic pattern and found it very difficult to change this; here are comments about the significance of the medium for them. These comments are extremely valuable and helpful to the therapist in gauging the person's insights and alertness to 'what is going on' (Pavlicevic, 1987).

An interesting tangent, though, is that even the most insightful persons do not always have access to the interactive dynamics of the improvisation itself, and this, perhaps, is more exclusively within the therapist's realm.

In terms of evaluating this richly textured process, the questions we seek to answer might include the following: What makes this improvisation between therapist (T) and person (P) different from, and more than, a merely musical event? What are the interactive features of this improvisation? How are these features occurring between the two players? How are the two players experiencing one another?

Music in Communication and Communication in Music

The features which characterise or define basic or direct human communication are essentially musical in character. They comprise time, in the sense of the (inter-) timing of the onset and duration of these gestures, as well as the timing within the gestures (i.e. their pulse and rhythm), intensity, in the sense of the force of a movement or of a gesture, which in musical terms is the energy or force embodied in music - this can be expressed through a crescendo, or a change in harmonic colour or texture. Then there is the contour of a movement, or gesture, which in musical terms can be embodied through melodic and rhythmic contours, or through contours evoked by changes of timbre. These features can be expressed through any of our modalities, such as through movement, vocalisations, facial expressions and posture, and are not restricted to a particular modality of expression, but are amodal or intermodal (Stern, 1985). Thus, for example, 'intensity' can be a feature of a frown (or a smile); of the timbre of a speaker's voice; or of the force of a rocking movement. Trevarthen has proposed another way of classifying these communicative features and offers three categories which convey qualitative information about gestures. These are kinematics, energetics and physiognomics (Trevarthen, 1986). Clinical improvisation, by its very nature, provides a powerful and immediate context for the sounding of these features of human communication. Not only is it a jointly created process, which provides the communicative and interactive context necessary for their activation and expression, but it uses the very ingredients with which human beings communicate with one another. Moreover, the constantly unfolding musical and creative process provides a fluctuating forum that potentially embodies these features and enables them to be shared, and developed and extended by both the therapist and the person.

Thus, any definition and evaluation of these communicative processes in clinical improvisation needs to address the critical information revealed in the inter-activation of musical phrases. The questions which need to be asked include these: Do the therapist and the person's musical phrases relate to each other in any way? Is this relating in timing, in duration, in the timing of the onset of phrases, in the intensity of the dynamic level. What is the nature of these relationships? Do the players imitate, partly imitate, or reflect only some features of one another's statements? Do the partners complement or dove-tail one another's melodies? Does one partner provide rhythmic or harmonic accompaniment to the other's statements? Is this relating consistent, fluid or halting?

It is these features that reveal the critical and direct information about the communicative nature of the interaction: whether the players really do take one another into account; whether their response to one another is direct or obtuse; whether the one is always imitating the other or whether there is a sharing of initiative, and so on. This is what I mean by verbal reporting in contrast to interpretation: the information is right there, within the improvisation. We need the sensitivity and astuteness to 'read' this information accurately - and that includes the integrity to acknowledge that it may be the therapist's lack of attunement to the person that is hampering the communicative process (and therefore hampering the person's communicative capacities from being revealed).

The Duality of Music and Communication in Clinical Improvisation

Figure 1 illustrates my understanding of the duality of the emotional/musical processes in clinical improvisation revealed within the context of human communication.

Figure 1: The duality of musical and emotional processes in clinical improvisation

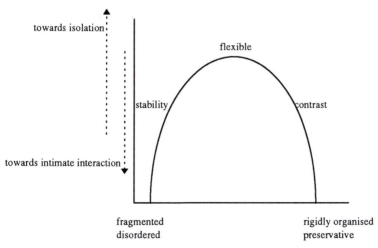

The y-axis represents the spectrum of communication, ranging from isolated, non-interactive experience, to mutually satisfying, reciprocal communication. The x-axis represents the contrasting limitations or restrictions on the interactive emotional/musical processes, ranging from fragmented, disordered patterns to rigidly over-organised processes. Here, of course, we may be speaking either of musical utterances within the clinical improvisation context, or we may be speaking of how someone is 'being in the world'. Thus fragmented musical utterances by one partner may make it far more difficult for the other partner to 'make sense' of these statements, and to 'join in' in a way that feels appropriate for both the players. Similarly, rigid musical statements, which, for example, may show no fluctuation in rhythmic form, will severely limit the interactive potential of the communication. The person may be rigid and over-organised (or fragmented and chaotic), and this will colour any interaction, as well as his or her experience and expression of feeling or emotion.

The individual's position at the non-interactive end of the communicative spectrum may be the result of either a conscious or intentional desire to remain isolated, or of a 'pathological' incapacity to participate fully in a communicative relationship, such as is found in chronic schizophrenic patients (Brown and Avstreih, 1989; Cameron, 1944; Condon and Ogston, 1966; Guntrip, 1977; Sullivan, 1944).

The inverted U-curve may be conceived as two arrows, moving towards the apex of flexibility, which is at the mutual and reciprocal end of the communicative spectrum. Here, the individual has the capacity and motivation to enter into a fully mutual interaction, and this is revealed by the flexibility and adaptability of his or her emotional processes (Winnicott, 1971; 1988). The use of the curve, rather than straight lines, symbolises the constant shifts of these qualities within us (Stern, 1985) . The interactive capacities of the individual can only be revealed within the context of human communication, as shown by the relationship between the curve and the y-axis. Also, the path towards interactive flexibility does not travel simply along the curves illustrated above. The person's performance may leap across to the other end of the x-spectrum: for example, a therapist's musical intervention may result in a chaotic person becoming rigid, or vice versa. Here, we are still at the non-interactive end of the spectrum, but this is a different polarity of non-interaction. The therapeutic process then involves allowing the person to experience both polarities, since both these exist within flexible communication, which is ultimately the direction towards which therapist and person move (Pavlicevic, 1991).

Briefly Evaluating Evaluation Models

How then are we to evaluate this complex process without losing its richness and fluidity of texture?

The interactive and communicative agenda, peculiar to music therapy, demands more than just a musical analysis. Thus, the perceptual and cognitive models developed by music psychologists such as (Deutsch, 1982; Dowling and Harwood, 1986; West, Howell and Cross, 1985; Pressing, 1984; 1988; Sloboda, 1985; 1988), while offering immensely valuable insights into the human experience of music, are incomplete for our purposes. They conceptualise and demonstrate the complex perceptual and cognitive processes involved in listening, playing and improvising music but, because of their predominately MUSICAL focus, do not address the dual agenda - i.e. the communicative/musical agenda - that is the critical feature of clinical improvisation. Similarly, Lee's (1989) admirably thorough musical analysis of clinical improvisation falls short of illustrating its dual nature: he is left posing the question as to whether there might be a correlation between the musical and the therapeutic processes. This question is based upon the premise that the two are separate aspects of the clinical situation, whereas my own premise is that they are two sides of the same coin. They cannot be separated, and it is this dual nature of clinical improvisation that a sound evaluating process needs to address.

The analysing and evaluating of the communicating dyad as a unit in order to glean information about one of its partners is fully justified (Buck, 1984), as studies in non-verbal communication have shown. Thus, by analysing the interactive processes between mother and infant, or between psychiatric patient and non-clinical adult, as Condon and Ogston described above (op. cit.), psychologists have learnt about the capacities of the individuals within the interactive unit.

We also need a simple but systematic framework to facilitate the reporting of our work to other professionals, since it is this instant access to the patient's inner world that provides us with a strong and immensely valuable role in the inter-disciplinary team.

The existing music therapy evaluation procedures developed by Nordoff and Robbins (1977), together with Bruscia's Improvisation Assessment Profiles (IAP) (Bruscia, 1987), offer some guidelines towards evaluating the communicative processes, although Bruscia's IAPs are complicated by their multi-dimensional structure. Furthermore, he separates intra- and inter-musical processes, as well as intra- and inter-personal, again offering a distinction between these, and I question whether this complexity renders it a feasible instrument for hard-pressed clinicians. Nordoff and Robbins' distinction between 'resistive' and 'participative' features has been questioned by Steele (1984), and its assessment of clinical improvisation with children limits its use for the more complex interactions which clinical improvisations with adults demand.

The development and application of the Musical Interaction Ratings (MIR) has been reported elsewhere (Pavlicevic and Trevarthen, 1989; Pavlicevic, 1991), and here I will simply present the essential considerations. I also draw attention to their having been developed primarily to define work done with patients suffering from chronic schizophrenia, so that their leaning is towards the lower end of the communicative spectrum.

The nine levels which comprise the Musical Interaction Ratings (MIR) illustrate where the individual is placed on the communicative spectrum (y-axis in Figure 1) irrespective of whether his or her position is determined by under- or over-organised musical/emotional form (i.e., irrespective of his or her position on the x-axis) . The nine levels of the MIR take as their basic premise that the therapist's (T) intention is to meet the patient/partner's (P) playing, since it is the therapist who, initially at least, has the musical skills and the facility to 'read' the communicative signals of the patient's musical utterances. Once T has met P's playing, T will attempt to establish the degree of flexibility in P's playing. She will do this by intervening clinically, or offering a potential musical direction, and note the timing, content and quality of P's response, i.e. she will note P's interactive responses. Also, because the emphasis, in this paper, is on T's responsibility and accountability to professional colleagues, the levels below evaluate P within the interaction, rather than T. However, their focus could be altered, so that the MIR could assess T. This is in keeping with the concept that an interactive dyad, provided it is analysed as a unit, reveals information about either partner.

The nine levels are as follows:

1) No communication

Here, the two players do not meet each other through the music. P's playing may be too disorganised for T to make sense of it; or T may be incapable of meeting P's musical statements.

2) One-sided contact: No response from P

The two players share some musical features, such as a common pulse or a joint rhythmic pattern, but it is T who is doing all the meeting, while P shows no sign of taking T's playing into account. Thus, when T intervenes clinically, P shows no sign of acknowledging T's intervention, and will continue to play in a self-centred, isolated world.

3) One-sided contact: Non-musical response from P

Here again, the two players share some musical features in the improvisation. P shows some alertness and response to T's clinical interventions, although P's responses are expressed outside the musical relationship. Thus, P may look up at T, frown, or may begin to speak, while within the musical interaction, it is still T who is doing all the meeting. Thus, while P is responding, it is not through the musical relationship.

4) Self-directed musical response from P

Here, P's response to T's intervention is to move away from the joint musical context. Ps response is not directed towards T, but is 'self' rather than 'other' directed. This makes it difficult for P and T to continue sharing the music, and it limits and may reduce the existing musical contact.

5) Tenuous musically-directed response from P

Here P's responses are within (in contrast to without) the musical relationship, although they may be tenuous or fleeting. This is the beginning of musical communication in the sense that the interaction is beginning to take place within a shared musical context.

6) Sustained musically directed response from P

Here, P's responses are more sustained, although P may remain in the imitative role, allowing T to take all the initiative within the interaction.

7) Establishing mutual contact

P begins to be musically independent, and at first this may be manifested in P not imitating everything that T does, but rather, being able to hold his/her own musically, and to contribute material to the improvisation.

8) Extending mutual contact

P begins to introduce variety, may initiate tempo changes and generally become more assertive, within the shared musical context.

9) Musical partnership

Here the two players take turns to lead in the improvisation, by using the musical components in a manner that acknowledges the other partner's use of them. The players share a reciprocity of musical intention and relate in a highly dynamic and intimate way.

These nine levels provide a useful starting point for attempting to understand the complex interactions which feature in adult communication. They address the interactive features of human communication which, as we have seen above, are essentially musical in character. They provide a profile for the quality of the person's motivation and capacity for engaging interactively, and provide a map for conceptualising and reporting to others on how the person is being 'in the world'.

The MIR is sensitive enough to distinguish between various adult psychiatric groups (Pavlicevic and Trevarthen, 1989), and to measure small changes within a population of chronic schizophrenics (Pavlicevic, 1991). It is simple and quick to use, which is a major consideration for music therapists in clinical practice, although it clearly needs to be extended in order to accommodate patients with a wider interactive range. The MIR also needs further validation through more widespread use.

Finally, a thorough understanding of how we work and play together with patients can only help to clarify our own clinical practice and offer professional colleagues some respite from their bewilderment. All of this can only enhance both our own and our patients' developments. Ultimately and essentially, it is thanks to them that we have the opportunity to practice this most exciting profession - we owe them our attempts at clarity.

Section 3: Music Therapy with Children

10

A Model of Assessment and Differential Diagnosis of Handicap in Children through the Medium of Music Therapy

Tony Wigram

For some parents, the experience of having a handicapped child comes as a sudden and shattering shock. Parents will react quite differently to this, but one thing they all have in common is an immediate realisation that they are going to experience many different problems in raising their children, problems that will be additional to the normal experience of parenthood. For other parents, their children do not immediately present as handicapped, and they experience a gradual awareness of some worrying problems that they seem to have with their child and their friends in the play group or local supermarket do not. Unusual behaviours, unusual or delayed language, unexpected tantrums, lack of affection and many other problems may emerge, and however much one may want to believe the friendly advice of a next-door neighbour saying 'Never mind, mine didn't talk till they were nearly two', the parents know that all is not well, and they must seek advice and help.

I am referring, of course, to parents who have children with autistic features, or autistic tendencies. They then embark on a process which can be even more difficult to cope with - finding a diagnosis for their child, and knowing what to do as a result.

This chapter begins by looking at the role of a specialist agency, The Harper House Children's Service[1] , and our work in evaluating the disabilities of children who have come with their parents for help. Because autism is such a difficult disorder to be clear about, front-line agencies such as general practitioners or community paediatricians are either reluctant to give such a label to a child, or on the other hand may give an intimation that the child has autistic features, thus suggesting to the parents that this is the direction in which they should look. The paper is going to examine the problem by looking at the musical behaviour and musical responsiveness of children as one means of providing some information to support, or not to support, a diagnosis of autism. The Harper House Children's Service consists of doctors, psychologists, physiotherapists, social worker, music therapist, art therapist and speech therapist, and all the professionals play a role as a team in trying to unravel the very confused picture many of the children who are

---

[1] part of Horizon NHS Trust and a sub-department of University College Hospital, London

referred present. The late Dr Derek Ricks founded the Service, and the ethos he created within the team, which still persists, was to put the parents at the centre of what was happening and work all the time with their co-operation. Ricks' own work looked specifically at verbal and pre-verbal communication (Ricks, 1975, 1978). Ricks believed that there were several aspects of diagnosis:

1. Finding out from the parents what they feel to be the matter with their child.

2. Attempting to discover or extending the evidence of his/her actual disability.

3. Presenting this evidence in as coherent a form as possible to the parents in an effort to reconcile what they feel to be wrong with the evidence available.

4. Thereby to equip the parents better to choose among several options available to their child.

Ricks, along with many other clinicians, has become well aware of the complexities and diversities of the disorder known as autism (Wing, 1976, 1979, 1981). The Autistic Continuum (Wing, 1988) has become a means of sifting out from the evident disability the degree of severity in the child. Many children present with autistic features and it is essential to identify the exact nature of their disability.

In the process of evaluating autistic disability in children for example, one is looking particularly for some impairment of social recognition, impairment of social communication and impairment of social imagination and understanding. At either a severe or mild level, all of these factors must be present for a diagnosis to be made of a disorder within the Autistic Continuum. Many children present the features of autism which are also features of other sorts of disorders and should be treated with some care until an overall survey concludes that there are enough evident features of autistic disability. Children may typically come to the Harper House Service described as isolated, withdrawn, with deviant behaviour and poor language development. Because these features are also compatible with autistic disability, one shouldn't necessarily ignore the fact that the child may have an expressive or receptive dysphasia coupled with a developed behaviour problem which causes them to present as autistic children. Similarly, children may present with unusual manneristic behaviour, obsessions, and a one-sided response to both their peers and to adults, whereby they may talk without listening. Within the Autistic Continuum one could identify such children as at the mild end; possibly bright children who have late onset disability. However, they should also be considered as having some of the clinical features of Asperger syndrome (Wing, 1981) which seems to be gaining recognition as a sub-set of autism but with different problems and a different prognosis. Children with dyspraxia can present with very particular behavioural symptoms and they try to cover up evidence of the features of the problem which are concurrent with a focal abnormality in the brain. Dyspraxia often demonstrates itself as a disorder of a voluntary act.

The differential diagnosis of autism and other handicaps associated with developmental language delay, was described by Patricia Howlin (1988) who considered that 'the important point to bear in mind is that accurate diagnosis cannot be reached on the basis of one or two isolated symptoms'. It is how symptoms cluster together and the patterning of deficits and skills that are the crucial factors for diagnosis . ' Other confusions can arise over bright autistic children who have been confused with maladjusted children, or autistic children who are so disabled, and have so many additional defects, that they have been regarded as a mobile, profoundly retarded child. We are also beginning to find quite a group of children who appear to be quite normal early on, then develop some autistic 'tendencies', but subsequently recover to some degree of normality, although remaining mentally handicapped. Finally, one can encounter children who are frequently described as autistic when they are referred, but in fact have other serious communication handicaps.

Unravelling the mystery of these damaged children is often a confusing and complex process for the professionals who are well skilled and experienced at doing it, so this must be magnified ten-fold for parents. Some parents actively seek a label of autism for their child, either because they are beginning to despair that anybody can clearly identify what is wrong, or because autism may seem to them to be a more acceptable or optimistic diagnosis than mental handicap or retardation. Other parents, when it is first indicated to them that their child may have autistic features, avidly read everything they can find on the subject and subsequently realise that autism is a very disabling disorder, and the prognosis can be extremely bleak. Parents who research the literature in the hope of understanding their children better often find themselves interpreting many of the child's behaviours as 'autistic features'. One also has to bear in mind that almost all children display autistic features as they grow up - i.e. they become very preoccupied with doing one thing over and over again, or for a need for security they like to do things in the same order and can become upset if their order is disrupted. However, for most normal children, or non autistic children, these features are only transient and they fade as the child grows up and adapts to new situations and new people. With autistic children, however, these features remain, and are often exaggerated in their manifestation.

In undertaking assessment work through music therapy, one has to consider a number of factors in terms of the child's general interaction and response, the abnormalities in their behaviour, their music behaviour and their general physical activity. One cannot ignore that in any assessment process in music therapy it is inevitable that one will see features of the disability or the pathology of the disorder in the musical behaviour, and it is important to isolate that and identify it in order to be clear about diagnostic evidence. It is equally important to isolate and identify evidence of normal musical behaviour or normal musical skills that are inconsistent with some diagnostic suggestions that may have been attached to an individual, and to write as accurately and eloquently about the abilities and responsiveness of an individual as one does about their limitations (Wigram, 1989).

The value of music therapy assessment was once described on BBC 2 by the late Dr Hugh Jolly, Consultant Psychiatrist and Paediatrician at the Charing Cross Child Development Centre. He estimated the value of a music therapy assessment as giving valuable evidence of what a child is able to do, and perhaps more importantly placing the child in a situation where, through the medium of music, they can be more in control, and even 'musically direct' the behaviour of an adult. The interactive feature of a music therapy assessment is going to give a clear indication of the child's receptive skills, their expressive skills and non-verbal communication, and their ability to play and engage in social relationships. But it will also give evidence of behaviour disorder, rituals or routines, lack of creative play and abnormal interaction that people would associate with autism.

More specifically, the assessment work the author has developed in music therapy as part of a multidisciplinary evaluation where a diagnostic opinion is required, always includes a close look at the way the child responds or behaves under the following five headings:

General interaction and response

Focus
Attention
Diverting behaviour
Body awareness
Response to physical contact
Response to verbal contact
Remoteness
Excessive friendliness
Response to direction
Ability to initiate and direct
Impaired sociability

Abnormal communication and behaviour

Language delay
Expressive dysphasia
Receptive dysphasia
Facial expression
Rigid and inflexible thought process
Resistance to suggestions
Strange interaction
Lack of awareness of the patterns of normal interaction
Talking without listening
Talking without waiting to answer
No desire to communicate
Using people as objects

Musical behaviour

No concept of rhythm and tempo
No concept of playing with therapist
No concept or limited awareness of turn-taking
Using musical equipment inappropriately

Transference of behaviours or features of pathology into musical behaviour interaction

1. Manneristic behaviour (twiddling, fiddling, twirling, plucking, spinning)
2. Obsessive behaviour: (sequencing, orienting to specific sounds continuously, perseverating, and organising therapist to respond in particular ways).

Physical activity and behaviour

Balance and posture
Dexterity
Handling equipment
Handedness
Synchronicity
Deviant Ambulation
Clumsiness

Looking in more detail at some specific cases, one can begin to find evidence in the behaviour of the child in the music therapy session which, together with observed evidence from other therapeutic assessments, adds weight to a clearer diagnosis. Many children who are referred to the Harper House Service (and probably to many other services in the country as well as to individual practitioners) come with a questionable diagnosis of autistic disability. Because we are beginning to discover the wide variety of disabilities that come within the Autistic Continuum, and are also beginning to take into consideration late onset autism, and the confusion between autism and closely related syndromes such as Asperger, this label can be inappropriately given.

Case 1

Allen presented as a child with a withdrawn and isolated manner. He had poor eye contact, poor comprehension and a clear and severe communication disorder which persisted despite progress in other developmental areas. In addition, he had middle-ear problems, and it was very difficult to disentangle the nature of his disorder as comprehension, expression and symbolic play appeared to be delayed to roughly the same extent.

In the art therapy assessment, Allen did show some communicative intent, particularly at the beginning of the session. He used art materials but did not explore their use for very long and avoided the therapist for much of the time he was in the room. He was capable of some interaction, marking round a circle that the therapist drew, and imitating the 'cleaning' as well as the use of the brush.

In the music therapy assessment, Allen wandered around the room, initially ignoring most of the equipment. Attempts to engage him by offering him sticks didn't work, and he discarded them. A game of 'peek-a-boo' gave us the first clue that Allen's interactive skills were certainly similar to those one might expect in a child with autistic disabilities. However, he did target on a length of 'plastic binding' which he found in the room and he fiddled with this several times during the session, holding it near his ear. Eventually we had to withdraw it and hide it as it was interfering with any attempts to engage him. He didn't object to things being taken away from him, such as this piece of 'play material' that he was fixating on.

Musically, there were short periods of interaction when he was playing the drum, and also when he came over to play the piano. He did seem quite interested in the piano, and using two or three fingers of each hand he played 'randomly' on the notes for about 1.05 to 2 minutes without having to be encouraged to continue. He did on several occasions respond to instructions, although he rejected quite a lot of suggestions during the course of the session. If I handed him a beater and pointed to an instrument and asked him to hit it, he would do so. He seemed to understand the game of 'turn-taking' and responded when I said that it was 'his turn to play'.

On some occasions I had more success in engaging him in an activity when I contained him in one place (i.e. on a chair) long enough for him to start using the equipment.

His vision appeared normal and he seemed to be able to hear well. However, there were several examples of him putting his hands over his ears, and on one or two occasions he showed a small anxiety of extremely loud sounds. His parents reported that he has a sensitivity to certain sounds, for example the sound the computer makes in the television game 'Family Fortunes'; when he hears this he screams and becomes upset until the television is switched off. However, they also commented that he likes some of the other computer sounds in other quiz games on television.

From this, one is beginning to build up a picture of a child whose resistance to activity, resistance to engagement and peculiarities are not consistent or sustained, and although he presented with many of the different features of 'funny behaviour' and resistance one might expect in an autistic child, he did not have the complete inaccessibility at a sustained level which one normally encounters.

The main difficulty seemed to be that he was unresponsive and had difficulty in being able to join in and make use of the situation at all. On the very few occasions in this assessment when I explored a therapeutic approach that I would use with him (i.e. containment, structure, etc.), it became apparent that one would need to develop a very structured style of session, and the need to use a fairly intrusive style of work would probably result in much better responses.

Although there was very little speech and he cut himself off from us frequently through the session, refusing to respond to our pleas for him to come and play or do something with us, he was an accepting little boy with whom quite a lot of work was possible. He seemed well able to take a certain amount of pressure and persuasion to be involved in activity and interaction, and this should be capitalised on.

Subsequent visits to Allen's home and nursery group impressed us, and we were able to observe him amongst a normal peer group. He seemed very attached to his welfare worker and was co-operative in structured play activities. The nursery said that they tried to keep a balance between free play and more structured activity, and this seemed to work well for Allen. Whilst he does like to wander off in a rather absent way, he did show signs of beginning to be interested in activities and exploring. When visiting the opportunity class, he appeared tired and unwell and yet was able to co-operate in a 'functional learning session', albeit with very little enthusiasm or interest. He seemed to be aware of our presence and looked at us watching him, although there were no signs of recognition that we were the two adults he had seen the previous day.

He was more enthusiastic in the home environment and we were able to observe some delightful play between Allen and his father.

The general consensus from the day assessment was that Allen was fairly difficult to interest and engage in constructive activities. There was no evidence of expressive language in his sessions, although some musical interaction had been noted and there were signs of communicative intent in the art session.

To this end, the team had concluded with the parents that they were no longer considering Allen's difficulties in terms of autism, giving a more hopeful prognosis for future development. Allen was three and a half years old at the time of the assessment, and by this age should have identified autistic disability, unless this was a case of late onset autism.

Case 2

Mark is a two-and-a-half year old boy with a variety of quite distressing behaviours, including self-mutilation, who was referred to the Harper House Children's Service by a consultant paediatrician who was seeking an opinion as to whether he was autistic, or had autistic features which were secondary to developmental delay. He was admitted to hospital when he was only seventeen months old due to self-mutilation (head-banging) and he was becoming aggressive, screaming and crying continuously. No definite diagnosis was reached and due to various unfortunate reasons, he was taken into voluntary care and fostered at the age of twenty-one months. Immediately prior to the assessment, his foster mother reported that eye contact was improving, and he was becoming responsive to sitting on knees and being cuddled. He had a notable feature of rocking, something he did almost all the time, but apparently this stops when he is being cuddled. His mother is on medication for depression and has had ECT in the past. She has two children from a previous liaison, both are said to be normal, but

Mark's father also suffered depression and committed suicide two months after Mark's birth.

All the behaviours described above, his impairments and social relationships, language development and his repetitive activities could be indicators for a diagnosis of autism. However, they can also have alternative explanations. In the music therapy assessment, he quickly became interested in the instruments and used sticks and beaters to hit them. He looked at what he was doing, and also looked across to his foster mother to see if she could see what he was doing. His vocal output was quite varied and there seemed to be periods when he would imitate and interact, vocally. However, he frequently used the same vocal sound, which did not necessarily either communicate anything or demand anything. His most meaningful vocal communication was when he was not permitted to do something, or something was taken away from him. Then his voice would turn to quite a harsh sound, and raise in both pitch and volume. He listened to me when I imitated his vocal sounds at first, but was most responsive when I called his name.

Although he rocked on occasions throughout the session, he would stop rocking for quite long periods of time when he was involved in playing. His playing was quite rhythmic and, although for most of the session I was matching musically with him, rather than him following my cues, there was a section of turn-taking in the middle of the session. Here he was using the drum, and I played short three or four beat rhythms to which he would respond by playing a few beats in response and then watching me for my response. After I had showed him where the instruments were, he would often seek them out. The cymbal, which was near the window, attracted his interest and he returned to it several times. He also connected the size, shape and sound of this instrument with the other cymbal near the piano and went from one to another playing them. Handling of the equipment was quite appropriate and he did not spin or fiddle with any of the instruments. There was a moment towards the end of the session when we played 'peek-a-boo'; this he enjoyed very much, causing him to smile and laugh out loud.

What conclusions can be drawn then from the evidence of this session? In terms of interaction, he responds better and better when he gets the response from adults that he wants. There was to some extent a danger that he turned everything into a game of which he is in control, and he can also become irritated and upset if he doesn't control what is going on. This supported the findings of other members of the team, whose overall impression was of a child who was unsure about social interaction and had only had limited learning opportunities generally. Although he occasionally appeared clumsy, there was no evidence that he had motor problems and the vocal interaction that he had in the music therapy session was reflected at other times while he was at Harper House, and noises he made were reported as being easily interpretable as cross, happy or requesting. In summary, it appears that Mark was a casualty of poor opportunities for learning and social interaction which have led him to present as a child who is withdrawn, delayed in developing speech and showing stereotype movements. When left to his own devices, he does revert to self stimulatory activity, such as rocking, and he is delayed in his general development. Almost all of these features are the result of sensory and stimulatory deprivation, and his musical behaviour and responsiveness certainly indicated a potential for learning, a potential for appropriate social interaction and relationship-building, and appropriate use of equipment - none of which one would expect to find in a prognosis for an autistic child.

Case 3

Sarah is a ten year old child who came to Harper House for an assessment when she was seven years old. She had previously been assessed in some depth at a Child Assessment Centre where they concluded with a diagnostic opinion that she was an autistic child. She has an older and a younger brother, all three children being delivered by Caesarian section. There were no neo-natal problems and she seemed to develop normally, feeding well and with no adverse reaction to the normal immunisations. Between fifteen and eighteen months she started to become detached and fretful, showing irritable behaviour, becoming upset (particularly in unfamiliar places) and often screaming. Up to this point she had produced normal babble, and also started to develop a few words, drawing attention to events and interests such as cats or lights. Autistic behaviour can be a striking feature in Rett's syndrome (Olsson, 1987).

Her parents began to become worried, particularly as Sarah continued to be fretful, seemed to have no development of vocabulary, and often roamed around randomly in an agitated way. After her second birthday she started to become even more remote and self-contained, sitting passively doing repetitive, pointless activities such as pulling off leaves or handling objects repetitively. Her hearing appears intact, but her listening seems to be selective, and in terms of communicating her needs she tends to pull people towards what she wants and then point out the objects. By the time she came for her assessment at Harper House, she still had quite limited self-help skills and although she was able to feed herself and help with dressing, she was not toilet-trained.

In this case, a music therapy assessment was followed by a series of music therapy sessions which are still continuing. Her general behaviour, and more specifically her musical behaviour and responsiveness, are much more typical of Rett's syndrome (see Hagberg et al., 1983; Kerr and Stephensen, 1985; 1986) than of autism. Although many of the disabilities that she appears to suffer from may also be attributed to autism, her ability to make personal contact is much more direct and is typical in autistic children. She is often very quickly stimulated and attracted by musical sounds, and enjoys engaging with the therapist in musical games.

In the assessment session and in subsequent music therapy sessions, Sarah did present with typical patterns of hand movements that are characteristic of Rett's syndrome. She clapped her hands together, occasionally tapping her face with them particularly around the mouth, and she had only limited hand use in the early sessions. She was most adept at picking items up, and depositing them with the therapist. She was not easily encouraged to play anything and when given beaters or sticks to use on the instruments she would quickly discard them. She often reached out to grab things and then pushed them away. Her ability to use her hands constructively was definitely impaired by her continuous plucking, and it has only been over the course of several therapy sessions that we have been able to see some change in this. Initially, by holding one hand apart and insisting that she used the other purposefully, we were able to break through the repetitive plucking movements and give her some structured use of her hands for a specific purpose. The results of this process have been that she will now hold beaters for quite long periods of time, and use them appropriately.

Sarah has not as yet shown any indications of the atrophy one expects in the lower limbs typical of Rett's syndrome. She is very agile, moves around quickly and prefers either to stand and move around the room or lie, rather than sit. She makes a variety of different vocal sounds, and it is possible to engage her at purely vocal levels. She will quite often gaze at you and make giggling or cooing sounds in response to similar sounds from a therapist, but she can also make distressed whining sounds when she is upset and is beginning to articulate words. We have definitely heard her use 'go' and 'bye-bye'. She also tries to say 'Mum' and other single syllable words. Sustained music therapy sessions over the last few months have resulted in much more positive activity by Helen. She now uses both her hands, whereas previously she could only be encouraged to use one. Part of the therapy process involved disrupting her repetitive activity and eliminating her habit of discarding objects indiscriminately. She has first been encouraged to pick up any object that she discards and give it to the therapist and this ultimately has resulted in her handing items to the therapist before she discards them. She can now be engaged in musical interaction using various instruments scattered throughout the room for up to ten minutes, and her level of interaction is very much aligned to the therapist's stimulus. The success of this process has partly been due to careful structuring and insistence on the part of the therapist, but also due to the ease with which one can engage Sarah at an interactive level, particularly through the medium of a musical 'game'. It would have been a very different situation if her disabilities had been primarily autistic.

Case 4

Simon was a five year old with obvious communicative disabilities, and he was referred to the Service for a second opinion on autistic disability, a diagnosis which had caused varied opinions during the educational statementing process. With Simon, the problems of differential diagnosis presented difficulties particularly in terms of the inevitable overlap between children presenting with autism and those presenting with specific expressive or receptive language disorders. In the final report, Dr Kugler pointed out that Simon's 'symptoms' clustered together, and that, on the basis of early history, Simon showed clear impairment in social interaction, and in verbal and non-verbal communication and social imagination. Yet in terms of social imagination, he had moved on from rather repetitive lining up of bricks along window sills at 2 to 2.6 years' of age, to appropriate use of toys such as bricks, trains, garages and cars, and is now able to play creatively and widely with these but shows more limited pretend or symbolic play with other toys. At Harper House, he tried to give a soft toy dragon a ride on the rocking horse. He is able to copy the symbolic play of others more readily than spontaneously initiating his own.

In the music therapy assessment, he initially became preoccupied with the process of being videoetaped and put on a 'performance' for the camera. Initially, he appeared indifferent to playing the instruments, and attempts to encourage him to sit on the floor and work from behind resulted in him wriggling away. He did reach out for the drumsticks, and he began to play when I offered him a large tambor. I used the tune 'Three Blind Mice', and he smiled and became excited when the music went faster, switching the beater to his right hand and playing vigorously.

He continued to play the drum for five to six minutes, and although I encouraged him to use two beaters, he preferred one. He started a game using his feet and pushing the tambor which I was holding. This resulted in me 'falling backwards', which he found very amusing and laughed loudly.

Moving on to the piano, he started three quarters of the way up the instrument and worked carefully down, playing every white note in sequence. He was very careful not to miss one out, and he had to reach right over me to get to the very bottom notes. In fact, he was almost lying across me to reach down to the very end of the piano. He then began to work all the way back up again to the top.

The session continued with Simon reverting to the television, and also resisting using some of the instruments. He found the large toy train in the room and began pushing it around. When using the cymbal, he found that he could balance it with his foot and hit it against the piano. He carried on playing the cymbal in this way, and on occasions he would glance across at me and smile while he was playing. It was, however, difficult a lot of the time to tell whether he was playing <u>with me</u> or just playing by himself.

Finally, he started to withdraw into himself, lounging on the floor. He crawled over to the train again and began to fiddle with the raised lettering on the back of the train which reads 'Baptist Church, St Albans, 1983 CWP'. He began to work with his thumb around the letters, starting at the bottom and working all the way up a line at a time. He then ignored any effort at communication that we were making, and when he got to the last letter of the top word he simply began to go all the way back down again.

It is easy to see from the described behaviours in this session that Simon presents as an unusual little boy who at one moment could be responsive and interactive, smiling and responding to instructions, and at the next moment would either be very resistant and opting out or would ignore one completely. Repetitive patterns of self chosen activity were evident both in this session and in other sessions with other therapists. In terms of language, Simon showed limited skill and quite a lot of echolalic acquisition. He had good memory skills though, and also good fine motor or manipulative skills. The mixed picture we obtained was of a little boy who was most responsive when rigidly or firmly structured and yet who could also show considerable flexibility. Looking at the overall picture presented, in terms particularly of reciprocity in social encounters, level of symbolic functioning, communicative intent and use of non-verbal forms of communication (gestures; facial expression) in initiating and maintaining social contact, Simon impressed us as an autistic child rather than as a child with specific language disorder.

Discussion

Sessions of assessment and diagnostic evaluation require from the therapist different protocol and procedure than in a therapy treatment session (Wigram, 1990). To be clear about this, one has to look at the purpose of the assessment:
- to evaluate with music the nature of the disorder
- to identify the child's responsiveness
- to highlight and identify the nature of resistance
- to look at positive and negative response
- to explore the physical, cognitive and perceptual abilities or deficiencies of the child
- to evaluate the benefit of a therapeutic approach
- to identify the appropriate therapeutic approach
- to explore emotional anxiety, distress and repressed feelings
- to explore the nature of the relationship between child and therapist, and child and significant offers.

In order to obtain the information that is so vital for a clear understanding of the child's needs, and also essential in determining the value of a therapeutic approach, the therapist probably has to adopt a number of different approaches to the child during the course of the assessment process. This assessment process at Harper House (by reason of the fact that the children often come from far afield) may have to happen in the course of one day, but often it is more preferable if it can take place over two or three assessments. Without categorising these points in any particular order, this is an attempt to describe some of the approaches and ideas the therapist would use in this process of diagnostic assessment:
- exploring the child's response to close contact and interaction
- exploring the child's response to distancing
- exploring the child's response to structure
- exploring the child's response to a free environment
- exploring the child's response to intrusive intervention and pressure
- exploring the child's response to an imitative/ intensive interaction approach
- investigating the child's response in conventional music situations, for example, their response to precomposed music, nursery rhymes, television tunes they may be familiar with etc.

- investigating the child's use of and response to instruments (including their handling and purposeful use of musical equipment)
- investigating the child's verbal, vocal and gestural communication skills
- assessing ways in which the child functions well that are inconsistent with the existing evidence of disorder or disability
- using music as a means of assessing the child's sociability, appropriate language, comprehension and interactive skills
- investigating the child's responsiveness to sound generally (with consideration to evidence of hyperacousis, pseudohyperacousis, over-sensitivity or preoccupation.

The therapist is attempting to explore and evaluate the nature of the child's disorder and to be clear about their level of responsiveness and functioning, and in so doing make comparisons both with an accepted norm and also with children with similar disabilities. The process may involve assessing the child's responsiveness to a therapeutic approach, and even evaluating and speculating on the nature of a potential therapeutic relationship. However, assessment does not entail or require the therapist to operate with the child in the same way as they would do within a normal therapeutic relationship begun and sustained during a course of therapy sessions.

In fact, it is more frequently desirable that the therapist retains an objective and evaluative stance when undertaking the process of diagnostic assessment, even though information may equally be gained from undertaking a more typically music therapy type of session. The reasons for this are that one needs to cover a broad spectrum within an assessment and be concerned with evaluating all aspects of the child's abilities and disabilities. In order to provide information and give an overall picture that can correlate or provide differential evidence to other assessments, the therapists may need to use many different approaches, and explore different facets of the child's character and personality. There is no reason why this cannot be done in a therapeutic and sensitive way but it probably needs to be done without the approach and aims of a therapy session.

In conclusion, these four quite different cases show how, in the process of assessing musical behaviour and musical responsiveness, one can tease out evidence of abilities, skills and characteristics of personality that are atypical of autism. Both Hugh Jolley and Derek Ricks have commented that the value of an assessment through the medium of music, by a music therapist, is enabling a child to demonstrate what they are able to do, much of which may have been hidden in other assessment work.

Language delay or disorder causes communication disabilities that are often confused with similar disabilities of autistic children, and perhaps the main value of the music therapy assessment is in reaching the child at a non-verbal level and enabling them to present their true potential for interaction through this medium.

11

Music Therapy and the Child with Cerebral Palsy: Directive and Non-Directive Intervention

John Bean

Introduction

The child with cerebral palsy, despite many difficulties, has great potential. S/he can be well motivated, creative in his/her ideas and thus, an exciting child to work with. For these dynamics to come into action, however, a sense of family support and care is necessary together with early intervention by various forms of treatment, each being specialised to meet the individual child's needs.

Cerebral palsy is a condition brought about before or immediately after birth by a lesion of the upper motor neurone of the brain. This brain damage interferes with normal childhood development particularly in areas of physical control. Disabilities common in cerebral palsy are:

(i) increased muscle tone causing stiffness in the joints of the body together with stereotype movements

(ii) insufficient muscle tone making the child 'floppy'

(iii) involuntary movements and constantly changing muscle tone (athetoid condition).

Additional disabilities may include poor vision due to a squint, and limited focusing ability of nystagmus. Hearing and speech patterns can also be affected, thereby further impairing communication skills. The child's general development is disorganised and abnormal; s/he lacks balance and control of postures such as sitting, standing and walking; s/he has restricted use of his/her arms and hands for support, reaching, grasping and manipulation. In order to achieve various skills s/he needs to develop compensatory muscle patterns (Finnis, 1974). Music therapy involves physical activity requiring varying levels of control and organisation. Being also a medium for interaction and musical self-expression it is a particularly relevant form of intervention for the child with cerebral palsy.

Through music therapy psychotherapeutic processes can develop in consequence to physiotherapeutic development. This can change a child's inner attitude to his/her body and awaken the realisation of some self-control being a possibility. Consequently a child's self-image may develop more positively. The relationship with physiotherapy is an important one. Elements of physiotherapy can be difficult and sometimes uncomfortable for children but may be a necessary part of their therapy programme. However, music therapy and physiotherapy can work together to provide a new dimension within which the child can work (Wigram and Weekes, 1985). The fun of musical activity can motivate a child to rise to new challenges presented to him/her. I should like to explore differing approaches of intervention at various levels. between highly-directive and non-directive. The type of intervention depends on a number of factors, namely; the condition responses and needs of the child, the initial music therapy assessment and the style of the therapist's approach in work. Two major areas will be explored; physical and emotional development, the latter by means of a case study.

Directive and non-directive approaches are by no means mutually exclusive. Some therapists hold strong views about these methods, particularly non-directive. However, the majority that I have discussed this issue with believe in using varying degrees of directive and non-directive therapy with their clients. It is valuable therefore to examine and articulate these differing approaches when considering the child with cerebral palsy.

Directive Intervention

There are a number of valid arguments against intervention that is highly directive. It can restrict the choice that the client may wish to take. It identifies itself with training and teaching models and can be viewed contentiously as a prescriptive approach to treatment. This runs contrary to the general philosophy of music therapy and also to the holistic approach that therapy can offer by treating the client as an entity of separate parts rather than as a whole person. Critics would argue that it presents a series of 'hurdles' for the client to surmount during the therapeutic process.

There are, however, good arguments in favour of using directive methods to some degree, especially in the case of the child with cerebral palsy. It can provide a sense of containment, security and clarity of purpose. The achievement of specific goals can have a direct and positive influence on the child's inner world. (Bailey, 1974). This can provide the child with information about his/her own abilities which may not be discovered so soon through a non-directive approach, especially when time-limits are imposed on a therapeutic programme by the education system comprising terms and the academic year. It is at this point that parents can make a vital contribution to the child's development by ensuring selected activities are continued during holiday periods. It may not be possible to have the same instruments available at home as in the therapy room but the therapist would be able to suggest alternative ways of working. Siblings too can support this work by sharing, encouraging and generating a sense of fun during the activities.

Developing a child's belief in his/her own capacity for control can be an exciting and positive contributory factor to development. Directive intervention, used sensitively, can still provide a framework for initiative and interaction to emerge.

Activities

The children for whom these activities have evolved are of the chronological age group 4-12 years with intellectual abilities upwards of 24 months. Of course many activities can be modified for the child with profound disability as well as the more able child. They are not intended so much for the ataxic or athetoid child, although some activities may be suitable for them also. Specific goals are suggested as part of the treatment. This organised framework is essential in order to avoid increasing spastic patterns. It is assumed that the music therapist is able to consult a physiotherapist on any aspects of the work. However, before embarking upon each aim, it must be emphasised that free exploration of the particular instrument should first be enjoyed between the child and the therapist.

The creation and control of musical sounds can bring great joy. In many cases excitement raises problems of tension and thus, loss of control. Problems that are typical when a cerebral palsy child becomes excited, are sudden increased stiffness of limbs often resulting in the loss of grasp and /foot position. The child then loses balance and functional posture. This inevitably creates a feeling of insecurity and a fear of falling. On the other hand, however, the child loses him/herself in the activity and gains great motivation and pleasure from it (Alvin, 1977). This sense of motivation is one of the most exciting dimensions of working with the child with cerebral palsy. S/he wants so much to create sound that, when directed clearly, will organise good motor control on his/her own volition. S/he can develop a degree of physical control without physical intervention and because of this, his/her belief in his/her ability can grow accordingly. Seating is of paramount importance; the physiotherapist should have made specific recommendations for a child's personal needs. This may be done by way of using additional padding and straps on the wheelchair or by fitting the child with a custom-made vacuum-moulded seat. Only when this has been done can the child be expected to maintain as symmetrical a position as possible which enables him/her to participate more fully. Body symmetry is a prerequisite for establishing balance and therefore important when developing awareness of hand/head activity in the midline position (an imaginary vertical line down the middle of the body). Exceptions to this are with children who have scoliosis or pelvic obliquity where postural symmetry is not physically possible. Ensure the child is securely seated with a balanced, functional posture prior to each activity (Finnise, 1974). It is important that, if possible, s/he has his/her face towards the therapist with hands and arms to the midline ready for participation.

The child needs a great deal of time to formulate responses; this may require much waiting on the part of the therapist. Indeed, hurried or awkward handling of the child with cerebral palsy results in stiffness and a sense of insecurity (Lubran, 1960). It is good to begin each session in a similar manner in order to orient the child, particularly if treatment is only once weekly. In each section, the 'suggested activities' (a), (b), (c), etc. are graded in order of 'difficulty', but need not necessarily be strictly adhered to.

Movement

Gross movement involves many aspects concerning the child; each stage naturally should be considered in relation to the severity of the child's problems. Firstly it is important to build self-confidence and body awareness. This can be achieved through exploring free movement to music, with the child lying on a carpeted floor. A two-way cassette player that plays either side of the tape solely at the touch of a button is useful to play contrasting styles of music in juxtaposition. A musical stimulus can be provided in two ways:

(1) Pre-prepared music on cassette, i.e. 'lively', such as popular music, dances or marches on the 'A' side of the cassette and 'calm', such as ballads, waltzes or nocturnes on the 'B' side, from one's own collection.

(2) Improvised music by the therapist who may wish to use familiar music as a basis for playing contrasting styles of music, as above. Alternatively he/she may prefer to improvise freely on any instrument to provide the music stimulus.

Suggested activities

(a) Listening: At first it may help to provide music that is familiar in order to assess the child's listening skills. The therapist can draw the child's attention, if necessary, to the difference between 'lively' and 'calm' music.

(b) Exploring movement: Invite the child to move in any way s/he wishes. Give the child time to move freely before encouraging him/her to reflect the style of music through movement.

(c) Starting and stopping: Children gain great pleasure from the element of surprise. 'Lively' music can release some of the excitement and energy that the child may be feeling. It is more exacting to stop when 'calm' music is played.

(d) Listening to the two styles juxtaposed.

(e) Moving to the two styles juxtaposed: The aim of these activities is to develop self-confidence and control of movement through a pleasurable medium. The child is secure on the floor so the demands made upon him/her are minimally stressful. Free movement is rarely 'correct' from a physiotherapeutic view of the child with cerebral palsy. However, positions and movements such as stiffening of the legs and hips or extension of the head and shoulders should be tolerated in order for him/her to enjoy body movement. From this the therapist can consider movements such as rolling and swinging.

(f) Role-reversal: This is only possible with live music and the child provokes consciously the style of music to be played i.e. lively or calm, by his/her movements.

Relaxation

Relaxation is one of the most difficult poses for the child to achieve. In music therapy s/he is so eager to play instruments that the concept of not playing can be hard for him/her to accept, (Smales, 1962). Relaxation demands great concentration, so bearing in mind that listening does not come easily, much time needs to be allotted in preparing him/her for it. Many children with cerebral palsy have difficulty in keeping their eyes closed when asked, a technique often used in developing relaxation. S/he may be helped, however, if the tenor of activities is reduced beforehand by preparing him/her posturally on the floor. Songs or recorded music in a slow 3/4 (e.g. Mull of Kintyre, Edelweiss) or 6/8 time (e.g. Speed Bonnie Boat, Greensleeves) and/or gentle humming would be appropriate in working towards this.

Head Control

The importance of developing good head control cannot be underestimated. Steps towards independence rely on the head leading in the sequence of movements required for turning, rolling and getting up from a lying position. (Finnie, 1974). Learning to focus gaze and to cross the visual midline requires practice with a variety of stimuli.

Suggested activities

(a) Follow the sound: Lying or seated facing the therapist the child is encouraged to follow a sounding musical instrument moved in front of his/her head, (a bell or maraca would be suitable).

(b) Up and down and side to side: Preparing these movements for 'Yes' and 'No' signs can be exercised in a similar manner. If the child tends to use his/her eyes more than the head, a song may be improvised using words to encourage a specific movement.

(c) Follow the silent instrument: This is similar to (a) but with the surprise element of the instrument making no sound.

(d) 'Look at the window' is a variation of the song 'Point to the window'. The child is asked to move his/her head to look deliberately in various directions according to the song. S/he is likely to enjoyed improvised variants such as 'Where is the window, where is the drum, where is the teddy, where are your shoes?!'

Control of Leg Movements

When the child has developed a reasonable level of head control, sitting posture and some independent movement it should be possible for him/her to develop more conscious control of the legs. It may be useful to revise free movement on the floor, encouraging him/her to move his/her legs together and separately. Once awareness of them as controllable parts has initially been established, it would be appropriate to develop this in a chair with arm rests.

Sitting passively the child has little problem with sustaining a correct leg position. However the moment any demand is made on the child physically (grasping or even speaking, for instance), s/he appears involuntarily to lose their control. The problem is not that the child lacks control, rather s/he ceases to apply conscious control over his/her legs when involved in another activity. It is possible to develop the child's belief that s/he has some control over the position of his/her legs. Inevitably, this will be a lengthy process but it is vital to offer the child the challenge, opportunity and guidance.

Music experiences and activities

(a) Listening: A short piece of music is played during which the child is asked to think only about his/her feet whilst they remain in the correct position. Improvised singing with words such as 'Can you keep your feet still? ' can reinforce this.

(b) 'Can you pull your foot back?' (song): Songs make repetition tolerable, enjoyable and can give the child time to execute the action. When for instance the foot is thrust forward, the following phrases can be sung, in many different situations.

(c) Kicking over the tambourine: In my experience, some children who have had problems with the above have no difficulty with this game! The child sits on a chair, with his/her feet resting on the floor. To clarify the idea, the tambourine can first be placed in front of each foot for the child to enjoy kicking over. The object of the activity is to knock over the tambourine with the heel, one foot at a time. Prefixing the activity with the count of three can give the child time to prepare consciously the correct muscular activity. A mirror at hand may satisfy the child's need for visual as well as auditory reward. It is important to clarify which foot is to be used, starting with the weaker one, if hemiplegic, and to encourage the child to return the foot to the correct position after each movement.

(d) Feeling the vibrations (guitar): Feeling vibrations with the hands whilst keeping the feet still immediately raises problems for the child. His/her attention is transferred from his/her feet to the instrument, and in his/her eagerness to touch it may easily lose foot position. It is for this reason that it is useful to ask the child only to feel the back of the guitar whilst it is vibrating. This experience can enhance the child's understanding of sound; that it is created by movement and that the child can have control over it by his/her own actions. This activity also demonstrates how sound can be perceived, not only aurally, but physically through touch.

(e) Gently strumming the guitar strings: Similar principles apply to this. The child may agree to strum the strings gently him or herself if, for instance, s/he is told the instrument is 'asleep' and wouldn't like to be woken up with a loud sound! The guitar is of particular value to the child with cerebral palsy. It can be held facing the child for him/her to play the 'open' strings with one or both hands. Very little effort is required to produce a sound that is mellow, sustained and immensely rewarding.

Arms

Hands and arms are inevitably going to be valuable tools to help the child to establish personal independence. Treatment will of course be tailored to the severity of the spasticity. With regard to the problem of arm extension my feeling is that because this is generally uncharted territory for the child, his/her stiffness is exacerbated by fear in reaching out. This psychological barrier can be surmounted by the attraction (and distraction) that music-making offers. The following activities often cause problems with loss of leg position, unless straps or stabilisers are provided.

Music experiences and activities

(a) Developing the awareness of each arm separately: This can be increased by placing a preferred instrument within reach of each hand, one at a time. The tambourine can be very stimulating for the child with limited movement, even a gentle hit will produce a sound.

(b) Bringing each towards midline separately: By following the above, the midline can be gradually achieved by bringing the instrument in front of him/her.

(c) Arm lifting: This is suitable for the child who is able to keep his/her arms on the chair rests. Improvised singing may be appropriate or following the words to the familiar theme from Schubert's 'Trout' Quintet. It gives the child time to prepare each movement. 'I lift up this arm carefully and down it goes again'.

(d) Stroking the auto-harp strings: Because of their sustained resonance, the auto-harp strings can be rewarding to play and encourage midline control, especially for the child who's lack of grasp limits his/her opportunity to play tuned percussion.

(e) Playing two maracas: The hemiplegic child invariably prefers only his/her stronger arm. If s/he is able to sustain a grasp with both hands it is important that s/he should do so when possible (Smales, 1960). If, when holding two maracas s/he plays only one, this is still a step towards using both hands and preferable to holding just one.

(f) Tilting the chocolo: The chocolo (shaker) is particularly useful for the child who is able to sustain a grasp with both hands simultaneously. Some instruments are made with each end sunk approximately 2 cm. into the cylinder. This can help secure the grip. A second instrument for the therapist can help to mirror the action. When tilted slowly the sound indicates a smooth flowing movement.

(g) 'Conversation' on the bongos: Problems with stiffness become very apparent when a banging movement is introduced. The desire and excitement in creating a loud sound only, of course, increases the problem. However, at first it is only reasonable to permit the child time to experience the fun of making a loud sound as it can release much tension. Engaging the child in a 'conversation' on the bongo drums (as above) can help him/her in basic social skills as well as motor activity. S/he will probably enjoy imitating the therapist's style of playing, so by deliberately playing each drum, s/he too will be stimulated to extend his/her arms.

(h) Playing the xylophone lengthways: Placing the xylophone as above offers the child the opportunity to extend to reach the higher notes. His sense of achievement is increased by the pitch of the xylophone bars rising the further s/he extends. Again the hemiplegic child should be encouraged to hold two beaters. As his/her confidence grows, so will the use of the weaker arm increase. Padded handles will help the child to grasp the beaters firmly.

(i) Pushing the bar-adapted concertina: A concertina is adapted as above. The child is assisted in grasping the bar either side with both hands, the therapist sitting opposite him/her, supporting the instrument. The child is then asked to pull the instrument so that it fills with air. (The removal of one valve will ensure this is possible and that no note will sound in the process.) The moment the child pushes the bar and begins to extend his/her arms, the therapist presses one or more of the note buttons his/her end so that the child makes the instrument sound. When the child pulls, the therapist releases the buttons so that there is no sound again. The purpose of making sound only for the extension is to act as a positive reinforcement to movement.

(j) Crossing the midline, drum and cymbal: These two instruments can be very loud! For the child they cause great excitement but at the same time can increase muscle tone to an undesirable level. Cymbal brushes go towards solving this problem yet still offer the child big movements; alternatively soft-headed beaters with shortened sticks can also help. Placing the instruments as above, the child can be encouraged to cross the midline with each arm. Improvised singing and imitation can be a valuable stimulus. This activity can be varied by using other instruments such as a tone bar or metallaphone.

(k) Vertical extension: An activity can be devised using claves and a suspended cymbal. Playing the claves whilst slowly raising the arms, the therapist can sing the 'woodpecker' song. This can be extended for 'coming down', as required, starting with the pitch high.

(l) Clasped stretch: Arm extensions with clasped hands can be exercised for example to the tune of 'Glory, glory, hallelujah' (from 'John Brown's Body') using the following words:

> 'Push your hands a little further (3 times)
> And hold them right out there!'

Summary

It is hoped. that, whilst this section does not cover a great many of the areas of the child's development, the suggestions will give specialists renewed ideas for treatments. Music therapy offers variety in having to perform similar activities and a music routine can lighten the task and thereby sustain the child's spirit in his/her continuing struggle towards more independence.

Non-Directive Intervention

Through non-directive intervention the therapist reflects the child's musical behaviour and provides positive reinforcement to his/her musical and personal experience, however negative or positive it may be. This may be a unique experience for the child and one that is unlikely to be attainable in the teaching situation. Nevertheless, there are some children for whom this approach is not altogether relevant. These include those who are particularly passive, who badly lack self-confidence or who become 'stuck' in obsessive patterns of behaviour. In these cases non-directive intervention may leave a child with a sense of isolation, being unsure of what to do, or what might be expected of them. These children may find freedom difficult to cope with. It may be that, in these cases, a directive bias provides a gateway towards more freedom. Boundaries need to be defined in any therapy programme, either through negotiation or directly by the therapist; avoiding damage to self or property being a typical example. Boundaries are created generally as a framework in order to provide an understanding of the limits within which to operate. The therapist may find that the child's needs are best met through non-directive intervention and that elements of direction are brought in later as therapy progresses.

What is paramount is that the needs of the child are being sought by the method of intervention and these needs will often alter during the course of a programme.

A case study follows to illustrate the course of a programme that is primarily non-directive. Examining this approach in the context of one individual can help us understand the purpose of considering the alternatives available to the therapist.

Case Study: Non-Directive Music Therapy

Jim's disabilities originated before birth. His mother, confined to a wheelchair, had a disabling degree of asthma and was dependent on a frequent supply of supplementary oxygen. He was born during an emergency Caesarean section at thirty-six weeks after signs of foetal distress during pregnancy. His condition at birth was poor, as he suffered from both hypoglycaemia and hypocalcaemia. He remained under observation in special care for five weeks and was found to be an irritable child requiring sedation. His initial medical assessment diagnosed him as having diplegic cerebral palsy with severe myopia and left alternating convergent squint. There was suspected global retardation and although he was multiply disabled, his hearing appeared to be within normal limits. His development was monitored on a regular basis by the health visitor and the paediatric team and he attended an assessment centre when he was four and a half.

Further assessment over the next two years revealed a clearer picture of Jim as he began to acquire basic skills. He made steady progress in a number of areas and good progress in language development. His vocabulary was above average and his understanding in the low average range. He was a likeable boy who made friends easily with his peers. He had a vivid imagination, loved dramatic stories and showed creative potential in contributing ideas to classroom stories. He was emerging more and more as an alert child and one that his parents felt learned quite quickly. His major difficulties at this stage were his limited mobility and his poor vision.

It was found that Jim became anxious very easily when he felt that an adult sounded annoyed. One reason for this was that he missed seeing a great deal of facial expression compared to the normal sighted child and relied heavily on the tone of the adult's voice for reassurance and guidance. He seemed to need increasing verbal feedback from staff working with him. Another aspect of his development that emerged was that he was easily distracted by the sound of things happening in his vicinity and this hindered the development of his concentration. His parents commented that although he was a sensitive boy he required sympathetic but firm handling. The educational psychologist felt that he was capable of rising to new demands made on him and that these should help his development, particularly in the area of self organisation.

Around the age of six he transferred to a school for children with physical disabilities. Sadly, his mother died just at this time and inevitably the emotional shock meant his development took a severe blow. In fact, there followed in relatively short succession two further losses. Both his grandfather, of whom he was very fond, and his family dog, another strong attachment, died. It seemed for Jim that at this time life was a series of traumas and disappointments. The trauma of family and maternal loss made a lasting impression on him, happening as it did at a critical time in his life. His problem of adjustment became a long-term one and one that was mirrored in his music therapy sessions in the future years.

Jim was aware of his own physical disabilities; despite being an active boy he was unable to run about outside at home like his neighbours' children or join in the football and other games they played together. He had difficulties learning to walk with his rollator and found manual and craft skills in the classroom dissatisfying because of his cerebral palsy. His poor vision compounded these difficulties and only served to add to his feeling of frustration and insecurity. He needed an appropriate medium in which to express these feelings. Active, improvised music-making in the therapeutic context gave him a dimension in which he could involve himself physically and expressively with much energy and satisfaction.

Directive intervention, in the form previously described, developed his capacity for some level of physical control and organisation. Over the months he became more aware of the control he had when he remembered to maintain a firm foot position to keep his balance. He also increased his ability to extend and use each arm independently.

Jim had a bus journey to and from school totalling two hours, as he lived on the periphery of the county. His father coped well considering the increased demands made upon him. As a keen sportsman, however, he was able to arrange to get out of the house some evenings and to meet with his friends, leaving Jim with a capable babysitter.

Initial Music Therapy Assessment

It was eighteen months later, when Jim was nearly eight that he was first referred for music therapy. Few details of the above information were known to me at the time of his initial assessment, other than that Jim's physical difficulties were compounded by the loss of his mother. It was felt that music therapy might provide the opportunity for him to work through the feelings he had with his situation. It was thought that in the long-term this might facilitate his education progress which was very slow and causing some concern.

General Behaviour

The first striking feature of Jim's behaviour in the therapy room was his considerable energy and exuberance when offered percussion instruments. He had no hesitation in playing, using his right hand in preference to his left, and making strong, irregular beats with great determination. He would talk a great deal during the session mainly asking questions about who I was, where did I live, what were the instruments called and whether I had some more. His playing was frequently interrupted by his talk and therefore lacked the fluency of musical expression. Although he was capable of asking 'sensible' questions, his timing of them was often inappropriate and without logical order. As with his comments he just seemed to say whatever came into his head. Whilst the questions might have indicated a desire for dialogue, his response to the answers showed that Jim's interest lay more in expressive monologue than in mutual conversation, e.g. 'Daddy go work', 'Can I have drink?' He was still very immature for an eight-year old; egocentric in demanding his choices of activity and not willing to co-operate in activities that were not self-directed. What hindered him considerably in his communication was his extremely poor concentration. He could aptly be described as having a 'butterfly' mind, settling on nothing for very long. Active music-making excited him very easily and there were few moments when he was still and silent. In this respect he was a challenging boy to work with.

Musical Behaviour

Engagement in musical activity was a very positive aspect of Jim's behaviour. His musical statements were usually loud, short bursts, interspersed with talking. What was clear was his great <u>need</u> to express himself; at first this appeared to be at an unconscious level through the music. He expressed much excitement together with a sense of frustration and aggression, through repetitive and heavily accented beating. Some of this was due to the limited gross motor control he had over his arms. However, it was the persistence of this style of playing that communicated these strong feelings.

It also suggested a strong desire to control the situation and mirrored an inner sense of insecurity he had about 'letting go'. It appeared to me that Jim's reluctance to have periods of silence in his improvisations was also a reflection of this. The adult world, it seemed, had let him down in depriving him of his mother. He feared a feeling of loss greatly, and overcompensated by clinging to what was immediately his, in this case his creative music. Another aspect of Jim's musical behaviour, influenced to a great extent by his visual limitations, was the difficulty he had in simple imitation. Since he lacked the clear visual clues most other children would rely on he found this an unrewarding task. It also meant that this was not a technique at his disposal for the musically interactive process of clinical improvisation.

Aspects of Therapy

Over the following months a therapy programme emerged that was essentially non-directive. The first noticeable change in his pattern of behaviour was the use of his voice. He loved songs and, although he could memorise only the first line or two of words, he developed a good knowledge of the tunes and could sing throughout. From this he began to improvise vocally (without words) with an energy that matched his instrumental playing. Rhythmically it was better organised than his physical playing and this later helped him develop better co-ordination in the use of his arms. It also increased the range of pitch he used over successive months. Perhaps the most significant aspect of his vocalising was that it began to displace the verbal statements made during his music-making and so became a part of the music rather than what seemed an interruption. There was a good stock of instruments in the therapy room and Jim would play most instruments if requested in any particular activity. However, over the next year his own preference was always the drum and the cymbal together. He would talk about these excitedly when walking with me to the session. One particular obsession that developed in his improvisation was the use of the rhythm pattern which sometimes, vocally, became a 'diddly um pum pum pum' pattern. One other difficulty for Jim was ending each session. He was aware that sessions took place only once a week, but he couldn't cope very well with saying or singing good-bye. He wasn't able to trust the fact that, unlike his mother, when people went away, they would come back again even if they assured him they would. The end of each session therefore, had to be carefully managed verbally and musically. Because he involved himself in such a dynamic way it was clearly important to 'bring him down' from the levels of intensity and excitement he felt and expressed. This had to be done gradually, sometimes taking ten minutes, to establish a calmer, quieter mood that he would accept. A practical way of achieving this was by removing one percussion instrument at a time from the set we were playing, leaving something like the bass metallophone till last. We would then talk about the next session instead of saying 'good-bye' and this helped Jim to look forward more positively. For most sessions this method worked, after he had absorbed it as part of his other rituals.

Interaction

As previously mentioned, this was an area of great difficulty for Jim. Although he had a limited vocabulary his expressive language was more than adequate to communicate his immediate needs and he had no difficulties with articulation. Most dialogue was initiated by him in the demand for a specific song, activity or 'the drum and the cymbal'. One encouraging aspect of his work however was that he was always happy to share musical improvisation, even though he did not seem very aware of my musical contribution. Very gradually he began to listen to my music and to accept it as part of our co-production. The development of his listening skills was an area of focus in the therapy. Jim liked dramatic and exciting sounds and would tolerate and attend more to different instruments being played for him. The effect that excited him most was that of the slow, gradual vocal crescendo coupled with a rising glissando between verses of 'Nellie the Elephant', sung with the guitar. This appeared to be one situation when he could best focus his attention for long enough to anticipate appropriately what was going to happen next. The excitement this generated in him was a great stimulus and of considerable satisfaction to him. This was one way, in fact, how he came to understand and participate in turn-taking without a verbal prompt, and it seemed that his musical play was beginning to take on an element of mutual exchange. Jim's music had always been regarded with significance and respect by me, even though for many months he was constrained by ritualistic behaviour and obsessive musical patterns.

It was questionable whether this approach was primarily a non directive one. I found over the four year period of therapy that, by maintaining a consistent non-directive start to each session, Jim was gradually more able to accept elements of direction at other moments in the session more as time proceeded. There were basic skills, such as active listening, waiting, watching, turn-taking and imitating that were valuable for him to become aware of consciously. His impaired communication skills could be enhanced by incorporating specific goals into his therapy programme, together with the freer and more liberating aspect of clinical improvisation. A great deal of work was done using the kazoo, which Jim played with relish. The tone of the instrument (rather like singing on comb and tissue paper) is unique in its nasal quality. This amused him and also motivated him to express more, vocally (his particular strength), in a playful manner. This was used in both non-directive and directive forms, incorporating some of his favourite tunes to focus his attention. The way that Jim was coping with more mutual give and take indicated that the relationship had grown, and that he could accept and trust my intervention.

While developments were slowly and gradually taking place over the first two years of music therapy, there was still concern about Jim's educational progress. This 'alert' boy was having difficulty in many areas of his school work, concentration appearing to be the main problem. Tearful outbursts and refusals to do the work requested were also becoming more frequent. What transpired later was that around this time his father was courting again and, understandably, his attention was distracted from his son more than usual. Over the following months Jim's music took on a more powerful quality of expression. What appeared to be happening was a delayed reaction to his mother's death. He began to grieve outwardly through anger and sadness in both his improvisations and his verbal outbursts. His unconscious processes were beginning to manifest themselves in a conscious way and music gave him a legitimate opportunity to express his anger. For this he turned to the cymbal and, together with me, would beat violently, increasing the intensity of sound until the combination of anger and excitement would bring him to scream cathartically at the climax of each episode. These episodes would be repeated three or four times during a session over a period of about six weeks, normally mid-session, during the course of his shared improvisation. I found that Jim's physical and vocal catharsis could be brought out at the appropriate moment in the session by a gradual crescendo on the cymbal. On several occasions Jim would break down into tears and express verbally some of his feelings, such as 'It's all my fault', 'Don't know where my Mum is', 'Why did she die?'.

The music had served as a catalyst to bring about verbal expression, reasoning and increased self-awareness. He carried a great guilt that he didn't save his mother from dying. He felt considerable anger that she had 'left' him and had much difficulty coping with these feelings. As a result of this and his related anxiety he experienced symptoms of a tight tummy', which he said, he hated.

There were times when I was able to reflect his feelings verbally and tried to help Jim talk through them. However, he was experiencing a complex set of emotions which he had great difficulty in understanding. His ability to reason was obviously clouded by these emotions. Around this time the school appointed a full-time counsellor and Jim took the opportunity of going to her regularly over the weeks to talk and spend some time. The counsellor and I met on a regular basis to discuss Jim's development and gain insights to the situation from new perspectives. The counsellor attended one of Jim's sessions and was able to witness at first hand his characteristic musical improvisation.

Evaluation

Music therapy was just one part of the treatment and education programme that Jim was being given. It was important to make some objective evaluation of this work. Informally this was being done during the course of treatment through contact and discussion with other professionals involved with Jim. Annual reviews and case conferences were particularly valuable, as the full team was able to discuss his situation together. One resource that served well in this respect was the video records that I kept. On a training day these were shown to the school staff of all departments. They were all very familiar with Jim and most had worked with him at some stage of his schooling. However, what they found the most revealing from the video was the intensity and duration of the feelings he was expressing through his improvisations. Subsequently, it was decided to allocate time available to Jim for counselling immediately after a music therapy session if he wished to take it up. This proved to be a purposeful outcome of the team consultation. One constructive criticism that also arose was that, after two years of music therapy, he was indulging in a rather narcissistic form of self-pity which was actually being supported and fed by his music. I did not agree that this was the case in Jim's situation. We had got to know and understand each other quite well over the years of working together. He was a boy who had a great need to express himself; he was rarely passive. It could be said that he had every right to feel sorry for himself. However, the emotions that he was expressing, principally through the music, and occasionally verbally, were certainly more powerful and consistent than those of mere self-pity. In music therapy Jim found an expressive dimension that was liberating and meaningful.

Jim's difficulties are by no means resolved. Major changes in the home situation with his father remarrying and new children arriving in the family have caused him to regress as a consequence at these critical events. There is evidence, however, in and outside his music therapy sessions that, despite his multiple disability Jim is developing a more mature attitude towards difficult situations and his life in general. At times he is able to see the positive side of his great energy and enjoy the sheer pleasure of his own exuberant music. Music therapy has been a partner to him over a wide range of personal experiences. One trusts that the effects of these events will serve him in the future as a meaningful experience.

Conclusion

In debating the issue regarding directive and non-directive intervention with the child with cerebral palsy, it is pertinent to consider how these approaches contrast and complement each other. Each has value when it meets the needs of the child. On the one hand, the freedom for musical expression that non-directive therapy offers is a vital component in the therapeutic process. The catalyst for the developing relationship between the therapist and the child is their mutual understanding of spontaneous interaction. Effective therapy exists because of this. On the other hand, freedom without clear boundaries, musically or behaviourally, is not always desirable or appropriate. The extent of these boundaries can be re-defined and renegotiated by the therapist and child as therapy progresses, according to the responses and needs of the child. It is not simply a question of whether a programme should be directive or non-directive. It may be important to incorporate different aspects of each approach with a bias towards one or other during the course of a balanced therapy programme. These timely decisions of the therapist are developed as part of the therapeutic and musical artistry in his or her work.

12

Music Therapy in the Education Service: Research with Autistic Children and their Mothers

Auriel Warwick

Introduction: Music Therapy in Education

Relatively few music therapists in Britain work for education authorities. This is due partly to the present economic climate where, though the value of music for children with special needs is recognised by teachers and therapists of other disciplines, financial administrators are often reluctant to see music therapy as a high priority. The other major factor is the lack of knowledge about music therapy - how it works and why it can be so effective. Perhaps therapy as a concept, particularly when related to the creative arts, is still viewed with suspicion by some in the education field. Music therapists must take on the responsibility for dispelling such suspicion and anxieties by being open about their aims and methods: talking in seminars to colleagues in schools, school governors, running workshops and presenting videos of individual and group work with children so that the value of the therapy can be seen in the context of the whole curriculum for the child. The approach is holistic, aiming to promote the balance between the emotional, physical, intellectual and social development of the individual.

Music teaching is concerned with the end musical product, whether as a classroom activity or a public performance. Of course, the sensitive teacher is aware of the non-musical implications such as initiative-taking, the building of self-reliance, self esteem and the ability to mix and negotiate within a social group. The changes in attitudes in music education over the past few years have meant that there is a broadening 'grey' area where therapy and teaching can meet on common ground. This is positive and needs to be acknowledged by therapists and teachers. So, in the light of this changing climate, what has the therapist to offer that the teacher does not?

Both professional groups know that music is special. Its meaning is individual to each listener and performer. It does not rely on language and has the power to reach out to the emotions, enabling us to feel and express something deep within us which cannot always be expressed in words. It can change our mood, it can make us laugh or cry. It can allow us to express ourselves publicly in music composed and performed for special occasions, or it can be very private. The problem is that music has seemed to become over-specialised. Rather than being central to our culture, it is too often considered only for those who are talented. How often do we hear, 'I love listening to music, but I'm not musical. I never learnt to play an instrument'. How many natural and instinctive musicians have we lost through this attitude? While we want our musically gifted to have every opportunity to develop their art, what about the majority who have a love of music, but not the aptitude or desire to become professional musicians in a crowded profession.

Fortunately, music educators in Britain are beginning to recognise the importance of music for all children - but unfortunately there is still a long way to go before all educators, administrators and politicians are as convinced. It remains to be seen how effectively the National Curriculum, with music as a foundation subject, can change opinion. Something must be done to rescue our musical heritage; not only that of Britain, but also to preserve the musical culture of the ethnic minorities, which provide vital resources for sharing and mutual understanding.

Music therapy and music education should be complementary while recognising the essential differences.

1. The therapist in training is concerned with the study of the psychology of music and the understanding of medical and paramedical pathologies in addition to maintaining a high standard of musical skills. The trainee teacher studies theories of education and teaching practices.

2. The therapist is trained to observe individual musical and non-musical responses closely in order to assess and diagnose needs.

3. The therapist is also particularly concerned with encouraging the release of emotions and the confronting of these emotions, providing musical support while the child may need to play, vocalise or sing at a level which would be tolerable in the classroom.

4. It is not the role of the therapist to teach musical concepts such as rhythm, dynamics, pitch or notation, although children often do learn some of these in the course of their experimentation and discovery using instrumental and vocal sounds. The teacher has specific objectives of teaching, including attainment targets, to be reached within a lesson or series of lessons, guiding the children towards the assimilation of knowledge.

5. The therapist must maintain flexibility in approach, to tune in to the individual needs and responses, following the child rather than leading; supporting and developing those responses in as equal a partnership with the child as possible. To be effective in this, the therapist works with individuals and small groups, ideally of no more than five or six, with adult assistance where necessary with profound and multiple disabilities.

6. In teaching, the music is the main objective; in therapy, the music is the tool for relating and communicating, not an end in itself.

Development of Music Therapy in Oxfordshire

After qualifying as a music therapist, I was employed on a full-time peripatetic basis by the Oxfordshire Education Authority. Work began in September, 1972, in five special schools with a range from moderate learning difficulties to severe with multiple handicaps. I was, and still am, responsible to the county music adviser; at that stage, a special needs adviser had not yet been appointed. It was a difficult period. Not only was I trying to find my feet as a therapist, but this was also the transitional period when the former Junior Training Centres under the administration of Health became schools under Education, following the 1970 Education Act. The schools needed qualified teachers, many of whom had had no specific training in working with children with varying special needs. It was more than enough for them to have to find the necessary levels for communicating with some very difficult children, let alone to work out suitable programmes of work. Put the demands of visiting therapists on top of all this and we have a recipe for mental, physical and emotional stress of a high order. I was very aware of the problems and felt that it would not be appropriate for an over-zealous input from me at that early stage.

Communicating with the teachers and other therapists was vital and I tried to make sure that there was some time, either between sessions when I took the children back to their classrooms, or at break times, when I explained what had happened during the sessions and what my aims were for each child. For example, where my predominant aim for a child was to build a relationship through shared music-making, I was able to report when the child made the first attempt to turn-take with me on a set of bongo drums. This was the time for discussion about any problems which might have arisen before or during the session and at this time I also had the opportunity to observe the children who had individual and group therapy. Feedback later in the day from the teacher about any carry-over effects from the therapy session helped me to decide the direction of the therapy. Where possible - this was the time before the video camera made a valuable contribution - a teacher would be invited to sit in on a session. The two-way communication was useful for both for us.

In those early days, expectations of the staff were often confused. Was music therapy another way of explaining music education? What was I teaching the children? Were they learning how to play instruments?

The adjustment to looking at music as a means of providing a channel for communicating seemed to be a difficult one to make. At the same time, teachers' own expectations of what they might teach their children, particularly in reading, writing and doing number work, were often unrealistic. It was not surprising that such an alien concept as expressing feelings through the use of instruments and voices could not be understood very readily.

Gradually, attitudes began to change as experience and opportunities for additional training grew. The needs of the whole child began to be recognised and the place of the creative arts seen as more relevant, not just as entertainment. My own attitudes also changed as I learnt to see how music therapy could complement the aims of individual children's educational programmes and form a valuable contributing partnership with speech therapy and physiotherapy. It was practical experience within the multi-disciplinary team that made the changes. The Annual Case Review was a further opportunity for discussion, not only with other professionals but even more importantly with parents. Meeting and talking with parents could change a whole perspective of working with the children and I became convinced that far more should be done with families - working with them, sharing and exchanging experiences and developing strategies for treatment. I was not convinced that we were supporting parents in education as well as we should.

Throughout the years I have been working for Oxfordshire, I have changed the schools where I have worked as a therapist so that a different geographical area could be covered.

Unfortunately, with government cuts in funding, a second music therapy post did not materialise. I am now based in the south of the county. With this move came the opportunities to work with autistic children: the first in a hospital school for children who also had severe learning difficulties and the second in a resource unit on a primary school campus. Having broadened my range of experience, I was able to make a fresh start, particularly in the area of staff communications, by giving series of workshops which included 'hands-on' experience for teachers, assistants and other therapists. How I was working and the effects of that work were now more easily understood and referrals were made for valid reasons - not 'because young John is so musical', but rather, 'John is so withdrawn and communication is extremely difficult'. Calls for help were also coming in from other schools - both special and mainstream - where there was a particular problem concerning a child with special needs and where a positive musical response had been noted. Could this be developed in any way? Eventually, this advisory work was recognised and has become part of my working week.

A maximum of two days each week, depending on demand, is set aside for covering all schools and units within the county where there are children with special needs. This includes mainstream schools. The work of an advisory teacher involves:

1. Working closely with teachers, giving advice about specific problems relating to a child's particular needs

2. Helping with suitable repertoire.

3. Planning of activities within the scope of each teacher's abilities, and developing those abilities through in-service training.

It is essentially a support service. Many teachers are drawn towards the therapeutic application of music and there is a great deal they can do in their own music sessions. I can teach them simple communicative techniques using instruments and voices which do not require high proficiency in musical skills. Lack of confidence in using music is very common and I often find it helpful for the teacher to be part of the group while I take a demonstration session. This is not a group music therapy session but music education with a therapeutic bias. The groups are class groups, often too large and complex in their needs for a therapy group. Musical skills may be taught as part of the music curriculum within the school. The emphasis is more on musical results while maintaining a balance with the non-musical aspects such as confidence-building and socialisation. The teacher is also given the opportunity to observe the responses of his or her children - and to question me about why some of the more unexpected responses might occur. Music can be a very useful tool for revealing a side of the child's personality not usually seen. The normally withdrawn child may show great energy when given a drum to play. Similarly, the hyperactive child may show sensitivity and an unexpected capacity for structure.

I do feel special concern for the mainstream teacher who is confronted by a child with special needs for the first time, having had no experience of such problems despite years of experience in education. As well as supporting the child in such an instance by giving therapy, it has been necessary to support the teacher, listening to problems encountered in the classroom, offering information about the particular pathology, and giving some practical ideas to work on.

But perhaps the most important aspect of my own personal development as a therapist can be seen through my work with autistic children. This is an area into which I went with considerable apprehension. Most of the children with whom I had worked were, despite a wide variety of problems, sociable. They were able to make a musical and personal relationship. What could I do for a child who existed with a high level of anxiety and who had great difficulties making a relationship?

The Challenge of Autism

There are differences of opinion and approach to the problem of autism. While these need to be recognised and evaluated, my experience is that no one treatment will be necessarily the right one for all people with autistic behaviour.

Michael Rutter has defined childhood autism in terms of four essential criteria. They are (1) an onset before the age of 30 months: (2) impaired social development; (3) delayed and deviant language development and (4) insistence on routine, shown by stereotyped behaviour patterns, such as spinning objects or flapping the hands, with strong resistance to change. In addition to this definition, the intellectual level, medical conditions and the psychosocial situation must be taken into account. There are theories about the possible cause or causes of autism but still we have no definite answer. Some knowledge of the pathology is one thing: how parents, teachers and therapists are to cope with the various manifestations of autistic behaviour is another.

There is an enormous range of behaviours; from very mild, where the autistic person may be described as odd or eccentric but reasonably able to cope with most aspects of everyday life, to severe, where lifelong support and care will be necessary.

The ethological approach - observing how the child behaves - is one which is readily appreciated by anyone working with autistic children. Both Tinbergen and John Richer have described the autistic child's avoidance of social interactions, a notable aspect of the impaired social development. Compared with non autistic children, autistic children seem to have a lowered threshold for avoidance. They may show this by moving away, looking beyond whoever has made the approach, or turning the head away. They will be found on the periphery of areas or activities. If a social approach is made by the autistic person, there seems to be conflict within that approach: the child may take some steps forward, then move back before approaching again. The autistic child will take flight if an over-intrusive approach is made. This does not mean that he or she will always avoid physical contact. Where trust has grown between the child and parents or another familiar adult, rough and tumble play can be enjoyed.

Interesting objects are easier for the autistic child to cope with than people.

Fifty per cent of autistic children do not speak and those that do show some characteristic oddities such as the reversal of the pronouns 'I' and 'you'. They may be echolalic, repeating the phrase or sentence they have just heard, particularly if there is a problem of understanding. Learnt phrases may be repeated in an inappropriate context. The voice is often marked by a strange, flat intonation, although it may be perfectly pitched in singing. An unusual perception of language can be apparent, such as one boy with whom I work who, at a stage when he was frightened of dogs and refused to say the word 'dog', referred to them instead as 'woof person'.

When the autistic child is in a state of conflict and extreme anxiety, stereotyped behaviour patterns may be seen. There will often be a favourite object to 'twiddle'. The difficulty for those coping with the child is the question of how to wean him or her away from the object which impedes anything else being approached, observed or learnt.

All these factors make up what can be observed in the autistic-type behaviour. As a music therapist, I had to learn how they would affect the musical and non-musical responses which could be observed in the therapy session. I also had to learn about the emotional responses and how difficult they might be for the autistic child to express.

The Role of Music for the Autistic Child

Juliette Alvin, at the beginning of her book, *Music Therapy for the Autistic Child*, describes music as a 'field of multifarious experiences which affect man's mind, body and emotions'. She goes on to show, through descriptive case studies, how music can penetrate the subconscious, revealing much of what can be hidden and how it can put us in touch with an environment. It is a very flexible medium in which to work. Its fluidity and ongoing movement of sounds and silences, through a structure of time and rhythm, provides a unique means of opportunity for two-way communication. It is this communicating and relating which is so difficult for the autistic child within the normal social interaction of language and gesture.

In my own initial period of discovering and learning about individual autistic children's responses to music, I found that the conflict behaviour of approaching and withdrawing was clearly observable. One of the most obvious was during a session with a six-year-old boy while we were involved in an activity called Bongo Talk, sitting on the floor opposite each other. Bongo drums were being used for turn-taking - a form of two-way communication through music. David had no problems with the concept of turn-taking, beating rhythmic phrases to me using his own drum or mine or a combination of the two. At this stage in our relationship, trust had grown so that I felt able to challenge him more. The activity had just begun. With a hand raised higher than usual, I made a slow, downward movement towards the drum - which might be interpreted as teasing or threatening. This challenge could not be made before a bond had been established. David watched my hand and just before it reached the drum, he moved away. But, quickly, he moved back to the drum to respond. This happened a few times until he allowed himself to be involved in the communicative play. Generally, his playing was energetic, matching me in his ways of using his hands, whether with the palm of the hand, fingertips or as fists. He was able to initiate his own rhythmic patterns and as he became involved, he initiated vocalisation, sometimes using repeated verbal phrases. I responded in kind, beginning with some imitation of what he had done, but also developing his vocal sounds into longer musical phrases. On this occasion, his range of pitches was varied. The approach/withdraw behaviour disappeared as soon as we were able to share a very real communication. Apart from emotional outbursts, David's conversation tended to be stilted, lacking spontaneity, often repeating some of the other person's words and phrases. Because he had some understanding of language, it was easy for others to believe him more intelligent than he was. Our interaction through rhythmic and vocal improvising bypassed the complexities of language. I felt emotionally close to him: such moments with a non-relating person are to be treasured as they may not happen with progressive regularity. For the autistic person, progress can be measured only over an extended period of time: years rather than months.

The other aspects of behaviour which particularly interested me were the stereotypes such as the spinning and repeated patterns of behaviour with objects, again manifest when the child was in a state of conflict. Careful observation was necessary to assess whether any of the instruments would be used in such a way. Apart from the cymbal, I have not experienced any specific problems with the large instruments. I don't use the snare drum, as fingers could become over-fascinated by the wires under the drum and the sharp, rattling sound is disturbing for some children. The cymbal is ideal for spinning and there have been a few instances when I have had to decide that the cymbal would not be in the room during successive sessions. However, I have known the sound to take precedence over the shape and the movement. The use of small, hand-held instruments needs watching. It is useful to have the opportunity to observe the children in the classroom and the playground so that potential problems may be avoided.

As I became more familiar with the observable behaviour, I began to conjecture more about why particular children responded to vocal and instrumental sounds in the ways they did and what it might reveal about the inner world of each child. There was also a rigidity in the behaviour of these children which prevented the exploration through play seen in normal child development. Gradually, some specific aims in music therapy for autistic children began to evolve. This did not mean that these aims couldn't apply to other types of learning difficulties but rather that they seemed very relevant, leading towards the overall aim of helping the children to relate to people and to their environment so that they did not always have to withdraw when confronted by new situations and change of routine.

Through the medium of sound discovery, sound making and music, I wanted to help the autistic child to relax, to feel safe enough to explore and enjoy success within the boundaries of not damaging self, other people or the instruments. I wanted the child to discover that when he or she produced sounds, those sounds would be responded to on his or her own level - the realisation of this was important to the growth of the relationship between child and therapist.

It was also very important to respect the child's silences and to give space, both physical and emotional, in which the relationship should develop. I wanted music to help the child towards some insight into him or herself, to develop self-awareness and to become aware of what it is like to interact with others and to share.

These central aims have remained with me throughout the ten years of working with autistic children or those with autistic features. Much of my present work with these children is carried out in the Chinnor Resource Unit which, at the time of writing, has three bases: Chinnor (primary), Thame (secondary) and Oxford (junior, middle and secondary). Each base is attached to a mainstream school into which the children may be integrated for particular subjects, with adult support, if and when they are ready. The strength of the unit lies in its belief in and practice of the co-existence of education and therapies and how each relates to the other. It is very forward-thinking, and therefore perhaps controversial. The staff is well prepared in the aims for the children both individually and as a group. But it is not only the children who are important but also the parents. Meetings with parents are regular. There is an open door so that they are welcome to come and discuss problems. Teachers are also prepared to go into the family home. There is not one overall approach, apart from as low a level of intrusion from teachers, therapists and helpers as possible. The philosophy is more psycho-dynamic than behavioural. What might work for individual children is tried and tested. This calls for flexibility, imagination, learning about new techniques and constant staff consultation.

In the Chinnor Resource Unit and Smith Hospital School in Henley-on-Thames (now closed) I took part in a research project which began in September, 1986, with Pierrette Muller, a research psychologist. The idea grew after discussions with Dr John Richer following a video workshop in which I showed some of my work with the Chinnor children. His main argument was that there were some lovely examples of communication between the child and me but what about involving the mother and making the duo into a trio? My reaction could well be described as typical conflict behaviour - a strong conviction that this was a direction in which therapists should be moving, i.e. involving families, combined with anxiety about my changing role in the trio; having to involve mother as well.

Within the existing climate of family therapy, we would like to have involved fathers. But from a practical point of view, this was not possible as we had to arrange the sessions during the day and all of our fathers were employed. However, they were involved in the questionnaires, designed by Muller, looking at any changes in attitudes and expectations as the project progressed.

The Research Project

Muller decided to define four hypotheses to be investigated.
1. Music therapy shows some positive effects in autistic children.
2. The effects will generalise into everyday life.
3. The mother's involvement will help the generalisation.
4. The mother's perception of and attitude towards her child will become more positive, so helping to build communication, through sound and music, because the communication begins on the child's level.

Ten children, divided into two groups, began the project with nine completing the research period of 20 to 22 sessions. There were two main ten session blocks, coinciding with the first two terms of the school year. For the first ten weeks, Group 1 received music therapy without mother present, while Group 2 had music therapy including mother. During the second block of ten weeks, the groups 'crossed over' so that Group 1 included mother and Group 2 was alone with me. As it was considered that the family home would provide a more consistent environment than the schools where unexpected changes often take place, we worked in the homes, with a video camera recording throughout.

As Muller is looking at the carry-over effects before and after music therapy, mothers were asked to play with the children for fifteen minutes before therapy and again for fifteen minutes after. The activity might be drawing, reading, playing games, doing puzzles or building with bricks or Lego. As long as the child was kept in the room, it didn't matter whether he or she was active all the time or not. In assessing the results of the project, it is hoped to measure:-
1. Short-term changes between the before and after therapy activities.
2. The longer term effects in the same situation, from week 1 to week 20, and also in the music therapy sessions over the period of the research.
3. An evaluation of the presence of the mother and her participation in the therapy session through a comparison between the two blocks of sessions - with and without mother.

Parents were involved in completing sets of questionnaires before the project began; in the middle of the point of cross-over and again at the end. For me, this was the beginning of two different partnerships; one with my psychologist colleague who, in addition to taking on the responsibility of the research and its writing-up, was always present with the camera, and the other with the mothers of the children. With some of the children I had already established a musical and personal relationship in the school setting. My anxieties centred on these already established relationships and how to involve mother so that she could be an active participant without feeling at a total disadvantage. Perhaps, given enough time, she might even take over my role. The other problem, more of a practical one, was having to limit the variety of instruments according to what could be transported. My main instrument, the piano, could not be considered since only two of the homes had one. The same instruments had to be offered for all. My personal instrument became the guitar which has some wonderful qualities, including its ease of access for the children to touch and play, strumming it while I changed the chords. I had to cope with missing the range of dynamics, expression and pitch of the piano. The electronic keyboard which I used with some of the children did not have enough amplification to act as a support instrument in therapy although those children who used it were fascinated by the different timbres of sound and variety of programmed rhythms.

Parents' expectation of music therapy varied. I suspect that in the initial stages of the programme, many thought that it must involve some form of teaching. As one of the questionnaires was concerned with what parents believed music therapy to be, with comparisons to be made between the three sets as already mentioned, I wasn't in a position to clarify what music therapy is and the way it works. Whether the lack of this knowledge has affected the results of the research remains to be seen. It may be very little. Even with the intervention from me with those mothers who felt that their children must be actively participating throughout the session and were over-intrusive because of their anxiety, the situation didn't change. They understood intellectually what I was saying - that they should avoid eye contact with the child and that the child did not have to participate all the time if he or she didn't want to - but the level of anxiety remained too high. My personal view is that they could not help their intrusion into the child's space and the number of sessions on the programme was too few for long-term changes to take effect. Although there were limitations while working under research conditions, the experience for me was very valuable.

From most of the mothers' points of view, there were two issues which were difficult for them. One was one of the main active ingredients of the music therapy session - improvising. The free and spontaneous use of music was particularly difficult for those who had any degree of traditional music training, either from private lessons or from their own school music education. The second issue was the presence of the video camera. It didn't seem to bother the children who were used to being filmed at school but the mothers were aware of it throughout the programme, especially during the music therapy sessions. This relates directly to the first problem - that most of them felt self-conscious participating in a different approach to music. This awareness of the camera was not so marked in the play activities which took place before and after the therapy.

The main initial problem for Muller and I to overcome was working in the family home. Professionals are very adept at sitting in their ivory towers and pontificating on what their clients and families ought to do. Too often there is a lack of any real understanding of how the dynamics of that family work and how the members experience their lives and their problems. I felt extremely vulnerable until I was accepted; i.e. when trust developed between us. Through this experience, my understanding of the problems of the mother/autistic child relationship was enhanced. I learnt to empathise with more than one point of view and gained first-hand knowledge of ways in which these children could control and manipulate their families. I have a great deal more respect now for those mothers who do have to battle against some tremendous odds - and I am impressed time and time again by their capacity to love in spite of it all. Perhaps the great challenge to therapy and to educational practice is to work within the environment of the home where there are problems. I am convinced it would change many attitudes: for professionals and parents alike, each learning from the other.

When the research period was over, three of the mothers wished to carry on: one for a further year, the second still continues in therapy with her child while the third, Pat with her son, Richard, had a further seven months. By the end of the seven months there had been a powerful resolution when Pat was able to take over my role as the therapist, both in her approach to Richard and through her music-making with him. A description of this case study follows.

Case Study: Richard and Pat

Pat had had one miscarriage before Richard was conceived. During the first three months of the second pregnancy she was worried that she might miscarry again. However, after that period was over, she was well and enjoyed being pregnant. When Pat was twelve days overdue, she was taken to hospital and induced, giving birth after a difficult nine hour labour. She was given pethidine which meant that Richard was sleepy and needed oxygen after he was born. Pat was told this was perfectly normal. He was a lovely baby.

Pat believed her husband was possessive about his son to the extent that Pat felt he resented the fact that she could breast-feed Richard and he couldn't. His arrival home from work each evening coincided with Richard's time for crying for a long period. This upset both father and son - father because he had had no experience of the father role model himself and became very demanding towards his baby son in the ways he tried to distract him from crying. Pat now feels that her husband felt rejected through his own childhood experience. This was a difficult period in the marriage.

Before Richard was ten months old, Pat began to realise that there might be something wrong. There were a lot of tantrums and he seemed to ignore her. Later, when they went to the local toddler group, he would go to the small pedal cars, turning them over and spinning all the wheels at once. He was obsessive about objects. Pat even though about the term 'autistic' although she had no real idea about what it meant. She found it painful to see the progress of her friends' children when Richard seemed to make none.

Two years after Richard's birth, a sister was born. At the same time, further difficulties were being experienced in the marriage. Eventually, Richard was referred to a main hospital where the paediatrician could find nothing wrong. Hearing and sight were tested. Often he appeared not to hear and he did odd things with his eyes where he would track along parallel lines or along the horizon. Finally a referral was made to Dr John Richer, Principal Clinical Psychologist in the paediatrics department at the John Radcliffe Hospital in Oxford. As far as Pat was concerned, here was someone who wasn't telling her that nothing was wrong or that 'he would grow out of it'. Dr Richer observed and filmed Richard on video at intervals in the family home. He also suggested that Richard should be seen by a neurologist. This took place but there was no neurological damage. A diagnosis of mild autism was made and practical suggestions were made for coping with management of the problems including diet. Nursery schooling had its ups and downs. Not everyone, including some of the medical fraternity, understood the problems, particularly as the child was attractive and looked normal. Pat had further discussion with Dr Richer when she decided to move back to Oxford so that Richard could attend first the nursery school attached to a first school. This school also provided the Oxford base for the Chinnor Resource Unit for autistic children and those with predominant autistic features, including obsessive behaviour and difficulties in making relationships. At this time, Pat and her husband finally separated.

When the research programme began, Richard was six years of age, a good-looking, fair-headed child with blue-grey eyes that searched out objects rather than people. The video camera, the audio cassette recorder and the video lamp were sources of great fascination for him. Richard spoke clearly with a slightly flat falling intonation in his voice and could hold a reasonable conversation. He read well although his level of comprehension was lower that his reading ability. He was in the group who, for the first block of sessions, had therapy with me alone.

During the first session, I had to discover Richard's personality; his ability to communicate and share as well as where he was in music. As the session opened, I called him to the guitar case. He told me there was a guitar in there and when I lifted the lid, he helped me take it out. Tuning had to be checked for which I used a tuning fork. When I held it to his ear, he wanted to hold it himself. He strummed the two lower strings before becoming distracted by the large cymbal on its stand. He commented that 'it's like a wheel' as he turned it. I called him back to the guitar, using it to accompany me singing a series of Hello's, leaving silences between in which Richard could respond. He chose not to although there were two quiet throaty sounds. He accepted the invitation to strum the guitar - when I lifted the lid, he helped me take it out. Tuning had to be checked for which I used a tuning fork. When I held it to his ear, he wanted to hold it himself. He strummed the two lower strings before becoming distracted by the large cymbal on its stand. He commented that 'it's like a wheel' as he turned it. I called him back to the guitar, using it to accompany me singing a series of Hello's, leaving silences between in which Richard could respond. He chose not to, although there were two quiet throaty sounds. When I introduced very short staccato chords, he began to interact with some turn-taking; the first indication of two-way communication. On brief occasions, there was eye contact between us.

When I put the bongo drums on their stand, Richard made car noises. I played a short drum roll. He responded on the cymbal. Further interaction followed with Richard showing that he was aware when the drum dynamics changed. Sometimes he was prepared to follow me. I indicated that he could play the drum as well as the cymbal if he wanted to. Our playing ended with my climatic beat on the drums to which Richard responded with two cymbal clashes.

I placed the smaller percussion instruments on the table - the tambour, tambourine, bells and maracas so that Richard could play and change when he liked. It became chaotic when he persisted in placing the tambour on top o f the tambourine, but the intention and the beating was definite. By this time it was coming to the end of the twenty minute session. I returned to the guitar. Richard counted the strings and ran his finger up and along them. I sang that it was nearly time for us to stop while he accompanied with some strumming. This led into the good-bye section. Richard sang one quiet 'Bye' before helping me put the guitar away in its case and fastening the catches for me.

From this session, it was clear to me that Richard had a desire to be dominant and in control. There was a strong will. Yet he was aware of changing dynamics between forte and piano and ready to use them, sometimes to respond to them. There were a few times when he smiled as he played. Pat was able to give me some feedback as well. She was listening as she worked in the kitchen. She was fascinated to hear what he was doing and in the following play session she found him more relaxed - and she felt more relaxed herself.

The determination to dominate was borne out in successive sessions leading to his final session with me alone. Other instruments were added to the collection: xylophone, chime bars and electronic keyboard. However, although Richard had problems with concentration, he did not flit between the full range of instruments available. By the final session in the first block of sessions, he preferred the keyboard, bongo drums and cymbal on stands and occasionally the tambourine. Given the choice, the keyboard was his favourite. He enjoyed changing the timbre of sounds by selecting the tone stops he wanted and he used the rhythm stops with great effect, mainly to control the tempi but also as a jamming, or blocking out device.

At the beginning of the session, Richard helped with the extension lead for the keyboard. He had a good understanding of plugs and switches. In the hello section, as usual, he did not respond vocally but played the appropriate rhythmic motif on the keyboard in response. I chose to play the drums and cymbal. There was a short period of turn-taking between us before Richard began to challenge me by his use of the rhythm section. He often watched what I was playing and there was some direct eye contact and a wicked grin whenever he turned the tempo switch to its fastest speed. His improvising varied between using the rhythm section on its own, playing single notes, often in a scale pattern and playing chord clusters, either with his fingers or with the whole forearm. As he became more involved, the music was more atonal. Richard was still in control musically but he accepted verbal direction from me when I suggested it was time for a changeover.

I took over the keyboard while he moved to the drums and cymbal. He chose to play with the brushes first, later changing to the beaters when he realised that he wanted a wider range of dynamics. However, within one minute of the new arrangement, he could not resist coming over to the keyboard to start the rhythm section before returning to the percussion.

We ended the session with both of us at the keyboard. Richard became inventive and quite imaginative. He discovered, by experimenting, that he could manipulate the Select rocker switch to produce octave leaps on a single note. He said this reminded him of a donkey's 'hee-haw'. Later, as his fingers moved in steps and hops up the keys, I commented that it sounded like someone going upstairs. He replied that it was him. Then he played high-pitched chord clusters which he announced was a baby crying. After the good-bye section, I explained to Richard that his mother would be with us in the following group of sessions. 'Is she?' was the reply. During this short conversation, he persisted in playing the keyboard so that, finally, I had to be very directive and tell him to turn it off. As usual, he helped me to dismantle the instruments and put them away. I found it necessary to be verbally directive with Richard so that he would move around the instruments rather than remaining at the keyboard. More of Richard was revealed to me when he was playing the percussion. He was too fascinated by the wealth of sounds produced by the keyboard for him to give himself time really to express himself. Later, he was more prepared to share the keyboard and to let himself be more involved with the other instruments. He had become more communicative verbally as the weeks progressed and was able to look at me more often.

The first session of the second block involved Pat for the first time. Richard looked to me a lot when the session started but gradually, as Pat was insistent through her musical improvising that she was there, he accepted the changed situation and began to enjoy it. During this session, I led the changes of instruments and activities and encouraged Richard to tell Pat the names of the instruments. At first he was reluctant but when we both quietly insisted, he complied. Laughter came early in the session and the musical interaction began when I was at the keyboard with Pat and Richard together on the drums and cymbal. When Pat joined her son on the cymbal, he allowed the intrusion and even briefly imitated her stroking movements with the brush around the circumference of the instrument. Soon, he abandoned the brush in favour of a beater and began a constant beat. Earlier, I had picked up the tambourine and Pat and I wove different rhythms around Richard's beat. There was good eye contact between mother and son but son was still determined to be the dominant member of the trio, playing with energy. When we ended, he claimed it made his ears ache. We agreed.

The next interesting interaction came when Pat had her turn at the keyboard. As he had with me, Richard couldn't resist interfering by changing stops and introducing the rhythms. Pat had inaugurated a 5/4 beat - 3:2 - a single note followed by one or two chords. Twice he stopped, leaving us to play as a duo.

I suggested that the two of them might like to play together on the keyboard. Pat changed to triple time. Richard was determined to use the rhythm section but complied when we commented that we needed a tune. He wasn't going to give in that easily however and soon invaded Pat's space in the bass. He played on one note before announcing that it sounded like a robot - 'I am a robot'. Pat suggested that he played the phrase. He repeated his note seven times. Pat responded by singing, 'I am a robot, I am'. I sang it after her. Richard then amended it to, 'I am a robot, are you?'

Pat sang and played the new phrase to which he answered, 'Yes' Richard thought the robot might run down, to which his mother sang, 'I am a robot, I'm sad', with a semitone fall on 'sad'.

There was mutual laughter during his improvisation, which continued when Pat held down a brass chord while Richard changed the stops. We listened to the different timbres. Richard had moved close to Pat so that he was leaning against her. When she asked if they should sing a robot song, he replied no. At this point, I intervened to introduce the good-bye section. During this, Richard took his mother's hand and guided it on to the keys he wanted her to play. When we arrived at the actual exchange of good-byes, Richard responded using a funny voice, probably suggested to him by the strange-sounding mandolin stop which Pat had imitated with her voice earlier. In the music therapy sessions, he rarely sang using his natural voice - he preferred to hide behind other voices. We had to meet him on the same ground, using a variety of vocal sounds.

As a result of this initial session of the second block of sessions, I felt that music could be a very positive mode of relating, sharing and communicating for Richard and Pat. Though she admitted to being untrained, Pat was a natural and instinctive musician, able to pick up and respond to musical cues. Because of circumstances in her personal life, she began to use the music-making as therapy for herself as well as for Richard. She could, and did, express a great deal of anger and sadness through her improvising. Richard became more aware of what his mother was expressing and showed that he was capable of empathy through his music, particularly in controlling his range of dynamics. This was not easy for him. As he was only mildly autistic, he did not have such great problems in relating to others as the other children on the programme. His problem was what he believed was his need and right to control his environment and all those in it. This was his way of coping with extreme anxiety. Often his music showed a determination to block us out, his mother in particular. I hoped that within the security and regularity of the music therapy he would begin to understand that sharing was fun and that nothing dreadful would happen if he did not have the upper hand all the time. He needed to feel secure in the fact that his mother was in charge, that she could direct without being over-intrusive, that he could accept this without feeling a sense of failure.

The resolution in the mother/son partnership came after the research period was over, when we were left to work together without the limitations of the research and the presence of the camera. Pat expressed her relief, although I think

Richard was disappointed for a short while that the camera was no longer there. During one of those later sessions, Pat was feeling very depressed, revealing this through her improvising modally on the chime bars. I supported her mood quietly with a counter melody on the xylophone. Richard could not play at all. He sat curled up on the settee watching her. When the improvising came to an end, Richard and I realised that Pat was crying. Together we held her until Richard became very matter-of-fact and man-of-the-house. He went out to the kitchen, coming back with a box of tissues. 'When you are crying, you need a tissue' was the emphatic statement. Such moments of closeness with a mother and her child were very precious.

It was following this experience some weeks later, that towards the end of the session, I realised that Pat had taken over the role of therapist. I was sitting on the floor, listening to them and watching them when suddenly I felt that the therapy was working between them. My support was no longer necessary. They were self-sufficient within their musical relationship at that time. In the previous week's session, Pat had met a musical challenge from Richard when he tried to drown her music by manipulating the rhythm section on the keyboard. Her response was to reach across and beat the cymbal with a tremendous crash. Richard had not expected such a powerful reaction. He was stopped and held by the assertive sound. Pat also realised during the following session that I felt able to leave them. She didn't mind, feeling confident that she could cope both musically and personally. This resolution came within a comparatively short time. With more severely autistic children it takes much longer. The mother and child I am still working with have achieved it during the last year - after two years of therapy. Music therapy was successful for Richard and Pat but it was only one aspect of the education and support team working with the family.

Conclusion

Good communication between school and home is vital. Education must allow for teacher and therapist contact time with parents as well as children, whether the children have special needs or not. Parent evenings and open days are not sufficient for real dialogue and support to take place. The school day is a busy and challenging one and staff are often too tired to give full attention to extra-curricular discussions and activities.

It has been stated that the roles of teacher and therapist should be complementary while acknowledging the differences. The therapist must make it clear that he or she is one member of the multi- and interdisciplinary team, that we all work together and that the education and therapy is child-centred. It has been known for teachers to feel resentful that the music therapist can give much more evidence of tangible results and effect then the teacher can. This natural resentment is more likely if the therapist chooses to isolate him or herself rather than becoming established as a team member with all the necessary communicative skills that entails. In the present climate of great changes in the education service in Britain and with the teacher morale low, keeping the channels of communication open isn't always easy.

Having the dual role of music therapist and advisory teacher for children with special needs has been helpful for extending my communication links but it raises a further issue. Should the music therapist working for an education authority also be a qualified teacher? In my particular role, it is essential, but not every therapist will want to take on advisory teaching work. It means that my training has spanned five years: three at university, one year for a post-graduate teaching qualification and one year for post-graduate therapy training. Without the teaching certificate, the therapist still has four years of music and therapy training. We consider that therapists should have similar status in schools to that of teachers. This is now under discussion by the Association of Professional Music Therapists.

Despite differences of philosophy and approach, music educators and therapists must unite to bring music back into our cultural heritage for all people, not just a privileged few. Music education should begin with parents cuddling their babies and singing to them, facilitating the bonding process for warm and secure relationships. When the children reach school age, the teacher then has a foundation on which musical responses and skills can be developed. Too much of our folk song heritage has disappeared. The world of pop music is over-reliant on modern technology - it, too, has become specialised in its own way. I believe that music therapy, with its emphasis on spontaneous, interactive music making, does present a challenge to conventional practice in music education. Music therapists need to be more assertive in making that challenge.

13

Communicating Through Music: The Balance Between Following and Initiating

Amelia Oldfield

Introduction

Even in the earliest stages of communication, there is a fine balance between following and initiating. When a small infant looks up at its mother and smiles, one could say that it is imitating its mother's smile. Alternatively, the infant may be expressing contentment and seeking to share that contentment in some basic way. Later, when a baby starts cooing and babbling it may well merely be experimenting with sound but it may also be consciously or unconsciously copying the sounds it has heard. The actions of following and initiating are often so closely intertwined that in many instances it is impossible to say who is the leader and who is the follower.

These different actions are also present in any verbal conversation between two people. They may be emphasised by the actual words used (for example: 'listen to me'....'pay attention'...) , or they may be more apparent in the two peoples' facial expressions or body postures. In most conversations, however, it is the meaning of the words and the contents of the verbal messages that are focused on and neither of the two people think about the other processes involved in their dialogue. Following and initiating processes are, however, occurring all the time. In some cases, words may 'mask' basic listening or leadership difficulties that a person may be experiencing because they lack self-confidence, for example.

For therapists working with people with communication disorders, all aspects involved in the communication between two people must be taken into consideration. The therapist must not only be aware of the exact nature of the communication difficulty of the child but must also consciously adapt his or her way of communicating to meet the needs of that child.

For music therapists using the medium of music, the non-verbal aspects of communication become particularly important. There are no words to interpret and no complex sentences to 'cover up' basic difficulties in concentration and listening. With no verbal content to focus on, the manner in which the music therapist chooses to communicate is going to be of particular importance. Does the music therapist initiate a sound herself, or does she wait until the child contributes a sound? Does the music therapist encourage a child to play with her or does she follow the playing of the child?

In the next section I will look at what is special about the use of music for communication. I will then go on to examine some of the literature regarding the different ways in which music therapists choose to communicate with their clients. My particular approach will be outlined and I will include some brief case studies of work with an autistic girl and an emotionally disturbed girl.

Why Music?

People with communication difficulties often show us that they enjoy music and sound and, in some cases, are clearly more alert and less isolated when music is involved in the communication process. The question I would like to pose at this stage is 'why?'. What is it about music or sound that motivates and interests people who are experiencing communication difficulties, and why music rather than another medium such as painting or gymnastics?

If one goes back to very early forms of communication, one could say that the speech that most mothers use with their young infants is 'musical' rather than verbal. The intonation of words is highly exaggerated and the accents on specific syllables are emphasised. Words or short phrases are repeated far more than in ordinary speech. The meaning of the words is unimportant. The infant reacts to the quality of the voice, the familiar sounds and the changes of intonation. If one believes that some communication disorders develop when a child is struggling to learn to speak, music, which is more like this earlier, simpler form of communication would be more accessible and appealing in such cases.

Another characteristic of both the early babbling exchanges of a mother and her infant, and a musical dialogue, is that unlike speech, the sounds used are non specific and can be interpreted in a variety of ways. An example of such a babbling exchange might be:

Baby: aaarreu...

Mother: (imitating the baby's sound) aaarreu, Paul... are you talking to me?

Baby: eu...aaaa.. daaa...

Mother: (joining in with the baby) daaa, dadada...

A child who is unsure about the meaning of words and what exact response is required from a spoken sentence will be more at ease using a less specific form of communication, such as music.

Unlike speech, which is normally intended to be heard by another person, music could be intended only for the player. A child can choose whether or not the player is trying to communicate, or whether the player is playing for themselves. Children who have grown used to isolating themselves and persistently rejecting any effort that is made to communicate with them can therefore take their time to respond to the therapist who can 'pretend' simply to be playing music to herself. On the other hand, it is impossible to shut sound out completely in the way that one can shut ones eyes or turn ones back on a silent activity one is uninterested in. The isolated child will, therefore, not be able to ignore the music altogether and can take as much time as he or she likes to respond to this non-verbal effort at communication.

Children's songs in England and a number of other European countries are characterised by simple harmonies, melodies that are easy to remember and above all simple rhythmic structures and plenty of repetition. 'London Bridge is Falling Down' and 'Frère Jacques' are two examples of such songs. Young children will often clap rhythms to songs and sing the correct sounds before they understand or use the actual words in the song. The ability to recognise and reproduce 'sound patterns' seems to be acquired very early and long before speech itself.

This would explain why music or repetitive rhymes with simple and predictable rhythmic patterns would be more accessible to children with communication disorders than ordinary speech. The fact that most children's' songs have a clear beginning and end is also a source of satisfaction to children who can feel that they have achieved and finished something. This is particularly important to a child who is confused by ordinary speech, and therefore needs the sense of achievement and satisfaction that can be derived from singing and clapping a simple song with another person.

The fact that music is often associated with movement and dance is also appealing to children. It is unclear exactly why a strong beat will give us the urge to get up and dance or tap our foot. However, this urge is developed very early on and seems to be a physical rather than an intellectual response. Very young babies will wriggle and 'dance' to music and will be particularly delighted if other grown ups or children take part too. This is an excellent way for children with communication difficulties to share and enjoy music with another adult. The common enjoyment of the music can bring a child out of its isolation. Once a rapport has been established between the adult and the child, the rhythm of the music and the impulse this rhythm produces to join in through movement can be channelled into a more elaborate form of communication.

The above mentioned explanations are mainly based on two suppositions:

1) the belief that the ability to respond and take part in musical activities precedes the acquisition and use of speech,

2) the belief that music can be more 'enticing' than speech and appeal to children who have isolated themselves and rejected all usual forms of communication.

There are other explanations which I would like to mention briefly, although more research is needed before they can be put into practice by the music therapist working with children with communication disorders. One of these is the idea that speech and music are processed by different parts of the brain (Damasio, 1977; Cook, 1973; McElwain, 1979). In theory, a person who had suffered brain damage affecting the area responsible for speech would be able to use a communication system based on music instead. Another explanation is based on the idea that music produces sound waves which can have a therapeutic effect on specific physical disorders and disabilities (Skille et al., 1989).

One last point needs to be made about the associative power of music. When we hear a song or a tune that we have not heard for a long time we will often remember immediately the situation we were in when we last heard that tune. The song will take us back to the past and we may experience the same emotions as we did previously. This evocative power of music needs to be taken into consideration, particularly when working with emotionally disturbed children. Signature tunes are used in this way on the radio and on television. Similarly, I have often found that children are reassured if the music therapy session starts off with the same tune every week. A greeting associated with a familiar tune can become an essential starting point for every session, providing familiarity and security.

Directive and Non-Directive Approaches

No therapist is completely directive or completely non directive. Even when one is asking a child direct questions one listens to the answer and when one is simply inviting a child to come into the room one is giving some direction.

Nevertheless, all therapists will be aiming for some kind of change in the child. This could be a physical improvement, a greater awareness of self or an increased ability to accept a difficult situation, for example. Some music therapists will have clearly defined objectives whereas others will focus on the exploratory aspects of the session with unconscious and more general aims. However, all music therapists have some 'direction' to their session and the work can therefore be said to be 'directive'. When I use the term 'directive', however, I am referring to the way in which the therapist chooses to achieve therapeutic objectives. For example:

- does the therapist suggest activities for the child or wait for the child to choose an activity?

- does the therapist steer the musical improvisation in a particular direction or simply mirror what the child has initiated?

- does the therapist lead the child or allow herself to be led by the child?

The way in which a music therapist works may be different during the early assessment stage than in later stages. Let us first examine what approach music therapists have during the first few sessions and then look at subsequent treatment.

Different Approaches During the Assessment Period

The first step for a music therapist is to establish a relationship with the child and gradually understand their personality and needs. The music therapist will not only be observing the child generally but will also be finding out about the child's musical preferences and abilities. Nordoff and Robbins talk about meeting the 'Music Child'. The emphasis is on the therapist finding the 'individualised musicality inborn in each child' rather than on directing the child in any way. However, the authors go on to say that with some children the 'Music Child' must be awakened and synthesised (Nordoff and Robbins, 1977). In this case the therapist will have to guide the child in some way and is not simply observing and following the child. Edith Boxhill clearly has to be a lot more directive during the assessment period as she is trying to answer a whole series of precise questions about the various abilities of the child (Boxhill, 1985). She says that the assessment should be administered over a series of weeks and that the therapist should use improvised or composed music for singing, chanting, instrument playing, and music-movement activities. Even if precise observations are made during relatively free, undirected activities, there is more direction here than in initial Nordoff and Robbins sessions.

Yolande Moyne asks her adolescents to do various 'tests' before commencing treatment, which include playing instruments, imitating rhythms and reading. Here again there is a lot of direction from the therapist (Moyne, 1988).

When working with verbal clients, many music therapists start off by talking to their client and explaining what sort of work might be undertaken (Munro, 1980). If the therapist is doing most of the talking this could be said to be a directive approach. If, on the other hand, the therapist spends her time listening to the client without steering the conversation in any particular direction, it is less so.

Many music therapists working in psychiatry start off by improvising with their clients (Priestley, 1975). Again this could be directive if the therapist is doing most of the playing and steering the improvisation in a particular direction, or it could be less so if the therapist mainly listens and reflects back what the client is playing. These examples show that different therapists may do very different things during the first few sessions. Even if the activities they suggest to the client are similar, the approach can still vary in directiveness. However, some music therapists are quite directive in that they structure the session around a series of questions they want to answer during the initial assessment period, whereas other music therapists direct very little and wait for a child to explore at his or her own pace.

Different Approaches after the Assessment Period

As the therapy progresses, approaches continue to vary. Nordoff and Robbins suggest that the therapist should determine clinical goals during each session according to the child's response (Nordoff and Robbins, 1977). The child is therefore the principal leader and the therapist is relatively non directive.

Edith Boxhill formulates precise treatment plans for her clients with short-term and long-term objectives. Her approach is both directive and non directive in that she uses 'reflection' (mirroring and matching what the client is doing) and 'identification' (feeding back the here and now of what is happening) in order to reach the 'contact song' where the therapist and the client share and communicate with one another (Boxhill, 1985).

Having administered her 'test' with her adolescent, Yolande Moyne works out a series of exercises to help the child to overcome difficulties. Here the therapist is quite directive while making sure that there is also room for self-expression and exploration (Moyne, 1988).

When working with terminally-ill clients, Susan Munro makes various suggestions which often involve listening to music rather than being actively involved in playing. Her approach is directive in that she makes suggestions to the client but non directive in that she follows up any preferences or choices the client might make (Munro, 1980).

In the chapter 'Aims of Music Therapy' Mary Priestley writes: 'When clients cannot communicate.... I do less and less and less. And finally more happens'. Clearly the emphasis is on containing and listening rather than on being too directive (Priestley, 1975).

It appears that those music therapists who have precise aims and objectives in their work tend to be more directive. When a therapist has a clear aim, there may also be less time for simply listening and following a child. For the same reason, long-term treatment is often less directive than short-term treatment where results are expected more quickly.

My Particular Approach

When a child is first referred to me with a view to possible music therapy treatment, I assess the child during two to three weekly half-hour sessions. The purpose of the assessment is mainly to determine whether or not the child will benefit from music therapy treatment and, if so, to determine rough objectives for the treatment. During the assessment period I will be building up an initial relationship with the child and I will also be finding out about the musical responsiveness and the musical skills of the child. I will listen for rhythmic and melodic characteristics in the child's playing, for example, and observe harmonic and tone colour preferences. How directive I am will depend very much on the type of child I am seeing and what the child's difficulties are.

When working with mainly non-verbal, isolated children who are either diagnosed as autistic or have a number of autistic tendencies (Rutter, 1985), I provide a clear starting and ending point for the very first session and allow the child as much freedom as possible in between. I will help the child to sit opposite to me for the first few minutes and sing a greeting to the child, possibly accompanied by the guitar. If necessary, I will physically help the child to remain seated for a few seconds. I will end the session in the same way by singing good-bye and often accompanying myself with the bongo drums which I will attempt to share with the child. In between, the child is free to roam around the room, exploring and discovering instruments on the way. I will support and encourage the child by mirroring the child's playing through song and instrumental accompaniment and at times identifying what we are doing by singing. For example: 'we are playing the piano together now' or 'I'm playing the drum and John is marching'.

Thus, I am extremely directive for the first and the last few minutes and much less so for the rest of the session. My rationale for this is that any child - but particularly a confused and isolated child - is reassured by a framework surrounding an event. When first meeting a new person children are used to being talked to and to the fact that attention is directed towards them. Even if an isolated child rejects this attention, it would be frightening suddenly to be subjected to a silent adult who waited for the child to do something before responding.

During the subsequent assessment sessions I continue with the same beginnings and endings, and even the most isolated children come to expect these familiar events. It is particularly important for the child who is very anxious to know how the session will end. Sometimes a child is so relieved by the sight of the bongo drums (signalling the end of the session) that he or she will relax for the first time at this point, and perhaps suddenly become aware of the therapist and the possibility of communication. The last few minutes of the session may then become crucial in the therapeutic relationship with that child. During the second and third assessment sessions I also gradually become more 'intrusive', showing the child instruments or verbally and physically guiding the child in some way. However, I will never be directive for more than a few minutes at a time and I will always intersperse my intrusions with 'free' periods. I find that if I am trying to assess whether a child will benefit from music therapy treatment I cannot simply mirror and identify what the child is doing but must suggest instruments and activities to be tried. In order for the isolated child to accept any suggestions and intrusions, however, all interventions must be very short and the child must have plenty of opportunity to retreat into it's own world in between these interventions.

If it is decided that the child should continue with music therapy treatment, I usually continue with the pattern established during the assessment period. The directive approach will be interspersed with the non-directive one. I find it is very important to make it obvious which approach one is taking at any given moment and to give every period of directive or non-directive interaction a clear shape with a beginning and an end. If the therapist starts an activity which is unsuccessful it is important not to stop suddenly but to make a proper ending (even if one does this very soon after one has started). There is nothing more confusing for a child than a therapist who keeps stopping and starting different activities. Sometimes I am very forceful and actually hold a child on a chair for a minute or two in order to attempt to help a child to concentrate for a little longer. At these times I might explain what I am doing by saying (or singing) 'I'm trying to help you, I care enough to hold you here'. Similarly, during the non directive times I might comment as I am accompanying a child's movements: for example: 'John is walking around the room'. At times it will become unclear whether I am accompanying John's movements or whether John is moving to my music. This means that I am communicating and helping the child in the non directive times as well as in the directive times. The non directive periods are no longer solely to allow the child to retreat into it's own world.

As the non directive periods become more meaningful, the child usually starts allowing the therapist to be more directive, both more often and for longer periods of time. This is very important not only for the progress of the therapy but also because any child has to learn to accept direction from adults at some times and the child has to learn to tolerate this direction.

I will now go on to a brief case study of Annie with whom this approach was used. (Both this and the subsequent case study are based on children I have worked with. The names of the children and some details have been changed for reasons of confidentiality).

Case Study: Annie

Annie was referred to music therapy by the paediatrician because her mother mentioned that she seemed particularly responsive to music. She was seven years old and diagnosed as autistic and severely mentally handicapped. She had no speech and seemed to live in a world of her own. She made no effort to communicate with those around her, preferring to wander around, endlessly twiddling small objects in front of her eyes. During our first session together she screamed and struggled when I tried to contain her by encouraging her to sit down with me at the beginning and at the end of the session. In between she wandered around the room aimlessly picking up small instruments such as bells and twiddling them briefly before dropping them and picking up another small instrument to twiddle. The only contact we made was when Annie briefly looked up at me a couple of times after I had finished singing : 'London Bridge is Falling Down' and 'Ba Ba Black Sheep'. During the next two sessions I sung 'Hello' to Annie using the tunes of: 'London Bridge is Falling Down' and 'Ba Ba Black Sheep'. I also cleared away all objects that I thought Annie was likely to twiddle as I felt that the twiddling was not constructive in any way and was helping Annie to retreat further away from me. By the third session Annie had become used to the structure of the session (starting and finishing on a chair opposite me and roaming around freely in between) and spontaneously went to sit down in 'her' chair as soon as she came into the room. She also became slightly less isolated as she roamed around the room, occasionally listening to snippets of music and looking up expectantly when a familiar tune ended.

As far as Annie's musical preferences and abilities were concerned I was able to discover that:

- Annie recognised quite a number of songs and was aware of phrase endings.

- Annie had an excellent sense of rhythm. She would clap her hands in time to simple songs, stop appropriately at the ends of phrases and follow gradual accellerandis or descellerandis.

- Annie had several characteristic short rhythms that she would repeat and particularly react to. These were:

- Annie would complete songs she knew such as 'Twinkle, twinkle ...' and 'Row, row, row your boat...', by singing a sound resembling the correct word in the song at the correct pitch.

- Annie enjoyed briefly hitting a large drum with her hand but would attempt to twiddle any instrument (or part of an instrument such as the bars of the glockenspiel or the beaters for the drum) that she could hold in her hands or obsessively twirl instruments like the cymbal.

After the first three assessment sessions I felt that Annie would benefit from further sessions. She appeared more interested in music than in anything else and I thought that I would be able to use this interest to encourage Annie to communicate with me.

I saw Annie for weekly half hour music therapy sessions for a year, at which point she moved out of the area and the sessions had to stop. I continued with the structure introduced during the assessment sessions and gradually introduced more short periods of directed work into the session. After a couple of months the sessions consisted of short periods of 'directed' activities (between two to ten minutes) alternating with short periods of 'free' activities. This pattern continued for the duration of Annie's treatment although occasionally both the directed and free periods would be longer as Annie become more communicative and her concentration increased. During the year she become a lot more communicative, playing and sharing bongo drums with me for up to ten minutes at a time, for example. She would enjoy playing clapping games with me and was also able to do this with her mother and with her teacher at school. As a result, her concentration and her ability to sit on a chair for longer periods at a time also improved. By the end of a year of regular music therapy sessions, she had just started to be able to use a stick briefly on a bass xylophone without twiddling the stick or attempting to take the notes off the xylophone to twiddle them. To me this indicated that she was more relaxed and more willing to communicate. She no longer felt the constant need to isolate herself through self stimulating, obsessive twiddling.

I am convinced that one of the reasons that Annie made so much progress, not only in music therapy but generally during that year, was the structure of our sessions and the strict and very clear alternating between directive and non-directive work. To begin with, the structure provided a predictable and safe environment within which to work. Annie was able to relax and retreat into her own world while I tried to follow her. At the same time I was able to steer her in certain directions and show that I cared enough about wanting to communicate with her to be quite firm and forceful when necessary. During both directive and non directive work Annie knew what to expect and knew what would follow.

Working with Emotionally Disturbed Children

I will now discuss some aspects of my work with children between the ages of six and twelve suffering from emotional disorders (Hersov, 1985). Most of these children are of normal intelligence, and verbal communication plays a greater part in the sessions than when working with children like Annie. During the first session I start off by singing a greeting to the child on the guitar and explain that this is the way I always start sessions. (This matter of fact explanation usually alleviates any initial embarrassment the child might experience). Once the greeting is over, I explain that we will take it in turns to choose instruments. I usually make the first choice and often choose percussion instruments for the child and provide a supportive accompaniment on the piano. This gives the shy, reticent child a chance to explore at his or her own pace and provides a solid, reassuring beginning for the chaotic, more extroverted child. I then encourage the child to choose an instrument for him/herself and for me. The session continues in this way with each of us taking turns to choose instruments and activities until five minutes before the end when I warn the child that the session is nearly over. I very often finish the session by asking the child what he or she enjoyed most. We talk generally about the session and what we might do in the future.

When using this approach it is important to make it very clear whose choice each activity has been. Some children will need encouragement to make choices for me and direct me as they may never have had the opportunity to do this with another adult. Other children have no difficulty telling me what to do but resent being directed in any way themselves. Many children find this structure extremely reassuring and their confidence is boosted by the fact that we are 'equal' and each have a say in what we will do in the session. As with the non communicating children it is important to give each activity a clear ending, and in some cases to prepare the child for the endings. Thus, the structure of the session allows me to alternate between directive (instruments or activities that I choose) and non-directive activities (instruments or activities that the child chooses). In some cases, however, a child will opt for activities where he or she is directed rather than taking the lead him/herself. In this case, if I wish to introduce a 'free' non directive improvisation, for example, I can choose this when it comes to 'my' choice. I can also vary the length of each activity depending on what the child's needs are.

During the assessment period this structure allows me not only to build up a trusting relationship with the child but also enables me to find out about a child's musical background, preferences and abilities. If it is decided that the child should continue with music therapy sessions I can continue to use the same structure initially but then gradually extend certain areas of work as the need arises. The following case study should show how effective this approach can be.

Case Study: Jenny

Jenny was an eight year old girl who had been referred to the psychiatric unit because of aggressive and very difficult behaviour towards both adults and children at school. Her parents also had difficulties managing her at home. It soon transpired that neither her parents nor any other members of her family either loved or wanted Jenny. As a result Jenny had very low self esteem and no confidence in herself. She craved adult attention but was incapable of trusting or confiding in anyone. She wanted to be loved but was incapable of showing any real affection herself.

During her first session with me she showed genuine surprise and delight when I sung a song especially to welcome her to the session. For the rest of the session she was eager to try out the instruments but also desperate to impress and charm me. She was unable to relax and enjoy any one activity for more than a few minutes at a time. At the end of the session she could not tell me what she had liked doing most, saying she had enjoyed everything. She appeared desperate to please me but unwilling to commit herself in any way.

The next two assessment sessions were very similar to this first session. She relaxed a little but generally remained meek and compliant. Occasionally, she would feel 'persecuted' and would complain that I was staring at her or even imagine that I was attacking her. She would ask me crossly to stop hitting her even though I had not even touched her. From a musical point of view, I was able to discover that she had a good sense of rhythm and pitch and that she felt she was 'good at music'. She mentioned that she had enjoyed learning to play the piano with her Grandad even though she did not seem to have acquired any piano playing techniques. She found free improvisations completely impossible and would start inventing rules for us to follow as soon as I suggested that we should play instruments together. After her assessment it was decided that she should continue with music therapy sessions as this was one of the few areas that Jenny felt positive about in any way and there was therefore potential to help restore her confidence in herself. It was also felt that I might be able to use the music sessions to help her to relax and relate to an adult in an ordinary way, rather than being either aggressive or superficially charming.

I saw Jenny for weekly half hour music therapy sessions for six months at which point she was discharged from the psychiatric unit. As Jenny got to know me better she allowed herself to relax a little more and enjoy playing more freely with me. I particularly remember some very enjoyable exchanges on the bongo drums when Jenny was very creative in her playing and was able to offer new ideas as well as to listen to my 'answers'. Because of the structure of the session I was able to choose instruments and activities that allowed Jenny to be creative in this way while at the same time giving Jenny the opportunity to make her own choices and share the responsibility for the session. As time went on Jenny started to rebel and gradually challenged the rules and limits surrounding the sessions. To begin with, she started to draw out our last activity or make sudden pleas for one more quick choice right at the end of the session. When I became firm about finishing our session on time she would refuse to leave the room and would lie down on the floor. I had to find a practical solution to this problem, as the end of the session was not a time when I could talk to Jenny in more depth about why she was behaving in this way. Therefore, I told her that I was pleased that she enjoyed the session so much that she did not want to leave but that we would have to stop playing and prepare for leaving ten minutes before the end of the session if she was experiencing difficulties in this area. This more or less solved the problem but then she started to refuse to take part in any of the activities that I suggested when it came to my choice. I gradually talked to her about why she might feel she had to 'spoil' our sessions because so many of her other 'good times' with adults had been spoilt in the past. Jenny seemed unable to listen or hear.

In spite of the difficulties I did not change the structure of the session. Jenny still enjoyed and took part in her own 'choices' so there were still enough positive elements in the sessions to keep us going. However, she continued to become increasingly challenging in her behaviour until one day she started playing the piano during my hello song, a moment she had chosen not to disrupt so far. Nevertheless, I continued to sing the song even though it was almost impossible to hear it. Then, one week, I told her that I was finding it too difficult to sing in tune while she was playing the piano and I would like to change the song a little to fit into her piano playing. Jenny looked at me in horror and told me firmly to continue and that she would like to listen again. From then on Jenny's disruptive behaviour diminished and she was able to talk a little about some of the previous comments I had made, which she had heard in spite of not appearing to. For Jenny, the clear structure of the session allowed her first to relax and enjoy making music with me, and then to rebel within a safe environment. She became able to face up to some of her difficulties. Without the directive parts of the session Jenny would have had nothing to rebel against. If, on the other hand, the whole session had been directive we would not have been able to continue as she would have refused to take part at all.

Conclusion

This chapter has focused both on why music is a useful way of communicating and on how it can be used to communicate.

In the initial sessions, the balance between directive and non directive work is very different when working with children with severe communication disorders and when working with emotionally disturbed children. However, as sessions progress, the distribution of directive and non directive work becomes much more similar. The non-communicating child becomes more able to accept direction and communicate and the emotionally disturbed child becomes more able to relax and concentrate on shared activities for longer periods of time.

Thus, I have tried to show how a very simple idea of alternating between directive and non directive work within individual music therapy sessions can be effective both when working with non communicating children and when working with emotionally disturbed children. Music therapists vary in how directive or non- directive an approach they like to have with their clients. Most music therapists focus more on the process of communication rather than particularly considering whether their approach is directive or non directive. I am suggesting that it can be useful and important for the therapist to make it very obvious whether he or she is using directive or non directive techniques. I have tried to show how the correct balance between directive and non directive work can be used towards therapeutic ends by the music therapist.

14

Elizabeth: A Case Study of an Autistic Child in Individual Music Therapy

Robin Howat

Introduction

Since Kanner first described the pattern of abnormal behaviour he termed 'early infantile autism' (1943) there have been widespread advances in our understanding of the nature of the condition. Kanner's initial view was that autism was a constitutionally determined developmental disorder. This soon gave way to the idea that it was a psychosis, an early manifestation of schizophrenia.

In the 1950s and early 1960s the popular theory was a psychogenic one centering on the hypothesis of the 'refrigerator' parent whose cold and unfeeling behaviour brought on a reaction or defence in the child. Psychogenic theories of autism fell out of favour and an increasing body of evidence pointed to autism as a biologically determined developmental disorder that involves serious and pervasive cognitive defects.

According to Howlin (1987) the diagnosis of autism should have three main criteria :
1. Delayed and deviant language development which is out of keeping with the child's non-verbal development and which affects non-verbal and abstract skills as well as spoken language.
2. Delayed and deviant social development, which again is out of keeping with the child's development in other areas.
3. The presence of rituals and routines and a general resistance to change.

Howlin goes on to point out that the cognitive impairment of autistic children 'ranges from moderate to severe mental retardation (in approximately 5,000 of cases) to normal performance on non-verbal tasks (in approximately 20%)'.

The aetiology of autism is generally considered in terms of organic and genetic factors. Continuing research aimed at finding the causes spans a wide range of experimental studies, biochemical and organic investigations, intervention programmes and clinical studies.

The Autistic Child and Music Therapy

An autistic child finds it very difficult to make relationships and to make sense of the world around him. He often seems cast in the role of an observer on life, unable to participate, trapped in an isolation not of his own making or choice. For the autistic child music offers a point of contact and a means of communication. It does not need either words as a mediator or require musical training on behalf of the child for him to respond.

Many autistic children are emotionally unawakened. Music speaks directly to the emotional life and is a powerful incentive for arousing and stimulating the emotional lives of autistic children. Others are emotionally confused and for them music can bring stability and consolation. For some older and more able autistic children music can go on to offer the challenges and wider scope of experiences that they often need.

At the beginning of this study of Elizabeth, an individual child in music therapy, I wish to stress that music therapy always begins with where the child is. The child's responses are the starting point for improvisation and remain central to the direction that the therapy takes. Out of the early interactions, general and often more specific goals can be formulated. The therapists' work with these in mind within the context of the improvised musical setting. In the work with Elizabeth her responses not only revealed her musical limitations but quickly revealed her underlying restrictions and emotional pathology. We were soon aware that in the context of music we were working directly with Elizabeth's inner life. The aim of this study is to illustrate how this happened; how the work began, evolved, grew and changed over nearly six years.

Elizabeth - A Developmental History

Elizabeth was born on May 25th 1975. The pregnancy and delivery were without complications. Elizabeth's mother described her as being 'very good' but noted that she did not smile. She crawled at a year but did not walk until two.

In early childhood Elizabeth showed selectivity in her responses e.g. an adverse reaction to noises such as the stripping sounds of sellotape. She liked to be carried by her mother in a certain way. Any attempt to change position was met with panic. Elizabeth developed selective visual attention e.g. gazing at very strong lights; pulling down lampshades to see the light; standing very close to the television to see the flickering shapes.

Over the years Elizabeth developed an obsessional interest in maintaining routines and special arrangements. To quote her mother:

'Elizabeth goes through the house checking rooms after us, putting things just so, checking lights, adjusting positions of chairs and furniture. If I move ornaments she will put them back as she likes them. Elizabeth prefers to take a non-direct route. If it is possible to circumnavigate furniture on her way she will do so. She often approaches things obliquely, we go a certain way to the local shops and any deviation in our route upsets Elizabeth. I always explain what we are doing and why, and reassure her that we will go to the shops. She copes quite well with changes to routine provided she is reassured.'

At two Elizabeth was diagnosed as 'a severely handicapped child with autistic tendencies' and from two and a half to three she attended a play group for children with severe learning difficulties.

From the age of three to seven Elizabeth attended a special class in St Paul's Wood Primary School, Orpington, Kent. At five she started to speak with short echolalic phrases (e.g.: 'That's all right' 'There you are').

At seven Elizabeth was referred to Rectory Paddock School for children with severe learning difficulties. At the end of her first year (July 1983) the report from Elizabeth's class teachers makes positive reading. I quote:

'Elizabeth has settled into the routine of her new school quite well. She knows her way to the classroom from the front door of the school, and makes her own way into the class each morning, carrying her own bag. Elizabeth is very energetic:- she likes to go out in the playground, where, although she does not 'play' in the way that some children do, she enjoys running around. Her habit of slightly dragging her feet when walking or running means that she has a tendency to fall over - she has done so quite a few times this year [special precautions are now being taken to prevent this]. In general, Elizabeth appears to be a happy child, and the rare occasions when she does cry are usually times when her undoubtedly strong will is frustrated. For example, when she has to wait for another child before the group moves off for another activity. She is also a solitary child, and, although she does approach adults and does relate to them, she rarely, if ever, approaches the other children. We hope to see her become more sociable in due course.'

The report from the music teacher reads:

'Music plays a big part in Elizabeth's life. She will often respond to things that are sung to her rather than said. She will pick up a tune or melody quickly and accurately. She enjoys music sessions and will join in with our percussion playing. She does have a sense of rhythm but does not always co-operate with rhythm work. A great deal of her language is sung rather than spoken and she enjoys moving to music.'

At the end of her second year (July 1984) Elizabeth's class teacher writes:

'Elizabeth can be very co-operative and agreeable in some situations but aggressive and uncooperative in others where she uses foot-stamping, nose-pressing and dancing about to show her displeasure'. Co-operation was obviously on Elizabeth's terms!'

In September 1985 Elizabeth was referred to the Nordoff-Robbins Music Therapy Centre for individual music therapy by her school, at her mothers request. Elizabeth has been coming to the Centre for individual music therapy since 1985. The journey to North London from her home in Kent takes up to two hours, involving a train into London then a tube to Kentish Town. She comes with her mother.

The sessions are taken by two therapists. One improvises music at the piano, the other is responsible for supporting Elizabeth in her music making if and when necessary. The co-therapist is also there to oversee the practical management of the instruments, the sticks and beaters, etc.

In this study I shall give a detailed description of certain sessions whilst summarising others. Relevant information about Elizabeth's home and school life are included in chronological order. Therapist - Robin Howat, Co-therapist - Jane Gibson

Early Exploratory Sessions: September to December 1985

Elizabeth came to the Centre for her first session on September 16th 1985. As she came into the room with the co-therapist I played simple open-ended music and sang 'Elizabeth, hello' gently. Elizabeth came and sat by me at the treble of the piano singing her name and 'hello' in the tonality of the music. She played clusters with alternate hands, loudly but often in the tempo of the music. She soon revealed a strong tendency to play insistent triplet rhythms and rhythmic patterns in compound time, for example:

We offered her a side-drum to play. Her first responses using one stick were similar to the clusters on the piano, i.e. fast, vigorous triplets and rhythmic patterns. These were accompanied by vigorous jumping from foot to foot. When we offered her a large cymbal on a stand Elizabeth became very interested in the central screw and with exploring the surface of the cymbal. She played triplets again but this time consistently in tempo with the music. At the end of the session I invited Elizabeth back to the piano. She sat at the treble again singing 'bye-bye' clearly, though tentatively. The music was diatonic with a simple melody.

It was clear to us from Elizabeth's reaction to the music and her general behaviour that she was often very unfocused, scattered and evasive, yet musically alert and at times engaged. The opportunity to use the musical instruments interested her. At times she was able to join with the basic beat/pulse of the music, though she preferred triplets and rhythms in compound time which were nearly always loud and with a driven quality. Having come in with Elizabeth, the co-therapist played a supportive but non-active role.

As therapists we felt that an initial contact had been made. Elizabeth had begun to accept us and the situation. She did not look at us directly at any time during the session. The session lasted for seventeen minutes.

September 23rd

Elizabeth comes in and goes straight to the piano. Initially tentative she soon begins to play loud rhythmic clusters and to sing 'hello' more to herself than to us. She sees the cymbal and becomes absorbed in fiddling with the screw and slapping the cymbal with her hand whilst dancing round wildly. After a while we remove the cymbal from the room as Elizabeth is becoming very over stimulated by the shimmering sound and the overtones. We are able to engage Elizabeth in vigorous tambourine playing to music in a Spanish idiom.

September 30th

Elizabeth is very caught up in her constant moving, leaping around and twirling her arms. However, she becomes quiet and with a stick beats rhythmically on the drum. Some of this is at the quieter dynamic, much of it is loud and driven. She touches my chin at the end of the session as she sits at the piano saying;

'Bye-bye Elizabeth'
'Bye-bye Robin'
'Bye-bye Jane'

She does not look at us.

October 7th

Elizabeth comes to the music in an obviously distressed state, crying and wailing. We do not know what has caused this but I meet it with strong music and singing. Throughout the session she vocalises wordlessly in a variety of ways - crying, whimpering, humming. Music in the Middle-Eastern mode catches her attention and she moves into strong rhythmic tambourine playing. Her distress surfaces again and strong Spanish music with increasing dissonance engages her in forceful playing of clusters at the piano. Quiet music enables her to become quieter and she sings softly with a voice that is now more centred. She goes back to loud rhythmically driven piano clusters and begins to sound distressed again as she leaves. Throughout the twenty-five minute sessions she makes no attempt to leave the room before the end.

October 14th

Initially Elizabeth cries and wails in a similar way to last week but this does not last long. A new song 'Welcome to Music' is improvised. This focuses Elizabeth as she plays the basic beat and melodic rhythm of the song on the piano. Much of her other instrumental work is very scattered and bears little relation to the music.

October 28th

Elizabeth shows no sign of the distress of October 7th and 14th. She touches my face and plays a conga drum with more rhythmic awareness of the improvised music. We bring the cymbal back into the session. Elizabeth shows interest but does not play it.

November 18th

Improvisation based on an American Indian dance accompanied by strong dissonant harmony draws Elizabeth into her most engaged drum beating to date.

November 25th

Elizabeth is very 'in and out' in her attention. She vocalises throughout the session in a teasing, evasive 'sing-song' way. I improvise music in a light mood, using the whole tone scale in the treble of the piano to reflect back to Elizabeth the tenuous, ambivalent teasing nature of these vocal responses. Apart from this there are moments of strong instrumental responses and at the end - quiet singing.

December 2nd

This proves to be a difficult session. Elizabeth is very scattered and evasive and we feel differently about the direction to take in response to this. Elizabeth senses our uncertainty and becomes wild and almost hyperactive. We hear much 'nonchalant' whistling. (She does this at home and at school.)

<u>December 9th</u>

Elizabeth comes in singing and 'chuntering' to herself. She plays the piano, cymbal and tambourine with either hand using a lot of triplet and compound rhythms. She wanders round the room a great deal. I try to focus her by singing her name and some of the music she has responded to previously. She sings the phrase 'here is a drum'. As the session progresses Elizabeth becomes increasingly distracted.

At the end of Term I we wrote the following summary: 'Elizabeth is a tall, slender and physically robust girl. Her face is strikingly pale and expressionless.

She never smiles and even when animated by the music, the animation seems to be a physical response as opposed to an expression of involvement or pleasure.

Elizabeth is rarely still except when sitting at the piano. Her movements include stamping her feet, dancing in big awkward movements round the conga drum or cymbal and flailing her arms and slapping her thighs. She vocalises a great deal when anxious and presses her hand into her face, particularly her nose. A diffuse anxiety seems to underline everything she does. However it seems clear that in her own way Elizabeth enjoys the sessions, perhaps in finding a channel for her energy.

Although many of her instrumental responses on the drum, cymbal, tambourine and tambour are loud and with a driven rhythmic quality, they reflect an underlying awareness of the basic pulse of the music and tempo change. She has an innate preference for playing in triplet and compound rhythms to the point of perseveration. Typical of these are:

Elizabeth also vocalises and sings in the greetings and goodbyes often finishing the '...lo' of hello as I wait for her, and bye-bye. Her singing is quiet, and not directed towards us. The uncentered, unfocused quality in her voice, the nature of her instrumental responses and body movement sum up her overall lack of personal integration and inability to sustain more than moments of involvement or concentration. However, we feel that music for Elizabeth offers something that <u>does</u> interest and engage her and is already providing a channel of communication for her to express some of her pent-up energy and feelings.'

A Period of Consolidation: January to December 1986

In Term II a second 'Welcome to Music' song became the focus of the musical activity. The two songs continued together in the sessions, offering a contrast of tempo, mood and dynamics.

January 20th

This is a short concentrated session. Elizabeth has never worked with us in the music so directly before. Her beating is clearly related to the music, sometimes in a quieter dynamic (which is new). She follows changes in tempo and beats not only her preferred triplets, but quavers and semi-quavers. As the new 'Welcome to the Music' is introduced she begins to play the melodic rhythm on the drum.

She is helped to concentrate by the fact that we encourage her to sit at the instruments for some of the time. Not every session saw Elizabeth as engaged as this but it became easier for us to distinguish when she was caught up in her body movements, rhythmic patterns and incessant repetitions of her name (which she did frequently), and when she was able to listen and be engaged by the music. The improvisation fluctuates between meeting Elizabeth's responses and inviting her to explore different tempi; dynamics and other ways of playing.

February 10th

I wrote after the session: 'Elizabeth is so quiet initially that you would hardly know she was in the room. She looks directly at us and waits. Very still. At the conga drum she plays with two beaters, she allows me to hold her finger and play the melody of the good-bye song as we end the session. This is most encouraging.'

The sessions continued into the Summer following the same basic pattern: Elizabeth would start by sitting at the piano, playing and vocalising. Nearly always she moved to the side drum or conga drum where much of her playing had a compulsive and driven rhythmic quality. I was able to give this back to her in music that met this energy, but was not always able to lead her into other musical experiences. In contrast to the early sessions she seemed wary of the cymbal appearing to find the sound rather threatening and overwhelming.

The sessions usually ended with Elizabeth coming back to the piano. As soon as I began to sing good-bye she would get up to leave. Often we could prolong these moments and encourage her to sing.

The final session of the year (July 16th) was positive. Our report of it reads:

'A communicative session. There are clear musical activities to which Elizabeth responds in a very direct way. There is a real sense of her beginning to share the music with us. Her compulsive rhythms are there but combined with others initiated from the piano which she follows sometimes. She seems to enjoy sharing the activity.'

Throughout the first year of therapy the role of the co-therapist was mainly one of offering Elizabeth verbal and sometimes physical encouragement and a steadying hand. This was important at times when Elizabeth had become unfocused and scattered. The co-therapist was frequently able to steady her enough to bring her back into the music. The school found Elizabeth's musical therapy reports encouraging and noted in her school music sessions (in groups of three or four children) that she could listen to a pulse on a metronome and keep time by stamping her feet with no difficulty. She elected not to sing with the others when asked to, a feature reflected in music therapy when Elizabeth would often sing the melody of the previous song or musical activity.

The school noted improvement in eye contact, a pleasure in stories and books and 'slow overall progress'. During 1986 Elizabeth was in short term care from time to time and by September she was living in a hostel during the week and coming home at weekends. Her mother reported that Elizabeth was talking about the therapists during the summer holidays.

September 8th

In the first session after a long break Elizabeth is anxious and evasive to begin with. She mutters to herself. On finding the cymbal behind the piano she plays very loudly and rhythmically with one hand, damping it with the other. She perseverates a great deal of quick and rhythmic:

and I meet the character of this in strong, equally rhythmic, music. This rhythm is transferred to the conga drum and in clusters at the piano. In response to this I introduce new music in 6/8 based on a theme from Nielsen's Fifth Symphony. Elizabeth immediately plays the melodic rhythm and follows some changes to slower tempi. She moves her body in time with the music and frequently from foot to foot.

September 15th

Elizabeth is very lively and sings back:

Good mor-ning.

She beats a pattern on the conga drum in a number of different tempi set by me at the piano. At a fast tempo Elizabeth loses concentration and goes into a flurry of rhythmic patterns and body movements. After work with the cymbal she indicates clearly that she has had enough.

September 29th

After some sensitive musical vocalising at the keyboard to a quiet greeting Elizabeth becomes distracted and unfocused. She whistles, hums, chunters to herself and resists our attempts to involve her further. She becomes caught up in a flurry of movements with loud rhythmic playing on the instruments. By introducing slow steady music loosely based in the Spanish idiom I attempt to focus and stabilise her responses. Elizabeth continues to play excitedly, ignoring my tempo. After some minutes the music changes to a rhythmic dance that suits her playing. She needs a great deal of encouragement from the co-therapist as we lead her into playing slowly with big arm movements.

After about fifteen minutes Elizabeth sings 'good-bye' urgently three times. Sensing a strength of emotion behind this I play slow music in D minor in 3/4.

There are strong tonal vocal sounds as she begins to sob then cry quietly. She stops, I sing her name and then finally bring the music from the Minor to a Major resolution. After this she continues to beat the drum and vocalise singing a very clear good-bye with us. This sessions lasts thirty minutes.

As the co-therapist and I listened to the recording of this session we felt that Elizabeth had shown more of her feelings than ever before and that they were predominantly feelings of anger and frustration.

October 6th

Elizabeth goes straight to the cymbal. She plays rhythmically and vocalises a little. At the drum she responds to dynamics and at one point plays a very controlled crescendo. Most particularly she responds to 'jazzy' music. This is her music today.

October 13th

Elizabeth spends some of the session playing the cymbal without purpose or focus. She responds to 'Welcome to Music' No.2 and the jazzy music from last week, following changes of tempo and dynamics on the drum.

November 3rd

We continue to work with music from recent sessions especially the slow cymbal music. I take every opportunity to offer her rhythmic patterns and tempi that contrast her preferred ones, with limited success. She is very stuck in certain rhythmic patterns and I make music with these too, e.g.:

Later there is sustained quiet cymbal playing, punctuated with bursts of loud rhythmic playing.

November 17th

Elizabeth is anxious at first. She comes into quiet, controlled playing. There is ample evidence of her musicality and she initiates:

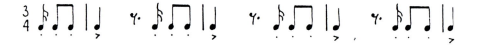

at the end of the session. At one point she cries. There is no apparent reason.

November 24th

This is a very interesting session. Much of the time Elizabeth is as though on automatic pilot', going through the motions. This may be a defence to her newly awakened involvement in the music. Later however she smiles and here is a sense of fun. We sense that inner changes are taking place.

December 1st

New march-like music in C Minor for the drum is improvised. We challenge Elizabeth to beat the rhythm of the words. She tries but cannot sustain her efforts. In complete contrast, this delicate music in the treble of the piano really seems to catch her imagination. She plays the cymbal quietly, following the rhythm throughout.

December 8th

Today's session is almost continuously instrumental. Elizabeth stands with her back to me as she plays, but is very communicative musically. Later, she sits on my knee of her own volition. All the drum beating is with the left hand and she does not want the co-therapist near or helping in any way.

December 15th

Elizabeth is evasive and scattered and remains so until the co-therapist comes behind her to encourage and support her. She plays strong slow beats on the cymbal with hands together for the first time. She also initiates (briefly), beating the side drum with alternate hands, something she has not done before. While singing good-bye, Elizabeth gives me the most direct look yet.

At the end of term we felt the following had emerged as clinical goals in our work with Elizabeth:

1. To encourage Elizabeth really to listen to the music.
2. To encourage her to find greater stability and involvement in shared music-making, leading to the expressively free, sustained, committed use of the instruments.
3. To encourage Elizabeth towards a more centred and communicative use of her voice through vocalising/singing.

After the Christmas holiday we asked Elizabeth's mother to write down what she thought were the benefits of music therapy. She wrote:

'I hope the following will help in your assessment of the effect music therapy is having on Elizabeth.

Firstly music therapy is relaxing Elizabeth, she is not nearly as tense and highly strung as she once was. Because Elizabeth is more relaxed she is beginning to be a little more confident in herself, she is more responsive and no longer so shut off. Her face is more animated and expressive and she is letting her feelings show through. It is so lovely to see her smiling at and with me and not into space or through me.

Secondly her language is improving, much of it is echolalic but we are getting more spontaneous speech from her and she is making more effort to express herself in speech.

Thirdly and just as important, Elizabeth looks forward so much to coming to music therapy that the effect after each session is quite noticeable. This is such a positive occasion for Elizabeth it must help combat so much in her that is negative.

Elizabeth has had a great many changes to cope with during the last year and although she has not yet adjusted to the changes I think that therapy has helped her cope.

I spoke to Elizabeth's care worker who has known Elizabeth for several years and she agrees that Elizabeth is a much calmer and relaxed child than she was before she commenced music therapy.'

Entering a Period of Change: January to July 1987

Over the next two months we worked with Elizabeth on alternate left hand/right hand beating with the drum and cymbal. We felt it was important for her to develop a sense of balanced co-ordination as a means of steadying her responses and deepening her involvement in the music. As we worked on this she insisted on the physical support of the co-therapist behind her, guiding the alternate beating. The co-therapist was always careful to keep to the supportive role, enabling Elizabeth to respond but not playing for her. This was often very difficult and Elizabeth fluctuated between over-dependence and wilful evasiveness. At this time she initiated more vocally. From the middle of March Elizabeth entered into a period of drawing back from contact and involvement. She became more evasive again and resistive. It was as though she was entering a new phase herself and needed time to make the transition. Increasingly she wanted the co-therapist's physical support to an over-dependent extent.

May 18th

She says good-bye from the beginning of the session. I continue to greet her with very open ended music and she begins to cry. She begins to sing in the tonality.

Elizabeth seems poised at the point of change - caught in an ambivalence of needing to retreat yet wanting to come out - wanting to avoid the close emotional contact yet somewhere responding to it. The tears were very real, she only wanted the cymbal with its less direct sound, she needed perhaps to remain 'hidden', yet to come out too. It is very noticeable how the lower pitches of her vocalisations have much more emotional content than the higher ones.

June 1st

Elizabeth is diffuse and ambivalent in her musical responses and general behaviour, constantly moving round the room making fleeting contact with the instruments. Her mother reported that a ten day holiday without her but with other children had been a great success for Elizabeth - despite high anxiety beforehand.

June 8th

Sitting at the treble of the piano Elizabeth allows me to pick out a melody with her left hand and index finger, she is very resistive at first. Her mother told us that Elizabeth is changing physically and growing into womanhood (she is twelve years old).

June 15th

This is the fourth session in a row when Elizabeth shows no interest in the instruments and sings good-bye from the beginning of the session. She plays some strong clusters on the piano and allows me to pick out a B Flat melody with her finger.

June 22nd - July 13th

We introduce Elizabeth to a variety of instruments including the bass metallophone and a reed horn. She shows no interest and is scattered in her responses. On July 11th Elizabeth's care worker visited the Nordoff-Robbins Centre; she told us that during this week Elizabeth came downstairs one morning singing Queen's 'I Need Somebody To Love Me' and in floods of tears. The staff at the home also noted that Elizabeth is very evasive and emotionally confused.

July 20th

We offer no particular direction musically in this session but create a quiet sustained and warm mood using simple open-ended music. She responds to this with a variety of vocalisations. She plays the instruments more vigorously using rhythmic patterns from some of her previous music. She seems glad just to be with us.

In August 1987 Elizabeth was seen by Dr Ricks - Consultant in Paediatric Mental Handicap at the Department of Paediatrics at the School of Medicine, University College London. This referral - made through the School Psychological Service -had been instigated by Elizabeth's mother, who was concerned to ascertain the extent of her autistic tendencies with a view to a clearer statement of her educational needs. Dr Ricks view was that Elizabeth's behaviour placed her in a sub-group of autistic children with suspect disorders of their purine metabolism known as 'purine autism'. He goes on to describe: 'they have the basic repertoire of social impairment, language disorder and manneristic activity found in autistic children but are different in various distinctive ways. They are often small for their age: they have delayed motor milestones and poor motor co-ordination which often affects their articulation, unlike the nimbleness, dexterity and clear articulation of conventional autistic children. They are prone to impulsive, occasionally aggressive, outbursts; they toe-walk, they frequently have hyperacusis or a hyper-sensitivity to certain sounds, usually of high frequency (like tearing). Certainly Elizabeth's motor unco-ordination which has a striatal quality is typical of purine autism and she also has impulsive 'winding up' episodes, often for inexplicable reasons, as many in the group do. Elizabeth's facial appearance to some extent reinforces this suspicion with its rather impassive facial expression which has a striatal quality as does her whole movement pattern.

The main point I would want to emphasise is that purine autism, a fairly recently defined sub-category of autistic children would explain in Elizabeth those features which are untypical of conventional autism. However, from the literature it does seem that this sub-group of children like other sub-groups within the autistic syndrome, do have the same learning problems with the broad autistic group. For this reason they benefit from the structured curriculum, the emphasis on intervention rather than instruction and to the highly predictable routines emphasised in schools for autistic children. Elizabeth's clinical disability has associated special educational needs, probably best met by this type of school setting. In a classroom aimed, however sympathetically, at retarded children, such autistic children often stand out as unresponsive and unrewarding in spite of the indications they give of much higher potential.

As a result of this report Elizabeth moved to a new class at school with a new teacher with experience of autistic children. She seemed happier, though she was described by the school as 'the odd one out'. In November, reports from the care placement were of Elizabeth in a 'regression'.

A Period of Steady Growth and Development as the Work Deepens: September 1987 to July 1990

September 15th

Elizabeth comes bounding in with lots of tense, diffuse energy. She says 'you do it' constantly. She is anxious. After improvising with her for a while we introduce a structured song by Paul Nordoff 'We'll Make Music' for drum, cymbal, reed horn and chime bars. Over the next weeks Elizabeth gradually becomes involved in this song, beginning to anticipate the changes from instrument to instrument but needing a lot of help. We use the song often as a preliminary to free improvisation.

September 25th

Elizabeth is very still for much of this session. Although quiet and rather withdrawn she seems to be listening to the music improvised for her.

October 6th

The beginning of the session features strong sometimes driven beating. 'We'll Make Music' really focuses her, as does an improvised 'Habanera'. Elizabeth sits down for much of the instrumental work.

November 10th

This is a difficult session. Elizabeth is very scattered and hard to involve in any way. If she sits she loses interest, if she stands she darts around. It is interesting that she doesn't revert to any of her rhythmic obsessions.

At this time the family were trying to get Elizabeth into a school for autistic children but with no success.

In 1988 there were a number of developments in Elizabeth's life. In her mothers words: 'February - Elizabeth's father started a new job which takes him away from home for varying lengths of time, Elizabeth frets when she doesn't see him for a while though she accepts and understands when told that Daddy is away working. April - Elizabeth becomes a young woman and begins her periods, coping marvellously at first. July - Children in the 'upstairs' left the house and half the staff left also. Four staff members remain and six new members started including a new 'Manager in Charge'. September - Reorganisation of the school, new class but same teacher. Classroom much larger with three separate groups in it. Elizabeth did not settle and was very distressed in this classroom mainly because of the noise level. November - Jeanette a senior staff member left - long-term staff member. Elizabeth was very upset at her leaving party and took a long time to accept her leaving.'

As we begin the new term in January 1988 Elizabeth combines making very firm musical statements of herself in the session with being very ambivalent and evasive, i.e. she seems to move from one extreme to another.

January 11th

Elizabeth is a complex mixture of ambivalence and extroversion. Her music making is characterised by her musical responsiveness, often obscured by anxiety and avoidance. Delayed echolalia abounds, for example 'bad girl', 'naughty', 'sit down'. At the same time we feel that she needs musical challenges as well.

In the spring term the work continues to evolve.

April 25th

This is a very important session. Elizabeth is eager to come and her drum and cymbal playing is loud and full of energy. She perseverates.

At one point she removes the drum and cymbal to the far corner of the room, she works there and, as the session progresses, she becomes more and more involved and is able to steady her responses which reach a new level of participation and commitment.

May 9th

This is another significant session. Elizabeth comes with many signs of anxiety, for example pressing her nose with her hand and agitated body movements. Unlike last week the session is full of compulsive and habitual 6/8 rhythms. Nevertheless, the impact of the music is such that it gives her stability and enables her to find, on her own, the other kind of beating. She is beginning to be able to come out of her habitual beating and participate more freely, more consciously. This is true of tempo and dynamic changes too. She sings quite a bit.

May 16th

Today's session sees a very anxious Elizabeth. She constantly repeats phrases such as you do it', 'sit down', 'listen', 'stand still', 'it's all right'. Despite the anxiety Elizabeth has enough inner emotional security to enable the music to hold her and bring her through into a place of shared music making. She is beginning to be able to overcome her own resistance.

In June I gave a short presentation of the work with Elizabeth to date concluding with the following quotation and comments. 'Adolescence is a time of crisis, crisis of identity, of 'making patent the latent self' (Dr M Marshak). Elizabeth is going through all the turbulence of adolescence. We believe that music is helping her develop an inner emotional security - that it is a 'safe place'. Music therapy has been important in bringing 'definition' into her life at a deep level. We believe that shape and structure in the musical improvisation have begun to enable Elizabeth to find shape and structure in her responses and in her inner life. This demonstrates again the essential place of improvisation in this work to meet the individual needs of each child. and how each child is an active partner in their own therapy. In three years of music therapy with Elizabeth there has been an 'ebb and flow' in our work. A step forward is followed by a step back or more often a step sideways. Nevertheless there has been an underlying growth and development.

September 15th

Back after the summer holidays Elizabeth is very active again, full of energy and playing many of her compulsive rhythms. She initiates:

She also initiates a pattern which she sings and plays on the drum. She leans physically on Jane for much of this session.

After a week of no therapy when I was away ill Elizabeth expressed her anger at home and just before the next session on September 22nd (though not in the session). I improvised a new song 'This is my song' and she happily lets me play the melody with one of her fingers.

October 3rd and 10th

Elizabeth spontaneously starts to sing 'This is my song'.

From here until the end of term Elizabeth again became generally more evasive and difficult to engage in any meaningful way. Nevertheless we were convinced that the music was holding her through these times and giving an important continuity.

Our end of term summary reads 'Elizabeth's voice is still very uncentered and unfocused. With the instrumental activities she still needs clear unambiguous music to engage her and channel her into music work. We feel that Elizabeth needs this challenge.

January 1989

At school Elizabeth goes into a new class with a new teacher. She seems to settle quite well. In Music Therapy the greeting song composed for her and an improvised drum march becomes the focus of the work. The quiet lyrical mood of the greeting appeals to Elizabeth and she sings fragments of it.

In time her singing becomes more sustained.

During January and February Elizabeth visits a possible new residential placement, but becomes extremely distressed. Any talk of moving upsets her so much that her parents stop talking about it. In music therapy a rhythmic yet lyrical drum song appeals to Elizabeth and she enjoys finding the melodic rhythm.

March

Elizabeth moves to a residential house run by the borough for five young people with special needs. The move goes well. Elizabeth settles into her new bedroom quite happily once the furniture is in the house. Elizabeth continues to go through a long difficult period though.

April 17th

This session sees nearly ten minutes of some of the most directed, strong and consistent drum beating Elizabeth has ever done. The music is in a jazz/blues idiom.

April 24th

Elizabeth is back to being very scattered and stuck in beating habitual rhythmic patterns.

June 12th

There is a photographer in the room today. Elizabeth shows a great deal of anxiety and is predictably very distracted. She talks about this constantly after the session.

June 19th

Today's session is very powerful. We witness co-ordinated energy in strong beating on the cymbal with big and extended arm movements. The music involved slow cymbal playing and then developed over the next nine months. The slow tempo, steady crescendo and use of first inversions continue to make strong supportive music. Elizabeth still needs the co-therapists presence behind her to support, though all the playing is hers. There is a delightful playfulness, even humour in her responses at the piano.

Having observed this session through a one-way mirror, Elizabeth's mother commented afterwards that although Elizabeth was hard to reach and remote, she noticed how the music drew Elizabeth out despite herself. 'Elizabeth is more relaxed when she leaves music - the music enables her to find an equilibrium. She is having a very traumatic time at the moment with her menstruation...'

Looking back over the year's work (September 1988 to July 1989) we recognised that the regularity of the music sessions involving the trip to London and back, as well as the sessions themselves, were an important focus for Elizabeth providing stability and always an opportunity for her to be herself and express herself freely in an accepting environment. We knew it was important to acknowledge and meet Elizabeth where she was emotionally and musically whilst offering the possibility for other experiences. Often at the piano and mainly at the end of the sessions, she would eventually sit quietly and sing fragments and short phrases of the songs with directness and purpose.

We recognised that music had given Elizabeth a powerful channel of communication in the context of a therapeutic context that acknowledged her need for space, to maintain distance and yet be close too. From our own experience as well as her mother's comments we sensed the importance of these weekly music therapy sessions for Elizabeth.

After the summer holiday the songs: 'Elizabeth is beating', 'Let's make some music', 'This is my song' were still important elements of the otherwise improvised music. The following music became very important over the coming months, enabling Elizabeth to develop a strong slow playing on a large free standing cymbal, playing with hands together and alternately.

September 18th

We move to a different music room within the Centre. Contrary to our expectations the change is stimulating for both Elizabeth and for us! This session confirms that we need to hold Elizabeth to musical work as well as offer her free improvisation. Today there is strong, directed, cymbal playing and singing. The co-therapist is actively encouraging and supportive.

October 2nd

Once again there is a proliferation of loud, fast, compulsive rhythms within a complexity and a wealth of drum beating. Elizabeth has a bad cold and is obviously unwell, She growls at me, when I growl at her she looks at me with surprise.

December

Elizabeth moves to temporary accommodation while repairs are carried out at the house. She is away four days. Her parents are away attending a family funeral at the same time.

Elizabeth's primary care worker leaves on maternity leave and Elizabeth misses her very much. Elizabeth's brother Timothy leaves home, and though not close to him she misses him too.

During 1989 there are constant staff changes at the house. In all, five staff leave and altogether there are six new members of staff. According to mother throughout 1989 Elizabeth has trouble coming to terms with menstruation and is troubled with pre-menstrual tension, becoming extremely irritable, very agitated and even aggressive at times. In retrospect we learn that the music therapy sessions when Elizabeth is most scattered, evasive and difficult to focus coincide with her pre-menstrual tension. Her behaviour in school and at home follow the same pattern.

January 1990

Elizabeth has a new teacher who is temporary until April while her usual teacher is on a course. Her father is back on the road after a month at home and there are more staff changes at the house and it is reported that Elizabeth still does not like school.

January 8th

This is a very important session. Twice Elizabeth says 'good-bye' at the beginning of the session. From the beginning her responses are strong and forceful. She becomes angry and expresses this on the instruments as well as by stamping her feet. At the drum she allows the co-therapist to support from behind again. At one point the co-therapist beats the drum herself inviting Elizabeth back into the music - a technique that has never worked before but does today.

February 5th

In a presentation of our work the co-therapist and I define our current working goals as follows:

1. To establish a working musical relationship consolidating Elizabeth's experience of the basic beat.

2. To help Elizabeth beat without a lot of extraneous movements that are distracting.
3. To continue to provide Elizabeth with an inner emotional security through music.
4. To continue the work of encouraging Elizabeth to sing.

Once again we asked Elizabeth's mother to write down what she thought were the benefits of music therapy for Elizabeth. She writes 'I am struck by the amount of change Elizabeth has had to cope with over the last year. Not only has she had to cope with circumstances around her but also changes within herself. Physically she is maturing fast and has all the turbulence of adolescence to cope with. The one thing that she has had that is constant in her life during all this change is her music therapy. She looks forward to her therapy each week and can't wait for her music therapy to start again when the school holiday ends. Elizabeth is a more confident person than she was and also a more communicative one. I feel that music therapy has helped her a great deal to achieve this. Although Elizabeth still gets high and worked up on occasions her moods can be very changeable, she has much more self control and is able to calm herself down.

I think her response to music therapy has gradually shown her that she has the ability to express her feelings and to calm down. As we left you last Monday Elizabeth said to me 'Robin is a good friend'. I agreed with her. I think that says it all.'

There are no sessions between March 6th and May 14th. This is a combination of Easter holidays and sickness.

May 14th

Elizabeth shows anger before the session and today she shows anger in the session with a lot of forceful playing of the instruments. We introduce 'The Old King' a story with music by Paul Nordoff the story was originally told to Paul Nordoff in a Camphill School by one of the children. The words are 'Once upon a time when the sun was rising there lived an old King. His father was dead and he had no mother. One day he found a big stone. He sat on the stone and lived happily ever after.'

This song involves chime bars, reed horn, drum, cymbal and a triangle. Today we sing the song for Elizabeth, without the instruments. She shows interest. We introduce 'The Old King' feeling that the emotional content of the music and words are appropriate for Elizabeth.

May 21st

Elizabeth is quietly interested and involved in 'The Old King' and she begins to play the instruments herself. We allow Elizabeth to respond freely within the structure.

For the last four sessions of term the co-therapist was away. Without her support Elizabeth was not able to sustain her interest in 'The Old King', and I returned to working in improvisation and structured instrumental activities. It was difficult to focus Elizabeth.

Recent Developments: September 1990 to November 1990

September 10th

After the long summer break and with the co-therapist back we wonder how Elizabeth will respond to us. It is a very positive session. A light-hearted 'hello' tune emerges. Elizabeth is caught by this and the three of us sing together. We note Elizabeth's physical animation in her playing and physical movements, an animation that is much less frenetic than it has been. At one level she is as elusive as ever and yet at another is really in touch with us through the music.

September 17th

Predominantly Elizabeth beats her compulsive and habitual rhythms. But these do not isolate her from co-activity, she is not nearly so stuck. She is 'mischievous' in the way she dances round the drum, tilting the drum so that the stick catches the wooden rim. Her nature is to 'circumnavigate' everything. Encouraging her to stand steadily on two feet and to beat firmly with a focus and directedness is one of our overriding considerations.

September 24th

We notice a growing physical freedom in her cymbal playing. The co-therapist is able to stand right back.

October 8th

A session combining the scattered, evasive habitual ways of playing with times of committed, direct communicativeness! At the end of this session Elizabeth sings:

In response to this a Good-bye Song is improvised. This remains important to Elizabeth. She sings it with us and week by week will start to sing it herself at the end of sessions.

November 5th

On entering the room Elizabeth is immediately involved at the drum, beating 'I can beat the drum' following a wide variety of tempi and dynamics. She is able to concentrate for about four minutes. We then lead on to slow cymbal playing; we encourage her in large free arm movements. Elizabeth finds this both exciting and upsetting; she is anxious yet is able to continue with loud strong beats, jumping up and down at the same time. Throughout this we see flashes of anger, anxiety, ambivalence, wilfulness, teasing and humour. In complete contrast, for much of the session Elizabeth chooses to play the drum quietly and delicately - I accompany this and the impression is of having an intense and intimate musical conversation. Elizabeth looks at the co-therapist frequently and wants her close but not actually to help her.

In the last three months we have noticed that Elizabeth has become more openly communicative and self-expressive. This includes more frequent displays of anger and new levels of evasiveness and resistance! In some of the most recent sessions Elizabeth has again perseverated the triplet and compound rhythms that were evident from her very first session. However, because she is functioning on a higher level of communicativeness in our sessions, we believe that in this latest phase of therapy we will be able to work very directly with whatever Elizabeth brings and accompany her into new areas of growth and development.

Conclusion

In drawing together this study of Elizabeth I will refer back to Howlin's three criteria and relate them specifically to her.

1. In the music therapy sessions the emphasis has naturally been on music as the means of communication. Working on speech and language has been a secondary consideration though we have noticed Elizabeth beginning to use language more spontaneously and appropriately. A repertoire of repeated phrases - frequently expressing anxiety - is still a feature of Elizabeth's speech. However it is very relevant that her musical vocalisations have become more centred and directed while certain songs have come to hold a special significance and meaning for her. The importance of song and the whole area of singing is illustrated in this extract from an article by Paul Nordoff:

'Pathological or developmental restrictions will clearly show themselves in a child's vocalisations - in the way he 'sings' or makes his sounds, and in his attitude towards singing; he may be unwilling to sing, he may be unable to summon enough freedom or courage to begin, or to try, to sing. Singing is an intensely human activity. To bring a child to wholehearted, unselfconscious singing, to free him into singing, is a therapeutic goal which cannot always be attained. Nevertheless, a child's vocal responses, his devotion to the songs improvised for him, and his singing - even when restricted - are both liberating and uplifting.'

2. In terms of Elizabeth's social development, we have developed a close relationship with her and the strength of the musical relationship between the three of us has given her continuity, stability and friendship.

3. The presence of routines and rituals is still a feature of Elizabeth's life but she is better able to cope with change in her surroundings. Adolescence is a time of transition and change, painful enough to negotiate without the complications of autism and severe learning difficulties. Music has enabled Elizabeth to find an inner emotional security, with the result that she has grown calmer, less tense and better able to cope with change both within and without.

Music has enabled her to express her feelings - often feelings of anger and frustration, yet music has also helped her discover and express a thoughtful, playful and certainly humorous side to her personality.

Section 4: Music Therapy with the Mentally Handicapped

15

Music Therapy and People with Severe Learning Difficulties who Exhibit Self-Injurious Behaviour

Chris Lawes and John Woodcock

This chapter describes a study of the efficacy of music therapy for four people with severe learning difficulties who exhibit self-injurious behaviour (SIB). The intervention consisted of 15 sessions of therapist interaction, followed by 28 sessions of music therapy. The findings revealed that there was no reduction in self-injurious behaviour as a result of the music therapy, nor an increase in communication skills, but that variation in self-injurious behaviour was significantly associated with the functions that it served for each person. Generalisation data supported these findings and conclusions are discussed for the role of music therapy. Several issues were raised during the study which illustrate the difficulties of evaluating music therapy. The results of the study and the implications for further research in music therapy are discussed.

Background

Music therapy has been used with handicapped people for the past 30 or 40 years. Many specific applications have been reported with a number of different groups of people: autistic children, people with mental handicaps, hearing impaired people, people suffering from brain damage and in forensic settings. Within the National Health Service (NHS) a proportion of adults with severe learning difficulties exhibit self-injurious behaviour (SIB - Oliver, 1989). Recently, self-injurious behaviour has been viewed as a maladaptive form of communication and interventions have often taken place involving a multidisciplinary team. It was within this context that a collaboration was formed between the two authors to identify research methods to evaluate music therapy.

Music Therapy and Learning Difficulties

Two major approaches have dominated the work of music therapists with people with learning difficulties in the published literature; the Nordoff-Robbins school and behavioural techniques. Nordoff and Robbins describe two techniques when working with subjects: first, the use of structured musical pieces; second, the use of improvisation. Nordoff and Robbins (1977) in a description of working with children with learning difficulties suggest that the therapist:

'Accompany any rhythmic body movement a musically inactive child makes; jumping, rocking, hand flapping, finger movements, etc. with music appropriate to it and its tempo. This can relate it for him to rhythmic-bound sound and possibly to some particular form of musical experience. His habitual movement may then become musically self-expressive, at a rudimentary level, in the musical context. This can be contributory to gaining an active contact. One result can be that he will change his movements to accord with changes in your playing.'

In this way the therapist can 'join' the world of the person, add musical structure, and incorporate rhythms and movements. Once this is achieved Goodman (1981) writes that self-confidence and control can be developed. Nordoff and Robbins argued that a number of concomitant changes may occur as well, including changes in musical tone of speech, musical rhythm of movement, awareness of therapist, musical interaction, and social function of communication via clapping or other behaviours. Goodman (1981) suggests that not only emotional development might occur: but also language and speech development through singing, the use of contact songs and improvisation.

Within the published literature there are no experimental validations of the Nordoff-Robbins techniques with people with severe learning difficulties, although there are reports of considerable clinical success. Within the behavioural tradition music is used in therapy as a reinforcer, as an extra-auditory cue, as a music learning experience, and to set the occasion for modifying non-musical behaviour. (Steele, 1968).

Music has been used as a contingent reinforcer of desired behaviour in several studies (Steele, 1968; Underhill and Harris, 1974; Harding and Ballard, 1982; Dorow, 1975). Steele used music as a reward to modify the aggressive behaviour of an eight year old child. Favourite music was played contingent upon the child remaining within a designated circle. Instruments were gradually introduced, and Steele reports that periods of co-operative behaviour increased from 4 to 23 minutes.

A number of studies have examined sterotypical behaviour. Soraci (1982) found that when a piece of recorded music was played at four different speeds to 11 children, rate of rocking or stereotypical behaviour varied with the speed of the record at between 33 and 45 rpm. Jorgensen (1975) reduced the average rate of stereotypic behaviour from 24 to 1 per session using a token economy programme of listening to favourite music as a condition of reduced rocking.

In the UK two studies have examined the outcome of music therapy in comparison to play therapy, the first with children, the second with adults. In a group of children with learning difficulties, Bunt (1985) found that music therapy was more effective in increasing positive vocalisation, turn-taking, looking at adults, and in reducing disruptive behaviour. For both therapies an increase in motor activity and context related vocalisation was found. Play therapy led to significant increases in object-centred play.

Oldfield (1986) studied four randomly selected adult subjects who received eight months of weekly music therapy followed by eight months of weekly play therapy. She found that there were some weak improvements in the music therapy condition but no strong conclusions could be drawn. She attributed this to the fact that the subjects only received 20 sessions of music therapy and so might have forgotten any gains. Both studies used cross-over designs but neither assessed the maintenance or generalisation of these changes, not any of the possible processes involved.

No studies have been identified which look explicitly at self-injurious behaviour, and very few which assess the process of therapy with handicapped people. Sloboda's (1985) analysis of the musical processes in a single case design of a child diagnosed as 'autistic' shows some of the complexities of the work.

Learning Difficulties and Self-Injurious Behaviour

Within the psychological literature a substantial array of literature has accumulated about people with severe learning difficulties, including those who exhibit self-injurious behaviour (Murphy and Wilson, 1985). However this population is not homogenous and the implications for cognitive and musical processes are little known or understood. Identified deficits may be due to physiological characteristics or environmental determinants or a combination of both. One interesting paper suggested that people with learning difficulties have a reduced ability correctly to label or understand emotional experiences as a result of these causes. This suggests that feelings and sensations can be re-labelled or identified by a therapeutic process. For people with very limited means of communication, this may be undertaken in ways which are little understood or difficult to identify.

Within learning difficulties the most prominent method of treatment has been behaviour modification. Self-injurious behaviour is a disturbing problem for care givers and for people with learning difficulties alike. Despite the seriousness of this problem, and the advance of behavioural treatments for this there is a severe deficit in the provision of treatments for this group both in the UK and the US (Griffen et al., 1986; Oliver, 1987).

A number of studies have reviewed possible factors maintaining self-injurious behaviour. Carr (1977) concluded that such behaviour is maintained by positive reinforcement such as attention, or negative reinforcement by escape from demands or aversive stimuli, or self-stimulation. But most interventions lack any formal analysis of reinforcers (Oliver et al., 1987), and most tend to employ mildly aversive methods such as overcorrection with a 'package' approach (Oliver, 1989).

Carr and Durand (1985) suggest that behaviour problems may be a form of communication. They argue that this hypothesis has not been applied in a systematic fashion either at a theoretical or empirical level. Carr and Durand suggest that with developmentally delayed children the social function of communication is not developed, and thus it might be expected that intervention programmes stressing broad communication competencies would displace behaviour problems. In one study, functionally equivalent communication was taught to a group of people with behavioural problems, which were then significantly reduced. They argue that the reconceptualisation of behavioural problems as communicative would be much more productive.

We chose to focus on self-injurious behaviour in this study because the most productive interventions from the psychological literature would suggest that a primary cause is maladaptive communication, a problem which music therapy apparently is able to address.

Evaluation of Music Therapy and Self-Injurious Behaviour

The evaluation of music therapy has been divided into two traditions qualitative and quantitative, with the former reflecting a concern to evaluate process, and the latter outcome. Little research in music therapy has been directed towards observing and describing the interaction between the therapist and client, with the exceptions of work looking at critical moments, psychoanalytical interpretations of musical meaning, or transcriptions of key musical passages (Sloboda, 1985; Ruud, 1980; Pavlicevic, 1990). However, as yet, no standard methods are available to identify this or describe the processes of music therapy for people with learning difficulties. One reason for this is the lack of agreement as to the nature of music therapy, and hence the disagreement about how to evaluate its efficacy. Various models of music therapy have been proposed, borrowing from a number of theoretical traditions; physiological, medical, cognitive, humanistic, psychoanalytic (Bunt, 1985). All of them have provided evidence for the effectiveness of music therapy from the basis of their traditions (Ruud, 1980; Pribram, 1982; Feder and Feder, 1981; Sloboda, 1985). However authors argue that music therapy cannot be described as analogous to a language based therapy (Chesney, 1987; Rudd, 1980). Minsky (1982), after Dennett (1978), in a discussion of the meaning of music argues that: 'there is simply no such theory as (music) at all; instead 'it' works in different ways at different times and all those ways have little in common for the usual sort of definition.'

Given these issues the question of how to evaluate the outcomes and processes of music therapy is raised. It is evident that to capture the richness of music therapy and evaluate these dimensions a multimodal method needs to be adopted, with multidimensional scaling. Such an approach would be flexible and meet the different questions that each study of music therapy raised. As yet, however, no such system exits, nor the scaling techniques to enable the applied music therapy researcher to assess the processes and outcomes of music therapy.

Previous studies of music therapy and handicap have stressed outcomes in terms of behaviours which can be measured (e.g. cognitive, sensory motor, etc.). Such outcome measures are typically the frequency of self-injurious behaviour, positive, negative and neutral vocalisation and engagement. The design of such studies are in the experimental or quasi experimental scientific tradition using comparison groups enabling an assessment to be made of outcome change attributable to the intervention. The studies of Bunt and Oldfield fall within this tradition. The weakness of this model is that it does not allow for individual effects which may confound the validity of this study. This latter problem is crucial for assessing outcome since group comparison designs often assume that change is in one direction (e.g. positive) and where therapy has different effects for all subjects then this may be lost when an average change is measured. Therefore single case experimental designs may be more useful.

As Nordoff and Robbins (1977) indicate, the key to therapeutic success is in the process of active participation. Such critical moments may only be apparent to the therapist. Usually these are recorded either using a diary giving an interpretation of events, or transcribed musically. Such ideographic approaches often provide a key to illuminating process, yet may not provide an easy method of 'capturing' the richness of the data, or a description of the musical process. An alternative method has been the use of Repertory Grid techniques (Hoskyns, 1987), to enable the therapist explicitly to state his construing of the process of therapy or 'beliefs tied to acts'. From this, key elements could be extracted, and presented as a dimensional representation of elements of the process as perceived by the therapist. It is proposed in this study that such an attempt is made.

The Study

The present study was designed to evaluate the effectiveness and generalisation of a music therapy programme for people with severe learning difficulties who exhibited self-injurious behaviour, and in particular whether any reductions in self-injurious behaviour were significantly associated with the functions of the self-injurious behaviour or an increase in communication skills. It differed from the work of Oldfield and others by providing an 'intensive' music therapy input within a shorter time period, assessing whether such gains generalised, and comparing the efficacy of the music therapy, not with other therapies but with that of the therapist himself. This was an attempt to isolate non-specific therapist variables. It extended such work by determining whether such gains were significantly associated with factors identified in the self-injurious behaviour and music therapy literature. The study was also designed to provide an evaluation of the process of music therapy by identifying key dimensions of the therapeutic process, and recording critical moments and transcribing them.

Design

An AB design was used with the A condition as a therapist only condition lasting 15 sessions, and the B phase (the music therapy condition) lasting 28 sessions. The music therapy condition (B) followed on after the therapist only condition (A). Measures were taken at the start and finish of the A phase (therapist condition), and at the end of the B phase (music therapy condition). Measures were also taken throughout the AB phases, and in a day centre in the hospital. The data from the three sessions were analysed using a time series analysis, and an analysis of the concordance of conditional and unconditional probabilities of the behaviours to determine if the outcome behaviour (i.e. SIB) was significantly associated with other behaviours (i.e. presence of therapist).

Subjects

Subjects were selected from a pool of people in the hospital who had exhibited self-injurious behaviour in the past four months, and who were thought by the music therapist as likely to benefit from music therapy. Several selection criteria were used:

a) No previous music therapy treatment (excluding subjects who had been in less than two sessions more than one year ago).

b) No current intervention by other staff for the self-injurious behaviour.

c) Subject approval to be gained where possible.

Four subjects were selected by the music therapist from the hospital. All four subjects were single, lived in the hospital, two were female, and their ages were 41, 51, 52 and 48 years respectively. Assessments were conducted by the speech therapy department using a schema developed by Uzgiris and Hunt (1975) and the Derbyshire Language Schema. None of the subjects used any formal means of communication to indicate their needs; e.g. signs, gestures, symbols or words.

Measures

The A and B phases of intervention involving the therapist were videotaped using a camera set in the corner of the room which was switched on by the therapist at the start of each session. In addition each of the subjects were separately videotaped at a set time, for one hour per week, in the day centre.

Measures were taken from direct observation of the videotaped data in the A and B phase as well as at the day centre. Direct observation was used to establish the frequency of self-injurious behaviour (i.e. hit head), during the videotaped sessions and to identify whether the self-injurious behaviour functioned as an escape from demands by staff (demand escape), escape from people (social escape), or to gain food or drinks (tangible reinforcement). In addition positive vocalisations (subject makes noise indicative of positive affect, or in response to elicited request), negative vocalisations (subject makes a vocalisation indicative of negative affect i.e. screaming) and neutral vocalisations (vocalisation not after any request with no particular affect), were recorded as well as stereotyped behaviour, and positive engagement (subject responds appropriately to staff demands). Data was collected for the behaviours using a procedure developed by Repp et al. (1983) using the Epsom HX20 portable lap-top computer which allowed continuous data recording. The chosen behaviours were coded using a schema and then recorded as either events or by duration. The data was collapsed into 5 second segments. The information was then downloaded onto a BBC master computer for later analysis using a programme written by Oliver and Crayton (1987).

A Music Therapy Rating Scale (MTRS) was developed using the constructs elicited from the therapist about the elements of therapeutic work with people with severe learning difficulties. The elements for the grid consisted of: the four subjects; two previous clients with best and worst outcomes; an ideal client and the worst possible client.

The elicited constructs were analysed using the GAB programme (Bannister and Higginbottom, 1985), and converted into 10 cm analogue scales.

A diary was kept after each session by the therapist, speaking to camera, of the major impressions of the session. If critical moments were identified (therapist and subject making therapeutic contact), then the musical process was transcribed.

Therapist and Music Therapy Condition

Music therapy sessions lasted on average 15-20 minutes. This period was chosen as the maximum amount of time subjects were considered likely to tolerate. For each of the two conditions (therapist and music therapy) each subject was brought from the hospital or day centre to the music therapy room by the music therapy assistant. At the start of the session the music therapy assistant would leave and come back at the finish to return the subject. During the A phase (therapist only condition) a number of procedures were followed:

a) Interaction with each subject corresponded to normal interaction during the music therapy sessions but with no music therapy being conducted e.g. if the therapist engaged in periods of silence or disengagement then this would be appropriate, and the session should last for approximately the same length of time.

b) One approach adopted was for the therapist to imagine that he was a volunteer trying to engage the subject with a familiar object.

c) Familiar everyday objects were used as a means of interaction.

During the music therapy phase the music therapist adopted a free improvisation style. This aimed to be 'client-centred' with the therapist responding musically to the output and perceived or intuited emotional state and 'presence' of the client. Events were viewed in terms of musical aesthetics and psychoanalytic theory (see Steele and Leese, 1987 for a further example of this approach).

A check was conducted after the completion of the study of the mean length of time that the subjects spent in each condition. It was found that the length of the therapist only session was shorter than the music therapy session for all subjects. The mean difference for each therapist-only (A phase) and music therapy (B phase) session for each of the four subjects was respectively: (Subject 1, 938:1,103secs; Subject 2, 823:1,138 secs; Subject 3, 918:1,057 secs; Subject 4, 883:1,005 secs).

Generalisation

To determine if any changes in behaviour occurred in another setting, subjects were observed throughout the whole period of the study in the day centre. Subjects were videotaped for one hour per week throughout the whole study. Here staff were asked to continue as usual and not to initiate any new programmes with the subjects.

Analysis of the Data

A sample of the videotaped sessions was analysed for the study. For the music therapy and generalisation conditions every other session was analysed (14 and 10 sessions). For the therapist session every two out of three sessions were analysed (10 sessions).

Inter-observer reliability

Inter-observer reliability was calculated by two observers rating the same samples of 10% of the videotaped behaviour selected at random. Both observers were trained in the procedure. For each piece of videotaped material a marked point was located and then separately observed. Inter-observer reliability was calculated using Cohen's Kappa, at the 5 second level. For the study the Kappa varied from .63 to .92, giving an overall figure of .74.

Time lag analysis

Analyses were conducted on the data using time lag sequential analyses (Sackett, 1978; Bakeman, 1978; Repp et al., 1983) to determine the relationship between the behaviours occurring at the same time as the criterion behaviour. A measure of the concordance of expected frequency between conditional and unconditional probabilities was calculated. From this a z index of significance was calculated. The functions of the self-injurious behaviour were determined by assessing whether staff demands, presence or tangibles occurred with self-injurious behaviour at the same time (lag 0).

Time series analysis

The data from the direct observation was plotted and a visual inspection of the data conducted. Where trends appeared in the data, tests for significance were conducted using a number of statistics for the time series analysis; the turning points and phase length test for non-randomness, the difference-sign test, Kendal's tau for correlation and Dufor's test for serial dependency (Morley and Adams, 1989).

Results

Self-injurious behaviour was measured as a percentage of occurrence in the therapist, the music therapy, and in the generalisation condition.

SIB and stereotypical behaviour

Subject 1 either punched his head, or pulled out his hair. Self-injurious behaviour occurred 8.62% in the day centre, 11.53% of the time in the therapist - only condition and 10.24% in the music therapy condition. Stereotypical behaviour occurred very infrequently in the therapist and music therapy condition (0.15%, 1.7%), but frequently in the day centre (18%).

Subject 2 displayed self-injurious behaviour by biting her hand. Self-injurious behaviour occurred 1.68% of the time in the therapist condition, 1.51% of the time in the music therapy condition, and 4% of the time in the day centre. Sterotypical behaviour occurred 48%, 60% and 30% of the time respectively for each of the conditions.

Subject 3 either slapped her head or picked her skin. Self-injurious behaviour occurred in the day centre for 1.5% of the time, but not in either of the therapy-only or music therapy conditions. Sterotypical behaviour occupied 100% of the time in both therapist-only and music therapy conditions, and 85% of the time in the day centre.

Subject 4 punched his head. Self-injurious behaviour only occurred in the day centre for 1.5% of the time. Sterotypical behaviour occupied 22% of time in the therapist condition, 18% of the time in the music therapy and 15% of time in the day centre.

For Subject 1 there was no change in self-injurious behaviour in the treatment condition, but a decrease in the generalisation condition. In Subject 2 there was a significant decreasing trend in self-injurious behaviour in the therapist-only condition (Kendal's tau =.53. $P<0.001$), but no significant change in the music therapy or generalisation conditions.

Positive, negative and neutral vocalisations

The percentage of occurrence of positive, negative and neutral vocalisations was measured for the three conditions. For Subject 1 there was an increase in neutral vocalisations for both the therapist and music therapy conditions. This was a positive trend (Kendal's tau=0.6 $P<0.001$) with significant oscillation at 3 lags. However, no explanation can be given as to why this might have occurred. For negative vocalisations no significant changes were evident. In the music therapy condition there was a non-random distribution for negative vocalisations ($T=4$, $P<0.05$), and neutral vocalisations varied at a non random pattern at 3 lags.

For Subject 2 there was no significant variation in trends for positive, neutral or negative vocalisation. However visual inspection of the data showed that positive vocalisation appeared to covary with self-injurious behaviour.

For Subject 3 no significant trends were found for vocalisation.

For Subject 4 negative and positive vocalisations occurred only in the therapist condition, and ceased entirely in the music therapy condition.

Thus it may be concluded that there was an association between therapist behaviour and vocalisations for Subject 1. For subject 2 they appeared to be associated with self-injurious behaviour, but for Subject 3 there appeared to be no association. For subject 4 vocalisations ceased entirely in music therapy.

Positive engagement

For Subject 1 little time was spent positively engaged in the therapist (1.91%), music therapy (1.03%), and generalisation (0%) conditions respectively. For Subject 2, more time was spent positively engaged in the day centre (12%) than was spent in the therapist (3.24%), or music therapy (1.61%) conditions. For Subject 3, 11.56%, and 25% of the time was spent positively engaged in the therapist, music therapist and generalisation conditions. For Subject 4, 53%, and 2% of the time was spent positively engaged in each of the three conditions.

As can be seen for all four subjects very little time was spent positively engaged in music therapy, but for Subjects 3 and 4 these figures were higher in the therapist condition than for Subjects 1 and 2.

Function of SIB

For Subject 1 direct observations revealed a significant association between the self-injurious behaviour and a function of social and demand escape (therapist demands $P < 0.05$; social escape in the therapist condition and day centre $P<0.05$).

For Subject 2 the function of her self-injurious behaviour was to gain tangible rewards in the day centre and in the music therapy setting ($P <0.05$), plus also social escape in the therapist condition ($P <0.05$).

For Subject 3 no functions of the self-injurious behaviour were identified between staff demands, escape, or tangibles, but self stimulation was proposed by exclusion of these categories and since she engaged in stereotypical behaviour (repetitive rocking, hair and finger flicking) for 100% of the time in both therapy conditions and 85% in the day centre.

For Subject 4 the function of self-injurious behaviour was identified as tangible reward. However self-injurious behaviour was also more likely to occur with staff presence and demands in the generalisation condition.

This latter finding may have been an artefact since the behaviour functioned to gain tangible reward (i.e. more cups of coffee, and so would occur when more staff were present). No self-injurious behaviour occurred in the two therapy conditions.

Music Therapy Rating Scale

because no behaviour changes were observed as a result of the music therapy, the ratings from the MTRS were not analysed and presented in this study.

Discussion

The aim of this study was to evaluate music therapy with people with severe learning difficulties who exhibited self-injurious behaviour. No previous study had addressed this group, or measured generalisation of gains when comparing music therapy to other therapies. Although this study focused on outcomes, a process measure was devised to account for any positive results. From the findings of this study it is evident that the hope that more music therapy with people with severe learning difficulties will necessarily lead to improvements is misplaced. No observable gains in positive engagement, vocalisation or self-injurious behaviour were made in this study as a result of the music therapy. A number of theoretical and methodological reasons may be suggested to account for these findings.

Three models have been proposed in the literature to explain self-injurious behaviour; the first suggests that self-injurious behaviour serves a number of functions; the second suggests that self-injurious behaviour is the result of broad communication deficits; the third that self-injurious behaviour can be modified by positive reinforcement.

When applied to the process of music therapy, the first model suggests that self-injurious behaviour might be varied if the therapist serves the function of the behaviour. Thus no long term change might occur, although a temporary decrease in the behaviour might result. This was shown by all four subjects; namely, that the self-injurious behaviour had different functions and so varied as a result of these. The implication is that the characteristics of the therapist are the critical variables in change, not the music therapy, a factor not considered in any other study of music therapy.

The second model would suggest that self-injurious behaviour is primarily communicative, and would not be reduced unless communication skills improved. Since in this study positive vocalisation did not change, this model remains as a possible line of investigation.

The final model is the one adopted by most music therapy studies to date whereby music is seen as a positive reinforcement for positive behaviour. If this happened in this study one would expect positive engagement by the subject to increase during music therapy, however this did not occur. From this perspective music therapy might become more effective if these factors were explicitly addressed.

A second reason for the failure of the study to demonstrate observable gains is that the nature of the music therapy itself was not appropriate. Use of improvisation based upon a psychoanalytical model may not be appropriate at this stage of the process, with this client group; this is discussed in detail later on.

A third reason for the failure of the study to show demonstrable gains may lie in the methodological approach adopted for this study. First, the experimental design may have interfered with the process of therapy since the therapist was required to deviate from his normal mode of working, and so the initial therapeutic alliance may have been changed. Second, the measures selected may have missed important facets of the process or fallen into the trap of type 1 errors, where minute changes were missed, or not even measured. Third, a problem which appeared during the study was finding subjects who exhibited self-injurious behaviour frequently enough during a 20 minute period. As a result subjects who exhibited self-injurious behaviour frequently were those with whom other interventions had failed, and who were severely handicapped. It may well be that such a study needs to be repeated with subjects who are less severely handicapped, and who are able to demonstrate some form of verbal communication prior to the study. In general the authors would recommend that with any study of music therapy attention needs to be paid to: (1) the initial screening and assessment (particularly for communication skills); (2) the means of gaining and maintaining the attention and motivation of the client; (3) a specification of the measurable aims and goals of therapy; (4) an acceptance that gains may be very small; and (5) that other non-music therapists could carry out some of the initial work of therapy (e.g. gaining the attention of the client, decreasing some of the functions of self-injurious behaviour, and gaining client motivation).

A number of competing models of music therapy have been identified in the literature, but a comparative study to date has not been conducted. However, it may well be that within a music therapy session each of these theoretical approaches might illuminate different aspects of the therapy, or even suggest that a number of processes are operating within a single session. In this case the best means of identifying key facets of the therapeutic process in future research would be to use a multidimensional approach. This would allow alternative models to be studied, and explore the possibility of different processes acting and interacting over time. A larger whole might be constructed from the findings of separate studies. Thus with this study it is evident that in future research the functions of self-injurious behaviour have to be identified, as well as the communication skills of the person. In other studies other factors will be important. One way to illuminate these factors might be to develop the Music Therapy Rating Scale, using the repertory grid technique, to clarify the underlying assumption of the therapist. This would allow for the generation of ideas about key issues in the processes being undertaken. The therapist as part of this process has an expert role not only because s/he is part of the relationship, but because s/he has knowledge about the music itself. Such a study could involve the active participation of the client where possible.

The value of such an approach can be seen when various studies are tied together to provide a temporal description of the process of therapy with people with learning difficulties. Behaviour modification techniques may well be useful in the first stages of therapy to gain attention, reinforce desired behaviour, and enhance the subject's perception of control and motivation by playing their favourite music. At the same time, on a physiological level, aspects of the music may have an effect on e.g. heart rate, endorphin levels, or muscle tone. During later stages of music therapy at a cognitive level the response to the music therapy may enable speech to develop, communication skills to be used, or intellectual processes to be assessed. During all stages of music therapy at a psychotherapeutic level, emotions may be labelled or 'tied by acts to physiological experiences', or the experience of the relationship between the therapist and client may enable transferences to occur. Throughout these stages the playing of music may help in ways which are as yet not understood. All or some of these processes may occur at all or some of the time, and as such open up our understanding of the benefits of music therapy. Such a perception would transform an assessment approach purely from a single behaviour to an assessment of a multiplicity of outcomes. Such a move would parallel a move away from a medical model to one which addresses a holistic view of the person, and asks questions about the impact of music therapy upon their quality of life.

The confusion in this field may have been linked to the notion that music therapy is a single entity with a single purpose which can be evaluated as such. Rather music therapy needs to be viewed as a communicative relationship between two people who do not know each other, but are trying to create a new understanding using a means that neither understands very well. This study has been one very small part in that process.

Acknowledgement

Part of this chapter is reproduced from *Clinical Psychology Forum* by permission.

16

Music Therapy Assessment for Developmentally Disabled Clients

Roy E. Grant

To assess or not to assess? This is seemingly a never-ending debate at formal and informal gatherings of music therapists. Included in such debates also, is whether we need a formal, standardised assessment instrument, or if an informal assessment will suffice to bring credibility to the profession. Indeed, the music therapy assessment is essential if we as music therapists are involved in the active treatment process, and if we function as a contributing member of an interdisciplinary team. In order for music therapy to stand at the threshold in the education/treatment of the developmentally disabled child, it must produce empirical evidence of its uniqueness on the cutting edge of active treatment. There is no other choice; we must establish our credence in contributing to primary needs of clients, or we do not have any credence. This process begins in the evaluative process in determining the primary needs, the strengths, the tomorrows.

In the USA, governmental accrediting and funding agencies require individualised programmes through an interdisciplinary effort, beginning with assessing strengths and needs within established parameters, then writing a programme of intervention. This is true for children in public schools or in residential facilities. The Intermediate Care Facility Guidelines (ICF-MR), designed for clients in residential facilities, specifically mention both formal and informal assessments in order effectively to evaluate an individual within 10 skill areas. Public Law (94-142) dictates free public education for handicapped children, mandates interdisciplinary programming, and mandates services in the least restrictive environment. This sometimes includes children in residential facilities, who also attend public schools. The American Council on Mental Retardation and Developmental Disabilities (AC MRDD) is an accrediting agency with volunteer participation, mandating high standards for those who are institutionalised, including the interdisciplinary process and beginning with the assessment.

Music therapists cannot afford to stand aside and wait for other disciplines to do the assessing and programme development, hoping that we can fit in somewhere and make the children happy. We must bring to the initial planning stages our uniqueness-music-and the students' unique responses to music stimuli. Parents of handicapped students hear repeatedly that their child functions on a low level, that certain skills are missing and that certain maladaptive behaviours are magnified, much of it a result of standardised tests comparing the child with normative data. The music therapist can bring to the evaluation information on

273

what the child can actually do in any number of skill areas, often including splinter skills or unique musical responses that surpass mental age level or other skills. It is the music therapist who often can prognosticate normalisation activities within the community, based on assessment results. We can evaluate many adaptive skills and programme intervention strategies to help meet needs in areas of deficiencies.

There are at least four areas in which the music therapist can make a unique contribution to the evaluative process: sensorimotor; cognitive, especially in the areas of visual and auditory perceptual skills; communication; and social. The author's assessment instrument addresses these areas and assists in identifying adaptive behaviours and skills within an interdisciplinary framework. It is intended that the instrument be adapted for use in a variety of settings, and for this reason parts of it may be used for some individuals and situations, but supplemented in others in accordance with philosophical or curricular content. More important than a score will be particular skills, how these skills can be used toward other learning, and how these skills can help the individual adapt to the environment and enjoy life to the optimal level. The exception might be in the sensorimotor area where a trend in the scores will be probable, thereby delineating a developmental level. Caution must be used in stating these levels, however, because severely handicapped individuals frequently have emotional problems which interfere with sensorimotor performance, the result often being non-performance, or what we consider maladaptive. The same is true in other areas, of course, but it has been most problematic in the sensorimotor area in the training of music therapists. This is most often evident in the first eight items; either the young therapist will ascertain a different rating for different items, or on consecutive days will determine a completely different set of ratings, declaring, 'Wow, 'Johnny' surely is inconsistent.' Indeed, 'Johnny' may be inconsistent, but not in his sensorimotor development; emotional problems are interfering.

Sensorimotor skills do not change moment by moment or day by day; neither do perceptual skills or communication skills, except in extreme cases of neurological impairment. This is one of the most difficult things to learn in becoming a therapist - pinpointing the specific behaviour desired, then programming that specific phenomenon, closing out all interference, and deciphering competing responses. We know that medications and certain malfunctions of the organism may affect any performance, but we get skilled in recognising these quite early in our careers.

The following explanations of the four areas included in the assessment, along with the testing items, are intended to help pinpoint particular behaviours, and contribute to the habilitation process.

Sensorimotor

Music therapists bring uniqueness to the sensorimotor assessment through music, especially rhythm. To complete an accurate assessment, the therapist must be creative and play music, to which most children will respond motorially. Too often, the young therapist in training will look at the assessment sheet, ponder it, painstakingly get a drum from the cart or box, and say, 'Johnny, play the drum.' No response. 'Johnny, I want you to play the drum.' Johnny drops the drum on the floor.... Poor, Johnny. If the therapist simply plays music, Johnny most often will get his own drum or preferred instrument (even better) from the cart and play it. In the creative encounter through music, few words are necessary.

During the sensorimotor assessment, play music and facilitate responses. Live and/or recorded music is appropriate, but only live music can be manipulated extensively, i.e. tempos, volume, different rhythmic structures, and other aspects. For this reason, live music is always preferable during the assessment. Duple meter is preferable, and the quarter-note and eighth-note structures will probably elicit more correct responses, although more rhythmic structures should be presented, including the chance for the client to be creative. By the different structures, I mean the beat-pulsation-division units, known in some circles as beat-division-subdivision. Also, the melodic rhythm of songs offers another avenue to explore, and specific patterns inherent in the melodic rhythm offer a chance to explore cognitive/sensorimotor skills. By all means, each individual must have the opportunity to be rhythmically creative during an assessment. Professional judgement must dictate the degree of syncopation employed, depending on the individual's responses. Most important, the end result, the written evaluation, must delineate the client's skills, limitations, and needs, not the therapist's limitations in assessment and/or creativity. If the instrument is used as a guide, and the assessment is administered over several days, the written evaluation will include strengths and needs in at least the following areas:

a. Co-ordination skills, agility, rhythmicity, both nonlocomotor (items 1-10, 13, 19, 22) and locomotor (items 25-28), in addition to both together (items 29, 30), in relation to rating scale.
b. Handedness. Differentiate between hand preference in particular tasks and hand dominance, or note absence of either.
c. Reach/grasp/release skills, including palmar (items 3, 4, 8-12, 17-24) and pincer grasps (item 7).
d. Bilateral co-ordination (items 2, 4, 5, 8, 10, 12). Nonlocomotor.
e. Eye-hand co-ordination (items 1, 2, 5, 8-24).

Cognitive

The written evaluation will address auditory and visual perceptual skills in areas of:

a. Awareness
b. Location
c. Tracking
d. Imitation
e. Visual discrimination and sequencing

f.   Auditory discrimination and sequencing
g.   Short-term auditory memory
h.   Object permanence

Further information and/or validation of skills may be obtained by being creative and providing more stimuli than given on the rating forms herein. For example, longer rhythm patterns may be used in echo-tapping. Also, whereas simple rhythms without syncopation are intended, more complex rhythms using syncopation may be used with higher functioning clients. The music therapist, as a member of the interdisciplinary team, may feel free to assess knowledge of numbers, colours, cause-and-effect, object permanence, or other information which may be programmed during the assessment process or later in the intervention stage. However, part of the interdisciplinary process is to rely on our peers in other disciplines to represent their areas of expertise.

The sensory modalities offering possible avenues for reinforcers must also be explored. Everyone on the interdisciplinary team has a responsibility to help identify possible reinforcers. Most often, the music therapist will find particular instruments or musical selections which are quite effective as rewards. Music preferences are important in this process, as stylistic preferences are often communicated by even the severely/profoundly mentally handicapped individuals. The musical reinforcers will be effective in eliciting both musical responses and desired non-musical behaviours such as reading, math, or particular social skills. Important also is whether the client can understand the work-reward concept. Contingent music is usually the place to start, and most students across all developmental levels will quickly understand this contingency. There will be some individuals who respond readily to non-musical reinforcers, which are effective in eliciting and extending participation in the music making. Frequently, a preferred sensory modality can be identified which opens up avenues for numerous elements in the auditory, visual, tactile, or olfactory modalities as reinforcers. These communication/cognitive functions will pay dividends throughout the music therapy intervention process. They are an indispensable part of the assessment.

Communication

Assessment in communication skills will include aspects of receptive and expressive skills. One of these areas, vocalisation, is peculiar to the music therapist, as probably no other discipline will provide information on vocal pitch control skills and vocal range, which limit all vocal expression. Our goal is not to produce opera singers, or even to identify them on the assessment, but to assess whether a child has the capacity to express basic needs and feelings, and to what extent beyond this basic level. Quite often, the decision to mainstream or not to mainstream can be determined primarily on these skills. Structured failure will bring embarrassment and further failure. The rating scale of three levels: non-singer, directional singer, and tuneful singer--offers sufficient criteria to evaluate the vocal skills on a simple but empirical basis.

Receptive language skills, including receptive labelling of instruments will offer possible avenues for future programming in following directions, overlapping with auditory processing skills already addressed. The music therapist should also assess expressive language skills, including labelling, grammatical structure, complete versus incomplete sentences, and evidence of particular dialect or cultural colloquialisms, then, in the true spirit of interdisciplinary function, discuss the findings with the speech pathologist. Joint programming often brings rapid positive results.

Social

It is my belief that developmentally disabled children progress through the four levels of play: individual, parallel, co-operative, and competitive (Moran and Kalakian, 1977), although sometimes it may be difficult to ascertain a clear progression from one stage to another, and the attainment of each progressive step may be delayed in comparison to normative data. Even severely handicapped adolescents can be quite competitive. It is possible, indeed imperative, to structure each activity in accordance with one or more level(s) of play, and it is then possible to observe empirically one's participation on any of these levels.

Most developmentally disabled children will have social deficits, and it becomes imperative to provide structure during which particular skills can be taught. The music setting offers a unique structure in which all four levels of play can be realised. The written evaluation will address the length of time spent in particular levels of play, observations of interaction with peers and adults, particular interfering behaviours, and strengths and needs peculiar to the individual.

MUSIC THERAPY ASSESSMENT

Sensorimotor Skills

Rating Scale:
1. Does not attempt to perform movement, even after prompt
2. Attempts to perform movement
3. Performs randomly/indiscriminately
4. Performs continuously but not rhythmically
5. Performs continuously and rhythmically
6. Synchronises movements with musical stimulus for several beats
7. Synchronises movements with musical stimulus for several measures
8. Synchronises movements with musical stimulus for entire selection
9. Not applicable; note reason

Apply to the following at pre-test and post-test, noting dates:

1. Plays drum with either hand.
2. Plays drum with both hands in parallel and alternating motion.
3. Shakes wrist bell or maraca with either hand.
4. Shakes wrist bell or maraca with both hands.
5. Claps hands.
6. Strums stringed instrument with open hand or finger(s).
7. Strums using pick.
8. Plays claves or rhythm sticks.
9. Plays resonator bells or xylophone bars (at least 5, placed together) with either hand, using mallet.
10. Plays resonator bells or xylophone bars (at least 5, placed together) with hands in parallel and alternating motion, using mallets.
11. Plays resonator bells or xylophone bars (at least 5, spaced apart), with either hand, using mallets.
12. Plays resonator bells or xylophone bars (at least 5, spaced apart), with both hands in parallel and alternating motion, using mallets.
13. Plays drum with either hand, using mallet, while in stationary position.
14. Plays drum with both hands in parallel and alternating motion, using mallets, while in stationary position.
15. Plays drum with either hand while drum is being moved horizontally across midline, vertically, and in circle within peripheral limits.
16. Plays drum with either hand when placed in different positions within 18' of centre line of chest.
17. Plays drum with either hand while drum is being moved horizontally across midline, vertically, and in circle within peripheral limits, using mallet.
18. Plays drum with either hand when placed in different positions within 18' of centre line of chest, using mallet.
19. Plays woodblock using mallet while in stationary position.
20. Plays woodblock using mallet while moving horizontally across midline, vertically, and in circle within peripheral limits.
21. Plays woodblock using mallet when placed in different positions within 18' of centre line of chest.
22. Plays resonator bell using mallet while in stationary position.
23. Plays resonator bell using mallet while moving horizontally across midline, vertically, and in circle within peripheral limits.
24. Plays resonator bell using mallet when placed in different positions within 18' of centre line of chest.
25. Stamps feet (standing, in place).
26. Walks/marches.
27. Jumps (lands on two feet).
28. Hops (lands on one foot).
29. Plays instrument and walks/marches simultaneously.
30. Plays instrument and stamps feet (standing, in place) simultaneously.

Cognitive, Auditory/Visual Perceptual Skills

Rating Scale:
1.   Does not perform task, even with assistance and/or prompts
2.   Performs task with assistance and/or prompts
3.   Performs task independently

Apply to the following at pre-test and post test, noting dates:
1.   Startles in response to loud musical stimulus.
2.   Changes activity momentarily when musical stimulus is presented.
3.   Focuses eyes on source of musical stimulus for 2-3 seconds.
4.   Turns head/eyes to left and/or right toward sound source.
5.   Moves head/eyes up and/or down toward sound source.
6.   Tracks auditory object horizontally to midline.
7.   Tracks auditory object horizontally across midline.
8.   Tracks auditory object in a circle in front of face.
9.   Imitates simple body movements of therapist (slap legs, clap hands) with and/or without verbal cues.
10. Imitates therapist playing single specified instrument, accompanied with verbal cue, 'Do this'. No visual distractors.
11. Imitates therapist playing single specified instrument, accompanied with verbal cue, 'Do this'. One visual distractor.
12. Imitates therapist playing single specified instrument, accompanied with verbal cue, 'Do this'. Two visual distractors.
13. Plays a sequence of two designated instruments, without visual distractors.
14. Plays a sequence of two designated instruments, with visual distractors.
15. Plays a sequence of three designated instruments, without visual distractors.
16. Plays a sequence of three designated instruments, with visual distractors.
17. Discriminates individual instrument sounds.
18. Discriminates and sequences 2 instrument sounds.
19. Discriminates and sequences 3 instrument sounds.
20. Echo-taps one-unit rhythm pattern.
21. Echo-taps two-unit rhythm patterns.
22. Echo-taps three-unit rhythm patterns.
23. Echo-taps four-unit rhythm patterns.
24. Echo-taps five-unit rhythm patterns.
25. Follows one simple verbal command.
26. Follows one complex verbal command.
27. Follows sequence of 2 simple commands.
28. Follows sequence of 2 complex commands.
29. Follows sequence of 3 simple commands.
30. Follows sequence of 3 complex commands.

Give comments on cognitive skills, instrument preferences and musical preferences.

Note. The visual distractors mentioned in Numbers 10 through 16 refer to the presence or absence of musical instruments which are extraneous to the given task.

Communication Skills

Rating Scale:
1. Does not vocalise
2. Vocalises isolated tones only; does not accurately imitate or use inflection or pitch
3. Directional imitation or vocalisation; some expressive skills (explain below)
4. Accurate or tuneful imitation or vocalisation, including singing

Apply to the following at pre-test and post test, noting dates:
1. Sings descending minor third interval using vowel sounds, nonsense syllables, or words (specify).
2. Sings descending scale pattern (minimum of 3 notes) on vowel sounds, nonsense syllables, or words (specify).
3. Sings ascending scale pattern (minimum of 3 notes) on vowel sounds, nonsense syllables, or words (specify).
4. Sings isolated phrases of songs.
5. Sings entire songs.
6. Vocal range: x to y (disregard rating scale).

Give comments, including receptive and expressive communication skills:

Social Skills

Rating Scale:
1. Participates for duration of 2 phrases (7-8 seconds)
2. Participates for duration of 4 phrases (15 seconds)
3. Participates for duration of 8 phrases (30 seconds)
4. Participates for duration of 8 phrases repeated (1 minute)
5. Participates for duration of 1 activity (2-3 minutes)

Apply to the following at pre-test and post test, noting dates:
1. Individual play
2. Parallel play
3. Co-operative play
4. Competitive play

Examples of Results

Example 1

Music Therapy Assessment Re: M12 (Male, age 12)
IEP Dually Diagnosed

Perceptual

M12's visual perceptual skills are among his strengths. He sequences two instruments with visual distractors present 100% of trials, and sequences three instruments with visual distractors present 50% of trials. Data indicate improvement in the short time he has been programmed. His auditory perceptual skills are also improving. He echo-taps a 4-unit rhythm pattern 75% of trials, an unsuccessful task during the first week. He follows two simple or complex commands, but does not correctly discriminate and sequence two instrument sounds.

Sensorimotor

M12 synchronises his movements with a musical stimulus for the duration of an entire activity while playing any of the instruments used in music therapy. He performs two tasks simultaneously, such as playing a drum while marching, although he has difficulty co-ordinating the tasks together and with a musical stimulus: the locomotor task takes precedence over the nonlocomotor task. He jumps in rhythm with a musical stimulus, but has difficulty hopping. Gross and fine motor skills, and eye-hand co-ordination are among his strengths.

Communication

M12 uses 4-word utterances when asked questions about group members or musical instruments. He is currently being programmed to increase the number of responses per session, along with volume and spontaneity. Data indicate progress has been made in his expressive communication. His ineffectiveness in communicating his wants often precedes tantrums which interfere with programming. Further work in this area is merited. Limited data indicate problems with vocal range and vocal pitch control skills, although a thorough assessment has not been possible; but with progress already seen in the short time he has been programmed, it is believed the latter skills will improve also.

Social

M12 participates for the duration of 1.4 parallel play activities per session, and is making progress on increasing the number completed per session. He rarely initiates interactions with peers or staff in music therapy, but responds appropriately when called upon or approached. He occasionally giggles at appropriate times, but does so at other times inappropriately, seemingly using his laughter as an avoidance technique, as he is off task when this occurs.

Strengths:
Gross and fine motor skills
Receptive communication
Visual perceptual skills

Needs:
Expressive communication skills
Improve social skills
Decrease maladaptive behaviours

Example 2

Music Therapy Assessment M7 (Male, age 7)
Annual Review Dually Diagnosed

Sensorimotor

M7 demonstrates good reach/grasp/release skills utilising palmar grasp. He uses his left hand more often than his right when playing the drum or xylophone but strums the autoharp with his right hand when told to keep his left hand in his lap. The drum appears to be his preferred instrument and he plays it continuously for up to two minutes and synchronises his playing with the therapist's singing for several measures. At other times, when the therapist plays the drum with him, he spontaneously initiates variations in the rhythm, tempo and dynamic levels. He plays with mallets for brief periods, during which time he often fails to make appropriate contact with the instrument in front of him. He does not play rhythm sticks and plays the drum with both hands in parallel motion for only two or three beats. Further work is needed in the areas of eye-hand co-ordination and bilateral co-ordination.

Perceptual

M7 demonstrates awareness of auditory stimuli by temporarily ceasing activity and tilting his head to one side. He also tracks an auditory object to the midline. He possesses emerging imitation skills as evidenced by his occasional imitation of the therapist's actions when given verbal and physical prompts.

Vocalisation/Communication

There are four nursery rhymes in M7's repertoire. He seldom signs an entire song, but vocalises one or more phrases with generally correct intonation and/or recognisable changes in melodic direction. He sings spontaneously but on command only after several prompts. The words of the songs he sings are recognisable approximations. He also speaks a few words appropriately (e.g. 'ball' and 'no'). Further work is needed in the area of verbal/alternate communication.

Social

M7 participates in parallel play with the therapist for up to two minutes and has on four occasions engaged in parallel drum play for five minutes. He makes eye contact with the therapist and sometimes becomes playful during drum duets. In music/movement group sessions he has increased his time spent within the group from 65% to 100% in three months; he no longer runs off to a corner of the room. He has been on task 98% of the time, a 79% increase since January.

Strengths:	Needs:
Reach/grasp/release (Palmer)	Eye-hand co-ordination
Agility	Bilateral co-ordination
Auditory-visual awareness	Pincer grasp
Improving social skills	Imitation skills
	Communication skills

Example 3

Music Therapy Assessment F13 (Female, age 13)
Annual Review Dually Diagnosed

Sensorimotor

F13 demonstrates excellent gross and fine motor co-ordination skills. She performs locomotor and nonlocomotor tasks with agility during music-and-movement sessions. She synchronises her movements with changing rhythmic structures and tempos of the music. Her previous assessment results noted the need for strengthening her bilateral co-ordination. Progress has been made as evidenced by her performance of two tasks simultaneously, each involving eye-hand co-ordination as well as bilateral co-ordination. The following examples illustrate this: She uses two mallets in playing instruments with hands in parallel and alternate motion; and in one activity she shakes a bell with one hand while tapping her knee with the other hand, simultaneously and alternately. Both movements are in synchrony with each other and with the music. Much progress is evident in all areas.

Perceptual

F13's perceptual skills are among her strengths. Her imitation of minutely varied movements is evidence of excellent visual discrimination skills. She echo-taps rhythm patterns of up to three units, either by clapping or by playing an instrument. She demonstrates keen auditory discrimination skills, distinguishing between individual instrument sounds, and matching vocal sounds performed by the therapist. Further work is needed in the area of auditory and visual sequencing.

Communication

F13 uses sign language and verbal approximations to express her needs and wants. She is currently labelling six instruments, using verbal approximations. She is also working on verbalising two- and three-syllable words (her own name and names of those with whom she has frequent contact). This is being done by having her play the rhythm of these names on the drum while saying the names. As part of her parallel play activities, her objective for the quarter is that she will sign the words of three four-phrase songs while the therapist sings. She is now half-way through the third song. Occasionally, she imitates the correct pitches presented by the therapist or makes isolated vocal sounds which approximate the pitches sung by the therapist.

Social

F13's aggressiveness toward the therapist has declined dramatically over the past two months. In the music/movement group it has been staff, rather than her peers who have been targets of her aggression. She participates in imitative tasks 64% of the time and in non-imitative tasks 86% of the time. During individual sessions she appears eager to play whichever instrument is assigned to her. When given the opportunity, she indicates her choice of instrument verbally. Recently, she has been expressing the desire to prolong an activity (2-3 minutes) or a session (15 minutes) by picking up and playing another instrument. These data reflect considerable progress.

Strengths:	**Needs:**
Motor skills	Improved Communication skills
Visual discrimination	Socialisation

Example 4

Music Therapy Assessment M11 (Male, age 11)
Annual Review Dually Diagnosed

Perceptual

M11's visual and auditory perceptual skills are among his strengths in music therapy. He imitates the therapist in motor movements and playing specific instruments, although he has difficulty when distractors are present in both visual discrimination and in visual sequencing tasks. In auditory tasks he echo-taps rhythm patterns up to four units, but is more successful in verbalising patterns of rhythmic syllables presented by the therapist than in playing the patterns on an instrument; however, he plays a sequence of three numbered bells after the therapist calls out the numbers. He follows one-stage simple and complex commands but has difficulty sequencing two or more.

Sensorimotor

M11 appears to have good gross and fine motor skills, but he has considerable difficulty co-ordinating his movements to an external stimulus. He plays instruments in rhythm with the music for only a few beats at a time. This same problem may be evident in the auditory tasks previously described, in that he verbalises rhythmic patterns more readily than he plays them on the instrument during imitative tasks. Also, M11's lack of participation and attitude skew the data somewhat in tasks demanding extended performance. Nevertheless, further programming seems merited in perceptual motor skills, including eye-hand co-ordination.

Social

M11's social skills remain a primary need. Data reveal little if any progress in music therapy groups. He is more co-operative during one-on-one interactions. Recently he has participated in the group during some individual tasks which he prefers, such as strumming the autoharp, but most often does not participate and often interferes with other group members' performance.

Communication

M11 has been programmed to use verb + object in expressing his preference for instruments in music therapy. The latest data reveal he has succeeded in at least close approximations 53% of trials. Expressive communication remains a primary need.

Strengths:	Needs:
Gross and fine motor skills	Expressive communication
Visual and auditory	Perceptual motor skills
Perceptual skills	Social skills
Receptive language	

Postscript

Persistence on the part of the music therapist in pursuing these assessment data and discussing the problems with other team members, especially the psychiatrist, finally led to the discovery of hyperlexia, which results in many changes in the child's programme. Interestingly, none of the indications were revealed in standardised assessments.

Example 5

Music Therapy Assessment M11 (Male, age 11)
IEP Dually Diagnosed, visual impairment from self-injurious behaviour

Perceptual

M11 focuses on a sound source for several seconds and often reaches to bring the source closer to him. He tracks an auditory object across midline and in a circle. He imitates the therapist in gross motor movements and in playing specified instruments with up to three distractors present. He visually sequenced two and three instruments with near 100% accuracy during the assessment. He needs further work in auditory perception. During the assessment he did not perform any auditory discrimination, auditory sequencing or short-term recall tasks correctly. M11 was quite distractible during the assessment and it was difficult to attain and maintain his attention; therefore, these data represent a minimal assessment of his potential.

Sensorimotor

M11 performs bilateral tasks, such as playing drums with both hands together and in alteration, and uses either hand during unilateral tasks. It has been difficult to ascertain hand preference. He has good palmar and pincer grasps as well as functional reach, grasp and release skills. He has good emerging eye-hand co-ordination skills, demonstrated by the fact that at times he performs sophisticated tasks in musical instrument play, while at other times he demonstrates some problems. Lack of attention effects his performance in these tasks. At times he evinces good nonlocomotor and locomotor agility, but frequently makes abrupt, jerky movements and occasional rocking movements that distract from his performance.

Communication

M11 follows simple verbal commands and establishes some eye contact with the therapist. He spontaneously vocalises and changes inflection, and he attempts to imitate vocalisations made by the therapist, but is unsuccessful. He does not communicate verbally or with the use of signs. Communication is identified as a major need.

Social

Mll participates in parallel play activities with frequent prompts and redirection. He is easily distracted and needs to increase time spent on task. M11 interacts with the therapist on a limited basis, but more so than with his peers. He sometimes shares an instrument with peers but often grabs instruments from them. His needs will include on-task behaviour and peer interaction.

Assessment Summary

Since M11's vision is deteriorating, it is imperative that a programme begins immediately to improve his auditory perception and auditory processing skills. Expressive communication is also a primary need.

Postscript

It was the music therapist in this case who identified the child's strength in processing information through the visual channel and the weakness in the auditory channel. Because the child was rapidly losing his vision, due to irreversible damage from self-injurious behaviour, most team members did not bother to assess the visual skills. It became imperative to develop skills in other sensory modes.

Example 6

Music Therapy Assessment F14 (Female, age 14)

IEP mild mental retardation, cultural deprivation, adjustment problems at school

Communication

F14 has a vocal range from G below Middle C to Bb2, just below High C, a fantastic range, and she has full control of the entire range, displaying vocal agility exceeding the norm for her chronological age. Her only weakness during the assessment was in the area of auditory processing: discrimination, sequencing, and short-term memory, which hinders her ability to learn new songs.

Postscript

F14 responded to a planned programme improve her auditory skills, including rote learning, and some phonetic reading skills. She returned to her high school after one year and was mainstreamed in chorus. She auditioned for and attained the leading role in a Christmas pageant during her first semester.

Summary

The preceding were a few examples of how the assessment instrument has been used for the IEP and the Annual Review process. In each case, the results indicated the function of the music therapist as an integral part of the interdisciplinary team in determining the strengths, needs, and the future of each student.

At times it becomes crucial to administer only a part of the assessment. For example, at one interdisciplinary team meeting, the team leader announced that F14 had only one goal to meet before meeting the criteria for release, that being buttoning and unbuttoning clothing. More broadly, she needed much work in bilaterality and finger dexterity. At that point it became crucial to assess these two areas and to plan a programme to help meet this particular goal. The music therapist was a leader and co-ordinator of team efforts to develop these skills, and F14 met the goal within the anticipated time frame. Individual needs are always the focal point, while also identifying the strengths that will enable one to attain the established goals.

This assessment instrument has been developed along with the curriculum parameters set forth by Grant (1989). Reference to the curriculum guide may facilitate greater understanding and flexibility in adapting the instrument to a particular model. Appreciation is expressed to all former music therapy interns who have studied with the author. Even without knowing it, perhaps, all have contributed toward the development of this assessment, even in their struggles. Special thanks must be conveyed to Lori Herbat and Marie DiGiamarino.

17

Perspectives on a Developmental Model of Music Therapy with Mentally Handicapped Adults

Steve Dunachie

Bunt (1985) suggests that it may become necessary to examine in detail the actual musical content of music therapy sessions, and perhaps develop a simpler approach to working with mentally handicapped clients. The implication of this suggestion is that there may be an element of musical redundancy in the input of therapists to their sessions, and that this may serve to obscure rather than enhance the musical rapport which is central to the therapeutic process.

This chapter seeks to explore some of these implications further and to sketch a possible approach to the practical music-making aspect of therapy, based on a developmental model of musical growth which may link in with the broader, psychotherapeutic understanding of the clients' problems and needs.

An assumption which seems to underlie much of what is currently written and spoken about music therapy in Great Britain is that the musical material which is produced by the client is in some way an abstract representation of the clients' 'inner' state (i.e. his/her emotions, thoughts, fantasies, anxieties etc.) and that the therapist, in facilitating or sharing in their expression, is relating directly to that part of the clients' psyche which is seeking expression through the music. Nordoff and Robbins in *Creative Music Therapy* (1977) identify various different sorts of beating which, it is claimed, are representative of various feeling/activity states (e.g. avoidance) which the therapist needs to identify and react to musically, using a variety of melodic, rhythmic and harmonic techniques elaborated in the course of the book and elsewhere. The rationale for this is that in doing so, the therapist is 'clothing' the clients' music in the forms and musical structures which (in the therapist's estimation) approximate the feelings that the client would like to express but lacks the musical facility to do so. This process is frequently referred to as 'meeting the child (or presumably adult) in the music.'

A central problem in working with mentally handicapped clients however, is that it is often difficult, if not impossible, to verify or confirm with the client whether the therapist's assumptions are valid (unlike similar approaches in psychiatric work, where the client may be able to confirm, deny or otherwise elucidate the 'meaning' or intention behind an improvisation. There may of course be other indications as to the client's emotional state, such as body posture, facial expression, vocalisations, etc. which would support the assumptions being made by the therapist and validate the subsequent musical character of the improvisation. However, the central problem remains of forming accurate or reliable hypotheses about the client's musical intentionality and the therapist's role in developing it.

Accepting for a moment however, the fact that in the absence of a more systematic model the therapist is forced to rely on his/her musical intuition to a large extent, the further problem then arises of deriving 'meaning' from the music.

It has been established through psychological studies of musical development in children that the capacity to understand and respond to music is a lengthy process of enculturation and exposure to the musical norms of the society. The stages of development from earliest infantile vocalisations to that of a young adult who is able to reflect upon, understand and identify with the music of his/her culture are complex and as yet only partially understood. The professional music therapist has not only been involved in this developmental process, but has additionally been through an exhaustive and rigorous training as a musician in order to achieve the standards necessary for acceptance onto a training course. The result is therefore a highly competent musician capable of extremely complex and subtle ways of thinking 'in' and 'about' music, and with an array of highly sophisticated, practical, musical skills at his/her command.

The mentally handicapped client, on the other hand, may be functioning at an inestimably low level of intellectual development, and (especially in the case of hospitalised clients) may have experienced little, if any, musical input other than that afforded by the ward environment (TV, radio, etc.). The whole complex web of interactions, understandings and experiences which contribute to our ability to invest music with emotional 'meaning' may therefore be partly or wholly absent.

The problems of 'assumption-making' about the client's playing (as outlined above) are therefore compounded by this further difficulty, i.e. that in choosing a set of musical formulations in which to express those assumptions (i.e. through the use of particular harmonies, rhythms, etc.) and in improvising accordingly, the therapist is further assuming that there is a shared understanding with the client as to the <u>meaning</u> of these particular musical formulations. To take a very simple example, a client plays with a slow, steadying beat on a drum; his/her face is expressionless, there is little body movement or eye contact with the therapist. The therapist may interpret this as follows: 'X gives the impression of being morose, perhaps depressed, certainly rather withdrawn and unwilling to make contact with me. I will accept that and attempt to reflect it musically by using a slow tempo, lower register, with modal or minor-key harmony, with a slow melody-line, synchronised with his/her beating, taking each of his/her beats as a crotchet unit.'

This is (deliberately) a gross oversimplification, but serves to illustrate the two points discussed so far:

1. there is an assumption that the musical output of the client is related to an interior 'feeling-state'.

2. there is an assumption that the client is at some level able to interpret the musical/emotional content of the therapist's material, and perceive it as being

'sad' or in some way reflective of his/her own state, and is able to identify with this.

An optimistic view of this might be that the therapist, through a combination of intuition, experience, empathy (and perhaps luck) 'gets it right' and a fruitful and satisfying musical interaction will result. Alternatively however, it may suggest a number of questions such as:

1. what are the 'norms' of this client's musical behaviour, i.e. what tempi, rhythmic features, melodic inventions, dynamic range etc. would the client use spontaneously, without any outside musical intervention?

2. does the above fit into any existing model of musical development (e.g. is X playing like a two-and-a-half year old child would play?)

3. if the client's playing does share a number of features with that of a small child, what are the implications for the client's level of musical <u>understanding</u>?

4. what are the implications of the above for the therapist in terms of choice of musical material, instrumentation, therapeutic goals etc.?

There is as yet no systematic procedure for determining these sorts of questions. My own current research project is an attempt to elucidate the first two questions, by studying the linguistic, artistic and musical levels of functioning of mentally handicapped adults, and comparing these with a set of normal children at different developmental stages (from six months to five years). It is hoped that as a result of this, and hopefully many other studies, it may be possible to view the musical output of these clients from the perspective of normal musical development. The only evidence available of this type, which is concerned with improvised music, is to be found in the music education literature.

In a study by Swannick and Tillman (1986) of children from 5 to 15 years, 'a musical developmental sequence is proposed, based on the psychological concepts of mastery, imitation, imaginative play and meta-cognition, drawing on the work of Moog (1976), Piaget and the observations of British writers. An interpretation of over 700 children's compositions is undertaken, yielding an eight-mode spiral of development that may have consequences for music teaching, for overall music curriculum planning, <u>for appropriate responses to individuals</u> (my emphasis) and for generating progression in a session or project.'

The children in the study were given a series of improvisation-based tasks and the results recorded. The tapes were then judged by an independent panel, who were asked to assess the ages of the children from their playing. A wealth of fascinating material is to be found in this study, but it is not appropriate in this context to attempt to reproduce the findings or summarise the theoretical content. The final model of development however is of importance to any discussion of musical ability since it relates very clearly to existing theories of child development proposed by Piaget and Bruner, and may be of relevance to the mentally handicapped population. Very briefly, the authors proposed four 'fundamental transformations' between the ages of three and fifteen years, which can be summarised as follows:

0 - 4   Mastery
4 - 9   Imitation
10 - 15   Imaginative play
15+   Meta-cognition

Within each of these stages there are recognisable characteristics in terms of the type of structural activity and thought content employed. In the 4 - 9 imitation stage, for example, the use of the vernacular is much in evidence, characterised by 'patterns, both melodic and rhythmic, which start to appear, marked by repetitions.' Other characteristics of this stage are also identified, defined and discussed.

The authors conclude that 'there is such a thing as musical development and that it takes place in a certain sequence.....in an environment where there are musical encounters, the sequence will be activated.....in an impoverished musical environment, development is likely to be minimal or arrested.'

While the methodology of this study and its findings may not be directly relevant to work with the profoundly handicapped individual (since the children in the study were of normal intelligence and with a full range of abilities), the comparisons drawn between handicapped adults and even <u>younger</u> children in my own study may perhaps afford some useful insights into the earlier stages of musical development not encompassed by the study above.

It should be noted however that while studies of spontaneous music-making with instruments are very rare, there does exist a considerable body of research evidence concerned with early singing and vocalisation. Many of these suggest that again there is a clear sequence, and that children progress from a very sketchy 'impression' of a song (usually approximating the intervals and melodic contours) through a series of stages in which the song is gradually 'brought into focus' until the intervals and rhythmic features are recognisable and accurate. A study of the vocalisations of handicapped clients in relation to this type of framework might be of considerable interest and yield insights into that aspect of their musicality.

In the area of receptive ability, a framework of understanding already exists for normal children but it is unclear whether it is also applicable to the handicapped population. Moog, for example, states in his study that children fail to register any preference between harmony and dissonance until five or six years of age; for the therapist working with a developmentally delayed adult client, it would be useful to know whether this finding also applied to the client, and would obviously be of importance in determining the type of musical material used by the therapist in improvisation.

It might be useful at this point to refer to the work of colleagues in other therapeutic media. Speech therapists, for example, have a wide variety of assessment procedures available (e.g. the Reynell Language Tests) for determining the developmental abilities of their clients, in both expression and comprehension of language. The range of test materials is constantly under review, and it has been agreed for a considerable time that tests developed for normal children are not necessarily very useful when applied to institutionalised, handicapped adults, and new materials are currently being researched and developed.

There is obviously a difference here between the two disciplines, since speech therapists are primarily concerned with improving language ability per se, whilst music therapists are not concerned with the acquisition of musical skills or fluency, but rather the use of the medium as a catalyst for the client's personal growth and development. This is perhaps to oversimplify the case however, and it could be argued that in some circumstances, the improvement or development of musical skills does in fact have concomitant benefits for the client. This is an area in which therapists have in the past seemed reluctant to linger, perhaps for fear that they may be confused with music educators. (Distinction between the two disciplines in some types of work may perhaps be more one of 'style' than 'substance').

In the field of art therapy, a quite clear developmental model also exists, with a body of research illustrating clearly the different forms of graphic representation produced by children from infancy to maturity. The art therapist therefore can view the client's work from a clear understanding of his/her artistic development, and is aware of the limitations within which the client is able to express him/herself. Obviously also, any deviation or change from this level can be viewed as possibly having importance or significance in the overall context of their treatment programme.

A similar situation pertains to dance/movement therapy, through the developmental studies of movement made by Dalcroze, Laban and others.

I am suggesting therefore that in the field of music therapy with mentally handicapped adults, a means of determining a client's musical functioning in developmental terms would be a useful asset in devising and carrying out therapeutic intervention. A number of issues need clarification however before this becomes possible. Some of these have been mentioned earlier, but could be summarised as follows:

1. Does a condition of mental handicap imply automatically that a person's musical development will have been curtailed at a particular developmental stage?

2. If this is the case, are both expressive and receptive aspects of musical experience similarly affected (i.e. does the client both play and perceive music at the same level of development)?

3. What, if any, connection exists between musical ability and other types of ability such as language, and what evidence is there that an improvement in one may produce a corresponding improvement in the other?

Assuming for the moment that a reliable means of musical-developmental assessment could be devised for this client group, the question arises as to how this would be of benefit to the client/therapist relationship and the progress of therapy.

One product of such an approach would be to provide the therapist with a baseline or 'snapshot' of the client's range of musical behaviours <u>prior</u> to any therapeutic intervention. From this baseline, any musical changes induced by the therapist's intervention could be accurately assessed. A profile, based on developmental data, would then emerge of the ways in which the client is able to use music. If, for example, it could be shown that a characteristic tendency of a particular stage of development was a tendency to loud, fast beating, then a client assessed to be performing at that developmental level would appear well within the expected musical 'norms' for his/her level of functioning, rather than perhaps being considered exhibiting 'driven' or 'aggressive' playing or some similar arbitrary label. A set of descriptors for a client's playing could therefore be formulated which were based upon objective analysis of musical events rather than subjective assessments of supposed internal states.

On the level of practical music-making, a developmental approach might be useful in determining the type of musical material to be used by the therapist. If the therapist can be said to be 'meeting the client in the music', it implies that the musical material used is appropriate for and accessible to the client. A speech therapist in an analogous position would be certain to ensure that the linguistic content of her/his sessions fell within the comprehension level of the client. Correspondingly, the music therapist might find it useful to have a clear model of the types of musical utterances common to the developmental level of his/her client from which to select the musical materials with which to improvise. If, for example, it could be shown that a client was functioning at a musical level of eighteen months, it would seem inappropriate to use musical structures (e.g. complex harmony or rhythm) which are beyond the grasp of an individual at that level. Also, it would be helpful for the therapist to know that his/her client's use of rhythm, for example, is entirely consistent with the level of maturation and should not be construed as a devious attempt symbolically to avoid contact with the therapist.

In therapy, the use of a developmental perspective, i.e. where a client is 'starting from', need not in any way conflict with or detract from a psychotherapeutic approach to the work. As the writings of Daniel Stern (1985) and others have shown, there need be no dichotomy between a developmental and psychotherapeutic understanding of a client's problems and needs. The assessment of the ways in which the client uses the music however, would be based on rational principles rather than supposition or speculation.

The immediate need however is for more thorough, detailed and systematic research into the musicality of mentally handicapped clients (both adults and children). In order to present as full a picture as possible, this could include investigations into areas such as rhythm, melody, harmony, timbre, instrumentation, dynamics, tempo, vocalisation, movement and the whole difficult area of affective responsiveness to both live and recorded music. The data thus obtained may then present us with a clearer understanding of the client as musician and enable us to proceed with him/her musically in the most effective way for his/her level of understanding and with a minimum of redundant musical input.

It has been my personal experience as a practising therapist in the field of adult mental handicap, that it is remarkably easy (and perhaps even unavoidable) to find in the course of improvising that the factors determining my musical input are actually aesthetic ones based on my own musical background and upbringing. The use of expressive dissonances or rhythmic syncopations may well be agreeable or stimulating to me as a musician, but may be wholly inappropriate or irrelevant to the needs of my client.

Sloboda (1987) discusses an article which describes a particular session in considerable detail, with notated examples from it; he questions why the therapist chose the particular pitches and rhythms that were used, and whether there was some underlying rationale behind her choice as regards the client's material.

At present there appears to be no such rationale, and each therapist is left to follow his/her own musical intuitions and responses as they occur and as the playing unfolds. Whilst this allows an admirable degree of flexibility and freedom of expression, the choice of musical material remains to some extent arbitrary and unsupported by any underlying principles of organisation (other perhaps than imitation or elaboration). To take a hypothetical example, it might be useful for a therapist to be able to infer from developmental data that his client is most easily able to understand simple diatonic melodies within the range of a fifth, with perhaps two or three different types of rhythmic patterns. This information would then provide the basis for the therapist's own contribution. This obviously oversimplified example may give the impression that a rigid prescriptive scheme of musical 'equations' is being suggested as an alternative to the spontaneous creativity of free improvisation. This, I suggest, would not be the result, but rather that the creative imagination of the therapist, being constrained by developmental guidelines, would be focused more intensely on appropriate material rather than becoming diffuse and tangential to the client's music.

In summary, I have suggested in this chapter that in music therapy with mentally handicapped adults, there is a need to develop ways of understanding and describing their musicality which are based on objective criteria, rather than subjective descriptions of musical behaviour, which may be ambiguous, vague and open to a wide variety of interpretations. One such conceptual framework is that of normal musical development, and one improvisation-based study has afforded new and exciting insights into the ways in which musical abilities develop among normal school-age children, thus linking closely with developmental psychology. By using a similar procedure but starting at a much earlier stage, (more appropriate to the levels of many mentally handicapped clients) my own study is exploring the possible correlations between the music-making of adult clients and small children. Further studies might serve to build a comprehensive developmental sequence of musical behaviours analogous to that which exists in art therapy and education.

For the specialist music teacher, this might afford a means of assessing progress in musical skills and charting a child's musical development over an extended period. For the therapist, it might provide a 'map' of the client's musicality and enable the therapist to proceed on the basis of a clearer understanding of the client's musical mind.

18

A Comparison of Mother-Infant Interactions and the Client-Therapist Relationship in Music Therapy Sessions

Margaret Heal Hughes

Introduction

Music therapists are working to develop models for understanding clinical music therapy practice. This often involves fertilisation from other fields (Bruscia, 1987, Rudd, 1980). Though there has been exploration of the application of psychoanalytic theory and technique to music therapy work, little has been written comparing the client-therapist relationship in music therapy sessions with mother-infant interactions (Pavlicevic, 1988; Steele 1986). Mother-infant observation serves as the foundation of much psychoanalytic training (Bick, 1964). Indeed it was Freud (1921) who sensitively described the child's experience of loss as explored with a cotton reel.

Excerpts from a two-year mother-infant observation will be compared with descriptions of client behaviour during individual music therapy sessions, and similar or different characteristics will be identified. The music therapy clients are adults with severe learning difficulties. The discussions are not attempting to provide a prescriptive dictionary for understanding client- therapist interactions, but rather a model for thinking about possible unconscious meanings that clients are communicating, a psychoanalytically-informed approach to music therapy.

Mother-Infant observation

Boston (1975) reviews some of the experimental methods employed in infant observation. She categorises them broadly into experimental and ethological approaches. The type of observation described here has an ethological base.

The mother-infant observation involves an hour-long, once-weekly visit to a family home with a new-born infant. The sessions are written up after the hour, away from the home. This allows the observer to concentrate on the interactions of the mother, baby and other family members, and minimises interference with the family's routine.

What sounds like a simple case of sitting back and watching can be an extremely draining experience. The observer has no task or function to serve during the hour, and so will tend to identify strongly with family members: baby, mother, father, or siblings. Infantile feelings may be triggered and the observer is forced to deal with her or his own childish state of mind. This provides an opportunity to develop a greater understanding of the family members' emotional experience. An example will clarify this.

Baby Jane was four weeks old. Mum was breast-feeding her. Baby looked lovingly at Mum's face. The eye contact was intense. She was feeding on the left breast, touching it with her right hand and holding the little finger of her mother's right hand with all the fingers of her left hand. I was aware of my jealousy of their intimacy through the strong desire I felt to interrupt this special moment. I wondered how Baby Jane's brother and sister were feeling.

My question was soon answered. The two began to fight over who would sit in which chair. Baby Jane's chair was the one that seemed to be desired. Mother continued to feed as she yelled at the boys. Their jealous quarrel had split the mother-infant couple.

I then felt panicked and slightly frantic. Baby Jane looked away from Mother, kicking and jerking her limbs slightly and focusing her eyes on the ceiling light. She had found something safe to hold her while Mother disappeared to be with the siblings.

During this excerpt we can see how the observer's feelings were identified with the jealous siblings, and then with the frantic Baby Jane. Perhaps a better name for the role of observer would be an emotional barometer.

Music Therapy Approach

Music therapy provides a framework in which a mutual relationship is set up between client and therapist. The growing relationship allows changes to occur, both in the condition of the client and in the form that the therapy takes. By using skilled and creative musicianship in a clinical setting, the therapist seeks to establish an interaction, a shared musical experience leading to the pursuit of therapeutic goals (Hoskyns and Odell, 1990).

Within this definition of music therapy each therapist finds a way of working suited to his or her character, temperament and personal style. As previously mentioned, the approach used in the music therapy sessions described in this chapter is informed by psychoanalytic theory (Heal 1989; 1990).

Sessions are held in the same room, at the same time each week, and are protected from interruptions and intrusions. Holidays are prepared for and their effects are taken into account. It is through using these boundaries that a musical framework can be provided in the same 'hello' and 'good-bye' songs each session. The same choice of instruments is available each session, though new instruments may be introduced (Heal 1989; 1990).

The therapist attempts to understand the meaning that the sounds, non-verbal and verbal, the movements, and the musical instruments have for the client, as well as for the developing relationship between client and therapist. These observations are made in the context of the sequence of events in the session and how this session compares with previous ones. The therapist seeks to understand, and to reflect and interpret either musically, physically or verbally therapeutic issues that have particular relevance for the client. This is providing the opportunity for real change to take place.

The main technique is clinical improvisation. Many British music therapists are informed by psychoanalytic theory in their work (Heal 1989 a, b, c; Heal and Morrison 1990; Priestley, 1975, 1989; Steele 1988, 1989; Steele and Leese, 1987; Towse, 1991; Woodcock, 1988). The author belongs to a work discussion group where there are music therapists with differing training and experiences, all of whom choose to understand their work through psychodynamic models. Over the past two years the group has begun to understand the common theoretical basis of its work, and the technical differences of approach.

Perhaps these technical differences can be understood by examining the medium through which music therapists choose to focus communications with their clients. A therapist may choose to express the countertransference in the form of a sound response. The client, choosing not to play an instrument or to remain in silence, is responding to using sound. Another approach is to focus on the sound but provide physical support for the client through the therapist or a second co-therapist, enabling the client to play. For example, the therapist or co-therapist may choose to pick up a beater when the client has dropped it. Other therapists may use words to reflect or interpret their understanding of the meaning of the musical and verbal relationship between the client and the therapist. Most therapists use different combinations of sound (including silence), movement and words in responding to their clients' communications. However, many who use a psychoanalytically- informed approach share a conceptual framework through which they try to understand the internal worlds of their clients: a mother- infant interaction model.

This approach to music therapy is best illustrated by a careful examination of material arising out of music therapy sessions.

Clinical Material

Client No 1:

Linda is a middle-aged woman with severe learning difficulties who has spent most of her life in an institution. She is verbal, but tends to be echolaic. She spends the day wandering the institution according to her own self-organised timetable. She is considered to have no ability to tell time. Linda attends music therapy sessions for forty minutes once weekly. In the early sessions she would attend for just ten minutes; but one year later she was able to stay to the end of the sessions. She now brings herself to the music therapy room, directly after breakfast on the given day. Interestingly, before the therapist's holidays she is very late in arriving for sessions. Her ability to use the time boundaries to express how she is experiencing my impending absence leads me to wonder about her true level of ability. This is an excerpt from a recent session.

Linda kept asking where a particular staff member was. I explained that Bert had left and was not coming back. Linda reached for the cymbal and spun it. She focused on it intensely for several seconds, twiddling her fingers under her chin at the same time, and then repeated her question, 'Where's Bert?' and answered herself, 'Gone to put his coat on'. I again tried to explain that Bert had gone away. Linda looked to the cymbal, gave it a good spin and focused on it intensely.

The painful news of Bert's departure had resulted in Linda seeking and finding a safe place to centre herself, on the cymbal. Later in the session the therapist was also able to acknowledge that not only had Bert left but that she too would be leaving for a holiday break. Did Linda wonder if the therapist would be coming back? Linda seemed to be struggling to deal with emotions that she felt over loss and separation. How can we begin to understand responses to loss? Where is the prototype for our experience of loss? Klein theorises that our model for partings in later life is in the same idiom as the emotional experience of being weaned from the breast, the original loss. The baby has to deal with waiting to be breast fed for longer and longer periods, and eventually is offered no breast at all. Various defences are brought into play to protect against the anxiety of being so helpless and dependent on another human being, mother. However, with a well-conducted weaning the baby is attracted to, and can enjoy, other food.

As mentioned earlier, one defence may involve the infant attempting to deny that the breast is missing at all. Is the baby able to imagine the breast in its absence? Baby Jane at the age of four weeks and two days, was observed struggling to wait to be fed.

Baby seemed to be fantasising the breast as she waited. She lay in her cot with her head turned to the left, the direction it was usually turned while she was feeding. Her upper lip was still as her lower lip moved up, down, and around. Her left hand clenched, open and closed in a sucking rhythm. Her right arm jerked up and down with a clenched fist. The grasping movements were like those she made when feeding on the breast. Baby Jane's eyes were focused on a spot on the wall. She seemed to be trying to summon the breast but was getting quite tired. She offered a big yawn. Her mouth movements increased. I expected her to cry out loudly, to demand the breast, but she yawned again and closed her eyes to go to sleep. It was as though she was able to conjure up the breast in mother's absence and so to find some satisfaction.

After weaning, this need to create the breast for herself found a more concrete expression in Baby Jane - sucking her thumb. This was a nipple that she had with her at all times, under her complete control. Though fantasising of the breast is seen as a defence against separation, Klein (1937) also sees this as a kind of mental activity, the beginning of imaginative thinking. It prepares the way for the later use of a transitional object. It is when the use of the defence becomes chronic, as in the case of Linda, that the individual's ability to experience the external world is severely limited.

How is Linda's behaviour similar to that of Baby Jane's? Linda's need to focus on and control the spinning of the cymbal when faced with emotions around the issue of loss reminded me of Baby D's struggle to survive when she wanted the breast. Her thumb served the same function as Linda's cymbal, and her sucking was under her control, as was Linda's spinning. Linda's illusion is that she is able to take care of herself, even when faced with overpowering anxieties. It is a denial of her need for the therapist and a denigration of what the therapist can provide for her. This behaviour is similar to that of Baby Jane who, by sucking her thumb, can defend herself against the experience of not being in control and of having to wait for mother to feed her. The need to be in control may explain why it is so difficult to decide to have therapy and then to make the journey to the therapist's room. The therapist has provided a safe consistent place for the sessions. She has commented on how Linda may be feeling about the relationship between the therapist and herself, and has used improvised music to reflect these emotions back to Linda. Linda has seemed less compelled to use the defence as described above. However, after any holiday break in the sequence of sessions, Linda reverts to the same frequency of this behaviour that she showed in the early sessions.

Client No 2:

Janet, a 25 year-old with severe learning difficulty was referred to music therapy as she suffered from an eating disorder. She seemed to struggle in communications with her family; they often chose to speak for Janet and to decide what her preferences were without consulting her. She is verbally able, but seems to think concretely. It is difficult to know whether this way of thinking is related to her learning disability, to her eating disorder, or to both. Spensley (1985) comments on how the slowness associated with learning disabilities 'may well be related to a diminished capacity for using symbolism which is as much a characteristic of psychosis as it is of subnormality or brain-damage.' Bruch (1978), in *The Golden Cage: The Enigma of Anorexia Nervosa*, explains how people who suffer with eating disorders tend to think in concrete terms.

When Janet was referred, she either somatised all feelings into a sore tummy, sore legs, and a sore head or expelled them from her body by sicking up food. Her refusal to eat resulted in severe weight loss, which threatened her health. An inability to digest painful emotions was clearly demonstrated in the music therapy sessions, where seemingly intolerable situations quickly became a sore tummy or a sore head. Janet did not seem to have the internal structures for modulating overwhelming feelings into a manageable form.

The aim of therapy was to help Janet deal with emotions in a creative way. Would she be able to find somewhere in the music therapy sessions to project painful affects so that she would no longer need to somatise them? Could she then take responsibility for these feelings? Would she be able to use clinical improvisation to express and symbolise her internal confusion?

Nolan (1989) has described music therapy improvisation techniques for the group treatment of bulimic patients and the value of this approach. He sees this model as facilitating the expression of affect in the here and now, as providing a successful experience in the mastery of tension regulation, as helping to identify intact areas of ego functioning that may not be apparent to the patient, as challenging cognitive disorders, and as providing a means for practising alternative interpersonal behaviours.

Example 1

The following excerpt is from an early session with Janet.

Janet chose to share the piano with me. She sat in front of the treble and I sat in front of the bass. She looked down at the keyboard and then up at me, indicating that she wanted to play the piano but needed some sign of permission to be given.

I played an open A minor chord in the bass. Janet rocked herself gently backward and forward twice and then began to play using her right hand. The movement seemed to provide the momentum for her to play. She played three successive notes in a triplet rhythm and then stopped to look tentatively at me out of the corner of her eye. It seemed that Janet needed further encouragement to dare to sound more notes. I played an open D minor chord, trying to imply some movement but within an harmonic form or container. Janet played another three-note triplet up the keyboard with her right hand.

It seemed that I had to provide a strong sense of form and rhythm for Janet. I decided to continue in a simple four-bar chord progression, modally based (white notes only), which would provide clear structure for Janet. It was a struggle to play with her as Janet was following my rhythmic direction as strictly as possible. I felt uncomfortable. Though Janet was musically doing something different from me it felt as if we were two accompanists sensitively striving to follow each other.

In this excerpt, Janet had seemed unable to use the harmonic form as a container for her own sounds, but had struggled to be sensitive and attuned to the therapist: to mirror her. The therapist was attempting to provide some structure to hold Janet's musical offerings. Perhaps Janet's emotions were so overwhelming that she feared no one could contain them, or so nebulous that she could not crystallise them into any form.

After several attempts at clinical improvisation, Janet still seemed unresponsive to the containing, holding situation which was being provided. Perhaps she had no strong internal model of a mother holding or containing and modulating into manageable form her explosive internal emotional life.

A similar-feeling situation was observed in the interactions of Mother and Baby Jane. Though single occurrences do not imply long- standing situations, they can be useful in helping to develop insight into primary relationships. Through successive observations it is possible to have a clearer idea of what the baby may be experiencing. As explained previously, the observer as an emotional barometer can gain insight into the dynamics of the family and the gamut of emotions experienced by a baby. In the following excerpt Baby Jane is just one year and two months old:

Baby Jane was in the playpen in her room. Mum had left the room to get a clean towel from the airing cupboard. Baby looked up at me, holding on to the bars of the playpen. After a slight pause she began to bounce up and down. Her response felt manic and a sudden change from her previous mood. She tantalised me with little looks and offered a conspiratorial look as she flipped around holding onto the bars tightly.

I was stunned by this burst of energy directed at me and wondered why Baby Jane was choosing to relate to me in this way. I did not feel like a third person whom Baby was wanting to engage. I felt that Baby's reaction to me was probably the one that worked most effectively with her mother.

Baby Jane's mother was a caring woman; but in her professional and personal life she tended to take on many things, wanting to be all things for all people. She often seemed to be overstretched and struggling to be emotionally in touch with her little girl. In previous observations her manic attempts to catch her daughter's attention had been painful to observe.

Mum had approached Baby Jane with a great deal of energy that did not seem to be in keeping with the mood of Baby Jane Baby had averted her gaze to the side, away from mum, or had focused intensely on the light. Now Baby Jane seemed to have developed a strategy for being with a manic mum: being manic herself! In psychoanalytic terms she was identifying with the object, the first stage in internalising significant figures of the external world.

Stern's (1985) idea of selective attunement supports the analytic theory of identification with and internalisation of external objects. Mother has conveyed to Baby Jane what mood is shareable with her by encouraging Baby to be manic. As Stern says, Through the selective use of attunement, the parents' intersubjective responsiveness acts as a template to shape and create corresponding intrapsychic experiences in the child. It is in this way that the parent's desires, fears, prohibitions, and fantasies colour the psychic experiences of the child (p.208).

Janet was trying to be with me in the music by mirroring me. What was her experience of mothering? Perhaps her mother had had difficulty in linking into her daughter's emotional needs? Mothers of babies with a mental handicap experience greater difficulty in coping with their babies (Bicknell, 1983; Solnit et al., 1961) and in fact show greater stress than those with chronically ill and neurotic children, being more preoccupied with their children and enjoying them less (Cummings et al., 1976).

Perhaps Janet had had a low level for tolerating frustration, so that she couldn't wait for her mother. Klein (1937) discusses the effect that the nature of the baby may have on its development. If an infant has a low tolerance for frustration and is unable to accept delayed gratification, it may be more inclined to develop defences that impede its mental growth.

Was Janet's need to be the same as the therapist in the music partly a denial of her handicap? Sinason (1986) discusses the intense denial that a client with a learning difficulty can have against accepting that they are different. This envy can result in the attacking of intact skills, creating what Sinason calls an 'opportunist handicap'. As long as Janet felt that the music she played was the same as the therapist's music, she was the same as her. She would then not have to face the painful emotions that she might experience if she were in touch with her awareness of being different, of being mentally handicapped.

Example 2

All the music therapy sessions had been audiotaped. Janet began to use the tapes in an unusual way.

In session fifteen, Janet slyly looked towards the cassette player that sat on a shelf behind the piano. It felt as if she experienced it as an impostor. I turned off the tape recorder and said that it was not necessary to tape the sessions: perhaps she felt the tape recorder was a spy listening to the sessions, or that tapes would go outside the sessions to be shared with workers and Janet's family. Janet agreed with this. We decided that she could control what was taped. She asked for the tapes that had been made to date. There were fourteen of these. Onto these tapes she had told of the terrible things that had been done to her and of the accusations that had been levelled against her by significant people in her life. The points she had chosen to record on the tapes had been counted out on the fingers of her hand. Any questions asked about these points had been met with groans of pain. She wanted to throw out several of the tapes. I explained that it was important to keep the tapes with all her stories and feelings on them in the room, but that they could be kept separate. Perhaps some day she might feel more able to think about these tapes. I gave her a cassette-carrying case into which she put the tapes in her own special order. She seemed relieved by this exercise.

To the following session Janet brought her own tape from home. She asked to use the recorder. Onto the tape she listed another catalogue of crimes that seemed to be upsetting for her, though she refused to accept any suggestion that she might be feeling angry or sad. As long as they were points that she could bounce off her fingers into the tape, she remained an empty person, happy displaying what Sinason (1988) has called 'the handicapped smile'.. As soon as she was encouraged to expand on her offered points, Janet would develop a head ache or a stomach cramp, or begin to cry with pain: 'No, that's not it'. The therapist felt as if she were persecuting Janet. This helped her to understand how Janet felt.

Each week when Janet arrived she would be relieved to see the tapes still in the box, and would rearrange them, perhaps adding a new tape. Outside the session, staff at her day centre, and her friends and family, commented on how much clearer she seemed. She had begun to gain weight.

A similar-feeling situation was observed with Baby Jane when she was one year and two months old. She had been playing quietly with her favourite container, shoving her hand in and out and peering into the red cylinder. Mother was busy in the kitchen.

Older sister looked at Mum who was busily cleaning up the kitchen. She decided now was the time to smother Baby Jane in kisses and hugs. Baby seemed to be trying to ignore the demonstration, though her brow was slightly knotted. Mum caught sight and told Sister to stop it. Sister complied.

For just a moment Baby seemed not to react to the incident. Then she stood up and trundled over to the gas fireplace. She began with a low growl and crescendoed into a high-pitched Red Indian war-cry, hitting the top of the fireplace with mighty blows from both arms in parallel motion. Five blows and she was finished with the bothersome fireplace.

Baby Jane had seemed unable to express directly to her sister how she felt about the sister's over-enthusiastic affection. Rather than being annoyed with her, Baby Jane personified the fireplace and then acted into it all her anger and frustration. She treated it as she would have liked to have treated her own sister - it was a safe sister that would not hit back.

Janet seemed to be using the tapes in a similar way. The tape recorder was personified, and into it, in the form of her stories, she poured all her feelings. The therapist was not seen as someone who could modulate Janet's overpowering anxiety into digestible bits.

This is related to Bion's (1962) idea of the mother providing an alpha function. The mother accepts the baby's overwhelming emotions and modulates them with the alpha function into a form that the baby can digest. The mother in her reverie intuits what to do as a result of unconscious thought. This seems to be a similar concept to Winnicott's (1971) idea of the mother holding the baby and making emotions containable in him/her.

Neither Janet nor Baby Jane seemed able to modulate the emotions that they were experiencing into manageable forms. The fireplace and the cassette tapes were concrete objects onto which the emotions could be dumped, but they did not serve as symbols for the emotions. Had the emotions been symbolised they could have been worked with and understood. At this time they were evacuated as anxiety into external objects.

Example 3

A year into therapy, Janet improvised alone for the first time. Janet sat quietly at the piano with her head bowed. I asked if she required more space between herself on the bench and the piano. She shook her head lightly and moved her left hand to the bass area. She began with the lowest note and moved up the keyboard playing groups of single notes in a distinctive fanfare rhythm. Having moved up well into the treble, she began again in the bass. This time the right hand played with her left as an equal, in the same rhythm but in contrary motion. There was a feeling of form in her improvisation and a potent sense of determination, a contrast to the weak little girl whose somatic complaints had often dominated the sessions.

At one point the hands seemed to lose each other and almost disappeared completely away. Then, after a half second of silence the two began again to work together in contrary motion. They found what seemed to be a chord that satisfied Janet. She repeated it several times, almost hammering the sound into the space of the room. This pattern was repeated several times: a fanfare followed by a repeated chord.

The improvisation lasted for over ten minutes. Janet explored the areas of the keyboard, playing with her hands in contrary and similar motion exploring juxtapositions of different pitches.

After this improvisation the therapist felt like a proud parent who had just witnessed the first steps of her child. The improvisation was named 'The Olympics' and reminded Janet of a sport at which she had been particularly good. She had decided to give up the event, partly because of the vulnerable physical situation in which it put her with a member of her family. This very powerful improvisation expressed the struggle she had had and continued to have in giving up, for her own feeling of safety, something that mattered to her very much.

No similar experience was witnessed with Baby Jane. Janet seemed able to express herself musically in a way that was much beyond the skills of Baby Jane, although when Baby Jane had first handed the observer a shoe saying 'shuz, shuz' the observer had felt terribly proud.

Janet in early sessions managed to get rid of painful emotions which she experienced as uncontainable anxiety, by emptying them into a tape recorder. This was a concrete way of dealing with them. In improvising 'The Olympics' she had been able to symbolise her feelings, to demonstrate a budding creativity. Winnicott (1971) wrote: 'It is creative apperception more than anything else that makes the individual feel that life is worth living. Contrasted with this is a relationship to external reality which is one of compliance, the world and its details being recognised but only as something to be fitted in with or demanding adaptation. Compliance carries with it a sense of futility for the individual and is associated with the idea that nothing matters and that life is not worth living.' Perhaps Janet could begin to be less compliant in her dealings with the external world - perhaps she could begin to believe more strongly that life was worth living.

Conclusion

This chapter has suggested a model for thinking about the unconscious meanings that clients are communicating through their movements and sounds during music therapy sessions. It has focused on regressive behaviours characteristic of earlier stages in life, as displayed by two clients with learning disabilities.

It is recognised that everyone depends on defences to manage anxieties aroused by the conflict between the requirements of one's internal world and those of the external world. However, when used chronically these defences can limit the individual's further development. Clients with learning disabilities, who lack the necessary cognitive or emotional structures and therefore have impaired symbolic function, show a greater tendency to resort to early defences. Linda and Janet have used these defences in response to the intolerable anxiety that they feel surrounding issues of separation.

Through understanding the client's unconscious fears and helping to hold, experience and think about them, we are providing the opportunity for internal change. By striving to comprehend the processes that promote such change, we are more likely to facilitate development.

Acknowledgements

I would like to thank Sally Box and the members of the Monday evening Mother-infant Observation Seminar, Valerie Sinason and members of the Thursday evening Work Discussion Seminar, and Dr H. Williams for his supervision of my case work.

Section 5: Music Therapy with the Elderly

19

Music Therapy as a Facilitator in Grief Counselling

Ruth Bright

Introduction

Music elicits a range of responses, physical, cognitive and emotional. These responses are influenced by a variety of factors such as ethnic origin, experience and education in music, family patterns of preference, peer-group influence and pressure, and so on.

One finds, for example, that an uneducated teenage refugee from a remote Indo-Chinese village, arriving in Australia in an open boat, has very different musical background, knowledge and experience as well as having different emotional and cognitive responses to music compared with those of a middle-aged British academic arriving by air to take up a University Chair!

Not only is the knowledge of and preference for music very different, the entire tonal, harmonic and rhythmic systems are also different, and yet the music therapist is responsible, should the need arise, for working in music with either person in a way which will help and not hinder his recovery from illness, and this will certainly involve counselling skills.

To be a designated counsellor implies that one has received some kind of formal training in facilitating problem-solving and counselling for people who are facing personal and family difficulties. This is different from being a clinical psychologist, a family doctor, a psychiatrist or a psychoanalyist. It is normal, however, for people in those and other helping professions to have had counselling skills, interviewing techniques etc. included in their professional training and expertise, as well as using counselling techniques in their daily work. Counsellors are trained at a variety of levels, and are employed in such fields as family therapy, marriage guidance, rehabilitation counselling, grief counselling, vocational counselling and so on (Kennedy, 1977).

Few, if any, music therapists are employed specifically as counsellors, but experienced therapists normally use counselling techniques in their work, e.g. when it becomes clear that a neurotic illness is linked with a major loss, when working with the 'significant others' of disabled children, (since we cannot work with a client in isolation but must see him as part of a community, whether this is a family or the community of an institution) and so on. We all need to know about the diseases and disabilities of our clients, the difficulties with which the patient and relatives are grappling, be they of body, mind, spirit or relationships.

The Skills of the Music Therapist

Although in practice the two areas overlap, it is convenient to sub-divide our skills into therapy skills and music skills. In 'Therapy Skills' we must ask ourselves whether we understand:

- Our own philosophy on illness, disability, dying and death.
- The client's philosophy on these issues.
- What the present illness, disability, weakness means to the client.
- What the probable outcome is for the client.
- How the illness/disability, etc. affects the client's life and relationships.
- How it affects those with whom he or she shares life.
  Under 'Music Skills', we should include:
- Appropriate practical music skills in our own instrument.
- Ability to play a portable instrument which can be taken to the bedside when necessary.
- Knowledge of the repertoire which is appropriate for the people with whom we work.
- Ability to select items which will fit the total therapeutic aims of the intervention.
- Ability to improvise and to help the clients develop their own ability to improvise in order to express feelings which are verbally inexpressible, etc.
- Ability to transpose at sight and on paper (e.g. for a person with limited vocal range or for one who plays a transposing instrument such as the horn or clarinet).

There are also many skills, usually impossible to label, which involve a combination of music and therapy, and it is in fact the combination of music with therapy which creates the profession of music therapy. The need for a diversity of skills will be seen from the case histories which follow.

The author's own approach is eclectic, based initially upon a Rogerian-style of empathy, reflection and affirmation (Rogers, 1961) expanded by 'Egan Skills Model' (Egan, 1976) but also including cognitive work, similar to the Rational Emotive approach of Albert Ellis (Ellis and Harper, 1975) and some features of Gestalt therapy such as 'Empty Chair' work (Fagan and Shepherd, 1970).

In Empty Chair work, the client is helped to get deeply into the reality of his or her relationship with the significant other, who may be a deceased spouse or parent, a living spouse or parent or any significant person with whom there have been difficulties in relationships.

Music is highly effective in this quasi-induction period, usually that which has been significant in the relationships, or which is familiar to the client and which carries emotional connotations, or - less commonly - music improvised by the therapist to induce a particular mood.

The client is then asked to address the empty chair as if the person with whom there have been difficulties is seated there. (The level of anger, grief, remorse, etc. which emerges is, to the beginning therapist, astonishing.) After there is a sense of completion in this stage - which may involve five minutes, ten minutes, half an hour - the client is then asked to change chairs and take the part of the other person. The reality of this identification is normally indicated by a major change of vocal tone, pitch and tension, expressiveness and style of speech, with, in some cases, changes even to syntax and grammar, and changes of posture.

By taking the role of the significant other, the client is then free to feel as that person felt, and perhaps gain deeper insight into the reality of the relationship, which may later be expressed musically.

The final stage is to put the person back into the original chair, reassure them that there was no ghost present, that the thoughts which emerged were only their own, thoughts which had previously been (for one reason or another - often guilt or emotional trauma) inaccessible to the client's conscious mind.

We must note that this is a most powerful psychotherapeutic tool and should never be used with persons suffering from hallucinations or delusional system of belief, since it will dangerously enhance both hallucinations and delusions. Empty Chair work must not be used by the inexperienced therapist, nor must it be used unless one has received some training in the methods. And even with these provisos met, we are wise to seek professional supervision as well as discussion of process and outcome with our colleagues.

The aim of this combined approach, using music together with counselling techniques, is to help the client to gain insight, through therapeutic applications of music, into the destructive aspects of his or her life and then help him to choose strategies to achieve change, also symbolised in music.

The vital unifying component is the music, which helps the client to relive relationships, symbolises emotion, and helps the client to understand his problem and then to achieve changes in attitude and behaviour.

This 3-fold approach can be expressed thus, (and I am deeply grateful to Sydney clinical psychologist Dr Brian Gray for this graphic representation).

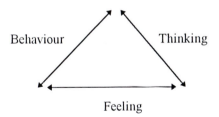

Behaviour   Thinking

Feeling

Each apex and each arm of the triangle is of equal value, and it will be noted that each line has double arrow-heads. This symbolises that:

- our behaviour is affected by both our feelings and our thinking.
- our thinking is affected by both our feelings and our behaviour.
- our feelings do not exist in a vacuum but are, in turn, affected by our thinking and our behaviour.

This model is highly appropriate for the use of music therapy in both the resolution of blocked grief and in other situations. We do not simply 'behave'; our total life is a mixture of all three and a therapy which looks at only one aspect of living neglects, to the detriment of the client, the other sides of his/her life.

Theoretical Background

What Are the Causes of Grief?

Grief is not concerned only with death or the prospect of death. We grieve over an enormous range of losses:

- loss of expectation in the baby born dead or disabled.
- grief over infertility when our hopes for children are unfulfilled.
- loss of expectation in the failure of relationships ending in loss of friendship in separation or divorce.
- loss of hope when illness or disability mars our plans for the future.
- loss of self-esteem when we are rejected or feel 'put down', lose our job or fail to achieve employment.
- when our upbringing of our children appears to have 'failed' and they are in prison, are substance-dependent, commit suicide etc.
- loss of self-esteem because we belong to an oppressed or rejected minority group.
- loss of material possessions through burglary or fire, or from political or religious oppression which forces us to leave our homes.
- loss of cultural and personal familiarity and feelings of security when economic or political difficulties force us into migration or into becoming unwilling refugees.

And these are only a few examples!

Why and How Does the Grieving Processing Become Blocked?

Almost all people who become psychiatrically ill and many who become physically ill or disabled have experienced loss. We see this in the loss of independence and competence resulting from a disability, the loss of self-esteem in the stigma attaching to psychiatric illness, and so on.

Although grief itself follows a wide diversity of losses, it seems that most instances of grief blocking come from only a small range of causes, all characterised by guilt. For example:

Guilt about the causes of the loss.

'Was it my fault that I lost my job? that the baby was born dead/suffers from Down's syndrome/died in childhood/became delinquent? that we didn't have children? that I had a car accident? developed cancer? had a stroke?'

Often, without justification, the secret answer is 'Yes'.

Guilty about the relationship which was lost, or about the reasons the relationship ended.

'It was such a difficult marriage, but I should have tried harder. What was wrong with me that he took off with his secretary?'

'I could never cope with my son's schizophrenia. I used to get angry with him but now he is in hospital I feel guilty that it is somehow my fault.'

'We always promised our retarded daughter that we would keep her at home but now we are old we just cannot cope any longer and have had to have her admitted to an institution, but we feel terrible about it.' 'And we are angry with that Home - they are not giving her the care we used to give!'

Guilt about the circumstances in which a significant person died.

'I did not take the illness seriously enough, didn't insist that he see the doctor, didn't phone soon enough for the ambulance.' 'I knew I ought not to have gone to the shops, he died while I was away, if I'd been home he wouldn't have died.' 'She died while I was in hospital - if I'd been home she would have lived.'

Guilt about the feelings which followed a death.

'It is awful! Our marriage was so unhappy that I just feel relieved that she is dead.'

'He had so many suicide attempts that now he finally managed it, I feel glad that all the anxiety and anger is over.' 'I always felt ashamed of being homosexual so that, though I loved her, it is a relief not to have to pretend any more.' 'All her life she was Mum's favourite, now it is my turn!'

Anger with consequent feelings of guilt.

'She promised she'd look after me, and now she's disabled.' 'How could he have been so stupid as to die from drugs?' 'I knew he always drove carelessly but he wouldn't listen.' 'She was too obstinate to get the car headlights fixed and now it has killed her and I am left alone.'

'The doctor told him he had to lose weight and give up smoking but he wouldn't do it.'

'We've always been good people, helping our neighbour - how could God let this happen to us?'

Many of these are caused by the relationship having been highly ambivalent, and long-term blocking of normal grief resolution may occur when it is impossible openly to acknowledge a sense of relief that the relationship is ended.

It is also true that a new loss 'hooks into' an old unresolved loss, so that people in whom the blocking has been established over many years need help urgently when a new crisis has reactivated the old feelings.

We also need to know that blocking may be in progress in recent losses unless we intervene to facilitate ventilation of feelings.

One may speculate as to why some people are able to resolve, emotionally and psychologically, major traumatic events whilst other people who are victims of similar circumstances 'break down'. A helpful paper (Rutter, 1985) discusses resilience in the face of adversity and suggests that those who survive have received adequate support whilst those who do not survive have failed to receive this necessary help.

When we work with children or adults, we have a responsibility (within the context of teamwork) towards parents, partners and siblings, as well as to the client, so that grief is not blocked, and we need to be aware of the hidden grief which lies behind the smiling mask of competence and control which so many relatives adopt to hide the reality of their feelings.

Those at risk include the families of people with major head or spinal injuries from motor vehicle accidents, (especially when there is anger about reckless driving), relatives of older people who develop Alzheimer's disease or other dementing conditions, relatives of stroke victims or of those who are suffering from terminal diseases, families of those suffering from congenital abnormality, etc.

Music therapy provides us with a suitable empathic milieu so that we help relatives to gain a sense of relationship with a disabled person through shared family music programmes, and meanwhile we 'drop' ideas into the conversation from time to time, e.g. 'I've often worked with parents who feel that having a child with Down's syndrome (or whatever) is somehow their fault, and I'm always sad for them if they can't talk about those feelings. It really is nobody's fault and yet some people really go through hell over this!' or 'Parents often blame themselves when a young adult has a major car accident, and yet to tie teenagers to your apron-strings is just as disastrous in its own way as letting them follow their own paths!'

This type of comment leaves the conversation open-ended, so that the relatives can respond then and there; ignore the opening that is offered, (perhaps by silence or perhaps by saying off-handedly 'Oh really?'); or they may come back to it at a future time.

How Do We Recognise Blocked Grief?

We may notice blocked grief by paradoxical responses to music, as, for example, when a group is enjoying a happy song but one person cries or walks out of the session. This indicates that there are personal, unhappy associations with the item which are at variance with the apparent mood of a song or a piece of non-verbal music, and we can assume that the person needs help.

This is 'Case Finding', in which one recognises people in need by chance observation. (We shall discuss with the team any plans we have for dealing with this situation, so that different therapists do not give conflicting messages to the client.)

Other referrals come from our colleagues who find that the history suggests there is an unresolved grief which needs help. (The story told in the referral may differ radically from the facts, so our assessment includes 'getting the story right'.)

The colleague may be puzzled by the patient and seek the music therapist's help, not because there is an identified problem of blocked grief but because we are known to be able to facilitate the ventilation of difficult feelings in a non-threatening milieu. Many people referred in this way are later found to be suffering the ill-effects of blocked grief.

Uncomplicated grief is defined (DSM IIIR, 1987) as a major depressive episode, manifested by changes to appetite and sleep, difficulty with concentration, loss of interest in normal activities, loss of libido, and other depressive signs and symptoms. But in a truly uncomplicated grief, these behaviours diminish gradually with the passage of time, although there may be flare-up of active grief at anniversaries: of the death, a wedding anniversary or birthday, the date of the final admission to hospital, the coming of age of a child, and so on.

We may, however, use the phrase 'getting over it' rather too glibly, and without any real thoughts as to what this involves.

When two elderly people have spent a lifetime together and the survivor is completely 'lost', when the death has been untimely (of child or young adult), when there was medical mismanagement, when the death resulted from murder, culpable driving, natural disaster, or other particularly traumatic events, when the outcome of a disaster has been not death but a life of extreme disability, (Gosling 1980) it is especially difficult to 'get over it' and there is likely to be a lasting emotional scar.

The 85-year old who had never been permitted to mourn over the death of her new-born son ('Crying is bad for you, the baby was so beautiful that God needed him more than you did, try to be brave for your husband's sake') had never 'got over' the death despite the passage of some 50 years, and it was only when the music therapist asked what music she would like to have sung to that baby if he had lived that she was, after all these years, at last able to cry, to gain relief and a sense of peace.

Time is not the great healer that the cliché would have us believe, unless we are able to use the time wisely, perhaps with support from a skilled counsellor.

Not all counselling is designated as 'Grief Counselling'; many counsellors work specifically in marriage guidance, child guidance, sexual counselling, rehabilitation counselling, but all deal with the grieving process since all the underlying problems are associated with disappointment and loss, and it is helpful to know what each area has to offer so that we can make appropriate recommendations.

Summary of Theoretical Background

Grief is complex and concerns losses other than death. Blocking of grief arises from various causes, which are usually associated with guilty feelings and/or anger.

Problems with blocked grief may never be resolved spontaneously. Resolution may be achieved through therapy, even after many years, with benefits emotionally and also biologically (Pennebaker, 1988).

Music therapy helps to facilitate resolution. (Bright, 1986). The music therapist needs a wide range of skills, in music and relationships as well as in the theoretical aspects of grief over all categories of loss.

Practical Application of Music Therapy to Grief Counselling

Case History 1

Miss A had been referred for music therapy by her physiotherapist, who came to believe that the intractable pain following a mastectomy, which caused her surgeon to refer her for physiotherapy, was probably of psychogenic origin, perhaps from the mutilating nature of the surgery. This surgery had taken place some weeks earlier, and it had appeared that she had made an uncomplicated recovery, coping well (with the assistance of counsellors from a mastectomy support group) with the emotional response to disfigurement.

Music was improvised to suggest feelings of sadness and anger. An assessment sketch was drawn of a steep rocky hillside, with trees and sunshine at the top, symbolising progress towards happiness and peace. She was asked where in this sketch she would place herself, and she put herself at the very bottom of the hill, a position which is noted to correlate with despair.

There was non-threatening conversation about the damage to femininity after a mastectomy, and also on possible fears of recurrence of cancer, since it is not unknown for such fears to be displaced onto the scar and the possibility of it collapsing.

Both these possible reasons for psychogenic pain appeared to be excluded, so Miss A. was asked whether she had recently lost someone close to her, being reassured that it is common to feel unwell in one way or another after a major loss.

She described the recent death of her de-facto (common law) husband. She had felt guilty that they were not married and she had therefore not felt able to grieve over his death. It was possible that the mastectomy had been perceived as punishment for her having 'lived in sin' but this aspect was not developed in this session.

The therapist clearly presented a non-judgmental attitude on the relationship, and asked whether there was any favourite music her partner had liked.

The immediate answer was that he had liked 'Phil the Fluter's Ball' and had whistled it all day! The music was played for her on a piano accordion, and she began to cry openly for some minutes, 'for the first time' she said.

The long-term nature of grief over a major loss was discussed. She was told that it seemed likely that her unbearable pain had been the expression of her unbearable bereavement, so that to work through some of her feelings would gradually bring about the diminution of that pain. It was emphasised, however, that this might take time and she was given as 'homework' the song 'Climb Every Mountain', with the instruction that she should sing the beloved Irish music to herself, allow herself to cry and then sing 'Climb Every Mountain' to symbolise hope. She was again reminded that it would take time to achieve resolution and freedom from pain.

She left at the end of an hour and a half, taking with her the sketch used in assessment, and an appointment was made for the following week.

It is the author's custom to suggest an item of familiar music for the client to take from the session as 'homework'; this will reinforce and remind her/him of what has been achieved. It also contributes to the client's sense of control over a situation, thus reducing the likelihood of a dependency state developing, since the 'homework' emphasises the part which the client plays in the therapeutic process, and diminishes the role of the therapist. (NB: the music must be thoroughly familiar to the client; improvised music is inappropriate since the music will not be accurately recalled after the session.)

Miss A arrived the next week promptly at the specified time and walked in briskly, with no trace of the hesitancy of the week before. She described how she had woken up on the morning following the first interview, and wondered where the pain had gone to.

There was shared rejoicing over this, and Miss A was asked whether she had had any important dreams that night. She described how in her dream someone had presented her with a plaque to go on the wall, and although she was not aware of what was written on it, when asked 'What would you like to have had written on it?' she said triumphantly 'Good for ME!'

She herself asked to sing her 'homework' song but changed the words to: 'Climbed every mountain... and I've found my dream!'

Miss A described how in the intervening week she had:
- Got a kitten
- Bought new clothes for winter
- Put down a deposit on a car
- Started to repaint her kitchen.

All of these symbolised a renewed interest in living. She was told of the possibility of grief flare-up on the anniversary of her friend's death, and given a contact phone number in case of need. (She did phone on the anniversary, but was coping well.) She then went to the physiotherapy department to tell them of her triumphant recovery for being written up in the patient's file and presented at the next Case Review meeting of the clinical staff.

This case history illustrates several important aspects of music therapy in grief counselling:
1. It is essential to have understanding of the ways guilty feelings can inhibit grief-work and we must be able to reassure the client.
2. We must not assume that the referring person necessarily has the full or the true story.
3. Depression can present as pain (Knorring, 1983).
4. Assessment only rarely includes music skills as such but focuses upon life needs and problems, in which symbolic expression of self-perception is more valuable than a check-list.
5. Improvised music can usefully reflect back feelings which the client has presented.

6. Pre-composed music which is familiar to the client can elicit even more helpful responses, giving permission to grieve because of its associations with the lost relationships.
7. Pre-composed music which is familiar to the client can be used as a memory aid and a behaviour-changing cue.

It often takes several sessions to build up sufficient self-esteem and trust before we are able to start work in depth; only rarely do we achieve instant success. The grief may have been blocked for so long that the person finds it impossible, or almost impossible ever to let go.

There may be a major depressive illness which requires medical intervention so that - although we may help the clinical team to identify the nature of the problem - we shall not achieve resolution without teamwork.

Grief resolution is especially difficult for persons with Post Traumatic Stress Disorder involving multiple traumatic loss situation, in which the emotional numbness so characteristic of the condition militates against successful resolution of the grief.

Case History 2

The patient in this instance was admitted to the same geriatric hospital as Miss A above, but as an inpatient. Mrs B had come from the psychiatric unit of a major teaching general hospital, where she had been admitted with acute agitated depression, with extreme hyperventilation. Other significant conditions included congestive cardiac failure and surgery for major cancer which had been carried out 12 months before this admission. Her husband had died from Alzheimer's disease a little over a year beforehand. She was included in a music therapy group, and a paradoxical crying response to one particular song had been noted. By coincidence, a referral for Mrs B to be seen for music therapy was received at the end of the session; in the referral the geriatrician asked for help because of Mrs B's sadness over her husband's death.

The conversation opened thus: 'That song, 'My Blue Heaven', obviously had special meaning for you. Can we talk about it?' Mrs B explained that this was the song her husband had sung to her during courtship. One may assume that the widow is crying because the song reminds her of lost happiness, but it is useful to express things ambiguously in case this is not so.

So the reply was 'It can be hard to look back over a marriage and the music can bring out all kinds of memories, can't it!?

Mrs B then explained that she cried over the song because, when her husband had sung it to her, it had symbolised her hopes for happiness. After some reassurance, she went on to describe how he proved to be an alcoholic who bullied and beat her, but never to the extent that the neighbours knew, so that when he died, people had been united in saying 'You must miss him!' Mrs B said she had replied 'Oh yes, I do' - but that she had not meant what they meant!

The music was repeated with patient and therapist singing together, partly to begin to desensitise her to the song, and explanations were given about the genetic basis for alcoholism, and Mrs B remembered that his parents had been heavy drinkers. She thus began to move towards a position of forgiveness towards her husband, with some thoughts as to whether she had been as supportive a wife as she might have been - she had found herself to be horrified by enjoying bossing her husband around as his dementia developed. 'Now it's my turn!'. (A common reaction.)

Despite a productive series of three sessions, it seemed possible that something else was hidden. Her feelings of being worthless were aired, and it was suggested that it was OK to see herself as a wonderful person for having remained loyal to an unkind husband. After hesitation, she then described the hidden grief which proved to be the main cause of her depression.

She described the close relationship with her sister, with whom she had made a pact that whichever of them survived the other would sing at the funeral the song 'The Garden of Tomorrow.' This song was totally unfamiliar to the therapist, so Mrs B was asked whether she would record it on tape, which she did - gaining joy in the knowledge that it might one day be used for someone else.

She described how her sister died unexpectedly while on a visit to relatives in a small country town, at a time when Mrs B had been in hospital for cancer surgery, so that she had not been there when her sister needed her, not been to the funeral (and therefore not kept her promise about singing the song), and since then had not been well enough to visit the cemetery.

It was highly significant that Mrs B's admission to the psychiatric unit had coincided exactly with the first anniversary of her sister's death. It seemed therefore essential that she should be taken to visit the grave-site in order to expiate her sense of guilt over the broken promise.

After discussion with Mrs B's physician and with her daughter the consensus was that even if Mrs B died in the process, it was better for her to go to the grave than continue bearing her (unjustified) sense of guilt. Mr B's grave was in the same cemetery, so it was decided to visit this also.

Mrs B's primary nurse came, in order to drive and to be available for any medical emergency, the location of both graves was determined, two posies of flowers were gathered, resuscitation equipment and a wheel-chair loaded into the hospital car.

Upon reaching Mr B's grave, Mrs B, said she felt able to forgive him, (but only spoke about him, not directly to him) placed the flowers in the niche provided, and said a prayer for the repose of his soul.

On reaching her sister's grave, Mrs B spoke directly to her sister, saying 'I can now believe that you really are dead, Joan. Thank you for all you meant to me, please forgive me for not being there when you needed me and for not keeping my promise about our song.' She then sang the song, The Garden of Tomorrow, in a strong voice, and we sat on a seat at the graveside. Mrs B then prayed aloud, and, after many minutes of quietness, said she was ready to return to the hospital.

The outing had taken over three hours but even at that stage it was clear that, despite being tired, Mrs B was greatly improved. She left hospital to go to her own home only three days later, with depression lifted, no trace of agitation or of hyperventilation, and with a feeling of hope for the future. Follow-up at six months showed that the change had been sustained despite two admissions to hospital for varicose ulcers needing repeated skin grafts.

This total series of interventions has lasted six weeks, each session being about one hour in duration, and the opinion of the clinical staff was that music therapy alone had been responsible for Mrs B's dramatic improvement, since anti-depressant drugs had been given for some weeks beforehand, with only moderate benefit.

The case of Mrs B illustrates a grief anniversary reaction presenting as a major depressive illness, in which music therapy was the means of achieving resolution.

Case History 3

The patient in this instance was a 17-year-old girl, looking younger than her stated age, dishevelled, poorly nourished, and in a state of suicidal depression. Her only words were 'I am dead' sometimes with the addition 'What shall I do?' These words were repeated constantly, at about thirty-second intervals, and she was on occasions found curled up in a foetal posture on the shelf of a dark cupboard.

She was seen for music therapy within 24 hours of admission, and her history showed that she had been a bright child at school, with one episode of school phobia and depression but no psychotic illness. Her mother (with whom she was living) was known to be a schizophrenic prostitute, living in a de facto relationship with a man about whom there was speculation re sexual harassment of Miss C by voyeurism. The girl's father had been intermittently a drug-user, and was a transsexual who had recently undergone gender-reassignment surgery.

Because of suicide risk, a few sessions of music therapy took place with the assigned nurse present at not more than arm's length, ('Care Level 1') but for the initial assessment and for most subsequent sessions the music therapist worked alone.

Weeks 1 and 2

Normal assessment was impossible because of the patient's elective mutism, and her failure to respond physically, verbally, musically or socially to any stimuli, so a variety of music was played which seemed appropriate for her age. Because of her apparently psychotic state no attempt was made to improvise music.

In the presence of hallucinations or delusional beliefs, improvised music (by promoting fantasy) may exacerbate and reinforce these to a dangerous degree, and although we had no evidence as to the girl's state of mind, the sole verbal behaviour, 'I'm dead' might well have indicated the presence of either hallucinations or psychotic delusions, so that improvisation was contra-indicated. Most staff believed that it was the loss of her father as a man which was probably/possibly the cause of her illness but that there might be other factors involved.

No response to music or conversation was perceived; the continual statements 'I am dead' continued unabated.

Week 3

Miss C was willing to move on request but in an automaton-like way. With the assigned nurse helping, a simple folk-dance was done, Miss C following the sequence of movements (clapping, swinging arm in arm, etc.) but without facial or body animation. At the end, however, she turned to look at a poster on the wall which showed a mother bird sitting on a nest with the male standing guard nearby.

'That is how we always think of family life, isn't it - the mother caring and the father protecting. But it doesn't always work out like that and you have been one of the unlucky ones.'

No reply.

Week 4

Sitting on the patient's bed, music abandoned in this session to see whether some other avenue would be more useful. Holding fashion magazines, the therapist tried to have a woman-to-woman conversation. 'I'd look really comic in that dress, I'm the wrong age, but you'd look really good in it!' etc. attempting to give the girl a feeling that she was attractive and would regain a normal teenage interest in clothes. No response.

Week 5

Played some lullabies; 'I used to sing my children to sleep with those...'

'Huh - my mother would probably have dropped me on the floor!'

This was the beginning of some verbal interaction but intermittently the remarks 'I'm dead' would return, to be dealt with by the therapist either by ignoring them or by using a tone of voice of: cheerful admonishment, mock-exasperation, or sometimes obvious irritation. Miss C talked with nurses and attended ward groups.

Week 6

First use of percussion instruments. Miss C invited to try to express some of her anger about life events while crashing chords and discords played on the keyboard. Miss C built up to a level of enormous anger, to the extent of damaging the top of a bongo drum, and was helped to reduce aggressive behaviour.

Over the next 20 weeks, weekly sessions in music therapy continued, with increasing extent of self-revelation but continued denial that anger and grief over her father's gender-change had any part in her illness. Miss C spoke of her mother 'Poor Mum, she just didn't know how to be a mother to me!'

Miss C had several episodes of manic behaviour and had to be in the Intensive Care unit for many weeks because of her risk of absconding, usually to the Red Light area of Sydney. Her behaviour was, however, so bizarre that the police returned her to the hospital before any adverse events had occurred, and she continued to participate in a varied music therapy programme.

Medication had been changed from anti-depressants to Lithium; this proved difficult to stabilise, but after many weeks, as a result of a combination of music therapy, daily living and social skills enhancement work through nurses and occupational therapy and with medication, Mrs C was ready for discharge to the care of her father, who gave up work in order to care for Miss C and was drug-free.

She returned for three out-patient sessions of music therapy because the team believed that it was this relationship which had been most important in the seven months of her treatment.

The final session focused on separation, and this included Miss C making a list of how the work had helped her to change. Her perception of the work included the importance of the therapist being motherly - i.e. not only kind but also telling her off if she behaved badly. It was decided to call this aspect of the sessions 'confrontation' since it involved looking critically at, and symbolising through music, many of the destructive aspects of her behaviour, feelings and thinking.

She also recalled the episode with fashion magazines, saying 'Do you know, I can't remember anything about that time except the day we looked at clothes in that magazine! That was really important for me.'

She then turned to her father, now living as and looking like a woman, and said 'Do you know, I used to get so mad at you for stopping being John and becoming Joanna that I actually went through the top of a drum!'

(This was an interesting indication that although Miss C had previously denied being angry with her father for changing gender, it had, as was suspected by staff, been a crucial issue in her illness).

They then talked together frankly about the issue and decided that the daughter could understand something of her father's needs in making the change, and that they could live together.

A 10-step self-rating scale was discussed; once Miss C's elective mutism had eased, this had been used as part of the on-going process of assessment. Miss C took the paper and drew the steps herself, saying with remarkable insight 'I have still got a manic depressive illness and I'll have to take lithium all my life so I can't put myself on the top step, but I reckon I'm on the 9th step!' On the list mentioned (about benefits of music therapy) she wrote a heading which said 'Changes from music therapy in a person with manic depression.'

At follow-up several months later, she has continued well, in stable employment, taking her own medication, and supported by the local community mental health team, despite the return to drug-use by 'Joanna', forcing Miss C to return to her mother.

This case illustrates the value of music therapy in a difficult major illness, probably having its origin in the loss of a male father-figure. A relatively long-term relationship was established through music therapy and counselling, in which the therapist was able to establish a quasi-parental role but without major dependency so that subsequent separation was successfully achieved.

General Comments

The technique of making low-key statements rather than asking questions has proved highly successful in facilitating, within the context of a music therapy session, the ventilation of 'forbidden' feelings. This approach is usefully supported by music improvised by the therapist in a Rogerian reflection of what has already been discussed, and is suitable for all ages.

One of the special blessings of music therapy is in providing a time for processing ideas. It can be frightening to take part in a direct conversation in which the only choice is to reply to a question or to remain in silence, and silence can be frightening in itself. To say merely that music helps to fill the gap is to downgrade its value, but there is reassurance in the careful use of music for the frightened client or relative, especially when that music is (as suggested above), improvised by the therapist to express the feelings which are below the surface.

In cases of blocked grief over bereavement, some clients benefit greatly from visiting the grave, symbolically to forgive and be forgiven, for failures in relationships, and to experience grief. We should note that blocked grief may present as alcohol or other substance dependency, but there is usually an underlying depression.

Summary

The three case histories described here demonstrate the diversity of music therapy as a facilitator in grief counselling. Music as a passport to the heart appears to offer many advantages over techniques which depend upon words alone, and also some advantages over psychodrama or art therapy techniques in that, in the initial stages, the client can take what seems to be an entirely passive role until confidence has been gained. People say 'I couldn't ACT it out!' but nobody has yet said 'I can't listen to music. I haven't got the skills!' As confidence and self-esteem improve, the sessions include more active participation by the client, both musically and verbally.

In all sessions, however, the expertise of the music therapist in aspects of obstructed grief and its resolution is of critical importance. It is not music alone which effects change, but music in combination with expert knowledge on such matters as illness and disability, social isolation, normal and abnormal responses to loss, etc. We need to have extreme sensitivity to people's needs (whether of client or significant others), and the gift of being able to assist the client to transfer (by one means or another) what has been achieved in therapy to the wider world of life and relationships.

It is this combination of knowledge, skills and empathy with skills in music which offers such a wide future to the music therapist who is willing to take the necessary time for additional study in counselling.

20

Listening and Accepting

Esmé Towse

'With the elderly, we have mostly been concerned with their physical care and socio-economic condition. This is essential , but it is not enough. We may too easily accept the problems and concerns of the elderly as purely a function of their age. The elderly have problems that they can be helped to cope with through psychotherapy.' Reiden Ingebretsen, 1977.

Background

In her excellent paper, 'Psychotherapy with the Elderly' Reiden Ingebretsen makes no distinction between those elderly people who are physically ill or disabled and those who are mentally ill. Indeed, the tone of the paper is less to do with treating conditions than with dealing with a group of people who continue to have life problems but who are often denied help, simply because of their age. Unfortunately, in the NHS in Britain, the provision of psychotherapy is erratic and is mainly offered to younger people. Not only is it rarely offered to those people attending units for the Elderly Severely Mentally Ill (ESMI) but it is even less readily available in medical geriatric units. 'Up to the 1950's, residential care for the elderly was provided largely in former workhouses. Most of this accommodation has since been replaced by small homes which are much better suited to the needs of the elderly and the quantity as well as the quality of provision has increased. But the demand far outstrips what is available, and there remain many problems of the quality of life for those who are accepted as residents.' (Arie and Jolley, 1982.)

Residential care may mix or segregate the physically ill/disabled elderly person and the mentally ill elderly person according to whether the residence is a local authority or private home or a hospital. During the last ten years, it has become more usual to integrate the mentally and physically disabled in homes. Whilst there is some evidence that such mixed environments can be beneficial to the morale of both residents and staff, the evidence available suggests that care staff are likely to be inadequately trained, particularly with reference to the psychological needs of the residents (Godlove et. al., 1980). In hospitals, medical geriatrics and psychogeriatrics are usually separate with differing training for the staff in each speciality. For example, doctors in ESMI units are generally psychiatrists, whilst geriatricians will have a medical background. Nurses too will have specialised in psychiatry or in geriatrics, rarely both. In many instances, hospitals which have a department of geriatric medicine will not have a department of psychiatry and so will have no psychogeriatricians on the staff. In spite of this, they may admit elderly people with serious psychological problems. If a health district has a large, old asylum as its psychiatric provision, elderly people who are mentally ill may be placed in an ESMI unit within that institution. In those cases there will be no medical geriatric provision.

Paramedical staff, too, tend to deal with either physically ill/disabled or with mentally ill elderly people. The main exception to this rule is the occupational therapist, who is trained to work in both settings. Recently, however, OTs have moved towards specialisation after qualifying.

The specialisation of pyschogeriatric medicine has been accepted in Britain since the mid 1970s , and, although there is a fairly standard provision of facilities and services, the style of service varies according to the ideas of the practitioners and the resources available. Thus, in some units, those people who suffer from a functional illness such as depression, anxiety, etc. will be separated from those suffering from a dementing illness, whilst in other units, they will be integrated . Some units will have the day hospital separate from theinpatient wards, whilst others will have the two facilities together. It is usual to have an occupational therapy department within a psychogeriatric service. Music therapy however, whose advent coincided with that of psychogeriatrics as a speciality, is by no means universally provided in spite of growing enthusiasm for its inclusion from other professions in the field.

Geriatric medicine is a longer established speciality and covers a wider range of disorders. The increase in developed countries, such as Britain, of the average life expectancy, has led to a large elderly population many of whom live alone. Two surveys conducted in the 1970s found that half the beds in medical and surgical wards in British hospitals were being occupied by elderly people, whilst 'chronic sickness hospitals' had been 'given over almost entirely to provide the bed base of geriatric medicine' (Brocklehurst, 1977) . Since then, there has been an increasing use of social service and private residential homes to accommodate people who would otherwise spend the last years of their life in hospital. Paramedical practitioners, particularly physiotherapists and occupational Therapists, have developed techniques which allow people to regain skills and independence. Twenty years ago many elderly people who had, for example, suffered a stroke, would have spent the remainder of their lives in bed. Today some 78% of stroke patients will return home even when living alone. However, although physical treatments have made considerable advances , there is as yet little consideration for the psychological aspects of being elderly and ill/disabled within geriatric services. Whilst large numbers of elderly people lived on long-stay wards in hospitals, some prominent geriatricians drew attention to the importance of the 'quality of life' and to the fact that elderly people were subjected to a life in which only the most basic needs (food and warmth) were met. However, as hospitals have begun to decrease their provision of long-stay accommodation, the problem of the unmet social and psychological needs of elderly people has been shifted to a variety of agencies, few of which provide therapeutic activities. Hospital departments with a rapid turnover of patients are unlikely to be able to cater for the psychological needs of the elderly and it is likely that few music therapists will be employed in such departments in the future.

Local Background

Manchester is perhaps unusual in that interest in music therapy came initially from geriatricians and psychogeriatricians and spread from these sources to general psychiatrists. Two part-time posts were established in the 1970s, one at North Manchester General Hospital and the other in the department of geriatric medicine at Withington Hospital. The author has worked in both these establishments and is presently employed in the latter, in the departments of geriatric medicine, psychogeriatrics and psychiatry.

A number of features make this particular music therapy post unusual, if not unique. Firstly, it is relatively unusual for a music therapist to be found in a District General Hospital. In the APMT list of places of work, 1989, there were only four such posts, the others being in more specialised settings such as psychiatric hospitals. Secondly, the therapist would not normally work for both physical and mental health facilities. Within each department there are some notable features also. The department of psychiatry is a relatively modern one and has no on site residential provision for chronic mentally ill people, although there are some day hospital places for this group.

In the psychogeriatric unit there are two wards , one for long-stay, mainly demented patients, the other an assessment ward, accepting both organically and functionally ill people. The ESMI day hospital has been built as an extension of the latter, with the result that people can begin treatment as inpatients and can continue to attend their sessions following discharge. Conversely, people who attend the day hospital who may require a period of hospitalisation can continue to attend groups or sessions whilst an inpatient. Finally, in the department of geriatric medicine, there exists a 'recreation unit' which, apart from being one of the first social therapy units for physically disabled elderly people is very unusual in both its philosophy and in the variety of services which it provides. The Recreation Unit was established in 1980, the brainchild of Jean Parker. A music therapist was involved in the formation of the present unit and the scheme was encouraged by Professor Brocklehurst, Withington's Professor of Geriatric Medicine. It provides 1-3 groups each morning and afternoon from Monday to Friday, in music, art, pottery, handicrafts , cookery, games, discussion, films and tai-chi. Those who attend the unit are primarily long-stay residents, most of whom are confined to a wheelchair following a stroke or because of severe arthritis. The unit aims to provide an environment in which people can take responsibility for themselves, can make choices and can develop relationships with both staff and other residents, relationships based on respect for each other. Although some entertainment is provided, the unit does not seek merely to entertain but tries to be a place where people can participate to whatever extent they choose. Residents work out a programme for themselves. Groups run on particular days at set times, so residents can choose to attend only the groups which interest them. Similarly, they have the right to withdraw from groups (although few do) if they feel dissatisfied for any reason. Even though various social therapy units exist in Britain, there are few, if any, which provide this range of interest, although many will contribute to reducing the boredom of hospital existence. The importance of choice and involvement, as opposed to entertainment, allows the recreation unit to provide not only activities which stimulate new interests and ideas. but also activities which allow time and space for reflection and for developing an understanding of the process of ageing and of approaching the end of life, and of the feelings which accompany that process.

A significant feature of the post is that a distinction exists between music as therapy and as entertainment. The latter is important and is available, but is not organised by the music therapist.

Music Therapy with Elderly People

There is little literature available describing music therapy with the elderly. The most notable author must be Ruth Bright, whose book, *Music in Geriatric Care* (1972), aroused the interest of geriatricians in Britain. In the introduction, Bright describes the specialisation of different aspects of treatment and comments that, in such a setting, it is easy for the therapist to lose sight of the 'patient as a person'. She goes on to describe the ways in which music can be used in connection with physical activities and as a means of providing an emotional 'release'. Much of the book is devoted to activity, with a detailed description both of instruments which can be used for specific purposes and exercises for specific conditions . Two chapters deal with the emotional aspects of ageing and give an indication of the author's interest in grief counselling using music , work which she has subsequently developed. In the chapter, 'Discussion group work' she illustrates the ways in which receptive techniques might be used as a stimulus to a discussion which may be personal or intellectual, according to the wishes of both the patients and of the therapist. Although she is clearly concerned about the boundaries of her work, (there are several references to it not being 'psychotherapy as such'), Bright's style is that of a counsellor. 'Any one piece of music may lead into several different trains of thought, and spontaneity will be dulled if the leader of the group wrenches the conversation around in an attempt to follow a predetermined pattern whenever it seems that a new line of ideas is being developed'.

In Britain, two articles by Dorothy Allen published in the *British Journal of Music Therapy,* indicated that she too considered the emotional as well as the physical consequences of ageing. However, the tone of her paper, 'Music therapy with geriatric patients' (1973) suggests that her concern was to promote positive values, such as sharing and succeeding, through remedial music rather than exploring and accepting feelings by using music to encourage catharsis. Allen's style is more behaviourally based, concentrating on the intrinsic 'rewards' of participating in active music-making. As the music therapist, she provides people with an enjoyable experience in an otherwise drab existence.

Music therapy training (at the time of the author's training) devoted only a small part of its curriculum to the illnesses or disabilities encountered in old age. Students who worked in large 'asylums' for either mentally handicapped or mentally ill people, would meet elderly people whilst on placement. However, such patients would almost certainly have spent the major part of their lives in that establishment . Although many were no longer ill (some, indeed, had never been ill or handicapped but had been placed in institutional care for 'moral' reasons), the level of social and intellectual functioning of these people was very low, due to the restricted and institutionalised life they had experienced. The musical techniques taught for use with elderly people concentrated on the playing of popular music of the period of the First World War and the 1920s. The therapist would play on either piano or guitar and would encourage active participation amongst the group by offering small percussion instruments and by encouraging singing. Theoretically patients would request songs which the therapist would be expected to perform.

Discussion of Techniques

Traditionally, the British schools of music therapy have emphasised active techniques particularly the use of free improvisation in which patients are given the opportunity to create musical sounds with the therapist on a variety of instruments, usually tuned and untuned percussion, either individually or in groups. In the opinion of the author, free improvisation is a central part of music therapy. The benefits of free improvisation are that the techniques allow exploration of feelings and the communication of these feelings in a non-verbal way, thus bypassing the restrictions, inherent in spoken language, created by pathology and culture. In this way, it can be used with people who cannot speak due to physical or neurological damage, and with people who either do not wish to use words or who cannot find the words in their vocabulary with which to describe and explore abstract ideas and feelings. It can be used in combination with words to explore interpersonal and intrapersonal issues and it is a powerful technique in both individual and group therapy which is psychodynamic in style. However, free improvisation produces sounds which are often atonal and generally unmelodic. To the lay person, it can sound like random noise. If it is to be musically effective and satisfying, considerable manual dexterity is required, combined with an appreciation of dissonance and of rhythms which are unusual to Western listeners. Whilst it may be regrettable, it is apparent from audience sizes that atonal contemporary music is not popular and seems to have little emotional appeal for the majority of people who are accustomed to Western music . Elderly people tend to have more limited manual dexterity than younger people. If they have suffered a stroke or are crippled with arthritis, their ability to play an instrument will be severely limited. Maracas, tambourines and various other small instruments can be played, but in a limited fashion. Professional musicians using such instruments are highly skilled. Instruments are used in combination, providing short bursts of colour. The techniques required to use these instruments in a musical and creative way are not available to most (elderly) people, particularly if that person is physically disabled. In addition, elderly people have a wealth of musical experience. At the present time it is unusual in our society for that experience to include atonal music. It is therefore unlikely that the creation of random sounds will seem relevant to someone who has been involved in diatonic music throughout his life, particularly if that person can see no reason for making such sounds.

Receptive techniques, on the other hand, are not widely used in Britain by music therapists, although many psychotherapists and occupational therapists use recorded music in, for example, guided fantasy exercises or for relaxation. Interesting work is being done in the Netherlands using receptive music with both depressed patients and with those suffering from anxiety disorders (Wijzenbeek and Nieuwenhuizen, 1989). Perhaps one reason for the lack of interest in receptive techniques is that music therapists fear to abandon their position as players who have developed a particular skill. Perhaps they believe that, since anyone can operate a record-player or tape recorder, the use of receptive techniques would fail to justify the long and expensive training involved in becoming a music therapist. Receptive techniques in reality, require the therapist to have access to a large repertoire of music of all types i.e. classical, jazz, popular, folk, opera, musical comedy, etc. They require thought and preparation before the session and knowledge and the ability to respond rapidly to changing conditions within the session. As well as using recorded music, the therapist may also at times wish to give a live performance which requires the ability to play well, to have a large repertoire available and possibly to sight-read well.

For elderly people there are several advantages in using receptive music, the most important of which is that the technique is drawing upon the persons abilities, rather than highlighting disability. This is particularly important when dealing with someone who has suffered a stroke as their ability to play may be affected by perceptual distortion as well the obvious physical handicap. The capacity to listen to and enjoy music, however, appears to remain intact.

Using receptive music that is familiar evokes memories and associations of people, places and events in one's life. Preoccupation with the past carries with it obvious dangers, but for elderly people who are aware of becoming increasingly dependent on others, descriptions of past events provide reassurance that they enjoyed the same independence as the (inevitably) younger therapist. The skills of the therapist should enable the conversation to move from the past to the present.

'Conventional' diatonic or polyphonic Western music can be beautiful and can provide the listener with a profoundly moving experience. However enthusiastic one may be about atonal music, it is difficult to imagine a free improvisation touching the soul with the sublimity of some composed music. Elderly people are often deprived of both beauty and of moving experiences. Beautiful objects (paintings sculpture etc.) are usually inaccessible to people who cannot go far from home. Beautiful literature is often inaccessible due to failing eyesight. The beauty of certain religious rites may be denied to people who can no longer get to church. For those who live in urban areas there may be little natural beauty and considerable drabness in their environment. Music can provide people with a rich emotional experience.

Finally, there is an advantage in using a technique which is not too primitive, but is one which allows people to use their intellectual capacities. Whilst it is recognised that intellectualising can be a resistance in therapy, it is important in some cases to allow people to use it as a defence. Free improvisation is a powerful tool for encouraging regression (to an earlier, usually infantile, state of relating), particularly if only untuned percussion is used. Elderly people who are dependent on carers to help with basic functions, such as bathing or going to the toilet are already in a state of enforced regression. It is not appropriate for a therapist to violate the defences of patients and it is unfair to withhold the opportunity to resist regression, particularly with people who may already feel humiliated and helpless. By using the intellect, an elderly person can remind himself and the therapist that he is not a child. He can choose to reveal personal material only if and when he feels ready to share his feelings, thereby retaining some control over feelings of exposure.

Case Material

Five small groups are held weekly with elderly members. Four are held in the recreation unit and one in the ESMI unit. The techniques used in all are essentially the same, although a piano is available only in the recreation unit. Discussion will focus on the ESMI group and one group from the recreation unit.

The ESMI. group was formed in the Spring of 1986, when the author was asked to spend two hours per week in the unit, funded by the Adult Education Authority. Although the job specified therapy, not education, a minimum number of ten people were required to be seen in two hours. Thus it was decided to run two one-hourly groups, one for demented patients and the other, the one in question, for functionally ill patients from both the assessment ward and the day hospital. Receptive techniques were chosen for the reasons outlined above and also for the practical reason that the only equipment available was a small cassette recorder.

The group runs on slow-open lines. People join and leave at varying times, usually according to admission and discharge from the ward or day hospital . However, four members joined as inpatients and now continue to attend as day patients. At the present time, this group consists of five members who have been attending for 1-3 years, plus one member who has recently transferred from inpatient to day patient status and 1-3 short-term members from the assessment ward. The group was run by the music therapist alone until early 1990 when she was joined by a junior member of the occupational therapy staff as co-therapist.

The ages of the members range from late sixties to mid eighties. Two regular members are men. Only one member lives with his spouse, but they have no children. The others are unmarried (1), divorced (1), or widowed (3) and live alone. None have a history of mental illness until later life (over 65 years). Two of the present membership were admitted to the assessment ward following serious suicide attempts. All suffer from anxiety and periods of depression.

The group meets at the same time and place each week. It is not described as a psychotherapy group but as an opportunity for people to listen to music and 'have a chat'. Consequently the therapists are careful to monitor the degree to which they challenge members, as they may not have established the 'contact' which is normally part of psychotherapeutic treatment. Similarly, although transference relationships do arise, the transference tends to be noted, rather than used as a central issue in the group. The group could well be considered to be supportive psychotherapy as it seeks to encourage the least maladaptive defences, rather than deal with unconscious material.

The music used in the group is taken from a broad range of styles. Excerpts usually last 2-4 minutes, although occasionally a longer piece is requested. Sometimes the group goes through a period of listening to old favourites . This can be interpreted as the safety of the familiar and so can lead to feelings around that issue. Usually the group will 'chat' for a few minutes before listening to the first piece. After this, another two or three pieces may be played in the hour's session, depending on the amount of discussion generated. Sometimes the second piece of music will follow on from the discussion, sometimes it provides a break. Vocal and instrumental music is used. Occasionally the words of a song will have a particular meaning, but often the group will maintain that they do not, or cannot hear the words. The group is usually silent while the music is being played.

The description given above is of the group as it is at present. However, it must be stressed that this particular form has evolved over the four years of the group's existence . When it began, the aims of therapy were unclear. A session had been provided for the unit by an outside agency. The music therapist was welcomed by the occupational therapists, who were pleased to have another group practitioner in their midst and regarded her as being from a closely related profession. Other staff were unaware of the role of music therapy, but were happy to see another group taking place. The general aim was to provide a pleasant, and therefore therapeutic, hour which might encourage people to leave the ward and participate in a social event. It was also understood that the group could be used to assess levels of concentration and social interaction of its membership, particularly with those who were inpatients.

The first groups involved a mix of inpatients and day patients. One of the day patients was a gentleman whom I shall call 'Bill' . Generally speaking Bill was uncommunicative and could be belligerent. He lived alone in inadequate conditions and his personal care was poor. In the group, however, he revealed his knowledge not only of music but also of literature and politics. He had travelled extensively and spoke of some of the places he'd visited. On one occasion he brought in a collection of dirty and battered cassette tapes for the therapist to look through and sort out for him. His cassette recorder was broken and his collection of tapes was one of his few possessions.. He seemed to want to share them with the therapist and, through her, with the group.

In response to Bill, the style of the therapist changed from being a leader who planned the group to one who tried to move with the group. The group as a whole started working at a deeper level ,with greater expression of feeling and personal material, which resulted in a couple of members leaving. However, since there were other opportunities for being in social, rather than exploratory groups this move was accepted.

The fact that all the music had to be brought into the unit by the therapist each week meant that some planning was needed. One of the anxieties of the therapist was that the group would be too influenced by her assumptions about the music which the group would 'like'. However, in a very short time, sufficient trust had developed within the group for the therapist to be able to bring music which the group disliked but would tolerate. Often, in fact, pieces which were disliked would generate interesting work. Some members would find it difficult to criticise the therapist's poor choice. They would wait until a leader had emerged from the group to take this step. If a piece of music was chosen by a member and disliked by another, it was rare for the latter to express his feelings. Usually he would show his dislike by bodily expressions of boredom and would need the therapist to help with a more direct, but tactful, expression such as, 'I wonder if some of the group found that a little slow/sad/long etc.' Such incidents would give rise to discussions about other situations when one feels unable to express feelings of dissatisfaction, a subject which appears to be particularly relevant to elderly people who often seem to feel that they should be grateful for services and carers and should not express dislike or dissatisfaction. At other times, the therapist could do no wrong. At the end of each group. she would ask if there were any requests for the following week and would be told that her choice was always just right, that she knew best, that she knew what they all wanted. At other times the group would be protective towards the therapist, treating her like a favourite grand-daughter. On one occasion, the therapist requested that the group listen to some music which she was going to use in an experiential session at an occupational therapy study day. The piece concerned was the first of 'Moods' for solo oboe, by Michael Berkeley, a piece which she considers to be haunting and atmospheric. The group listened with unconcealed dismay. What would these professionals think? Why didn't she play something 'nice'? Great concern was shown that her session would not be a 'success' and that she would be criticised and misunderstood by her 'audience'. The next week they were very anxious to know what had happened and how she had been received.

In the early days of the group, the therapist was concerned that, by using taped music, she would be imposing her assumptions about the particular music which might be meaningful to elderly people onto the group. In order to try to overcome this problem, she decided to choose music around an external theme (such as an event) following the style of Ruth Bright, thereby making an attempt to keep her own feelings out of the group. However, as she developed in confidence, she found that the theme could arise out of group material. Finally, the idea of a theme diminished almost entirely as the therapist learned to deal with the material arising in the 'here-and-now'.

One of the features of the group is that, in addition to 'chatting', people are able to speak of their thoughts and feelings. Possibly this is due to the combination of long and short-stay members, the 'core' group, indicating that it is safe to reveal feelings. The psychodynamic background of the therapist also allows her to indicate that it is appropriate to talk about feelings and that people will be heard when they speak. The group is generally supportive, rather than challenging, particularly when people describe feelings of loneliness and their fears of increasing dependency, feelings which they all share. Occasionally the therapist, or another member, will point out some maladaptive defence strategy, but it is always done gently. The main themes discussed by the group are loneliness and the associated feelings of bitterness (I spent my life caring for others, who now cares for me?), fear (who will care for me when I can no longer manage?) helplessness (nothing that I do makes it better) and hopelessness (what has life been about?). Sometimes people will reveal their ambivalence about being in hospital or day hospital. They need it, they appreciate it's availability, yet they don't want to need it; the presence of demented people is frightening because they too might 'end up like that'. The process of ageing is generally regarded with dislike.

Issues Arising from the Group

Two problems have arisen with the group. The first is not insurmountable but is to be expected in a unit which is not predominantly psychotherapeutic. In one instance, the therapist heard by a round-about route that a group member had complained to another member of staff that there was, 'too much talking and not enough music'. In a psychotherapy unit, she would have directed him back to the group, explaining that it was one of the tasks of the group to deal with such problems. The therapist dealt with this in the next session by wondering aloud if people felt that the balance of music and talking was acceptable. There was some discussion and the person concerned gave the opinion that there should be more music. It was then pointed out that members were free to suggest at any time that it was time to listen to another piece of music. The group focused on being too timid to ask directly. Since that time the ratio of listening to discussion has remained the same, but occasionally the person who complained will say that it is time for more music. In a more formal group, the therapist could have focused on the breach of boundaries or could have looked at the implied hostility. However, she felt that it would be too stern to tell the group that she'd heard that someone had been complaining outside the group, and chose to introduce the subject indirectly.

The second problem is that none of the 'core' group appear to wish to leave the group, which could eventually cause the group to become full and closed. Part of the reason may be a type of institutionalisation caused by the normal psychotherapy practice of sticking to a regular day, time and place. Possibly there are some dependency issues involved which have not been addressed. However, the reason for continued attendance at the day hospital is that the people concerned are at risk. The fact that they have coped at home for three years is evidence of the success of the day hospital and of the groups (including the music group) which make up the day hospital programme. Discharge from the day hospital may precipitate a crisis which would lead to greater dependency than exists at present. With younger patients, too, there is always a risk of relapse or recurrence of an illness. However, they do not have the additional frailties of the elderly and so the risk is perhaps more acceptable.

Comparison Group

The second group is held weekly in the recreation unit. There are six regular members, all of whom have attended a music group for several years, before the author took over the group. The group is joined at intervals by a man who comes in for a fortnight's 'holiday admission'. The eighth member is a lady who has spent several months on a rehabilitation ward, following a cerebral haemorrhage which affected her right side and her speech. The six regular members are long-stay residents in the hospital. Two have been inpatients for longer than twelve years , one having been admitted whilst only in her late forties, suffering from multiple sclerosis. The remaining members have each suffered a stroke and are unable to walk. One has no speech as a consequence of the stroke, although she tries very hard to communicate with noises and gestures, one is very deaf and one lady can speak only with difficulty. Three are unmarried, one is divorced and the others are widowed, all with families. There are two men in the group. All attend other groups in the unit, two people attending every morning and afternoon.

There are many similarities with the ESMI music group. Sessions last approximately one hour and are held at the same time, on the same day and in the same room. The music therapist is the sole leader, although she is assisted by two volunteer staff, both of whom are retired men. The volunteers will run the group whenever the music therapist is absent. Group members can choose to attend or not, though few miss sessions willingly. Exerpts from music of all types are played, interspersed with discussion. Again, exerpts usually last for 2-4 minutes.

There are two major differences in the running of the group. One is that a good quality piano is available in the music room, so the group has the opportunity to listen to a live performance if it wishes. Secondly, a large record and tape collection has been built up in the unit, mainly from donations. Obviously it is not limitless, but the therapist has a large repertoire instantly available.

Another difference between the two groups is the expectation of the medical team. In the psychogeriatric unit, the music therapist is seen as a clinician running a group which provides treatment and an opportunity for assessment. The groups run in the recreation unit are not seen as treatment, although their contribution to the quality of life of the residents is recognised and appreciated.

As with the ESMI group, the therapist tries to plan the group as little as possible and tries to follow, rather than lead, the discussion. Also, she is mindful that members have chosen to attend a music group and not a psychotherapy group, although her style is influenced by her psychodynamic orientation. Unlike the ESMI group, members are not treated equally. In this group there are three members who speak spontaneously and, now, need no help or encouragement from the therapist to voice their opinions and thoughts. Those with the additional handicaps of dysphasia or deafness need more attention and help from the therapist who consequently spends time with them, often repeating things said by another member.

Discussions in the recreation group tend to be less personal and more anecdotal than in the ESMI group. Occasionally a member will choose to talk about a deeply personal issue, but, when this happens, it is usually told quietly to the therapist, and not to the group as a whole.. Personal issues discussed by the whole group tend to focus on hospital life often with ventilation of the frustrations of being dependent , of being told what to do and when to do it or of being unable to escape from other residents who may irritate, upset or distress a group member. Another issue is the anger and resentment which members can feel about being the victims of a crippling condition. Most agree that, in their youth and middle age, they never considered the possibility that they would spend their old age in a wheel-chair, on a long-stay ward. The feelings expressed are carefully monitored by group members. Anger is expressed about powerful figures, such as doctors and nurses, but is rarely openly expressed concerning the therapist or each other. Although two members go home, or to a relative's home on occasions, none of the others has expressed envy or self-pity. It seems important to hold the group in a positive regard, to make it a place where people can laugh together as well as cry together. The group members have been forced by circumstances to live a communal life and they have to adapt to that in a way which suits each one of them.

The one feeling which is discussed by the recreation unit group but rarely by the ESMI is sexual love. The topic sometimes arises from an association of a piece of music with a partner. Two of the unmarried ladies make it clear that they have experienced love affairs and that they chose to remain single. Exploits are remembered and sometimes laughed about in a light-hearted way. However, an underlying dynamic is that the myths and fantasies about unmarried elderly ladies are dispelled. It is clear that the two group members were in full control of their lives and knew what they wanted. On other occasions, the subject of love and romance arises from listening to a piece of music which 'sends' a member (the group's word for feelings of nostalgia, seductiveness or sexual desire generated by some music). Often pieces will be chosen because a member wishes to feel 'sent' . Current guarantees are the songs, 'Passing Strangers' and 'The Rose', sung by Bette Midler. Instrumental music includes some pieces of modern jazz.

The striking feature of the recreation unit group is the social interaction which it generates. Opinions are voiced and compared regarding the quality of performances; memories of incidents or events are shared. People are aware of the effect of a particular piece of music on a particular person. One member will remember that a particular piece is special to another member. People can be quite confrontational if they feel that another person has made a mistake about a fact. When it comes to personal choice , however, such as requesting a piece of music, members show tolerance and sensitivity to each other's feelings.

The relationship between the group members and the therapist is more reality-based than with the ESMI members, perhaps because it is difficult not to reveal details of personal life within the unit. Some hostility was expressed when the author first took over the group, by a lady who dislikes change and knows that she finds change difficult. The previous music therapist was held in high regard and it felt difficult for the author to live up to her standards. However, it now seems that the music therapist is liked and is credited with abilities (particularly regarding piano playing) which she feels are not always justifiable. The lady who was initially hostile now shows her affection for the therapist by occasionally giving objects she has made in the pottery class, or by requesting music which she knows the therapist likes if an entertainer is in the unit. She has no family and probably needs a special person more than the others do.

The music used with this group is again chosen from a wide range of styles, but generally is geared to the preferences of at least one member. Occasionally the therapist will choose something completely new, or will try to be provocative in some way. Generally, however, it is the pure experience of hearing something moving or else the pleasure of an association or a shared memory that is important to the members. Their lives encompass pain and discomfort and, for some, the music group is a time when they can push that pain and discomfort aside for a while.

The Music

Emphasis has been placed on the need to choose music from a wide range of styles. It is also, the author believes, inappropriate to refer to the group as a 'class' or a 'music appreciation' group. Such titles imply that the therapist will, firstly, be directing the group and secondly, will be more concerned with the music than with the group dynamics and the relationships. Similarly, a group which concentrated on one particular style of music would be excluding and would lose the qualities of tolerance and of willingness to hear something new. Much of the music used does, admittedly, come from the 'popular classics' category, including the famous operatic arias, music from operettas and shows, music found in collections such as 'Your 100 Best Tunes', orchestral music by Johann Strauss, etc. In addition however, movements from sonatas and symphonies are used. Folk music from both Britain and abroad is used. Jazz, particularly traditional jazz is popular with some members. Rock music has been used with the ESMI group, generating discussion about aspects of modern life, such as violent crime, which is very relevant to that group. Songs from the 1950s and early 1960s are popular with the recreation unit group, particularly those sung by Nat King Cole, Sarah

Vaughan or Jim Reeves . Elvis Presley and the Beatles are sometimes requested. Hymns are rarely played, unless sung by a special choir, such as the Glasgow Orpheus Choir. Other religious music is used. Many people are very familiar with the 'Messiah'. Gregorian chant can evoke recollections of the atmosphere at Lourdes, to which some of the recreation unit group have been on several occasions. Singers and performers vary and most people have opinions about the quality of a voice. The timbre of a voice seems to be very important. Local connections are also important . The recordings of Isobel Bailey and Kathleen Ferrier never fail to cause a reaction in both groups, either because of the particular and easily recognisable qualities of their voices, or because of personal memories of the two singers.

References have been made throughout this chapter to the ways in which music elicits feelings, memories, associations and desires. Occasionally the author is asked to recommend music to soothe, to facilitate relaxation or to give pleasure. Having observed the two groups and the differing reactions in each, she is now of the opinion that it is not possible to prescribe music with any accuracy, because the ways in which we react to music are influenced by our projections. Someone who is mentally well may, for example, find a particular slow movement (such as the fourth movement of Mahler's 5th symphony) exquisitely beautiful and soothing, whilst someone who is depressed may well describe the same music as dreary and death-like. One person may smile and move to an Irish jig, whilst another may be irritated by its speed and liveliness. In the ESMI group there is a man who goes through periods of depression. One of the indications of his mood is the way in which he will describe certain pieces of music. On one occasion, he found Kathleen Ferrier's singing of ' I know that my Redeemer liveth' unbearably gloomy, yet at another time he found the same performance quite pleasant. In today' s society, there are many demands for prescriptive music. Supermarkets and shopping malls play music which is supposed to encourage spending. Airports play music to decrease anxiety and fear of flying or else anger about waiting for flights. Elderly people are subjected to prescriptive music in hospital wards and in homes. People seem to assume that elderly people will be stimulated and made happy by certain music. Music Hall songs, Max Bygraves and Mrs Mills seem to be high on the list of choices. There is no indication, in the two groups described in this chapter, that any of these styles of music are particularly welcomed by elderly people. In the author's opinion, such prescriptive music has nothing to do with therapy and everything to do with the assumptions and needs of staff.

In this respect, though, the author has set herself apart from the majority of music therapists in Britain, many of whom are concerned with physical or behavioural responses to sounds or music. Many music therapists spend time analysing the sounds they use in great detail in an attempt to ascertain which sound, or which aspect of the sound, caused a particular reaction, so that that reaction may be understood and, if desired, repeated. The style of the author, however, is to use the reaction as it happens, whether or not it has been anticipated. Reaction in itself is desired by the therapist, not a particular reaction.

This leads directly to the question, why music? If the medium is simply used to provoke a reaction, why not use art or literature or any other activity? The author is unaware of any studies involving the use of different media with this particular group of people. However, many activities take place in the recreation unit and it is possible to make observations and to get subjective information from the group members. One of the important aspects of receptive music is that it is different from a creative activity which involves making something, and it is also different from entertainment, which is entirely passive. In groups such as pottery or art, discussion does take place during the class, but, on the whole, participants are concentrating on the task in hand. They are absorbed by the skills involved or the details of their work. People who are not physically disabled may be able to create an object and think about the various implications of the activity but this would seem to be more difficult for elderly people, especially if they have only limited use of their hands. Entertainment, on the other hand, is not personal and gives no space for discussion. When entertainers come to the recreation unit, there are often several people in the audience who fall asleep. Receptive music, like entertainment, does not ask the recipient to do anything except listen. Thus there is no distraction or need to focus full attention on a skill. On the other hand, there is space for discussion. Whilst listening to the music, the group members can each engage in 'free-floating attention', a particular combination of concentration and letting the mind wander which then gives material for discussion. It is perhaps unfair and invalid to compare a group which is led by a therapist with one led by a teacher. However, the author believes that the fact that one can participate in music without having to be physically active gives music a particular quality. It is difficult to imagine a group of people being engaged and emotionally affected by looking at a piece of pottery or craftwork. Many will admire the skill and workmanship; many will regard the piece as a beautiful object. However, in the opinion of the author, there is no comparison between admiring such a work and being emotionally affected by it. Great works of art can be emotionally moving, but such works are inaccessible to those of us who do not live near a major gallery, and reproductions are generally a poor substitute. Perhaps poetry is closest to music in its accessibility and capacity to arouse feelings. It would be interesting to compare the effects of music with the effects of poetry or story-telling, preferably with the same therapist as group conductor.

Another advantage of music seems to be its quality of timelessness, in the sense that one can move freely around past, present and future whilst listening to music. Many people talk of the memories evoked by music. It is also possible to dream whilst listening to music and it is possible to hear the music as an immediate, here-and-now experience. For a therapist, this has a real advantage, particularly if one is working with people who have suffered a bereavement or loss, as many elderly people have, and are tending to dwell on the past, or with people who are anxious about the future and spend their time preoccupied with worrying about events which may never happen.

In the end, however, is it necessary to prove that music is more effective than any other medium? The therapist believes that this particular way of using music is effective with the particular groups of people described. Subjective reports from some of the patients encourage that belief. The opinions of the staff in both the units concerned are that the music groups are beneficial for a variety of reasons. Perhaps dissatisfaction with 'good', as opposed to 'the best' is a particular problem for the author. Perhaps it is in the nature of musicians to strive to be 'the best' and all music therapists are musicians. Music therapy also has a long way to go before being generally accepted as a form of treatment and so it is tempting to overstate its value in an attempt to gain recognition.

Conclusion

References have been made throughout this chapter to the influences of psychotherapy on the particular style of the author. It must be clearly stated that neither group described is considered to be pure psychotherapy for the following reasons. Firstly, no contract has been established with the group members. They have not identified areas in their lives which they wish to change. Secondly, no-one has been referred for psychotherapy and the idea of psychotherapy being available in the elderly unit may well be regarded with disapproval. Thirdly, the therapist has not asked for supervision for these groups and makes little use of the transference and counter-transference. Finally, regression is not encouraged. However, Ingebretsen stresses that the approaches used with elderly people should not necessarily follow classical technique. She points out the necessity of a realistic attitude to possible change, and the realisation that a positive outcome may be acceptance rather than change. She accepts supportive forms of therapy in which there is not a direct interpretation of the transference saying, 'If the person experiences acceptance and respect and feels that another takes his feelings seriously, this situation produces a real increase in the individual's capacity for self-determination and self-esteem. ' As well as dealing with feelings about death, she talks of the importance of feelings about life prior to death and the need which some people have to review their lives in the knowledge that there is limited time left to them. Finally, she describes the methods of Rechtschaffen (1959) who modified his classical approach in order to prevent complete regression. 'Encouraged to complete regression, the individual may not be able to work with the material that emerges and is overwhelmed by self-criticism and guilt.'

Ingebretsen also takes the view that psychotherapy with elderly people is valuable for us all because it gives us an insight into and an understanding of the last years of the life cycle. 'To learn more about the problems of the elderly is not only of relevance for the elderly as a group, but to our concept on life as a whole.' The implication is that psychotherapy should be seen not only as a form of treatment, but as an opportunity to think about existential questions and to become more at peace with one's self.

The music therapy groups described fulfil some of the criteria used by Ingebretsen. People are listened to, people work through issues of increasing dependency, loss and loneliness, people look back on their lives and draw conclusions about its meaning. There is no doubt in the author's mind that the groups are psychotherapeutic. The use of music makes it possible to run such groups in environments which are not geared to psychotherapy, and the author could be accused of introducing psychotherapy by the back doorway. However, the use of music also makes it possible for the therapist to modify the groups according to the needs of the members. The ESMI group usually operates at a psychologically deeper level than the recreation unit group and is more open to discussing the psychic pain felt by its members. The people who attend the recreation unit group, however, live in a situation where they feel obliged to deny certain painful feelings for the benefit of others, including the staff. It is not appropriate to push people towards insight and understanding if that leads to greater difficulties in dealing with an often unpleasant reality. The use of music allows the group to monitor the extent to which it wants to look at painful issues in particular, and allows the therapist to respect that need for control.

Using music also allows patients to be introduced to psychotherapy via the back door. Analysis and psychotherapy is increasingly sought out in Britain today. However, many elderly people are unaware of psychotherapy, whilst others would regard it with suspicion. For many people, psychotherapy is regarded as a dangerous, or perhaps ridiculous, dredging up of past events, events which cannot be changed. The exclusive nature of psychoanalysis has perhaps not helped people to understand that psychotherapy is concerned with every day human feelings. For it seems that people do have a need to talk about themselves and their feelings and people do ponder about the meaning of their lives. Both the ESMI group and the recreation unit group could choose to operate differently. They could choose to have more music and less talk. They could vote with their feet if they were unhappy with the way in which the group was working. But they choose to come and to talk and to have the music. In the words of one lady from the elderly unit, 'I really look forward to coming. The music gives me something; nothing else gets to me like music does.' She went on to describe free-floating attention perfectly. 'You can be really listening when you suddenly remember where you heard that before and who you were with and it all snaps back in your mind.' She also confirmed to the author that, in residential care, there is practically no opportunity to talk about herself, although she pointed out that that is true of other situations also, and that it can happen in any relationship.

Dynamic psychotherapy with elderly people has evolved more slowly and is less frequently available than with younger people, partly due to Freud's reluctance to treat people older than 45 years, and partly due to limited resources and financial considerations. Yet there seems to be an increasing acceptance that older people can use psychotherapy and can be helped by it. Psychogeriatric medicine is a comparatively recent specialisation and practitioners are open to new ideas. Hopefully, psychodynamic music therapy can develop in this setting. If it is to develop, it will be with the help of those people who, like Ingebretsen, believe that concern for physical care and socio-economic conditions, although essential, is not enough. Unfortunately, at the present time, the psychic well-being of elderly people is often ignored. Such denial of elderly people's needs is both heartless and, in many ways, short-sighted. Elderly people can enrich the lives of younger therapists or nurses. They have experience of life and of the joys and the difficulties of life. They are experiencing a part of life which most of us will have to experience. If we listen to elderly people and attempt to share their experience, we can acquire some of their wisdom and we can perhaps deal with problems in other areas with increased understanding. We can, perhaps, work more effectively. For, although the author believes that her interest in dynamic psychotherapy, which developed as a result of work with younger psychiatric patients, has influenced her way of working with elder people, she believes too, that her experience of working in the two elderly units has influenced her style of work with younger people, people who can recover from illness or distress and lead a life in which they can contribute to society.

Perhaps such opinions are too idealistic in a society in which cost-effectiveness and proven results are greatly valued. Perhaps we need to look at the benefits of therapy to society as a whole, rather than simply to the individual person. Unfortunately, it is at the present time impossible to prove the benefits of this particular form of music therapy. However, in the ESMI group, in the four years of its existence only one long-standing member from the day hospital has required a period of inpatient treatment. He suffers from recurring bouts of depression and has, in addition to the one very bad episode, experienced periods of depression which, although serious, have been survived without the need for hospitalisation. Another member, who made a very serious suicide attempt three years ago, has coped with her lonely life with minimal support (day hospital attendance once weekly). Day care is, in addition to being preferable to most individuals, considerably cheaper than residential care. Naturally, the author is not claiming that such results are due to music therapy alone, but she does feel that her group contributes to the effectiveness to the overall treatment. In the elderly unit it is more difficult to prove the merits of both the recreation unit and music therapy to sceptics. One survey indicated the reduction of incontinence in people who were engaged in an enjoyable or meaningful activity. Such results are medically and socially desirable. Generally speaking, though, it is not possible to justify the use of psychotherapy, music therapy or recreation with elderly people if one is looking for either economic benefits or of objective evidence of cure or progress. Such yardsticks should not be the only ones used. It should be enough to accept that elderly people seem to feel better when such therapies are available to them.

21

Retrieving the Losses of Alzheimer's Disease for Patients and Care-Givers with the Aid of Music

Suzanne B. Hanser and Alicia Ann Clair

'Music gives me life!' These are the words of Mr B, a victim of Alzheimer's disease, just prior to his entering a nursing home. Mr B and his wife attended a music therapy group in Palo Alto, California before the burden of caring for his daily needs resulted in placement in residential care. Mr B's story is one of many who have appreciated the meaning of music in a life otherwise fraught with confusion, anger, sadness and loss.

This chapter presents music therapy programmes which have been employed successfully with patients who have dementia of the Alzheimer's type and their family caregivers. It is based on research and clinical work with individuals functioning in a wide range of levels from community-dwelling patients at early stages of Alzheimer's disease to inpatients at the later stages of the disease process. Our work represents programming in two geographic regions of the United States, specifically, in the states of California and Kansas.

The chapter describes the etiology, prevalence and course of Alzheimer's disease as well as those who provide their care. We introduce the goals of music therapy with Alzheimer's patients, and demonstrate how music therapy enhances the lives of both patient and caregiver. We present three specialised programmes which comprise a variety of structured music experiences, and offer case studies to demonstrate their impact.

Dementia of the Alzheimer's Type

Mrs H has had a long day at the office. Suddenly, she finds herself looking at her appointment book without being able to recall why she is checking it. When her secretary comes in, Mrs H snaps at her, ''Return to your desk!' 'But, you just called me in,' the secretary states in defence. Mrs H, known for her mild personality and polite style, throws down the book in anger and rushes out of the room. Outside, in the parking lot, she wanders around the perimeter, looking for her car. She cannot seem to remember where she parked that morning. This has been happening lately, but now, she cannot seem to tolerate the frustration. Finally, she finds the car and starts out for home. After driving several blocks, Mrs H realises that she is lost. Tears keep her from driving, and she pulls over, not able to understand what could possibly be happening to her.

Those who suffer from Alzheimer's disease experience a slow and progressive deterioration in their mental abilities, often accompanied by personality changes and other behavioural manifestations. This is evident in the increasing difficulty and eventually, the impossibility of finding the words to express a simple idea. Recent memory is vastly impaired as time goes on, and learning new material becomes unrealistic. The speed with which the eyes and ears take in information slows, and the messages processed by the brain are significantly delayed. As the disease progresses, depression and delusions are not uncommon, and problem behaviours such as agitation and wandering often pose challenging concerns in managing the individual.

Alzheimer's disease, known more formally as dementia of the Alzheimer type, was identified by Alois Alzheimer (1907) in a woman who died at age 55 with progressive, presenile dementia. At age 51, this woman had experienced a progressive dementia, a deterioration in intellectual functioning which eventually resulted in gross interference with daily functioning. At autopsy, her brain was observed to have unusually abnormal nerve cells. Specifically, the nerve fibres were tangled and nerve endings had died off. Called neurofibrillary tangles and neurotic plaques, respectively, these biological markers identified Alzheimer's disease. But, unfortunately, it was only at autopsy that these abnormalities could be seen. Today, the diagnosis of Alzheimer's disease is still impossible to determine with complete certainty until autopsy. With continued study of dementia, however, it has been estimated that a complete neurological, psychiatric, and medical profile may reveal a diagnosis of ''probable' or 'possible' Alzheimer's disease with 90% accuracy (Katzman, 1986).

The identification of this syndrome actually led to more questions than answers regarding the nature of memory lapses associated with normal ageing as opposed to the pathological characteristics of dementia. It is now clear that dementia has many manifestations and causes, and that Alzheimer's disease is only one type. Many dementias are reversible, but at present, there is no known cure for the Alzheimer's type. The etiology of the disease is, likewise unsure. Some theories link the disease with genetics, acetylcholine levels, abnormal proteins, slow viruses, the presence of aluminium, decreased blood flow, and the prevalence of head injuries. However, inconsistent research results have only confirmed the hypothesis that the condition is multifaceted and caused by a complex interaction of factors.

A sharp increase in the prevalence of Alzheimer's disease has led to increased attention to this major world-wide problem. Epidemiological studies in the United States, Great Britain and Scandinavia estimate that 5 to 7% of those over age 65, and 20% of those over age 80 are afflicted (Mortimer, in press). In addition, over half of the US nursing home population is said to have Alzheimer's disease (Terry and Katzman, 1983).

Mrs H is not alone. Hopefully, family and friends will urge her to have a complete diagnostic evaluation and, if Alzheimer's disease is suspected, help her cope with this devastating and degenerative condition.

Stress and Burden in Family Caregivers

Mr C knows he needs help. Soon after his retirement, he learned that his wife had probable Alzheimer's disease. Now, two years later, his life consists of dressing and diapering his wife, cleaning her, feeding her, and caring for her every need. If unattended, she wanders, and last week, she walked right out of the house and across a busy street while Mr C was asleep. The police officer who brought her home believed that she was fortunate not to have been hit by passing traffic. During the night, Mrs C weeps and occasionally screams out. Mr C feels powerless to console her. In fact, he feels powerless all the time now, out of control, anxious, depressed, beyond being able to cope.

Asking for help is difficult for Mr C, who was always so self-sufficient. But, now, he is feeling suicidal, and the only thing to keep him from committing the act is the thought that his wife needs him so much.

Family members caring for Alzheimer's patients undergo unbelievable strain in lives that are no longer their own. The burden of care giving may cause both psychological and physical impairments. At least 50% of caregivers experience depression, anxiety, frustration, and sleeplessness to a moderate or severe degree. They are at risk for stress-related physical illnesses, often making massive changes in their social, professional and family lifestyles. Research has shown that caring for the Alzheimer's patient may have devastating effects, including increases in the need for psychotropic drugs, major decreases in social and recreational activities, and large increments in the number and severity of stress symptoms. Even placement in a nursing home or residential care facility does not completely relieve the strain of having a family member with Alzheimer's disease. It is now recognised that the burden of care giving is a major world problem requiring as much attention as the disease itself (Light and Leibowitz, 1989).

Mr C recently heard a radio advertisement for the local chapter of the Alzheimer's Disease and Related Disorders Association. Calling the Association, he learns that there are support groups for caregivers like himself and that respite care programmes serve people with Alzheimer's disease living in the community. The support group will urge Mr C to have a physical exam himself, seek further treatment for his psychological distress, and take care of himself for part of his day while his wife is in respite care. In addition, he will be invited to take part in a music therapy group with his wife.

Music Therapy for People with Alzheimer's Disease and Related Disorders

'Music therapy has let me communicate with dad once again. We have fun singing together just like we did before he started showing signs of Alzheimer's disease. It is amazing that he can hardly talk to me or recognise me, but singing is a great joy!'

Music therapy is widely practised with older adults in the United States in such facilities as institutions, convalescent hospitals, respite programmes, day care, and adult day health care centres. The work of music therapists is sufficiently extensive to warrant the publication of many books for the clinician (see Bauman, 1987; Bright 1972, 1981; Douglass, 1989; Grant, 1979). Furthermore, employment opportunities for music therapists have expanded and will continue to grow with the needs of a larger older adult population (Palmer, 1989).

Music therapy offers opportunities for the individual to use some of the few skills which have remained relatively intact. Beatty et al. (1988) report the case of a man with global cognitive deficits confirmed by neuropsychological testing who was able to preserve complex musical abilities, namely performing classical piano music. There are many musical activities which can be accomplished successfully with ease and enjoyment well into late stages of Alzheimer's disease. Mastery of a complex task and enjoyment of pleasant and creative activities may contribute greatly to an enhanced sense of self, so severely diminished in the individual with Alzheimer's disease.

Research reviews by Gibbons (1988) and Prickett (1988) support strong and varied effects of music therapy. Notable is a study by Riegler (1980) which found that a reality orientation programme with music was significantly more effective than the same programme without music in hospitalised geriatric patients. In controlled experimentation with Alzheimer's patients (Smith, 1986), a musical activity significantly increased scores on the Mini-Mental Status Questionnaire. Musically cued reminiscence and verbally cued reminiscence were not as effective in improving cognitive functioning as the music activity. In a study by Olson (1984), behavioural responses i.e., smiles, body movement, extremity movement and rhythm attempt, increased when patients in a retirement centre listened to player piano music. In subjective interviews, patients also reported an enhanced state of well-being and youth. Experimental research by Millard (1989) demonstrated that group singing resulted in significantly more social and physical behaviours in Alzheimer's patients when compared to their behaviour in a discussion group. Vocal and verbal participation was significantly higher in the singing group as well. It is noteworthy that many patients who can no longer talk coherently are able to sing lyrics to familiar songs quite well (Novick, 1982). Although this may demonstrate the persistence of an over learned response, it supports the use of music with patients with a history of enjoyment or practice in musical endeavours. The persistence of rhythmic responsiveness has been noted in several studies (as reviewed by Gibbons, 1987). Music has also increased attention and alertness without increasing agitation in the demented patient (Dietsche and Pollman, 1982).

In a recent research study, Clair and Bernstein (1990a) discussed the decrease and eventual termination of singing behaviours over the latter stages of probable Alzheimer's disease in severely regressed persons with dementia. The results of their study demonstrated that these persons no longer sang even when given the encouragement and the opportunity to do so with songs their families indicated they liked. Though these persons did not sing, they participated actively in playing a large, flat drum. That drum playing was of longer duration when the drum was held in the person's lap to provide vibrotactile stimulation than when it was held in front of the person within ready reach.

Clair and Bernstein (1990b) also found that severely regressed persons with a probable diagnosis of Alzheimer's disease tended to participate in rhythm instrument playing activities, in watching others participate, and in sitting for a duration of 30 minutes in music therapy sessions. These persons tended not to sing even when their preferred music was used. Clair and Bernstein's research indicates that severely regressed persons with dementia will likely participate in musical rhythm activities even when they no longer sing. Therefore, music therapy is a viable approach to promote meaningful and purposeful activities even into the last stages of dementia.

In another controlled experimental design, Wolfe (1983) observed improved scores on a self-designed questionnaire when geriatric nursing home patients experienced sensory stimulation including sound and music. Control subjects failed to improve. In a similar study, Vander Ark et al. (1983) demonstrated significant changes in quality of life (self-concept, life-satisfaction, socialisation, and attitude) as a function of music therapy at a skilled nursing facility. Other effects of music therapy are discussed in the literature on older adults, including greater involvement with the environment (Kartman, 1977), expression of feelings (Shapiro, 1969), awareness and responsiveness (Liederman, 1967; Oke, 1979), positive associations (Gilbert, 1977; Hodges, 1980); socialisation (Katzman, 1986; Isenberg-Grzeda, 1978), grasp strength and task performance (Cofranesco, 1985), and rhythm and consistency of gait (Staum, 1983).

The advantage of using music is that it focuses on the Alzheimer's patients' strengths and abilities. It can be experienced and enjoyed by those who are functioning at a deficient cognitive level while offering a relaxing respite from the concerns of the day. The role of music in palliative coping with stress is supported by a considerable amount of research. This holds implications for the Alzheimer's patient who is coping with the prospects of declining mental abilities.

For the individual who has reached regressed functioning levels in the later stages of the disease, music can provide opportunities for social interaction through nonverbal communication. Music may be one of the only media through which social interaction with others occurs in meaningful ways (Clair and Bernstein, 1990b). As an element of nonverbal communication, music provides opportunities for emotional response and expression (Gfeller, 1990). In addition, music can influence changes in mood (Radocy and Boyle, 1979). These responses can take the forms of vocalisations and facial expressions and may or may not require words. They can also be formalised through musical instrument playing, physical movements and dancing which are acceptable within the music therapy framework.

Although no music therapy research with caregivers is known to be published, Hanser (1989;1990a) has investigated the use of a music-facilitated stress reduction programme with depressed older adults, many of whom were caring for demented family members. This programme included a series of body relaxation techniques (body movement and gentle exercise to music, facial massage and progressive muscle relaxation) and guided mental imagery strategies which were practised along with familiar and preferred music. Over time, listening to music provided a stimulus for relaxation and pleasant visual images. Results of an experimental research design demonstrated successful relief of anxiety symptoms and depression while improving self-esteem for those involved in an eight-week music therapy programme (Hanser, 1990b).

Music Therapy for Alzheimer's Patients and Caregivers: Two Clinical Practice Protocols

To facilitate communication between colleagues and to test music therapy approaches across facilities and geographic areas, the authors developed individual clinical practice protocols in the hope that these would serve as replicable research models, if shown effective in a single setting. The effectiveness of both clinical protocols was determined through field research. Data were collected during the clinical practice efforts in both protocols. Protocol A was developed and implemented by Suzanne Hanser in a clinical research effort supported by the National Institute on Ageing of the US Department of Health and Human Services. Protocol B was developed and implemented by Alicia Ann Clair and Barry Bernstein in a clinical music therapy programme at the Colmery-O'Neil Veterans Affairs Medical Centre in Topeka, Kansas. Both protocols were tested through music therapy sessions with persons with possible or probable diagnosis of Alzheimer's disease.

Music Therapy for Patients in Early Disease Stages and their Family Caregivers: Protocol A

Protocol A included several music therapy techniques for small groups including persons in the early stages of possible or probable Alzheimer's disease accompanied by their caregivers or family members. This protocol provided a positive, creative experience for both the afflicted person and caregiver while offering a means of verbal and nonverbal expression. The stress reduction skills learned during sessions were practised as homework assignments to encourage a daily pleasant event while limiting anxiety and any underlying depression. The most important goal was to provide a shared experience to unite the family and offer opportunities for caregivers and individuals with dementia to enjoy and appreciate new ways of communicating with one another.

First, Hanser met with each family to compile a list of assorted potentially relaxing musical selections. The therapist requested that the family members identify music from their own collections which were most familiar and enjoyable. She recommended that they find music with positive associations and meanings particular to the family. She also asked them to select music which was soft, slow, repetitive and full of long, flowing melodies.

The primary caregiver in the family designated other family members who could attend music therapy groups regularly with the patient. In all cases, the primary caregiver was a spouse or daughter. Although the primary caregiver always attended with the Alzheimer's patient, in some cases, children and grandchildren also participated in the group. Group size varied from 6 individuals (3 families) to 10 individuals with no more than 3 with Alzheimer's disease.

Each one-hour session followed the same general outline and procedures to facilitate the greatest recall and familiarity with the routine. There were four distinct parts to each session: music listening for stress reduction; singing; improvising; and music listening with discussion. Music-facilitated stress reduction exercises developed and adapted from Hanser's research with depressed older adults, constituted the first part. Singing, as used successfully by Millard and Smith (1989) followed. Third, active participation with percussion and improvisation (Palmer, 1977) offered opportunities for creative expression within a structured environment. Finally, an experience led by one of the families focused on that particular family's strengths and talents. Families attended eight weekly, one-hour sessions.

Part I: Music-facilitated Stress Reduction

All families were requested to bring selections of quiet, soothing music to each session. Every family introduced the musical selection they brought by describing the associations one or all of them had with the music and how it made them feel. Based on the presentations and ensuing discussion, caregivers and patients collaborated to choose the first piece of the day which was used to facilitate stress reduction. The therapist then instructed the group in one of eight stress reduction techniques (adapted from Hanser, 1990a).

Technique I was a gentle exercise to music. Participants took turns leading the group in body movement after the therapist modelled circles and smooth lines guided by the music. Body tension was identified as the participants breathed to the music and moved tight muscles in slow and naturally flowing patterns. Next, family members were encouraged to interact in their movements. Some caregivers mirrored patients' movements and some preferred to use familiar dance patterns. The group was urged to try new ways of moving and dancing with each new musical phrase.

Technique II was a self-massage of facial muscles. Participants learned simple massage techniques that they could use on themselves and each other to relieve muscle tension. This gave family members the chance to touch each other with tenderness and love while helping each other to overcome tightness of facial muscles. The therapist recommended that participants try massage at home in any ways that they felt appropriate, once again guided by relaxing music.

Technique III combined progressive muscle relaxation with music listening. In this case, therapist-selected music of a slow, deep breathing tempo was used to cue relaxation of distinct parts of the body. The group practised this in the session and at home while experimenting with new pieces of music from their own collections.

Technique IV was a guided imagery experience employing programmatic classical music. This technique was designed to replace dysfunctional thoughts and worries with pleasant, familiar visual imagery. Listeners were asked to visit a place in the mind's eye where they would like to be, reminiscent of calming and peaceful scenery. The caregivers expressed their satisfaction with the beneficial results obtained with this technique. Many of the patients were no longer capable of this type of imagery, but they appeared to enjoy the relaxed state they were able to achieve while listening to music. The therapist used clinical judgement to determine when the level of confusion and the lack of reality content contraindicated use of this technique.

Technique V was a special imagery suggestion based on a particular source of anxiety or depression. In it, slow music with long, flowing phrases was used to cue positive images, for example, changes in physical symptoms such as tension floating away from the body. Some group members visualised themselves performing enjoyable activities which they never seemed to have time to do. Once again, family members were able to gain the most from this technique. However, the patients also enjoyed the opportunity for relaxation, and sometimes reported pleasant visual images. The same precautions for lack of reality content were exercised to insure that patients who could not identify the boundaries of reality would not be encouraged to use this technique.

Technique VI provided tips for sleep induction. The participants were instructed to listen to their favourite music or that which was the most successful in inducing a relaxed state. They were encouraged to use this music to enhance relaxation and clear thinking at bedtime.

Technique VII was a music stimulation programme that gave the participants ideas for physical exercise at the start of the day or at a low point in the daily routine. Rhythmic music which evoked a positive mood or pleasant associations was used as the group identified an appropriate pace for enhancing energy. Group members took turns leading.

Technique VIII added other modes of creativity such as art, dance, and drama to express feelings and thoughts. It engaged the participants more thoroughly in successful mastery of a new skill or talent, focusing on healthy aspects of each individual.

At the end of each exercise, the group discussed whether or not the music served to evoke a mood which was incompatible with tension and anxiety. Caregivers were asked to interpret the afflicted person's moods, and the afflicted persons were asked to describe their caregivers' moods. This encouraged families to use nonverbal cues to interpret moods and feelings. In this way, caregivers and family members learned skills to facilitate understanding without verbal communication.

Group members also decided when, where and how they would use these skills at home. By taking some control in the decision making process, participants learned to discriminate the most and least helpful elements of each music therapy programme and how to apply them when they needed them most.

Over time, they mastered relaxation skills and were able to use them in a co-operative and creative manner.

Part II: Singing

In the next part of each session, songbooks were passed out and family members assisted the patients as necessary in locating favourite songs. At every session, participants were asked to identify songs that described how they felt after the relaxation segment or songs that represented something about themselves, their pasts, or their families. Often, when a caregiver selected a piece, and presented the reasons for its choice, an important memory would be cued in the person with dementia.

Singing songs proved to be enjoyable, even by the shyest members of the group. Many had fine voices, and were able to 'star' in a solo, were applauded by others, or recalled experiences such as singing in a choir, at a party, for religious occasions, or even during sing-alongs at camp or retreat. Although it was difficult for some patients to follow written words, there were many familiar songs everyone could sing from memory.

For those who were interested, autoharp accompaniment provided another way to enhance the singing experience. Most of the time, it was appropriate to teach the caregiver or family member the chords for a song and have the demented person strum in rhythm. This offered a chance for the two to co-operate effectively and successfully in the accompaniment of singing. Starting with songs which required only one chord and gradually introducing more difficult chord patterns, every group member was capable of participating at a level commensurate with individual abilities. In addition, simple percussion instruments were used to provide rhythmic accompaniment. Mastery of these skills was designed to provide another example of accomplishment in individuals who, generally, were experiencing less of it day by day.

Part III: Improvisation

Using the approach to music education and therapy by Carl Orff, the musical rondo form structured opportunities for individual improvisation interspersed with a group chant or melody. For most of these activities, group members used xylophones tuned to the pentatonic scale to create their own melodies (Bitcon, 1977).

One popular chant was, 'How do you feel?, How do you feel? Reach inside and pull it out. How do you feel?' After chanting this as a group, one participant played the xylophone to express a feeling. The chant was repeated and the next person had a chance to play. A pattern was repeated around the circle of participants until everyone played the xylophone. Then, possible interpretations of each other's improvisations were discussed. This not only gave family members a chance to express and share their feelings with supportive others, it also provided a way for them to hear their loved one's feelings expressed in a new way.

The next improvisational technique involved a musical conversation between caregiver and patient. The therapist modelled this approach with a caregiver in such a way as to demonstrate the natural give-and-take of a conversation. First, the music therapist played a melody, and waited for a response. Then, the music therapist imitated certain of the caregiver's notes and patterns. Next, the music therapist played a new simple pattern. After group members attempted this in patient-caregiver dyads, the similarities between musical and verbal interchanges were discussed.

Frequently, caregivers were struck by the metaphor. In one case, the frustration the caregiver felt when her husband failed to listen to her, and instead, talked on and on, was witnessed in the 'musical conversation'. She realised the source of her frustration, and was able to express this in the supportive group atmosphere. She and her husband tried the improvisation again after talking, and she said that during the second trial, she focused more carefully on the feelings expressed by her husband, and practised a more patient response to him than she did during the first attempt.

Part IV: Closure

At the end of every session, one family would collaborate with the music therapist in leading the group in a music listening experience. Usually the family would select the background music and suggest a structure for expressing something about the session. They often suggested using another art form such as drawing, painting, movement, or drama, or identified a theme which was important to them. At other times, a family chose a new type of activity, such as song writing or learning to play an instrument.

Song writing was extremely popular because it enabled the group to co-operate in a meaningful creative endeavour. They used this opportunity to describe how they felt about one another and to express common concerns and sources of support.

The sessions always ended with a song which requested input from the participants. This information included what they liked best, how they felt, and what they planned to do musically during the week ahead.

Music Therapy Group: Case Study A

Mr B was diagnosed with probable Alzheimer's disease three years ago, when he was 54 years of age. Mrs B cared for him at home until his wandering and incessant talking became unmanageable. One year ago, unable to cope with his deteriorating condition Mrs B reluctantly placed her husband in the Alzheimer's Inpatient Unit of the Palo Alto Department of Veterans Affairs Medical Center. Currently, he comes home on weekends and for special holidays. He is able to verbalise coherently when asked a specific question; but then, perseverates and rambles, preoccupied with details. On the unit, he has been either withdrawn or extremely aggressive towards other patients.

Mr and Mrs B participated in the eight-week music therapy programme along with their 32-year old daughter, never missing a session. The entire family attempted every activity, from the passive listening and relaxation techniques to more active ones, such as learning to play the autoharp.

The stress reduction techniques were particularly appreciated by the B family. The women enjoyed the chance to relax and participate for an hour which had been eagerly anticipated. Even Mr B reported vivid imagery, but he seemed to take a greater interest in the content of his wife's experience. When she related a visit to a favourite place in her mind's eye, he elaborated with pleasant memories, many of which the daughter was hearing for the first time. This met with laughter and a renewed sense of sharing life as a family.

Singing provided another opportunity for the B family to reminisce. Mr B remembered the lyrics to many songs. Some songs were completely new to their daughter, having been popular before she was born. Mr and Mrs B were able to talk about what they were doing when they heard or sang these songs early in their marriage, again, sharing in the education of their daughter. This experience of reliving a more carefree, fun-filled time in their lives was extremely meaningful to the Bs.

The two women were most pleasantly surprised to discover musical abilities they had not known previously. Although somewhat reticent at first, they became more and more confident in their autoharp abilities, until they were the first to volunteer to lead the group in song.

Improvising was another new experience for the whole family. Because Mr B was able to verbalise his thoughts, and showed some confusion related to new things, however, this activity was not as successful as it was for other families. Music listening, likewise, was not consistently appropriate for Mr B who became agitated after sitting too long. But, even in these less preferred activities, Mr B was consistently co-operative and appeared to enjoy himself immensely. This surprised both his family and the staff on the unit.

During the final sessions, the family composed a song about the characteristics they enjoyed most about one another. The verses, each one written by Mr B, Mrs B or their daughter about the other two, was set to Mr B's favourite song, *San Francisco*. In the last several weeks of the programme, Mr B appeared considerably calmer, both in and outside of sessions. His wife brought him a cassette player, and he enjoyed listening to it during unstructured times of the day. The staff reported hearing him singing on the unit, and there were no instances of aggression towards others. Mr B was observed to initiate conversations and appeared far less withdrawn.

In a post-programme interview, Mrs B and her daughter claimed to gain a new sense of their husband and father. Both of them reported greater self-esteem through developing their own abilities, and being able to see Mr B performing so positively and creatively. They had not dreamed that it would be possible to enjoy their family time together like this ever again. Yet, during these eight weeks, they all had learned new skills and shared experiences which were some of the richest in their lives.

Music Therapy for Institutionalised Patients in Late Disease Stages: Protocol B

This protocol is the culmination of two years of clinical work with persons who were in the later stages of dementia with a probable diagnosis of Alzheimer's type. The music therapy programme was introduced with a group of four male patients at the Colmery O'Neil Veterans Affairs Medical Centre in Topeka, Kansas. All patients were severely dysfunctional and in need of total care. One was completely nonverbal and had not spoken for three years. The other three were verbal but spoke, generally, in brief responses to others, though occasionally each spontaneously initiated brief, verbal comments.

The sessions with these four patients were conducted by Alicia Ann Clair and Barry Bernstein, two registered, board-certified music therapists, in the visitor's room on the medical centre care unit where these patients resided. Each participant's wife was informed about the music therapy programme and was invited to join the group whenever it met.

Sessions were held once weekly for approximately 30 minutes. In initial sessions, taped recordings of big band music were used in an effort to stimulate responses in men who had been young adults when the music was popular. It was assumed the music was familiar to them. They were given rhythm instruments to play, or they were asked to make large arm and leg movements in rhythm to the music. Most generally, the patients responded by becoming increasingly more agitated as the music played. This was evidenced in their movements while seated in their chairs, their efforts to get out of their chairs and wander around the room and their facial expressions of apparent distress.

After several sessions it was decided to discontinue the tape-recorded big band music, except when it was used just prior to the session as participants entered the room. Instead of taped recordings, piano accompaniment was used while singing and playing rhythm instruments was encouraged. The piano was somewhat effective in stimulating responses, but it placed an unsatisfactory distance between the music therapist who played it and the group participants.

After trying these approaches and different activities, it was decided the sessions would be conducted with the music therapists seated on chairs with rollers which allowed them to move freely among the patients. The therapists used acoustic guitars and singing to promote responses and they incorporated participants' singing and instrumental playing responses into the songs whenever possible.

After a number of rhythm instruments were used in the group sessions, it seemed that three types were particularly successful in encouraging responses. These included: tambourine, maraca, and hand drum. These three instruments might have been successful in stimulating responses because each is easy to hold, large enough to attract attention and pleasing to hear. It is important to note that the pleasing characteristics of these instruments are dependent upon the quality of the instruments. The instruments were all professional type instruments which were purchased at a music store. They were not toys. Toy instruments can be perceived as insulting to adults who find them a threat to their dignity.

Following several months of sessions, it was determined that the singing and rhythm music activities were quite viable for all the patients involved and that these types of activities would form the framework for the music therapy sessions. Gross motor, rhythmic movement activities were not included since they were provided on a regular basis by the recreation therapy staff.

Part I: Greeting

Each session began with a spoken greeting to each patient as the music therapists found them on the unit. As patients were located, they were taken to the visitor's room on the unit where chairs had been arranged, previously. After all patients were seated in the usual configuration, the music therapists began the session with a greeting song that was adapted to include each patient's name in turn. This segment of the session was usually five minutes long.

Part II: Familiar Songs

Following the greeting song, two or three songs were sung by the music therapists and all group members were encouraged to sing. These songs were selected from those suggested by family members or caregivers as those songs which were familiar and well-liked by the patients. These were usually well-known folk songs and popular songs of the patients' young adult years.

While the music therapists sang, they moved about the group seated on roller chairs. This allowed them to make eye contact readily with patients as they moved into close proximity. The music therapists accompanied the singing with acoustic guitar which seemed to attract the attention of the group members. This segment of the session ranged in duration from five to ten minutes.

Part III: Rhythm Participation

To initiate this portion of the session, each individual group member was presented a choice of two rhythm instruments and asked to choose one. The instrument for which the participant reached was considered his choice. Participants were encouraged to explore their instruments and how they might be played. All responses which included holding, striking or rubbing the instrument were accepted as viable playing, even if the responses did not include traditional playing forms and/or styles. Some individuals participated in instrument playing by simply holding the instrument. They also participated in non-traditional ways which included rubbing the drum head with a mallet rather than striking it or by rolling the mallet around the periphery of the drum head. These non-traditional drum playing behaviours were typical of patients as they became more regressed in the latter stages of dementia.

During the course of the session, each participant was requested to play an instrument in imitation of simple rhythm patterns presented by the music therapist. In this process, several rhythm patterns were presented to each individual before going on to the next person. The following patterns among others were successful:

```
Pattern 1:    1         2         3         4
              /         /         /         /
Pattern 2:    1         2         3         4
              /                   /
Pattern 3:    1         2         3         4
              /                   /         /
Pattern 4:    1         2         3         4
              //        //        //        //
```

These patterns were presented one at a time with ample time for the response. Each pattern was presented several times to allow sufficient opportunities for successful responses.

Not only were participants asked to imitate the rhythm patterns provided by the music therapist, the participants were asked to provide rhythm patterns for the music therapist to imitate. In addition, each participant was requested to play his instrument for other group members to imitate.

During the rhythm imitations, those persons not directly involved in the activity observed the participants. This was particularly noteworthy since these patients were so demented that they generally did not see others in their environments. They often walked down the hall bumping into persons who they apparently did not see, but in the music therapy sessions, they appeared as interested observers.

For the remainder of the rhythm participation, group members were asked to play their instruments in a rhythm ensemble while the music therapist accompanied with a drum, or with singing and an acoustic guitar. This instrumental ensemble was quite successful, and often participants were very attentive as indicated by their active participation. There were some instances in which they participated for as much as 17 minutes.

When the music therapists sang with guitar accompaniments, the group members were encouraged to sing with them. Participants were given the options to 'scat sing' or to use a syllable such as 'la' to sing the melody of a song when they could no longer sing the words. Again, only very familiar, preferred songs were used. Sometimes, these songs were blues songs which were quite repetitive. On several occasions one group member showed his residual creativity when he sang the verse of a blues song. Some phrases of the song had come from popular blues tunes and some he seemed to invent on the spot.

The rhythm portion of the session was generally 15 minutes long. It culminated in the collection of the rhythm instruments.

Part IV: Closure

After rhythm instrument playing, it was considered important to stay in close proximity to the group members and to sing some music either with them or to them. Again the music therapists used every opportunity to move close enough for each member to notice and make eye contact. The singing segment usually included two or three familiar, well-liked songs that were different from those used earlier in the session. This part of the session lasted approximately five to ten minutes.

The last song of the session was one which Alicia Clair and Barry Bernstein had composed as a 'good-bye' song. It was done in a rock style and included simple lyrics focused on saying farewell. At the conclusion of the song, each group member was thanked for his participation and all were assisted in leaving the room.

Throughout the music therapy session, participants' responses and subsequent successful experiences were facilitated through repetitious presentations and adequate time allowed for them to respond. Along with repetition and adequate response time, appropriate structure and support were integral to successful experiences. The predictability provided through the structured routine seemed to contribute to the participants' comfort, and the music therapists' attitudes of acceptance and kind respect encouraged participants to tap their residual abilities and skills.

Music Therapy Group: Case Study B

The four male participants in this protocol each had been hospitalised for at least one year prior to the initiation of the programme. They ranged in age from 54 to 81 years and were selected randomly from a population of 12 severely regressed, demented patients with probable diagnoses of Alzheimer's type dementia. All subjects were very low functioning and were placed in the total care category. All subjects were physically mobile and observations on the unit showed that subjects wandered aimlessly around the day room and up and down the halls, or sat in chairs in the day room in front of the television with eyes closed or apparently staring. These patients seemed confused and did not have orientation to place, time or person. They maintained their confusion even when given simple directives such as where to find the toilet, or where to be seated for meals. None of these patients initiated verbal conversations with others and one did not respond to any interactions unless another patient physically assaulted him. All subjects sometimes approached nursing staff on the unit, and accompanied staff when requested to do so.

Two of these patients could feed themselves at meal times; the other two required assistance. One was completely mute and had been for three years. One patient made one-word responses when spoken to directly and was often confused as indicated by his frequent requests for clarification. His verbal content indicated active hallucinations. Two patients spoke in short responses and any other verbalisations usually did not relate to time or place. Their reality contact was often questionable and one of these patients was clearly delusional.

Once weekly when Alicia Clair and Barry Bernstein approached these patients on the unit and asked them to come to the session, they did not acknowledge the invitation verbally but accompanied the music therapists to the session when escorted by them. After they were seated in the room, these patients tended to look at the floor and to make eye contact only when requested. One tended to wander around the room in initial sessions and did not participate for more than a few seconds at a time. After the first two months of the protocol, however, all patients sat in chairs for the duration of the sessions.

In initial sessions, various activities were attempted and group members were not always eager participants. The first time drums were presented as rhythm instruments however, all participants took the drums and the mallets and proceeded to play without any instructions or demonstrations from the music therapists. This instrument seemed one that all participants received well and were eager to play. They seemed to know what to do with it immediately, and their participation was successful from the first attempt. This playing was consistent throughout the course of the clinical sessions and did not decrease as the patients deteriorated in the disease process. They participated in drum playing together as a rhythmic ensemble for as long as 17 minutes upon occasion. Using drums or other rhythm instruments, they could focus their attention by playing for long periods of time, 7 to 10 minutes of playing was quite usual. But, while on the unit they were unable to concentrate on anything for more than a few seconds. No matter how long they played, their playing always seemed purposeful and not just a matter of repeated movements. This was evident when they started to play or stopped playing when asked by the music therapist. Through the instrument playing, the patients interacted and communicated nonverbally with one another. The music therapy sessions, particularly the rhythm playing, provided the opportunities to participate together in activities which were suited to their ability and skill levels and which promoted in them an awareness of others.

In addition to playing instruments together in a rhythmic ensemble, two of the group members learned to imitate rhythm patterns and could play a rhythm solo when asked to do so. This imitative and solo playing was maintained as a skill throughout the 15 months of the protocol, but it decreased after that time. Eventually, the participants did not imitate rhythm patterns or provide rhythm pattern models for others to imitate. Even so, they maintained their abilities to play instruments in rhythm which allowed for interaction with others.

All participants were encouraged to sing throughout the sessions. One group member, age 65, who probably had symptoms of the disease for three years and had been hospitalised for a year, sang in initial sessions. His singing decreased, however, over the 15-month period until he did not sing at all. Even when songs were used that were particularly familiar to him, he did not sing. Instead, he made eye contact with either Alicia Clair or Barry Bernstein as they sang to him. Initially, he learned to inhibit his impulses and to play a rhythm instrument when asked to do so he learned to imitate rhythm patterns and he readily played in the rhythm ensemble.

Three years after his initial involvement in music therapy sessions, this patient no longer plays a rhythm instrument except with physical assistance. He holds a drum or a tambourine, though, and makes eye contact with the music therapist during singing and playing activities. He also holds a maraca when it is given to him, but he tends to put it in his mouth as if it were an ice cream cone or a lollipop. Even with his functional deficits and continued deterioration, music still attracts this patient's attention and is one means of involving him with others.

One patient was mute throughout the course of the 15-month protocol study. At age 54, he had been hospitalised at the Veterans Affairs Medical Center for three years and had the disease for approximately 8 years. His condition was quite deteriorated. Yet, he participated in rhythm instrument playing. He did not imitate rhythm patterns due to his deterioration, but he participated by rhythmic playing with both hand drum and maraca. This patient became progressively more physically ill and by the end of the study, he had been transferred to the medical unit of the hospital. The music therapists visited him during his stay of several weeks there. At first, he opened his eyes at the sound of Alicia's voice. Then, eventually there was no response. His wife had been told he had pneumonia and that it was unlikely that he would survive. As she maintained a vigil beside his bed, he became less and less responsive to anyone. She talked to him but still there was no response. She said she was certain that he would not be with her much longer. One day after many weeks, she sang his favourite hymn to him, he opened his eyes, he looked at her for a moment, and then he closed them again. A few hours later, he died. She said that her last memory of him was his look at her while she sang, and though she had tried other ways to make contact with him, it was music that reached him at the end.

One of the patients who was 67 years old had been hospitalised for one year and had had a possible diagnosis of Alzheimer's type dementia for four years. He had been a singer all his life, and though he did not sing professionally, he sang at church, at home and any place there was singing activity. He liked all types of songs and knew the lyrics to many popular songs of his young adult years. From the beginning of the sessions, he often responded spontaneously by singing with the music therapists, and even if he could not remember the lyrics, he sang the melodies of familiar songs. This man was an active drum player in the group and responded readily in most activities. Upon occasion, however, he was quite confused and could not function physically. In these times, he could not remember how to walk and had to be in a wheelchair for several days until he could get up and walk again. He was quite delusional and often thought he was 'on the job' as a construction worker. One day when he was approached for the music therapy session, he said he could not go anywhere until he finished the work. The music therapist tried to orient him to time and place only to elicit a hostile response. He insisted that he was at work. When asked if he was a union man, he said he was. Then, when asked if he had taken his break for the morning, he said he had not.

The music therapist then told him that he would have to take a break and it would be just as well that he take it in the music therapy session. He agreed and accompanied her to the session where he participated actively for the next 30 minutes. Even when he was most delusional and confused and could not be oriented to reality, the music was successful in capturing his attention and persuading his participation.

In the last year, this patient was discharged to a residential care facility. His condition had deteriorated to the point that he did not need the highly structured environment of the special long term care unit of the Veterans Affairs Medical Center. His musical participations since his discharge from the hospital are not known.

The fourth man who participated in the music therapy protocol sessions was the oldest group member. At age 81, he had been demented for several years and had a very short attention span. He tended to grab other persons and to interfere with their activities, so he was placed in a geri chair with a tray across it for the duration of each session. The chair provided enough freedom for him to participate readily while it maintained him at an appropriate distance from the other group members.

This man did not sing during the sessions. His verbalisations were very brief and usually unintelligible. He required frequent assistance from the music therapists to participate. Over the course of the 15-month protocol, it was noted that his interactions were not typical of the other group members in that he tended to be less attentive to the music therapy activities and looked around the room as music was being played rather than at the other people in the room. He seemed to avoid the social contact with others. His behaviour was also noticed by the unit staff and the unit physician. Due to the lack of progression in his dementia, the unit physician decided that the diagnosis of probable dementia of the Alzheimer's type was in error and that a diagnosis of organic brain syndrome was more appropriate. Over a period of three years, this patient's behaviour did not change appreciably. There was not a continual deterioration and his condition was quite stable. It seems quite possible that this patient was misdiagnosed initially and that he did not have a dementia of the Alzheimer's type.

During the sessions in which this protocol was conducted, video tapes were made of the sessions. They were analysed for data which could provide information concerning the participation of persons with possible or probable Alzheimer's type dementia. It was evident from these data that persons could maintain participation in music, particularly in rhythm activities until late in the disease. These results are fully described elsewhere (Clair and & Bernstein, 1990).

There were also some observations made by those who periodically visited the sessions. Nursing staff who saw the patients participate in music exclaimed that the interaction was far more sophisticated and functional than they would have ever thought possible judging from the usual day to day behaviours on the unit. Wives of the group members commented that they saw for the first time in a very long time, sometimes years, a glimmer of the man they had known and loved, the person who was really their husband, the man whose personality they only remembered. They said that music was the only way they had to make contact with that loved one, to capture a moment in which they could again belong with one another.

Conclusion

Based on the observations and the data collected from the music therapy clinical protocols presented here, it is clear that music therapy is a viable approach with persons who have a possible or probable diagnosis of dementia of the Alzheimer's type and for their caregivers. These clinical evaluations offer convincing evidence that music therapy is flexible in providing therapeutic services for a wide range of abilities at all stages of the disease process. Further, it accomplishes a variety of goals for both victims and caregivers coping with Alzheimer's disease, making it a treatment of choice for this population. Music therapy may provide one of the only ways that those afflicted with Alzheimer's disease and their caregivers may retrieve some of the many losses associated with this devastating, degenerating condition.

Acknowledgement

Dr Hanser's contribution was supported by a National Research Service Award (AG05469-02) from the National Institute on Aging, US Department of Health and Human Services.

Section 6: Specialised Areas of Work in Music Therapy

22

Music Therapy for Hearing Impaired Clients

Alice-Ann Darrow

Introduction

The term 'therapy' usually implies the remedial treatment of a disease or other physical or mental disorder. Because of this connotation, there are many hearing impaired individuals and professionals in the field of music therapy that could, and understandably so, take exception to the title of this chapter. The deaf community has made great strides in recent years to depathologise their disability. Deafness is no longer viewed as a medical condition, a deficit in need of treatment. The only true handicap related to deafness is being cut off from the usual means of acquiring and transmitting language. As a result, most deaf individuals communicate manually rather than orally. They regard this alternative form of communication as their only 'difference.' Consequently, one can understand their resentment in being considered a client in need of therapy, music or otherwise. Music therapists do not offer or provide services for other non-native speaking populations; solely on the basis of their communication status. The loss of hearing, however, has many implications for the development of communication skills. It is during the process of acquiring communication skills that music therapists can contribute to the development of hearing impaired individuals.

The ability to adapt music therapy procedures to the learning characteristics and communication styles of hearing impaired individuals requires specialised preparation. There are some prerequisite skills and considerable background information that the music therapist must have in order to work successfully with hearing impaired individuals. Background information in the following areas should be particularly helpful to the music therapist: speech and hearing science, audiology, aural habitation, manual and oral communication methods, and the impact of hearing loss on speech, reading and language development. Probably no other area of information is more important, however, than deaf culture. Sensitivity to and respect for the culture of the deaf community is essential to working successfully with hearing impaired individuals.

Deaf Culture

Culture has been defined as a way of life that differentiates a specific group of people. Deaf people in the United States have customs, mores, and institutions which differ from those of the hearing culture. Existing within and in continual relationship with the larger society, the deaf community adopts many of the characteristics of the hearing populations; yet, because language is the foundation of culture, the deaf community, which communicates in sign language, is also unique in many ways. 'Taken as a whole, the deaf community emerges as a distinctive societal entity, marked by the satisfaction deaf people usually find in the company of each other' (Schein, 1978, p.511).

The deaf population has grown, doubling its proportion of the total population in the last 40 years. The balance of adventitiously to congenitally deaf persons has shifted: a greater portion of the deaf population now is congenitally deaf. Changes in the nature of the deaf community are happening along with external events, such as the practice of mainstreaming, which dramatically reduced enrolment in residential schools. In the past, state schools for the deaf were the cornerstones and centres of the local deaf communities (Schein, 1978).

Other educational influences on the deaf community have been the practices of oral only programmes and the implementation (by hearing educators) of English sign systems, which differ greatly from American Sign Language, the language of the deaf community (Padden, 1980). Hearing impaired children educated by these sign systems and those who have oral skills only, often find it difficult to communicate with other members of the deaf community. Because of these educational practices, hearing impaired children are often caught between the hearing society and the deaf community, resulting in a lack of personal identity with either group (Sacks, 1989).

Political factors have also influenced the deaf community. In the spring of 1988, after demonstrations, protests, and boycotts, Gallaudet University, the only university in the world for hearing impaired students, inaugurated its first deaf president. This was a pivotal moment in the history of the deaf community. The Gallaudet experience clearly demonstrated the power of advocacy and fuelled the 'deaf pride' movement. Legislative acts in the past ten years have also influenced the deaf community by protecting their legal, personal, and educational rights (Kannapell, 1980; Prickett, 1989).

Though the deaf culture is a part of the larger society , it remains enigmatic to most of the hearing population. Knowing little about other cultures often results in ethnocentrism - the tendency to judge other cultures by the standards of one's own. This tendency has often been apparent in regard to the deaf community. Historically, the hearing have taken a paternalistic attitude toward the deaf; making decisions on their behalf for such important issues as speech instruction, the composition and use of various sign systems, as well as academic instruction and administration.

It is necessary for hearing professionals to recognise, be sensitive to, and respect the ways in which the deaf react to their social environment. In deaf culture, subtle facial expressions and gestures are often used to communicate specific information such as comprehension or confusion. The deaf are also more physical when attempting to secure attention. They may stomp on the floor or table, flicker lights, or grasp the individual with whom they are attempting to communicate. The deaf are also sometimes considered rude by hearing people because of their candid, straightforward manner. Their directness has been attributed to a desire to reduce the misunderstandings that have occurred throughout their lives due to problems in communication (Schmitz, 1990). Because of the difficulty in using traditional telecommunication devices, the deaf are more apt to visit without calling. Acquiring knowledge of these and other cultural characteristics, which may differ or have alternative meaning from the hearing society, can avoid misunderstandings between music therapists and their hearing impaired clients. Until recently, information regarding deaf culture was primarily limited to those who lived within the culture. There are now several excellent resources on the deaf community and the social characteristics of its people (Padden and Humphries, 1988; Sacks, 1989).

Background Information

Client Description

There are many terms associated with the hearing impaired disability; those associated with the type and degree of hearing loss, the measurement of hearing loss, the language status of the individual at the time of hearing loss, and the methods of communication used by hearing impaired individuals. Without a basic understanding of these terms and their effect on clinical practice, the music therapist is at a tremendous loss. There are a number of other variables, unrelated to the disability, that influence the hearing impaired client's communication skills and consequently, interactions with the environment: native intelligence, personality, family background, age at onset of deafness, language environment, use of residual hearing, listening skills, speechreading and speech production abilities, and educational placement.

Terms Related to Types of Hearing Loss

There are two basic types of hearing impairment, conductive and sensorineural. A conductive hearing loss results from obstructions or interference in the outer or middle ear; the pathways for sound to reach the inner ear. Fortunately, these conductive obstructions can often be corrected by surgical treatment; and hearing aids are usually helpful. A sensorineural hearing loss results from damage to the auditory nerve fibres or other delicate mechanisms of the inner ear. These hearing losses can range from mild to profound. They often affect certain frequencies more than others, resulting in distorted sound perception even when the sound level is increased. Amplification, simply making the sound source louder, is very often of little or no benefit to the hearing impaired individual with a sensorineural loss.

Terms Related to Degree of Hearing Loss

Hearing impaired - is a global term used to described all degrees of hearing loss ranging from hard-of-hearing to profound.

Hard-of-hearing - is a term used to describe those individuals with a significant hearing loss, yet are still able to process speech through the auditory channel, with or without the assistance of a hearing aid.

Deaf - is a term used to describe those individuals whose hearing loss is so severe that it is impossible to process speech through the auditory channel alone. Additionally, it is also a term usually reserved for those who communicate manually rather than through lip-reading and speech.

Residual hearing - refers to the remaining amount of hearing. Very few hearing impaired individuals are totally without hearing.

It is particularly helpful for the therapist to be familiar with those terms which describe the age at onset of a hearing impairment. This information has considerable implications for the communication style, language background, and social experiences of the hearing impaired individual.

Congenitally hearing impaired - refers to those individuals who acquired their hearing loss at birth.

Adventitiously hearing impaired - refers to those individuals who acquired their hearing loss after birth. This group of hearing impaired individuals can be broken down further by defining the language stage at which their hearing was lost.

Prelingual - refers to hearing impairments which were present before the acquisition of language.

Postlingual - refers to hearing impairments which were acquired after language and speech were developed through the normal sense of hearing. These terms have important implications for choosing a rehabilitative or habilitative approach in music therapy. Habilitative approaches for the prelingually hearing impaired usually focus on the acquisition of language and communication, while rehabilitative approaches for the postlingually hearing impaired usually focus on the conservation of speech and continued development of language.

Terms Related to the Measurement of Hearing

Music therapists are concerned with the response of the human ear to music stimuli; therefore it is helpful to know those terms which relate to the measurement of hearing. Sound consists of vibrations that travel in waves, generally through the air. Sound waves can vibrate at different speeds as they travel through the air. The faster the wave vibrates, the higher the pitch. Frequency is the number of vibrations produced per second and is measured in Hertz. One vibration per second equals one Hertz. The frequency of a sound is a physical reality while pitch is our subjective judgement of its frequency. Table 1 gives familiar frequency ranges.

Table 1: Familiar frequency ranges

Frequency range	Hertz
normal hearing	20 - 20,000
normal speech	500 - 2,000
the piano	27.5 - 4,186

The duration of sound has to do with its continuance in time. The aural discrimination of varying lengths of sound is the basis of rhythm perception. Intensity is the amount of energy in a sound wave. Intensity is a quantitative measurement of sound. Loudness is our subjective judgement of this measurement. The intensity of sound is measured in decibels. Zero decibels (0 dB) is the quietest audible sound while sounds above 120-140 dB can actually cause pain to the ears. Table 2 gives some common decibel ranges.

Table 2: Common decibel ranges

Decibel levels	Sound source	Musical levels
0 dB	just audible sound	
20 dB	soft rustle of leaves	
30 dB	quiet whisper	background music
40 dB	soft speech	*p*
50 dB	normal conversation	*mp*
60 dB	loud conversation	*mf*
80 dB	shouting	*f*
90 dB	heavy traffic	marching band
100 dB	riveter 35 feet away	
120 dB	jet engine	

Audiology, the science of hearing, has made great strides in the development of instruments which assist in the detection and assessment of hearing loss. Audiologists measure the degree of hearing loss by generating sounds at specific frequencies and intensities on an audiometer, and then measuring an individual's response to these sounds. By viewing these responses displayed graphically on an audiogram, the music therapist can determine the aural accessibility of music stimuli and the degree of amplification required in the clinical setting.

Effects of Hearing Impairments in the Clinical Setting

An individual's hearing impairment is generally described in terms of slight, mild, moderate, severe, and profound, based on their average hearing level, in decibels, throughout the frequencies most important for understanding speech (500 to 2,000 Hz). Each level of hearing loss will have a differential effect on the client's interaction with the clinical environment. Table 3 outlines the effects each level of hearing loss will have on the clinical environment.

Table 3: Effects of hearing loss

Hearing level	Effect on the clinical environment
Slight loss (27 to 40 dB)	May have difficulty hearing faint or distant speech. May experience some difficulty with language arts.
Mild loss (41 to 55 dB)	Understands conversational speech at a distance of 3 to 5 feet. May miss as much as 50% of conversation if not face-to-face. May have limited vocabulary and speech irregularities.
Moderate loss (56 to 70 dB)	Can understand loud conversation only. Will have difficulty in group discussions. Is likely to have impaired speech, limited vocabulary and difficulty in language use and comprehension.
Severe loss (71 to 90 dB)	May hear loud voices about 1 foot from ear. May be able to identify environmental sounds. May be able to discriminate vowels but not consonants. Speech and language likely to be impaired or to deteriorate.
Profound loss (91 dB or more)	More aware of vibrations than tonal patterns. Relies on vision rather than hearing as primary means of communication. Speech and language likely to be impaired or to deteriorate. Speech and language unlikely to develop spontaneously if loss is prelingual.

From Heward, W. and Orlansky, M. (1988) Exceptional Children. Columbus, Ohio: Merrill Publishing Co. © Bell and Howell Co. Adapted by permission.

Fortunately for us as music therapists, our medium, music, is usually more aurally accessible to hearing impaired individuals than speech. Music is generally more intense than conversational speech, employs many more frequencies than normal speech, and is composed of notes which are longer in duration than speech sounds; which is why even individuals with a severe hearing loss will still be able to listen to and enjoy music, yet may have difficulty in aurally processing speech.

Skills and Information Necessary for the Music Therapist

In any therapeutic relationship, communication is essential. Miscomm-unication is inevitable when two individuals are not conversing in the same language. This may mean that the music therapist will need to learn a new form of communication in order to work successfully with hearing impaired clients. In the United States, hearing impaired persons use a variety of methods and symbol systems for communication; these include:

American Sign Language

American Sign Language (ASL) is the native language of most deaf adults. It is a natural language with its own grammar and syntax. It is a beautiful and graceful visual-gestural language created by deaf people and used widely in the United States. The signs in ASL have both abstract and concrete meanings. Signs are based on concepts rather than words. They are made by either one or both hands assuming distinctive shapes in particular locations and executing specified movements. The use of spatial relations, direction, orientation, and movement of the hands, as well as facial expression and body shift make up the grammar of ASL.

Fingerspelling

A manual alphabet is merely an alternative form of a written alphabet with hand shapes and positions corresponding to the letters of the written alphabet. This form of communication is sometimes called the 'Rochester Method.'

Manual Communication

The term 'manual communication' includes a combination of sign language and fingerspelling used for both expressive and receptive communication. A number of manual communication systems combine sign language and fingerspelling with the grammar and syntax of standard English. There are four major systems in this group: (1) Seeing Essential English, (2) Signing Exact English, (3) Linguistics of Visual English, and (4) Signed English.

Oral Communication

This term denotes the use of speech and speechreading as the primary means for the transmission of thoughts and ideas with deaf persons. Educators who believe in the oral communication philosophy, in their work with deaf children, emphasise, exclusively, the teaching of speech and speechreading together with amplification and the use of whatever residual hearing remains.

Cued Speech

Cued speech is a system of communication in which eight hand movements supplement the information being spoken. This is not a form of sign language. The hand 'cue' is used to indicate, visually, the exact pronunciation of every syllable spoken. With cued speech, a hearing impaired person can see all the words a hearing person hears. It is a speech-based method whose purpose is to communicate the nearly two thirds of speech not visible on the lips.

Simultaneous Communication

This term is used to denote the combined use of speech, signs, and fingerspelling. Receptively, an individual receives the message both by speechreading and what is being said and by reading the signs and fingerspelling simultaneously.

Total Communication

Total communication is often confused with simultaneous communication. It is, however, more of a philosophy of communication which implies acceptance, understanding, and use of all methods of communication to assist the hearing impaired child in acquiring language and the deaf adult in understanding.

Adaptations in the Music Therapy Setting

There are two primary areas of adaptation that should be made in the music therapy setting in order to meet the special needs of hearing impaired clients. These areas are the physical environment and the communication environment. In the physical environment:
1. The speaker's face must be clearly seen.
2. Optimal speechreading distance should be kept at 6 feet.
3. Unnecessary noise such as air conditioners or outdoor traffic should be eliminated or minimised.
4. The clinical setting should have good lighting.
5. Clinic room fixtures such as draperies, carpeting, and upholstery should be used to absorb unnecessary noise.
6. Seating should be in a circle for group activities.
7. Hearing impaired clients should be positioned with their hearing aid toward the group.

Adaptations in communication should also be made; they include:
1. Articulation should be clear, though not exaggerated.
2. Communication should be face-to-face.
3. Pacing and other unnecessary movement should be avoided during communication.
4. Facial expression and body language should be used as cues for message content.
5. Other communication cues to include:
    use natural gestures to convey meaning
    use visual aids when possible
    write down key/topic words
    look at other clients when they are speaking or signing

6.   Discuss new vocabulary before sessions (unfamiliar words are difficult to speechread; unfamiliar signs will not be understood).
7.   Watch for signs of confusion.
8.   Repeat questions or comments if necessary.
9.   Be sure major points are understood.
10. Encourage clients to ask questions.
11. Restate phrases differently if they are not understood.
12. Provide a note taker for important information.
13. Use complete sentences in sign or speech.
14. Use an interpreter if necessary.
15. Make sure clients wear their hearing aids.

Inclusive information regarding hearing impaired clients can not of course be included within this chapter. Music therapists working with hearing impaired clients should request in service as needed. Suggested topics for further information might include the following:

1.   Sign language instruction
2.   Introduction to hearing aids and other assistive listening devices
3.   Care of hearing aids.
4.   Psychosocial aspects of deafness.
5.   Seminar offerings in basic hearing science.
6.   Current literature in deaf culture.
7.   Hearing impaired musicians.
8.   Speechreading concepts.
9.   Language assessment and development.
10. Methods of nonverbal communication.
11. Causes and prevention of hearing impairments.
12. Parts and functions of the ear.

Music Therapy Objectives

The ear is one of our most vital sense organs. It is difficult to imagine how different our world would be without our ability to hear. Most individuals with normal hearing take for granted the enormous importance of auditory experiences. Hearing is the sense upon which we are most dependent for nearly every aspect of our daily existence. The loss of hearing is a disability; a physical deficit. The associated handicap, however, lies in communication, not in the actual loss of hearing. Helen Keller felt that blindness is an environmental handicap that keeps us from things; and that deafness is a communication handicap that keeps us from people. She believed that the resulting isolation was the far greater handicap. Communication is the basis of our social and cognitive being; therefore music therapy objectives should include those related to the development of communication skills: auditory training, language acquisition and development, reading, writing, and, for clients capable of oral communication, speech production and comprehension (Darrow and Gfeller, 1988). Other objectives should include the social and musical development of hearing-impaired children.

Attention to these objectives can also contribute to the leisure skills of the hearing impaired client.

Auditory Training

The goal of auditory training is to teach the complex task of listening. The ability of individuals to use their hearing for the purpose of listening varies. Good hearing does not necessarily insure skilled listening; conversely, poor hearing does not necessarily indicate an inability to listen. Listening is a mental process; hearing is a physical process. It is the function of the ear to collect auditory stimuli and deliver them to the brain; at which time the brain takes over and hearing becomes listening (Darrow, 1990c). The development of good listening skills allows the hearing impaired individual to use their residual hearing to the maximum extent possible. When hearing impaired individuals learn to interpret the sounds around them, they also increase the rate and quality of their social and communicative development.

Training the ear to listen requires: (1) analysis of the desired auditory task, (2) the structuring of successive approximations to the desired goal, and (3) regular and systematic evaluation of the client's auditory skill level. Auditory training should consist of sequential listening exercises. Nearly all auditory tasks can be broken down into four very basic levels of aural processing (Erber and Hirsh, 1978). These levels of aural processing follow, as well as ways of integrating music to determine a client's present level.

1. Detection - the listener determines the presence or absence, initiation or termination of music stimuli.
2. Discrimination - the listener perceives differences in music stimuli (such as fast and slow, high and low).
3. Identification - the listener appropriately applies labels (such as forte or piano, woodwind or brass) to music stimuli.
4. Comprehension - the listener makes critical judgements regarding music stimuli (such as judgements concerning form, harmony, or texture).

Most hearing impaired individuals develop detection and discrimination skills through normal interaction with the environment. It is the third and fourth levels of auditory processing, discrimination and comprehension, that require the attention of the music therapist.

There are a number of other listening behaviours which are subsumed within these four basic levels of auditory processing. These additional listening behaviours are prerequisites to auditory comprehension. Derek Saunders (1977) developed a hierarchy of auditory processing which should assist the music therapist in developing sequential listening objectives for a wide range of clients. The hierarchy was developed with the processing of the speech signal in mind; however, music applications can be made and are given in each of the hierarchical steps. Speech and music contain many common properties, though perhaps identified by different names. In music, reference is made to intonation, tempo, accent, and rhythm. Speech counterparts are speech inflection, rate, stress, and speech rhythm. Once again, proficiency at the first four levels of the hierarchy is usually acquired naturally. The remaining six levels of auditory processing should provide a guide for music listening experiences.

1. Awareness of acoustic stimuli: is the client aware that music is in the environment ?
2. Localisation: Can the client identify the location of the musical sound source ?
3. Attention: Can the client attend to the music over time ?
4. Discrimination between speech and non speech: Can the client discriminate between music and non music sounds ?
5. Auditory discrimination: Can the client discriminate between the timbre of different instruments or the entrance and exit of specific instruments within the total music context (figure/ground discrimination) ?
6. Suprasegmental discrimination: Can the client make discriminations about the expressive qualities of the music (dynamics, tempo, phrasing)?
7. Segmental discrimination: Can the client make discriminations about changes in pitch ?
8. Auditory memory: Can the client remember what instruments were heard ?
9. Auditory sequential memory: Can the client remember in what order the instruments were heard ?
10. Auditory synthesis: Can the client make critical judgements regarding form, texture, harmony ?

There are controversial views regarding the transfer of music listening skills to linguistic use; however, teaching a client to develop a focused and analytical attention to sound will undoubtedly transfer to the development of good listening habits, regardless of the source of sound stimuli. Unfortunately we can do little to improve hearing impaired individuals' ability to hear; we can however, do much to improve their ability to listen. Our goal is to increase the amount of information they receive through the sense of hearing. We do this by teaching them to interpret the sounds they hear. Listening, like any other skill, must be practised through regular, sequential listening exercises. The ear is a valuable listening device; and music, a powerful medium through which listening skills can be taught, practised . . . and rewarded.

Language Acquisition and Development

Language is the means by which people communicate. Native languages are generally learned through listening, with ease, and over a relatively short period of time. Aural exposure to language is the most important ingredient in the development of communication skills. Without adequate aural exposure to language, hearing impaired children essentially learn a 'foreign' language with only the assistance of nonverbal cues such as facial expression, body language, and small movements of the lips - on which approximately only one third of all speech is visible. It is understandable that, without alternative forms of communication such as sign language, hearing impaired children are at a tremendous disadvantage during the process of language development. Even children with mild hearing impairments experience difficulty with the fine discriminations that must be made in comprehending language.

Other more subtle forms of language, such as sarcasm and play-on-words, are dependent on the aural processing of speech. Many verbal behaviours are also learned by listening; some of these include social customs such as 'please' and 'thank you', use of compliments, and avoidance of inappropriate questions. Young children are generally able to comprehend various words or phrases long before they are able to use them appropriately; demonstrating the importance of exposure as an antecedent to expression. Every professional involved in the habilitation of young hearing impaired children, including music therapists, should have among their objectives, the acquisition and development of language.

The two fundamental components of language with which the music therapist is most likely to work are vocabulary knowledge and word-class usage (Gfeller and Darrow, 1987). Receptive and expressive skills, as well as reading and writing skills, should be employed as a part of instructional strategies. In order to foster language development to the fullest extent possible, methods of achieving these goals should not be confined solely to lesson objectives, but to every procedure employed in the music therapy setting. The music therapist can make most interactions an opportunity for learning language (Rickard et al., 1990). For young hearing impaired clients, the most important language objective will be the increased and appropriate use of vocabulary. Developing vocabulary skills is not as simple as defining words. Word meaning in a single context measures only one component of vocabulary knowledge. Words often have multiple meanings and serve separate language functions. Hearing impaired children tend to know fewer words and to use them in a singular context (Davis and Hardick, 1981). A hearing impaired child may know the word 'kid' in its noun form, a child or young goat, but not in its verb, adverb, or adjective form. It is the therapist's task to introduce vocabulary words, their multiple meanings, and their proper use in as many circumstances as possible: in song texts, song writing, informal conversation, and contrived situations. The therapist's choice of target words should be made in consultation with the child's classroom teacher or professionals who specialise in the language development of hearing impaired children.

Hearing impaired children may also experience difficulty with word-class usage. Less severely hearing impaired children tend to use most word classes adequately with the exception of adverbs, pronouns, and auxiliaries; more severely hearing impaired children use fewer words in all classes than normal hearing children. A characteristic of most hearing impaired children's language is a tendency to overuse nouns and articles; thus, the speculation that impaired hearing interferes with the function of words as well as the understanding of their meaning (Davis and Hardick, 1981). The music therapist must attempt to provide good models of word usage, opportunities for variety of word use, and corrective feedback. Again, this can be accomplished through the study of song texts, informal conversation, or contrived situations. Additional approaches are activities such as song writing, song signing, and small group ensembles where communication is essential (Gfeller, 1987, 1990). Gfeller and Baumann (1988) give suggestions for the assessment of language skills in music therapy.

Speech Production and Reception

Speech production is acquired and controlled through the auditory system. Children learn to speak by imitating the sounds of others. The degree to which these sounds are available to the hearing impaired child will directly influence the quality of speech production and the ability to receive the speech signal. The aspects of speech which are most severely affected by impaired hearing are phonation, rhythm, and articulation. Hearing impaired children often do not associate breath control with the power source needed for fluid speech; consequently, they may breathe in the middle of words or phrases. Errors of rhythm constitute one of the most deviate aspects of hearing impaired individuals' speech. The speech is generally slower, the syllables prolonged, and stress placed on inappropriate syllables. Speech intelligibility varies widely among hearing impaired individuals; however, even individuals with very little hearing are capable of developing intelligible speech.

Hearing one's own voice allows the speaker the aural feedback necessary to self correct pronunciation of words, adjust vocal inflection and imitate speech rhythm. Hearing impaired children are dependent on corrective feedback and instruction in remedial strategies from others. The music therapist can provide assistance in both of these areas. Music therapy objectives may include, though not be limited to, the following: vocal intonation, vocal quality, speech fluency, and speech intelligibility. In speech, the melodic elements such as rhythm, intonation, rate, and stress are referred to as the prosodic features of speech. These prosodic features convey important contextual information. Music activities such as singing can aid in the recognition and development of these melodic aspects of speech (Darrow and Starmer, 1986). Appropriate procedures include free vocalisation, vocal imitation, rhythmic vocalisation, and work on vocal phrasing and dynamics. Traditional music activities such as pitch matching practice, singing songs and vocal exercises, and following notated melodic contours are also helpful (Bang, 1977).

The remediation of poor vocal quality can also be enhanced through traditional music activities. A breathy quality can be alleviated by vocalising which exercises the diaphragm; a nasal quality can be minimised by incorporating vocal exercises which utilise the head voice. The volume of a client's voice can be monitored during music therapy by teaching and practising the use of expressive terms such as *piano* and *forte*, *decrescendo* and *crescendo*.

Speech fluency and articulation are not as easily influenced by the use of music therapy techniques. Speech fluency can be improved by the rhythmic chanting and singing of syllables, syllable combinations, words, word combinations, phrases, and finally complete sentences. Articulatory problems constitute the greatest challenge for speech and music therapists. Problems with articulation usually involve sound omissions, such as final consonants; substitutions such as 'thoup' instead of 'soup'; interjections such as 'boyee' instead of 'boy'; and mispronunciation of sounds such as 'sh', 'th', or 's'. The music therapist can carefully select song literature which focus on specific speech sounds or words. The therapist should also maintain a record of the number of intelligible words in a given song. Consultation with the client's speech therapist can be extremely helpful in selecting appropriate and realistic objectives. In addition to directed music activities, feedback regarding a client's speech intelligibility should be given by the music therapist during everyday interactions in the clinical setting. Traditional assessments used in speech therapy can also be of use to the music therapist.

The aforementioned objectives and procedures are by no means inclusive. The music therapist should work in conjunction with the goals of the hearing impaired client's speech therapist, audiologist, and language specialist. It is the music therapist's challenge to provide unique and exciting supplementary training in communication skills.

Music Objectives

Some people believe that to be musical, one must have good hearing; however, many hearing impaired individuals are indeed musical. The degree of interest in music among hearing impaired individuals varies as it does among those with normal hearing. Many hearing impaired individuals enjoy participating in musical activities. Their education in the arts should not be forfeited for entirely academic study (Birkenshaw-Fleming, 1990). Music objectives for the hearing impaired should follow those that are often outlined for normal hearing individuals. Objectives should include various forms of music participation:

1. Listening to music   4. Moving to music
2. Singing   5. Creating music
3. Playing instruments   6. Reading music

Objectives should also include knowledge about masterpieces of music and the elements of music. rhythm, melody, harmony, form, and expression. Traditional approaches to teaching music concepts can be employed with hearing impaired individuals (Ford, 1990; Schatz, 1990). Because of their visual and movement components, music educators of hearing impaired students have indicated that Orff and Kodaly approaches are particularly useful (Darrow and Gfeller, in press). Special attention should also be given to amplification of music stimuli (Dalgarno, 1990b), the quality of recording equipment and instruments, as well as the suggestions given earlier for adaptation of the physical and communication environment. Every individual, regardless of hearing status, deserves the right to participate in the musical arts and, as a result, experience a part of our culture. Some hearing impaired individuals do not consider music a part of deaf culture and consequently, look upon musical study as a 'hearing value.' Many hearing impaired individuals, however, do find music to be an important part of their lives (Darrow, 1991c).

There are some generalisations that can be made regarding the musical characteristics of hearing impaired individuals based upon research in music perception and performance (Gfeller, in press).

1. Rhythmic abilities tend to be stronger than pitch related abilities.
2. Discrimination of or production of rhythmic patterns are more difficult than beat reproduction.
3. Music stimuli must be presented at an appropriate level of amplification.
4. Tactile perception can, in part, compensate for auditory deficits.
5. Visual cues, such as tapping the beat, are particularly helpful.
6. Music skills may be delayed rather than deviant.
7. Pitch discriminations can be made more easily in lower frequency ranges.
8. Pitch discrimination skills can be developed with training.
9. Discrimination skills may be misjudged because of language problems which interfere with hearing impaired individuals' ability to describe what they hear.
10. The vocal range of hearing impaired individuals is often lower and more limited in range.

Research on Music and the Hearing Impaired

Considering the substantial history of anecdotal literature on music and the hearing impaired (Darrow, 1990b; Darrow and Heller, 1985; Edwards, 1974; Solomon, 1980), a paucity of data based research exists in this area. There are a number of probable reasons for this lack of available data:

1. Hearing impairment is a low incident handicap; therefore, an adequate sample of subjects is difficult to secure.
2. The research must often be conducted in a foreign language, that of American Sign Language.
3. The hearing impaired population is heterogeneous in regard to degree and type of hearing loss; therefore, matching subjects is difficult, if not impossible.
4. Other variables that are difficult to control are: use and type of amplification, educational history (manual, oral, aural, or total communication), age of onset, and auditory training background.

In reviewing the research, most of the literature falls into one of three broad categories: music perception, music performance, and therapeutic uses of music. Descriptive studies in the first two areas are primarily concerned with hearing impaired subjects' performance and/or perception of rhythm as compared to their normal hearing peers. Rhythm is a likely area of investigation since the tactile perception of rhythmic vibrations is possible even for children with very little hearing.

Music Performance

Two of the studies in the area of rhythm performance investigated subjects' reproduction response to a given beat. The propensity toward beat response is usually considered a reaction to auditory rhythmic stimuli (Kaufman, 1940), suggesting a connection between the auditory sense and temporal sequencing. Fraisse (1963) labelled hearing the 'time sense'. Consideration has also been given, however, to beat response as a subjective reaction. Though generally established and supported by objective stimuli (sounds), the sense of pulse may exist subjectively (Cooper and Meyer, 1960).

In a study by Darrow (1979), normal hearing and hearing impaired subjects were asked to reproduce a given beat. Hearing impaired subjects were asked to reproduce a given beat. Hearing impaired subjects demonstrated a significantly greater temporal deviation. Normal hearing subjects responded more accurately, though tended to play faster than the given beat while hearing impaired subjects tended to play slower than the given beat. A significant difference was also found among the four selected tempi. Deviation scores were the greatest for both groups at the slower tempi. Hearing impaired subjects performed most accurately the tempi approximating the human pulse. A similar study by Squires (1982) examined the effect of performance media on the beat accuracy of hearing impaired subjects. No significant difference was found regarding performance media, though hearing impaired subjects did respond more accurately with sustaining instruments which corroborates earlier research by Roelofs and Zeeman (1949) on 'filled' versus 'empty' beat intervals.

Rileigh and Odom (1972), concerned with the relationship between hearing and rhythm performance, asked hearing impaired subjects to reproduce rhythms on a telegraph key. No significant differences were found due to hearing status; however hearing and hearing impaired subjects yielded different developmental curves of rhythmic skills. It appears from these data that hearing deprivation may delay, though not necessarily impair the developmental process. Korduba (1975), also found no significant difference between the rhythm reproduction errors of hearing impaired and hearing subjects. Darrow (1984) also found no significant performance difference between these groups when asked to maintain a given rhythm pattern, as in an ostinato. Other data (Darrow, 1984; Sterritt et al., 1966) did, however, reveal a significant difference between hearing ability groups in rhythm reproduction accuracy and melodic rhythm duplication of familiar children's songs. The conflicting data among the studies are most likely due to subjects' varying ages and past experiences with music, as well as the studies' selected performance media and rhythm patterns.

In the studies above, subjects were asked to reproduce a given rhythm or beat; consequently, subjects' performance was dependent on their perception of the stimuli. In a study by Darrow and Bolton (1988), an attempt was made to control this variable by testing mainstreamed hearing impaired children's ability to read and perform selected rhythms. Results indicated no significant difference between the rhythmic performances of hearing and hearing impaired subjects.

Music programmes and research studies involving hearing impaired children have centred primarily around rhythm activities with little attention given to vocal performance. This has been because the hearing impaired are not considered 'singers' given the unusual quality of their voice. Darrow (1987) found that the mean range of hearing impaired children's singing voice was significantly smaller and the midpoint significantly lower. This conflicts with common tonal characteristics of deaf speech which generally include a higher fundamental frequency than normal speech and frequently no variation in pitch. Several studies examined techniques for modifying the vocal intonation of hearing impaired singers. Darrow (1990) found that adjusting the frequencies of auditory stimuli to accommodate the individual audiological curves of subjects enabled them to reproduce pitches vocally with significantly greater accuracy. Darrow and Cohen (in press) found that private instruction and programmed pitch practice on the Pitch Master, a device used to give visual and numerical cues regarding pitch accuracy, were also effective methods of improving the pitch matching skills of hearing impaired children.

Music Perception

The *Primary Measures of Audiation*, a music aptitude test for young children, was administered to hearing impaired children through a portable audiometer at 35 dB above the subjects' speech reception threshold (Darrow, 1987). Results indicated that hearing impairment adversely affects rhythm and tonal perception with the greater deficit in tonal perception, although results of an earlier perception study indicated that hearing impaired subjects perceived specific rhythmic characteristics (beat, tempo change, and meter change) within a musical context as well as normal hearing subjects (Darrow, 1984). Darrow (1987) found that hearing impairment does adversely affect tonal perception. Gfeller and Lansing (in press) investigated the melodic, rhythmic, and timbral perception of adult cochlear implant users and also found that performance for temporal contrasts was better than for melodic contrasts. Leach (1982) found that the degree of hearing loss had no significant effect on the melodic, rhythmic, and timbral discriminations of hearing impaired subjects.

Several investigators have examined the utility of supplementing the auditory sense with vibrotactile stimuli. Music educators have often suggested that auditory stimuli be supplemented with direct physical contact with the musical source (Buechler, 1982; Dalgarno, 1990a; Barrow, 1985; Fahey and Birkenshaw, 1972). The additional sensory channel adds complementary and/or redundant information to that which the child is already receiving auditorily. Complementary information results in an increase in the total amount of available information; redundant information allows the child to solidify concepts. In addition, the level of concentration required to receive, understand, and use auditory information is decreased by the supplementary sensory input. Several recent studies have provided data which support the use of vibrotactile stimuli in the music instruction of hearing impaired students.

Results of a study by Gfeller (1988) indicated that tactile stimuli assisted in rhythmic discrimination. Studies by Darrow and Goll (1989) and Darrow (1991b), employing the SOMATRON, a vibrotactile platform, also found vibrotactile stimuli to be an effective tool in communicating rhythmic and tonal concepts to hearing impaired children. Fisher, Baker and Darrow (1989) and Weibe (1989) found that vibrotactile stimulation and adjustment of stimuli frequencies did not improve the tonal perception of their subjects, indicating that unusual adjustments in subjects' listening conditions may be distracting or interfere with perception judgements. An early study by Madsen and Mears (1965) speculated that sound vibrations might also cause the skin itself to vibrate and that this might be a factor in a hearing impaired person's perception of music. Data from the study indicated that: 1) sound vibration does have a significant effect upon the threshold of the tactile sense; 2) a 50 Hz tone at both high and low pressure levels desensitises the skin and raises the tactile threshold; and 3) a 5,000 Hz tone at both high and low pressure levels seemed to sensitise the skin, although not significantly.

Ford (1985) investigated the ability of hearing impaired children to discriminate the pitch of complex tones. The research was designed to study the effects of age and school musical experiences on pitch discrimination and to identify possible relationships between pitch discrimination and other variables such as hearing levels, academic achievement, and home music background. No significant differences were found on the basis of age and school music programmes. High correlations were found between pitch discrimination abilities and hearing levels among younger subjects. Results suggested that hearing impaired children may benefit from appropriate pitch related activities. Pitch related activities were also suggested by Gengel (1969) who found that hearing impaired children can improve their ability to discriminate small differences in frequency with structured practice.

Miscellaneous Music Studies

Several studies examined hearing impaired subjects' preference for listening conditions, intensity levels, musical instruments, and timbre. The purpose of a study by Baird (1979) was to determine what decibel level of music stimuli would maintain a response in young hard-of-hearing children. The study produced an accurate assessment of sound intensity preference for music. Darrow (1991a) examined hearing impaired children's propensity for various musical instruments and timbre. Little agreement was found among three measures of preference, though independent measures indicated that hearing impaired subjects tended to prefer instruments with vibratory feedback and on which aural feedback was immediate, such as string instruments; or instruments which were unfamiliar to them, such as the trombone. Data, which was similar to that of Gfeller and Lansing (in press), revealed no group preference for specific timbres, but data for individual subjects did indicate preferences for various timbres. Woike (1987) investigated hearing impaired subjects' preference for listening conditions produced by different graphic equaliser settings. A significantly greater number of subjects preferred a flat frequency response curve over that of a frequency response curve adjusted to accommodate the hearing impaired subject's individual audiological curve.

Several studies investigated the involvement of hearing impaired students in music classes. A study by Gfeller, Darrow and Hedden (1990) found that hearing impaired students were perceived by music educators to be one of the most difficult exceptional student populations to mainstream into the music classroom. Darrow and Gfeller (in press) examined the status of public school music instruction for hearing impaired students and the factors which contribute to the successful mainstreaming of hearing impaired students in the regular music classroom. Results of the study revealed the following: (1) more than half of all hearing impaired students attend regular music classes; (2) of those students mainstreamed, over half receive no music education in the self-contained classroom or otherwise; (3) many music educators are lacking in the educational preparation necessary for teaching hearing impaired students; (4) important instructional or administrative support is often not available; (5) several factors, such as lack of communication with other professionals, were identified as obstructions to the successful mainstreaming of hearing impaired students; and (6) only 35% of the respondents reported that they have the same objectives for hearing impaired students as for normal hearing students.

Several related studies examined the scope and sequence of music programmes in residential and day school educational programmes for hearing impaired students. These studies (Ford and Shroyer, 1987; Shroyer and Ford, 1986; Spitzer, 1984) investigated the extent to which day and residential programs for the hearing-impaired offer music programmes and the methods and objectives most commonly employed in these programmes. Results of these studies revealed that only a little over half of these residential and day school programmes offered music. The most commonly cited reason was lack of a qualified teacher. Other findings were: lack of participation by many students in schools where music was offered; programme objectives were commonly concerned with speech improvement as well as the development of music concepts; music teachers often had degrees in academic areas other than music and often had additional teaching responsibilities other than music.

A study by Darrow and Gfeller (1987) examined the verbal identification of music concepts by hearing impaired children. Analysis of the data indicated that only the terms 'fast' and 'slow' were selected appropriately and consistently. Information regarding the language development of hearing impaired children offers a rationale for these findings.

Only two studies utilising historical research methodology could be found. The purpose of Solomon's study (1980) was to support the hypothesis that music played an important role in hearing and speech development in early special classrooms before 1930. Evidence includes pictures of classrooms in the first schools for the deaf in the United States showing music activities and musical instruments. Early diagnostic uses of music to determine hearing capacity and an analysis of texts written in the nineteenth and early twentieth centuries covering the uses of music in the special classroom to develop speech are also presented. A historical study by Darrow and Heller (1985) recognises the early efforts of William Wolcott Turner and David Ely Bartlett on behalf of music education for the deaf. In an 1848 article in the *American Annals of the Deaf and Dumb* (now called *Americans Annals of the Deaf)*, these two pioneers showed that a hearing impaired student could learn music and that sound reasons existed to support such an endeavour. The research confirmed both the authenticity and credibility of Turner and Bartlett's work, with biographical information on the two authors and a critical analysis of the contents of their article in light of subsequent research on music for the hearing impaired.

Therapeutic Uses of Music

Research has indicated that music instruction may also affect a number of non-musical behaviours. These secondary outcomes of music participation are particularly beneficial to the hearing impaired child. Studies have shown that music instruction can be a useful tool in auditory training, speech production, and language development. Amir and Schuchman (1985) investigated the effects of auditory training within a musical context on how severely to profoundly hearing impaired pre-school children use their residual hearing. A significant improvement was found in the children's ability to discriminate and recognise auditory stimuli. However, the lowest level in the hierarchy of auditory perception, detection, and the highest level, comprehension, were unaffected. Data suggested that group auditory training through music cannot replace training with speech and environmental sound; however, this type of therapy may serve as a useful adjunct to other techniques for maximising the use of residual hearing in hearing impaired pre-school children.

Several studies examined the effect of music performance on non-musical behaviours. These studies were concerned with the effect of music involvement on the melodic aspects of hearing impaired children's speech. Darrow and Starmer (1986) examined the effect of vocal training on the fundamental frequency, frequency range, and rate of hearing impaired children's speech. Students spent equal amounts of time per class session singing songs and participating in vocal exercises. Post-test results indicated a significant reduction of fundamental frequency and a significant increase in frequency range following vocal training. There was no significant reduction of fundamental frequency and a significant increase in frequency range speech rate. Gfeller (1986) investigated the efficacy of musical speech rhythm training on the intelligibility, rate, intonation, and length of hearing impaired children's speech. Results indicated improvement in most measures of speech production. Klajman, et al. (1982) also found that musical instruction resulted in significant improvements in the articulation, speech rhythm, breath regularity, and phonation of hearing impaired children. The purpose of Staum's study (1987) was to determine whether a treatment programme using music notation would improve the verbal rhythmic and intonational accuracy of hearing impaired children, and to determine the degree of transfer to other reading and verbal skills. Results indicated that, while all children learned a substantial number of rhythmic and inflectional patterns, subjects capable of reading made the greatest gains in transferring their skill to novel verbal material. It is suggested that the use of music notation written below printed words could be a beneficial visual cue for verbal, rhythmic, and intonational accuracy in reading tasks with hearing impaired children.

A number of articles exist regarding the use of music in teaching language to hearing impaired children; however, only two research studies could be found which empirically examine the effect of music activities on the development of language skills of hearing impaired children. Galloway and Bean (1974) studied the effect of music action songs on body-image and body-vocabulary development in pre-school hearing impaired children. Body-image was defined as the child's awareness and knowledge of the physical and spatial characteristics of his/her body upon request. Results indicated that music may be helpful in teaching selected vocabulary words to hearing impaired children. The purpose of Gray Thompson's (1985) study was to examine empirically the validity of using picture-song books as a tool to teach sight vocabulary to hearing impaired children representing three language skill levels. Thirty words from songs were selected by classroom teachers as appropriate to the vocabulary needs of their students. Pictures depicted these 'key words'. Sight vocabulary was divided into word recognition and concept recognition. Following six weeks of intervention, all three groups scored significantly higher on the post-test for word recognition and concept recognition. No significant pre/post-test differences were found among groups. It was concluded that picture-song books are an effective tool for teaching selected components of sight vocabulary.

Therapeutic Implications

Though the extent and scope of music therapy research with the hearing impaired is more limited than in the areas of musical perception and performance, existing studies have produced a number of findings relevant to the music therapy setting. These findings have both general and specific implications for music therapists working with hearing impaired clients. Some of these are:

1.   Hearing impaired individuals can benefit both musically and academically from participation in music activities.
2.   Hearing impaired individuals are more responsive to the rhythmic aspects of music than the tonal aspects.
3.   Hearing impaired individuals may require greater exposure, both in duration and intensity, to music stimuli than normal hearing individuals in order to meet therapeutic objectives.
4.   Sustaining instruments may provide more useful aural feedback to hearing impaired individuals than do percussive instruments.
5.   Use of moderate tempi assist in greater rhythm performance accuracy by hearing impaired individuals.

6.   Hearing impaired individuals may perform more accurately by reading standard music notation than by relying on the ear to imitate or learn by rote.
7.   Hearing impaired individuals can improve their vocal intonation, both in singing and in speaking by participating in vocal activity.
8.   The vocal range of song literature should be taken into consideration with hearing impaired singers.
9.   Hearing impaired individuals are as capable of improvements in ear training as are normal hearing individuals.
10. Vibrotactile stimuli comprise a useful supplemental tool in the music instruction of hearing impaired individuals.
11. As with normal hearing individuals, hearing impaired individuals can develop a more sensitive ear over time.
12. Hearing impaired individuals could benefit from instruction in the use of musical vocabulary.
13. Hearing impaired individuals exhibit certain musical preferences in regard to sound source, intensity, and listening conditions.
14. Amplification and sound quality of the musical media should be given particular attention when instructing hearing impaired individuals.
15. Music instruction can assist in the development of a number of nonmusical behaviours such as speech production, listening, language, social, and academic skills.

23

The Functions of Music in Music Therapy

Henk Smeijsters

Introduction

Music-psychological research in the seventies and eighties mainly concentrated upon the way in which people use music (de la Motte-Haber, 1970; Gembris, 1981; Smeijsters, 1993). Researchers tried to give an answer to the question of how music is used in everyday life, and what functions music has and can have.

Some forms of use have been around for centuries. For example, music has always been used in religious ceremonies and in the medical treatments which often accompanied them. Music in the shape of working-songs was used to support the working rhythm and it served as a battle song. Other uses, on the other hand, are typical of our age.

Among the first is probably the phenomenon of background music, be it as a way of decorating the room, as a means to stimulate 'buying' behaviour in supermarkets, to prevent fear and loneliness or something else. What is especially striking is that music is present on a large scale and always has some function or other which can go hand in hand with the conscious intention of the music listener and producer, or can come about unnoticed. Nowadays it seems as if music is much more consciously used with the aim of influencing mental reception. Research in many cases concentrates on the functions that are consciously experienced. People are asked why they listen to music, what they do while listening or why they make music. The same questions could be put to music therapists: 'To what purpose do you use music? What psychic or social changes do you expect to realise through music?'

The answers given by a music therapist will not completely correspond with those which non-music therapists give, and what is more, a music therapist uses music in a much more systematic fashion. Research on ways of using music could add to insight into the possible uses of music in therapy. It is implicit that the conscious use of music influences aspects of the individual which are larger than the musical experience in itself. People listen to or make music in order to re-store or enlarge their general sense of well-being.

Research into the Use of Music

Perhaps the best known classification of ways of using music comes from Adorno (1981). Firstly he mentions the *expert* and the *good listener*, who can follow exactly, by expertise or by intuition, what goes on in the music. In this classification we next find the individual who takes part in musical life in order to demonstrate a 'good taste' and culture (the *educational consumer*). Adorno describes the listener who seeks compensation in music, who tries to escape from his problems in daydreaming and, while listening, allows feelings to enter which in everyday life would be inadmissible (the *emotional listener*). Instead of escaping into daydreams, the individual can be looking for structure and obedience in music. This listener or performer attaches high value to music being performed exactly as it is noted down, including the surroundings existing at the time the music was first created (the *resentment listener*). Another one, according to Adorno, uses music to protest against society (the *jazz expert*) and then there is the individual who uses music merely as a background (the *amusement listener*).

Adorno's classification is far from complete, and not the result of empirical research. The idea that a person belongs to one category only, seems contestable from the very start; a person can belong to more categories at the same time or change in the course of his life. As an ideal-typology the division will serve the purpose, however, for we recognise a number of ways of using music in it. Whether one should cling, as Adorno does, to the standard in which only the expert and the good *listener* are deemed favourable, is highly questionable.

Formann-Radl (1980) examined psychiatric patients and discovered Adorno's types among them. In particular the *good listener*, who spontaneously follows the music, and the *amusement listener* were found.

Behne (1986b) developed an empirical *'Hörertypologie'* to which division in ways of using music belongs. The sentence *'When I listen to music...'* was completed by pupils in many different manners. For instance with *'...I would like to move'* (motor), *'...it changes my heartbeat'* (vegetative), *'...I think of something different'* (diffuse), *'I experience emotions'* (emotional), *'...I would like to cry'* (sentimental), *'...I get visual impressions'* (associative), *'...I try to follow the musical themes'* (distanced).

By subsequently coupling the ways of using music to the verbal and auditory preferences for music (after the mentioning of or listening to music, respectively) Behne found a typology of youthful listeners.

Usually several functions were found with one specific preference. This way, lovers of only pop music listen motorially, vegetatively and compensatorily as well as emotionally. Some clusters of musical preferences were only tied to one single function however.

Next Behne (1986a) investigated whether young people in a specific mood choose music with specific qualities. Four moods were examined: anger, sadness, joy and contentment. With anger he found a group that picked aggressive, fast and exciting music and tried to let off steam by these means, a second group that picked music which radiated not only aggression but also pain and sadness, and a third group that mainly looked for comfort in music, and had a preference for sensitive, soft and slow music.

With sadness Behne found only one group. Everybody who is sad wants music that fits the sadness; one does not try to take away the sadness by cheerful music. Joy and contentment were not linked to any clear preferences. It is striking that the strategies with anger rather differ.

A survey carried out by the Allensbach Institute (1980) found that only 25% of those questioned claimed that music calmed them down and that a number of the categories later described by Behne were not found: vegetative, associative and distanced. An obvious outcome is that young people dream more and that older people remember more. Motor and compensatory listening in cases of loneliness can occur at any age; diffuse and emotional listening are strongest with the young. Moreover the social and the aggressive/protesting element turn out to be important with the young.

Kleinen (1985, 1986) carried out a study in which 153 essays were elicited on the subject of 'My musical life'. The essays were supplemented with questionnaires. The statements and notions were classified with the help of computer-controlled content analysis. The psychic functions of music which were found were: background ('*I listen to music with everything I do*'); relaxation/conflict-control ('*Music helps me with frustration and stress*'); social ('*I make contact through music*') actualisation ('*I can put a lot of myself into music*'); joy ('*Making music is fun*'); and nuisance ('*Music disturbs me when I have to concentrate on my work*').

An Essay-Based Study on the Functions of Music

From the research described it does not always follow that the same functions which are found. This fact necessitates the repetition of similar research. A primary target of the research described here is whether the functions found in a new investigation in The Netherlands will be the same or whether they will be different.

To start resolving this question a preliminary investigation was conducted, following Klein's research method, with the question: '*What functions does music have for students at a college for music therapy in The Netherlands?*'.

Second year students of music therapy at the Hogeschool Nijmegen wrote one-page essays with the title '*My musical life*'. There were 11 participants.

Results

In this preliminary investigation, a content analysis of the essays of 11 music therapy students resulted in the classification rendered in Table 1.

Table 1: Analysis of the essays of 11 music therapy students

Category	Statements
Sentimental	'music works like a dream, it evokes pleasant worlds, but also nightmares and repulsion; music is addictive'
Associative	'film and music go hand in hand'
Social	'doing something together for fun; pleasant atmosphere'
	'losing oneself in music and being one with others'
	'contact with other people'

	'making music together is fun'
	'conflict and solidarity'
	'sharing emotions with others by playing together'
Compensatory	'I associate music with freedom and getting away from everyday concerns
	'music improves the atmosphere and the mood'
	'music makes me forget about things and really live it up'
	'forgetting the surroundings'
	'diversion'
	'relaxation'
	'releasing images by abstraction; relaxing'
	'safety valve for emotions (making music)'
	'an upper when I'm feeling tired or down'
	'a partner in life who helps to keep me going'
Emotional	'I recognise parts of myself in it'
	'communicating with myself'
	'music stimulates a feeling I already have and enables me to brood once more'
	'coming to myself'
	'music supports the expression of emotions or moods'
	'music intensifies emotions/unrest'
Tension/ relaxation	'music evokes tension and relaxation'
	'worlds in which you can discover exciting things'
	'music brings relaxation'
	'music takes and replenishes energy'
	'it can have a relaxing effect'
Motor actualisation	'music activates movement'
	'shaping myself'
	'in music I can express myself'
	'spirit and intuition'
Joy	'having fun'
	'enjoying something beautiful
	'drugging effect'
Nuisance	'functional music is irritating'
	'noise pollution by my neighbours disturbs my own peace and mood'
Background	'an ordinary way of spending the time'
	'music is the background to my life'
	'background music stimulates me while working and fills the silences in contacts with persons with whom I do not feel at ease'
	'there is always some music around me'
Preparation	'after making music I can concentrate more easily'

In the above table the terminology regarding the functions was derived from research by Behne and Kleinen. With every function you can find statements discovered in the essays. Each entry represents one test subject.

Discussion

In this small sampling survey we come across many of the functions discovered in other research. When we compare the results with Behne's categories it turns out that the vegetative and the distanced function are lacking. There is no reference to physical reactions like respiration or heart-beat. Perhaps these reactions do occur, but are they either not noticed or not deemed important.

Not much is made of the musical structure either. The latter fact is interesting in the light of Adorno's classification, in which the music expert takes first place, and music therapy according to Formann-Radl (1980), in which it is the intention that the emotional listener be changed into a good listener, who pays attention to the musical structure.

Both the previous statements and Kleinen's categories, which were all discovered in the results of this experiment, show that following the musical structure is, also with students of music therapy, far from a primary function. Only the category actualisation in hindsight points somewhat in this direction, even though it does not follow from the statements that it is a matter of clear purpose.

Striking, on the other hand, are the numerous statements in the social, compensatory, emotional and tension/relaxation categories.

Conclusions based on these data can only be made with the utmost care, but these categories do point in the direction of certain human needs which play a part in the use of music:

- the social needs
- the need for compensation and/or release
- the need to experience emotions
- the need for tension and relaxation.

A Questionnaire Study on the Functions of Music

A questionnaire was formulated on the basis of the above research, consisting of questions related to functions in the use of music. The questions were formulated in the shape of statements, for instance, '*When I listen to music I would like to cry*'. The list consisted of 41 questions in all. Each statement could either be marked or left open.

At the end of the questionnaire some questions followed on age, education, number of years of musical education, attending concerts, purchasing music, listening to music, making (performing) music, alone or in the company of others, and musical behaviour of the parents.

With the help of this query sheet the following questions were answered:
1. What are the functions of music and to what degree can they be found?

2. Is there any connection between function and age, education, musical education, attending concerts, purchasing music, listening to or performing music (alone or with others) and the musical behaviour of the parents?

In this investigation 57 students of further education (MBO: intermediate vocational education) and 17 students of music therapy at the Hogeschool Enschede, Conservatory sector, participated. This non-representative sampling survey necessarily limits the validity of the questions about variables, like for instance education, because some school types are not included. Therefore, when generalising the outcome to the entire population some caution is required. It became apparent from previous research however that the functions are independent of education. In the German Federal Republic, Kleinen (1986) discovered students of vocational education, grammar school pupils and students of music at colleges in virtually every category. Students at vocational education could, in other words, be taken as representative as far as functions of music are concerned. One exception is the category actualisation, which is found with music students exclusively.

Against this background it is an interesting question as to whether there are any differences between students in secondary education who are not potential music students and music students:

3. Can any function differences be pointed out between music therapy students and students in secondary education when variables like age and musical education are kept stable?

4. How can the functions of music be subdivided? Can they be reduced to a few large categories?

Results

Table 2 shows subjects' responses relating to the functions of music for them arranged in order of importance.

Discussion

If one compares the scores on the questions to Behne's 'musikalische Umgangsweisen' then it turns out that the motor function (singing, moving) can be discovered and that it has a very high score. The compensatory function (getting into a better mood, being pepped up, forgetting, letting off steam, feeling more at ease and less lonely, filling the silence) is strongly represented.

The vegetative function (goose flesh, stomach, heart, respiration) is also discovered. The great difference between getting goose flesh and the other vegetative reactions raises the question of whether, in getting goose flesh, we are dealing with a vegetative reaction or with the proverbial meaning of the phrase.

Music is not often said to serve as a background (doing other things, only half listening, paying no attention to the music) and it is relatively often mentioned that music can sometimes be a nuisance.

The emotional function (paying attention to the feelings expressed in music, discovering one's own feelings, getting cheerful or sad) scores less high than the compensatory function. With the sentimental function, remembering is more strongly present than crying. The difference between dreaming and living in a world of ones own creation is remarkable. The latter fits in with the low scores on actualisation.

Table 2. The functions of music arranged in order of importance (question numbers are in brackets)

When I listen to music ...	No (%)	Yes (%)
I sing, hum or whistle along (24)	27.0	73.0
I can really live it up (11)	31.1	68.9
I want to move or dance (23)	32.4	67.6
I get into a better mood (13)	35.1	64.9
I (sometimes) get goose flesh (36)	37.8	62.2
It sometimes disturbs me (29)	48.6	51.4
I experience pleasure (26)	50.0	50.0
I get cheerful (21)	50.0	50.0
I get pepped up (16)	52.7	47.3
I follow the melody and the rhythm (39)	54.1	45.9
I pay attention to the feelings expressed by the music (18)	56.8	43.2
I can forget about things (10)	56.8	43.2
I can vent my frustrations (15)	59.5	40.5
It reminds me of things from the past (3)	59.5	40.5
I feel more at ease (9)	60.8	39.2
I also do other things (30)	64.9	35.1
I feel free (12)	66.2	33.8
It is as if I were dreaming (2)	67.6	32.4
I discover my own emotions in it (17)	67.6	32.4
It fills the silence around me (32)	68.9	31.1
I experience tension and relaxation (22)	71.6	28.4
I experience something beautiful (27)	73.0	27.0
I pay attention to the style of the music (38)	73.0	27.0
I feel connected with other people (5)	74.3	25.7
I try to understand the composition of the piece (40)	74.3	25.7
It is like a film being shown (4)	75.7	24.3
I do so together with other people (6)	77.0	23.0
I feel less lonely (8)	77.0	23.0
I get sad (20)	77.0	23.0
I can live in a world of my own creation (14)	78.4	21.6
I pay attention to whether the piece is well performed (41)	78.4	21.6
I would like to cry (1)	79.7	20.3
I only listen to the music with one ear (31)	79.7	20.3
I can be myself (25)	85.1	14.9
It is like I am addicted (28)	87.8	12.2

I do not pay any attention to the music (33)	89.2	10.8
I can express myself better in contacts with others (7)	90.5	9.5
I can feel it in my stomach (37)	90.5	9.5
I can feel it in my heartbeat or in my respiration (35)	91.9	8.1
I can better prepare myself for things (34)	93.2	6.8
I get to know myself better (19)	95.9	4.1

The associative function (film) and the distanced function (following melody and rhythm, minding style, structure and performance) are both present. The question remains whether the answer to the following of melody and rhythm can be indicative of music-directed structural listening. The other scores for distanced listening are much lower.

Behne's functions can all be discovered. But also functions lacking in Behne's description occur. With living it up, which scores very highly, in all probability something different is meant from letting off steam, experiencing freedom or being able to be oneself.

Having fun (see Kleinen's classification) has a very high score. The social function (sense of solidarity, being together with others, expressing oneself in contacts) is found, but its scores are not very high. The experience of tension and relaxation is also mentioned.

It is remarkable that some of the scores on the actualisation function are very low. Only feeling free and experiencing something beautiful have a somewhat higher score.

Type of Training

Further analyses of the data by Chi-square tests of significance reveal that, in comparison with MBO students, students of music therapy at a conservatory indicate that they are more often inclined to cry when listening to music (1), are reminded of things from the past (3), are feeling solidarity with others (5), are able to discover their own emotions in music (17), can be themselves (25) and experience something beautiful (27). We can gather from this that students of music therapy have a special developed emotional bond with music and place a strong emphasis on what music brings about in people. Possibly this strengthens their conviction that music can help people, and it may be because of this they chose their profession in the first place. That music students listen to music together with other people (6) more often is, of course, hardly surprising, but from the answer to the question on loneliness (8), it follows that making music together meets a specific socio-emotional need. The answer to question 40, trying to understand the composition of the piece, is obvious with music students. Students at a conservatory are a little bit older and usually have had a higher preliminary musical training than most students at the MBO. Is it possible that the differences that were found can be explained from the fact that students of music therapy are both older and have enjoyed more musical education?

To this end the answers to the function were re-examined. Both age and musical education were kept constant. Do differences between students of music therapy and students at the MBO continue to exist with an age of 19 years or older and a musical education of 3 or more years?

In the previous part it was ascertained that differences were found in questions 1, 3, 5, 6, 8, 17, 25, 27, 40.

It was found that, concerning the matching of age, with the exception of questions 6, 27 and 40, the differences continue to exist. This way most differences in the answers to the questions can not be traced back to an age difference.

But holding the musical education variable constant did have the effect of eliminating the differences among functions. There are therefore strong indications that it is not so much the type of vocational training which influences the results the most but the musical education.

Those who enjoyed three or more years of musical education are said to be reminded of the past (3), to be pepped up (16) and to experience something beautiful (27). Two answers coincide with those found with training; what is new is being pepped up. That people who have had music lessons for a longer time are pepped up by music and experience something beautiful could be explained from the fact that because music props these people up they were stimulated to make music themselves, that being the reason they took music lessons for a longer time. Another explanation is that by taking music lessons for a considerable period of time they learned to master more of it and are getting more fun out of it because of that.

Some other variables

Those who do not go to concerts say that they have no inclination to cry (1) when listening to music, experience something beautiful (27) less and that they are less involved in other things (30). Those who attend more than 5 concerts answer that they feel more solidarity with others (5) and that they feel this in the stomach more.

The latter two facts are not hard to interpret. Attending a concert involves the sensation of being together and being part of a special manifestation. The individual is absorbed into the masses and experiences a 'we-feeling'. Because of this being together, connected by moving and listening to loud music, it is not surprising that this is felt in the gastric region. We are speaking of an enervating, social, psychic and physical experience.

Questions 7, 10, 15 and 25 are answered positively more often by people who claim to attend a concert 1-5 times a year.

Young people who buy more long playing records/CDs experience more tension and relaxation in music (22). Those who never buy records say that they only half listen to music (31). These individuals are probably less selective, have less of a bond with music and for that reason do not buy LPs/CDs, but rather listen to music on the radio, which chiefly serves them as a background. This corresponds with the answer to the last question. Those who buy a lot of LPs/CDs pay attention to whether the piece is well performed (41).

The Reduction of Functions

Factor analysis showed that the items could be reduced to six factors: 'Psychosomatic self-experience,' 'Aesthetic experiencing and compensation', 'Compensation by isolation', 'Background and diversion', 'Sentiment/melancholy/nostalgia' and 'Social enjoyment'.

Conclusion

People use music in different ways. How students of schools without a music teaching programme and students of music therapy use music has been the topic of the reported research. Students of music therapy are, more than other pupils, influenced by music in an emotional, social and aesthetic way, but the duration of musical education seems to be more important than the type of professional training.

Functions of music can be used by the music therapist to specify the goals of music therapy. They can also be helpful in describing the different fields of work: psychotherapeutic, rehabilitational, developmental, actualising, recreative and palliative.

24

The Skille Musical Function Test as a Tool in the Assessment of Psychological Function and Individual Potential

Maria Sikstrom and Olav Skille

The Musical Gesture

Musical practice and gesture are profoundly related to each other - and the musical gesture, which controls the quality of the sound is constantly in interaction with the sonorous perception received by the ear. But it is not only the ear that perceives the sound; the whole body can sense it as a vibration.

Making music makes possible the creation of an interaction between sensory and motor experiences, especially when we can discover the relationship between what the ear perceives and the motor activity that produces the sound. According to a French scientist and musician Francois Delalande, musical gestures can be transformed into an interpretation expressing an intention.

Working first on the hand, the mouth, or the breathing, this pleasant sensorimotor experience can develop into musical symbols resulting in an interpretation which will be linked to the musician's emotional life.

Delalande proposes a theoretical model of musical play drawing on the work of developmental psychologist, Jean Piaget. This approach to musical practice also forms the theoretical bases of the Skille Musical Function Test (SMUFT).

In Delalande's approach to musical play, three dimensions can be distinguished as described below.

a. Sensorimotor Play

In the sensorimotor aspect of play, emphasis is put on the gesture. The motor movement and the motion are the beginning of all musical production. The control of the gesture permits first of all a functional assimilation but it will also always be profoundly related to musical practice.

When we talk, for example, the vocal gesture is forgotten because we are concerned with the meaning of the speech. But when we sing or make music, the vocal or motor gesture is deliberate and conscious. The gesture permits the feeling of the sonorous vibration but supports also the control of the sonorous form and also gives it its significance. The musician emphasises the motor control of the sound. He intervenes in the emission of the sound by working on the movement of the hand, the breathing, the mouth, etc. Touching the instrument is for him a source of pleasure in itself.

Sometimes the motor control involved in musical production is considered as a goal in itself. The music then becomes a play of precision, of virtuosity that relates to the dimensions of effort and satisfaction. But this experience of touching the instrument or the sensation of the vocal gesture is completed by a sonorous perception received by the ear. Due to the physical/corporal dimension of musical production, a relationship can be established between the sensation and the motion. The music is perceived as gesture and sound; reception and production happen at the same time. The sensation of the body position strengthens the auditory perception.

According to Piaget the sensorimotor dimension is fundamental to the development of the cognitive functions in childhood. The evolution of practical intelligence is based on sensorimotor experience, concerning especially the hand and the mouth. For the musician there is no reason to distinguish the gesture that produces the sound from the perception of the body position. The musical object remains both sonorous and tactile, but for the listener, the musical object is only sonorous.

b. Symbolic Play

When analysing symbolic play, it is the interpretation or the intention that is considered. In order to refine his interpretation, the musician, starting with the motor gesture, develops little by little a symbolic gesture. This concerns a precise manner of producing the sound which forms the musical phrase, the nuance and all other formal aspects of the execution. He intervenes in the different aspects of the sound like the intensity, the tempo, the timbre, the pitch, in order to refine his intention or his emotion. We could also say that the motor function organises itself in time following the melodic or rhythmic movements.

But the motor function and the muscle tone are each deeply tied to the interpreter's/musician's emotional life. The motor schemata are not the same in a state of depression or excitement, for example. The motor symbolism reflects the affective life and the intentional expression as well.

Sentimental expression intervenes at this level, which gives the motor activity its humanised aspect. Therefore the way in which we produce the sound, determines the affective content. When using the word symbolism in the sense of evoking an absent object or psychological reality, we can state that musical play offers a privileged playground to evoke and elaborate our conflicts, our dreams and desires.

c. Play as a Game Governed by Rules

This aspect concerns play as a game governed by rules, and music is analysed here as an artistic creation. Music obeys rules. The sounds are not organised haphazardly, but according to a certain order. In classical music we can suggest that it is the first intervals of the harmonic series that have organised and structured the musical artwork. These intervals are the octave, the fifth and the fourth. The third is the following, and this interval was introduced in European music only in the 15th-16th century. During the 18th and 19th centuries the composers started to emphasise the expressive aspect of music.

A common experience is that the introduction of the third changes the emotional value of musical expression. But rules also reflect social context and relationship, in short the communication with others. Musical play as a game governed by rules is especially a social activity and when a child starts to play with these 'social material and schemata' he also begins to assimilate the rules.

In this context, the issue is not about moral rules, but about rules that refer to a stability, a normative tendency, a regularity which assures the transmission of a message; in short, the communication. But the rule can also be to transgress the previous rules and create a new law or organisation. Modern composers may often work in this way.

The source of satisfaction thus resides in the very applying of the rules that govern the game. The musical object is understood according to its cultural and social context, and the sense of the musical form is analysed in its dimension of interaction.

The Traditional Concept of Musicality and Skille's Psychological Music Functions

The way a musicality test is carried out will depend on the manner in which the musical phenomenon has been defined. In the past the first tendencies were to have traditional musicality tests that considered musicality mainly as a quality of the ear: a capacity to perceive and structure sonorous material.

These auditory capacities were supposed to be specific talents, more or less innate. They concern the individual's ability to discriminate and identify different sounds and time durations.

In this context, music is considered according to its acoustic aspects and the four qualities of the sound (pitch, timbre, intensity, duration) determine the content of the subtests.

More recently, tests of 'psychological sensitivity' to the dynamic structure of the sounds or the tones has been introduced. This sensitivity is sustained by mental activities, and musicality is not only considered as the sum of specific talents, but as a psychological process as well.

This approach leads us to define music not only as an acoustic phenomenon, but also as an art governed by rules referring to certain cultural values.

Musicality is here considered as a psychological process that reflects the capacity to integrate the rules of our tonal system. This process is called 'musical acculturation' and explains the way an individual integrates and assimilates the music-cultural phenomenon. Music education or musical stimulation facilitates this kind of assimilation process. Consequently, people who have had the opportunity to receive an appropriate music education would be expected to be more 'musical' than others!

According to Skille, music is not only to be analysed as an external event, but its origin will this time be the individual who uses sonorous productions in order to express a part of his psychological and corporal functioning, his inner psychological and body experiences.

Music has its acoustic/physical aspects and its artistic/qualitative aspects; but above all, it has a functional place in human life and thus becomes a specific mode of expression.

Music is not a separate phenomenon, but a lively part of a human activity, a type of action. Art does not exist for its own sake but fulfils a function in relation to human need for communication and self-expression.

Skille considers music to be a specific form of expression conveying emotions, intentions, moods and feelings, but also corporal experiences and sensations. Music is thus considered to be a kind of communication system, using musical stimuli in order to transmit a message containing emotion and having a specific meaning. Moreover, several persons can be involved at the same time in an exchange by musical means: meaningful interactions with others as with the music, can be created simultaneously. This is impossible when we talk to each other, because communicating by words implies alternately speaking and listening. Making music implies notions of succession and simultaneity.

Skille underlines the importance of taking part in musical activities, especially in our age when music has become more and more an object of consumption ('canned music'). The effects of music are the most beneficial when they are integrated and personal, and not limited to a specialised training that is only concerned with a certain technical perfection.

The tendencies today are to consume music, to specialise, but the essence of music is revealed when there is integration and participation.

Skille's psychological music functions differ from the traditional musicality concept in the sense that they refer to elementary functions used even in situations of everyday life. These functions are necessary for everyone in order to be able to live a meaningful life. Basic functions (motor, sensorial, mental, affective, cognitive, etc.) used in ordinary situations are called upon in different kinds of music activities. The starting point is not only the capacity of the ear but also the body and its natural performances.

Details of SMUFT

Psychological Music Functions

Skille postulated approximately 12 basic functions necessary for producing sounds that are musically acceptable. These functions constituted the starting point for SMUFT.

The psychological music functions are supposed to be independent of the learning of schemes relating to a given musical system. The learning process is included in the test situation. It is more a question of basic functions called upon even in non-musical situations.

1. A perceptual function, concerning the capacity to perceive sonorous stimuli but also to organise them into 'Gestalts' or forms. This perception is auditory,

but other perceptual levels can intervene (such as visual, tactile, kinaesthetic). The test is built up progressively, starting with a central note that serves as a point of reference. This permits the subject to structure and to organise the sonorous material.

2. A motor and psychomotor function which is characterised by the capacity to control movements and gestures in order to produce or reproduce perceived sonorous stimuli.
3. A capacity to organise and structure motor activities. The movements are considered as the capacity to transform sensorial, affective, cognitive stimuli into musical gesture. The gestures are used in order to produce rhythms and melodies. A comparison could, in this context, be made with the praxis as defined by Piaget in the sense that one is able to have a psychomotor project in order to express an intention. This praxis plays an important role in the development of intellectual capacities; it permits the structuring and the co-ordination of our motor activities.
4. A capacity to imitate and to respond in the test situation by observing the tester's musical behaviour. The learning of adequate musical conduct will also depend on the capacity to imitate.
5. A cognitive function that permits the transformation of symbols into cognitive activities.
6. Intellectual resources are called upon in the sense that one considers the capacity to apprehend, understand and to resolve an event.
7. The creativity function in this context not only refers to the capacity of imagination and exploration, but to the creation of new sonorous forms and to the way in which the sonorous material is organised.
8. In order to create a musical relationship a certain conscious level of the self is needed. The self should be sufficiently differentiated from the environment so that paying attention to one's owns actions becomes possible (self-control).
9. The capacity to evaluate one's own performances (self-criticism).
10. Social activity; the capacity to integrate rules so that a certain stability in social exchange can be assured.
11. Adaptability; this function refers to the way in which the subject is able to adapt to a new situation.
12. Need for communication; the emotional state will sustain the need for communication and determine the means called upon in order to express and canalise affects.

These basic functions, when sustaining musical expression, are connected to three principal characteristics of musical expression considered by the test: rhythm, melody and dynamics.

These functions, fundamental even in everyday life, intervene also in sonorous productions. The individual, with his personal possibilities, will be at the origin of musical phenomena. He will sustain all musical expression.

SMUFT is a systematic observation process of psychological music functioning and provides three kinds of information.

1. The evolutionary level: understanding the way a child expresses his basic music functioning actively, permits an orientation of the therapeutic project, at which level one should start a musical activity for example.
2. The functional level; certain of the observed functions will be more or less developed. This indicates which functions should be considered when establishing the therapeutic (or pedagogic) music programme.
3. The individual's sensitivity and receptiveness to music.

Analysing the Different Communication Areas

SMUFT is an individual, non-verbal test, that takes about 20 minutes, and is used to evaluate a child's potential and musical functioning in a situation of active music playing.

The test starts with a contact item. In order to enter into contact with the child, he is invited to play with the tester on the drum. The beating is first very slow, and the tester then 'pulls up' the tempo. This item gives initial information about the child's rhythmical flexibility, his physical and psychological limitations, his capacity to co-operate and to establish a relationship in his beating compulsive, persevering, or does he adapt himself to the situation by entering into a relationship with the tester.

I. Rhythmical Communication

The starting point of this subtest is the most simple and elementary musical element - a single beat on the drum. To begin with, the beats are not organised in structures, but the child repeats a series of single beats that do not yet have any form of 'Gestalt'. Skille defines this capacity as a possibility to perceive, contain, memorise and repeat a given quantity of rhythmical elements - an 'auditory perception of quantities'. Four, seven and twelve beats are given, by dictation, and in each case the child is asked not to count. The reproduction should be 'instinctive', completely spontaneous.

The second part of this subtest concerns rhythmic patterns organised into structures or 'rhythm cells'. After the dictation, the child repeats several combined beats, this time presented as rhythmical Gestalts, but which can be perceived as a whole. The auditory (or even visual) perception of these forms requires attention, and reproduction requires precise motor control.

II. Dynamic Communication

In this subtest the complete dynamic scale between a diminuendo and a crescendo is presented to the child. During the dictation, as when he reproduces the sonorous material, his emotional reactions are observed. The way he receives the dictation (with fear, anxiety or excitement for example) and the way he reproduces the dynamic content, will reflect his ability to canalise emotional reactions into an adequate music/dynamic expression. Inhibited children with difficulties expressing their emotional reactions seldom use the full dynamic scale from piano to forte.

III. Melodic Communication

The single beat is also used here, but this time associated with a tone on the alto xylophone. The rhythmical beat is associated with a melodic element, and the performance requires greater precision and motor control of the hand movements. At the same time, a tonal reference system is built up (G tone). Different pitches are added one by one until a pentatonic scale at five tones is obtained. The sonorous material is thus built up according to auditory and visual criteria.

One considers the child's capacities of visual/auditory control of the dictations and his own reproductions. This visual/auditory motor control expresses the possibilities he has to learn adequate musical behaviour by referring himself to imitation and his own discoveries. Clinical practice has shown that dyslexic children often fail in this subtest - the more information channels there are, the more complicated the task becomes. Complexity induces confusion, because the succession of the movements seem not to be rhythmically organised.

IV. Auditory Discrimination

This subtest is meant to analyse the capacity to discriminate, identify and orient sounds coming from different sources (xylophone side, drum, floor, xylophone). No visual support is given, because the child is asked to close his eyes. The identification of the sources will depend not only on the capacity to discriminate, but also on the way he experiences distances in space (near/far - up/down). Children with severe problems in organising their sonorous space will reveal their difficulties in this subtest.

V. Improvisation

The child is invited to play something that he invents himself. This activity should be completely spontaneous so that one can appreciate his creativity, his ability to work out his own ideas and to organise sonorous material into meaningful forms at a rhythmic and dynamic level. The improvisation should be recorded in order to facilitate the evaluation that is made in relation to the presence and the absence of certain rhythmical melodic and dynamic aspects.

VI. Vocal Communication

The child is asked to sing a song he knows, and his production is scored in function of tune quality - is he in tune or not. Skille proposes here the concept of 'socialised singing' and when analysing this subtest, different underlying factors should be considered.

Singing is a complex experience of inside and outside - the body simultaneously produces and analyses the sound. The first contact with the voice is the maternal voice and using the voice, as well as singing will also contain relational aspects.

Problems in this subtest can be of a relational or affective nature, but also related to sensorial/perceptive or motor difficulties (the vocal organ is undeveloped for example).

VII. Movement Communication

In this subtest the whole body expresses the different movements of music. The child is here invited to improvise movements to three different musical examples (Hansen, Brahms, pop music).

The way he uses his body is observed, but also his sensitivity to different kinds of music. Is he aware of and able to adapt his expression according to the changing aspects of music, are the body reactions spontaneous, free, co-ordinated with the musical stimuli, etc. This subtest has an important correlation with the sum of SMUFT, but it is not significant when used in isolation.

Results Obtained with SMUFT

The diagnostic value of SMUFT first of all lies in its ability to describe deviations from normal musical behaviour. The scoring sheet and testing manual were first printed in the book *Music in Medicine* (Spintge and Droh, 1987). Experience from about 30 years of work with music therapy has shown that music therapy is suffering from a lack of concise concepts and exact observation procedures.

In this test we are not primarily interested in the final score - expressed in numbers - of the tested person. We want to observe **how** the person is making his/her mistakes.

Factor analysis of SMUFT has shown that there are several underlying dimensions:

1. A pure rhythmical factor, which consists of parts 0, I, and III.1. The factor explains 7.3% of the total variance and 12.6% of the co-variance.

2. A melodic factor which consists of part III.1-5. This factor explains 16.6% of the total variance and 28.7% of the co-variance.

3. A general SMUFT factor, explaining 21.9% of the total variance and 37.8% of the co-variance. The factor contains part I, II, V and VII. The main features seem to be rhythmical in nature, but, as part V also concerns melodic criteria, there is at least a vocal melodic component in this factor.

Reliability and Validity of SMUFT

A study examining the reliability and validity of SMUFT was carried out on 131 children from a normal elementary school (Grades 2, 3 and 4) in Levanger, Norway. There were 67 boys and 64 girls.

Reliability was measured by retesting 30 randomly chosen subjects 6 months after the first testing. The time interval was too long for optimal measurement, but test-retest correlation was 50 ($p = .003$). Split-half reliability is 0.97.

In assessing the validity of SMUFT the following tests were used:

1. Teacher assessments were used in music, arts, maths, language and social sciences. SMUFT scores did not correlate highly with music assessment but there were positive correlations of between 0.2 and 0.6 with assessments in other subject areas.

2. A linguistic function test was used from the department of School Psychology in Trondheim (spelling and reading). The overall SMUFT score and in particular the rhythmic subscale correlated well (above 0.5) with reading ability.

3. A questionnaire to the families was used to estimate some common social variables, including the music activities of the family. SMUFT scores correlated positively with: presence of guitar in the home , presence of wind instruments in the house, family going to concerts, members of family practising music, the subject playing an instrument, the subject receiving music education, parents thinking the subject sings well.

4. The Wechsler Intelligence Scale for Children (WISC) was used. Correlations between SMUFT subscales and subscales of the WISC were generally higher than 0.4. The rhythmic and melodic subtests showed the highest correlation with intelligence.

5. The Wartegg Zeichen Test (WZT) of personality. Correlations with the SMUFT were low but statistically significant for neurotic tendencies (negative association) and intellectual control (positive association).

6. The WZT and the Torrance-Heikkila Circle Task (THCT) were used as tests of creativity. The SMUFT subscales did not correlate with scores on this test.

7. The Frostig Development Test of Visual Perception (FDVP) was used. Correlations between the SMUFT and this test were low.

8. The Goodenough-Harris Drawing Test was used to test maturity.

9. The Grooved Peg-Board Test from Lafayette Co was used to determine hemispheric dominance.

10. Standard audiometry screening procedures were used. Hearing loss was recorded separately for each ear in the area between 250 Hz and 4,000 Hz. This did not correlate with SMUFT scores.

11. Standard evaluation procedures for perimitory were used involving the Master Ortho Ratar from Bausch and Lomb. There was no association with SMUFT scores.

12. The Elementary Music Achievement Test (EMAT) was used as a test of musicality. Correlations with subtests of the SMUFT were in the range 0.04 to 0.18 which reveals that there is little correspondence between SMUFT scores and conventional musicality scores.

A Follow-up Study

A longitudinal study of the use of SMUFT as a diagnostic tool for evaluating progress in a group of mentally retarded youths and adults was carried out at Akershagan Central Institution between 1976 and 1978.

There were two objectives:

1. To see if SMUFT could be used as a tool for evaluating the effect of music therapy
2. To see if SMUFT could be used to assess progress in non-musical areas. (Skille 1980).

A pre and post test were made, the interval between which was 1.5 years. The test group got one music therapy lesson per week during this period. The control group got no such stimulation.

We found a rise in SMUFT functions of 70% in the test group. In the control group the same functions rose by 18%. There were also markedly better scores in the non-musical functions in the test group than in the control group, especially in sociability and contact ability. Linguistic functions also improved.

SMUFT has been used on many occasions and follow-up projects have been carried out in Germany, Austria, Italy, Finland, France and England.

The results tend to support Skille's hypothesis that there is close correlation between SMUFT scores and basic educational functions.

Some Aspects Concerning the Use of SMUFT in Clinical Work

When using SMUFT in clinical practice, the test situation is usually experienced by the children as play. They generally do not feel as though they are taking part in a test, but rather as taking part in a process in which they can express themselves. This is also one of the aims when one is choosing SMUFT - it is not mainly the results (scores) that interest us, but the way in which the child is organising itself in the test situation, and how it structures the musical activities.

The aim is not to test each child systematically, but to evaluate the skill level and personal potential, when this has a sense and meaning in the elaboration of the therapeutic project.

The fact that an important connection between SMUFT and WISC (and linguistic functions as well) has been found, is particularly interesting when assessing a child's potential in order to refine the diagnostics or to orient music and therapy programmes.

This means that we, by observing the way in which a child uses his potential in a situation of active musical play, should be able to estimate his intellectual potential as well.

Traditional efficiency tests are often difficult to use with children suffering from severe verbal expression problems. This also concerns children who are traumatised by so called typical 'school-situation', where communication is mostly verbal and the answer given is often felt as being judged 'right' or 'wrong'. These children are often penalised by the WISC results.

In clinical practice we have met children with severe learning problems and low IQ levels, who have been able to respond as normal children of their age, when they have been observed by SMUFT. This information can be important when establishing therapy and training programmes. It will also influence the estimation of a child's potential, when considering his ability to integrate into normal school systems.

Thus we can wonder if 'basic' musicality, when considered as a psychological function, might have its roots in biological manifestations and body functions, expressed through what we can experience as rhythms and sound. Such rhythms and sounds are, for example, the rhythms of the heart, breathing, sucking, balancing movement, walking, crying, the mother's voice, etc.

The artist creates, but he needs and uses material. Perhaps he has been inspired by the human being's natural performances when creating his first work of art.

25

The Role of Music Therapy in the Effective Use of Stress

Pixie Holland

Introduction

Stress can play both a positive and a negative role in people's lives. Currently, music therapy is recognised for use in the treatment of specific conditions where stress is experienced, e.g. autism, mental handicap, psychiatric illness and ageing. This chapter will concentrate on the role of music therapy in an entirely new area of application - namely, <u>preventive</u> work; providing a means of diffusing stress and tension during the sessions themselves, but most importantly, enabling people to learn the tools and methods necessary to control and manage their <u>own</u> stress and tension; to recognise the signs and to respond accordingly.

From running music therapy sessions on stress management with 'well' people I have found that people can learn, through music, to live with stress and tension and to <u>control</u> whether stress has a positive or a negative role in their lives. They are able to use the music to change the <u>perspective</u> from which to view the stress in their everyday lives.

Within my work I am to view stress from a positive standpoint. I recognise that negative stress can be a part and parcel of life, but I encourage my clients to release their negative stress whilst improvising on musical instruments, and to re-cycle the energy then available into positive action.

I will tell my clients they can either drown in the depths, wallow in the shallows or get up on the surf board, learn how to control it, ride on the crest of the wave, and let the stress carry them to wherever they want to go.

I will argue that music therapy is successful in controlling and managing stress and tension. It is unlike other methods of stress management because it gets straight to the emotions, bypassing language. Music therapy strips bare the soul revealing particularly difficult or private anxieties, concerns and problems, and helps people rebuild their responses.

The Use of Music Therapy in the Treatment of Stress-Related Mental and Physical Conditions

This section draws on two case studies to show how music therapy was used in the treatment of two clients suffering from stress-related illnesses - one illness mental, the other physical - and shows the potential for using music therapy to help people to see these problems and prevent them developing into serious mental and physical conditions.

Case Study 1: Guy

Guy is a wealthy Indian businessman aged 62. Both his parents are dead. He was referred to me by a consultant psychiatrist, having been in analysis for many years and with a long history of psychiatric illness, which he described as 'my three nervous breakdowns'. I ran five music therapy sessions with Guy in hospital, and six individual sessions after he returned home.

Session 1 After a few minutes of introductory questions and talk I suggested to Guy that he might like to choose an instrument and play how he was feeling at this moment. I said I would choose an instrument and do the same. He chose a pair of hand cymbals and a large drum. I chose a large drum. He started playing tentatively, short erratic rhythms, on the drum. He then picked up the cymbals and started crashing them together very loudly for at least two minutes. I quietly supported his initial drumming on my drum, and then I had to play very loudly and rhythmically, with strong definite 4 beats in a bar, accenting the first and the third beat in each bar. I had to do this in order to keep the music contained, safe and steady for Guy to continue his cymbal crashing. During the cymbal crashing I sensed the emotion of anger coming very strongly from Guy. I realised he was exhausted when we both stopped playing. There was a long silence and then he told me that he was very frightened of his feelings. He said that he was very angry and that he wanted to kill me, and was I frightened that he might kill me? I replied that I was not. He accepted this and we resumed.

Before our next session his analyst contacted me. He told me that during analysis Guy had related this anger episode to him. He was very excited about Guy expressing his anger and was anxious that Guy should explore these feelings further as he had been unable to get in touch with them before. He repeated that Guy was extremely worried that he might kill me if he experienced these angry feelings whilst playing on musical instruments, and he asked me how I felt about continuing. I said that I was not worried that he would harm me, and that naturally I would continue working with him.

Session 2 Guy asked me if he frightened me, and he appeared disappointed when I replied that he did not. Guy then told me that in order for him to feel safe, and to protect me, he had arranged for a 6'4' male nurse to join us. The male nurse was present for three sessions, numbers 2, 3 and 4. During these sessions we all three of us visualised situations and played on instruments to express many different feelings of emotion, including anger. Nothing untoward happened. I was aware of the fact that Guy continually praised the playing and expertise of the male nurse.

Without fail at the beginning of every session Guy would say 'I find it very hard to accept that my mother did not love me.' From the things that he told me it was obvious to me that his mother <u>did</u> love him.

Session 5 There was no male nurse present and neither Guy nor I referred to him nor to the anger again.

Session 6 Guy started off with the same sentence about his mother not loving him and about twenty minutes into the session I felt that it was time for him to know that his mother had loved him. I asked him to visualise a conversation with his mother, and then I suggested that he take on the mantle of his mother and just play the sounds of what he was feeling whilst thinking about it. He chose the autoharp, I the piano. The music we played was quite beautiful. Gentle, loving, peaceful and calm. I returned to the chair opposite him and he said 'That music was beautiful' and I added spontaneously 'and loving'. He agreed. He moved the conversation on. A little while later he said 'If that music was beautiful and loving, that means that mother loved me'. I remained silent.

Session 7 His first words were 'I find it very hard to accept that my mother really loved me'. He never referred to this again.

Session 11 On his last session we discussed his living out of England for two months and improvised on parting, how he would cope without analysis and music therapy. The music was solemn, contemplative but strong. When we finished the session, I stood up, faced him squarely, put out my hand to shake hands and say good-bye and wish him luck. He shook hands, looked me clearly in the eye, bent down and kissed me gently on the cheek, and left. I have not seen him since.

Lessons for me from working with Guy

1.   For the whole of his life Guy believed his mother did not love him. He was very angry that she did not love him. Through music he got in touch with these angry feelings which he projected on to me. Fear of the anger was so intense, that he thought he would kill me.

2.   Strong emotions such as anger (or the fear of the anger) can be experienced, worked with, and overcome in a music therapy session, and therefore incorrect beliefs, held for 62 years, can be changed very simply and quickly, through visualisation and music (a visualisation is an event experienced in the imagination. It can be an actual past experience or an invented experience).

3.   Music succeeded where many years of analysis had failed.

Case Study 2: Harry

Harry is a partner in an international firm of chartered accountants, working in the City of London. He is aged 52. Harry had had a heart attack two years prior to my seeing him. Joining a stress management with music group was part of his overall plan of recovery from his heart attack. He had never been in any 'group' before, and was clearly apprehensive about this.

Harry attended 12 music therapy sessions, and during these sessions the following picture emerged:

1. Over a period of six years he had visited two specialists, complaining of several symptoms of feeling unwell. He was told that there was absolutely nothing wrong with him.

2. He then had a heart attack. At his final visit to the cardiologist he was told no further appointments were needed and that he was to go home and lead a normal life.

3. He said he still did not feel at all well, and he had no idea what a normal life was - he thought he was leading a normal life when he had his heart attack.

4. As he could find no more help from the medical profession, he read every book he could find on heart attacks, high blood pressure, and Type 'A' personality. (Dr Friedman's diagnosis of the high-risk Type 'A' personality. He successfully treated hundreds of patients through the Recurrent Coronary Prevention Project). Amongst many things Harry learned was that the original symptoms he felt when he first went to his own doctor were listed in every book under the heading 'Stress' and that many people experienced such changes prior to stress-related illnesses, e.g. a heart attack.

5. Due to reading these books, he realised that to survive without having a further heart attack, (which in 75% of cases meant instant death) he had to make major changes in his life. He stopped commuting and lived in the City, he worked out in a gym daily, he was careful over his diet and he was trying to learn to change his reactions to certain stressful situations. He had noticed that he had difficulty in dealing with his emotions and had been told that the music therapy group might help him.

In Session 6 the group were discussing what stressed them, and one member said 'confrontation'. I asked the group to visualise a real-life confrontation and then to choose an instrument on which to make sounds about how they were feeling during the confrontation. I then asked them to do an action replay of the event making the sounds on the instruments. Harry chose a small tambour (tambourine without metal discs). During the improvisation he got up and changed this for a large drum! Afterwards he said that he suddenly realised he got very angry during the confrontation and had to have a larger drum to make more noise. He seemed very surprised to learn that he felt angry during a confrontation.

Several sessions later Harry came in smiling. Before we started the session he said that earlier in the day he had been in confrontation with someone. He suddenly felt his anger rise, then he remembered that during the session he had had to express the anger on a larger drum. Then something had happened. He said, inside himself he laughed and the anger suddenly subsided. He has said since, that now when he is in confrontation, the situation is no longer charged with the emotion of anger.

Lessons from working with Harry

1. Harry recognised there was something wrong with him and reported this to the medical profession six years before he had a heart attack. At that time the medical profession had not connected the symptoms of stress with any serious illness, and he was given no support.

2. After his heart attack Harry was unable to find the help he so badly needed from the medical profession which told him to lead a normal life, but did not give him any guidelines.

3.   Harry took a deliberate decision and made profound changes in his lifestyle, following his heart attack. These changes, however, did not affect his emotional responses. It was through the visualisation of an emotional situation, whilst playing on an instrument in a music therapy session, that he was able to start examining his emotional reactions, and to begin to deal with them.

4.   Emotions, such as unresolved anger, can be diffused through visualisation and improvisation; and can be prevented from recurring even in highly stressed situations.

Extending the Use of Music Therapy to the Management and Control of Stress and Tension and the Prevention of Stress-Related Mental and Physical Conditions

This section describes the work I have undertaken in extending the use of music therapy by setting up specialist individual and group sessions to work with stress-related symptoms before their development into stress-related illnesses.

Whilst working with children and adults who have been diagnosed as having a variety of mental and physical conditions, I observed early on, that the music therapy sessions were found to be helpful to others present, such as nursing staff, parents, and siblings, who are classified as 'well'. These experiences helped me to see the role that music therapy has to play in the prevention of stress-related illnesses - one thing that the nursing staff, parents, and siblings had in common was a highly stressed and responsible position.

This section of the chapter will concentrate on four different types of sessions I have run.

1. Sessions at Conferences

Some years ago I attended a conference at Edinburgh University run by the International Stress Management Association. I ran two workshops at the Conference. Each workshop was 1 1/2 hours in length. For 20 minutes I talked about music therapy, myself, stress management and how I applied this to the structure of a session, and followed this by involving workshop members in a group session.

People attending the workshops were astounded by how quickly they could get in touch with themselves and their feelings in a music therapy session. In fact, 14 people from these workshops contacted me over the next 12 months and this led to the setting up of a number of further workshops with organisations including Health Education Departments, the Church and a self-help charity.

I have arranged many workshops for conferences run on similar lines to the Edinburgh Conference ranging from the Open University to an International Symposium on Hyperventilation.

I feel attendance at these conferences has been very important to extending the role of music therapy and developing its use to new areas and institutions. Music therapy is generally unknown, possibly viewed with suspicion and thought to be only available to children and people in the back wards of psychiatric hospitals. Running the workshops practically meant that delegates could experience music therapy themselves and come to their own conclusions about its effectiveness. In this way the conference workshops have, I feel, helped to raise the profile of music therapy alongside other recognised therapies.

2. Sessions for the Media

An interesting development of my work with music therapy has been the broadcast of music therapy sessions on television and over the radio. In all I have been involved with eighteen radio broadcasts and three television broadcasts. I set up volunteer groups for each broadcast, because I did not feel it was ethical to ask clients receiving therapy to be filmed. One radio broadcast is worth mentioning in detail: the Johnnie Walker Show for Greater London Radio broadcast on 19th December, 1988. I had been asked to do a session live with stressed British Broadcasting Corporation employees, after I had done three or four 'interviews' between records.

I took about thirty instruments into the studio. I was very fortunate in that I was asked all the right questions, and the interviews generally went well. I had arranged the chairs in a circle and the instruments on a table. Seven men and women came in one minute before we were due to start. Johnnie Walker told the listeners what was going to happen and then handed over to me.

I introduced myself and asked the members of the group to say who they were and what jobs they did at the British Broadcasting Corporation. One by one they reeled off their jobs: producer of this show, news reader, reading news in nine minutes time, presenter of a one hour show, due to go on air in nine minutes, secretary, research assistant, etc. I decided we had to use this energy - we only had seven minutes! -everyone chose an instrument and played how they were feeling. It was very fast, lively and I had to keep a safe, loud secure rhythm going so that it did not run away with itself.

During the feedback they all said it was great fun, and they felt more relaxed. (I did not think they looked more relaxed.) I then suggested we might use voices and make vowel sounds. I said there were no expectations, no rights and no wrongs they could move their voices where they liked and when they liked, and if they did not want to join in, they need not, but that they would enjoy it more if they did. We started off quite beautifully - the harmonies were natural, resonant and everyone sang. Suddenly on my left, amongst all the vowel sounds I heard 'Oh I do like to be beside the seaside' being sung, and opposite me 'Any time you're Lambeth Way'. I nearly died - it was all going wrong - I remember frowning and at the same time feeling my frown was inappropriate.

Suddenly we halted. Johnnie Walker was my Guardian Angel. He said 'Hey Pixie, it sounded as if some of them were taking the mickey out of you. But you did say they could do anything they liked, didn't you?'. I replied 'Yes, I did say that they could do exactly as they liked'. Johnnie then said 'What about the chaps singing the songs?' and I said 'It is up to them to decide why they had to do that'.

I then turned to one of them and said 'You were one of the people who used words, could you tell us why you did that?' and he said 'Everything was fine to start off with, and then I suddenly realised I was feeling very vulnerable, and singing about myself and feeling unconfident. I didn't know what I was doing. I wanted to sing something I knew and felt confident with'. This was the man who was about to present a one hour show. All his defences were up and he was geared to 'give out'. Going into himself to learn seriously about his own feelings was dangerous ground for him when he had to be on the air for one hour. So he chose to sing something familiar, something that did not affect him. I felt he was very courageous to have replied so honestly.

An Australian Television Channel 9 broadcast was also very significant. Eight sessions were arranged in total. A volunteer group was set up consisting of a health education officer, a relaxation specialist, a chartered accountant, a company secretary of a firm of architects, a psychologist, a landscape architect, a merchant banker, a stockbroker and a managing director of a sales business. These people were in highly-stressed jobs but had in no way approached me for music therapy.

Television recordings were made of the first and the last sessions. The producer made two news items about stress reduction through music. These were shown in April and May, 1989 on two news programmes.

In the last session the conclusions drawn by the programme producer were:
- It was hard to find anyone looking stressed
- One person had learned to understand and control his temper
- One person had enjoyed himself, and he had not expected to do so
- The atmosphere of the group was lively, spontaneous and there was a great deal of laughter
- Everyone had agreed that they had had time for themselves, time to 'have a good bash on something', think about their own lives, how they reacted to situations, and perhaps re-assess things.

Six months later I invited the members of the group to meet to see the two films and to thank them for being guinea-pigs. Only one person was unable to be present. It is important to note that none of these people had felt they needed help with the management and control of their stress and tension and they had all offered themselves as volunteers for the broadcast.

However, it is also very significant that members of the group felt that the music therapy sessions had helped them to make important decisions and changes in their lives. They said that the music helped them to go much deeper into their thoughts than if they had just been talking. Music, and the shared feelings that the music evoked, using themes such as anger or love, provided a common link between people. The fact that people got together with strangers, played on musical instruments and talked reasonably freely together helped them to express deep-set emotions.

After the first session, for example, one person said that he certainly had not expected to talk about the intimate things in his own life in the way that he did, neither had he expected others to talk so freely. 'It must have been the music that made it happen.

Another person emphasised the power of music therapy in enabling him actually to feel he was reliving a situation of 20 years ago. He said that he saw, heard and experienced all the feelings and emotions he had then. I had asked the group to think of a time when they felt totally at peace with themselves and, through reliving this experience, this group member was able to rediscover parts of himself and certain emotions he thought were gone forever.

One man in the group was due to retire four months after the group disbanded. His retirement present had been a large electronic keyboard. Apparently his wife had realised the significant changes in him whilst he was coming to the sessions and so she suggested this retirement present to his partners.

There was a couple in the group. It was significant to me that it was the wife who told me that her husband really was changing and that he had not been in a process of change at the start of the sessions. Sometimes it can take time to realise that you are changing - it can take other people to notice it first.

The managing director's company was about to go public - during the sessions he began to realise what he really wanted from the company and was now making these things happen.

One woman had decided her life was too frenetic and had decided to cut down and do a job share. (Twelve months later she retired early, sold her house and moved to live in a community project in Devon.)

One man said he had always been angry with himself because in a one-to-one confrontation he seemed unable really to push his point through to the bitter end. He usually allowed himself to weaken his resolve by becoming too involved himself in the other person's point of view. The sessions had given him the time and space to change in this response, and he was now able to be rock solid in his interaction with other people.

In general people looked well, happy, bright-eyed and very pleased to see one another. A great deal of caring had developed during the existence of the group.

3. Specialist Individual and Group Sessions

One of the most important aspects of my work has been the development of individual and group sessions in the management and control of stress and tension. These sessions took place in a quiet room, either in my flat or in the workplace.

It was during my music therapy sessions for professional clients suffering from stress and tension that I began to notice a pattern emerging, particularly with the men. Most of them had an 'up-front', confident strong exterior to present to the public, but when they improvised on instruments about how they felt deep down inside, they were unable to present a facade. In the sounds I heard an extraordinary beautiful quality, a vulnerability, a creative spirituality; and all this was being kept tucked out of the way so that nobody else could see it, least of all themselves. I had the feeling that these people would feel better if they were able to get in touch with experience and express their hidden inner feelings, and I created different ways of doing this during the following months.

This memory of the strong exterior coupled with a vulnerable secret spirituality remained in my mind, and while preparing a paper on 'The Role of Music Therapy in the Effective Use of Stress' I kept on coming up with questions that remained unanswered. I realised that all those questions were basically a single one:

'Was man losing touch with his spiritual side - his soul - due to the many pressures of living in the 1990s?'

Several months later I was reading C. G. Jung's *The Holy Men of India* and suddenly realised that what he said also applied to my clients and the conclusions I had drawn. Jung speaks here of an Indian going to a Holy Man to play out the drama of his own personal ego-consciousness 'in opposition and indissoluble bondage to the self or non-ego'. Jung suggests that this conflict is known to the Westerner as the relationship of man to God. In Jung's opinion, the goals of Eastern religious practice and Western mysticism are the same: 'The shifting of the centre of gravity from the ego to the self, from man to God'. The ego then disappears into the self, and the man in God (i.e. psychic wholeness). Man's unconscious aim is to try and keep the scales balanced between ego and self, resulting in endless compromises having to be made.

For existence everything requires its own polar opposites: hot-cold, long-short, etc. otherwise the words have no meaning. And so the ego and self continually negotiate with one another. It is this pursuit that Eastern man has studied endlessly, and Western man is only beginning to start to contemplate. Jung suggests that Indian sages such as Ramakrishna and Ramana Maharshi should perhaps be looked upon as modern prophets. 'These lives and teachings form an impressive warning not to forget the demands of the soul in all the new things of Western civilisation and their materialistic-technical and commercial concerns of the world. The breathless impulse to obtain and possess in the political, social and intellectual fields rummages the apparent unappeasable passion in the soul of the Westerner... The externalisation culture of the West can truly clear away many evils, the destruction of which seems to be very desirable and advantageous. But, as experience has shown, this progress is bought too dearly with a loss of spiritual culture.'

Modern man forgets that for all his wordly successes he still remains the same inwardly. So Jung says that the inner man 'raises his claim which cannot be satisfied by any external goods; and the less his voice is heard in the hunt for the 'wonderful things' of this world, the more the inner man becomes a source of inexplicable bad luck and incomprehensive unhappiness in the midst of conditions of life from which one would expect something quite different.' Man does not realise that 'the one-sidedness of the diet of his soul ultimately leads to the most serious disturbances of balance. It is this which forms the illness of the Westerner.'

Jung's observations seem highly relevant to the psychological problems of professional people in relation to stress. Only now, after working for six years with businessmen and women, do I begin to realise the magnitude of the problem: exactly how and why they are stressed. The need is for a musical approach that restores equilibrium and balance, thereby reducing negative stress and enabling people to talk more openly about how such stress affects them.

In March 1990 I was asked if I would undertake six half-day sessions of work for a government retraining scheme organised by Arts Psychology. Music therapy was part of an intensive six weeks of counselling, career analysis, personality measures and psychometric ability tests. This involved working with a group of out of work Classical, Jazz, Rock and Pop Musicians, Dancers, Actors, Entertainers, Writers, Artists, Designers, Film-makers, Photographers and creative staff. The levels of stress were high as I was working with problems of low self esteem, fear of success, creative blocks, burnout, unemployment, maintaining standards, stage fright, perfectionism, fear of auditions, and fellow-professionals and anxiety.

All these people were suffering high levels of stress and tension. Twelve months later I am still there!

The first thing that struck me were the incredible musical improvisations. The level of creativity, spontaneity and imagination was something new to me in a session. Each improvisation 'took off' and was a very exciting experience.

I remember with the first improvisation I had asked everyone to choose from a selection of about 35 untuned percussion instruments and then to think about the child within them, have fun and just play. If they felt like looking at anyone in the group and smiling together, that was quite in order. The music was exciting, rhythmical, exploratory and creative, it had a life of its own. The improvisation lasted a long time, nearly thirty minutes, and when, in its own time, the music ended, everyone was smiling and excited. I remember in the feedback I thought I had misheard one poet when his comment on his experience had been:

'My spirit danced up here. (He pointed upwards to the centre of the group) even though my arse was stuck to the seat.'

At the end of the session we sat together quietly for a long time. There was the feeling of peace and nobody wanted to break up the group and leave. It was such a good feeling that we all shared - creating thirty minutes of exciting uplifting music.

It was at the end of sessions such as this that I realised how invaluable music therapy is to people who work in the creative arts. An artist is essentially a very lonely person and these group improvisations not only provide a space for artists to create their own individual sounds, but also to share in a whole sound, thus breaking down their isolation.

I soon noticed that sometimes within the improvisations two people would start up a rhythmic 'conversation'. In the feedback later they would both say how much they enjoyed the sharing together, supported by the rest of the group. Another time I remember an actor saying how agitated he was that day, and a poet's playing on a Chinese cymbal had been very calming. The interesting part I found was that the sounds from the cymbal represented the cymbal player's inner man and in effect the agitated actor was saying that the poet himself had helped him calm his agitation. This could not have been executed in words. They smiled at one another, and at the end of the session I left them talking enthusiastically together in the room. In other words the instruments brought these two men together and had broken barriers. The agitated man felt calmer, the man playing the cymbal felt good, as he had been appreciated for his playing.

The first 10 minutes of the sessions were taken up with my asking how they were feeling. If the reply was 'OK,' or 'Fine' I would say that I wanted a 'feeling' please. Then I would hear words like 'angry', 'sad', 'frustrated', 'depressed' 'unsure', 'blocked'. After a few sessions they soon began to realise their underlying feelings, and I could begin to work with them.

I have found that my best tool in this work has been using visualisation whilst improvising and then feedback. At the beginning of the session when I enquire about their feelings, I gradually form an idea of the general picture of the problems they are experiencing that day. For example, one morning I experienced feelings of 'blocks' on all fronts, creative, personal, and with these blocks the inability to get to a new position. They appeared to me to be 'stuck'. They seemed to be unable to do anything on their own, so I suggested that whilst they played on instruments they visualised a cross country race track, that they were riding a horse and that they knew the horse could take them over all the jumps. They could choose the type of horse, size of jumps and materials from which the jumps were made. I asked them to be aware of colour, texture, sounds, smells.

In the feedback these were some of the experiences people had:

'It was wonderful, I felt the horse's strength beneath me as he took me over all the jumps. I clung to his mane and I watched his ears twitching. I could hear the bit click in his teeth. I felt so good. I now know I could do anything'.

'My horse jumped over four jumps with me on his back, and then he grew wings. I watched these strong wings as they carried me up over the trees. I could see the coast and the sea ahead as we soared upwards. Then we got up to the blue sky and we jumped over clouds, we lay on clouds, and as the music began to end we descended, floating downwards until we landed on the grass. It was great'.

'My horse ran up to the first jump, but the jump was all thorny and too high, so he stopped and turned to the left and went round the side of it. He did this all around the track.' Then after a pause - 'You know, I think I do avoid issues'.

'My horse galloped up to the first fence, took off, but on the other side there was thick mud and he got stuck in it, and I fell off. I stayed there'.

'I couldn't even get onto my horse'.

I realised we needed to do some further work on this, so I suggested that perhaps 'going over' the hurdle was insufficient. What perhaps they needed to do was to go 'through the hoop'. I gave them directions to see a large hoop covered in thin paper in front of them, put themselves on the back of a horse, put their heads down on the neck of the horse, and whilst they played on instruments, let the horse carry them through the very thin paper hoop.

In the feedback these were some of the replies:

'My horse walked slowly through the hoop. When I was the other side I wondered why I had been so fussed about it all'.

'My horse galloped up to the hoop and went straight through. The thing was, I forgot to get on him'.

'My horse trotted up to the hoop, and then stopped'.

'I never got on my horse'.

At the end of this improvisation I was beginning to feel that most of the group had been able to visualise and improvise on the subject of 'creative blocks', thus allowing a different perspective for each of them to have on their own personal blocks.

One middle-aged actor had very vivid visualisations. I remember once we were improvising with instruments on 'the Moon'. We had had all sorts of sounds from the night, owls, shrieks, wind rustling, etc., and suddenly from his voice came the most incredible sort of half cries; half calls, - primordial sounds. They always came in 'the right place' in the music and were very exciting to anticipate. As soon as we finished he got out pen and paper and started writing poetry - poetry from the soul. When it came to the feedback everyone said how wonderful his vocal sounds had been. He seemed surprised and said that he had never made sounds like that before. He said they felt very good to him, very primeval. After this session he wrote poetry immediately after the improvisations. After three or four weeks he said he was seriously considering changing his profession to writing instead of acting.

Another morning I remember experiencing the feeling that the members of the group were unable to get in touch with their creativity.

I suggested to them that their creative energy was contained in some sort of cooking pot - perhaps a pressure cooker - and that the creativity came out of the pot with the steam, there was no stopping it and it was always available to them. They chose their instruments and off we went.

In the feedback, these were some of their replies:

'I was in a big black cauldron and gradually with my right shoulder I could push the lid off. The steam and creativity went out together. It was an effort to push the lid up, but when I succeeded it was a wonderful feeling'.

This comment was from a young musician in his early 20's with a young son of 3 and a wife who appeared to me to be controlling him. They lived in a small flat and he seemed to have no space to be creative, to compose or practise, his wife was always around and his son disturbed his concentration. 'I was in a pressure cooker, my wife and son were stoking up the fire beneath me, it was intolerable. Every so often my wife let a little steam escape from the weights on the top of the cooker. I could hear my son running and dancing around the cooker on the fire. I couldn't do anything'.

I think this visualisation was a turning point in this young man's life. He really understood that he was allowing certain things to happen which he found intolerable. After 5 more weeks of intensive input on the course, and many more musical improvisations based on changing perspectives, 'changing low self esteem' etc. he was able to understand that it is possible for him to make changes and take control of certain areas in his life.

'I didn't know what you meant'.

'I knew I had the creative energy in the pot, but I didn't know how to go in and get it out for me to use'.

This last statement made me move onto a further improvisation and visualisation. I asked the group to imagine their creative energy in the 'cauldron' and then asked them to visualise how they were to get it out.

Feedback comments were 'I saw it [creative energy] down at the bottom of a deep well. There was light down there; the moon I think. I had a huge leather bucket, with brass joints and handles. I was able to control the rope to lower and raise the bucket. It was wonderful cool water, and I was in control, I felt the heavy bucket had value as I lowered it into the well'.

'I had a wicker-work basket to carry my creative energy in. As I walked away the water all ran out of the basket. I repeated the journey umpteen times, but I couldn't keep any water in the basket'.

'I put a teaspoon in occasionally'.

'I siphoned it out with a hose pipe. It was long and narrow and when I got it out I could direct it with the nozzle on the end of the pipe. I didn't realise it was so concentrated and strong'.

Over the weeks I noticed how people changed. I asked if friends and relations had noticed any changes in them, and gradually this started to happen. One photographer in his late 30s said that he never stuck at anything. This course was the first thing he had taken seriously and attended each day. As weeks went by they gradually felt safer with each other, and were able to reveal more about themselves. I learnt that one artist had spent 2 years in a large psychiatric hospital, another was struggling with the discovery that he was gay, another lived in a squat and stole milk, bread, etc. from office doorways. Another musician had been in the 'Marchioness' river boat disaster that sank in the Thames. He very nearly drowned, all his friends and business colleagues had drowned, and due to the trauma of this he had been unable to work and had become bankrupt and homeless. Gradually they learnt that the way they reacted in their improvisations and visualisations was generally the way they behaved in 'real life' (e.g. the man whose horse went around each jump and never faced the jumps said he realised he avoided issues). I was always very careful not to draw their attention to these insights until I felt that they were quite ready to face up to the knowledge.

Suggested Guidelines for Individual or Group Sessions

This section outlines the way I run a session using music therapy practices and techniques in the management and control of stress and tension, and then looks at two case studies to show the effects of these sessions on an individual basis.

The overall plan is divided into three sections:

1. Group awareness
2. Exploration of emotions
3. Relaxation and visualisation

I plan to have a structure but to be free within that structure.

I work with a maximum of seven people in a group session. I place the chairs in a circle, as the dynamics of a circle are very important when sound is used. On a table out of the circle I arrange about forty small musical instruments (tuned and untuned percussion): autoharps, glockenspiels, drums, bells, flutes, recorders, rattles, cymbals, 'bangers, beaters and scrapers'.

People are quite naturally apprehensive when they arrive, usually nervous, talkative and wondering what is expected of them. Some say they feel embarrassed or silly, others say they have been sent along by someone else. I will usually use this nervous energy for a group rhythm to start the session.

Before we start the first session I will run through some ground rules:

1. Clients will be given permission to 'PLAY', to remember the feelings of playing, as they did as children.
2. The musical instruments will be used for their SOUNDS and are not going to be used for PERFORMANCE.
3. There are no right and no wrong ways of playing any of the instruments, and people can stop whenever they wish to do so.
4. There are no expectations.
5. Clients will be asked to express FEELINGS in the sounds they make on the instruments.
6. The session will consist of SOUND and SILENCE.
7. Clients will learn to be honest with themselves and with the group, in order to learn about themselves.
8. There will be feedback during the session, and clients have a choice about what they reveal to the group.

Group Awareness

To form group awareness everyone chooses an instrument.

1. **Rhythmic attunement** (heartbeat basis of life, cell growth, the seasons, the stars)

   a. Therapist starts a safe, steady rhythm, then each client joins in playing their own rhythm, one by one, until all are playing together.

   or

   b. Everybody starts playing together, and is asked to be aware of each other in order to try and form a group rhythm.

   People can stop when they feel like stopping.

   Feedback. Each person in turn says something about their experience.

2. **Pitch attunement**

Clients are asked to close their eyes and hum and try to find their place in the harmony of the group.

Feedback (as above).

These two methods of creating group awareness also facilitate a feeling of security and safety for the clients. This is absolutely necessary in order for the session to move on the Section 2.

Exploration of Emotions

Each client is asked to choose an instrument on which to play how they feel, everyone playing together. Then feedback is obtained or clients play on their own and the other members of the group comment. It is during the feedback or from comments people make that the therapist can pick up on feelings or emotions that she feels need to be specifically expressed (e.g. sadness, loneliness, depression, love, anger). Some explorations have included 'change', 'letting go', 'confrontations', 'regression to childhood' (playing with toys, family meal-times). Sometimes an improvisation will start with, say, irritation, go on to feeling cross, then to anger and possibly fury. The anger will not last for long, and in my experience the improvisation has without fail ended itself in calm peaceful sounds.

If it seems necessary to explore this emotion, the therapist will then ask the clients to think about a time when they felt sad, lonely, loving, angry (whichever emotion is chosen) and choose an instrument they feel will make the sounds of that emotion. Then everyone is asked to visualise the remembered episode and whilst they are remembering the episode, just to move their hands over the instrument and make sounds. These feelings expressed in the sound have usually been suppressed within the client, so to remember these feelings, express them in sound, hear the sounds, seems to give the client permission to be sad, lonely, etc. Expressing the hidden feeling seems to be very beneficial. It also appears to me that making the sounds of the feelings enables the client to let go of their feelings a little bit and so to begin to change the perspective from which they view these feelings.

I find that the situation of change, and the imagined consequences recur frequently. I often suggest that in the group we should do two improvisations, one after the other. The first one is to think about something in their lives they would like to change, and just play how they were feeling whilst they were thinking about the change. Then for the second improvisation they have to think about the same change, but not play how they were feeling. Instead they are asked to play a very definite strong rhythm of their choice - i.e. change the rhythm but have the same thoughts. (This means the thoughts do not have the same power, rhythm or pattern to them, enabling people to shift away from old thinking habits, giving them the understanding that a change is taking place). If people understand that a change is possible in the music therapy session, then there is a possibility that they might think a change is possible in reality.

Relaxation and Visualisation

The plan of this section varies with each session. I might, for example, spend the whole of the session on relaxation if I feel it is necessary. On another occasion I might just ask people to close their eyes and breathe in slowly through their noses to a count of three and out slowly through their mouths to a count of six. It is possible at this stage that I may also introduce a group vocalisation with vowel sounds - I may use the Brazilian Rainmaker as well.

I ask clients to close their eyes and try to let the sound become part of them, or for them to become part of the sound. I explain that I will start with a vowel sound and when each person feels they have attuned themselves to this sound, I suggest that they join me with any vowel sounds they feel like making. The sounds may move freely wherever they wish to go to, and the music will end in its own time.

When starting this improvisation I sit quietly to attune myself to the room and the group. I then concentrate on the group feelings and make my vowel sound. It just comes. Sometimes the music can be very beautiful with rich harmonies, ebbing and flowing from one person to another. People are amazed to find they have 'beautiful voices' and are surprised at the sheer musicality of the improvisation. I impress upon everyone that we all have this music inside us. As a therapist, I note that if some clients are unable to make any vowel sounds, it is a warning to me that perhaps all is not well with that client - that perhaps they are not truly in touch with themselves.

To end the sessions I suggest that the clients visualise a memory of a time when they felt really happy, content, and at peace with themselves. I will then put in a few ideas - perhaps childhood times, walking in the woods, being with a loved one or walking on a beach. I then ask them to choose an instrument to make sounds on whilst they are reliving this happy time. This is to ensure clients leave the group with a good memory, a clear brain and their blood pressure lowered. Sometimes there is feedback after this improvisation, but more often than not I feel it is more appropriate to leave the client with his or her own good memories to take away from the group. I would like to thank Mary Priestley for her basic structure for a session.

Conclusions Drawn from the Sessions

A number of conclusions have emerged from my use of music therapy in control of stress. People who are well, but stressed, do very little about changing their situation. Even when there are many stresses, held for long periods, they seem to think this is part of life and feel unable to change anything.

Men particularly fall into this category and it is usually the women in their life who suggest that they 'do something about their stress'. The men then perhaps start by doing something physical, like jogging, playing squash, working out in the gym and swimming. They tend to ignore the fact that there are also mental and emotional aspects of stress.

Women appear to be more open to the fact that they may have a problem over handling their stress, once it has been pointed out to them.

When it comes to stress at work and people knowing about it, there is the great fear of becoming vulnerable, loss of status or advancement at work, or loss of the job itself.

These fears seem to prevent people from actually doing something or even knowing that they can do something about the situation and so then lead them into a downward spiral.

People find it hard to pay money for sessions when they are not ill but are coping with life.

Most clients who come to the groups have never attended a group before.

People who are well are able to work out for themselves what is happening to them when they improvise, and also what is happening to other members in the group.

Clients are able to get in touch with feelings very quickly, actually feel these feelings, within the improvised music.

In my experience, however powerful the sounds are, they are always resolved into peaceful, quiet gentle music.

When the session ends with clients visualising a time or a place when they felt happy or at peace with themselves (walking on a beach, in a wood, reading a book or with people they loved) clients have often turned to me and said things like 'thank you for letting me remember that occasion. I had completely forgotten how happy I was then, and it was wonderful to feel like that again'.

Many clients have said that after a music therapy session they have slept very deeply that night and for several consecutive nights. One client said he was having unbroken nights sleep for the first time in years.

Some clients notice an improvement in their skin.

Others say they get a surprise when they look in the mirror. They see a smiling hopeful face instead of a rather withdrawn sad face.

Realisations that clients have during music therapy sessions may take several weeks to become actualities.

Some clients have top positions in their professions or jobs, and are thus very isolated. To be in a group is quite threatening at first, but very soon they relax within the safety and security of the group. When they discover that in the group there are no expectations and that they are able to communicate in a different way, non-verbally, they appear to relax, have fun and flourish.

I have noticed that in groups that are only verbal, members of the group will often pick on one another, sometimes really attacking that person for being what he is or thinking what he does. I have never experienced this in a music therapy group. Members are entirely supportive towards one another. When members of a music therapy group improvise together there is a coming together of individual sounds which makes a total whole sound that seems to heal in itself; something words are very often unable to do. Perhaps it is during this musical improvisation that they have in some way shared in each others' pain, fear, anger, sorrow, and do not feel the need to attack one another, only be there to support and encourage.

Sometimes I will notice group members exchanging telephone numbers before or after a session.

If members of the group have to miss some of the sessions it does not seem to matter if one or two are missing from a group of nine. But one week six were missing and two of the three were quite angry that the others were not there and had not told them they would not be there. <u>They</u> had made a commitment to be there and appeared to feel let down by the others. The interesting thing was that because there were only three of them that week, each person contributed a great deal to the session and worked at very great depth; they then took this into the next session, leading the rest of the group into more in-depth work.

I find the getting in touch with the emotions connected with a stressful situation leads clients back to what created the emotions, whether thoughts or the situation itself - what was the cause. We improvise on the whole gamut of that emotion moving from one area of experience to another, staying in each for a time to experience where we were, but understanding that we can move freely from one to the other. This exercise results in clients realising that they are able to <u>control</u> the amount of emotion that they could feel at any one time, and that they are perhaps able to go to 'Middle Ground' sometimes and not experience the full-blown emotion if it is not necessary. This is particularly applicable to the emotion of anger. We improvise on irritation, or frustration within ourselves, then visualise coping with that feeling facing someone else also feeling irritation and frustration, then full-blown anger. The improvisation on anger ends two ways - either by everyone laughing and then stopping playing; or by beautiful calm peaceful sounds, as if the storm had blown itself out.

Techniques and Instruments

I have found that certain music therapy techniques can help people to manage, control and use the stress and tension in their lives.

Once the problems of a client have been heard and understood by the therapist, a musical intervention can be designed to aim to deal with that problem, thus enabling the client to draw his own conclusions from the sounds he makes himself. I consider the silence after the improvisation to be of vital importance. It is the assimilation of information period, and it is here that the healing process, which was started during the improvisation, really takes place. The sound and the silence are the tools of the music therapist. The methods with which the therapist handles these tools must be flexible and versatile, the intuition, creativity, spontaneity and empathy are all part of the process of an interaction with a client.

Obviously, it would be inappropriate to claim that the following points constitute a blueprint for managing and controlling all stress and tension in any individual. However, the work I have carried out with a range of different people experiencing specific conditions of stress and tension has led me to draw a number of tentative conclusions, which are outlined below.

People who are suffering from stress and tension exhibit many different sorts of conditions. Specifically, I have worked with the following conditions, and noticed some very positive results:

1.   lack of confidence
2.   suppressed anxiety
3.   lack of decision making
4.   loss of identity
5.   feeling out of control
6.   feeling out of rhythm with life
7.   panic attacks and hyperventilation
8.   isolation, loneliness
9.   frustration
10.   anger
11.   exhaustion

Generally speaking I will not work with these conditions until we are at least two-thirds of the way through the session. The reason for this is for the client to feel safe and secure with me, the music and the group (if they are in a group).

Each session, whether individual or group, starts by building a relationship of awareness and trust between client(s) and therapist. I usually do this with rhythm (for rhythm attunement) and by vocalising, sometimes humming or with vowel sounds (for pitch attunement). I work on the 'here and now', that is, on the feelings that the client(s) bring to the session on that particular day. I do not ask the client(s) to explore any feelings or emotions until I am entirely confident that they are feeling safe and secure in our therapeutic relationship. I will not attempt any explanation of feelings if I sense that the client(s) is not ready to do so. Each client is different and therefore there are no hard and fast rules. Some clients are ready to explore their innermost feelings ten minutes into their first session. Others take five or six sessions, and are 40 minutes into a session before I feel that they are ready to move on to work with their own feelings. If one member of a group appears to me not to be ready to look at certain issues I will change direction and work with something else. I am extremely careful over this issue as I feel it is vital in the therapy to do things when I sense the client is ready to do them - the right time - and not before.

1. Lack of Confidence

The most successful way I have found of working with lack of confidence is with visualisation. I suggest to the client to think of a time in their lives when they felt confident and sure of themselves, and choose an instrument that would make the sort of sounds of them feeling confident. I will also choose an instrument on which to express confidence, and we will both visualise and play together. Afterwards the client will usually smile, look happier, sometimes say things such as 'I had completely forgotten what it <u>felt</u> like to be confident. I really <u>did feel</u> confident whilst I was playing - I hope I can feel this away from the music therapy session'. I have found that some people only need to do this exercise once. Having re-lived the <u>feelings</u> of confidence they seem to be re-charged with this feeling and can accept that it is possible to be more confident, and then be more confident.

2. Suppressed Anxiety

I think that the ability of music therapy to reach through to fundamental emotions is most significant in dealing with suppressed anxiety, as the following example shows.

This episode is interesting because it took place during a one-off group session for a radio broadcast. The client concerned was a volunteer and just came to make up the numbers in the group.

Two-thirds of the way through the session I asked the group to do two consecutive improvisations. These were my directions:

'Think how you are NOW, choose an instrument to make the sounds of how you are feeling, and then we will all play together'.

THEN

'Think how you are feeling <u>deep down inside</u>, choose an instrument and we will play again'.

The client said that she chose one instrument for the first improvisation and a different one for the second. In the first improvisation she said she seemed as if she was fairly all right, she thought. But in the second improvisation, she changed instruments and played how she felt <u>deep down inside</u>. She said all sorts of anxieties and worries surfaced and then suddenly she discovered that underneath these anxieties was an incredible strength. All the anxieties were only on the surface. She then found out that the instrument she had chosen made the wrong sounds, so she got up and chose another instrument which would make the right sounds of this newly discovered hidden strength. She said she also discovered that this strength had hardly been touched.

Nine months later she told me that this was a most incredible experience for her. Finding out her hidden strength had completely changed her attitude to her anxieties. Discovering that she had this hidden strength seemed to give her supreme confidence over her anxieties. She said she had discovered that whatever happened now, she knew she had this hidden resource to cope with 'absolutely anything'.

4. Loss of Identity

I have found that a group is best for someone suffering from loss of identity. In this case it is the first part of the session that is important. As I mentioned in the format of the group session, to create group awareness, and for each member to feel safe within the group we usually start with a rhythm. I start the improvisation with a safe and steady rhythm. (Before I start I sit quietly turning my mind's eye inwards towards myself, and pick up the speeds of the members of the group. I then intuitively pick up on a rhythm which sets a common theme for the group, allowing each person to weave in and out creatively with their own individual rhythms.)

The instructions are that each person is to choose an instrument on which to express a rhythm. I explain that instead of speaking to each person in turn, we are going to use non-verbal communication. I will start the improvisation with a safe, steady rhythm, then I will look to each person in turn around the group, inviting them to join me in the rhythm. I ask people to try not to play the same rhythm as anyone else, because they are stating who they are in the improvisation, and who they are in the group, and of course no two people are the same. I suggest if they want to look at one another, and smile, that's all right. Sometimes I find that people look awkward, embarrassed and unsure at their first session. As the weeks go by they learn to find their own identity in this small group, and then they seem to be able to gain in confidence to find their own identity outside the group.

5. Feeling Out of Control

The following example shows what I have found to be a very important aspect of music therapy - its ability to help people change the perspective with which they view their lives.

I had only one session with this client. She told me that she felt completely out of control of her own life. Events had overtaken her, and at the time I saw her she had taken a very serious decision. She was petrified as she was not sure if it was the right decision to have made. She told me she had three days in which to change her mind. She told me she felt that her life was out of control.

We talked and improvised on various things. It seemed to me that order was needed in her life as her feelings and emotions appeared unbalanced. I asked her to think of the word 'balance', choose an instrument, and play whilst she was thinking of what balance meant to her. She chose my Brazilian Rainmaker. It is a stout bamboo 5' in length, 3' in diameter. It has tiny stones inside and as it is eased up and down or rotated the stones move and rest on many wooden nails driven into the bamboo. The sounds are likened to water, the sea lapping the shore, a waterfall or a clear stream. I chose two Chinese bells either end of a rope and I held the rope up with the balls hanging down.

We both played together. I swung the bells on the cord, made them hit each other, altered the length of cord and the bells missed each other, etc. My client moved the Rainmaker up, down, sideways - sometimes making wonderful rushing water sounds, sometimes silent. Then she suddenly stopped and shouted out '<u>I've got it!</u> Look, when I hold the Rainmaker up here it's balanced (no sound), when I hold it out here, or down there, it's balanced (still no sound). It is the perspective that has changed. I have only seen my problem from one angle, if I change the perspective it looks different - I know I can now cope with my problem.

The following week she telephoned me. She said that whilst she was moving the Rainmaker in all directions she was able to control whether or not it made any sounds. She could balance the making of sound or silence. 'I suddenly realised I could balance my feelings if I wanted to. On the one hand I had to accept the decision I had already taken, on the other hand was this terrible panicky fear that it was the wrong decision and it was irreversible. In my thoughts I remained there balancing between the two. My terrified fears of my decision came racing up in me, and beside it there was the acceptance. I realised I had changed the perspective of the situation,

I had made my decision and I would stick by it. I was not going to run away from my fears'. I have not seen her since.

6. Out of Rhythm

People complain that they are stressed because they feel 'out of rhythm - out of the rhythm of their life - out of step with themselves and with other people'.

For this condition both client and I choose instruments on which to improvise rhythms. We start and I fit my rhythms into the pattern of my client. I then realise what is happening - it may be that the client will have two bars of regular four beats in each bar. Then the next bar will have five beats. The next bar seven, and then four again. (This 'out of step rhythm' is quite common with autistic people. I have tried the following techniques with autistic people with a small amount of success). I am then very directive. I usually choose a large drum that can produce louder sounds than my client. I very deliberately match my client's four beats in the bar, and keep this going very loudly and accented. I can usually anticipate his 'extra beat' bars so make a very strong first beat of the next bar. The client finds it very difficult to keep to their 'odd' rhythm bars and slips into my manipulated four regular beats in each bar. Sometimes I have been too strong and the client has obviously felt overpowered by me and has just stopped playing. We start again and I try to temper my beats more carefully and the improvisation seems to take off. I keep this going for as long as the client is able to do so. This is to ensure that the rhythms form a new pattern in the client's mind. The structure of the rhythm provides a basic structure of life for the client to identify with. We will do this every session.

7. Panic Attacks and Hyperventilation

These problems are both to do with irregular breathing. I watch and listen to the breathing of the client. We both choose instruments on which to improvise. I will start to breathe at the same speed as my client. I will then start to make vowel sounds vocally, then move on to singing still keeping the same speed as my client. I will then ask the client to join me on the instrument of their choice. I will still be singing, but add the instrument of my choice. All the time I will be manipulating the beat of the music to be slow, even and deliberate. I will keep this going for as long as possible. Finally, I will ask the client to join in vocally. By this time, the clear definite secure rhythm is safe enough for the client to be vocalising with me in a steady rhythm. We will do this each session.

8. Isolation, Loneliness

The mere fact of attending a group, playing music together, and talking to the group about one's feelings means sharing and creating beautiful sounds together. The fact of sharing creativity with someone in itself defeats the feelings of isolation and loneliness.

The more responsible a job is, the more isolated the person doing that job can become. I have watched people who have responsible positions in their work look very lonely and isolated when they first attend a group. After several sessions they all seem to warm to each other - the improvised music brings out the best in people - they are no longer isolated or lonely in the group. Clients tell me that sharing creativity in the group prepares them for communication and possible sharing outside the group. In other words they are able to make changes whilst in the group which they can carry over to everyday life.

After an improvisation on isolation and loneliness we have often sat quietly and ended the session, even though that was perhaps not the intention. It appeared too significant and profound an experience to move away from. People needed to finish with the memory of this shared experience, and carry this with them away from the session.

A person who is isolated and lonely is usually unable to move out of that state and move towards somebody and make contact. The following is a visualisation exercise I have used which seems to create an inner awareness and feeling of love from each member of the group enabling an outward gesture. Each time I have used this exercise, the members of the group have needed to hug each other and me. (This does not usually happen in a session.)

I ask the group to visualise a water lily, one flower floating on top of the water. I then go on to say 'Put whatever else you want to into the picture, but be aware of the <u>WATER</u> that is all around the lily, supporting the flower. Is the flower a bud - half open or fully open? See if the water is deep, is it still, or are there ripples? Is it clear or muddy? Do you visualise the water lily just floating there, or are there roots? If so, how thick are they and where do they go to? Put whatever you want to into the picture. Put in any colours you want to - if the lily has a colour, what is it?' Then I asked them to chose one or more instruments to play on whilst they are thinking about their picture.

With some people the music has been quite 'surface' and possibly jolly to start with (i.e. people thinking about ordinary things happening to them in everyday life). Perhaps bright quick sounds on chime bars, or decisive rhythms on a drum. Very quickly the music changes, perhaps the clients need to change their instruments to make a different sound. It is quieter, contemplative, introspective, serious, lacking in rhythm - perhaps idly letting the sticks run up and down a xylophone or glockenspiel, tiny fragile sounds from a cluster of bells being shaken - the haunting floating notes from a wooden pipe - all these sounds tell me, the therapist, that the clients are making sounds to represent their 'INNER WORLD'. They are really in touch with how they are feeling deep down inside. The real truth about their innermost feelings is being allowed to flow in the music out into their conscious minds. The music is safe and secure for them to come to terms with the hidden depths of themselves. The music gradually subsides, perhaps there will be the occasional shimmer from the bells, or one or two sounds from the xylophone, but the sounds fit into the time and space of this improvisation. Nothing intrudes. The silence that follows is very long and profound. I look at people's faces. People seem to have taken on a wisdom they did not appear to have had earlier. It is as if they have experienced and learnt something very profound and meaningful. I do not encourage people to talk about this experience, as it is very personal. I just look around at people, smiling at them, perhaps with an eyebrow raised encouraging anyone to say something if they need to do so. The lily has been described as being half open and grey and black, fully open and pink and white - another had no roots - another had flowers all around the one lily until the water was nearly covered. I leave the reader to draw their own conclusions, as I and the group did.

9. and 10. Frustration and Anger

I do not attempt to work with these emotions until the client feels entirely safe with me, or if it is a group until I feel all clients feel safe within the group. I ask the group to visualise a real-life situation when they feel frustrated, to think of the feelings and to choose an instrument on which to express these feelings. I say that if the feelings move on to anger, not to worry, but to move with the feelings. (I have always noticed that when an improvisation has moved to anger, when the anger is spent it moves to slow, calm, quiet sounds.)

When improvising with emotions of frustration and anger, I make sure that I have availability to the loudest sounds in the room. I feel this is necessary to support and contain the sounds of anyone who expresses very loud anger, to make them feel safe.

11. Exhaustion and Lack of Energy

The client and I both choose instruments on which to express exhaustion. I will probably use my voice as well, with lots of sighing sounds. I match my sounds with my client's and we will just express the sounds of exhaustion vocally and then add instruments when needed.

Most clients say that in the session it is good to feel they are allowed to be exhausted, as all the time they are perpetually trying to buck themselves up and do something. The fact of allowing themselves to feel exhausted takes the guilt away from the feelings.

Lack of energy was a specific complaint many people had. Clients were asked to visualise a hard dark rock-like substance of energy, which was situated just below the navel. They were told this energy was always there and could never be depleted. They were asked to choose instruments and make sounds on them as they visualised an energy spiral with 3 1/2 turns coming out of the dark object. They were to start with no energy, and build up. Nearly everyone reported a feeling of more energy. Some people got very hot and had to remove shoes, socks and jackets. Even very depressed people reported feeling some energy generated.

This gives the client a different perspective on their feelings, allowing the possibility of change.

The Instruments

In my work I have found that certain types of music and certain types of instruments can work for specific conditions. For relaxation the two 'tools' I use are my voice, and the 'Rainmaker' described earlier. The sounds clients hear from the Rainmaker can be a gentle drip of water, a stream trickling, a torrent, a waterfall, the sea lapping a beach (shingle or sand), the scrunch of coarse sand under the feet and the sea as it laps over the ankles, hand clapping, and landslides of pebbles. All these descriptions of sounds can create incredible pictures in people's minds of peaceful beaches, leafy woods, vast trees, brightly coloured kingfishers, and sparkling streams.

I will usually start by asking clients to close their eyes and go into themselves quietly and relax. I might do a complete body relaxation and take time over it, or it might be a short relaxation. I then very gently either use my voice with vowel sounds, or I gently rotate the Rainmaker with small sounds. I have found that using them together is confusing for the clients, but frequently I will start with my voice and then move to the Rainmaker. I invite the clients to concentrate on the sound and let the sound become part of them, or for them to become part of the sound. I do not decide when to stop, the music stops when it is ready to do so. When the music stops there is always a long silence.

After only one twenty minute session of this type of relaxation one client wrote me a letter to say that she normally found it extremely difficult to relax her pelvic region. She said that during this short relaxation, she had experienced a tingling in this area which was then followed by the sort of relaxation she had not experienced for years. She said that several days later when she wanted to relax she thought about the sessions, the sounds made, and she was still able to experience a relaxation.

As a therapist, I put myself, my very self, my person, on the line, into that interaction, into that communication and in so doing I can find out what is wrong/right with the other person by listening to their music - what feelings, emotions go into the sounds, into the music.

As a music therapist I work from my calm centre, aiming to communicate, through music, with the calm centre of my client. I first of all have to encourage the client to realise they have a calm centre. When I feel they are beginning to realise that they, like everyone else, have this calm centre within them, we improvise musically on this centre recognising it is there and allowing it to be there, giving it permission to be there. When I sense the client has accepted this - I think it is my intuition at this point - I suggest they give this calm centre a shape out of nature - a flower or a tree, and whilst improvising on an instrument, allow it to grow. I ask them to see the type of flower or tree, be aware of the colours and the textures, <u>listen</u> to the <u>SOUNDS</u> they are making on their instruments. If it is a group session I explain that nobody will listen to <u>them</u>, as everyone will be too busy and involved with their own thoughts and sounds. I suggest to them that they think about the word LOVE at the same time - try and have the <u>FEELINGS</u> of LOVE in terms of compassion, care, respect, honour, friendship, empathy about them as they watch the flower grow from the very centre of their being.

I consider that when I work with a client I undertake to accompany that client on part of their Journey of Life. I consider that it is a great privilege to share in part of this Journey, and I will give all I am capable of giving to ease the pain of this Journey.

I am learning that there is <u>always</u> a musical answer, a musical solution to the problems presented, certainly the problems that I am able to pick up on. I think of a solution and a way to adapt it into musical language. I have also learned that I can introduce 'techniques' which have worked in one session into other areas of my work, perhaps initiating something which may not otherwise have come up.

Conclusions

In this chapter I have outlined that music therapy can be used in preventive medicine and that 'well' people can benefit from short term music therapy in the management and control of stress and tension.

When promoting stress management with music, rather than offering 'therapy' - or 'music therapy', I feel that it would be advantageous to concentrate on the fact that the music session will provide a safe space for people to look at themselves, look at their lives, make changes or accept situations. In this way the focus is taken away from the thought that perhaps 'People will be having things done to them' and moved towards 'People will have the time and the opportunity to re-plan their lives, observe their reactions, implement changes if needed. This change of perspective on people's lives encourages spaces providing room for creativity'.

As music relaxes you, so it can also work at a deeper level and release the stress patterns that have built up over the years. The stress patterns are subconscious, sometimes they are blocks to understanding how you are functioning. They can be released by working with music and discussion.

When I initially set out planning my work with a view to managing and controlling stress and tension through music I saw stress as 'something to get rid of'. I now see the stress as an essential part of life, and the work I do as building on inner resources for coping with the stress.

As I perceive the situation, self knowledge through sound can enable changed perspectives and values. The healing process is <u>within</u>, available to all. This healing power can be accessed through music.

The healing process takes time, sometimes weeks or months. I find that I will notice a client is changing and on the road to recovery before they notice it themselves. At first I found it hard not to tell them, but now I just smile outwardly and inwardly as I see them getting better.

'The self is the sum of all the divergent forces, energies, and qualities that live within you and make you who you are - a unique individual. The self is the balanced, harmonious, symmetrical unity at the very centre of one's being, which each of us senses within. But we rarely experience the self without conscious mind; we rarely have that sense of unity and wholeness. We feel ourselves usually as a chaotic mass of conflicting desires, values, ideals and possibilities, some conscious and some unconscious, pulling us in many directions at once.'

This quote from Robert A Johnson's *The Psychology of Romantic Love* gives an idea of musical improvisation in music therapy. The improvisation can start with a jumble of rhythms, expressing conflicting emotions, (sadness, anger, frustration, fear, isolation) and out of the chaos comes order, a harmony, a beauty of sound, a peace, a feeling of at-oneness, a unity, a wholeness. Amazingly, this always happens, which leads me to conclude that the human instinct is to resolve conflict, to create harmony from disharmony.

I experience this harmony of mind, body and emotions as 'Healing' of the self and the improvisation as 'Music and the Healing Process'.

26

The Integration of Mental Health Science Concepts in the Education of the Music Therapist

Paul Nolan

Introduction

Within forty years the profession of music therapy has grown dramatically. In the United States alone there are 3,100 registered music therapists as active members within the National Association for Music Therapy (NAMT) and approximately 300 active music therapists who are certified by the American Association for Music Therapy (AAMT), a somewhat younger professional organisation. There are currently 72 colleges and universities which offer a degree in music therapy. In addition to being the oldest creative arts therapy organisation within the United States, music therapy was the first arts therapy profession to develop a certification exam which tested the body of knowledge required for the entry-level music therapist. Currently, music therapists in the United States work with numerous treatment and educational populations of virtually all ages. The music therapy literature continues to illustrate new horizons of clinical applications pertinent to the needs of society.

Many aspects of music therapy education in the United States have been documented, including the content of the separate standards developed by the NAMT and the AAMT. For an excellent review of the literature on music therapy education and training in the United States the reader should consult Maranto's (1987) review of the literature. She cites 72 references and states that the 'responsibility of educating and training the music therapist has been, perhaps, the most controversial area in the profession for almost 40 years' (p. 1).

When music therapy began as an organised discipline the entry level credential for many health care professionals (including psychologists) was the bachelors degree. Today it appears that many of these professions have increased the academic requirements for an entry level credential due to the expansion of knowledge within health care. Due partly to the ever-expanding body of knowledge available to music therapy students and to the knowledge, skills and abilities required for quality clinical work, both music therapy organisations are testing the development of more than one level of certification. The AAMT has recently added an advanced credential which requires a minimum of a masters degree. In 1989, the NAMT developed a Task Force on Levels of Certification based upon the recommendations of the California Symposium on Education and Training (Maranto, 1989). As of this writing the NAMT is determining criteria for an advanced level of registration and is simultaneously investigating a competency based system for education. It appears that the profession, after 40 years of expansion within clinical, research and educational areas, is re-examining its place within health care and is attempting to grow to meet the needs of the health care consumer. It is this author's contention that a major area of focus in this re-examination process should include the development of an in-depth understanding of how psychological factors, or the more inclusive paradigm of 'mental health sciences', relate to the use of music therapy.

This chapter will address the importance and function of mental health science concepts in music therapy education and training. Suggestions for their integration into the music therapy curriculum will be described. The relationship between mental health science concepts and music therapy education has not yet appeared in the literature available to this author. The topic is important in the light of the current movement within the American music therapy profession to consider the levels of music therapy practice, such as activity therapy, behaviour modification and music psychotherapy. The results of this organisation of levels of clinical practice will undoubtedly impact upon music therapy education. It is this author's premise that current NAMT and AAMT educational guidelines need to be further broadened and extended to meet the sophisticated needs of professional music therapists, specifically in regard to their current clinical realities. Because many music therapists are not trained to integrate their understandings of music therapy with mental health science concepts, they often remain in a relatively low position in the clinical and administrative hierarchy. This is especially so in mental health and developmental treatment environments where most other professional treatment disciplines obtain credentials beyond the bachelors degree level.

In clinical practice, when the therapist is able to link clinical phenomena with mental health science concepts, she or he possesses the necessary foundation upon which to develop appropriate goals and courses of action. The therapist may also be able effectively to communicate findings to treatment team members in a manner which is clinically relevant and affects team treatment decisions. These skills may influence how the music therapist is regarded by clients, physicians, psychologists and administrators.

When the music therapist is unable to link music therapy experiences with current mental health science concepts, it has the potential to affect negatively the development of a positive professional identity and clinical competence. This issue, which has roots in the educational process, seems to be related also to the high rate of burnout among music therapists (Glider, 1987).

Relationship to Clinical Practice

In the practice of clinical music therapy most interventions relate to a pre-existing approach of psychotherapy regardless of whether the therapist is aware of the connection or not (Wheeler, 1981). Knowledge of this connection may not necessarily be required for successful treatment outcome. However, knowledge of treatment approaches and methods would seem to be linked positively with successful treatment outcome.

Music therapists apply interventions within an interpersonal context. This context relies upon psychotherapeutic and developmental understandings. Therefore, knowledge of the specific population and treatment relationships/dynamics serves as the foundation upon which all interventions rest. This includes knowledge of client abilities, disabilities, reasonable therapeutic goals and objectives, relevant clinical or educational approaches, and verbal communication to report progress to all levels of the treatment staff.

These areas of knowledge and skill fall into the category of mental health sciences and relate to the development, restoration, and maintenance of mental health. Areas of study within mental health sciences include psychology, group dynamics, modalities of psychotherapy (creative arts therapies, family therapy, etc.), theoretical orientations (psychodynamic, gestalt, behaviourism etc.), neurosciences, psychopharmacology, and normal and abnormal psychological development. Some combinations of these knowledge areas are essential ingredients within every therapeutic encounter. Whether these topics are taught in the university, practicum/internship site, or acquired on the job is currently a question for debate among educators, clinical supervisors, and clinicians (Maranto and Bruscia, 1988). Also, the question concerning who should teach these areas to music therapists has not yet been addressed.

Limitations of Current Educational Guidelines

Recent authors have begun to address the issues related to the acquisition of knowledge and skills of the mental health sciences in music therapy training. Goldberg (1989) recommends a graduate degree in music therapy for clinical work in all psychiatric practice, as this population requires expertise in the previously listed knowledge areas. Bruscia (1986) cites that beyond undergraduate training, music therapists are frequently called upon to expand their professional roles thus allowing for recognition as primary therapists as well as adjunctive therapists. He lists eight broad categories as areas for advanced competencies in music therapy training. Within the described category of Advanced Clinical Skills over 66% require specific knowledge of mental health science concepts, for example, all aspects of normal and abnormal psychological development and related treatments. More than 70% of the items listed by Bruscia as Theoretical Skills require knowledge of mental health science concepts.

Current Emphasis of Mental Health Science Studies

Within the United States the music therapist's means for acquiring the education necessary for the development of this clinical knowledge rests within the educational guidelines set forth by the NAMT and the AAMT. The NAMT undergraduate requirements for music therapy are very similar to most other music degrees with music course requirements compromising 45% of the degree. Fifteen percent of the degree requirements focuses upon music therapy and psychology of music courses along with clinical practicum and internship. Mental health science courses are categorised with other courses in health and natural sciences (human anatomy, etc.), which comprise an additional 15% of the degree. Of the courses related to mental health sciences only abnormal psychology and exceptional children are identified areas which are required specifically (Scartelli, 1987). The AAMT lists specific competency areas which must be addressed in undergraduate education, however, the clinical foundations only include exceptionality, dynamics of therapy, and the therapeutic relationship as required areas (Scartelli, 1987). Programme directors of NAMT and AAMT approved schools face the difficult chore of adding elective courses in mental health science areas (when available) to a curriculum which is already bursting at the seams.

From the educational guidelines of both associations and from a review of university catalogues it appears that many of the music therapy foundations include, or require, knowledge areas of mental health sciences. If this is the case then music therapy faculties are forced to teach mental health science concepts. The question remains then, if other mental health science educators are involved in the overall educational process or if the music therapy instructor is alone in these instances. This area will be addressed later in this chapter, but at issue is the problem that music therapists move into clinical settings where additional education and training is desirable in the mental health sciences.

Unfortunately, graduate training in music therapy is not always the answer for the professional music therapist who finds a need to increase his or her clinical knowledge beyond undergraduate training. Both the NAMT and the AAMT construct their graduate training closely around the criteria set by the National Association of Schools of Music which includes mental health science related courses as areas, along with such academic areas as social or health sciences, research, management, humanities, and creative arts therapies (Scartelli, 1987).

Research Emphasis In Graduate Education

University catalogues from graduate music therapy programmes list specific courses regarding training in music therapy research. Beyond required electives in music and listings for music therapy seminar, graduate students must choose from course offerings outside of their department for education in mental health science topics. Although attempts are made by faculty to design a curriculum based upon the individual needs of the student, the emphasis seems to be focused upon the development of research skills in most of the programmes. In terms of the relevance of graduate training to necessary skills for working music therapists, it appears that guidelines for advanced training in music therapy do not address the issues which music therapists face in their clinical environments. The great majority of music therapists still make their living through clinical and supervisory work. Although some level of skill in research is pertinent to the clinical setting, perhaps the degree of emphasis placed upon research skills in masters degree education should go further in addressing the professional need of the music therapist. Academic emphasis in research areas may integrate into the functional life of the music therapist through the development of research consumer skills. An example of this skill is the ability to evaluate the findings and conclusions of a research article in relation to the methodology and to relate these results to theory and practice. In some settings music therapists may become part of a team research project or may perform their own research. However, academic emphasis in research areas should not outweigh the development of knowledge and skills in clinical areas required to function as an important, contributing member of an interdisciplinary treatment team.

The Role of Internship

Although many music therapy programme directors believe the clinical internship experience is the appropriate forum for the development of specific areas of knowledge (Maranto and Bruscia, 1988), there is no standardised curriculum within the NAMT clinical training guidelines which suggests or guides the process of integrating mental health science concepts with the process of music therapy. The NAMT internship requirements specify that the undergraduate student perform their clinical internship after all academic requirements are completed. In almost all cases this occurs away from the university setting. Although the process through which integration occurs between the internship site and the university is not clearly specified within the current educational guidelines, the NAMT programme directors develop systems which maintain contact with the intern through written assignments sent through the mail and other forms of communication.

The AAMT has attempted to maintain the student's link with the university by requiring the internship to occur during the last academic year locally to the university. Competencies which include some ability in integrating music therapy with mental health sciences are measured. Guidelines for where and how integration is taught are not specifically stated. Many programme directors use the group supervision class for integration.

By understanding mental health science foundations the music therapist finds contexts, in addition to their own subjective understanding, upon which to comprehend and work with clinical phenomena. Although this integration process matures over time, the initial exposure to these concepts should occur within the academic environment where the program director can insure the process through co-ordination with other faculty.

The Function of Mental Health Sciences Integration with Music Therapy Education

Dulicai et al.(1989) have addressed the issue of identification in the integrative education of the creative arts therapist. By stressing the concept of identification with more experienced clinicians during the education process, students begin to link themselves with concepts and areas of knowledge from interdisciplinary sources. This process encourages the seeking out of knowledge and the discovery of mentors throughout the professional life.

Through interaction with faculties of various treatment modalities (psychiatrists, psychologists, other arts therapies, family therapists, etc.), students can begin to 'see themselves as part of a system rather than outside of it' (Dulicai et al., 1989, p.12). Through this process the students understand that their own modality offers a unique perspective and 'will perceive their involvement as primary rather than adjunctive' (p. 13).

Within the United States all but two music therapy degree granting programmes are housed within the school of music and are usually part of a music education programme. Courses in mental health sciences in undergraduate and graduate curricula are taught by another department, usually psychology. In these cases the class material is not necessarily specific to the training of music therapists, or other clinicians. Usually the material is designed to accommodate the wide variety of students enrolled in the course. The instructor is not in a position to address questions concerning the clinical experiences of the music therapy student, thereby the opportunities for the promotion of integrative thinking in the student are missed. In addition to this problem, the instructor's area of expertise may reside outside of clinical areas (e.g. educational psychology, experimental psychology) or, as in undergraduate training, the course may employ a graduate assistant with little or no practical experience. Maranto and Bruscia (1988) report that many of the concepts related to mental health sciences are actually taught by the music therapy faculty. This may reflect the need, as determined by the music therapy educators, to link mental health science concepts with music therapy methods. The question is raised by this author if these educational programmes are suggesting by this practice that guidelines should stress this integration and suggest a means by which it can be accomplished? The issue at hand is not to have structure and course content dictated to the university from without, but to set a standard from which a music therapist may : 1) develop a broad foundation of clinical understanding which will provide the best possible application of treatment to the client; and 2) become encouraged to present findings in a manner which communicates the multi-levelled psychological processes inherent within the music therapy relationship.

The process of integration presented in this chapter relies upon additional faculty in some cases. Current programmes are clearly attempting to integrate the world of developmental and clinical concepts with the student's music therapy understandings.

Instructors are constantly in search of current readings, and in many cases even seek out additional education in areas which enhance their own development as a clinical educator. The need for an additional faculty (if possible from another modality) is based upon the value of offering mentors to students. This encourages the identification and intellectual interaction with experienced clinicians who could represent a future treatment team colleague. With standards set by certifying agencies to encourage this approach to clinical integration, programme directors will have some support with which to make budgetary proposals to university administration.

Integration

The integration of mental health science concepts with music therapy theory and practice occurs through the simultaneous exposure to:

1. music therapy courses (theoretical and clinical)
2. mental health science courses
3. clinical experiences
4. individual supervision (psychiatric and music therapy)
5. music therapy group supervision
6. clinical case presentation experiences

Music therapy courses involving the link of clinical practice with theoretical influences generally include literature written from a particular philosophical orientation. These may include clinical affiliations with known models of therapy such as behaviourism, psychodynamic, gestalt, or eclectic combinations. It is most likely that an instructor would teach from the perspective from which they have had training and clinical experience. With additional chosen part-time faculty on hand the programme director could increase the likelihood that students would become directly introduced to a variety of clinical orientations through which they could integrate mental health concepts with music therapy experiences. Students may become more interested in comparing and contrasting the relevance of psychological theories to their own growing understanding of therapy and to their professional role. Within the course of music therapy training the student develops clinical methods which are based upon their personality and those theoretical orientations which are congruent with their values and beliefs. Ultimately, students should conclude this area of training with the belief that research and clinical findings in music therapy will eventually broaden and enrich existing psychological orientations (Johnson, 1984; Noy, 1967).

When designed specifically for the music therapy student, courses in mental health sciences should contain context-related material and allow the opportunity for the student to make direct links with their own clinical experiences and understandings of music therapy theory. Although the instructor is not actually a music therapist, the course could be designed to allow the opportunity for the student to apply the information verbally or through example. The instructor offers feedback on the application of the class material by determining if the student demonstrates awareness of the mental health science concept and evaluates the overall clinical soundness of the example. Generally, the mental health science instructor does not advise on the musical elements unless they obviously enhance or detract from the class concept, and/or the instructor has an additional professional background as a music therapist. This process is handled by the music therapy faculty within the clinical or supervisory courses. The assurance of integration of mental health science concepts with music therapy principles rests in the careful co-ordination of course content in both areas. The process can be tracked within music therapy group supervision, through student case presentation, by frequent communication with clinical supervisors, and through the student evaluation process. Mental Health Science faculty selection for courses within music therapy education is often limited by the resources of the training environment. If the psychology faculty is unavailable to the music therapy students, the programme relies upon adjunctive or part-time faculty . This option provides the opportunity to select a faculty whose interest and expertise serves a dual function: as instructor who can design course content specifically for clinicians in training; and as an object of identification for the future professional.

Before these issues are addressed further, a profile of the typical mental health sciences course instructor from our graduate programme will partially illustrate the capacities which serve the integration of mental health concepts with music therapy concepts. First, the instructor is well established in clinical knowledge and is clinically active. The emphasis is usually in psychotherapy, developmental therapy, or clinical research. Second, there is a belief in the creative arts therapies as primary treatment modalities. The instructor has usually worked with a creative arts therapist, or knows the process well through indirect routes, such as having had an editorial board position in an arts therapy related journal, if she or he is not a creative arts therapist. Ultimately, the instructor demonstrates a genuine interest in the arts therapies and has a concern in the development of the student's transition from musician to a music therapist. In many cases the mental health science course instructor has experience within one of the arts and finds the connection between the arts and healing to be quite a natural relationship.

In the early stages of integration the music therapy faculty must keep abreast of the course outline within the mental health science courses in order to respond to students' questions on the linkage of theory with practice. This requires that music therapy faculty maintains a working knowledge in current theoretical, clinical, and research areas.

The carry over to music therapy courses allows for the repetition of concepts which are usually new and complex to music therapy students. Abstract ideas take on musical form and are guided into an approach which is potentially applicable to the fieldwork/practicum or internship experience of the student.

Within the professional world the music therapist then presents an understanding of music therapy within a biopsychosocial framework. The result of this integration affects the client, the treatment team, and the professional self concept of the music therapist.

Conclusion

Our profession has experienced tremendous growth over the past decades partly due to developments in: 1) knowledge of the effect of music upon behaviour; 2) the refinement of methods for music therapy interventions within an increasing array of physical and mental health applications; and 3) an increased self assessment of our role and function within health care and special education. With the expanded methodology and technology available to music therapists, we are capable of activating emotional, cognitive, and neurological responses at a level, or of a quality, currently unreachable through more traditional therapeutic approaches.

The next developmental milestone for the profession is to secure and expand the foundations of music therapy within the rapidly growing mainstream of health care. We must identify, as a profession, additional methods of integration to understand and communicate further the processes and results of our work. It is upon us, from within the profession, to demonstrate to our clinical and educational colleagues the vitality of our findings as a mental and physical necessity within health care. This process must begin within the educational institution.

The education and training methods to date have provided the profession with the nourishment and fortification necessary to develop music therapy from a collective idea in the late 1940s to a large organised profession which has served many thousands of patients and clients. As the contemporary practice of music therapy approaches its fiftieth anniversary, at the end of this century, we hold the option of contributing toward the future development of psychological theory and the direction of health care.

References

American Psychiatric Association (1987). *Diagnostic and Statistical Manual of Mental Disorders - Revised edition.*

Abrams, R. & Taylor, M. A. (1981). Cognitive dysfunction in schizophrenia, affective disorder and organic brain disease. *British Journal of Psychiatry, 139*, 190-194.

Achterberg, J. (1985). *Imagery in Healing: Shamanism in Modern Medicine.* Boston: New Science Library.

Adams, M. (1987). Measurement problems in applied music therapy research. *British Journal of Music Therapy, 1,* 6-10.

Adorno, T. W. (1981). *Einleitung in die Musiksoziologie.* Frankfurt-am - Main: Suhrkamp.

Aldridge, D. (1989). A Phenomenological Comparison of the Organisation of Music and the Self. *The Arts in Psychotherapy, 16,* 91-97.

Allen, D. (1975). Music therapy with geriatric patients. *British Journal of Music Therapy, 8,* 2-6.

Allensbach, D. (1980). Institut fur Demoskopie. *Die Deutschen und die Musik.*

Altshuler, I. M. (1948). *A psychiatrist's experience with music as a therapeutic agent.* New York:

Alvin, J. (1975). *Music Therapy (Revised edition).* London:

Alvin, J. (1976). *Music for the Handicapped Child (second edition).* Oxford University Press.

Alvin, J. (1978). *Music Therapy for the Autistic Child (2nd edition).* Oxford University Press.

Alvin, J. (1978). Principles of music therapy. *Physiotherapy, 64,* 77-79.

Alvin, J. & Bryce, J. (1978). Physiotherapy and music therapy for physical handicap. *British Society for Music Therapy.*

Alzheimer, A. (1907). Uber eine eigenartige Erkrangkung der Hirnrinde. *Acta Psychiatr., 64,* 146-148.

Amir, D. & Schuchman, G. (1985). Auditory training through music with hearing impaired pre-school children. *Volta Review, 87,* 333-343.

Ammon, K. (1968). The effects of music on children in respiratory distress. *American Nurses Association Clinical Session,* 127-133.

Arie, T. & Jolley, D. (1982). *Making services work. In the Psychiatry of Late Life.* Oxford: Blackwell Scientific Publications.

Assagioli, R. (1969). Symbols of Transpersonal Experiences. *Journal of Transpersonal Psychology, 1,* 3-16.

Assagiolo, R. (1965). *Psychosynthesis.* New York: Viking Press.

Atkinson, R. C. and Shiffrin, R.M. (1971). 'The control of short-term memory'. *Scientific American, 225,* 82-90.

Baacke, D. (1985). An den Zauber glauben, der die Freiheit bringt. Bastian, HG (Hrsg) Musikpadogogische, Forschung. Arie, T. & Jolley, D. (1982). Making services work, organisation and style of psychogeriatric service. In The Psychiatry of Late Life (1982) Ed. Levy, R & Post, F, Oxford, Blackwell.

Baddeley, A. D. (1983). Working Memory. *Philosophical Transactions of the Royal Society B, 302*, 311-324.

Baddeley, A. D. (1984). The fractionisation of human memory. *Psychological Medicine, 14*, 259-264.

Baddeley, A. D. & Hitch, G. (1974). *Working Memory.* New York: Academic Press.

Baddley, A. D. Thomson, N. & Buchanan, M. (1975). Word length and the structure of short-term memory. *Verbal Learning and Verbal Behavior, 14*, 575-589.

Baddley, A. D. & Warrington, E. K. (1970). Amnesia and the distinction between long- and short-term memory. *Verbal Learning and Verbal Behavior, 9*, 176-189.

Bailey, L. M. (1983). The effects of live music versus tape-recorded music on hospitalised cancer patients. *Music Therapy, 3*, 17-28.

Bailey, P. (1974). *They can make music.* Oxford: Oxford University Press.

Baird, S. (1979). A technique to assess the preference for intensity of musical stimuli in young hard-of-hearing children. *Music Therapy, 6*, 6-11.

Bakeman, R. (1978). *Untangling streams of behaviour: Sequential analyses of observational data.* Baltimore: University Park Press.

Bang, C. (1977). *A Music Event.* Hicksville, NY: M Hohner, Inc.

Bannister, D. & Higginbottom, P. (1985). *G.A.B. Grid Analysis for Beginners.* Department of Psychology, Leeds University.

Barger, D. A. (1979). The effects of music and verbal suggestion on heart rate and self-reports. *Music Therapy, 16*, 158-171.

Barman, I. W. (1981). Musical functioning, speech lateralisation and the amusias. *South African Medical, 59*, 78-81.

Bason, P. T. & Celler, B. G. (1972). Control of the heart rate by external stimuli. *Nature, 238*, 279-280.

Bauman, K. (1987). *Music and Memories.* In St Louis: MMB, Inc.

Beatty, W. W. Zavadil, K. D, Bailly, R. C. Rixen, G. J. Zavadil, L. W. Farnham, N., & Fisher, L. (1988). Preserved musical skill in a severely demented patient. *International Journal of Clinical Neuropsychology, 10(4)*, 158-164.

Beaumont, J. G. & Dimond, S. J. (1973). Brain disconnection and schizophrenia. *British Journal of Psychology, 123*, 661-662.

Beebe, B. Feldstein, S. Jaffe, J. Mays, K. & Alson, D. (1985). *Interpersonal Timing: The Application of an Adult Dialogue Model to Mother-Infant Vocal and Kinetic Interactions.* In T. M. Field and N. Fox (Eds) *Social Perception in Infants.* Norwood, NJ: Ablex.

Behne, K. E. (1986). *Die Benutzung von Musik.* Wilhelmshaven: Florian Noetzel Verlag.

Behne, K. E. (1986). *Horertypologien, Zur Typologie jugend lichen Musikgeschmacks.* Regensburg: Gustav Bosse Verlag.

Behrens, G. A. (1982) *The use of music activities to improve the capacity, inhalation, and exhalation capabilities of handicapped children's respiration.* Unpublished master's thesis, Kent State University.

Benenzon, R. O. (1981). *Music Therapy Manual.* Illinois: Charles C. Thomas.

Bentley, A. (1966). *Musical ability in children and its measurement.* London: Harrap.

Bever, T. G. & Chiarello, R. J. (1974). Cerebral dominance in musicians and non-musicians. *Science, 185,* 137-139.

Bick, E. (1964). Notes on Infant Observation in Psychoanalytic Training. *International Journal of Psychoanalysis, 45,* 558-66.

Bicknell, J. (1983). The psychopathology of handicap. *British Journal of Medical Psychology, 56,* 167-178.

Bion, W. (1957). The differentiation of the psychotic from the non-psychotic part of the personality. *International. Journal of Psychoanalysis, 38.*

Bion, W. (1962). *Learning from experience.* London: Heinemann.

Birkenshaw-Fleming, L. (1990). Music can make a difference. In A. A. Darrow (ed.), *Second National Conference on Music and the Hearing Impaired .* Gallaudet University, The University of Kansas: Lawrence, K.S..

Bitcon, C. (1977). *Alike and Different.* Santa Ana: Rosha Press.

Bob, S. R. (1962). Audioanalgesia in paediatric practice, a preliminary study. *Journal of American Podiatry Association, 52,* 503-504.

Bollas, C. (1986). *The Transformational Object.* London: Free Association Books.

Bonny, E. (1988). *Clinical Treatment of Adult Children of Alcoholics with Guided Imagery and Music.* Salina, KS: Bonny Foundation.

Bonny, H. (1975). Music and Consciousness. *Music Therapy, 12,* 121-135.

Bonny, H. & Tansill, R. (1977). Music Therapy: A Legal High. In Waldorf, G. (Ed). *Counseling Therapies and the Addictive Client.* Baltimore, MD: School of Social Eork and Community Planning.

Bonny, H. (1978). *Facilitating GIM Sessions.* Salina, KS: Bonny Foundation.

Bonny, H. (1978). *The Role of Taped Music Programs in the GIM Process.* Salina, KS: Bonny Foundation.

Bonny, H. (1980). *GIM Therapy, Past, Present and Future Implications.* Salina, KS: Bonny Foundation.

Bonny, H. L. (1983). Music listening for intensive coronary care units: A pilot project. *Music Therapy,* 4-16.

Borchgrevinck, H. M. (1980). *Cerebral lateralisation of speech and singing after intracarotoid amytal injection.* Stockholm: Almquist Wicksell.

Borchgrevinck, H. M. (1982). *Music, Mind and the Brain: The Neuropsychology of Music.* New York and London: Plenum Press.

Boston, M. (1975). Recent research in developmental psychology. *Journal of Child Psychotherapy, 4,* 15-34.

Boxhill, E. H. (1985). *Music Therapy for the Developmentally Disabled.* Rockville, Maryland: Aspen Publications.

Bright, R. (1972). *Music in Geriatric Care.* Lynbrook, New York: Musicgraphics.

Bright, R. (1981). *Practical planning in music therapy for the aged*. Lynbrook, New York: Musicgraphics.

Bright, R. (1986). *Grieving*. St Louis: MMB Publications.

Brocklehurst, J. C. (1977). *Geriatric Care in Advanced Societies*, MTP, Lancaster.

Broner, A. (1978). *The Effects of Low Frequency Noise on People*.

Brook, E. (1984) *Soothing music during the active phase of labor: Physiologic effect on mother and infant*. Unpublished master's thesis, University of Florida.

Brook, P. Degun, G. & Mather, M. (1975). Reality Orientation, a therapy for psychogeriatric patients: A controlled study. *British Journal of Psychiatry, 127*, 42-45.

Brown, F. M. & Graeber, R. C. (1982). *Rhythmic aspects of behavior*.

Brown, J. J. & Avstreith, Z. A. K. (1989). On Synchrony. *The Arts in Psychotherapy, 16*, 157-162.

Bruch, H. (1978). *The Golden Cage: The Enigma of Anorexia Nervosa*. London: Open Books.

Bruscia, K. (1986). Advanced competencies in music therapy. *Music Therapy, 6A*, 57-67.

Bruscia, K. (1987). *Improvisational Models of Music Therapy*. Springfield, Maryland: Charles C. Thomas.

Bruscia, K. E. (1989). *Defining Music Therapy*. Pennsylvania: Spring House Books.

Bryant, W. (1987). *Occupational therapy with E,M,I, people at Fulbourn Hospital*.

Buchsbaum, M. (1977). Psychophysiology and schizophrenia. *Schizophrenia Bulletin, 3*, 7-14.

Buck, R. (1984). *The Communication of Emotion*. New York: Guilford Press.

Budzynski, T. Stoyva, J. & Adler, C. (1970). Feedback-induced muscle relaxation: Application to tension headache. *Behavior Therapy and Experimental Psychiatry, 1*, 205-211.

Buechler, J. (1982). *Music for handicapped children: Hearing impaired*. Washington. D/C: National Association for Music Therapy.

Bunt, L. (1985) *Music therapy and the child with a handicap: evaluation of the effects of intervention*. PhD, City University, Department of Music.

Bunt, L. & Hoskyns, S. (1987). A perspective on music therapy research in Great Britain. *British Journal of Music Therapy, 1*, 3-6.

Bunt, L. Pike, D. & Wren, V. (1987). Music therapy in a General Hospital's Psychiatric Unit - a pilot evaluation of an eight week programme. *British Journal of Music Therapy, 1*, 22-27.

Burt, R. K. & Korn, G. W. (1964). Audioanalgesia in obstetrics: White noise analgesia during labor. *American Journal of Obstetrics & Gynecology, 88*, 361-366.

Byrne, M. T. (1971). On a geriatric ward. *British Journal of Music Therapy, 2*, 5-7.

Caine, J. (1989) *The effects of music on the selected stress behaviors, weight, caloric and formula intake, and length of hospital stay of premature and low birth weight neonates in a newborn intensive care unit.* Unpublished master's thesis, The Florida State University, Tallahassee, Florida.

Cameron, N. (1944). *Experimental Analysis of Schizophrenic Thinking.* In J. S. Kasanin (Ed) *Language and Thought in Schizophrenia.* Berkeley and Los Angeles: University of California Press.

Carr, E. G. (1977). The motivation of self-injurious behaviour: A review of some hypotheses. *Psychological Bulletin, 84*, 800-816.

Carr, E. G. & Durand, V. M. (1985). *The social-communicative basis of severe behaviour problems in children.* New York: Academic Press.

Cassity, M. D. (1976). The influence of a music therapy activity upon peer acceptance, group cohesiveness and interpersonal relationships of adult psychiatric patients. *Music Therapy, 13*, 66-75.

Chalmers, I. Enkin, M. & Keirse, M. (1989). *Effective care in pregnancy and childbirth*

Chapman, J. S. (1975). *The relation between auditory stimulation of short gestation infants and their gross motor limb activity.*

Chesney, J. (1987). Is psychotherapy research possible? In *Starting Research in Music Therapy, Proceedings of the Third Music Therapy Day Conference.* The City University, London.

Chetta, H. D. (1981). The effect of music and desensitization on pre-operative anxiety in children. *Journal of Music Therapy., 18*, 74-87.

Clair, A. A. & Bernstein, B. (1990). A comparison of singing, vibrotactile and nonvibrotactile instrumental playing responses in severely regressed persons with dementia of the Alzheimer's type. *Journal of Music Therapy, 27*, 119-125.

Clair, A. A. & Bernstein, B. (1990). A preliminary study of music therapy programming for severely regressed persons with Alzheimer's type dementia. *Journal of Applied Gerontology, 9*, 299-311.

Clark, D. H. (1981). *Social Therapy in Psychiatry.* Edinburgh: Churchill-Livingston.

Clark, M. E. McCorkle, R. R. & Williams, S. B. (1981). Music therapy-assisted labor and delivery. *Journal of Music Therapy, 18*, 88-109.

Codding, P. A. (1982) *An exploration of the uses of music in the birthing process.* Unpublished master's thesis, The Florida State University, Tallahassee, Florida.

Cofranesco, E. M. (1985). The effect of music therapy on hand grasp strength and functional task performance in stroke patients. *Journal of Music Therapy, 22*, 125-149.

Condon, W. S. & Ogston, W. D. (1966). Sound Film Analysis of Normal and Pathological Behavior Patterns. *Nervous and Mental Diseases, 143*, 338-347.

Connolly, J. F. Gruzelier, J. H. Kleinman, K. M. & Hirsch, S. R. (1979). Lateralised abnormalities in schizophrenic, depressed and non-psychotic patients in hemispheric specific tachistoscopic tasks. In H. J Gruzelier & F.H.P (eds), *Hemisphere Asymmetries of Function in Psychopathology.* Amsterdam: Elsevier/North Holland Biomedical Press. pp. 647-672.

Conrad, R. & Hull, A. J. (1964). Information, acoustic confusion and memory span. *British Journal of Psychology, 55,* 429-432.

Cook, R. B. (1973). Left-right differences in the perception of dichotically presented musical stimuli. *Music Therapy, 10,* 59-63.

Coons, D. H. & Weaverdyck, S. E. (1986). A residential unit for persons with Alzheimer's disease and related disorders. *Physical and Occupational Therapy in Geriatrics, 4,* 29-53.

Cooper, G. W. & Meyer, L.B. (1960). *The Rhythmic Structure of Music.* Chicago: The University of Chicago Press.

Corah, N. Gale, E. Pace, L. & Seyrek, S. (1981). Relaxation and musical programming as means of reducing psychological stress during dental procedures. *Journal of British the American Dental Association, 103,* 232-234.

Cosgriff, V. (1986). Music and Parkinsonism. *British Journal of Music Therapy, 17,* 13-18.

Coutts, C. A. (1965). Effects of music on pulse rates and work output of short duration. *Research Quarterly, 36,* 17-21.

Crago, B. (1980). *Reducing the stress of hospitalization for open heart surgery.*

Cummings, E. & Henry, W. (1961). *Growing Old: The process of disengagement.* New York: Basic Books.

Cummings, S. T., Bayley, H. C., & Rie, H. E. (1976). Effects of the child's deficiency on the mother: A study of mothers of mentally retarded and chronically ill children. *American Journal of Orthopsychiatry, 46,* 246-255.

Curtis, S. L. (1986). The effect of music on pain relief and relaxation of the terminally ill. *Journal of Music Therapy, 23,* 10-24.

Dainow, E. (1977). Physical effects and motor responses to music. *Research in Music Education, 25,* 211-221.

Dalgarno, G. (1990). A computer-based music system for the hearing impaired. In A. A. Darrow (Ed). *Proceedings from the Second National Conference on Music and the Hearing Impaired at Gallaudet University* (pp. 31-42). Lawrence, KS: The University of Kansas.

Dalgarno, G. (1990). Technology to obtain the best music sound for hearing impaired listeners. In A. A. Darrow (Ed). *Proceedings from the Second National Conference on Music and the Hearing Impaired at Gallaudet University* pp. 45-59. Lawrence, KS: The University of Kansas.

Damasio, A. R. & Damasio, H. (1977). *Music faculty and cerebral dominance.* London: W Heinemann.

Darrow, A. A. (1979). The beat reproduction response of subjects with normal and impaired hearing: An empirical comparison. *Journal of Music Therapy, 16,* 6-11.

Darrow, A. A. (1984). A comparison of the rhythmic responsiveness in normal hearing and hearing impaired children and an investigation of the relationship of the rhythmic responsiveness to the suprasegmental aspects of speech perception. *Journal of Music Therapy, 21,* 48-66.

Darrow, A.A. (1985). Music for the deaf. *Music Educators Journal,* 71(6), 33-35.

Darrow, A.A. (1987). An investigative study: The effect of hearing impairment on the music aptitude of young children. *Journal of Music Therapy, 24,* 88-96.

Darrow, A.A. (1987). *A comparison of vocal ranges of hearing impaired and normal hearing children.* Unpublished manuscript, The University of Kansas, Lawrence.

Darrow, A. A. (1989). Music therapy in the treatment of the hearing impaired. *Music Therapy Perspectives,* 6, 61-70.

Darrow, A. A. (1990). *Development of rhythmic concepts and skills.* The University of Kansas. Lawrence, KS:

Darrow, A. A. (1990). The effect of frequency adjustment on the vocal reproduction accuracy of hearing impaired singers. *Journal of Music Therapy, 27,* 24-33.

Darrow, A. A. (1990). *Proceedings from the Second National Conference on Music and the Hearing Impaired at Gallaudet University.* Lawrence, KS: The University of Kansas.

Darrow, A. A. (1990). The role of hearing in understanding music. *Music Educators Journal, 77(4). 24-27.*

Darrow, A. A. & Bolton, B. (1988). A comparison of rhythmic performances by hearing and mainstreamed hearing impaired children. In *Music Educators National Conference,* Indianpolis, Indiana.

Darrow, A. A. & Cohen, N. (in press). The effect of programmed pitch practice and private instruction on the vocal reproduction accuracy of hearing impaired children: Two case studies.

Darrow, A. A. & Gfeller, K. (1987). Verbal identification of music concepts by hearing impaired children. In *National Association for Music Therapy Annual Conference.* San Francisco, California.

Darrow, A. A. & Gfeller, K. (1988). Music therapy with hearing impaired children. In C. Furman A, (eds). *Effectiveness of Music Therapy Procedures: Documentation of Research and Clinical Practice.* Washington, D, C. NAMT. pp. 137-174.

Darrow, A. A. & Gfeller, K. A study of public school music programs mainstreaming hearing impaired students. *Music Therapy.* In Press.

Darrow, A. A. & Goll, H. (1989). The effect of vibrotactile stimuli via the SOMOTRON on the recognition of rhythmic concepts by hearing impaired children. *Music Therapy, 26,* 115-124.

Darrow, A. A. & Heller, G. N. (1985). William Wolcott Turner and David Ely Bartlett: Early advocates of music education for the hearing impaired. *Research in Music Education, 33,* 269-279.

Darrow, A. A. & Starmer, G. J. (1986). The effect of vocal training on the intonation and rate of hearing impaired children's speech: A pilot study. *Music Therapy, 23,* 194-201.

Davies, A. & Snaith, P. (1980). The social behaviour of geriatric patients at mealtimes: An observational and an intervention study. *Age and Ageing, 9,* 93-99.

Davis, J. M. & Hardick, E. J. (1981). *Auditory training.* New York: Holt, Rinehart, & Winston.

Davis, J. M. & Hardick, E. J. (1981). *Rehabilitation audiology for children and adults.* New York: John Wiley & Sons.

Davis, W. B. & Thaut, M. H. (1989). The influence of preferred relaxing music on measures of state anxiety, relaxation, and physiological responses. *Music Therapy, 26,* 168-187.

Dawes, S. A. (1987). The role of music therapy in caring in Huntingdon's Disease. *British Music Therapy, 18,* 2-9.

De Mare, P., & Kreeger, L. (1974). *Introduction to group treatment in Psychiatry.* London: Butterworth.

deBoer, E. (1976). *On the "residue" and auditory pitch perception.* Berlin: Springer-Verlag.

DeJong, M. A. van Mourik, K. R. & Schellekens, H. M. (1973). A physiological approach to aesthetic preference-music. *Psychotherapy and Psychosomatics, 22,* 46-51.

Demeskopie, A. (1980). Die Deutschen und die Musik.

Dennett, D. (1978). *Brainstorms Philosophical Essays on Mind and Psychology.* Montgomery: Bedford Books.

Desoille, R. (1968). *The Directed Daydream.* New York: Psychosynthesis Research Foundation.

Deutsch, D. (1970). Memory and attention in music. *In "Music and the Brain".* London: R. A. Heinemann.

Deutsch, D. (1970). Tones and numbers: Specificity of interference in short-term memory. *Science, 168,* 1604-1605.

Deutsch, D. (1972). Mapping of interactions in the pitch memory store. *Science, 175,* 1020-1022.

Deutsch, D. (1982). *Grouping Mechanisms in Music.* In D Deutsch (Ed). *The Psychology of Music.* New York: Academic Press.

Deutsch, D. & Fereo, J. (1981). The internal representation of pitch sequences in tonal music. *Psychological Review, 88,* 503-522.

Dickens, G. & Sharpe, M. (1970). Music therapy in the setting up of a psychotherapeutic centre. *British Journal of Medical Psychology, 43,* 83-89.

Dietsche, L. & Pollman, J. (1982). Alzheimer's disease: Advances in clinical nursing. *Journal of Gerontological Nursing, 8,* 97-100.

Dorow, L. G. (1975). Conditioning music and approval as new reinforcers for imitative behaviour with the severly retarded. *Music Therapy, 12,* 30-40.

Douglass, D. (1989). *Accent on rhythm - Music activities for the aged* (3rd edition revised edition: St Louis: MMB Music, Inc.

Dowling, W. J. (1978). Scale and Contour: Two components of a theory for melodies. *Psychological Review, 85,* 341-354.

Dowling, W. J. & Fujitani, D. S. (1971). Contour, interval, and pitch recognition in meory for melodies. *Journal of the Acoustical Society of America, 49*, 524-531.

Dowling, W. J. & Harwood, D. L. (1986). *Music Cognition*. Orlando, Florida: Academic Press.

Dulicai, D. Hays, R. Nolan, P. (1989). Training the creative arts therapist: identity with integration. *The Arts In Psychotherapy, 16*, 11-14.

Edgington, E. S. (1980). *Randomisation Tests*. New York: Marcel Dekker.

Edwards, E. (1974). *Music education for the deaf.* South Waterford, Maine: The Merriam Eddy Co.

Egan, B. (1976). *Interpersonal Living*. Brooks/Cole, Monterey. CA, USA.

Eisner, B. & Cohen, S. (1959). Use of Lysergic Acid and Diethylamide in a Psychotherapeutic Setting. *American Medical Association Archives of Neurological Psychiatry, 81, 615-619.*

Ellis, A. & Harper, R. A. (1975). *A New Guide to Rational Living*. New Jersey: Englewood Cliffs.

Ellis, D. S., & Brighouse, G. (1952). Effects of music on respiration and heart rate. *American Journal of Psychology, 65*, 39-47.

Epstein, L. Hersen, M. & Hemphill, D. (1974). Music feedback in the treatment of tension headache: An experimental case study. *Journal of Behavior Therapy and Experimental Psychiatry, 5*, 59-63.

Erber, N. P. & Hirsh, I.J. (1978). Auditory training. In H David and S R Silverman (Eds). *Hearing and deafness.* New York, NY: Holt, Rinehart & Winston.

Fahey, J. & Birkenshaw, L. (1972). Bypassing the ear: The perception of music by feeling and touch. *Music Educators, 58*, 44-49.

Farrell, D. (1984). Musical therapy case studies of patients in a regional medical center.

Feder, E. & Feder, B. (1981). *The Expressive Arts Therapies*. New Jersey: Prentice-Hall Inc.

Felce, D. & Jenkins, J. (1979). Engagement in activities by old people in residential care. *Health and Social Services, 2*, 23-28.

Feldstein, S. & Welkowitz, J. (1978). A chronography of conversation: in defense of an objective approach. In A. W. Feldstein (Eds) *Nonverbal Behavior and Communication*. Hillsdale, N.J. Erlbaum.

Finnie, N. R. (1974). *Handling the young cerebral-palsied child at home*. London: Heinemann.

Fisher, J. Baker, B. & Darrow, A. A. (1989). The effect of two selected variables on the tonal perception of hearing impaired children. In *National Association for Music Therapy*, Kansas City, Missouri:

Fitszimmons, M. (1987). Drama therapy with E,M,I, people at Fulbourn Hospital.

Fleiss, J. L. (1975). Measuring agreement between two judges on the presence or absence of a trait. *Biometrics, 31*, 651-659.

Flor-Henry, P. (1969). Psychoses and temporal lobe epilepsy; a controlled investigation. *Epiliepsia, 10,* 363-395.

Flor-Henry, P. and Yeudall, L. T. (1979). Neuropsychological investigation of schizophrenia and manic-depressive psychoses. In: J. Gruzelier and P. Flor-Henry, eds. *Hemisphere Asymmetires of Function in Psychopathology.* Amsterdam: Elsevier/North Holland pp. 341-362.

Flor-Henry, P. & Koles, Z. J. (1980). Studies in right/left hemispheric energy oscillations in schizophrenia, mania, depression and normals. *Psychopharmacology Bulletin, 16,* 52-53.

Flor-Henry, P. & Yeudall, L. T. (1979). Neuropsychological investigation of schizophrenia and manic-depressive psychoses. In G. J. & F.H. (eds), *Hemisphere Asymmetries of function in Psychopathology.* Amsterdam: Elsevier/North Holland. pp. 341-362.

Ford, T. A. (1985) *The effect of musical experiences and age on the ability of deaf children to discriminate pitch of complex tones.* Unpublished doctoral dissertation, North Carolina, Greensboro.

Ford, T.A. (1990). Development of rhythmic concepts and skills. In A. A. Darrow (Ed), *Proceedings from the Second National Conference on Music and the Hearing Impaired at Gallaudet University,* (pp 21-30). Lawrence, KS: The University of Kansas.

Ford, T.A. & Shroyer, E.H. (1987). Survey of music teachers in residential and day programs for hearing impaired students. *Journal of the International Association of Music for the Handicapped, 3,* 16-25.

Formann-Radl, I. (1980). Musiktherapie im Rahmen eines verhaltenstherapeutischen Gesamttherapiekonzeptes. *Zeitschrift psychosomatische Medizin, 26,* 282-295.

Forster, A. & Palastange, N. (1985). Clayton's Electrotherapy Theory and Practice. In A. Forster & N. Palastange (eds), London: Balliere Tindall: pp. 165-180.

Fraisse, P. (1963). *The Psychology of Time.* New York: Harper and Row.

Frank, J. (1985). The effects of music therapy and guided visual imagery on chemotherapy induced nausea and vomiting. *Oncology Nursing Forum, 12(5),* 47-52.

Freedman, A. M. Caplan, H. I. & Sadock, B. J. (1976). *Modern Synopsis of Psychiatry/II.* Baltimore: Williams and Wilkins.

Freud, S. (1921). *Beyond the pleasure principle, group psychology and other works of the Standard Edition of the Complete Works of Sigmund Freud.* London: Hogarth Press. 1-64.

Froelich, M. (1984). A comparison of the effect of music therapy and medical play therapy on the verbalization behavior of paediatric patients. *Journal of Music Therapy., 21,* 2-15.

Furst, P. (1977). The Roots and Continuities of Shamanism. In A Brodzdky, R. Daneswich, and N. Johnson (eds). *Stones, Bones and Skin: Ritual and*

Shamanic Art. Toronto, Canada: Rome Artscanaca Society for Art Publications.

Galev, A. & Monk, A. F. (1982). Verbal memory tasks showing no deficit in schizophrenia - fact or artefact? *British Journal of Psychiatry, 141,* 437-548.

Galloway, H. F. & Bean, M.F. (1974). The effects of action songs on the development of body-image and body-part identification in hearing impaired pre-school children. *Journal of Music Therapy, 11,* 125-134.

Gardner, H. (1981). Do babies sing a universal song? *Psychology Today, 14,* 18-27.

Gardner, W. J. & Licklider, J. C. (1959). Auditory analgesia in dental operation. *Journal of American Dental Association, 59,* 1144-1150.

Gaston, E. T. (1968). *Music in Therapy.* New York: Macmillan.

Gaston, E. T. (1951). Dynamic music factors in mood change. *Music Educators, 37,* 42-44.

Gembris, H. (1981). Teilprobleme der Forschung und Praxis in der rezeptiven Musiktherapie. *Musiktherapeutische Umschau, 2,* 93-105.

Gembris, H. (1989). Zum Verhaltnis Musiktherapie-Musikpsychologie. *Musiktherapeutische Umschau, 10,* 4-16.

Gengel (1969). Practice effects in frequency discrimination by hearing impaired children. *Journal of Speech and Hearing Research, 12,* 847-855.

Getsie, R. Langer, P. & Glass, G. (1985). Meta-analysis of the effects of type and combination of feedback on children's discrimination learning. *Review of Educational Research, 55,* 9-22.

Geula, M. S. (1986). Activities for AD: Music encourages self-expression. *Alzheimer's Disease and Related Disorders Newsletter, 6,* (2), 7.

Gfeller, K. (1986). Music as a remedial tool for improving speech rhythm in the hearing impaired: Clinical and research considerations. *Music Education for the Handicapped Bulletin, 2,* 3-19.

Gfeller, K. (1988). *A comparison of hearing aids and tactile aids in facilitating accuracy of profoundly deaf children on rhythm subtest of the PMMA.* Paper presented at the Music Educators National Conference, Indianapolis, Indiana.

Gfeller, K. E. (1990). Music as communication. In R. F. Unker (ed). *Music therapy in the treatment of adults with mental disorders: theoretical bases and clinical intervention* (pp. 50-62). New York: Schirmer Books.

Gfeller, K. & Baumann, A. (1988). Assessment procedures for music therapy with hearing impaired children: Language development. *Journal of Music Therapy, 25,* 192-205.

Gfeller, K., Darrow, A.A. & Hedden, S. (1990). The perceived effectiveness of mainstreaming Kansas and Iowa schools. *Journal of Research in Music Education, 38,* 90-101.

Gfeller, K. & Darrow, A. A. (1987). Music as a remedial tool in the language education of hearing impaired children. *The Arts in Psychotherapy, 14,* 229-235.

Gfeller, K. & Lansing, C.R. (in press). Melodic, rhythmic, and timbral perception of adult cochlear implant users. *Journal of Speech and Hearing Disorders.*

Gfeller, K. Logan, H. & Walker, J. (1988). The effect of auditory distraction and suggestion on tolerance for dental restorations in adolescents and young adults. *Journal of Music Therapy, 27,* 13-23.

Gibbons, A. C. (1977). Popular music preferences of elderly people. Journal of *Music Therapy 14,* 180-189.

Gibbons, A. C. (1987). Music therapy with the elderly: Research review and practice implications. In *Annual meeting of the National Association for Music Therapy,* San Francisco, CA.

Gibbons, A. C. (1988). A review of literature for music development/education and music therapy with the elderly. *Music Therapy Perspectives, 5,* 33-40.

Gilbert, J. P. (1977). Music therapy perspectives on death and dying. *Journal of Music Therapy, 14,* 165-177.

Gilliland, A. R. & Moore, H. T. (1924). Immediate and long-time effects of classical and popular phonograph selections. *Applied Psychology, 8,* 309-323.

Glass, G. McGaw, B. & Smith, M. (1984). *Meta-analysis in Social Research.* Beverly Hills, CA. Sage Publications.

Glider, J. S. (1987). Trainee distress and burn-out: threats for music therapists? In C.D. Maranto & K. Bruscia (eds). *Perspectives on Music Therapy Education and Training* (pp. 195-207). Philadelphia: Temple University, Ester Boyer College of Music.

Godfrey, K. E. (1967). Metamorphosis of an LSD Therapist. In Abramson, H.A. (ed.). *The Use of LSD in Psychotherapy and Alcoholism.* Indianapolis, Indiana: Bobbs, Merrill.

Godlove, C. Dunn, G. & Wright, W. (1980). Caring for Old People in New York and London; the 'nurses' aide interviews. *Psychological Society of Medicine, 73,* 713-723.

Goldberg, F. S. (1983). *Music Psychotherapy.* Paper presented at the annual conference of the National Association for Music Therapy, New Orleans.

Goldberg, F.S. (1989). *Music psychotherapy in acute psychiatric inpatient and private practice settings.* Music Therapy Perspectives, *6, 40-43.*

Goldberg, F. S. Hoss, T. & Chesna, T. (1988). Music and Imagery As Psychotherapy With a Brain Damaged Patient: A Case Study. *Music Therapy Perspectives, 5, 41-45.*

Goldstein, A. (1980). Thrills in response to music and other stimuli. *Physiological Psychology, 8,* 126-129.

Goldstein, J. L. (1973). An optimim processor theory for the central formation of the pitch of complex tones. *Journal of the Acoustical Society of America, 54,* 1496-1516.

Goloff, M. S. (1981). The responses of hospitalized medical patients to music therapy. *Music Therapy, 1(1),* 51-56.

Goodman, K. D.(1981). Music Therapy. In A., Brodie (ed) *American Handbook of Psychiatry 2nd edition Vol. 7, 565-583.*

Gordon, H. W. & Bogen, J. E. (1974). Hemispheric lateralisation of singing after intracarotid sodium amylobarbitone. *Nuerology, Neurosurgery and Psychiatry, 37*, 727-738.

Gosling, P. (1980). Mourners without a death. *British Journal of Psychiatry, 137*, 397-398.

Gottsman, L. & Brody, E. (1975). *Psycho-social intervention programs within the institutional setting. In Long-Term Care: a Handbook for researchers, planners and providers.* New York: Spectrum.

Graeber, R. C. (1982). *Alterations in performance following rapid transmeridian flight.* Hillsdale, NJ: Lawrence Erlbaum Associates.

Grant, R. (1979). *Sing Along Senior Citizens.* St Louis: MMB Music, Inc.

Grant, R. (1989). Music therapy guidelines for developmentally disabled children. *Music Therapy Perspectives, 6*, 18-22.

Gray-Thompson H, (1985). *The use of picture song books on the vocabularly development of hearing impaired children.* Unpublished masters thesis. The University of Kansas, Lawrence.

Greenbaum, D. (1970). Music program at Kingsbridge Veterans Hospital. *British Journal of Music Therapy, 1*(4), 3-8.

Griffin, J. C. Williams, D. E. Stark, M. I. Altmeyer, B. K. & Mason, M. (1986). Self-injurious behaviour: A statewide prevalence survey of extent and circumstances. *Applied Research in Mental Retardation, 1*, 105-116.

Group, H. & Wigram, A. (1985). *Music Therapy - Applications in Mental Handicap: The Contribution of a Music Therapy Service in hospitals and to the transfer process of residents from long stay institutions to community placements.* Cambridge: A.P.M.T.

Grunefield, F. (1974). *Peter Ilyich Tchaikovsky.* Alexandria, Virginia: Time-Life Records.

Grundy, A. (1989) *The effects of music and the Somatron on the physiological and speech responses of head injured and comatose subjects.* Unpublished master's thesis, The Florida State University, Tallahassee, Florida.

Gruzelier, J. (1979). *Lateral asymmetries in electrodermal activity and psychosis.* Amsterdam: Elsevier/North Holland.

Gruzelier, J. (1981). Cerebral laterality and psychopathology: fact and fiction. *Psychological Medicine, 11*, 219-227.

Gruzelier, J. & Hammond, N. (1979). *Lateralised auditory processing in medicated and unmedicated schizophrenic patients.* Amsterdam: Elsevier/North Holland.

Gruzelier, J. & Venebles, P. H. (1974). Bimodality and lateral asymmetry of skin conductance orienting activity in schizophrenics: replication and evidence of lateral asymmetry in patients with depression and disorders of personality. *Biological Psychiatry, 8*, 55-73.

Gruzelier, J. (1981). Cerebral laterality and psychopathology: fact and fiction. *Psychological Medicine, 11, 219-227.*

Guntrip, H. (1977). *Psychoanalytic Theory. Therapy and the Self.* London: Basic Books.

Gur, R. E. (1978). Left hemisphere dysfunction and left hemisphere overactivation in schizophrenia. *Abnormal Psychology, 87,* 226-238.

Gur, R. Resnick, S. Alavi, A. Gur, R. Caroff, S. Dann, R. Silver, F. Saykin, A. Chawluck J. Kushner, M & Reivich, M. (1987). Regional brain function in schizophrenia 1: A positron emission tomography study. *Archives of General Psychiatry, 44, 119 - 125.*

Gur, R. Resnick, S. Gur, R. Alavi, A. Caroff, S. Kushner, M. & Reivich, M. (1987). Regional brain function in schizophrenia 2: Repeated evaluation with positron emission tomography. *Archives of General Psychiatry, 44,* 126-129.

Hass, F. Distenfeld, S. & Axen, K. (1986). Effects of perceived musical rhythm on respiratory pattern. *Applied Physiology, 62,* 1185-1191.

Hagberg, B. Aicardi, J. Dias, K. & Ramos, O. (1983). A progressive syndrome of autism, dementia, ataxia and loss of purposeful hand use in girls. *Annals of Neurology, 14,* 471-9.

Hagen, R. L. Thomas, T. & Shannon, D. (1977). Administration of digit span on the Wechsler and Binet: Differences that matter. *Clinical Psychology, 33,* 480-482.

Haisch, E. (1974). History of the treatment of mental disorders with music. *Nervenarzi, 45,* 50-53.

Halpern, S. (1978). *Tuning the human instrument: An owner's manual.*

Hamel, P. (1979). *Through Music to the Self.* Boulder: Shambala.

Hamilton, M. (1960). A rating scale for depression. *Neurosurgery and Psychiatry, 23,* 56-62.

Hanks, K. (1985). *The Therapeutic Use of Music and Imagery.* Saline, KS: Bonny Foundation. Unpublished manuscript.

Hanser, S. B. (1988). *Music therapist's handbook.* St Louis: Warren Green, Inc.

Hanser, S. B. (1989). Music therapy with depressed older adults. *Journal of the International Association of Music for the Handicapped, 4(4),* 15-26.

Hanser, S. B, (1990). A music therapy strategy for depressed older adults in the community. *Journal of Applied Gerontology, 9,* 283-298.

Hanser, S. B. (1990). Two investigations of the impact of music on older adults in the community. In *International Society for Music Education XIX.* Helsinki, Finland:

Hanser, S. B. Larson, S. C. & O'Connell, A. S. (1983). The effect of music on relaxation of expectant mothers during labor. *Journal of Music Therapy, 20,* 50-58.

Hanser, S. B. Martin, P. & Bradstreet, K. (1982). *The effect of music on relaxation of dental patients.*

Harding, K. & Ballard, K. D, (1982). The effectiveness of music as a stimulus and as contingent reward in the promoting of spontaneous speech of three physically handicapped pre-schoolers. *Music Therapy, 192,* 86-107.

Harrer, G. & Harrer, H. (1977). *Music, emotion and autonomic function.* London: William Heinemann Medical Books.

Hass, F. Distenfeld, S. & Axen, K. (1986). Effects of perceived musical rhythm on respiratory pattern. *Applied Physiology, 62,* 1185-1191.

Heal, M.I. (1989). *In Tune with the Mind.* Surrey: Good Impressions Publishing Ltd.

Heal, M.I. (1989). Psychoanalytically-informed music therapy in mental handicap: two case studies. In *5th International Congress: Music Therapy and Music Education for the Handicapped, Developments and Limitations in Practice and Research.* The Netherlands.

Heal, M.I. (1989). The use of precomposed music with a highly defended client. *Journal of British Music Therapy, 3,* 10-15.

Heal, M.I. & Morrison, J. (1990). Music Therapy at Leytonstone House, Community Services Unit.

Hensor, L. (1985). Emotional disorders. In M Rutter and L. Hensor *Child and Adolescent Psychiatry: Modern Approaches, 2nd edition.* London: Blackwell.

Herman, N. (1987). *Why Psychotherapy?* London: Free Association Books.

Hinde, R. A. (1976). On describing relationships. *Child Psychology and Psychiatry, 17,* 1-19.

Hitch, G. J. & Halliday, M. S. (1983). *'Working memory in children'. B302,* 325-40.

Hodges, D. A. (1980). *Handbook of music psychology.* Lawrence, KS. National Association for Music Therapy.

Hoffman, D. H. (1978). Arts programming for the elderly. *Education in Gerontology, 3,* 17-33.

Hoffman, J. (1974) *Management of essential hypertension through relaxation training with sound.* Unpublished master's thesis., University of Kansas.

Holden, U. & Woods, R. (1982). *Reality Orientation; Psychological approaches to the 'confused' elderly.* Edinburgh: Churchill Livingstone.

Horowitz, M. (1978). *Image Formation and Cognition.* (Revised edition). New York: Appleton-Century-Crofts.

Horowitz, M. (1983). *Image Formation and Psychotherapy.* New York: Aronson.

Hoskyns, S. (1988). Studying group music therapy with adult offenders: research in progress. *Psychology of Music, 16,* 25-42.

Hoskyns, S. (1982). Striking the right chord. *Nursing Mirror,* June 2nd, 14-17.

Hoskyns, S. & Odell, H. (1990). *Artists and arts therapists: A brief discussion on their roles within hospitals, clinics, special schools and in the community.* Contribution to document prepared by the Standing Committee for Arts Therapies in Britain, St Albans College of Arts and Design.

Houts, D. (1981). The Structured Use of Music in Pastoral Care. *Journal of Pastoral Care, 35,* 194-203.

Howlin, P. (1988). *The Differential Diagnosis of Autism and other Handicaps Associated with Developmental Language Delays.* London: The National Autistic Society.

Huck, S. W. Cormier, W. H. & Bounds, W. G. (1974). *Reading Statistics and Research*. New York: Harper & Row.

ICF-MR (1989). *Interpretive Guidelines for the Application of Standards for Institutions for the Mentally Retarded or Persons with Related Conditions.*

INC. A. S. (1975). *Instruction manual for the Autogen 1100.*

Ingebretsen, R. (1977). Psychotherapy with the elderly. *Psychotherapy: Theory, Research and Practice, 14*(34), 319-332.

Isenberg-Grezda, I. (1988). Music therapy assessment: a reflection of professional identity. *Music Therapy, 3*(25), 156-169.

Isenberg, G. C. (1978). Music therapy: Its implications for the mentally impaired aged. *Journal of the Canadian Association for Music Therapy, 6*, 2-6.

Jacobson, E. (1938). *Progressive Relaxation.* Chicago: University of Chicago Press.

Jacobson, H. L. (1957). *The effect of sedative music on the tensions, anxiety and pain experienced by mental patients during dental procedures.* Lawrence, KS: National Association for Music Therapy Inc.

Jellison, J. A. (1975). The effect of music on autonomic stress responses and verbal reports, 206-219.

Jenkins, J. Felce, D. Lunt, B. & Powell, L. (1977). Increasing engagement in activity of residents in old peoples homes by providing recreational materials. *Behavioural Research Therapy, 15*, 429-434.

Jenkins, J. Felce, D. Powell, L. & Lunt, B. (1978). *Measuring client engagement in residential settings for the elderly.* (No. 120).

Jindrak, K. & Jindrak, H. (1986). *Sing, clean your brain and stay sound and sane.* New York: Jindrak.

Johnson, D. M. & Trawick, M. (1938). Influence of rhythmic sensory stimuli upon the heart-rate. *Psychology, 6*, 303-310.

Johnson, D. R. (1984). Perspective: The creative arts therapists as an independent profession. *The Arts In Psychotherapy*, 11, 40-43.

Jorgenson, H. (1975). *The use of contingent music activity to modify behaviours which interfere with learning.* New York: Teachers College Press.

Kamin, A. Kamin, H. Spintge, R. & Droh, R. (1982). Endocrine effect of anxiolytic music and psychological counselling before surgery. In I. R. D. &. R. Spintge (Eds), *Angst, Schmerz, Musik in der Anasthesie.* Basel: Editiones Roche. pp. 163-166.

Kannapell, B. (1980). Personal awareness and advocacy in the deaf community. In W. C. Stokoe (Ed), *Sign language and the deaf community.* Silver Spring, MD: National Association for the Deaf.

Karpas, M. (1987). *Art Therapy with EMI People at Fulbourn Hospital.*

Kartman, L. (1977). The use of music as a program tool with regressed geriatric patients. *Journal of Gerontological Nursing, 3.*

Katsh, S. & Fishmann, C. (1984). The musical metaphor: A model for music therapy in community practice. In *A.P.M.T. Conference proceedings.* New York:

Katzman, R. (1986). Alzheimer's disease. *New England Journal of Medicine, 314,* 964-973.

Kaufman, H. L. (1940). *You can enjoy music.* New York: Reynal and Hitchcock.

Kay, D., Beamish, P. & Roth (1964). Old age mental disorders in Newcastle-upon-Tyne. *British Journal of Psychiatry, 110,* 146-158.

Keiser, L. (1979). *The Release of Written Expression Through Guided Imagery and Music.* Unpublished manuscript. Olney, MD: Archedigm, Inc.

Kellog, R. (1919) Analyzing Childrens' Art. *National Press.*

Kennedy, E. (1977). *On Becoming a Counsellor.* USA: Seabury Press Inc.

Kenny, C. (1988). Music and Life: The Field of Play. In *National Association of Music Therapy Annual Conference,* Atlanta, Georgia.

Kerr, A. & Stevenson, J. (1985). Rett Syndrome in the West of Scotland. *British Medical, 291,* 579-582.

Kerr, A. & Stevenson, J. (1986). A study of the natural history of Rett Syndrome in 23 girls. *American Journal of Genetics, 24,* 77-83.

Kibler, V. E. & Rider, M. S. (1983). The effect of progressive muscle relaxation and music on stress as measured by finger temperature response. *Clinical Psychology, 39(2),* 213-215.

Kimura, D. (1961). Some effects of temporal lobe damage on auditory perception. Journal *of Psychology Canadian, 15,* 156-165.

Kimura, D. (1964). Left-right differences in the perception of melodies. *Experimental Psychology Quarterly, 16,* 355-358.

Kimura, D. (1967). Functional asymmetry of the brain in dichotio listening. *Cortex, 3,* 167-178.

King, F. L. & Kimura, D. (1972). Left - ear superiority in dichotive perception of vocal non-verbal sounds. *Journal of Psychology, Canadian, 26,* 111-115.

Klajman, S. Koldej, E. & Kowalska, A. (1982). Investigation of musical abilities in hearing-impaired and normal-hearing children. *Folia Phoniatrica, 34,* 229-233.

Klein, M. (1937). *Love, Guilt and Reparation.* London: Hogarth Press.

Klein, M. (1952). *Notes on some schizoid mechanisms.* London: Hogarth Press.

Klein, M. (1959). Our adult world and its roots in infancy. *Human Relations, 12,* 291-303.

Kleinen, B. (1985). Musik in deutschen Wohnzimmern. *Jahrbuch der Deutschen Gesellschaft fur Musikpsychologie, 2.*

Kleinen, B. (1986). Funktionen der Musik und implizite asthetische Theorien der Horer. *Jahrbuch der Deutschen Gesellschaft fur Musikpsychologie, 3.*

Knorring, L. von, et al (1983). Pain as a symptom in depressive disorders. *Pain, 17,* 377-384.

Koffer, U. E. (1969). Music therapy within the rehabilitation program of group therapy. *Zeitschrift fur Psychotherapie und Medizinische Psychologie, 19,* 24-27.

Kohut, H. (1971). *The Analysis of the Self.* New York: International University Press.

Kohut, H. (1988). *The Analysis of The Self.* New York: International University Press.

Korduba, O.M. (1975). Duplicated rhythmic patterns between deaf and normal hearing children. *Journal of Music Therapy, 12,* 136-146.

Langer, S. (1980). *Philosophy in a New Key.* (third edition 1957). Cambridge, MA: Harvard University Press.

Latner, J. (1974). *The Gestalt Therapy Book.* New York: Bantam Books.

Lawes, C. J. (1989) *An evaluation of music therapy for people with learning difficulties and self-injurious behaviour.* Unpublished M.Sc, Polytechnic of East London.

Leach, K. (1982). *Discrimination of musical elements made by hearing impaired residential school children.* Unpublished masters thesis. University of Kansas, Lawrence.

Lee, C. A. (1989). Structural analysis of therapeutic improvisatory music. *British Music Therapy, 3*(2), 11-20.

Lee, C. A. (1990). Structural analysis of post-tonal therapeutic improvisatory music. *British Music Therapy, 4,* 6-21.

Lehikoinen, P. (1987). Vibro-Acoustic Treatment to Reduce Stress.

Leonard, G. (1978). *The silent pulse.* New York: Elsevier-Dutton Publishing Co.

Leuner, H. (1969). Guided Affective Imagery: A Method of Intensive Psychotherapy. *American Journal of Psychotherapy, 23,* 4-22.

Levine-Gross, J. & Swartz, R. (1982). The effects of music therapy on anxiety in chronically ill patients. *Music Therapy, 2,* 43-52.

Levy, B. A. (1978). *Speech processing during reading.* New York: Plenum Press.

Levy, B. A. (1981). *Interactive processing during reading.* Hillside, New Jersey: Lawrence Erlbaum Associates.

Liederman, P. C. (1967). Music and rhythm group therapy for geriatric patients. *Journal of Music Therapy, 4,* 126-128.

Light, E. & Leibowitz, B. D. (1989). *Alzheimer's disease treatment and family stress: Directions for research.* Rockville, MD: U.S. Department of Health and Human Services.

Lininger, L. (1987) *The effects of instrumental and vocal lullabies on the crying behavior of newborn infants.* Unpublished M.Sc thesis, Southern Methodist University, Dallas, Texas.

Livingood, A. Kesic, K. & Paige, N. (1984) *A study of families to determine of effect of sedate music on their state anxiety level while they await the outcome of surgery.* Unpublished study. Eastern Kentucky University, Richmond, Kentucky.

Locsin, R. (1981). The effect of music on the pain of selected post-operative patients. *Journal of Advanced Nursing, 6,* 19-25.

Lonergan, E. C. (1982). *Group Intervention.* Northvale, New Jersey: Jason Aronson.

Longrove, T. H. (1963). Music and the social rehabilitation of the adolescent spastic. *British Society for Music Therapy.*

Lovell, G. & Morgan, J. (1942). Physiological and motor responses to a regularly recurring sound: A study in monotony. *Experimental Psychology, 30,* 435-451.

Lubran, A. (1960). Music therapy and the spastic child. *Society for music therapy and remedial music.*

Luce, G. G. (1971). *Biological rhythms in human and animal physiology.* New York: Dover Publications.

Lyman, B. Bernadin, S. & Thomas, S. (1980). Frequency of Imagery in Emotional Experience. *Perceptual and Motor Skills, 50,* 1159-1162.

Madsen, C. H. J. & Madsen, C. K. (1981). Teaching/discipline: a positive approach for education development.

Madsen, C. K. & Mears, W.G. (1965). The effect of sound upon the tactile threshold of deaf subjects. *Journal of Music Therapy, 2,* 64-68.

Mandler, G. (1984). Consciousness, Imagery, and Emotion-With Special Reference to Autonomic Imagery. *Journal of Mental Imagery, 8,* 87-94.

Mann, C. (1990). Meta-analysis in the breech. *Science, 249,* 476-480.

Maranto, C. D. (1987). Continuing themes in the literature on music therapy education and training. In C.D. Maranto & K. Bruscia (eds.) *Perspectives on Music Therapy Education and Training.* Philadelphia: Temple University, Ester Boyer College of Music.

Maranto, C. D. Bruscia, K. (1988). *Methods of Teaching and Training the Music Therapist.* Philadelphia: Temple University, Ester Boyer College of Music.

Maranto, C. D. (1989). The California symposium: summary and recommendations. *Music Therapy Perspectives, 6,* 82-84.

Marley, L. (1984). The use of music with hospitalized infants and toddlers: A descriptive study. *Music Therapy, 21,* 126-132.

Martin, M. (1987). *The influence of combining preferred music with progressive relaxation and biofeedback techniques on frontalis muscle.* Unpublished M.Sc thesis, Southern Methodist University.

Mason, C. (1978). Musical activities with elderly patients. *Physiotherapy, 64,* 80-82.

Matarazzo, J. D. (1972). *Weschler's Measurement and Appraisal of Adult Intelligence (5th edition).* Baltimore: Williams and Wilkins.

McClure, A. (1983). *Guided Imagery and Music With Children.* Salina, KS: Bonny Foundation.

McDonald, R. (1986). *Healing Parasitic Infection Through a Partnership of Guided Imagery and Music and Applied Kinesiology.* Unpublished manuscript. Salina, KS: Bonny Foundation.

McDowell, C. R. (1966). Obstetrical applications of audioanalgesia. *Hospital Topics, 44,* 102-104.

McElwain, J. (1979). The effect of spontaneous and analytical listening on the evoked critical activity in the left and right hemispheres of musicians and non-musicians. *The Journal of Music Therapy, 16,* 180-189.

McKee, G. Humphrey, B. & McAdam, D. W. (1973). Scaled lateralisation of alpha activity during linguistic and musical tasks. *Phychophysiology*, *10*, 441-443.

McKinney, C. H. (1990). The effect of music on imagery. *Journal of Music Therapy*, *27*, 34-46.

McNiff, S. A. (1987). Research and scholarship in the creative arts therapies. *The Arts in Psychotherapy*, *14*, 285-292.

Meddis, R. (1980). Unified analysis of varience by ranks. *B.J. of Mathematical and Statistical Psychology*, *33*, 84-98.

Meier, C. (1967). *Ancient Incubation and Modern Psychotherapy.* Evanston, Illinois: Northwestern University Press.

Metzler, R. & Berman, T. (1991). *The effect of sedative music on the anxiety of bronchoscopy patients.* Washington, D.C. National Association for Music Therapy, Inc.

Meyer, L. B. (1956). *Emotion and meaning in music.* Chicago: University of Chicago Press.

Millard, K., A., O. (1989). The influence of group singing therapy on the behavior of Alzheimer's Disease patients. *Music Therapy*, *26*, 58-70.

Miller, E. (1977). *Abnormal ageing: the psychology of senile and pre-senile dementia.*

Miller, G. A. (1966). The magical number seven plus or minus two: some limitations on our capacity for processing information. *Psychological Review*, *63*, 81-97.

Miller, L. (1984). *Spontaneous music therapy sessions for hospitalised children.*

Miller, H. et al. (1991). *P.S.E. Therapy Services Booklet.*

Milligan, E. (1986). Will you join the dance? *Physiotherapy*, *72*, 475-477.

Minors, D. S. & Waterhouse, J. M. (1981). *Circadian rhythms and the human.*

Minsky, M. (1982). *Music, Mind and Meaning.* New York: Academic Press.

Monsey, H. L. (1960). Preliminary report of the clinical efficacy of adioanalgesia. *Journal of California State Dental Association*, *36*, 432-437.

Montague, J. (1988). *Music Therapy and the Treatment of Rett Syndrome.*

Moog, H. (1976). *The Musical Experience of the pre-school Child.* Schott & Co. England.

Moran, J. & Kalakian, L. (1977). *Movement experiences for the mentally retarded or emotionally disturbed child.* Minneapolis: Burgess.

Moreno, J. J. (1988). The music therapist: creative arts therapist and contemporary shaman. *The Arts in Psychotherapy*, *15*, 271-280.

Morgan, O. S. & Tilluckdarry, R. (1982). Presentation of singing function in severe aphasia. *West Indian Medical Journal*, *31*, 159-161.

Morley, J. E. (1989). An Approach to the Development of Drugs for Appetite Disorders. *Neuropsychobiology*, *21*, 22-30.

Morrison, J. & Cometa, M. (1980). A Cognitive, Reconstructive Approach to the Psychotherapeutic Use of Imagery. *Journal of Mental Imagery*, *4*, 35-42.

Mortimer, J. A. & Hutton, J. T. Epidemiology and etiology of Alzheimer's disease. In J. T. Hutton and A. D. Keeny (Eds). *Senile dementia of the Alzheimer's type*. New York: Alan R. Liss, Inc.

Motte-Haber, H. de la (1970). Typologien des musikalischen Verhaltens *Musica, 24,* 136-139.

Moyne, Y. (1988). *Musique pour Renaitre*. Paris: Desciee de Brouwer.

Munro, S. (1978). Music therapy in palliative care. *Canadian Medical Association, 119,* 1029-1033.

Munro, S. (1980). *Music Therapy in Palliative/Hospice Care*. New York: Maganmusic-Baton.

Murphy, G. & Wilson, B. (1985). *Self-injurious behaviour: a collection of papers on prevalence, causes and treatment in people who are mentally handicapped or autistic*. Kidderminster: BIMH.

Murray, D. J. (1968). Articulatory and acoustic confusability in short-term memory. *Experimental Psychology, 78,* 679-684.

Murray, L. (1988). *Effects of postnatal depression on infant development: direct studies of early mother-infant interactions*. In R. Kamar and I. Brockington (Eds). *Motherhood and Mental Illness. Vol. 2, pp. 159-190.* London: John Wright and Sons.

Murray, L. & Trevarthen, C. (1985). *Emotional Regulation of Interactions Between Two-month-olds and their Mothers*. In T.M. Fields and N.A. Fox (eds.). Norwood, N.J.: Ablex.

Naeser, M. A. Levine, H. L. Benson, D. F. Struss, D. T. & Weir, W. S. (1981). Frontal leucotomy size and hemispheric asymmetries on computerised tomographic scans of schizophrenics with variable recovery. *Archives of Neurology, 38,* 30-37.

Neisser, U. (1967). *Cognitive Psychology*. New York: Appleton-Century-Crofts.

Nicholson, R. (1981). *The relationship between memory span and processing speed*. New York: Plenum Press.

Nolan, P. (1989). *Music Therapy Improvisation Techniques with Bulimic Patients*. New York: The Guilford Press.

Nolan, P. (1981). *The Use of Guided Imagery and Music in the Clinical Assessment of Depression*. Unpublished Master's Thesis, Hahnemann University, Philadelphia

Nolan, P. (1983). Insight Therapy: Guided Imagery and Music in a Forensic Setting. *Music Therapy, The Journal of the American Association for Music Therapy, 3,* 43-51.

Nolan, P. (1989). Music as a Transitional Object in the Treatment of Bulimia. *Music Therapy Perspectives, 6,* 49-51.

Nordoff, P. & Robbins, C. (1971). *Therapy in Music for Handicapped Children*. London: Gallanct.

Nordoff, P. & Robbins, C. (1977). *Creative Music Therapy*. New York: John Day.

Norris, A. (1987). Reminiscence with elderly people. London: Winslow Press.

Norris, A. (1987). Clinical Psychology with E,M,I, people at Fulbourn Hospital. *Personal communication.*

Novick, L. J. (1982). Senile patients need diverse programming. *Dimensions in Health Service, 59*(9), 25-26.

Noy, P. (1966). The psychodynamic meaning of music. *Music Therapy, 33, 4,* 126-135.

Noy, P. (1967). The psychodynamic meaning of music-part 5. *Journal of Music Therapy, 4,* 117-125.

O'Connell, A. S. (1984). *The effects of sedative music on test of anxiety in college students.* Unpublished master's thesis, University of the Pacific, Stockton, CA.

Odell, H. (1982). Music therapy with adolescents within a multi-disciplinary team. In *Music Therapy Annual Conference Proceedings.* London: B.S.M.T. Library.

Odell, H. (1985). Music therapy treatment with the mentally ill, and student training.

Odell, H. & John, D. (1985). Music Therapy Department; Mental Health Unit No. 2.

Odell, H. (1986). Music Therapy. *The Methodist Recorder, 15.*

Odell, H. (1987). *Music therapy and the elderly mentally ill.* Unpublished M. Phil. thesis. The City University, London.

Odell, H. (1988). A music therapy approach in mental health. *Psychology of Music & Music Education, 16,* 62-70.

Oke, D. (1979). Developing music stimulation programmes in long term geriatric settings. *Bulletin of the Australian Music Therapy Association, 2,* 5-9.

Oldfield A. (1971). The assessment of handedness, the Edinburgh Inventory. *Neurophsychologica, 9,* 97.

Oldfield, A. (1986). *The effects of music therapy on a group of profoundly mentally handicapped adults.* M.Phil, The City University, London.

Oliver, C. (1989). *Self-injurious behaviour in people with a mental handicap: A review of the literature between April 1987 and March 1988.* (In press).

Oliver, C. Murphy, G. H. & Corbett, J. A. (1987). Self-injurious behaviour in people with a mental handicap: a total population study. Journal of *Mental Deficiency Research, 31,* 147-162.

Oliver, C. Murphy, G. & Crayton, L. (1987). *The functional analysis of challenging behaviour.* Paper presented to the British Psychological Annual Conference.

Olson, L. K. (1984). Player Piano music for the elderly. *Journal of Music Therapy, 21,* 35-45.

Orton, M. R. (1953). *Application of the iso-moodic principle in the use of music with psychotic and "normal" subjects.* Unpublished master's thesis, Lawrence, Kansas.

Overall, J. E. & Gorman, D. R. (1962). Brief Psychiatric Rating Scale. *Psychologial Reports, 10,* 799-812.

Owens, L. D. (1979). The effects of music on the weight loss, crying, and physical movement of newborns. *Journal of Music Therapy*, 16, 83-90.

Oyama, T. Hatano, K. Sato, Y. Kudo, M. Spintge, R. & Droh, R. (1983). Endocrine effect of anxiolytic music in dental patients. In R. Droh &. R. Spintge (eds.), *Angst, Schmerz, Musik in der Anasthesie* (pp. 143-146). Basel, Editiones Roche.

Padden, C. (1980). The deaf community and the culture of the deaf people. In W.C. Stokoe (Ed). *Sign language and the deaf community.* Silver Spring MD: National Association of the Deaf.

Padden, C. & Humphries, T. (1988). *Deaf in America: Voices from a culture.* Cambridge, MA: Harvard University Press.

Palmer, M. D. (1977). Music therapy in a comprehensive program of treatment and rehabilitation for the geriatric resident. *Music Therapy*, *14*, 190-197.

Palmer, M. D. (1989). Music therapy in gerontology: A review and a projection. *Music Therapy Perspectives*, *6*, 52-56.

Papousek, M. & Papousek, H. (1981). *Musical elements in the infant's vocalization: their significance for communication, cognition and creativity.* Norwood, NJ: Ablex.

Parker, J. (1986). A life worth living. *Occupational Therapy*, *11*, 7-9.

Pavlicevic, M. (1987). Reflections on the Pre-Musical Moment. *British Music Therapy*, *1*, 22-24.

Pavlicevic, M. (1988). Describing critical moments. In *The Case Study as Research*. City University Music Department, London.

Pavlicevic, M. & Trevanthen, C. (1989). A Musical Assessment of Psychiatric States in Adults. *Psychopathology: 22, 325-334.*

Pavlicevic, M. (1990). Dynamic Interplay in Clinical Improvisation. *British Music Therapy*, *4*, 5-9.

Pavlicevic, M. (1991). *Music in Communications Improvisation in Music Therapy.* PhD Thesis. University of Edinburgh, Department of Psychology & Music..

Peach, S. (1984). Some implications for the clinical use of music facilitates imagery. *Music Therapy*, *21*, 27-34.

Perls, F. Hefferline, R. & Goodman, P. (1951). *Gestalt Therapy.* New York: Dell.

Pennebaker, J. W. et al. (1988). Disclosure of Traumas and Psychosomatic Processes. *Social Science Medicine*, *26*, 327-332.

Perry, J. (1974). *The Far Side of Madness.* Englewood Cliffs, NJ: Prentice Hall.

Pickett, E. (1987-88). Fibroid Tumors and Response to Guided Imagery and Music: Two Case Studies. *Imagination, Cognition and Personality, 7,* 165-176.

Pignatiello, M. Camp, C. J. Elder, S. T. & Rasar, L. A. (1989). A psychophysiological comparison of the Velton and Musical Mood Induction Techniques. *Music Therapy*, *26*, 140-154.

Pippard, A. B. (1978). *The Physics of Vibration (Vol. 1).* Cambridge: Cambridge University Press.

Pitt, B. (1982). *Psychogeriatrics; An introduction to the psychiatry of old age.* Edinburgh: Churchill Livingstone.

Plutchik, R. (1984). Emotions and Imagery. *Journal of Mental Imagery, 8,* 105-112.

Pontvik, A. (1955). *Heilen durch Musik.* Zurich: Rascher Verlag.

Powell, L. Felce, D. Jenkins, J. & Lunt, B. (1979). Increasing engagement in a home for the elderly by providing an indoor gardening activity. *Behavior Research and Therapy, 17,* 127-135.

Powell-Proctor, L. & Miller, E. (1982). Reality Orientation; A critical appraisal. *British Journal of Psychiatry, 140,* 457-463.

Pressing, J. (1984). *Cognitive Processes in Improvisation.* Amsterdam: Elsevier. In W. R. Crozier & A.J. Chapman (eds). *Cognitive Processes in the Perception of Art.*

Pressing, J. (1988). *Improvisation: methods and models.* Oxford: Clarendon Press. In J.A. Sloboda (Ed). *Generative Processes in Music: The Psychology of Performance, Improvisation and Composition.*

Pribram, K. H. (1982). Brain Mechanism in Music: Prolegoma for a Theory of the Meaning of Meaning. In D. Deutsch (ed), *The Psychology of Music.* New York: Academic Press.

Prickett, H.T. (1989). *Advocacy for deaf children.* Springfield, IL: Charles C Thomas Publisher.

Priestley, M. (1975). *Music Therapy in Action.* London: Constable and Co. Ltd.

Priestley, M. (1976, 9th Dec). Music, Freud and the port of entry. *Nursing Times,* p. 1940-1941.

Priestley, M. (1989). Transference and countertransference in music therapy.

Quittner, A. L. (1980) *The facilitative effects of music on visual imagery: A multiple measures approach.* Unpublished master's thesis, Florida State University, Tallahassee, Florida.

Radocy, R. E. & Boyle, J. D. (1979). *Psychological foundations of musical behavior.* Springfield, Illinois: Charles C. Thomas.

Radocy, R., E., & Boyle, J., D. (1988). *Psychological foundations of musical behaviour (2nd ed).* Springfield, Illinois. Charles C. Thomas.

Reason, P. & Heron, J. (1981). Human Inquiry. John Wiley, London.

Rechtschaffen, A. (1959). *Psychotherapy with geriatric patients,* 73-84.

Reigler, J. (1980). Comparison with a reality orientation program for geriatric patients with and without music. *Music Therapy, 17,* 26-33.

Reinhardt, U. & Lange, E. (1982). Effects of music on depressed patients. *Psychiatrie Neurologie und Medizinische Psychologie, 34,* 414-421.

Repp, A. C. Harman, J. L. & Felce, D. (1983). A real time parallel entry, portable computer system for observational research. Dekalb: Northern Illinois University. Illinois.

Rett, A. (1966). *Uber ein cerebral atropisches Syndrome bei Hyper-ammonamie.*

Richer, J. (1979). Human ethology and mental handicap. Psychiatric illness and mental handicap, ed. by F E James and R P Snaith. Gaskell.

Ricks, D. M. (1975). *Vocal communication in pre-verbal normal and autistic children*. London: Butterworths.

Ricks, D. M. (1978). *Making sense to make sensible sounds*. Cambridge: Cambridge University Press.

Rider, M. S. (1985). Entrainment mechanisms are involved in pain reduction, muscle relaxation and music-mediated imagery. *Journal of Music Therapy, 22*, 183-192.

Rider, M. S. Floyd, J. W. & Kirkpatrick, J. (1985). The effect of music, imagery, and relaxation on adrenal corticosteroids and the re-entrainment of circadian rhythms. *Journal of Music Therapy, 22*, 46-58.

Riegler, J. (1980). *Comparison of a reality orientation program for geriatric patients with and without music.*

Rileigh, K.K. & Odom, P.B. *Perception of rhythm by subjects with normal and deficient hearing.* Developmental Psychology, 7, *54-61.*

Roberts, C. (1986) *Music: A nursing intervention for increased intracranial pressure.* Unpublished master's thesis, Grand Valley State College.

Roelofs, O. & Zeeman, W. (1949). The subjective duration of time intervals. *Acta Psychologica, 6,* 289-336.

Rogers, C. (1961). *On Becoming a Person*. Boston, Houghton-Miffin.

Rogers, P. J. (1988). A comparison of short-term verbal and musical memory in a single case study. Mini-project submitted for M.Sc degree.

Roter, M. (1957) *The use of music in medical reception rooms.* Unpublished master's thesis, University of Kansas.

Rutter, M. (1985). *Infantile autism and other pervasive developmental disorders.* In M. Rutter and L. Hensor, *Child and Adolescent Psychiatry: Modern Approaches,* 2nd edn. London: Basti, Blackwell.

Rutter, M. (1985). Resilience in the face of Adversity. *British Journal of Psychiatry, 147,* 598-611.

Rudd, E. (1980). *Music Therapy and its relationship to current treatment theories.* St Louis, USA: Magnamusic-Baton.

Sackett, G. P. (1978). Measurement in observational research. In Sackett, E., P. (ed). *Observing behaviour, Volume II, Data collection and Analysis Methods.* Baltimore: University Park Press.

Sacks, O. (1989). *Seeing Voices.* Berkeley, CA: University of California Press.

Salame, P. & Baddley, A. D. (1982). Disruption of short-term memory by unattended speech: implications for the structure of working memory. *Verbal Learning and Verbal Behavior, 21,* 261-273.

Sammons, L. (1984). The use of music by women in child-birth. *Journal of Nurse-Midwifery, 29,* 266-270.

Samuels, M. & Samuels, N. (1975). *Seeing With the Mind's Eye*. New York: Random House.

Sanderson, S. (ed.). (1984). *Music therapy with a terminally ill cancer patient.* Unpublished research manuscript. The Florida State University:

Sanderson, S. (1986) *The effect of music on reducing preoperative anxiety and postoperative anxiety and pain in the recovery room.* Unpublished master's thesis., The Florida State University, Florida.

Saperston, B. M. (1989). Music-based individualized relaxation training (MBIRT): Sequential stress reduction techniques for the behaviorally disturbed mentally retarded. *Music Therapy Perspectives, 6,* 26-33.

Saunders, D. A. (1977). *Auditory perception of speech.* Englewood Cliffs, NJ: Prentice-Hall Publishers.

Savage, B. (1984). *Interferential Therapy.* London: Faber.

Scartelli, J. P. (1982). The effect of sedative music on eletromyographic biofeedback assisted relaxation training of spastic cerebral palsied adults. *Journal of Music Therapy, 19,* 210-218.

Scartelli, J. P. (1984). The effect of EMG biofeedback and sedative music, EMG biofeedback only, and sedative music only on frontalis muscle relaxation ability. *Journal of Music Therapy, 21,* 67-78.

Scartelli, J. (1987). Accreditation and approval standars for music therapy education. In C.D. Maranto & K. Bruscia (eds.), *Perspectives on Music Therapy Education and Training.* Philadelphia: Temple University, Ester Boyer College of Music.

Schatz, V. (1990). Using percussion to teach music concepts and enhance music and movement experiences. In A. A. Darrow (Ed). *Proceedings from the Second National Conference on Music and the Hearing Impaired at Gallaudet University* (pp. 85-92). Lawrence, KS: The University of Kansas.

Schein, J.D. (1978). The deaf community. In H. Davis & S.R. Silverman (Eds). *Hearing and deafness.* New York: Holt, Rinehart & Winston.

Schieffelin, C. (1988). A case study: Stevens-Johnson Syndrome. In *Annual Conference, Southeastern Conference of the National Association for Music Therapy Inc.* Tallahassee, Florida.

Schmitz, K. (1990). An explorer's guide to cultural understanding. *NTID Focus, 26-29.*

Schneider, F. (1982) *Assessment and evaluation of audio-analgesic effects on the pain experience of acutely burned children during dressing changes.* Unpublished doctoral dissertation, University of Cincinnati.

Schoenberger, L. & Braswell, C. (1971). Music therapy in rehabilitation. *Rehabilitation, 37,* 30-31.

Schouten, J. F. (1940). *The residue, a new concept in subjective sound analysis.* The Journal of Auditory Research Publishers, 1969.

Schubert, E. D. (1980). *Hearing, its function and dysfunction.* New York: Springer-Verlag.

Schuster, B. L. (1985). The effect of music listening on blood pressure fluctuations in adult hemodialysis patients. *Journal of Music Therapy, 22,* 146-153.

Schuster, D. H. & Guilford, J. P. (1962.). The psychometric prediction of problem drivers. *Traffic Safety Research Review., 6.,* 16-20.

Schutz, J. & Luthe, W. (1959). *Autogenic Training: A Physiologic Approach to Psychotherapy*. New York:

Schwabe, C. (1981). Music therapy in geriatric rehabilitation. *Zeitschrift fur Gesamte Hygiene und ihre grenzgebiete, 27*, 937-940.

Scott, M. John, D. & Woodcock, J. (1987). *Music therapy with EMI people.*

Scott, M. Odell, H. & John, D. et al (1986). *Music Therapy and Mental Health.* APMT publication, Cambridge.

Seashore, C. E. Lewis, D. & Saetveit, J. (1960). *Seashore measures of musical talents' manual (revised).* New York: Psychological Corporation.

Shallice, T. & Warrington, E. K. (1970). Independent functioning of the verbal memory stores: neuropsychological evidence for a phonological short-term store. *Experimental Psychology Quarterly, 22*, 261-273.

Shankweiler, D. (1966). Effects of temporal lobe damage on perception of dichotically presented melodies. *Journal of Comparative Physiological Psychology, 62*, 115-119.

Shapiro, A. (1969). A pilot program in music therapy with residents of a home for the aged. *Geronotological Society, 9* 128-133.

Shapiro, A. G. & Cohen, H. (1983). *Auxiliary pain relief during suction curettage.* In R. Droh and R. Spintge (eds.). *Angst, Schmerz, Musik in der Anasthesie (pp. 89-93).* Basel: Editiones Roche.

Shatin, L. (1957). The influence of rhythmic drumbeat stimuli upon the pulse rate and general activity of long-term schizophrenics. *Mental Science, 103*, 172-188.

Sheikh, A. (1978). *Eidetic Psychotherapy.* In J. Singerof & K. Pope (Eds). *The Power of Human Imagination: (pp.197-224).* New York: Plenum Press.

Shepherd, G. (1988). *The History of Fulbourn Hospital.*

Sherwood, J. Stolaroff, M. & Harman, W. (1962). The Psychedelic Experience - A New Concept in Psychotherapy. *Neuropsychiatry, 4*, 69-80.

Shoenberger, L. & Braswell, C. (1971). Music therapy in rehabilitation. *Rehabilitation, 37*, 30-31.

Shroyer, E.H. & Ford, T.A. (1986). Survey of music instruction and activities in residential and day schools for hearing impaired students. *Music Education for the Handicapped Bulletin, 2,* 28-45.

Siegel, S. L. (1983) *The use of music as treatment in pain perception with post surgical patients in a paediatric hospital.* Unpublished master's thesis, University of Miami, Florida.

Silverstein, M. L. & Meltzer, H. Y. (eds). (1983). *Neuropsychological dysfunction in major psychoses: relation to premorbid adjustment and social class.* Amsterdam: Elsevier Science.

Sinason, V. (1986). Secondary handicap and its relationship to trauma. *Psychoanalytic Psychotherapy, 2*, 131-154.

Singer, J. & Pope, K. (eds). (1978). *The Power of Human Imagination.* New York: Plenum Press.

Skille, O. (1967). *Rapport fra studiereise i Danmark inngitt til Kirke-og Undervisningsdepartmentet.*

Skille, O. (1968). Coloured Music. *British Journal of Music Therapy.*

Skille, O. (1968). Misikk i den spesialpedagogiske behandlingen. *Adresseavisen som kronikk.*

Skille, O. (1968). The Wingfield Music Clubs. *Arbeidsterapeuten nr 4,* 14-18.

Skille, O. (1969). *De musikalske problembarn.* Artikkel publisert i Spesialpedagogikk.

Skille, O. (1969). *Musikken gir ny styrke.* Liv og Helse nr 3, 65-67.

Skille, O. (1969). *Teorier innen klinisk og pedagogisk musikkterapi.* Foreleaning ved Nordisk konferanse om musikkterapi som et ledd i den spesiaipedagogiske behandlingen. Knebel, Danmark. Unpublished paper.

Skille, O. (1970). *ADL-trening som skolefag. Trinnvis uavhengig undervisningsopplegg.* Foreleaning ved spesialpadagogisk kus for skolelederlaget i Nord Trondelag. Unpublished paper.

Skille, O. (1970). *Music Therapy. Essay based on articles appearing in Nordisk* Tidsskrift for Spesialpedagogikk nr 1. Unpublished.

Skille, O. (1970). *Skjemaundersokeise om musikkterapeutiske aktiviteter i norske spesialskoler og inatitusjoner.* Forskningarapport til Kirke-og undervisningsdepertmentet.

Skille, O. (1970). *Stromninger i europeisk musikkterapi.* Foreiesning ved musikkterapisaminar i Helsinki. Unpublished paper.

Skille, O. (1971). *Report on the use of the Skille system of combining colours and music in the elementary music education.* (Private publication 1971).

Skille, O. (1973). *SMUFT-prosjektet - Jyvaskyla Universitet spesialpedagogiske publikasjoner.*

Skille, O. (1974). *En musikalitetsfunkejonstest.* Etterskrift fra Nordisk Musikkpedagogisk Unions X kongress. Trondhelm s.77.

Skille, O. (1975). Musikalitetsfunksjon som bakgrunn for spesialpedagogisk behandling og observasjon. *Nordisk Tidsskrift for Specialpadagogik, 1,* 88 - 99.

Skille, O. (1975). Musikalitetsfunktioner som baggrund for secialpadagogisk behandling og observation (SMUFT). *Musik og terapi - Tidsskrift for Dansk forbund for Musikterapi, 1,* 4-16.

Skille, O. (1977). SMUFT-prosjektet - sluttrapport, del 1. Moss 1979.

Skille, O. (1979). SMUFT-prosjaktet - sluttrapport, Tabel 1 del. Moss 1979. .

Skille, O. (1980). *Differential Diagnosis of Musicality Functions as found in Normal and Mentally Retarded Children.* Unpublished paper.

Skille, O. (1981). The Musical Behaviour Scale (MUBS). Theoretical background and description. In *European Music Year,* Wein.

Skille, O. (1982). "Musikkbad": Oket tilgjengelighet hos de svakeste. *Rapport nr 6,* 209-212.

Skille, O. (1982). MUSIKKBAD for oket aktivitetsniva. *Rapport nr 5,* 175-177.

Skille, O. (1982). Musikkbadet - anvendt for de avakeste. Nordisk Fidsskrift for Spesialpedagogikk 4, 275-284.

Skille, O. (1982). Musikkbadet - anvendt for de svakeste. *Nordisk Tidsskrift for Spesialpedagogikk*, 275-284.

Skille, O. (1982). Musikkbadet - en metode for de aller avakeste. *Spesialpedagogikk nr 1*, 12-15.

Skille, O. (1982). Musikkbadet - en musikkterapeutisk metode. *Musikkterapi*, 24-27.

Skille, O. (1982). Musikkbadet - en musikkterapeutisk metode for de aller svakeste, 3 de og siste del. *Musikkterapi 4*, 22-29.

Skille, O. (1982). Musikkbadet - en musikkterapeutisk metode for de aller svakeste, del 2. *Musikkterapi 3*, 6-10.

Skille, O. (1982). Musikkbadet - Teoretisk grunniag. *Spesialpedagogikk 9*, 19-22.

Skille, O. (1982). Musikkbadet. Psykisk utvecklingshamming, 16-22.

Skille, O. (1982). Musikkbadet. Virkemate og metodikk, anvendt for de svakeste. *Spesialpedagogikk nr 10*, 24-29.

Skille, O. (1982). Praktisk bruk av SMUFT i andasvakeomsorgens institusjoner.

Skille, O. (1985). MUBS - ein diagnostisches Hilfsmittel.

Skille, O. (1985). *The Music Bath - Possible Use as an Anxiolytic. In Spintge/Droh (eds.) Music in Medicine*. Berlin: Springer Verlag.

Skille, O. (1986). Manual of Vibroacoustics. Private publication Steinkjer.

Skille, O. (1986). Musikkbadet v/Olav Skille. *Musikkterapi 1*, 30-41.

Skille, O. (1987). *Low Frequency Sound Massage - The Music Bath* - A follow-up Report. (In Spintge/Droh (Eds) Music in Medicine (Springer Verlag 1987, 257-259).

Skille, O. (1987). Rapport fra symposium. *International Society for Vibroacoustics Bulletin, XVL*, 118-123.

Skille, O. (1987). Samierapport fra VibroAkustisk seminar, Skogn.13-15.

Skille, O. (1987). Vibratory Motor Stimulation. *Australian Journal of Physiotherapy Rapport fra symposium 13-15*, 118-123.

Skille, O. (1988). VibroAcoustics and Sport - The Beginning of a New Approach to Muscular Stress. (In Spintge/Droh (eds) Schmerz und Sport 150-156.

Skille, O. (1988). VibroAkustisk stimulering - et godt tilbud til de aller svakeste - og til oss alle.

Skille, O. (1989). Vibracoustic Therapy. *American Journal of Music Therapy, 8*.

Skille, O. (1989). Vibro Acoustic Therapy. *Music Therapy, 8*, 61-77.

Skille, O. (1992). Vibroacoustic Research 1980-1991. In: Spintge & Droh (Eds): MusicMedicine. *MMB Music Inc.*, 249-266.

Skille, O., Wigram, T. & Weeks, L. (1989). Vibroacoustic therapy: The therapeutic effect of low frequency sound on specific physical disorders and disabilities. *Journal of British Music Therapy.*, *3*, 6-10.

Sloboda, J. (1985). *The Musical Mind. The Cognitive Psychology of Music.* Oxford: Oxford University Press.

Sloboda, J. (1988). A discussion of case study research in psychology of music: Implications for music therapy. In *The Fourth Music Therapy Research Conference*. London: City University Music Department pp. 24-30.

Sloboda, J. A. (1988). *Generative Processes in Music: The Psychology of Performance. Improvisation and Composition.* Oxford: Clarendon Press.

Smales, G. (1960). Music with physically handicapped children. *Society for music therapy and remedial music.*

Smales, G. (1962). How music helps the handicapped. *Society for music therapy and remedial music.*

Smeijsters, H. (1993). *Listener responses on a graded scale between opposite semantic descriptors of 30 musical excerpts.* St Louis, Mo: MMB Music.

Smith, G. H. (1986). A comparison of the effects of three treatment interventions on cognitive functioning of Alzheimer's patients. *Music Therapy, 6A*(1), 41-56.

Solomon, A. L. (1980). Music in special education before 1930: Hearing and speech development. *Journal of Research in Music Education, 28,* 236-242.

Solnit, A. J. & Stark, M. H. (1961). Mourning and the birth of a defective child. *Psychoanalytic Study of the Child, 16,* 523-537.

Soraci, S. (1982). The relationship between rate of rhythmicity and the stereotypic behaviours of abnormal children. *Journal of Music Therapy, 14,* 46-54.

Spellacy, F. (1970). Lateral preferences in the identification of pattern stimuli. *Journal of the Acoustical Society of America, 47,* 574-578.

Spensley, S. (1985). Mentally ill or mentally handicapped? A longitudinal study of severe learning disorder. *Psychoanalytic Psychotherapy, 1,* 55-70.

Spielberger, C. Gorsuch, R. & Lushene, R. (1970). *State-trait anxiety inventory test manual.*

Spintge, R. (1982). Psychophysiological surgery preparation with and without anxiolytic music. In R. Droh. &. R. Spintge (eds). *Angst, Schmerz, Music in der Anasthesie* (pp. 77-88). Basel: Editiones Roche.

Spintge, R. & Droh, R. (1982). The pre-operative condition of 1910 patients exposed to anxiolytic music and Rohypnol (Flurazepam) before receiving an epidural anesthetic. In R. Droh & R. Spintge (eds). *Angst, Schmerz, Music in der Anasthesie* (pp. 193-196). Basel: Edotpmes Roche.

Spitzer, M. (1984). A survey of the use of music in schools for the hearing impaired. *The Volta Review, 86,* 362-363.

Spreen, O. Spellacy, F. & Reid, J. R. (1970). The effects of interstimulus interval and the intensity of ear asymmetry for non-verbal stimuli in dichotic listening. *Neuropsychologia, 8,* 345-250.

Standley, J. (1986). Music research in medical/dental treatment: Meta-analysis and clinical applications. Journal of *Music Therapy, 23,* 56-122.

Standley, J. (1992). Meta-analysis of research in music and medical treatment: Effect size as a basis for comparison across multiple dependent and independent variables. In R Spintge & R. Droh (eds). *Musical Medicine* (pp. 364-378). St Louis: MO, MMB.

Staum, M. J. (1983). Music and rhythmic stimuli in the rehabilitation of gait disorders. *Journal of Music Therapy, 20,* 69-87.

Staum, M. J. (1987). Music notation to improve the speech prosody of hearing impaired children. *Journal of Music Therapy, 24*, 146-159.

Steele, A. L. (1968). Programmed use of music to alter unco-operative problem behaviour. *Journal of Music Therapy, 5*, 103-107.

Steele, P. (1984). Aspects of resistance in music therapy: theory and technique. *Music Therapy, 4*, 64-72.

Steele, P. H. (1988). Children's Use of Music Therapy. In *Music Therapy one day conference: Music and the Cycle of Life*, .

Steele, P. & Leese, K. (1987). The Music Therapy Interactions of One session with a Physically Disabled Boy. *British Music Therapy, 1*, 7-12.

Steele, P. H. & Dunachie, S. (1986). Towards a musical process model of research.

Stern, D. (1985). *The Interpersonal World of the Infant. A View from psychoanalysis and developmental psychology*. New York: Basic Books.

Stern, D. Dore, J. Hofer, L. & Haft, W. (1985). Affect Attunement: the Sharing of Feeling States between Mother and Infant by means of Inter-Modal Fluency. In T. M. Field and N. Fox (eds). *Special Perception in Infants*. Norwood, N. J. Ablex.

Sterritt, G.M., Camp, B.W. & Lipman, B.S. (1966). Effects of early auditory deprivation upon auditory and visual information processing.

Stokes, S., J. (1985). Guided Imagery and Music (GIM) as a Synergistic Approach. Unpublished manuscript. Salina, KS: Bonny Foundation.

Storr, A. (1976). *The Dynamics of Creation*. London: Penguin.

Stratton, V. N. & Zalanowski, A. H. (1984). The relationship between music, degree of liking and self-reported relaxation. *Music Therapy, 21*, 184-191.

Sullivan, H. S. (1944). *The Language of Schizophrenia*. In J.S. Kasanin (Eds) *Language and Thought in Schizophrenia*. New York: Norton.

Summer, L. (1981). Guided Imagery and Music with the Elderly. *Music Therapy:* Journal of the *American Association for Music Therapy, 1*, 39-42.

Summer, L. (1985). Imagery and Music. *Journal of Mental Imagery, 9*, 83-90.

Summer, L. (1988). *Guided Imagery and Music in the Institutional Setting*. St Louis: MMB Music.

Swallow, M. & Sutton, J. (1993). Music Therapy in Parkinson's Disease. Unpublished paper for 1993 World Conference of Music Therapy, Spain.

Swannick, K. & Tillman, J. (1986). The Sequence of Musical Development: A study of childrens composition. *British Journal of Music Education, 3*, 305-339.

Symington, N. (1986). London: Free Association Books.

Tanioka, F. Takazawa, T. Kamata, S. Kudo, M. Matsuki, A. & Oyama, T. (ed). (1985). *Hormonal effect of anxiolytic music in patients during surgical operations under epidural anaesthesia. In R Spintge & R. Droh (eds),* Music in Medicine *(pp. 285-290)* Basel: Editiones Roche.

Tart, C. T. (1969). *Altered States of Consciousness*. Garden City, New York: Anchor Books.

Teirich, H. R. (1962). *On Therapeutics through Music and Vibrations. Postscript to: Gravesaner Blatter (1959).* Ars Viva, Mainz.

Terdhart, E. (1974). Pitch, consonance and harmony. *Journal of the Acoustical Society of America, 55,* 1061-1069.

Terry, R., D., & Katzman, R. (1983). Senile dementia of the Alzheimer type. *Annals of Neurology, 14,* 497-506.

Thaut, M. H. (1990). *Physiological responses to music stimuli. Music therapy in the treatment of adults with mental disorders.* New York: Schirmer Books.

Tobin, S. & Lieberman, M. A. (1976). *Last home for the aged.* San Francisco: Jossey-Bass.

Tomkins, S. (1962). *Affect Imagery Consciousness. Volume 1: The Positive Affects.* New York: Springer - Verlag.

Towse, E. (1989). Do music therapy techniques discourage the emergence of transference? In *5th International Congress: Music Therapy and Music Education for the Handicaped Developments and Limitations in Practice and Research.* Noordwijkerhout, the Netherlands:

Towse, E. (1991). *Relationships in music therapy: Do music therapy techniques discourage the emergence of transference?*

Trevarthen, C. (1984). *Emotions in infancy: Regulators of contacts and relationships with persons.* Hillsdale, N.J.: Erlbaum.

Trevarthen, C. (1986). *Development of Intersubjective Motor Control in Infants.* Dordrecht: Martinus Nijhof.

Trevarthen, C. (1987). In R Steele & T. Threadgold (eds.) *Language Topics: Essays in Honour of Michael Halliday.* Amsterdam and Philadelphia, John Benjamins.*Sharing Makes Sense: Intersubjectivity and the making of an infant's meaning.*

Trevarthen, C. (1990). *The Foundations of Intersubjectivity: Development of Interpersonal and Cooperative Understanding in Infants.* New York: Norton.

Tronick, E. Als, H. & Adamson, L. (1979). *Structure of early face-to-face communicatived interactions.* In M. Bullowa (ed). *Before Speech.* Cambridge, Cambridge University Press.

Tsao, C. C. Gordon, T. F. Maranto, C. D. Lerman, C. Murasko, D. (1991). The Effects of Music and Biological Imagery on Immune Response (S-IgA). In C.D. Maranto (ed). *Application of Music in Medicine* (pp.85-121). Washington, D.C.: The National Association for Music Therapy, Inc.

Tsao, C. C. Gordon, T. F. Maranto, C. D. Lerman, C. & Moraski, D. (In press). *The effects of music and directed biological imagery on immune response.* Washington, DC: National Association for Music Therapy.

Tyson, F. (1981). *Psychiatric Music Therapy.* New York: Creative Arts Rehabilitation Center.

Underhill, K. K. & Harris, L. M. (1974). The effect of contingent music on establishing imitation in behaviourally disturbed retarded children. *Journal of Music Therapy, 11,* 156-166.

Vance, C. L. (1989). *An Exploration of the Possibilities of the Use of Guided Imagery and Music in the Treatment of the Traumatically Brain Injured Population.* Unpublished Manuscript. Salina, KS: Bonny Foundation.

VanderArk, S. Newman, K. & Bell, S. (1983). The effects of music participation on quality of life of the elderly. *Music Therapy, 3,* (1), 71-81.

Ventre, M. (1981). *Guided Imagery and Music and the Autistic Child: A Pilot Study.* Unpublished manuscript. Bonny Foundation, Salina, KS.

Walker, R. (1984). Musical Perspectives on psychological research and music education. *Psychology of Music, 15,* 167-186.

Ward, L. (1987) *The use of music and relaxation techniques to reduce pain of burn patients during daily debridement.* Unpublished master's thesis, The Florida State University.

Washco, A. (1948). *The effects of music upon pulse rate, blood pressure, and mental imagery.* New York: Columbia University Press.

Wasserman, N. M. (1972). Music therapy for the emotionally disturbed in a private hospital. *Music Therapy, 9,* 99-104.

Watson, C. S. & Kelly, W. J. (1981). *The role of stimulus uncertainty in the discrimination of auditory patterns.* Hillsdale, N.J. Erlbaum.

Watson, C. S. Wroton, H. W. & Kelly, W. J. (1975). Factors in the discrimination of tonal patterns: I. Component frequency, temporal position and silent intervals. *Journal of the Acoustical Society of America, 57,* 1176-1186.

Wehr, T. A. (1982). *Circadian rhythm disturbances in depression and mania.* Hillsdale, NJ: Erlbaum.

Weibe, J. (1980). *The effect of adjusted frequency on the tonal perception of older hearing: impaired adults.* Unpublished masters thesis. The University of Kansas, Lawrence.

Weiner, L. S. (1985). *Relationships: Encountering the Self and Other.* Unpublished manuscript. Salina, KS: Bonny Foundation.

Weiss, D. S. & Billings, J. H. (1988). *Behavioral medicine techniques.* Norwalk, CT: Appleton & Lange.

West, E. D. (1984). Right hemisphere dysfunction and schizophrenia. *The Lancet p. 5, February 11.*

West, R. Howell, P. & Cross, I. (1985). Modelling Perceived Musical Structure. In P. Howell, I. Cross and R. West (eds). *Musical Structure and Cognition.* London: Academic Press.

Wever, R. A. (1979). *The circadian system of man: Results of experiments under temporal isolation.*

Wexler, B. E. (1986). A model of brain function: Its implications for psychiatric research. *British Journal of Psychiatry, 148,* 357-362.

Wheeler, B. (1981). The relationship between music therapy and theories of psychotherapy. *Music Therapy. The Journal of the American Association for Music Therapy, 1, 9-16.*

Whyke, M. (1977). Music ability and neuropsychological interpretation. In M. Critchley & R. Henson A, (eds). *Music and the Brain* London: W. Heinemann.

Wickelgren, W. A. (1969). Context-sensitive coding, associative memory and serial order in (speech) behaviour. *Psychological Revue, 86,* 44-60.

Wightman, F. L. (1973). The pattern transformation model of pitch. *Journal of the Acoustical Society of America, 54,* 407-417.

Wigram, A. (1987). *Report on a two-day conference on the effective use of vibroacoustic therapy (Levanger, Norway).* International Society of Vibroacoustic Therapy, Steindjer, Norway.

Wigram, A. (1988). Music Therapy developments in mental handicap. *Society for Research in Psychology of Music and Music Education, 16,* 42-52.

Wigram, A. (1989). Processo De Diferenciacao Do Autismo E Outras Mentais. (The Significance of Musical Behaviour and Music Responsiveness in the Process of Differential Diagnosis of Autism and other Handicaps). In *International Conference on Music Therapy:* Sao Paulo, Brazil. Unpublished.

Wigram, A. (1990). Processes in Assessment and Diagnosis of Handicap in Children through the medium of Music Therapy. In *APMT Conference,* Severalls Hospital, Colchester: Unpublished.

Wigram, A. & Weekes, L. (1985). A specific approach to overcoming motor dysfunction in children and adolescents with severe physical and mental handicap using music and movement. *British Journal of Music Therapy, 16,* 2-12.

Wigram, A. & Weekes, L. (1989). Collaborative Approaches in Treating the Profoundly Handicapped.

Wigram, A. & Weekes, L. (1989). *A project evaluating the difference in therapeutic treatment between the use of low frequency sound (LFS) and music alone in reducing high muscle tone in multiply handicapped people, and oedema in mentally handicapped people* - Paper (Unpublished) to the Internasjonale Brukerseminar Omkring Vibroakustisk Behandlingsmetodikk in Steinkjer.

Wijzenbeek, G. & Nieuwenhuijzen, N. (1989). *Receptive music therapy with depressive and neurotic patients.* Noordwijkerhout, Netherlands.

Wilkinson, R. T. (1982). *The relationships between body temperature and performance across circadian phase shifts.* Hillsdale, NJ: Lawrence Erlbaum Associates.

Wing, L. (1976). *Early childhood Autism.* Pergamon Press.

Wing, L. (1979). Differentiation of retardation and autism from specific communication disorders. *Child care, health and development, 5,* 57-68.

Wing, L. (1981). Asperger Syndrome - A Clinical Account. *Psychological Medicine, 11,* 115-129.

Wing, L. (1981). Language Social and Cognitive Impairments in Autism and Severe Retardation. *Autism and Developmental Disorders, 11.*

Wing, L. (1988). *The Continuum of Autistic Characteristics.* New York: Plenum publishing Co. Ltd.

Winnicott, D. W. (1953). Transitional Objects and Transitional Phenomena. *International Journal of Psycho-Analysis, 34,* 89-97.

Winnicott, D. W. (1971). *Playing and Reality*. London: Tavistock.

Winnicott, D. W. (1975). *Through Paediatrics to Psychoanalysis*. London: Hogarth Press and the Institute of Psychoanalysis.

Winnicott, D. W. (1988). *Human Nature*. London: Free Association Books.

Winnie, J. F. & Schoonover, S. M. (1976). Diagnostic Utility of WISC digits forward and backward. *Psychological Reports, 39*, 264-266.

Winokur, M. A. (1984) *The use of music as an audio-analgesia during childbirth*. Unpublished master's thesis, The Florida State University.

Wolfe, J. R. (1983). The use of music in a group sensory training program for regressed geriatric patients. *Activities Adaptation and Aging, 4*, 49-61.

Woodcock, J. (1987). Towards group analytic music therapy. *Journal of British Music Therapy, 1*, 16-22.

Woods, R. T. (1977). Psychological approaches to the treatment of the elderly. *Age and Ageing, 6*, 104-112.

Woods, R. T. (1979). Reality orientation and staff attention: A controlled study. *British Journal of Psychiatry, 134*, 502-507.

Woods, R. T. (1983). Specificity of learning in reality-orientation sessions: a single case study. *Behavior Research and Therapy, 21*, 173-175.

Wright, P. (1989). Music Healing. Journal of *British Music Therapy, 3*, 22-26.

Wylie, M. & Blom, R. (1986). Guided Imagery and Music with Hospice Patients. *Music Therapy Perspectives, 3, 25-28.*

Yalom, I. D. (1970). *Theory and practice of group psychotherapy*. New York: Basic Books.

Zenatti, A. (1969). Le development genetique de la percetion musicale. *Monographs Francais de Psychologie, 17.*

Zimmond, N. A. & Cicci, R. (1969). *Auditory Learning*. Belmont, CA: Fearon.

Zimny, G. H. & Weidenfeller, E. W. (1963). Effect of music upon GSR and heart-rate. *American Journal of Psychology, 76*, 311-314.

Zuckerkandl, V. (1973). *Man the Musician*. Princeton, NJ: Princeton University Press.

Index